THE OXFORD HAND

CW01582205

ORAL HISTORY

THE OXFORD HANDBOOK OF

ORAL HISTORY

Edited by

DONALD A. RITCHIE

OXFORD
UNIVERSITY PRESS

OXFORD
UNIVERSITY PRESS

Oxford University Press is a department of the University of Oxford.
It furthers the University's objective of excellence in research, scholarship,
and education by publishing worldwide.

Oxford New York
Auckland Cape Town Dar es Salaam Hong Kong Karachi
Kuala Lumpur Madrid Melbourne Mexico City Nairobi
New Delhi Shanghai Taipei Toronto

With offices in
Argentina Austria Brazil Chile Czech Republic France Greece
Guatemala Hungary Italy Japan Poland Portugal Singapore
South Korea Switzerland Thailand Turkey Ukraine Vietnam

Oxford is a registered trade mark of Oxford University Press
in the UK and certain other countries.

Published in the United States of America by
Oxford University Press
198 Madison Avenue, New York, NY 10016

© Oxford University Press 2011

First issued as an Oxford University Press paperback, 2012.

All rights reserved. No part of this publication may be reproduced, stored in a retrieval system, or transmitted, in any form or by any means, without the prior permission in writing of Oxford University Press, or as expressly permitted by law, by license, or under terms agreed with the appropriate reproduction rights organization. Inquiries concerning reproduction outside the scope of the above should be sent to the Rights Department, Oxford University Press, at the address above.

You must not circulate this work in any other form
and you must impose this same condition on any acquirer.

Library of Congress Cataloging-in-Publication Data
The Oxford handbook of oral history / edited by Donald A. Ritchie.
p. cm.
Includes bibliographical references and index.
ISBN 978-0-19-533955-0 (hardcover); 978-0-19-994506-1 (paperback)
1. Oral history—Handbooks, manuals, etc.
2. Oral history—Methodology.
3. Interviewing—Handbooks, manuals, etc.
4. Historiography. I. Ritchie, Donald A., 1945–
D16.14.O95 2010
907.2—dc22
2010008196

9 8 7 6 5 4 3 2 1

Printed in the United States of America
on acid-free paper

To everyone who has ever given an oral history interview

Acknowledgments

The forty contributors to this volume, from five continents, reflect the global nature of oral history. The international and interdisciplinary nature of the undertaking produced copy in a variety of styles, spellings, and citations that the editor has sought to standardize, but the intellectual substance of each essay belongs to each author exclusively. Although widely separated geographically, we have followed each other's work through scholarly journals, documentaries, Web sites, and electronic communication. We have especially benefitted from the biennial meetings of the International Oral History Association, where oral historians from many nations meet to deliver papers, participate in discussions, and converse between sessions, often over memorable servings of local food and drink. As the only historians who deal exclusively with the living, oral historians have a reputation for conviviality that makes their gatherings livelier than most professional meetings and that has forged strong friendships among practitioners around the world. We owe special thanks to the organizers of those international meetings, as well as to those who have sponsored the numerous regional, national, and local oral history meetings and workshops, for spreading an awareness of the practice, raising its standards, and encouraging its technological and intellectual advancement. This volume would not have possible without the extensive network they have fostered. Our thanks also go to Nancy Toff of Oxford University Press. As an editor and an oral historian, she inspired this collaboration. By reviewing the past and reflecting on the future, we hope that the *Oxford Handbook of Oral History* will reinforce those already in the field, and serve as a welcoming introduction to those considering oral history interviewing, using interviews in their research, preserving the recordings and transcripts in libraries and archives, and incorporating oral history in their public presentations.

Contents

Contributors, xiii

Introduction: The Evolution of Oral History, 3
Donald A. Ritchie

PART I. THE NATURE OF INTERVIEWING

1. The Dynamics of Interviewing, 23
   Mary Kay Quinlan

2. Those Who Prevailed and Those Who Were Replaced: Interviewing on Both Sides of a Conflict, 37
   Miroslav Vaněk

3. Interviewing in Cross-Cultural Settings, 51
   William Schneider

4. Case Study: Oral History and Democracy: Lessons from Illiterates, 65
   Mercedes Vilanova

PART II. MEMORY AND HISTORY

5. Memory and Remembering in Oral History, 77
   Alistair Thomson

6. Can Memory Be Collective?, 96
   Anna Green

7. Case Study: Rome's House of Memory and History: The Politics of Memory and Public Institutions, 112
   Alessandro Portelli

8. How Does One Win a Lost War? Oral History and Political Memories, 124
Federico Guillermo Lorenz

9. Disappointed Remains: Trauma, Testimony, and Reconciliation in Post-Apartheid South Africa, 142
Sean Field

10. Case Study: Memory Work with Children Affected by HIV/AIDS in South Africa, 159
Philippe Denis

Part III. Theory and Interpretation

11. The Stages of Women's Oral History, 169
Sue Armitage

12. Race and Oral History, 186
Albert S. Broussard

13. Remembering in Later Life: Generating Individual and Social Change, 202
Joanna Bornat

14. The Proust Effect: Oral History and the Senses, 219
Paula Hamilton

15. After Action: Oral History and War, 233
Megan Hutching

16. Case Study: "Above all, we need the witness": The Oral History of Holocaust Survivors, 244
Jessica Wiederhorn

17. Case Study: Field Notes on Catastrophe: Reflections on the September 11, 2001, Oral History Memory and Narrative Project, 255
Mary Marshall Clark

Part IV. The Technological Impact

18. Doing Video Oral History, 267
Brien R. Williams

19. Case Study: Opening Up Memory Space: The Challenges of Audiovisual History, 277
Albert Lichtblau

20. Achieving the Promise of Oral History in a Digital Age, 285
Doug Boyd

21. Oral History: Media, Message, and Meaning, 303
Clifford M. Kuhn

22. Messiah with a Microphone? Oral Historians, Technology, and Sound Archives, 315
Robert B. Perks

23. Case Study: Between the Raw and the Cooked in Oral History: Notes from the Kitchen, 333
Michael Frisch and Douglas Lambert

PART V. LEGAL, ETHICAL, AND ARCHIVAL IMPERATIVES

24. The Legal Ramifications of Oral History, 351
John A. Neuenschwander

25. Medical Ethics and Oral History, 372
Michelle Winslow and Graham Smith

26. The Archival Imperative: Can Oral History Survive the Funding Crisis in Archival Institutions?, 393
Beth M. Robertson

27. Case Study: The Southern Oral History Program, 409
Jacquelyn Dowd Hall, interviewed by Kathryn Nasstrom

28. Case Study: What Is It That University-Based Oral History Can Do? The Berkeley Experience, 417
Richard Cándida Smith

PART VI. PRESENTING ORAL HISTORY

29. Toward a Public Oral History, 429
Graham Smith

30. Motivating the Twenty-first-Century Student with Oral History, 449
Glenn Whitman

31. Oral History in Universities: From Margins to Mainstream, 470
Janis Wilton

32. Case Study: Engaging Interpretation through Digital Technologies, 490
Rina Benmayor

33. Oral History in the Digital Age, 499
Kelly Schrum, Sheila Brennan, James Halabuk, Sharon M. Leon, and Tom Scheinfeldt

Index, 517

Contributors

Sue Armitage, professor emerita of history and Women's Studies at Washington State University, is known for her work in women's oral history. She is co-author, with Kathryn Anderson, Dana Jack and Judith Wittner, of "Beginning Where We Are: Feminist Methodology in Women's Oral History" (1987), edited *Women's Oral History: The Frontiers Reader* (2002), and co-edited with Laurie Mercier *Speaking History: An Oral History Reader of the United States, 1865–Present* (2009).

Rina Benmayor teaches oral history, literature and Latina/o studies at California State University Monterey Bay. She is a former president of the International Oral History Association and vice-president elect of the Oral History Association. She co-edited with Andor Skotnes *Migration and Identity* (2005) and has written on oral history and Puerto Rican women, cultural citizenship, and digital storytelling.

Joanna Bornat is professor of oral history at the Open University and joint editor of *Oral History*. She has an interest in older people's remembering and has researched and published on oral history and gerontology themes.

Doug Boyd is the director of the Louie B. Nunn Center for Oral History at the University of Kentucky Libraries. He previously managed the Digital Program for the University of Alabama Libraries, served as the director of the Kentucky Oral History Commission and as senior archivist for the oral history collection at the Kentucky Historical Society.

Sheila Brennan is the senior digital history associate in the Public Projects division at the Center for History and New Media and a doctoral student in history at George Mason University.

Albert S. Broussard is professor of history and the Cornerstone Faculty Fellow in the department of history at Texas A&M University. A former president of the Oral History Association, he has published *Black San Francisco: The Struggle for Racial Equality in the West, 1900–1954* (1993) and *African American Odyssey: The Stewarts, 1853–1963* (1998).

Mary Marshall Clark is the director of the Columbia University Oral History Research Office and the co-founder and co-director, with Peter Bearman, of the

Master of Arts in Oral History at Columbia University. Clark and Bearman also directed the September 11, 2001, Oral History Narrative and Memory Project.

PHILIPPE DENIS is professor of history of Christianity at the University of KwaZulu-Natal and director of the Sinomlando Centre for Oral History and Memory Work in Africa.

SEAN FIELD is senior lecturer in the Historical Studies Department and the director of the Center for Popular Memory, a training, research, and archiving center committed to the dissemination of marginalized people's stories, at the University of Cape Town. His research interests include the traumatic, emotional, and visual aspects of popular memories of the apartheid and post-apartheid eras in South Africa, and the genocide in Rwanda.

MICHAEL FRISCH is professor of history and senior research scholar at the University of Buffalo. The author of *A Shared Authority: Essays on the Craft And Meaning of Oral and Public History* (1990), he also created the consulting firm, The Randforce Associates, LLC, within the university's Baird Research Center Technology Incubator.

ANNA GREEN is a member of the history department at the University of Exeter and the public history editor of *Oral History*. History and theory, oral history, and public history are the focus of her teaching, research, and publications.

JAMES HALABUK is the project manager of the Bracero History Archive at the Center for History and New Media and a doctoral student at George Mason University.

JACQUELYN DOWD HALL is the Julia Cherry Spruill Professor of History and director of the Southern Oral History Program at the University of North Carolina at Chapel Hill. She is the founding president of the Labor and Working Class History Association, past president of the Southern Historical Association, and the Organization of American Historians, the author of *Revolt Against Chivalry: Jessie Daniel Ames and the Women's Campaign Against Lynching* (1979, 1993), and the co-author of *Like a Family: The Making of a Southern Cotton Mill World* (1987, 2000).

PAULA HAMILTON is associate professor of history at University of Technology, Sydney, where she works with oral history projects with community groups, museums, heritage agencies, and local councils. She has also edited, with Linda Shopes, *Oral History and Public Memories* (2008).

MEGAN HUTCHING is a freelance oral historian in Auckland, New Zealand. She has published a number of books using oral history interviews, including a six-volume series on New Zealanders in the Second World War.

Clifford M. Kuhn is associate professor of history at Georgia State University and a former president of the Oral History Association. He is the author of *Living Atlanta: An Oral History of the City, 1914–1948* (1990).

Douglas Lambert is project manager for the HistoryMakers project conducted by the Randforce Associates.

Sharon M. Leon is director of public projects at the Center for History and New Media and research assistant professor at George Mason University.

Albert Lichtblau is an assistant professor in the department of history at the University of Salzburg in Austria, where he teaches contemporary history. His fields of scholarly expertise are Jewish, genocide, and migration studies, oral history, and audiovisual history.

Federico Guillermo Lorenz is a historian who works for the Argentine Ministry of Education. His writings include *Fantasmas de Malvinas. Un libro de viajes* (2008), *Las guerras por Malvinas* (2006), *Los zapatos de Carlito. Una historia de los trabajadores navales de Tigre en la década del 70* (2007), and *Combates por la memoria. Huellas de la dictadura en la Historia* (2007).

Kathryn Nasstrom is associate professor of history at the University of San Francisco. She is an editor of the Oxford Oral History Series and the author of *Everybody's Grandmother and Nobody's Fool: Frances Freeborn Pauley and the Struggle for Social Justice* (2000).

John A. Neuenschwander is an emeritus professor of history at Carthage College and the municipal judge for the city of Kenosha, Wisconsin. He holds a PhD in history from Case Western Reserve University and a JD from the Illinois Institute of Technology-Chicago-Kent College of Law. He is the author of *A Guide to Oral History and the Law* (2009).

Robert B. Perks is curator of Oral History and director of National Life Stories at the British Library in London. He is a visiting professor in Oral History at the University of Huddersfield, secretary of the Oral History Society, co-editor of the *Oral History Journal*, co-editor of *The Oral History Reader* with Alistair Thomson (2006), and an editor of Oxford University Press's oral history series.

Alessandro Portelli teaches American literature at the University of Rome "La Sapienza," Italy. He is the founder and president of the Circolo Gianni Bosio for the study of oral history and people's cultures, and the author of a number of books on oral history including *The Death of Luigi Trastulli: Form and Meaning in Oral History* (1991), *The Battle of Valle Giulia Oral History and the Art of Dialogue* (1996), *The Order Has Been Carried Out: History, Memory* *and Meaning of a Nazi Massacre in Rome* (2003), and *They Say in Harlan County: An Oral History* (2010).

Mary Kay Quinlan is associate professor of journalism at the University of Nebraska-Lincoln. She was a Washington newspaper correspondent for fifteen years and has been involved in oral history for more than twenty-five years as a teacher, workshop leader, and editor of the *Oral History Association Newsletter*.

Donald A. Ritchie is historian of the United States Senate. A former president of the Oral History Association, he is the author of *Doing Oral History: A Practical Guide* (2003) among other works.

Beth M. Robertson is manager of preservation at the State Library of South Australia, and was the library's foundation oral history curator from 1987 to 1999. Her *Oral History Handbook* is in its fifth edition and is regarded as the Australian standard. She won the Australia Oral History Association's Hazel de Berg Award for Excellence in Oral History in 2006.

Tom Scheinfeldt is managing director of the Center for History and New Media and research assistant professor of history in the Department of History and Art History at George Mason University.

Kelly Schrum is the director of educational projects at the Center for History and New Media and an associate professor at George Mason University.

William Schneider is curator of oral history at the University of Alaska, Fairbanks, where he has had the pleasure of living and traveling extensively and working with some wonderfully knowledgeable elders.

Graham Smith is a senior lecturer in oral history in the Department of History, Royal Holloway, University of London. He is also Chair of the Oral History Society.

Richard Cándida Smith is professor of history at the University of California, Berkeley, where he directs the Regional Oral History Office. A past president and executive secretary of the Oral History Association, he is the author of *Utopia and Dissent: Art, Poetry, and Politics in California* (1995), *Mallarmé's Children: Symbolism and the Renewal of Experience* (1999), and *The Modern Moves West: California Artists and Democratic Culture in the Twentieth Century* (2009).

Alistair Thomson is professor of history at Monash University in Australia and formerly professor of oral history at the University of Sussex in England. His publications include *Anzac Memories: Living With the Legend* (1994), *The Oral History Reader*, with Rob Perks (1998 and 2006, with Rob Perks), and *Ten Pound Poms: Australia's Invisible Migrants*, with Jim Hammerton (2005).

Miroslav Vaněk is director of the Oral History Center at the Institute of Contemporary History in Prague, lecturer at the Charles University, and the founding president of the Czech Oral History Association.

Mercedes Vilanova is Catedrática emérita of contemporary history of the University of Barcelona, founding editor since 1989 of the journal *Historia, Antropología y Fuentes Orales*, and first president of the International Oral History Association. Her main publications use statistics, oral history, cartography, and classical historiography to deal with the democratic process, revolution and civil war during the 1930s in Catalonia, Spain.

Glenn Whitman directs the American Century Oral History Project at St. Andrew's Episcopal School in Potomac, Maryland. He is the author of *Dialogue with the Past: Engaging Students and Meeting Standards through Oral History* (2004) and a recipient of the Oral History Association's Pre-Collegiate Teaching Award.

Jessica Wiederhorn is cofounder of the Narrative Trust, a partnership dedicated to capturing the oral histories of institutions, communities, and individuals. She was associate director of the Oral History Research Office at Columbia University and manager of academic affairs at the Shoah Foundation, where she reviewed hundreds of Holocaust testimonies, providing guidance and coaching to interviewers worldwide.

Brien R. Williams, a former university professor of mass communications, is a Washington-based oral historian and video producer who has conducted, advised, and directed oral history projects at various institutions, including the Smithsonian Institution and the American Red Cross.

Janis Wilton has taught oral history to undergraduate and postgraduate students at the University of New England, Armidale, Australia. A past president of the International Oral History Association, she has conducted community workshops and community-based public history projects. Her books, exhibitions, and Web sites include *Different Sights: New England Migrants* (an online database and thematic study, 2009) and *Golden Threads: The Chinese in Regional NSW 1850–1950* (a traveling exhibition, Web site and book, 2001–2004).

Michelle Winslow is a research fellow within the Academic Unit of Supportive Care, University of Sheffield, UK. She has worked extensively as an oral historian in health and medicine, with both patients and health care professionals, specializing in palliative care.

THE OXFORD HANDBOOK OF

ORAL HISTORY

INTRODUCTION: THE EVOLUTION OF ORAL HISTORY

DONALD A. RITCHIE

ORAL history is as old as the first recorded history and as new as the latest digital recorder. Long before the practice acquired a name and standard procedures, historians conducted interviews to gain insight into great events, beginning at least as early as Thucydides, who based his account of the Peloponnesian wars "partly on what I saw myself, partly on what others saw for me." Efforts to collect and preserve oral reminiscences predated the tape recorder, and they exist in archives today in various forms, from interrogations recorded by church scribes during the Inquisition, to veterans' pension applications for American Revolutionary War pensions, and interviews with former slaves conducted by unemployed writers hired by the Works Progress Administration (WPA) during the Great Depression.[1]

In the eighteenth century, Samuel Johnson commented that "all history was at first oral," but the term "oral history" was first used in reference to troubadours and oral traditions.[2] Oral history did not attach itself to interviewing until an article appeared in the *New Yorker* in 1942 about Joe Gould, a Greenwich Village bohemian who claimed to be compiling "An Oral History of Our Time." Gould told of interviewing the "shirt-sleeved multitude" in saloons and on park benches, because "what people say is history." Gould's quest earned him many free meals, but was later revealed to be a figment of his imagination. He left behind no manuscript. The label stuck, however, and in 1948, when the Columbia University history professor Allan Nevins established the first archives to conduct and preserve interviews, he called it the Oral History Research Office.[3]

Nevins had turned to history after a career in journalism, where interviewing direct participants in events was a mainstay of the reporter's trade. A prolific writer, Nevins plumbed the traditional archival sources, manuscripts, memoirs, and newspaper accounts, but he grew concerned that modern communications and transportation were lessening the impetus for letter writing and diary keeping. Funded by modest grants from the university and a private foundation, Nevins set out to record the reminiscences of major players in important events, politicians, jurists, business executives, and military officers.[4]

His innovative approach to history swam against the tide within the profession. A leading research primer of the 1950s, *The Modern Researcher*, written by two of Nevins's colleagues at Columbia, Jacques Barzun and Henry F. Graff, acknowledged his oral history project in a single footnote, observing confidently that "The written word is still so compelling, however, that these recordings are transcribed and the typescripts filed like books." Barzun and Graff called for scholarly skepticism and verification of evidence, dismissing eyewitness testimony as biased and unreliable, and linking interviews to sociology rather than history. (In the 1920s and 1930s, sociologists at the University of Chicago had pioneered in the use of ethnographic interviewing for studying urban life.) The walls of the library and archives defined the historian's world, rather than going out "in the field," to interview participants.[5] Historians had been strongly influenced by the work of Leopold von Ranke, the nineteenth-century German scholar who emphasized archival documentation for greater accuracy in history. Even Ranke regarded eyewitness account as "the most genuine and direct sources," but since he was dealing with the distant past he meant the documents that participants had left behind.[6]

The news media, reflecting its own reliance on interviewing, gave more credibility to the emergence of oral history. A 1950 editorial in the *New York Times* mused about what it would be like to have recordings of George Washington describing the Battle of Trenton, or Abraham Lincoln discussing his Gettysburg Address, and urged other universities to follow Columbia's lead. Thanks to Columbia's oral histories, the editorial predicted, "history students in 2050 will know more about this generation than we know about the year 1850."[7] During the 1950s, oral history archives were developed at the University of California at Los Angeles and at Berkeley. Over time, more universities followed this lead, as did presidential libraries, government agencies, corporations, labor unions, and religious orders, which sponsored their own oral archives.

Where the first oral history projects in the United States started with a "top down" focus on political, economic, and cultural elites, European oral historians were more rooted in social and cultural history, and allied with political movements on the Left. They reexamined history from the "bottom up," intending to include the voices of those previously excluded from national narratives. A sense of social responsibility motivated this approach, which challenged the social and intellectual status quo by interviewing those who had been overlooked or oppressed. By creating a history of everyday lives, they aimed to contribute to the larger movement to improve those lives, and, as Ronald Grele put it, "to radicalize the practice of history."[8]

In 1966 British historians founded the History Workshop at the trade union–sponsored Ruskin College, on the belief that history should be a collaboration of the efforts of researchers, archivists, curators, local historians, and "the 'do-it-yourself' enthusiast." Oral history was one of the tools that fit all. The radical adult education movement combined with women's history and community history to shape British oral history, which also received a boost from Ronald Blythe's widely acclaimed *Akenfield* (1969), a portrait of an East Anglian village drawn from his interviews with rural agricultural folk. In 1978 Paul Thompson's *The Voice of the Past: Oral History* helped give scholarly credibility to the "hidden histories" that interviewing revealed.[9] In the United States, the "bottom up" approach also took hold in the 1970s, with American oral historians increasingly turning their attention to race, class, gender, and local communities. Promoting this trend were the best-selling oral histories by Studs Terkel, *Hard Times* (1970), *Working* (1974), and *The "Good War"* (1984), which made the method far more widely recognized. A veteran of the WPA's Federal Writers' Project, Terkel was a radio interviewer who based his books on the long interviews he had conducted on the air. An earlier television career might have reduced him to sound bites except that he was blacklisted for his leftist politics and returned to the radio, where he spent the next half century talking to people in a medium that tolerated long interviews.[10]

Oral historians debated the merits of "elite" versus "non-elite" interviewing, but many came to appreciate that the same methodology fit both approaches. The British emphasis on working-class interviews had led to the observation that a fisherman was more likely to be interviewed than a Member of Parliament. But over time the focus expanded and, for instance, social historians approached "the City" (the oldest part of London) to record from the inside the transformation of London's financial establishment.[11] Interviewers could record generals or privates, managers or workers, activists and the apolitical, and projects that recorded multiple perspectives from different levels developed a more comprehensive picture of the actions and counteractions, motives and results in human events. Oral historians collected the recollections of soldiers and antiwar protestors, women in the war industries, Holocaust survivors, civil rights demonstrators, political refugees, immigrants, and those grappling with their sexual identity.

Oral history projects became a staple of college campuses and community organizations, but governments also saw the value in collecting interviews. During World War II, the U.S. military began dispatching interviewers to war zones, where they recorded soldiers' combat experiences immediately after battle. Interviewers later followed the troops across Europe to Korea, Vietnam, Afghanistan, and Iraq. War-related projects interviewed combatants on both sides, whether in Japan and the United States after World War II or in Great Britain and Argentina after the Falklands War. They sought military planners, prisoners of war, conscientious objectors, and defense workers. Intelligence agencies, whose personnel were prohibited from speaking openly to outsiders, conducted internal interviews to create their own archives. On the domestic side, national parks collected oral histories for their historic sites, using the testimony for reconstructing buildings, preparing orientation films, and providing information for visitors.

The oral history movement spread worldwide, with a proliferation of oral history projects and national associations. Beyond the United States and Western Europe, it expanded into Eastern Europe, Africa, Asia, and Latin America as they were undergoing social and political upheaval, and where the written archives reflected discredited regimes. Oral historians recorded the testimonies of those who overturned the old order, along with those who had suffered under those regimes. In South Africa, where racial apartheid collapsed and a multiracial democracy emerged, oral historians noted that their George Washingtons and Thomas Jeffersons were still living and available to be interviewed. Eastern European oral historians recorded those who toppled and replaced the Communist regimes, but having lived with a one-sided history under the old regime they set out to interview both the victors and the vanquished. Other societies found oral history useful for confronting and understanding old injustices. Australians have reexamined their relations with Aboriginals, just as American and Canadian interviews with Native American and First Peoples helped explain their diverse cultures.[12]

Milestones in Sound Recording

Advancements in recording equipment made all these developments possible. But technology has challenged as well as propelled the field of oral history. Practitioners have benefitted from and must also cope with their technologically driven methodology. Interviewers, constituting a tiny segment of the consuming public, could exert little influence on the developing technology, and instead have adjusted their practices to fit whatever the recording industry produced. In purchasing equipment, oral historians have had to "follow the music," since the most popular ways of playing music dominated the markets for recording equipment, regardless of their suitability for recording and preserving interviews. Equipment that is compatible with the technology most widely used for music sales will be likely to last the longest, even if some other technologies are superior, the way Betamax lost to VHS. Projects that failed to keep current with technology quickly became outmoded, restricting the usefulness of their collections. Others changed with the times, seizing upon new opportunities to conduct and disseminate interviews in ways that not long ago would have been unimaginable.

In the late nineteenth century, sound was first recorded on wax cylinders, some of which still survive and have been copied onto tape and digital formats. Other audio formats, from gramophones to vinyl records, replaced wax cylinders, but were generally impractical for field work. When the WPA dispatched unemployed writers during the Depression to conduct interviews, most simply made notes on paper. Their stenography was notoriously uneven, and a few apparently used their writing talents to embellish their transcripts.[13]

Rudimentary wire recorders dated back to the 1898 but became more practical in the 1940s. Even then their cumbersome size generally limited their use to office dictation. At Normandy Beach, military historians used the wire recorders for debriefings on hospital ships but feared that the bulky wire recorders would draw sniper fire on shore. Wire recorders used steel piano wire to make recordings. These were durable for archival preservation—some lasted for a half century after the war—but the wire could also tangle and break, and it was difficult to edit.

As soon as wire recorders became less expensive and more readily available for consumer purchase, they were rendered obsolete by the introduction of magnetic tape recorders in 1948. Magnetic tape had been developed in Germany, and it was only after the Allies invaded during World War II that they acquired any tape recorders. While wire recordings were fine for voice, magnetic tape was much more popular because of its portability, high fidelity, and ability to accommodate stereo music recordings, which accounted for its postwar popularity. Reel-to-reel tape recorders became the mainstay of the first oral history archives. They combined improved recording facilities with archival-quality tape.

The first commercial tape recorder went on the market in 1948, the same year that the Columbia Oral History Research Office opened. Columbia recorded its interviews on reel-to-reel and then transcribed them, allowing interviewees to correct the transcript, practices, and principles that influenced other oral history archives. Because the edited transcript varied from the spoken word, Columbia regarded the recordings as irrelevant once they had been transcribed. To save money, always in short supply, it recorded other interviews over its original tapes. When a scholar raised objection to this policy in 1962, then director Louis Starr doubted the practicality of storing hundreds of hours of recordings that "would have to be indexed to be of much use, and that in itself would be pretty expensive." He also noted that only one of the hundreds of people who had used the oral history collection had ever asked to hear a tape.[14] Columbia's cost-saving elevated practice into principle and promoted the transcript over the recording. Other projects recognized the importance of the "aural" nature of interviews and began saving their recordings. The Columbia practice of downgrading the recordings in favor of transcription influenced American practices but was not adopted in Europe, due to its origins among linguists and folklorists, and also because the British oral historians Raphael Samuel and Paul Thompson took an early stance in favor of the value of the tape as documentation.[15]

The first Columbia transcripts also turned the dialogue of the interview into an autobiographical monologue by deleting all the questions. The responses therefore appeared as a long, uninterrupted narrative, implying that interviewing was generic and that interviewers were interchangeable. This format, by omitting the give-and-take of the interview, obscured the relationship between the interviewer and interviewee, which can significantly influence the discussion. When answering questions, people talk about issues and provide information that they might not have volunteered unprompted. Interviewees often adjust their responses depending on the age, race, gender, and status of the interviewer, providing what they think the interviewer wants to hear, and also to shape the interpretation of the interview. The practice of omitting questions from the transcript was challenged by other oral historians, notably those at Duke University, whose methodologies called for more active involvement of interviewers in the interview process, warning that passive interviewers surrendered too much of their professional capacity. Rooted in social history and influenced by the social sciences, this school of thinking called for more thorough research and scholarly analysis of interviews.

The next milestone in oral history occurred in 1963, when the Netherlands-based Royal Phillips Electronics, Inc. (otherwise known as Phillips) introduced the compact cassette tape recorder. Portable recorders using cassette tapes eliminated the need to thread large reels. Since they were less expensive and easier to carry, cassette recorders quickly supplanted the reel-to-reel recorder, despite the longer archival shelf life of reel-to-reel tape. For years afterwards, the National Archives continued to request that oral histories be submitted on reel-to-reel, requiring some donors to copy their cassettes onto reel-to-reel. The copy became the "original" for preservation purposes, while the cassettes was designated the "copy" for research use. Over time, as the manufacturing of reel-to-reel recorders declined, oral history archives either had to maintain obsolete equipment to play back their interviews or to go through the expensive process of transferring their recording to cassettes. Veteran interviewers clung to their antiquated recorders, feeling comfortable with them, and cannibalized old machines for parts to keep a few of them operating. By 1984 cassette tape recorders had become so prevalent that for the first time music cassettes surpassed the sale of LP records.

Portable cassette recorders vastly expanded the number of oral history practitioners and facilitated field-based interviewing that better suited the growing "bottom up" approach to history. Extensive interviews were conducted regarding racial segregation and the civil rights movement, and with environmentalists, jazz musicians, Hispanic farm workers, folk crafts artists, and any number of other groups. When the military sent historian interviewers into Vietnam in the 1960s to conduct postcombat debriefings, they carried cassette recorders. Soldiers in Vietnam, and their families back home, often exchanged cassettes of chat and music, many of which have survived under the worst possible conditions before being donated to archives for preservation. It was still relatively expensive to record and preserve oral histories, and projects tended to be located in larger institutions.

In 1966 American oral historians held their first national colloquium at Lake Arrowhead, California, as a result of which they founded the Oral History Association the following year. Among the participants at that first meeting were professors of history, economics, and speech, journalists, archivists, and librarians, government historians, folklorists, psychoanalysts, state and local historical society directors, and a number of people connected with medical history and medical libraries.[16] British oral historians held their first meeting in December 1969 at the British

Institute of Recorded Sound (now the British Library Sound Archives), launched the journal *Oral History* in 1971, and founded the Oral History Society in 1973. In 1979 the British Oral History Society hosted the first International Conference on Oral History at the University of Essex, and other international meetings were held over the next decade in Western Europe. In 1996 the International Oral History Association (IOHA) adopted a constitution and began holding biennial meetings beyond Europe, from Latin America to Africa and Australia. The same years saw the formation of national oral history associations, among them Canada (1974), Australia (1978), New Zealand (1986), Argentina (1996), Brazil (1998), Japan (2003), South Africa (2004), Italy (2005), Argentina (2005), Czech Republic (2007), and Ukraine (2007). Each ran its own meetings and workshops and published journals, further encouraging oral history interviews.

The Digital Revolution

It may have been coincidental that formal organization of the IOHA occurred in 1996, a year of explosive growth in the newly emerging Internet, but the enterprise likely would not have succeeded without the digital communications revolution. Between biennial meetings, its council grappled with concerns about finances, publications, translation, education, connections to national oral history associations, and scholarships to encourage diversity at the meetings. Spread out across the world, its members met electronically and distributed their announcements and newsletters online. Without email and the Internet, this multitude of tasks would have been insurmountable. At the same time, oral history projects everywhere established Web sites to advertise and disseminate their collections.

Digital electronics broke like a wave over the analog world during the 1980s. The first digital recordings, on compact discs (CDs), were introduced to the market in 1982. Five years later, digital audio tape (DAT) recorders appeared. By 1988 CDs topped record sales, and over the next decade they replaced cassettes in sales. As the music world changed, cassettes survived primarily through the sale of books on tape. Once the audiobooks were transferred to disk, however, cassette tapes went the way of reel-to-reel. While analog tape recorders are still used by projects that invested heavily in older equipment, oral historians have trouble finding merchants who still stock cassette tapes.

Minidiscs came on the market in 1992. In 2001 Apple introduced the iPod, which students began using for interviews, since all they needed was to purchase inexpensive microphones to adapt them to oral history. Older practitioners preferred more substantial digital recorders, although the correlation between size and sound quality had disappeared. Military historians in Iraq recorded postcombat interviews on compact flash audio recorders, emailing the sound files back to their headquarters for transcription.

Paralleling the changes in recording equipment were the electronic communications that linked oral historians and enlarged access to their collections. Email became available in the 1980s, and by the 1990s the Internet opened a world of possibilities. Oral historians established the H-ORALHIST listserv to post announcements, pose questions, and share answers. Some oral history archives posted their catalogs online, while others put up entire transcripts, along with sound and video recordings. Research use multiplied exponentially, reaching new audiences of teachers and students, genealogists and local historians, and casual Web browsers. Where previously archivists had lamented that not enough researchers consulted their oral histories, they now worried that too many might use them, perhaps improperly. They would lose their "guardianship relationship" with the interviews in their collections if anyone could read them online. Archivists grew concerned about protecting interviewees' privacy and whether their original consent agreements permitted Internet posting, and many have taken care to consult with interviewees before posting anything about them. As sites began to include both the recording and the transcript, they also highlighted the differences between the two, reviving the debate over whether transcripts should be strictly verbatim, or whether interviewees should be able to edit them. Some projects resisted transcripts entirely, preferring that researchers listen to the sounds of the interview. Research in sound recordings was facilitated by the development of spoken-word indexing. Another unexpected result of placing interviews on the Internet was that for the first time oral historians were likely to access interviews done by their colleagues, opening the possibility of worldwide peer review.[17]

The marriage of oral history and digital electronic technology has bred creative uses for interviews. Oral history has been used to provide commentary for audio walking tours of historical areas. Some universities are offering oral history courses online, or as distance learning through video links, with faculty and students communicating electronically, and student projects being published on CD-ROMs. One oral historian at the Regional Oral History Office in Berkeley has used text messaging to interview a man with severe disabilities that affect his speech.

Digital recording also facilitated video interviews, adding what the Impressionist artist Paul Gauguin called the "listening eye." As early as the first oral history colloquium in 1966, a participant advocated recording interviews on 16mm motion picture film to preserve the "intangibles" of appearance and expression. By then Sony had already introduced its first consumer video cameras, and in 1969 the first videocassettes went on the market. Experts warned oral historians not to conduct video interviews by themselves because video cameras still required lights and a crew to record at a decent quality, and to reduce the number of distractions for the interviewers. By 1996 DVD cameras were introduced in Japan, and soon afterward the same experts were reporting that without the need for additional lighting and bulky equipment, they were able to conduct interviews and keep an eye on them through discreet monitors held in their laps. While the debate has continued over whether interviewees would be intimidated by the cameras, advocates argue that those with a story to tell will tell it regardless of the equipment being used, particularly if the equipment is placed unobtrusively. In a notable demonstration of people's willingness to be interviewed on camera, even about the most painful memories, the Shoah Visual History Foundation project since 1994 has amassed an archive of more than fifty thousand video testimonies in thirty-two languages from Holocaust survivors.

The migration of sound recordings from analog to digital has additional costs for older projects, both in terms of purchasing new equipment and in converting extensive collections to the new medium. New equipment appears on the market so quickly that recent acquisitions may approach obsolescence and discontinuation before the interviewer has gotten used to operating it. DAT recorders and minidiscs have already been relegated to the shelves with eight-track players and VHS tapes. Fortunately, once in the digital domain the whole act of transferring data becomes simpler, quicker, and more automated. The constant changes in technology have generally kept oral historians, like Alice through the looking glass, running as fast as they can just to stay in place.

The Intellectual Evolution of Oral History

The strata of technological development have been matched by multiple layers of interpretation. As a method of collecting and interpreting information, oral history has attracted a remarkable diversity of disciplines, from historians to archivists, curators, journalists, sociologists, anthropologists, ethnographers, folklorists, and educators at all levels. This multidisciplinary foundation has constantly expanded to incorporate the interests and needs of new practitioners, encouraging them to consider each other's different methods and uses of interviewing. As a sign of this diversity, graduate and undergraduate courses in oral history taught at universities are often offered outside of history departments. Many fields consider interviewing a valuable skill as well as a teaching tool that engages students through "active learning."

Oral history's big tent incorporates both the humanities and social sciences, and methodological debates have ranged among its dissimilar constituents. For instance, anthropologists and sociologists have a long tradition of participatory observation and the use of anonymity and pseudonyms for the individuals and communities they study, while historians expect verification through identifiable sources. Although one approach may be unconventional by the other's standards, oral historians have tried to respect and learn from these differences. Indeed, the great strength of both oral history meetings and literature has come from the intersection of disciplines, with practitioners including ideas from multiple fields in their citations, although too often other fields omitted oral history sources from their own notes. Over time, this one-way traffic also began to change and "oral history" began appearing in the titles and notes of scholarly articles in diverse fields, such as medical journals, which carried articles considering not only the evidence gathered from oral history but the therapeutic value of doing interviews with patients.

Like Allan Nevins, historians have generally conducted interviews to acquire information that would otherwise not have existed, since their subjects were writing fewer letters and diaries. This approach seeks in interviews the small but telling details that previously escaped notice and were overlooked in the historical narrative. They do interviews to hear the observations and perspectives of eyewitnesses, even if the testimony confounds their own assumptions. Information gained from interviews can force historians to rethink what they thought they knew, and there will often be unexpected discrepancies between the written and oral sources. Much of the initial scholarly resistance to oral history had to do with its "subjective" nature. Memory can change over time and is dependent on perception. Documents were unchangeable and therefore seen to be "objective." Although oral historians recognize the fallibility of memory, they do not put more weight on a source just because it has been written down. They have found that memos have been written to obscure rather than illuminate what happened; that memoirs can be notoriously self-serving; and that newspapers sometimes get the story wrong. Contradictory oral testimony has forced interviewers to reexamine the written sources and sometimes alert them to documents they might not have consulted, or that the archives might not have collected. More than one oral historian has been rewarded by an interviewee with a box of pertinent letters, photographs, or artifacts long stored in an attic, which verify the narrator's version of events.

Anthropologists, folklorists, linguists, and others have been attracted not only by the details that interviewees recall but also by what they fail to remember, get wrong, or choose to remain silent about. Memory studies have examined autobiographical memory (unique to a particular individual), collective memory (the historical consciousness of a group), and public memory (the ways in which communities remember and commemorate their past), pursuing the patterns of memory among many narrators. Oral history and memory studies differ but are compatible. Oral history relies on people's testimony to understand the past, while memory studies concentrate on the process of remembering and how that shapes people's understanding of the past. Memory studies are often more interested in how facts are remembered and in distortion of facts than in the facts themselves. But since oral historians deal so directly with long-term memory, they have incorporated memory studies into their own methodological discussions.[18]

While people are interviewed at different stages in their lives, many are more comfortable giving reflective interviews in their retirement rather than at mid-career. It is not simply a matter of having more time on their hands. In the 1960s, the gerontologist Robert Butler put forward the notion that as people grow older they go through a mental process of "life review." Long forgotten earlier memories return and grow vivid as people sort through their successes and failures. Such life review can cause depression and despair in some, and candor and serenity in others.[19] Though Butler's theories immediately appealed to oral historians and to those working with the elderly in nursing homes and hospitals, psychologists and gerontologists and those working in "reminiscence therapy," given their preference for quantified studies, did not begin studying "autobiographical memory" until the 1980s.[20]

Social scientists generally depended on structured and standardized questionnaires to obtain the maximum amount of valid, reliable information, while minimizing distortions of what respondents knew. Others, influenced by the "linguistic turn" of social inquiry, felt that this approach failed to question where their informants' knowledge was coming from, and how it was derived. What sociologists have called "active interviews" transformed their interviewees from "subjects" into "constructors of knowledge in collaboration with interviewers." They argued in favor of more conversational interviews whose means are cooperatively reached and interpreted. The interviewer's objection should not be to dictate the interpretation through a predetermined agenda but to provide a conducive environment for people to address relevant issues in their lives.[21]

Robert Butler's concept of "life review" significantly influenced oral historians, although Butler himself remained skeptical of oral history. He found it a shame that oral historians did not use a standard questionnaire. Rooted in scientific methodologies, Butler wanted quantifiable data for generalizable research. Emerging from the humanities, oral historians have generally rejected questionnaires, except for specific issues, reasoning that no single set of questions could encompass the diversities of experiences, observations, and opinions that their projects record. Oral history interviewers often find that the best material they collect was volunteered by the interviewees with little prompting, sometimes covering subjects they had not anticipated and about which they had prepared no questions. "I didn't know that, can you tell me more about it?" being the best response they could make.[22]

An aggregate of individual memories forms the collective memory of a group or community. Often organized around an anniversary, oral history projects have focused on the history of businesses, unions, religious orders, military units, faculties, alumni, townspeople, activists, and volunteers. In some cases, the institution or the structure at the heart of the project survives only in the memories of the participants. Collective memory can record tragedy as well as triumphs, and in some cases plays a role in a community's attempts to emerge from a difficult past. Since the end of World War II there have been repeated efforts to air past atrocities and heal a nation through Truth and Reconciliation Commissions. Seeking amnesty, the accused are required to provide "full disclosure" of their past actions, and what they recall is matched against the testimony of their surviving victims. Oral historians have carefully studied the testimonies elicited by these commissions, recognizing that a large gap between their methodology and those of the more politically motivated commissions.[23]

Oral historians have also discovered that whole communities have rearranged their recollections collectively to make them more convenient and relevant to the present, a phenomenon that has been highlighted in the influential work of Alessandro Portelli.[24] In these cases, interviews remain meaningful, despite their errors in fact, by revealing how the community has made sense of a troubled past. Communal forgetting sometimes involves deliberate efforts to expunge unpleasant events from the record. Inhabitants of Centralia, Washington, for instance, resisted the efforts of public historians to install any historical markers or visitor information about the bloody battle that took place there in 1919 between members of the International Workers of the World (the IWW) and the American Legion. A researcher in Salonika, Greece, looking for signs of its Jewish community, which had been the majority of the city's population before World War II, interviewed one of the few remaining Jewish residents. The woman regretted how the city had eliminated all references to that part of its history. "There is nothing in the historical institutes. Nothing in the city's museums. Hardly a book in the Greek bookstores. Nothing. As if we were never here."[25]

Collective memory suffers bouts of amnesia. Even such traumatic events as the great influenza epidemic that claimed twenty million lives worldwide followed World War I have faded into obscurity into obscurity. The historian William McNeil was just a year old when his mother and newborn sister came down with the flu in December 1918. He later observed that his parents made no written record of the event and expunged the most dreadful experience of their entire lives from family memory, so that exactly what happened and how they survived remain completely unknown to him. What the family did mention was that they had survived by going to a grandmother's farm in Canada, meaning that the tale survived in the family's oral tradition only "because the story had a happy ending." McNeil concluded that perhaps there was "nothing much to say or remember after such an experience," which may explain why the influenza epidemic left so few traces in human memory.[26]

More recent catastrophes, however, have inspired oral historians to work at the "intersection of grief and history." An increasing number of projects have combined an interest in recording major events of the immediate past, broaden the scope of voices of history, and provide a cathartic release for the victims. Natural disasters have also generated major oral history efforts. When Hurricane Katrina devastated the Gulf Coast in August 2005, oral historians immediately began implementing their methodology to document the storm and its aftermath, both with those who stayed behind and those who were evacuated to other areas. The projects ranged from on-the-spot interviewing in Mississippi and Louisiana to refugees spread out from Tennessee to Texas, focusing on different aspects of the events, from rescue efforts during the flooding to medical assistance, religious responses, and the memories of specific groups, such as "Katrina's Jewish Voices." As it became clearer that the same events affect different segments of the population in different ways, oral historians in Central Florida interviewed the homeless about their experiences with three hurricanes that ripped through the state, comparing the effects of the storms on them as opposed to property owners. With fewer material concerns, the homeless received shelter and food after the storm and found work in the cleanup. The same traumatic events caused less disruption in their lives and allowed them to contribute to society.[27]

Interviewing soon after such a traumatic event created new considerations for oral historians and initiated extensive discussions about the issues of historical distance, objectivity, reflection, and emotional trauma. After the terrorist attacks in New York and Washington on September 11, 2001, oral historians began recording a wide cross section of people affected by the events, in part to preserve a multitude of experiences and observations, and in part to study what memories people take away from such events and how long they retain them. Most oral histories have been conducted long after the events, when people have had the benefit of hindsight, and when later experiences caused them to revise their earlier stories. Interviews taken in the immediate aftermath of September 11 will likely be different from those recorded years later. An oral history project conducted at Columbia University has followed this progression by returning to interview the same people at regular intervals. Other projects have ranged from the efforts of New York City Fire Department to record interview with firefighters, paramedics, and emergency medical technicians on the events of that day, to the U.S. Army Corps of Engineers interviews with the boat crews who evacuated panicked New Yorkers from lower Manhattan. They noted that in the hectic days following the attacks, written records were sparse and contained mostly "dry, official documentation of any disaster response," while the interviews they collected recorded the human drama.[28] Beyond direct participants, the American Folklife Center at the Library of Congress also instituted a September 11 project to document the thoughts and concerns of citizens from across the country.

Outside of the academic world, oral history has become a mainstay of genealogists, community historians, and others. Thousands of individuals have been encouraged by the Library of Congress's Veterans Project to conduct and submit interviews with relatives and friends who were veterans of various wars or had experiences on the home front. Hundreds of others have visited the StoryCorps booths in New York's Grand Central Terminal, in order to record short interviews with each other. Founded by a radio producer, StoryCorps also dispatches mobile booths around the United States, inviting people to record their own brief interviews, highlights of which are broadcast on National Public Radio. One journalist who reviewed the recordings concluded that "part of the appeal of the clips was that in less than five minutes, each of the interviews gave a real sense of someone else's experience. We are storytellers and listeners by nature, but we are also, by nature, curious about other people." While such brief narratives are entertaining to listeners and satisfying to the tellers, they are little more than snapshots, not as substantial as full scale oral history and therefore less likely to be woven into the historical narrative.[29]

Whether as professionals or amateurs, all oral historians need to respect the dignity and autonomy of those being interviewed. Every oral history project should use legal release forms that define the interviewee's wishes for the recording and transcript and meet the copyright needs of archives and publishers. Oral historians have debated, created, and promulgated ethical and legal standards of practice, in addition to guidelines for evaluating oral history projects. Rather than being carved in stone, these standards have been periodically revised to accommodate new developments and new technologies. Funding agencies regularly use such standards for judging professional competency. Complicating this effort has been the emergence of academic requirements for human subject review. Although designed for medical and behavioral science research with the potential for inflicting harm, some of these rules have deemed oral history as a form of human interaction. For the most part, oral history standards more than meet requirements for human subject review. However, some review boards have set inappropriate requirements, instructing interviewers to avoid asking embarrassing questions, to erase tapes, and to cite interviewees anonymously rather by name, procedures that ran contrary to the canons of the field.

"Oral history has never had more currency," *US News & World Report* declared in a 2007 cover story on the Veterans Project at the Library of Congress.[30] Technologically, the equipment available for conducting, preserving, and disseminating interviews in audio or video form has become more diverse and affordable. Academically, oral history has moved from the margins into the mainstream, as a readily accepted—and rigorous—method in a multitude of disciplines, as well as a proven teaching tool. Universities and the United States and Great Britain have begun offering graduate degrees in oral history and life history research. The International Oral History Association attracts hundreds of oral historians, from within and without the university, from dozens of countries at meetings that have traveled from Rome to Sydney, Rio de Janeiro, and Istanbul.

The Oxford Handbook on Oral History weaves together these many threads to display the intricate fabric of oral history worldwide. While basic interviewing skills remain fundamental to all forms of oral history, uses of the practice vary widely by nation and discipline. Oral historians may interview within a community or cross-culturally. They question the educated and the illiterate, the victors and the vanquished, those at the center of events and those on the periphery. Oral historians must be attentive to what people remember and why they forget or rearrange events of the past. They record both triumph and tragedy, whether immediately after the events when emotions still boil, or after they have simmered and individuals can reflect on their lasting impact. They experiment with modes of interview, in audio and visual formats, and apply the latest technology to conduct, preserve, and disseminate their work. They cope with legal and ethical issues that affect the doing and the using of oral history, and the relationship between interviewers and narrators, as well as archivists and researchers. They offer case studies of projects, new and well established, some undergoing transformation as new generations of oral historians reconsider what has been collected, what needs to be done, and what new equipment can offer. They evaluate implementation of oral history in education and pubic presentation. The articles in this volume reflect the past and project future directions. Having grown more widely used and accepted than ever, oral history will continue to evolve with the latest technologies and spawn new interpretations, testing practitioners' creativity in their applications.

NOTES

1. Emanuel Le Roy Ladurie, *Montaillou: The Promised Land of Error* (New York: Vintage, 1979); John C. Dann, ed., *The Revolution Remembered: Eyewitness Accounts of the War for Independence* (Chicago: University of Chicago Press, 1980); Ira Berlin, Marc Favreau, and Steven F. Miller, *Remembering Slavery: African Americans Talk About Their Personal Experiences of Slavery and Emancipation* (New York: New Press, 1998); Donald A. Ritchie, *Doing Oral History: A Practical Guide* (New York: Oxford University Press, 2003), 19–23.

2. Paul Thompson, "Britain Strikes Back: Two Hundred Years of 'Oral History,'" *Oral History Association Newsletter* 15 (Summer 1981), 4–5; see the uses of "oral history" in "Ancient North Americans," *New York Times*, Dec. 13, 1879; and "Norse Discovery of America Held Proved in Manuscripts," *New York Times*, Sept. 29, 1923.

3. "Joe Gould Dead; 'Last Bohemian,'" *New York Times*, Aug. 20, 1957; Joseph Mitchell, *Joe Gould's Secret* (New York: Viking, 1965).

4. Allen Nevins, "The Uses of Oral History," in *Oral History at Arrowhead: The Proceedings of the First National Colloquium on Oral History*, ed. Elizabeth I. Dixon and James V. Mink, Sept. 15–28, 1966, 25–37 (Los Angeles: Oral History Association, 1969).

5. Jacques Barzun and Henry F. Graff, *The Modern Researcher* (New York: Harcourt, Brace, and World, 1957), n132, 213.

6. Antony Grafton, *The Footnote: A Curious History* (Cambridge, Mass.: Harvard University Press, 1997), 51.

7. "History on a Sound Track," *New York Times*, Jan. 14, 1950.

8. Ronald J. Grele, "Oral History as Evidence," in *Handbook of Oral History*, ed. Thomas L. Charlton, Lois E. Myers, and Rebecca Sharpless, 48 (Lanham, Md.: AltaMira Press, 2006).

9. Paul Thompson, *The Voice of the Past: Oral History* (New York: Oxford University Press, 2000 [1978]); Alistair Thomson, "Oral History and Community History in Britain: Personal and Critical Reflections on Twenty-Five Years of Continuity and Change," *Oral History* 36 (Spring 2008): 95–104; Ronald Blythe, *Akenfield: Portrait of an English Village* (London: Allen Lane, 1969); Lynn Abrams, "Revisiting Akenfield: Forty Years of an Iconic Text," *Oral History* 37 (Spring 2009): 33–42.

10. John de Graaf and Alan Harris Stein, "The Guerrilla Journalist as Oral Historian: An Interview with Louis 'Studs' Terkel," *Oral History Review* 29 (Winter/Spring 2002): 87–107.

11. P. Thompson, *Voice of the Past*; Thompson with Tony Wailey and Trevor Lummis, *Living the Fishing* (London: Routledge and Kegan Paul, 1983); and Cathy Courtney and Paul Thompson, *City Lives: The Changing Voices of British Finance* (London: Methuen, 1996).

12. A. Dunlap-Smith, "South African Oral History Taped to Preserve Spirit of Movement and Its Leaders," *Columbia University Record* 25 (Dec. 10, 1999); Philippe Denis and Radikobo Ntsimane, *Oral History in a Wounded Country: Interactive Interviewing in South Africa* (Pietermaritzburg: University of KwaZuli-Natal Press, 2008); Coral Edwards and Peter Read, *The Lost Children: Thirteen Australians Taken From Their Aboriginal Families Tell of the Struggle to Find Their Natural Parents* (Sydney: Doubleday, 1989); Sean Field, "Imagining Communities: Memories, Loss and Resilience in Post-Apartheid Cape Town," and Maria Nugent, "Mapping Memories: Oral History for Aboriginal Cultural Heritage in New South Wales, Australia," in *Oral History and Public Memories*, ed. Paula Hamilton and Linda Shopes, 47–64, 107–24 (Philadelphia: Temple University Press, 2008).

13. Leonard Rapport, "How Valid Are the Federal Writers' Project Life Stories: An Iconoclast Among the True Believers," *Oral History Review* 7 (1979): 6–17.

14. *Oral History Association Newsletter* 24 (Spring 1990): 2.

15. Paul Thompson, "Raphael Samuel, 1934–96: An Appreciation," *Oral History* 25 (1997): 30–37.

16. A roster of those who attended is provided in Elizabeth I. Dixon and James V. Mink, eds., *Oral History at Arrowhead: The Proceedings of the First National Colloquium on Oral History* (Los Angeles: Oral History Association, 1969), 92–95.

17. Rob Perks, "The Challenges of Web Access to Archival Oral History in Britain," *International Association of Sound and Audiovisual Archives Journal* 32 (Jan. 2009): 74–82.

18. See, for instance, Alessandro Portelli, "What Makes Oral History Different," Popular Memory Group; "Popular Memory: Theory, Politics, Method," and Alistair Thomson, "Anzac Memories: Putting Popular Memory into Practice in Australia," in *The Oral History Reader*, ed. Robert Perks and Alistair Thomson, 33–53, 244–54 (New York: Routledge, 2006).

19. Robert N. Butler, "The Life Review: An Interpretation of Reminiscence in the Aged," in *New Thoughts on Old Age*, ed. Robert Kastenbaum, 265–80 (New York: Springer, 1964); and Butler, *Why Survive? Being Old in America* (New York: Harper and Row, 1975).

20. See Joanna Bornat, ed., *Reminiscence Reviewed: Evaluations, Achievements, Perspectives* (Balmoor, UK: Open University Press, 1994); Joanna Bornat, Robert Perks, Paul Thompson, and Jan Walmsley, eds., *Oral History, Health, and Welfare* (New York: Routledge, 2000); Douwe Draaisma, *Why Life Speeds Up As You Get Older: How Memory Shapes Our Past* (New York: Cambridge University Press, 2004).

21. James Holstein and Jaber Gubrium, *The Active Interview* (Thousand Oaks, Calif.: Sage, 1995).

22. Robert Butler conversation with the author, Apr. 19, 1988, at a dinner at Georgetown University's Intercultural Center commemorating the twentieth anniversary of Eugene McCarthy's maverick presidential campaign.

23. See Claire Moon, *Narrating Political Reconciliation: South Africa's Truth and Reconciliation Commission* (Lanham, Md.: Lexington Books, 2008).

24. Alessandro Portelli, *The Death of Luigi Trastulli, and Other Stories: Form and Meaning in Oral History* (Albany: State University of New York Press, 1991); *The Order Has Been Carried Out: History, Memory, and Meaning of a Nazi Massacre in Rome* (New York: Palgrave Macmillan, 2003).

25. Robert R. Weyeneth, "History, He Wrote: Murder, Politics and the Challenges of Public History in a Community with a Secret," *Public Historian* 16 (Spring 1994): 51–73; Robert D. Kaplan, *Balkan Ghosts: A Journey Through History* (New York: St. Martin's Press, 1993), 237.

26. William H. McNeil, "Weapon of Mass Destruction," *New York Review of Books* 51 (Apr. 8, 2004), 3–4.

27. Stephen Sloan, "Oral History and Hurricane Katrina: Reflections on Shouts and Silences," *Oral History Review* 35 (2008); Luke Leonard and C. Reider Howe, "How The Homeless of Central Florida Experienced Three Hurricanes: Charley, Frances, and Jeanne," *Public History News* 26 (Fall 2005): 3.

28. http://graphics8.nytimes.com/packages/html/nyregion/20050812_WTC_GRAPHIC/met_WTC_histories_full_01.html; John Lonnquist, "The U.S. Army Corps of Engineers Office of History Since 9/11," *Federalist: Newsletter of the Society for History in the Federal Government* 7 (Fall 2005): 3.

29. Kiera Butler, "Other Voices," *Columbia Journalism Review* 42 (July/Aug. 2006): 28–32.

30. Alex Kingsbury, "Making History," *U.S. News & World Report* (Sept. 24, 2007), 49–53.

BIBLIOGRAPHY

Charlton, Thomas L., Lois E. Myers, and Rebecca Sharpless, eds. *Handbook of Oral History*. Lanham, Md.: AltaMira Press, 2006.

Grele, Ronald. *Envelopes of Sound: The Art of Oral History*. New York: Praeger, 1991.

Perks, Robert, and Alistair Thomson, eds. *The Oral History Reader*. New York: Routledge, 2006.

Ritchie, Donald A. *Doing Oral History: A Practical Guide*. New York: Oxford University Press, 2003.

Thompson, Paul. *The Voice of the Past: Oral History*. New York: Oxford University Press, 2000.

Yow, Valerie Raleigh. *Recording Oral History: A Guide for the Humanities and Social Sciences*. Walnut Creek, Calif.: AltaMira Press, 2005.

PART I

THE NATURE OF INTERVIEWING

CHAPTER 1

THE DYNAMICS OF INTERVIEWING

MARY KAY QUINLAN

INTERVIEWS are everywhere.

"Senator, you ran on a platform of ending the war. How do you explain your vote to authorize more money for troops?"

"Did you know that State U. is in the top twenty in U.S. News and World Report's latest college rankings?" "I don't really put much credence in those rankings." "Oh. [Telephone solicitor for the alumni association pauses. My response clearly isn't on her script.] But isn't it great?" "If you say so."

"Sir, do you have any idea how fast you were driving?"

"What did you do in school today, honey?" "Oh, nothing."

"Would you like fries and a medium drink with that?"

From the profound to the perfunctory, question-asking permeates modern society. While we generally do not dignify the fast food cashier's inquiry about an order by calling it an interview, it is, in fact, a purposeful attempt to get information, however limited, by asking a particular question in a particular, if prescribed, way. Sometimes, of course, the questioner does not want information, like the alumni association solicitor. At other times, the respondent, wise to the conventions of culture, knows that a question—*How are you today?*—is not really a question at all but an alternate way of saying hello. Nonetheless, the purposeful exchanges of questions and answers—these commonplace mini-interviews—characterize our days.

Beyond such conversational exchanges are the more formal, conscious interviews that dominate some professionals' lives. Search the keyword "interviewing" in a university library's online catalog and be prepared to scroll through hundreds of entries. There're *88 Mistakes Interviewers Make* and *Conversations at Random* and the Social Security Administration's manual for interviewing applicants for old-age, survivors, and disability insurance, and the Army Public Affairs Office's guide for radio and television interviews. There're *Questions and Answers in Attitude Surveys* and *The Executive's Guide to Handling Press Interviews* and *Interviewing Victims and Witnesses of Crime* and scores of manuals aimed at nurses, social workers, teachers, child support enforcement workers, police interrogators, telephone solicitors, law firm recruiters, market researchers, mental health professionals, counselors, and all manner of other helpers. One library has nineteen books on radio talk show interviews alone and several dozen on interviewing child abuse victims. There's a book on "computer-assisted interviewing" and another about "active" interviews. (What, one wonders, is an inactive interview?)

Everyone, it seems, is an interviewer—but not everyone is an oral historian. Tucked in among the entries listed under "interviewing" are a few references to oral history interviews. Perhaps the scant number of entries signifies nothing more than a gap in the library's collections policy, since there are plenty of print and online resources aimed at audiences interested in doing oral history interviews. Indeed, oral history, in its generic sense, has become wildly popular—in classrooms and community clubs, state fairs and railroad stations, corporate headquarters and homeless shelters. StoryCorps will allow you and your grandmother to record your stories in a traveling booth.[1] Or you can go online to find all manner of audio and video oral histories, ranging from energetic middle school classes with access to high-tech equipment and easy-to-use computer software, to professional oral history archives, fully transcribed and featuring photos and links to related information you did not even imagine you wanted to know.

What sometimes gets lost in oral history practitioners' enthusiasm over the vastly expanded and readily available mechanisms to *do* something with oral history interviews is the reality that at its core, the oral history interview has changed little since the earliest days of wire recording devices. It remains an intensely interpersonal exchange between a prepared interviewer and a willing narrator who set out purposely to record the narrator's first-person information and experiences in a structured interview setting and to make that information available to others. The interview may be part of a large project whose planners intend to carry out elaborate forms of online publication. Or it may be an intensely personal effort by a student to document a beloved grandparent's life for the purpose of creating a family keepsake. Whatever the motive and whatever the end product, the oral history interview itself is the bedrock upon which all the rest depends, and understanding the dynamics of an oral history interview is essential to creating one whose depth and substance contribute to the public record in a meaningful way.

Interview-Based Research

To many people, the word *interview* conjures up an image of a television journalist peering knowingly into the camera ready for verbal engagement with some politician whose behavior has raised eyebrows, the grief-stricken parents of a drive-by shooting victim, or the athlete whose press agent has arranged a self-serving appearance. The common denominator in all such interviews is its entertainment value. It is, of course, possible to find broadcast interview programs in which thoughtful, if necessarily abbreviated, exchanges occur between reporters and news sources, and viewers can come away with new information and insights. Many fine documentaries include excerpts from longer interviews. But the reality for most television reporters is that only rarely do they have the luxury of conducting extensive background interviews, like the two-hour session state nursing home regulators in Nebraska once spent with student print reporters who were preparing to profile all the senior care centers in one rural county. What made for authoritative reporting would not have made compelling television. But the distinctions between interviews conducted for television and for the print media are increasingly blurring as newspapers cut staff and send reporters out with video cameras so they can post interview excerpts online; such in-depth background research may be on its way to becoming a luxury for print journalists as well. The convergence of print and broadcast techniques often leads to ever shallower reporting on both sides.

While broadcast interviews offer a poor model for would-be oral historians in their premium on snappy answers, some similarities between journalistic approaches to interviewing and oral history approaches are worth noting. All in-depth interviewers, whether news reporters or oral historians, do their homework first, rely heavily on open-ended questions, probe for details, and seek to verify unclear points. Reporters, like oral historians, are likely to record the interview, but there their practices diverge. Journalists seldom have the time or reason to create complete verbatim transcripts of an interview nor are a reporter's interviews usually archived in a public repository, as oral history interviews often are. The fundamental difference between the two approaches lies in the distinct purposes for which the interviews are conducted. Journalists usually conduct relatively short interviews, often with little advance notice to the interviewee, for a narrow, short-term purpose—a news or feature story that will be published or broadcast within hours or days at the most. Oral historians, ideally with considerable advance planning, usually conduct longer, in-depth interviews whose immediate product may be a verbatim transcript deposited in an archival collection and listed in a finding aid many weeks or even months after the interview. Those distinct purposes set journalistic and oral history interviews apart.

Ethnographic interviews, another scholarly form of qualitative research, also bear some resemblance to oral history interviews but, like journalistic interviews, also feature important distinctions. Ethnographers may conduct in-depth, recorded interviews but generally focus less on historical events than cultural folkways. An ethnographer may not record interviews in any formal way, but instead take the role of participant-observer, making copious notes after a day's encounters with people in the community being studied. Unlike oral historians who seek interviews with specific individuals because of their involvement in the topic at hand, ethnographers may take the approach of talking to whomever seems willing. The scholarly standard for ethnographic writing customarily also encourages the researcher to create pseudonyms for persons who were interviewed and observed, while ethical standards for oral historians and journalists require using the real names and identities of those they interview, except in extraordinary circumstances.

While these three interview-based research methods share certain similarities, and their practitioners can learn constructive techniques from each other, their differences are more notable. So also are lessons likely to be learned by studying techniques of all those other question-asking professions. An oral history interview is not quite like the others.

What, then, are the dynamics of an oral history? What are the forces that move and change within an interview setting? The short answer is: *Every* aspect of an oral history interview, including a number of factors preceding the interview itself, affects the intense relationship that develops between those engaged in the interview.

The evolution of the nomenclature applied to an interview's players provides some clues to the dynamics of an interview and to oral historians' sensitivity to what is really going on when two people sit down to record an oral history. The person asking the questions is customarily called the "interviewer." While that term is widely accepted, some scholars have objected to calling the person being asked the questions an "interviewee" or "interview subject," suggesting that such words imply an unequal power relationship, with the interviewee's role being that of a person to whom something is being done. As a consequence, some oral histories refer to the person being questioned as the "informant," a term common to ethnographic research. But that term has connotations that others find objectionable. An oral history project created by the Society of Former Agents of the FBI settled on "interviewee," because the retired agents they wanted to interview equated "informant" with an insider who reveals a group's secrets. The term "narrator" has also been used for the person answering the questions or telling the "narrative." This synonym for storyteller has become popular in other spheres as well, with everything from feature stories to art exhibits being described as narratives. The choice of words for the participants in an oral history interview is more important to some scholars than others, but most agree that the oral history process is a collaborative one in which both players make equally important contributions.

Factors That Affect Interviews

Just as the choice of titles may have some bearing on the way the players approach the interview, so also the purpose of an oral history project can contribute to the interview itself. Some community-based oral history projects, such as those involving the homeless, migrant workers, and other disenfranchised groups, use the oral history process as well as the content of the interviews to achieve an explicit political or social end. The interviewer and those being interviewed might be committed to a common goal and therefore will engage in the interview process with a fervor they might not have if they did not believe the project would result in some demonstrable improvement in the lives of those involved. Whether such mission-oriented oral history projects reach their political or social goals, sharing an overarching political or social mission establishes a purpose for the interview that affects the process.

Even if political or social change is not an overt purpose, and an oral history project is dedicated to a more neutral goal of fleshing out the historical record for an archival collection, narrators who agree to participate generally share the project organizers' conviction that preserving information about their concerns is worthwhile as a benefit for future generations. While they may have less missionary zeal, they nonetheless are likely to approach the project in a positive manner, which will likewise affect the interview dynamics. In short, they *want* to tell their stories. Narrators, in fact, sometimes like hearing themselves tell their own stories more than the interviewers do.

The specific end product for which an interview is being conducted can affect an interview even before the recorder is turned on. The Oral History Association's *Principles and Standards* and *Evaluation Guidelines* advise oral historians that respect for interviewees—and a commitment never to exploit them—is fundamental and must guide all aspects of an oral history project. Some projects are driven by plans to create a video or an elaborate Web site featuring either interview excerpts or full-text transcriptions and audio. Oral history narrators, like anyone else engaged in talking to another person, consciously self-edit for a wide variety of reasons, but faced with the prospect of digital fame, some may be tempted to elaborate their roles, while others may be less than forthcoming. Still others may not care about how their words are used. Each of these reactions affects the interview dynamics.

Access to online oral history collections has dramatically improved the ability of scholars to locate new primary sources related to their research. At least in theory, there is no difference between an oral history collection that deposited its interviews in a library or archives, and one that has posted full transcripts or full audio or video recordings online. But the traffic volume of researchers requesting oral history transcripts at a library is far smaller than the online finders and users. Some participants in oral histories argue unequivocally that online access is a positive development. They want as many people as possible to have access to their information. Others, however, have expressed concern that the increased potential for misuse of oral histories online poses a risk of harm for narrators, which ought to be considered. Decisions on end products and final disposition of oral history materials have a bearing on the interview dynamics, too.

Before the interviewer presses "record," another factor influencing the interview relates to the circumstances that led to the project in the first place. Increasingly, oral historians have adopted a journalist's sense of urgency in their efforts to document the aftermath of manmade and natural disasters, from the September 11, 2001, terrorist attacks to the hurricanes that devastated the U.S. Gulf Coast and other "emerging crises." That very sense of urgency—the notion that oral historians must begin immediately to document the experiences of those involved in a catastrophic event before the fire is out—creates a dynamic within the interview setting that cannot be ignored. The drive to get the stories down right away may contribute to a focus on the drama of the situation, just as immediacy marks the defining characteristic of breaking news. Yet, the type of distance over time from the event, which is the more usual approach of an oral history and most clearly distinguishes it from journalism, allows for more reflection and analysis. Columbia University's September 11 oral history project provides an effort to combine the two, interviewing immediately after the events and re-interviewing the same narrators after some time has passed. Project managers found that some of the original narrators declined to be re-interviewed because they needed "time *not* to talk about it."[2]

Outside the interview itself, the physical environment in which the interview takes place will affect the exchange. The location may evoke important memories for the narrators and contribute to the depth of their recollections and responses. For both the narrator and interviewer, the physical features of the place—the temperature, room size, light level, ambient noises, chair comfort, visual distractions, and the like—all create an environment that can make an interview more or less challenging to complete. Whenever interview participants have to vie with their surroundings to focus on the topic at hand, the dynamics of the interview will change. Experienced oral historians try to examine the interview setting in advance to minimize potential distractions and disruptions.

Another environmental factor may be the presence of additional individuals. Oral history interviews customarily involve only two participants. Some projects use multiple interviewers, but they still question one person at a time. Sometimes, despite the interviewer's best efforts to limit the interview to one person, a family member or friend will join in, which will significantly alter the relationship between the interviewer and interviewee. With two or more persons serving as narrators, the most outspoken person in the group will almost always dominate the discussion and set the agenda for permitted topics or comments. The group members may argue among themselves, which may yield some interesting insights to the topic at hand, but it will complicate the effort to transcribe the interview and may not be the best use of limited interviewing time. Occasionally, an interview with more than one person yields unexpected rewards. An interview had been arranged with the former mayor of a small, farm-dependent community that had seen livelier days. At the last moment, the mayor's wife joined in, and the interaction between them led to rich recollections. Between them, they reminded each other of details about the community's past that likely would not have surfaced otherwise.

Having multiple players in the interview setting is sometimes unavoidable. One community history project used a visually impaired volunteer interviewer who needed an assistant to operate the recorder. As the two volunteers worked together, the equipment helper gradually evolved into a second interviewer, asking follow-up questions and suggesting avenues to pursue that the first interviewer welcomed because it expanded the content and quality of the interview. Also unavoidable are those occasions when a translator is needed. The translator's skills and relationship to the narrator will be critical elements in the interview dynamic. Relying on a family member as the translator can significantly inhibit what the narrator says. Having a translator with less than fluent skills in both languages can lead to confusing back-and-forth side discussions about vocabulary and meaning in the question-answer process.

Beyond the players at the table in an oral history interview, the recording equipment sitting on the table will affect the process. In the early days of recording oral histories, the unwieldy size of the recorders was seen as an impediment to narrator candor. The machine was like a bulky, intrusive eavesdropper in what was intended to be an open, frank exchange. Succeeding generations of recorders—now video as well as audio—have become smaller, and succeeding generations of oral history narrators have become more conversant with technology, reducing the intrusion factor. Even older people, often assumed to be reluctant technology adopters, are likely to be familiar with equipment like telephone answering machines, even if they play no video games and send no text messages. The recording technology, small and unobtrusive though it may be, can still be an impediment if the interviewer cannot operate it adeptly. The machine itself can become the center of attention because the interviewer is constantly tending it. Video interviews, which many narrators find more intrusive than audio-only recording, can actually improve the interview dynamics by using additional staff to handle the camera, microphones, lights, and any other necessary equipment, thus freeing the interviewer to focus on the narrator's story.

The Well-Prepared Interviewer

Many of the factors affecting interview dynamics will be beyond one's control, while other elements will be well within the interviewer's purview. The most important—and controllable—factor is the amount of research that goes into preparing for an oral history interview. Journalists, for their part, are accustomed to dropping work on one story and dashing off to tackle breaking news with no time for preparation beyond what they recall from their accumulated storehouse of knowledge, and an instinct about what questions to ask honed from their experience. Oral historians, by contrast, can take more time to study general background information about the topic at hand as well as to gather biographical information about the person being interviewed. Thorough research is a critical element in the interview dynamics.

A well-informed interviewer can more easily establish rapport with a narrator. This shows that the interviewer was interested enough to learn about the topic and the individual beforehand. Research also identifies new lines of inquiry not already on the public record. A prepared interviewer can use the interview time effectively by not dwelling on areas that are already commonly known but can probe for more details, and ask for interpretation and analysis that the narrator may not have revealed previously.

An interviewer who is already conversant with the topic or with the narrator's background can readily fill in the blanks if the narrator's memory falters over dates, places, and people's names. Such memory lapses unnerve narrators. During an interview with a retired college administrator, the dean stumbled over trying to recall the year he had finished graduate school. The interviewer was not prepared to supply the year (which could have been determined readily from biographical materials) and did not say, "Don't worry, we can look that up later." Instead, the interviewer harangued the dean with questions aimed at trying to figure it out: Was it before this? Was it after that? Would it have been right when such-and-such? This exchange derailed the interview and nothing of substance emerged thereafter. The transcript even reflects the narrator calling out to his wife, apparently in another room, in case she could remember the date. A poorly prepared interviewer (or one who regards the interview as a quiz with right and wrong answers) can offend and embarrass the narrator and decrease the prospect that another interviewer would be given a second chance.

Even when thoroughly prepared, interviewers walk a fine line between earning a narrator's respect by showing that they've done their homework and evoking enmity by showing off about how much they know. Appearing to be the know-it-all in an oral history interview can set up a destructive dynamic. If narrators perceive that interviewers are not really interested in anything they have to say, they become intimidated or offended and unresponsive. Sometimes oral history projects use interviewers who had a role in the topic at hand themselves. The interviewers' firsthand knowledge can be an advantage in guiding the narrators to deeper levels of detail and analysis. But these participant-interviewers will also have to struggle against the temptation to argue with narrators or offer their own versions of the past, which may be sharply at odds. Interviewers should, of course, probe narrators about divergent interpretations of the matter at hand, but oral history interviews are not debating forums, where those asking the questions clash with those being asked to recall and respond. Some oral history project planners try to forestall this possibility by first interviewing the interviewers. That way, the interviewers have had a chance to put their own versions of the past on the record, which may make them more willing to listen to their narrators' views rather than express their own.

The degree of preparation determines how skillfully an interviewer will be able to ask questions. It is the nature of the questions themselves that make an interview uniquely "oral history" and not any of the other types of question-asking exchanges. An oral history interview is not a conversation with a more-or-less equal exchange of ideas. Both the narrator and interviewer have equally important *roles* to play in the collaboration, but they usually do not contribute equal amounts of *information*. An oral history transcript should reflect a few lines from the interviewer, whose responsibility is to question, followed by many lines of response from the narrator, given ample time to respond.

An oral history interview's success hinges on questions that are neutrally framed, open-ended, and asked one at a time. Similar questions may be part of a journalist's question-asking repertoire, but because a journalist, operating on deadline, tends to have an immediate focus that is considerably narrower than that of an oral historian, the journalist's questions are likely to be much more narrowly framed. Both journalists and oral historians are trained to listen carefully, ask follow-up questions, clarify inconsistencies, probe for additional details, and ask for interpretation. Journalists, however, usually fill the silent spaces in interviews by quickly asking new questions rather than waiting through the narrators' pauses to see if they will volunteer something more. Quite often, given more time, narrators will tell the story in more detail and reveal things they might otherwise have held back. A narrator's silence, or struggle to frame a response, is actually part of the information gathered in the oral history interview and may warrant follow-up questions.

Like political pollsters, thoroughly prepared oral history interviewers are keenly aware of the subtle ways that the wording of a question can suggest the "right" answer. A responsible oral historian would be unlikely to ask: "You didn't like living there, did you?" A more open-ended version might be: "How did you like living there?" Even that phrasing presumes a "liking" by the narrator. Instead, "Tell me about living there" allows the narrators to take the lead in choosing how to answer. Perhaps they neither liked nor disliked the place; it was just a temporary home considered so ephemeral as not to warrant liking or hating.

While most oral historians advocate asking neutrally framed questions to avoid signaling to the narrator what answers are expected, some have noted that the choice of questions to ask, like the choice of narrators, inevitably reflects biases. Even asking neutral questions about a person's background signifies that the interviewer believes it is important to know about the narrator's upbringing, which in itself reflects a value judgment.[3] It is worth noting, however, that asking questions about a person's background also serves a practical function in an interview setting. Most people can speak freely and comfortably about their backgrounds, so they start talking, and the interview unfolds.

An interviewer with a clear plan, knowledgeable questions, and respectful listening skills can put a nervous narrator at ease, increasing the likelihood that the narrator will be open and forthcoming in responding to questions. Awareness of body language cues—arms crossed, nervous laughter, fingers drumming the arm of the chair, head turned away—can also help the interviewer recognize when the oral history has crossed into troublesome territory for the narrator. This may prompt additional follow-up questions or a change of subject. Prepared interviewers will be able to judge when they need to abandon their planned interview structure altogether because the narrator's more interesting stories turn out not to be the ones the interviewer expected. In some cases, an interview structured chronologically may be an ineffective approach for a narrator who recalls details by association rather than by time sequence.

Attention to "reading" people is a key to an oral historian's ability to guide the interview. From the initial greeting between interviewer and narrator, the personal characteristics of each one will contribute to how the relationship evolves during the interview. They move from strangers to historical collaborators—a relationship in which narrators may well come to tell the interviewer things they would not normally say. People participate in an oral history because they *want* the story preserved, but they still need to be reassured that the process will not exploit them.[4] The challenge for the oral historian is to build a level of trust that will facilitate openness, whether the two players share most personal traits or are distinctly different. Relative age, gender, race or ethnic background, educational background, social status, religion, regional identity, relationship to each other, and even relative degree of emotional commitment to the project are among the key factors that can affect the interview dynamics. How such characteristics play off against one another is a matter of endless debate, but attempts at ideal pairings of interviewer and narrator are seldom practical, given the limitations of time and staff.

For some oral historians, the biggest challenge related to personal characteristics centers on the race or ethnic background of the interviewer and narrator. The United States has a long history of blacks and whites being unable "to deal with one another in open, candid ways."[5] This reality manifests itself in interview settings, as scholars have observed of the Federal Writers' Project's 1930s interviews (precursors to modern oral history) with former slaves. The Depression-era Federal Writers' Project must be understood in the context of what it was: a mechanism to employ *writers*, among out-of-work, white-collar, educated people, who were perhaps more interested in hearing a great story than in documenting actual life experiences.[6] During the 1930s African Americans were treated as inferior, particularly in the South, which became an unavoidable part of the unspoken communication in the interviews and an overarching reality that affects their subsequent use. Two interviews with the same elderly African American woman illustrate the point. One interviewer was a white woman, the other a black man. The accounts she offered each of them differed dramatically. In other interviews, former slaves quite openly acknowledged their lack of candor with white interviewers: "Oh, I know your father en your grandfather en all of dem. Bless Mercy, child, I don't want to tell you nothin' but what to please you."[7]

More recently, in one midwestern city with a small black population, a young, white woman involved in an oral history project aimed at documenting early African American life in the community interviewed an elderly black woman, long a resident of the community and the granddaughter of slaves. Both women were acquainted before being involved in the oral history project, but their first formal oral history interview revealed considerable discomfort for both of them when racial issues were the focus of questions. Rather than relate a story about her slave grandmother, the narrator said: "Well, I'll skip that." The interviewer, for her part, passed up many opportunities to ask follow-up questions related to Ku Klux Klan activity in the town, relationships with people of other races, education, and the like. After critiquing her first interview, the young woman came to terms with her own discomfort at causing discomfort for a woman she deeply respected. She wrote an introduction to their next interview in which she acknowledged the difficulty both of them had in speaking frankly about racial issues but emphasized the value of creating a record of an African American woman's experience growing up at a time of entrenched, institutional racism. "You can teach us what it was like, and we can put together a document for others to learn from and gain a better understanding of what it was like for you go grow up here," the interviewer said, adding: "It may be difficult for me to ask you certain questions, and difficult for you to answer, but I hope we can try.... Right now I am available and would like to see what you and I can accomplish."[8]

Subsequent interview sessions revealed greater willingness by the interviewer to ask race-related questions and an apparent greater openness by the narrator to respond with more candor as the relationship between the two of them evolved. Would the interview have been different if a young African American woman had been asking the questions? Undoubtedly, as it would have been if the interviewer was an African American man or a Hispanic woman. The possible theoretical combinations are endless, but under the circumstances there was only one actual combination. The pair talked about their initial discomfort on the record for future readers to make of it what they will.

Here are some examples of how other combinations of personal characteristics affect the interview dynamics:

1. An oral history project planner puzzled over the best person to interview a long-retired faculty member noted for disjointed conversations, even in her younger, professional days. Her normal approach to discourse frequently involved shorthand references to people and places about which she assumed her listeners knew. Such truncated discussions can be a danger in an oral history when the two players know one another well and share a common knowledge base. Without realizing it, they may resort to speaking in code: "Do you remember when what's-his-name...oh, you know the fellow I mean. Had short hair and long sideburns." "Oh, sure. Can't think of his name right offhand, but his office was next to mine. Always argued in faculty meetings about the SAB. And never did think the ACE plan made any sense." What does that mean? Hoping to avoid such an exchange, the planner suggested an oral history student as the interviewer, someone to whom the narrator would have to explain the details of her stories. The retired faculty member refused, however, insisting she would only be interviewed by someone she already knew.

2. Another oral history project planner wondered if it would be best for an emeritus faculty member to be interviewed by a seasoned professional. The man was popular with students and enjoyed working with them during his teaching career,

so a project adviser suggested that having a trained student interviewer conduct the oral history might add a spark of energy to the interview dynamic that otherwise could be lost.

3. Familiar relationships between narrator and interviewer can be a double-edged sword. Interviews with family members close to one another often are not as candid as interviews between more distant family members. Martha Ross, who taught oral history at the University of Maryland, was fond of telling her students that grandchildren could conduct effective interviews with their grandparents because they "shared a common enemy."

4. Gender pairings can be a challenge in some oral history settings, especially if family or cultural codes prevent women from sharing certain kinds of information with men and vice versa.

5. Educational background and social status, characteristics that often are related, can pose additional challenges to the dynamics of an interview. Some oral historians with advanced college degrees take on projects with low-income or illiterate narrators. But their efforts will falter because the narrators interpret the interviewers' questions—by word choice or falsely familiar mannerisms—as condescending or patronizing.

6. Educational background and social status can align the other way, too. Some oral history projects seek to interview highly educated, wealthy, busy, sophisticated professionals, some of whom attempt to intimidate everyone they meet. Interviewers who may not share such social standing can conduct effective interviews by being thoroughly prepared and confident in their ability to be equally professional in their role as oral history interviewers.

7. Regional identity of either the narrator or interviewer can also enter into the interview dynamic. Dialect, colloquialisms, slang, and insider lingo can create a wall between the participants in an oral history, as well as complicating the transcription efforts.

8. Strongly held religious or political beliefs, particularly if they are integral to an interview, can create yet another layer of complexity if the participants do not share the same beliefs. An oral history can yield greater insights and depth of understanding about the topics at hand as long as the participants remember that the purpose of the exchange is to explore and document ideas, not engage in arguments or ad hominem attacks. Even ideas an interviewer may consider abhorrent are worth documenting and probing for greater historical understanding.

9. Aspects of the players' physical appearance or mannerisms—weight, body piercing, gum chewing, nail biting, smoking, hairstyle, attire, physical disabilities—also can influence the interview. Narrators might be put off by characteristics they consider peculiar in an interviewer, and the reverse might also be true. The Artists With Disabilities Oral History Project at the University of California, Berkeley's Regional Oral History Office, illustrated how narrators with pronounced physical disabilities and a respectful interviewer could develop engaging relationships, yielding important insights about the narrators' life experiences.

Documenting the Interview Experience

With so many variables affecting the interview dynamics, what is an oral historian to do? Most importantly, interviewers need to recognize them, document them, and take them into account in conducting and analyzing the content of oral history interviews. Preservation and documentation are what ultimately distinguish oral history interviewing from the many other forms of interviews we encounter in everyday life.

Oral historians have noted that no research, not just oral history, is a value-free process. While scholars do not customarily comment on their reactions to documents, even the search for documents involves personal experiences that readers are entitled to know as part of the context within which to understand a scholar's work.[9] Journalists, while not considered scholarly, do this quite frequently. A news organization will call attention to its "exclusive" interview or make a show of reporting that it took a court order to get documents requested under the Freedom of Information Act. What journalists may not as readily acknowledge, however, is that sometimes the documents or the exclusive interview yielded little of importance. As a result, the dramatic circumstances involved in obtaining the information often leads to overplayed news stories.

Oral historians come to the table with a perspective. They are never really neutral. As the oral history pioneer Saul Benison noted: "There is no such thing as writing objective history. It's like reading the telephone book, if you were going to write objective history. It would be a series of names. It would be meaningless."[10] Yet, an oral history interview is about making meaning, and all parties to the process—including those who will use the interviews years after they were created—come with a personal perspective that will affect its meaning. It is not the same as a chemistry class in which the textbook tells students how to do the lab experiment, with a reasonable expectation that the results will be the same each time. Oral history interviews will not come out the same because each is a unique encounter between two individuals undertaking a conscious, purposeful effort *today* to reconstruct a past they did not share in an effort to explore and understand its meaning for *tomorrow*. Because they are unique encounters, the players need to acknowledge their individuality and document the circumstances surrounding the interview. Only in that way will those who encounter the interview in the future have a chance of understanding the layers of meaning the oral history collaborators have created through that commonplace, yet complex, process of asking and answering questions.

NOTES

1. http://www.storycorps.net
2. Columbia University's Mary Marshall Clark, quoted in "Documenting Sept. 11, 2001: Two Years Later," *Oral History Association Newsletter* (Winter 2003): 9.

3. Ronald J. Grele, ed., *Envelopes of Sound: The Art of Oral History* (New York: Praeger, 1991), 85.

4. Valerie Raleigh Yow, "Ethics and Interpersonal Relationships in Oral History Research," *Oral History Review* 22 (Summer 1995): 51.

5. James West Davidson and Mark Hamilton Lytle, *After the Fact: The Art of Historical Detection* (New York: Alfred A. Knopf, 1986), 185.

6. Bruce M. Stave, "'The Doctor Told Us What He Wanted': Sam Koenig's Instructions to WPA Ethnic Group Survey Interviewers," *Oral History Review* 34 (2007): 17–25.

7. Davidson and Lytle, *After the Fact*, 191.

8. Quoted in Barbara W. Sommer and Mary Kay Quinlan, *The Oral History Manual* (Walnut Creek, Calif.: AltaMira Press, 2009), 71.

9. Valerie Raleigh Yow, "'Do I Like Them Too Much?' Effects of the Oral History Interview on the Interviewer and Vice-Versa," *Oral History Review* 24 (Summer 1997): 70.

10. Grele, *Envelopes of Sound*, 85.

BIBLIOGRAPHY

Frisch, Michael. *A Shared Authority: Essays on the Craft and Meaning of Oral and Public History*. Albany: State University of New York Press, 1990.

Grele, Ronald, J., ed. *Envelopes of Sound: The Art of Oral History*. New York: Praeger, 1991.

Ritchie, Donald A. *Doing Oral History: A Practical Guide*. New York: Oxford University Press, 2003.

Sommer, Barbara W., and Mary Kay Quinlan. *The Oral History Manual*. Walnut Creek, Calif.: AltaMira Press, 2009.

Yow, Valerie Raleigh. *Recording Oral History: A Guide for the Humanities and Social Sciences*. Walnut Creek, Calif.: AltaMira Press, 2005.

CHAPTER 2

THOSE WHO PREVAILED AND THOSE WHO WERE REPLACED: INTERVIEWING BOTH SIDES OF A CONFLICT

MIROSLAV VANĚK

"WE are not masses; we are people!" Of all the slogans we heard on Prague's Wenceslas Square and Letná Plain in November 1989, this is the one I remember the most, because it contains the core of oral history. It is possible to incorporate a "mass" into statistics, to indicate it more or less precisely as the "agent of history," and to generalize its role and meaning in important historical events, but people live their own private lives in calm as well as in stormy times. Their experiences, attitudes, and evolving opinions allow us to see the living side of history, which is constantly reminding us of itself even in the present. Oral history should not be seen as the opposite of written sources in archives but as two sides of the same coin. A coin, to be valid, needs to be minted on both sides. Similarly, history should include both the facts about events and occurrences as well as the personal experiences of individuals who lived through these events, who reacted to them, and whose attitudes helped shape their pace and direction.[1]

In order to understand modern Czech history, we can begin with a simple arithmetic problem: For how many years in the twentieth century was Czechoslovakia (or the Czech lands) truly free and independent? That small cultural and industrial Central European country comprised part of the Habsburg or Austrian empire until 1918, when the first independent Czechoslovak Republic was established. Following twenty years of freedom this republic was occupied in 1939 by Nazi Germany and became the Protectorate of Bohemia and Moravia. The great international conferences at Yalta and Potsdam in 1945 incorporated Czechoslovakia into the Eastern bloc of countries led by the Soviet Union. When the Communist Party of Czechoslovakia (CPC) took power in February 1948, the country's fate was sealed for the next two decades. Then came the "Prague Spring" of 1968, when reformers in the Czechoslovak Communist leadership introduced a program of broader democratization and liberalization in an attempt to humanize the socialist system. These steps toward greater openness were quashed by the Soviet-led invasion of the Warsaw Pact armed forces in August 1968, after which another two decades of oppression ensued. This final period of Communist rule, officially referred to as *normalizace*, "normalization,"ended with the November revolution in 1989. At that time, the country was reborn as a democratic, independent republic and an integral part of Western civic society. All in all, the country experienced only thirty-three years of freedom during the twentieth century. During the forty years of Communist rule, Czech historiography found itself in a situation similar to that of the Czech people. It could not develop freely and was isolated for many years from modern world trends and developments. This was also the case in the field of oral history.

We Czech historians who are investigating our country's contemporary history using oral history methodology have made research into the development of society during the Communist era, including the period of normalization, one of our top priorities. In general, the only accessible sources for historians of the normalization period are archival documents of official provenance. In the stormy days of November 1989, however, many of these documents were lost, hidden, or destroyed. What was left presented our history only from the perspective of the former regime. Before 1989, the only half-hearted attempt historians made to utilize individual memories as a historical source came in the late 1960s with the organization of "informal discussions" with groups of prewar Communists and Czech partisans from World War II. These witnesses were asked direct questions about their memories and were expected to give presupposed, ideologically acceptable answers. Moreover, these interviews were partly-recorded, partly stenographed, and partly transcribed from notes made by interviewers whose education was ideological, not historical. During the decades of normalization, even these rare and methodologically helpless experiments had to be abandoned.

Immediately after the fall of the Communist regime in Czechoslovakia, a newfound freedom appeared in academic scholarship, opening up fresh possibilities, approaches, and opportunities for the development of historiography and historical research methods. At that time, our ideas about the theory, fieldwork, and results of oral history research in the West were underdeveloped and vague, due to our limited access to Western scholarship in this field and our almost complete lack of experience with the methodology before 1989. In the early 1990s, a small group of Czech historians took the chance provided by the new political atmosphere to expand our field, not just by exploring topics and events in our contemporary history that only recently had been officially taboo but also by seeking out new concepts and methods for doing research itself.

From the very beginning, our group encountered discouragement, warnings, and even ridicule from those colleagues who made up the conservative majority of Czech historians with their traditional ways of thinking. A number of historians who had worked under the previous regime had "changed their coats"—or switched allegiances—after 1989, and had begun examining and judging the period of normalization. Still, they remained skeptical of new methods of research. Dissidents and historians who had returned from exile were better informed about the new research methods coming out of the West (including oral history), but they were far from familiar with Czech society and its particular atmosphere, problems, and contemporary demands. Almost all of them had been educated in the Marxist-Leninist school of history. They retained their long-held beliefs about research methodology and expressed doubts about the reliability and validity of oral sources. They were convinced that it was almost impossible to obtain real and objective facts and information from an individual, or that a person's subjective opinions, views, and experiences had anything to do with "great history," which dealt exclusively with political developments.

In spite of these obstacles, those of us working at the Institute for Contemporary History (ICH) in Prague did our best to become informed about and trained in the current theories and applications of oral history methodology being used in the United States and Western Europe. Here I would like to express our gratitude to the Oral History Association (OHA) and International Oral History Association (IOHA) as well as to the several universities in the United States that hosted members of our team on various research trips. With their abundant experience, these groups enriched our knowledge of the literature on oral history and supported our first steps in the field.

One Hundred Student Revolutions

By late in the 1990s, we were ready to begin our first oral history project. The topic offered itself: We decided to record the narratives of approximately one hundred young people who, as university students in the crucial November days of 1989, had been a driving force in the popular uprisings that swept through Czechoslovakia in the first few days of the revolution. From a methodological perspective, the ex-students were an ideal choice because our sample of narrators comprised a homogenous group connected by age, education, and life experience. We published the results of this three-year project in *One Hundred Student Revolutions*, which included transcribed and edited versions of approximately two-thirds of the interviews or autobiographical stories.[2] It also contained our first attempts at analyzing and interpreting the narratives, because we felt that the historian's task was not complete after "only" recording, collecting, transcribing, editing, and publishing the interviews. In our efforts to provide evidence for the validity and reliability of oral history itself, we considered the analysis and interpretation of the interviews a necessary component to our work. Thanks to the success of this project, in 2000 our small but growing group of historians founded the Center for Oral History (COH), as part of the Institute for Contemporary History. Two years later the Center became a member of the International Oral History Association. In January 2007 the Czech Association of Oral History was established, expanding its activities through courses and seminars at various Czech universities.[3]

At the same time, we published several methodological and practical guides and articles on oral history for the growing numbers of university students and faculty from various disciplines in the humanities who were becoming interested in the subject.[4] These books discussed not only the technical aspects of doing oral history, from field work to analysis and interpretation, but also trends in the theoretical and methodological developments of the field.

Political Elites and Dissidents

The main purpose of the Center for Oral History has been to carry out large-scale projects that are fundamental—at least from our point of view—to obtaining a deeper and broader understanding of the years of normalization. Our most extensive project to date has been the three-year undertaking: "Political Élites and Dissidents in the So-called Normalization Period in Czechoslovakia: Autobiographical Interviews." This project was designed to contrast the narratives of the former power-holders with their opponents. We interviewed forty-three Communist functionaries who held office during the previous regime, along with seventy-seven dissidents or opposition activists—people who had openly and publicly opposed the regime, exposing themselves to various forms of oppression, including imprisonment in Communist jails. The edited transcripts of many of these interviews were included in the two-volume publication *The Victors? The Vanquished?*, which has enjoyed much interest from readers and provoked some heated discussions in academic circles.

At the present time, the scope and concept of this project remains unique among the countries of the former Eastern bloc. While there have been various attempts to interview the leading personalities of the new political and social orders in some post-Communist countries, these usually have dealt only with the perspective of the victors, those who prevailed. What we have added is to take into account the vanquished, those who lost.

In the atmosphere of anti-Communism in our country that was intensifying as we started our work, we were often asked why we had decided to do such a project at all. The unspoken implication was that we were compromising ourselves by allowing the former Communist functionaries to speak. We felt, however, that such questions were motivated ideologically rather than by a historical or academic concern about our work. We were also aware that our topic diverged from the current focus of oral history projects in many other countries, which has concentrated on minorities or on other specific groups on the edge of society. However, when studying Western literature on oral history, we discovered that the first oral history projects in the United States dealt with high-profile social and political actors such as politicians and outstanding personalities from various professions. We felt that the techniques and trends employed there, and in Western Europe, could provide a model for the development of oral history in our country. The previous scholarship gave us inspiration and a solid methodological foundation, and we were able to adapt some of these procedures and objectives to our own criteria. One of our most important objectives has been to study Czech society under normalization and to do so *sine ira et studio* ["without anger and fondness"] as much as possible. When deciding where to begin this research, we chose to explore the two main opposing viewpoints in politics during this period.

Redefining "Dissident"

We began the interview process with the former dissidents by establishing contacts not only in the capital, Prague—but also in small towns around the country, using the efficient snowball technique and the abundant literature available at the time.[5] The majority of them agreed to give us interviews, which were usually divided into two or more sessions with each narrator. At the first meeting, we asked them to speak freely, which they usually did, beginning with their family backgrounds and continuing up to the present. The second session (and, in some cases, the third) was conducted as a semistructured interview. We returned to interesting points that had been mentioned during the first meeting and stimulated the interviewees to express their opinions and viewpoints, and to provide more precise comments, deeper insights, and judgments about the present day, based upon the trust previously established between interviewer and interviewee.

One of the most important questions we asked the interviewees concerned the source of their hopes during the two oppressive decades following the August 1968 invasion: that the Communist regime would eventually fall and that change would occur. We posed this question to former dissidents of various ages, political opinions, and ideological orientations, including Václav Havel, the famous Czech dissident who became president of the Czech Republic. He replied:

> I have written many times that I understand hope as a spiritual state. The way I see it, someone does something simply because he thinks it's the right thing to do, and he doesn't worry about whether the effect will come earlier or later. Naturally, everyone is happier when there is an effect and the sooner the better. But that does not mean that if something is risky, that if the effect is small and it comes only after a long time, we should not do anything. It's done more as an expression of self-cleansing, of the state of a person's own spirit, mind or soul. With hindsight, it suffices to consider the climate in the dissident circles, in the so-called dissident's ghetto, which was created particularly around Charter 77... but it was basically cheerful.[6]

It is interesting to see how quickly and easily an original idea or term can be rendered sterile or cliché. Academic circles in the 1970s and the '80s in Czechoslovakia, as well as during the Velvet Revolution, frequently refer to a "dissident ghetto," an "underground ghetto," and even a "functionaries' ghetto," in spite of the fact that the term "ghetto" has, at least in Europe, a precise and clear meaning. Starting in the medieval era, a ghetto was the part of a town where Jews were *forced* to live. A ghetto was not a synonym for the isolation of an oppressed minority group fighting against a dominating and ruling majority. A ghetto was the place one was born, or in modern history where one was imprisoned because of race and family background. The dissident, the underground rock musician, and the functionary of the Communist Party of Czechoslovakia all *chose* to become members of their respective circles. They were not born dissidents, underground rockers, or Communist functionaries. For them, to be enclosed in such a ghetto was rather a question of exercising one's free will. In the case of the dissidents, life in the ghetto could represent a kind of exclusiveness (because of one's bravery) and at the same time a separation from the rest of society, which often resulted in the dissidents' inability to appreciate or share the everyday problems and worries of the majority.

If the quote above represents Václav Havel's opinions, we must take into account that in dissident circles his viewpoint was not shared by everyone who came out openly against the Communist regime. The first and most important dissidents' movement, Charter 77, was not a compact body that expressed one unified opinion. It was composed of individuals who formed roughly three groups, each with very different convictions: ex-Communist "reformers" expelled from the Party after 1968, religion-oriented people, and liberal (open-minded) thinkers and artists. Listening to their stories, we came to the conclusion that it had not been their individual political orientations, but rather their individual human qualities and features that had allowed their hope to survive during an oppressive regime. But to have and hold that hope was only one aspect of a broader problem. Working to change the regime was not just a question of ethics or spirituality; it had a practical component that could be called everyday political work. In general, as a political aim this goal was shared by the majority of dissidents. When we asked our narrators from the various dissident circles and civic initiatives about such an aim, we received a broad range of viewpoints and opinions, depending often on the age of the interviewee. Among the youngest of our narrators was Petr Placák, the leader and spokesman of an initiative called Czech Children. Placák told us quite openly:

> It was somewhat a matter of generations . . . we were not concerned with the opposition against the Communists, because that would have meant somehow giving them credit, acknowledging them as a legitimate power of sorts. That wasn't our goal. . . . To hold any kind of dialogue with the Communist power, that would have been like legitimizing them, so the Czech Children, it was an opposition against the renowned opposition [Charter 77] . . . we acknowledged what it had done, but for instance their idea of human rights, it sort of irritated me personally. From today's perspective, however, I think that what they did was the only possible thing to do, the only good program. Yet at the time it seemed to me an absurd idea, to try to convince the regime to be consistent to its own rights and rules. . . . And it was irritating for us too that core of ideas of the older dissidents generation, of those connected with the year 1968 as well as of those liberals, who spoke only about the first [prewar] Republic, as if there had not been anything before that.[7]

The young men and women in Prague who had created Czech Children were inspired by the idea of a Czech kingdom. As Petr Placák described: "We were interested in this idea naturally. . . . It could be fun, of course, a happening, yet it was also an expression of our protest against that simplification of the Czech dimension."

Although these words might sound somewhat wild and fantastic, they demonstrate the broad differences between various dissident groups. The generational divide he mentioned became more visible in the second half of the 1980s, especially in the last few years before November 1989. The new generation of young men and women, born around 1968, were growing up and coming of age, eager to speak their minds. Since they did not experience the events of 1968 personally, they were not frightened by the memory of the hardest years of the normalization period, and they took the concept of human rights as a matter of fact. It was a foundation upon which they wanted to build their more modern version of civic society. These younger dissidents did not want a slow, gradual "democratization" of political conditions, supported by a *perestroika* imported unwillingly from the Soviet Union. They wanted democracy and civic society of the standard West European type.

Even though more than twenty diverse civic initiatives existed during the final months leading up to the events of November 1989, each one claimed only a few dozen, at most a few hundred, members. They lacked sizable influence on the broader public, and in many cases even without strong contacts with it. Communist counterpropaganda against these groups portrayed them as bands of hooligans, alcoholics, and drug abusers, which cannot be discounted, since that message especially affected the country's older citizens. Many of these younger groups had started their activities for nonpolitical reasons, such as seeking "islands of freedom" where they could pursue punk rock or New Wave music, or could criticize the regime's gradual destruction of the environment and nature. Persecution by the state's security forces had driven them into opposition against the whole regime.

At the other end of the dissident spectrum stood the reformed Communists, those who had been expelled from the Communist Party after 1968. Twenty years later, a group of them formed an initiative called Revival (*Obroda* in Czech), whose objective was to return to the ideas of 1968 and finally achieve "socialism with a human face." In many respects, a broader gap in mentality existed between dissidents from the older and younger generations than between the dissidents in Revival and the younger, progressive functionaries who took their positions in the final years of the Communist regime.

After November 1989, many of the former dissidents returned to their previous professions and disengaged from politics. Another group, however, tried to participate in politics at the district, regional, or national level. Their attitude toward the post-November changes often depended on how successful they were in these attempts. There were also those who had subordinated their private and family lives to their activities in opposition to the old regime, but who were so disappointed after 1989 that they asked themselves whether it was all worth it. Some of the older dissidents had become important actors in governmental or parliamentary circles immediately after the revolution. When they found themselves being replaced by a younger generation of politicians, they felt undervalued and injured.

After collecting the interviews with this range of dissidents, we felt it necessary to reexamine the term "dissident" itself and to redefine it in light of the specific conditions of the 1970s and the 1980s. "Dissident" signified those individuals and members of independent civic initiatives who expressed their discontent with the Communist regime in public forums. Those who did so could expect to face persecution of various sorts, including imprisonment. Yet, the dissidents' level of activism and repression was not necessarily determined by their proximity to the center of power. We interviewed true opponents of the regime in small towns around our republic, who were unknown to the broader Czech public, not to mention to the Western mass media, such as Radio Free Europe, the Voice of America, and the BBC. These nearly anonymous heroes had sometimes been more vulnerable to repression than the better-known dissidents, who had greater access to the media because of their prominence or social contacts, and could thus publicize their plight to a world audience.

The interviews we conducted reminded us that no dissident or Communist functionary could be a "dissident" or "functionary" twenty-four hours a day. While both groups shared a sort of a workaholism, we expanded the focus beyond our narrators' political activism and encouraged them to talk about other aspects of their lives as well. As the project progressed, we became more convinced that even though the political or professional sides of the narrators' lives were the most visible, there also existed an almost hidden realm of everyday life. This encompassed their personal concerns, families, worries, friendships, and hobbies, issues that are usually not included in official biographies but that comprised an indispensable aspect of their lives, perhaps the most important aspect, if only on a subconscious level.

From their earliest memories up to the present, individuals in both groups lived not only in politics but also as members of their families, clubs and social organizations, or friendship circles. When speaking about the flow of everyday life, we first tried to gain the narrators' trust, after which they clearly showed us that their life was not based primarily on political (or social) connections.

Interviewing Ex-Communist Functionaries

At the beginning of the project we were uncertain (perhaps because of the skepticism of our colleagues) about whether we would be able to obtain sincere and useful interviews from the ex-Communist functionaries. Quite easily, we found a list of district, regional, and Central Committee members with contacts and addresses, but the next step was much more difficult. As a team, we discussed how to reach the former functionaries—by letter or by phone—and ended up using both of these methods. Instead, the most important factor for us turned out to be the role played by our "gatekeeper," an ex-Communist who was a professor of sociology at a regional university. He proved willing to help us contact his friends, comrades, and acquaintances. We took great care in drawing up the legal section of the interview consent form, promising the anticipated narrators that nothing from the interview would be published without their signed authorization, which we obtained both before the interview and again after the interviewees had read the edited version of their transcript.

We wanted to talk to functionaries from various levels in the party's organizational hierarchy, from the district and regional committees all the way to the Communist Party's Central Committee, including the general secretary, Miloš Jakeš. We were admittedly concerned about whether these powerful functionaries, representing "the defeated," would be willing to give us their candid opinions, viewpoints, and life stories at all. We knew that these mostly aging individuals had grown up in a climate of instinctive and mutual distrust. They had been educated to use the clichés of their ideology and were experienced in giving only formal, official, and self-censored autobiographies—if any at all.

Almost 40 percent of the contacted functionaries refused our request for an interview. Only two of them did so because of ideological reasons; the rest excused themselves for health issues. Some of those who participated agreed only after a period of hesitation, during which we visited them to explain the project more fully. Hearsay and conversations with other potential interviewees undoubtedly played a role in some narrators' evaluations of our project. The former functionaries had experienced some negative experiences with the mass media, particularly in relation to the recently founded Institute for the Documentation of the Crimes of Communism, whose main concern was investigating cases of repression by the Communist regime rather than collecting the life stories of that regime's former representatives. After dealing with all of these issues, we could finally begin the interview process with the ex-Communist functionaries.

As in the case of the dissidents, we divided our interviews into two sessions (more if necessary). The first meeting consisted of a free-form recollection of the narrator's past; the second was a sort of semistructured interview without any pressure on the narrator to talk about topics he or she preferred to avoid. We had to assure our narrators that we would not judge them or test their knowledge, education, or attitudes. These interviews were rarely conducted at the Institute of Contemporary History. More often they took place at the narrators' homes, where they felt more comfortable. These meetings were valuable insofar as they informed us of our narrator's lifestyle, hobbies, and most treasured objects. For one narrator this was a collection of photos; for another the medals and souvenirs he had gathered from his frequent visits to the Soviet Union during the 1970s. They showed us bookcases full of treasured objects and pictures, information that helped us conduct as free and friendly an interview as possible. It provided a bridge for obtaining their trust and provided many neutral topics to discuss before, during, and after the interview. The home environment also showed us the desolate loneliness of an elderly, widowed man, keeping in mind that some twenty years ago he was one of the pillars of a repressive regime. Sometimes we felt our narrator was pleased that we were keeping him company, giving him the opportunity to speak and be heard.

Finally, we were very surprised to discover how open and fruitful an interview that a well-prepared interviewer could obtain. In many cases, the interviews provided richer and more colorful narratives than some of these ex-Communists had published in their memoirs after November 1989.

Some functionaries spoke openly about their personal relationships, about their private and family lives, and about small events from their childhood and careers. The renowned oral historians Alexander von Plato and Alessandro Portelli have argued that the most successful interviews occur when the interviewer provokes the narrator into a confrontation of viewpoints. Even if we accepted this approach theoretically, we found it unsuitable for speaking with either the ex-Communist functionaries or the dissidents who were their former opponents. These men and women, who had been accustomed their whole lives to subordinating themselves to authority, censorship, and self-censorship, were not ready for a confrontational interview.

Nevertheless, we were satisfied with the statements our narrators made quite spontaneously. Even those on the district and regional levels gave us information "from the inside," information that no written material could have provided us. The factions, lobbies, and intrigues that a functionary dealt with on the job indicated that the Communist Party of Czechoslovakia had never been the monolith it was traditionally believed to be. The Communist Party of Czechoslovakia's Central Committee had a suffocating climate where genuine friendly contact was almost out of the question. In the final years before November 1989, such tensions existed that, as one narrator told us, "nobody even wanted to have lunch with anybody else." When the Big Brother of the Soviet Union stopped paying attention to its satellites, it left those in the Central Committee feeling uncertain and helpless. Thus, it was Mikhail Gorbachev and his *perestroika* program that our functionaries hated most of all. The new Soviet model put them in a paradoxical situation. Habituated as they were to being obedient and disciplined vassals, they literally did not know what to do (cf. the emancipated slaves in the Deep South: after the war and emancipation, many simply did not know what to do or how to do it, leaving them in a never-never land in which they could neither follow nor lead). To follow the new Soviet model would necessarily lead to liberalization in Czechoslovakia, which would in turn have resulted in the replacement of those in power in the CPC. And yet open disapproval of anything "from the Kremlin" was unimaginable for the Czechoslovak Communist establishment, which knew only too well that its true power and ability to rule depended on the presence of Soviet troops. As a consequence, the Soviets' *perestroika* and *glasnost* worried the top leaders of the CPC much more than any opposition at home.

Miroslav Štěpán, who headed the Communist Party's powerful municipal organization in Prague, spoke about the opposition's activities with absolute arrogance:

> And I really came to the conclusion that as far as content was concerned, they were far behind, especially in comparison to all the well-established positions in other socialist states. They were the weakest. Definitely the weakest. Therefore I drew the conclusion that these people couldn't overthrow us. They could only come after the Soviets had decided to sell out. That was clear. And also, if Soviets hadn't done what they did, they would have continued to go to demonstrations, and then what? Some demonstrations would have become legal and they would have gone round in circles. The opposition was really frivolous. They were set up externally.[8]

When Miloš Jakeš was asked about the main reasons for the collapse of the Communist regime, he unhesitatingly replied: "*International conditions*... *Without a doubt.*" While the opposition as a whole was generally underestimated by the top leaders of the CPC, Jakeš did consider negotiating with at least one part of it:

> With Obroda. Holding dialogue with Obroda. At the moment when it was decided to talk to [Prague Spring leader Aleksandr] Dubček, etc. Or to be more precise, with the left-wing movements outside the Party that we wanted to have on our side, because the politics of perestroika only made sense if the group of socialist supporters expanded. That was its point. And searching for approaches and debates. Therefore, I would say, it was pointless to cooperate with such an opposition as was represented by Havel and his group. Because we knew them and we knew their goals and connections. We knew they had connections with the West, with Western intelligence, that the West provided them with money, etc. Therefore cooperation with the people who actually wanted to overthrow socialism by using the politics of perestroika and liberalization didn't make any sense.[9]

The Communists' proclaimed willingness to open up dialogue with at least one of the increasing number of civic initiatives changed substantially after November 17, 1989, when a peaceful student demonstration in Prague was violently broken up by armed police forces. The protests that followed drew not only young people but also their enraged parents out onto the streets. In his interview, Miloš Jakeš was asked about the leadership's reaction to the unexpected burst of public unrest in the capital. Although his answer sounds like a mixture of George Orwell's *1984* and bad burlesque, it describes in detail the ethical and mental level of the Communist Party leadership at that time:

> We decided to invite the militia in order to demonstrate strength in Prague. Fighting strength with strength. To demonstrate. This can't happen, I would say, without somehow being noticed. It can't happen through surrender. That's just the way it is. That was our approach. Unfortunately, everything was messed up. Messed up in that on the one hand, the Head of the Prague Communist [Party] Štěpán wasn't in on the session, when everything had been decided . . . and the Presidium decided to give the task to Novák, the Chief of Staff of the People's Militia, to execute this decision. During the night, because it was a hectic situation Mr. Novák came to my house and told me simply what he had to do. The controlling party in Prague was against inviting the People's Militia. So, I was there in my pajamas, sitting by the telephone thinking about what to do. What to do then? Ask him again, but how? So I was deciding what to do, what to do about this situation. The city committee tried to persuade the head secretaries in the regions who were refusing [to act] that they alone would be able to handle the situation. This inflicted a frightful blow. What should I do? If the head secretaries of the Prague district are against it, what significance would their arrival in Prague have when simply there are those here who are able to support it and who are able to organize it. I'm telling you, I decided that whoever was on the way to Prague, they should arrive. And they would be assigned to certain posts and lodged at those posts. And the ones who weren't on the way, they wouldn't come to Prague. That was the decision I made.[10]

None of the ex-Communist functionaries with whom we spoke had renounced their former ideology, even though some of them, usually the younger ones, had carved out new places for themselves as prosperous businessmen in the transformed economic system. We did not find anyone among the narrators who suffered from a bad conscience or expressed regret over previous activities. The former functionaries from various levels only oscillated between the need for self-defense and the feeling that despite their petty mistakes and faults, they were the ones who had been unjustly harmed. The most frequent slogan they used was this: The system collapsed, but not the idea of socialism or communism.

When asked about the privileges they took for granted, such as special shops with imported goods and luxury vacations, they answered in a way that could be misinterpreted as genuine, even if it was more of a bad joke. "Special shops? Never," said one. "I have never been there. And when I needed something, I sent my chauffeur for it."[11]

After finishing this project, we found it necessary to direct our attention to the very core of the Czech population in order to further study life during normalization. Living one's life though politics was a special feature of the establishment and the opposition (legal or illegal). We also realized that changes in society had influenced the criteria for evaluating the fortunes of various social groups. Immediately after the November revolution in 1989, it was clear who had won and who had been defeated. Two decades after the revolution, it now no longer seems that clear. The former Communist functionaries undoubtedly lost in the struggle for power, yet some of them, while remaining stubbornly dedicated to their ideology, managed to adapt quite well to the new economic conditions and rules. If they constitute a new branch of the bourgeoisie, are they still "defeated"? The former dissidents who lost in the national elections in the early 1990s, and are now retired or even unemployed—where do they belong? Can they still be counted among those who prevailed, or do they belong in a new group that has been replaced? Did the substantial changes in the political regime and social system bring about more or less harmony between a person's moral beliefs and his standard of living?

This oral history project explored only a few of the many perspectives in Czech society during the normalization era. We are learning more about society during that period through a subsequent project focusing on the lives of manual workers and the intelligentsia, for which we have collected 115 interviews. This additional testimony has advanced our theoretical knowledge as well as our methodological approaches. At the same time we are dealing with information that could, to a certain extent, alter our views of the twenty years of Czech history prior to November 1989. Our interviews have repeatedly confronted us with the fact that the great events of history do not form the main axis of individual life for the majority of our population. Historical periodization that derives from important, mostly political events seems to be absolutely unimportant to the man on the street. The structure of individual life presents quite a different phenomenon, which will serve as the basis for further research into the broad array of social groups in contemporary Czech history.

NOTES

1. See Miroslav Vaněk, introduction to *Oral History in the Research of Contemporary History [Orální historie ve výzkumu soudobých dějin]* (Praha: ÚSD AV ČR, 2004).

2. Milan OttÁhal and Miroslav Vaněk, *One Hundred Student Revolutions: Students in the Period of the Fall of Communism—Life Stories [Sto studentských revolucí: Studenti v období pádu komunismu životopisná vyprávění]* (Praha: Nakladatelstvi Lidove Noviny, 1999).

3. More on this at http://www.oralhistory.cz.

4. Miroslav Vaněk, *Oral History: Methodological and "Technical" Advances [Orální historie. Metodické a technické postupy]* (Olomouc: FF UP Olomouc, 2003); Vaněk, *Method of Oral History in Contemporary History Research*; Miroslav Vaněk, Pavel Mücke, and Hana Pelikanová, *Listening to the Voices of Memory: Theoretical and Practical Aspects of Oral History [Naslouchat hlasům paměti: Teoretické a praktické aspekty orální historie]* (Praha: Ústav pro soudobé dějiny AV ČR, 2007).

5. See Michael Frisch, *A Shared Authority: Essays on the Craft and Meaning of Oral and Public History* (Albany: State University of New York Press, 1990); Ronald J. Grele, *Envelopes of Sound: The Art of Oral History* (Chicago: Precedent Publishing, 1975); Jaber F. Gubrium and James A Holstein, *Handbook of Interview Research: Context and Method.* (Thousand Oaks, Calif.: Sage Publications, 2002); Steiner Kvale, *Interviews: An Introduction to Qualitative Research Interviewing* (Thousand Oaks, Calif.: Sage Publications, 2007); Luisia Passerini, *Fascism in Popular Memory: The Cultural Experience of the Turin Working Class* (Cambridge: Cambridge University Press, 1987); Robert Perks and Alistair Thomson, eds., *The Oral History Reader* (London: Routledge, 1998); Alessandro Portelli, *The Death of Luigi Trastelli and Other Stories: Form and Meaning in Oral History* (Albany: State University of New York Press, 1991); Donald A. Ritchie, *Doing Oral History: A Practical Guide* (New York: Oxford University Press, 2003); and Paul Thompson, *The Voice of the Past: Oral History* (New York: Oxford University Press, 1978).

6. Václav Havel, interview by Miroslav Vanek, Sept. 2004, Oral History Center, IHC, "Interviews" collection.

7. Petr Placák, interview by Petra Schindler, Oct. 2004, Oral History Center, IHC, "Interviews" collection.

8. Miroslav Štěpán, interview by Miroslav Vaněk, Oct. 2004, Oral History Center, IHC, "Interviews" collection.

9. Miloš Jakeš, interview by Miroslav Vaněk, Sept. 2004, Oral History Center, IHC, "Interviews" collection.

10. Miloš Jakeš, interview by Miroslav Vaněk, Oct. 2004, Oral History Center, IHC, "Interviews" collection. During the night of November 21 state organs were deciding whether to send out the Peoples Militia. It was the first and the last attempt to surpress the demonstrations by force. In the end a path of dialog was chosen.

11. Zdeněk Čermák, interview by Miroslav Vaněk, Sept. 2004, Oral History Center, IHC, "Interviews" collection.

CHAPTER 3

INTERVIEWING IN CROSS-CULTURAL SETTINGS

WILLIAM SCHNEIDER

IT is fair to begin by asking: "What are cross-cultural interviews and what special considerations should be made when doing such work?"[1] Cross-cultural interviews involve an interviewer and an interviewee who come from different backgrounds and have different experiences. They may not share common assumptions about meaning, and both must work to establish understanding of what they mean by what they say. Usually, the person interviewing comes from a literate tradition and is conducting the interview to create a record that they or others will analyze and reference in their work. The person interviewed often is from a group whose primary reference is their oral tradition and narratives based on personal experience. This is not to infer that they are illiterate; instead it emphasizes that the most important source of their knowledge comes from what they have learned through oral narrative, what my African colleagues call "the oral information system."[2] In the examples that follow, I refer to stories in the context of interviewing, which is often the way interviews go with people whose first frame of reference is a highly developed oral information system. Stories teach at multiple levels and are flexible to be used in different ways. They do not just answer the question asked; they provide a framework for answering many similar questions, particularly in the areas of ethics, relationships between people and animals, and the environment.

In cross-cultural settings the interviewee or narrator is creating narrative from his or her oral tradition and personal experiences, while the interviewer is working to make a record for reference after the recording session. In order for the recording to be understood, not just by the interviewer and interviewee but also by future listeners who were not present at the recording session, they need to know how the stories were used at that time to convey meaning. They will also want to know something about the way the story has been used in other contexts. There will be room for misunderstanding at each step, from narrative voiced to narrative interpreted, and then to narrative referenced.

Protocol issues often influence how a cross-cultural interview goes. Long periods of silence are common and allow both the interviewer and the interviewee time to figure out how they want to formulate a response.[3] Too often inexperienced interviewers will rush from one question to the next while the interviewee is still thinking about the previous one. The complexity of such cross-cultural settings and the importance of spaces of silence has been described by Barre Toelken in his work with the Navajo storyteller Yellowman. Analyzing the beginning of a storytelling session, he wrote, "A period of friendly silence occurs while the guests and hosts enjoy each other's proximity."[4]

To really understand and preserve an accurate record, one must recognize not only the conventions and the protocols but also the symbols and the beliefs that inform the speakers in their lives. I can illustrate this point with three examples, one from South Africa, one from Alaska, and one from a Mexican American in Oregon. The first example is taken from a colleague, Ike Matibhe, a South African librarian. He told the story of the African king who sided too much with European ways, "mixed the traditions of the people." Showing their discontent with the new order, the ancestors made the crops to fail, the water in the river to dry up, and discontent to fester between the people. Only after the king changed his ways did the water return, the crops flourish, and the people were at peace. In this story one has to know that in the African traditions ancestors, even though they have passed on, continue to influence people's lives; water is a social barometer of well-being; without water nothing lives. The ancestors' withholding of water was their way to tell the king to change his relations with the Europeans and to restore balance and order in the lives of their descendants. The crop failures and dry streambed were indications that the elders were calling for change.[5]

The second example comes from research by a colleague in a small Yup'ik community in Southwest Alaska and involves a place called "The Giant Footprints."[6] This is a depression in the tundra believed to be the place where two young pubescent girls were drawn into the ground, "lost to the world of the living," when they disobeyed a cultural taboo against leaving their house during their menstrual seclusion. In traditional Yup'ik culture, it is believed that women who are menstruating are powerful and potentially dangerous to hunters. Contact with men or their hunting equipment may make it impossible for the men to get game. Therefore, strict rules govern women, particularly when they are menstruating. Even though this event is believed to have occurred many years ago, the site remains a barometer for some members of the community. Some believe that changes in the appearance of the site indicate the health and well-being of the community. When people make reference to this place they know the history, which imparts a cautionary warning based on the original event that is believed to have occurred, and the history of references to events in the community since then. Knowing the history and use of the site, just like knowing the African meanings of how ancestors and water play a part in peoples' lives, are keys to understanding each of these different "oral information systems."

The third example comes from research that Joanne Mulcahy has done with Eva Castellanoz. Eva's roots are in Mexican American culture; she is a healer, an artist, and a social activist who seeks to help youth in the Mexican American community find meaning and support in their lives. Using the metaphor of wood and trees in her stories to show people how to live, Eva says, "I learned that when the root is ruined, the limbs are sick, like our heritage that has been stripped and bitten away."[7] In one of her stories, she implores the young people to take care of their roots, not to abandon who they are, for like a tree, their roots must be nourished if they are to survive and be healthy. While the metaphor works well to our European and Western ears, Mulcahy explores the religious and healing power of wood as recognized in Mexican culture and how it fits into a heritage of references to wood and its healing qualities. Mulcahy writes: "In stories about the tree, the bark, and faith, Eva links her 'inner being' to historical narratives about 'where we come from.' For the Day of the Dead celebration, Eva's emphasis on faith and family reinforces the importance of Mexican beliefs and rituals."[8]

Even with knowledge of the culture, many interviews involve a fair amount of ambiguity, and we are left wondering what people really meant by what they said. In biblical tradition, the tower of Babel was destined to failure not only because people spoke different languages but also because they had different experiences, backgrounds, and standards, and that meant different ways of understanding. Basic to cross-cultural understanding is the way the narratives are heard and processed. Then, beyond the questions of understanding are issues about how the narratives can and should be used, questions about what is private, what is public, who "owns" the recording, who has rights to retell, and where, and how. As an oral historian, I have wrestled with these questions, and will share some of my experiences, starting with understanding.

Communicating in the Cross-Cultural Context

I have had the pleasure of living and working in Alaska for more than thirty years, and I was fortunate to spend ten months living and working in South Africa where I helped to set up an oral history program. These experiences broadened my appreciation for the importance of hearing and experiencing stories told not once, but over many times. I have two favorite examples, both based on linguistic terms that hold multiple and complex meanings. Beginning with the African Xhosa term, "ubuntu," roughly but not completely translated as "a person is a person through other people." I first heard this term in a university lunch room in South Africa where one of my colleagues was describing the traditional practice of sharing the same vessel of beer. The point in this context was that by sharing, no one gets more than the other, and our success, health, well-being, and fate are interlinked. The second reference to the term comes from Archbishop Desmond Tutu, who used the term in a biblical sense: Since everyone is made in the image of God, no one is superior to anyone else.[9] There have been other popular uses of the term to illustrate the notion of common destiny based on common effort. The term is so deeply ingrained in the cultures of South Africa that it is reflected in different languages and in the workings of government. In the post-Apartheid period, it represents a strong yearning to build a multi-ethnic nation from all sectors of the society.[10]

My second example is drawn from interviewing Chief Peter John, the traditional chief of the whole Tanana Chiefs' region, encompassing all of Interior Alaska. The traditional chief is an honorary position, chosen for his wisdom and guidance. I was fortunate to visit with him on several occasions. Chief Peter John talked a lot about the term "Ch'eghwetsen'," roughly translated as reflections on acts of love. On some occasions he would talk about memorial potlatch songs, lovingly composed by family members to recognize and speak of a loved one who had passed away. The potlatch songs draw strong images of the person and how they are remembered. They are meant to capture the qualities of the deceased. But, the term is used in other contexts as well. Once, in frustration over my not understanding, Chief Peter John said to his granddaughter, "Go get Chief Andrew Isaac's necklace." When she returned with the necklace, which he had inherited from his predecessor, he put it on and said, "See this, when I wear this everyone knows it belonged to Chief Andrew Isaac and when they see it on me they are reminded of his wonderful qualities; that is Che'ghwetsen'."

In both the African and Alaskan cases, the meaning of the term takes on a fuller form as we experience the story's reflection over many tellings. Meaning takes time and is dependent on our experience. But when do we ever really get it? Stories are not fixed entities. They represent our attempts to relate past experience to create meaning in new contexts. This is true in all cultures but becomes particularly problematic in cross-cultural contexts where we may not have the extensive experience base to weigh and interpret meaning. This is where oral history, the recordings of past tellings become so critical. It can help fill in our background on how the story was told, to whom, and why. The oral record gives us references to how interviewers' questions may prompt particular stories. The variations are critical to seeing how the story is offered and the range of meanings. Of course, answers to these questions depend on how well the recorder has documented the circumstances of the particular telling, what folklorists call the performance. Unlike the written record, stories are not static, they are re-created each time they are told. In order to understand, we need to know what prompted the story.[11]

We do not always get immediate answers. In cross-cultural interviewing there is an important place for ambiguity. At times, we do not understand and must wait, living with questions in our minds. When the Oral History Association came to Alaska for its annual meeting in 1999, I asked Chief Peter John for an appropriate quote to set the tone for the program. He thought for a while and then said, "In between the lines is something special going on in their minds, and that has got to be brought to light, so they understand just exactly what is said."[12] The quote was perfect because it reflected two important themes in oral history: the subtlety of metaphor and how people use stories to indirectly instruct; and the tension between a story told and a story written.[13] Was he pointing to the differences between a story told and a story written, and the challenges in both cases of determining meaning? This is what I got from what he said, and it fueled my thinking about the differences between oral performance and written text. Yet, I have no assurance that this was what he meant. So many times I would leave his village scratching my head for meaning as I drove the long road back to Fairbanks. I often concluded that I could not distinguish between Chief Peter John's intent and my interpretation. Since many of his stories were instructional about how to live, I decided that they were meant to be applied and interpreted broadly. It would distort the power of the story to try to draw a line between his intent and the meaning I derived from the story. That seemed fine as long as I made it clear where I was sure and where I was interpreting. I realized that I needed to hear the stories in different contexts to test my interpretations, particularly with stories that are meant to teach by example. Central to this is my need to ask why the story was told to me.

This was illustrated by the work of Aron Crowell and Estelle Oozevaseuk, who wrote about the 1878–80 famine and epidemic on St. Lawrence Island. Theirs is an excellent example of how context influences when and how a story is told. Their work also models how to analyze narrative for meaning. The setting for the telling of this story was a gathering of Yupik elders at the Smithsonian Institution where they were examining artifacts from their home, an island in Northwest Alaska. One of the items they identified was a seal-intestine parka, and that prompted Estelle to tell a story about the St. Lawrence Island "die off." In her version of the story, islanders died because they mistreated walrus, cutting chunks of meat from live animals. For this mistreatment of the walrus, they were told they would die and were instructed to put on new clothes and prepare themselves. The parka that they examined at the Smithsonian was the same kind that the islanders wore as they prepared to die, and that prompted Estelle to tell the story.

Estelle's account of the disaster is strikingly different from the written accounts of whalers and Revenue Cutter Service personnel who attribute the deaths to alcohol and Eskimos missing the opportunity to hunt migrating animals. We are left with questions about what really caused the disaster. Did the people starve because they were drinking and missed the seasonal hunt of walrus migrating up the coast, as reported, although not observed, by the Western travelers? Or was the cause of the massive die-off linked to the mistreatment of the walrus by hunters, as reported by some Yupik Eskimo descendants? We can attest to the fact there was indeed a disaster and many people died. We know that whalers made alcohol available to the Natives. We know that the flu and other epidemics were a common plight when ships came to remote communities. Yet we do not know the ultimate cause of this disaster. The claim by some Natives that hunters had mistreated the walrus by cutting off pieces of flesh from live animals and therefore must die cannot be empirically proven, but it should not be dismissed. The story explains what some people felt happened, instructs about the consequences of mistreating animals, and provides a local Native perspective and voice that had not been part of the record. The fact that the story was retold at the Smithsonian, a seat of the nation's "literate" knowledge, sends a powerful message about Native participation in the historic narrative.[14]

Whatever ultimately is "proven" to be the cause of death, the story's power is a message that goes beyond the proven facts, that can be retold again and again to instruct new generations about proper treatment of animals. The lesson in moral instruction is timeless in significance and must not be missed in the consideration of the historic event. The job of oral historians is to sort out what lends itself to empirical testing and what does not.

The story told may leave us with some moral instruction, but applied over and over it gives us a range of how people create meaning in the present, what has been called the "production of history."[15] Past, present, and future tellings become part of the meaning and purpose of the story.[16] Unlike interviews in a Western or European context where we intuitively know through familiarity something of the background of the speakers, in the cross-cultural interview we ask ourselves not only what is said but also how are people using narrative to create meaning. This ongoing endeavor is less conclusive and more tentative than a strictly historic analysis. But how much should we interpret and assign meaning to people's use of a narrative? In an interview context, we usually hear the story only once. Unless we can refer to older recordings, we lack a range of tellings for interpretation.

Elsie Mather, a Yup'ik elder and scholar, and her collaborator, Phyllis Morrow, an anthropologist, struggled with the question of how much stories should be interpreted or left to listeners to take what they can from the sharing.[17] Morrow, trained to interpret, seeks to find the meaning, while Mather encourages people to live with the stories. Underlying this discussion is the question of whether the story informs our life on an ongoing basis. Recording and writing about stories may fix their meaning in place, and without other recordings and context, meaning can get sandwiched and packaged in ways that distort meaning. The oral tradition is timeless; the written record seeks closure. Sensitive to each other's perspectives, and modeling the type of dance necessary to sensitively and ethically treat oral narrative, Mather and Morrow's work together forms a healthy tension and represents the type of exchange that has become the hallmark of "dialogic anthropology," where stories are discussed over time, where the perspectives, backgrounds, and inclinations of the interviewer and interviewee are part of the discussion, with the intention not to lock in meaning but to expand appreciation for how the story is understood and used.[18]

Cross-cultural interviewing is susceptible to possibilities for conflicts. Interpretation is an area where outsider and insiders may simply "get it wrong," in terms of the facts, the interpretations, and the rights to use the story. For the curator of a collection of recordings, the minefield of possibilities for mistakes expands exponentially. I feel this acutely because when I do an interview I am making a public record for the world to hear and must be sure that the interviewee realizes this as well. It is easy for some interviewees to forget that after they are recorded; they have little control over how future listeners may interpret them, although some people realize this right away. Early in my career, I wanted to interview a woman in a senior center about horse-drawn scows, which were used on one of our northern rivers. She said that I did not know enough to get it right. I often think back on her statement and the difficulties of explaining to someone who did not know the river and the activity. Perhaps she was questioning her ability to relate a complicated concept to not only me but to future listeners, people who would access the recording in the collection and would know even less than I did. She never gave me the story, and the incident illustrated how careful both the interviewer and interviewee must be.

Robin Barker wrestled with the question of interpretation in her analysis of Maggie Lind's story, "How Crane Got His Blue Eyes." At first read, the story resembles the *Boy Who Cried Wolf*, but Barker demonstrates that for her Yup'ik friends the story has other elements, such as being observant, seeing wisely, reciprocity in the natural world, correct behavior, and humor.[19] The story is about how Crane went berry-picking and took out his eyes, put them on a stump, and told them to watch out for danger. Several times the eyes called to him to come, and each time he put the eyes in his eye sockets, he looked around and declared nothing was wrong. Finally he was called by his eyes yet again, and when he got there the eyes were gone. Eager to see he tries several types of berries in his eye sockets and finally settles on blueberries and declares them just right. The conclusion of the story is "That is how Crane got his blue eyes."[20] Of course, interpretation depends on how we experience the story told over many tellings. One can imagine that a young child might focus on one aspect of the story and an adult on something else. Learning how to use a story depends both on how we have heard it used and the opportunities we have to retell it. This story resembles others from the Native traditions because it points to a physical characteristic or natural feature. In this case, the color of Crane's eyes are a visual reminder of the story and its potentially more complex meanings. Those of us who work in cross-cultural contexts must exercise great care both in how we record the story told and in how we represent the story in our own analysis. We must also hold open the possibilities for different interpretations, even within a population of people who share the same tradition.

Learning how to use a story also involves establishing the right to use it. Establishing rights to use a story is complicated in the cross-cultural context because, beyond the individual, the community may have a strong investment in how they are represented, and the lines between private and public shift according to the community and the topic. A standard release form is just the first step. In the Western tradition, we ask the individual who is recorded to sign a release form to make the recording available to the public, but we also recognize that the individual may not be able to speak about certain topics that are controlled by their cultural group.

When I was just starting out my research in Alaska, I visited the village of Beaver to see how Indians and Eskimos learned to live together. Beaver was of particular interest because it was settled by Eskimos from the Arctic Slope and the Kobuk region of Alaska and two linguistically different Athabascan groups: one from down river, one from up river. When I presented my research, the people told me I would be welcome to come and work as long as I did not put them under a microscope. I had to find a way to accommodate the community. The solution turned out to be a series of personal life histories of individuals, where they informally narrated the stories of their lives. From that I determined the collective history of the community as well as the Indian and Eskimo history. This allowed me to assess the impact of the different backgrounds and to draw some conclusions about how their history of joint activities and intermarriage allowed for a peaceful and relatively conflict-free coexistence. I was fortunate that the approach was acceptable to most members of the village. It gave me a way to let individuals tell their story, avoided the ethical problem of my probing questions, and provided me a window into cultural patterning and historic roots of identity.[21] This developed in a rather informal way, but in other cases, the establishment of public and private has been more formal and problematic.

A few years ago, I interviewed a Tlingit man in Southeast Alaska. In their cultural tradition, many of the stories belong to clans or groups of related people, who actually own the stories, tell them on special occasions, and consider them property. In the interview, the man talked in general terms about how the community was settled and where people came from. He did not tell the clan origin stories but merely alluded to them and the broad outlines of their content. When he mentioned the interview to other members of the community, however, there was sufficient concern that he decided he did not want us to have the recording. Generally, if someone is talking about their own experiences it is considered to be their business, and they can tell it to anyone. In this case, we did a new recording and avoided the controversial parts. In cases like this, clan ownership helps to insure that the stories are told only in the proper cultural contexts and by appropriate people, but as this example shows, it is not always a clear cut issue.

Transcribing a recording in part or whole into a book raises issues of credit. If the entire story is published under the name of the "writer," this is viewed as a flagrant violation. If the narrator is referenced or quoted, then it is expected that he or she will be referenced properly. In the Alaskan context, narrators wish to be mentioned by name and credited. "Oral biographies" or life histories based on recordings with a knowledgeable person, raise the question of authorship. In some cases the author is the narrator, the person who tells their stories.[22] In other cases, it is the "writer."[23] In still other cases, the credit line is shared, as in "told to."[24] Much depends on the level of collaboration between the writer and the narrator, and how they choose to represent themselves.

In doing oral biographies, the individuals tell their life stories, and my role is to help contextualize and arrange them for a reading audience. The term "oral biography" points to the "shared authority" involved in producing the volume.[25] This genre of writing raises all sorts of opportunities for both the writer and the narrator to work together. For instance, the story that is produced is influenced by the relationship between the writer and the narrator and the experiences they have had together. After I finished a book with Waldo Bodfish Sr., an Inupiaq Eskimo from the Arctic coast, a colleague approached me and said, "Well, you certainly didn't do him justice." I have thought back on those comments, and they have forced me to consider how the biography would have been different if someone else had written it. It would not have been better or worse, just different. The book that Bodfish and I produced was based on the stories that he had shared with me over the years.[26] It is also the case that the life history reported at one time in a person's life can change with time. Margaret Blackman, in the second edition of her work with Florence Edenshaw Davidson, reported that after she became a mother she could see new avenues of discussion with Mrs. Davidson; their relationship had evolved. She wrote: "Aside from the opportunities not taken, the changes in my own life were a powerful lesson in how life experiences of the interviewer can affect the course of life history interviewing."[27]

Integral to authorship are questions about editing, arranging, and contextualizing. These are collaborative decisions between the interviewer and interviewee. There will be things that the interviewee just does not want in the life history, and the writer must remain sensitive to these points. In Moses Cruikshank's life history there were whole parts of his life that he did not want included in his story. I had to accept that he had the first and last word on inclusion. In Waldo Bodfish's book, there were a few cases where dates or numbers did not correspond to the written record, and I noted these in footnotes, so not to interrupt or usurp the story he was telling.

Collaboration in a life history extends to the actual book design. In the first life history I worked on with Turak Newman, I failed to check the illustrations with him.[28] Their inaccuracy was a serious mistake that could have been avoided by review. In the second biography, Moses Cruikshank and I worked together, even going so far on one illustration to get an old-fashioned dog pack, find a suitable dog to wear it, and take a picture of the dog with the pack sitting just right on his back. The picture was then used by the artist to render a sketch for the book.[29]

Collaboration Is the Hallmark of Cross-Cultural Interviewing

Most of the interviews that I have done in Indian and Eskimo communities have either been life histories or focused on a particular theme. In both cases, collaboration was the easiest and best way to get good interviews. The interview is a shared product of both the interviewer and the interviewee, and requires mutual support or it will not work. In thematically focused interviews, more than one person will be asked about a topic such as local history, place names, climate change, or subsistence activities. Their interviews become part of a collection, and their observations are weighed against others, providing a rich comparative record, reinforcing the idea that meaning can expand as we gain different perspectives.[30]

In a multiyear project with Eskimo reindeer herders on the Seward Peninsula in Northwest Alaska, the interviews sought to gain an understanding of how herders were responding to the influx of caribou on their reindeer ranges.[31] The complexity of the situation and the variety of responses to the intrusion could not have been learned from one interview, nor could we have determined the range of responses to the problem. Several herders told us that their elders had warned them that "the caribou would come back sometime." For one herder, this was demonstrated to him through witnessing their return. For another, it was a question of reasoning that the caribou would run out of grazing land and have to expand their range and would eventually move onto the reindeer ranges. For a third, it was a question of knowing that there were old caribou bones and reasoning that if they were there once they could come again.[32] The herders were using the elders' expression, "the caribou would come back sometime," in slightly different ways that provided subtle clues about how individuals derive meaning from oral tradition. It was important to consider the particular tellings, the way each person made sense of the elders' prophesy, and the collective record of tellings—one gave a personal insight, collectively they gave a range of meaning. The meaning is both *all* of the explanations and *each* of the explanations provided at the particular time of the interview.

A thematic approach gives the chance to expand our understanding of how the story is used. It is also the case with thematic interviews that the later interviews build on what you learned from earlier ones, giving opportunity to show a variety of responses and depth of information on a subject. In the case of the herders, the economics of herding, the physical conditions of travel on the ranges, equipment needs, changes in technology, and the impacts of moving to a settled village life provided a complicated mix of variables that influenced how herders responded to the damage done by the caribou. Throughout the several years of interviewing, we continued to brief the herders at their annual meeting on what we were learning, and we coordinated with the director of the herders association on our research directions. The answer to our questions about how herders were responding to the decline in their herds could not have been answered in fewer interviews because of the complexity of each herder's situation and the large number of variables. Collaboratively, the herders taught and guided us throughout the process. Without their endorsement and interest, this project would not have been as successful. By posting the interviews on the Web, we created a record of our findings. But even here, the decision to post was discussed collectively and decided individually by each herder.

A key question in this research, and in all cross-cultural interviewing, concerns the role of heritage. In the case of the herders, this is reflected in the ways they see themselves and envision possibilities for the future. Their experiences with good and bad times in herding help them realize the possibilities for herding in the future, even as many now—for the time being—must turn to other ways of making a living. In examining the role their heritage plays in future decisions about herding, researchers will want to consider how they draw on their oral tradition and personal experiences to inform those decisions.

Heritage is both how we remember and what from the past nourishes us in the present. Far from my Alaskan and African experiences, two examples illustrate the role of heritage, particularly where it relates to people who rely heavily on oral narrative. The first is from the backwoods of Maine, the second from Pullman porters. Edward Ives's book, *George Magoon and the Down East Game Wars* (1988), documents stories of the notorious Maine moose poacher, George Magoon.[33] Ives points out that these stories continue to be told as a way for a disenfranchised part of the population to express their resentment against the laws that have been stacked in favor of those who come to hunt for sport. The stories not only express their feelings about the laws, but also allow them to feel a sense of power in recalling a character who outwitted the authority. George Magoon is the culture hero whose ability to outmaneuver the game warden provides, in the retelling of stories about him, some sense of satisfaction for the teller and the audience in a world that is largely beyond their control. He is in a way, a Robin Hood figure. The second example is drawn from Jack Santino's book, *Miles of Smiles, Years of Struggle*, a study of the black railroad porters who served passengers on the main train lines across the country. The stories that the porters told demonstrated the values they held and the ways they maintained a sense of dignity in a job that in many respects treated them poorly. One story that continues to be told is of how A. Philip Randolph, representing the porters, refused to accept a blank check from the company in exchange for giving up his fight for the porters' rights. Santino wrote, "The principles of honesty, integrity, and dignity are epitomized in it. The man could not be bought, bribed, moved, cajoled, threatened, or otherwise corrupted. These qualities are central to the porters' image of themselves."[34] The "blank check" story is a central part of the porters' heritage.

Both the rural Mainers and the aging black porters continue to retell their stories because they represent the experiences and values that shaped their lives. When heritage fails to speak to us, the stories fade into obscurity, becoming artifacts of the past. The oral tradition thrives when a group knows the old stories, values them, and finds reason and occasion to retell them to later generations.

Impact of Cross-Cultural Interviewing on Interviews Within One's Own Culture

Cross-cultural interviews broaden our appreciation for how people use oral narrative to express meaning. This can have a direct impact on interviews we do within our own cultural group. It can force us to question whether we really understand what is meant by what is said, and it can make us more sensitive to the nuances of expression. It makes us more conscious of the role of context and how circumstances affect construction of narrative. And it forces us to consider tradition, what people bring to their understanding and discussion of the present. These are aspects of dialog that we take for granted in familiar surroundings. In our translation of oral narrative to literate prose we often miss the nuances of meaning specific to the oral performance, the setting, the questions that came before, and the relationships between the present and past history.

Do you hear Chief Peter John saying: "In between the lines is something special going on in their minds, and that has got to be brought to light, so they understand just exactly what is said"? If we can imagine living with our stories, not just as facts but also as part of a creative process that brings our past forward and shapes our understandings of that past to address the questions and issues of the present, then we may see more clearly how narrative is used in our own culture to convey meaning. We ask ourselves over and over again: What do we need to know by way of background to understand? One of the gifts we get when we work in cross-cultural settings is that things may seem so different that they force us to question what is "between the lines" and to try to determine what people really mean.

NOTES

1. Because this is a summary article and because I believe they are the best personal examples to emphasize the points, I have used many of the old stories and examples from my previous work. At first it bothered me a bit that I was retelling old stories, but now I think it speaks more to the power of the particular stories and how deeply they have influenced me personally and professionally. I often tell students that to do good oral history one has to think and live one's life like a story. It is no coincidence that this is the main theme of Julie Cruikshank's classic work, *Life Lived Like a Story: Life Stories of Three Yukon Native Elders* (Lincoln: University of Nebraska Press, 1990). It is also no coincidence that the old stories would come to me as I sought examples to illustrate my own experiences interviewing cross-culturally.

2. William Schneider, *So They Understand: Cultural Issues in Oral History* (Logan: Utah State University Press, 2002), 31.

3. See, for instance, Ronald Scollon and Suzanne B. K. Scollon, *Linguistic Convergence: An Ethnography of Speaking at Fort Chipewyan, Alberta* (New York: Academic Press, 1979).

4. Barre Toelken, *The Dynamics of Folklore* (Logan: Utah Sate University Press, 1996), 129.

5. Schneider, *So They Understand*, 131–32.

6. Holly Cusack McVeigh, "The Giant Footprints: A Lived Sense of Story and Place," in *Living with Stories*, ed. William Schneider, 18–30 (Logan: Utah State University Press, 2008).

7. Joanne Mulcahy, "The Weight of Faith: Generative Metaphors in the Stories of Eva Castellanoz," in Schneider, *Living with Stories*, 103.

8. Ibid., 108.

9. M. Battle, "The Ubuntu Theology of Desmond Tutu: How Desmond Tutu's Theological Model of Community Facilitates Reconciliation among Races in a System of Apartheid" (PhD diss., Duke University, Department of Religion, 1995), 46–47.

10. Schneider, *So They Understand*, 55–57.

11. Ruth Finnegan, *Oral Literature in Africa* (Nairobi: Oxford University Press, 1970), 2.

12. Chief Peter John to the author, June 1999.

13. Walter Ong, *Orality and Literacy: The Technologizing of the Word* (London: Methuen, 1982), 113–14.

14. Aron Crowell and Estelle Oozevaseuk. "The St. Lawrence Island Famine and Epidemic, 1878–80: A Yup'ik Narrative in Cultural and Historical Context," in Schneider, *Living with Stories*, 36–67; Aron Crowell and James Clifford, "The St. Lawrence Island Famine and Epidemic, 1878–80: A Conversation with Aron L. Crowell and James Clifford," in ibid., 68–73.

15. David William Cohen, *The Combing of History*, (Chicago: of Chicago Press, 1994), 5.

16. See, for instance, Julie Cruikshank, "'Pete's Song': Establishing Meanings through Story and Song," in *When Our Words Return: Writing, Hearing, and Remembering Oral Traditions of Alaska and the Yukon*, ed. Phyllis Morrow and William Schneider, 53–75 (Logan. Utah State University Press, 1995).

17. Elsie Mather, "With a Vision Beyond our Immediate Needs: Oral Traditions in an Age of Literacy," in Morrow and Schneider, *When Our Words Return*, 13–26; Phyllis Morrow, "On Shaky Ground: Folklore, Collaboration, and Problematic Outcomes," in ibid., 27–51.

18. Dennis Tedlock and Bruce Mannheim, eds., *The Dialogic Emergence of Culture* (Urbana: University of Illinois Press, 1995).

19. Robin Barker, "Seeing Wisely, Crying Wolf: A Cautionary Tale on the Euro-Yup'ik Border," in Morrow and Schneider, *When Our Words Return*, 79–97.

20. Ibid., 81–83.

21. William Schneider, "Beaver Alaska: The Story of a Multi-Ethnic Community," (PhD diss., Bryn Mawr College, 1976).

22. For instance, in Moses Cruikshank's *The Life I've Been Living* (Fairbanks: University of Alaska Press, 1986); and Waldo Bodfish's *Kusiq: An Eskimo Life History from the Arctic Coast of Alaska* (Fairbanks: University of Alaska Press, 1991), the narrators are the authors, and I am listed as compiler or editor.

23. Margaret Blackman, *During My Time: Florence Edenshaw Davidson, A Haida Woman* (Seattle: University of Washington Press, 1992).

24. Sidney Huntington, as told to Jim Rearden, *Shadows on the Koyukuk: An Alaskan Native's Life Along the River* (Anchorage: Alaska Northwest Publishing, 1993).

25. Michael Frisch, *A Shared Authority: Essays on the Craft and Meaning of Oral History and Public History* (Albany: State University of New York Press, 1990).

26. Bodfish, in Schneider, *Kusiq*.

27. Blackman, *During My Time*, 160.

28. Turak Newman, *One Man's Trail* (Anchorage: Adult Literacy Laboratory, n.d.).

29. Cruikshank, in Schneider, *Life I've Been Living*.

30. Carrie Nobel Kline, "Giving it Back: Creating Conversations to Interpret Community Oral History," *Oral History Review* 19 (1996): 9–39.

31. www.uaf.edu/library/jukebox.

32. Schneider, "Lessons from the Storytellers," in *Resilience in Arctic Societies*, ed. Lawrence Kaplan and Michelle Daveluy, papers from the Third IPSSAS Seminar, Fairbanks,

Alaska Native Language Center, 2005, 112–13. [IPSSAS: International PhD School for Studies of Arctic Societies]

33. Edward "Sandy" Ives, *George Magoon and the Down East Game War: History, Folklore, and the Law* (Urbana: University of Illinois Press, 1988).

34. Jack Santino, *Miles of Smiles, Years of Tears: Stories of Black Pullman Porters* (Urbana: University of Illinois Press, 1989), 61.

BIBLIOGRAPHY

Blackman, Margaret. *During My Time: Florence Edenshaw Davidson, a Haida Woman.* Seattle: University of Washington Press, 1992.

Bodfish, Waldo. *Kusiq: An Eskimo Life History from the Arctic Coast of Alaska.* Compiled and edited by William Schneider. Fairbanks: University of Alaska Press, 1991.

Cohen, David William. *The Combing of History.* Chicago: University of Chicago Press, 1994.

Cruikshank, Julie. *Life Lived Like a Story: Life Stories of Three Yukon Native Elders.* Lincoln: University of Nebraska Press, 1990.

Cruikshank, Moses. *The Life I've Been Living.* Compiled and edited by William Schneider. Fairbanks: University of Alaska Press, 1986.

Finnegan, Ruth. *Oral Literature in Africa.* Nairobi: Oxford University Press, 1970.

Morrow, Phyllis, and William Schneider, eds. *When Our Words Return: Writing, Hearing, and Remembering Oral Traditions of Alaska and the Yukon.* Logan: Utah State University Press, 1995.

Ong, Walter. *Orality and Literacy: The Technologizing of the Word.* London: Methuen, 1982.

Schneider, William, ed. *Living with Stories.* Logan: Utah State University Press, 2008.

———. *So They Understand: Cultural Issues in Oral History.* Logan: Utah State University Press, 2002.

Scollon, Ronald, and Suzanne B. K. Scollon. *Linguistic Convergence: An Ethnography of Speaking at Fort Chipewyan, Alberta.* New York: Academic Press. 1979.

Tedlock, Dennis, and Bruce Mannheim, eds. *The Dialogic Emergence of Culture.* Urbana: University of Illinois Press.

Toelken, Barre. *The Dynamics of Folklore.* Logan: Utah State University Press, 1996.

CHAPTER 4

CASE STUDY: ORAL HISTORY AND DEMOCRACY: LESSONS FROM ILLITERATES

MERCEDES VILANOVA

THE "discovery" of illiteracy and its defining characteristics should be a main focus of oral history, since it is the only way to integrate the illiterate population into mainstream written history.[1] The difficulties in reaching illiterates, the communication problems, and their frequent silences, especially in societies that have suffered civil wars and harsh political repression, challenge historians. The experience of interviewing them allows us to measure the degree to which the historian is anchored in the literate culture and complicit in the power of writing. But if we ignore this segment of the population, we lose a necessary counterpoint to understanding literacy, and we refuse to look at much of the past; thus we lose the complete memory of what we have been.

Through an oral history comparative study we researched the voting and social behavior of illiterate workers in Barcelona, Baltimore, and the Nazi death camps. This case study presents some results, a comparison between the samples, and the theoretical challenges about the role of democracy and illiteracy in situations of social and political upheaval. The research centers on proving that *illiterates are not disruptive* in these situations and that they show a *moderate response*. As a conclusion, future research is presented in the form of four conjectures that follow from these two theses and the field work conducted.

Main Questions, Field Sites, and Interviewees' Sample

The main research question was: Why do democracies fail in situations of social and political upheaval? Other questions were: What are the voting characteristics of illiterates and what does it mean to not be able to read or write? Three sites were chosen (see table). In Barcelona we approached workers who lived during the 1930s and lived through the Republic, civil war, social revolution, and the Franco dictatorship.[2] In Baltimore we approached workers who had gone through the New Deal in the 1930s and the civil rights movement in the 1960s and '70s.[3] And in Germany we interviewed Spanish Republicans who had been deported between 1940 and 1944 to Mauthausen, Buchenwald, or Ravensbruck; in these camps we did not find any illiterates among the survivors, yet some of the key findings of our research come from the comparative analysis stemming from these interviews. The Spaniards in the camps were militants, had fought against Franco, and all were literate.[4]

The story behind this research began when I interviewed an illiterate woman worker in a metallurgy factory collectivized during the Spanish civil war (1936–39). She used to vote and belonged to an anarchist trade union. This interview made me review the affirmation that literacy was a prerequisite for membership in a trade union or political party.[5] My interviews prove that illiterates were indeed members of trade unions, political parties, and other organizations such as the Masons, but they were never disruptive within the values of the organizations they belonged to.

Illiteracy is further obscured by the fact that many of them know how to mask their inability, partly because they do not use speech codes different from those used by the literate population, and it is hard to distinguish them in casual conversations. They can get a driver's license and travel long distances: "I gets me a map and study for about a month, or maybe more. I study that route, the way I was going." They can open a bank account: "When I opened the account I did not know how to read or write. I did not tell them a thing. They didn't care. I signed my name." They can order in restaurants: "Most of the restaurants I used to go they would come and say we have so and so." They can even join the Masons: "I am Mason since 1939; the Masons did not know that I could not read or write, no." On the job, they sometimes hire a literate worker to perform tasks they are unable to do.

The interviewees told me their life stories, while also focusing on the meaning of their vote, ideology, religious beliefs, and their concept of social change, reform, or revolution. The men talked more and were more anxious to learn in Baltimore; while in Spain many women learned how to write in order to communicate with their companions who were in the army, in jail, or in exile. In Baltimore women had experienced greater violence, which they revealed in their many stories of drugs, alcohol, and isolation. Many in both Baltimore and Barcelona had lived in shanties or in the open. All started to work at an early age picking grass or cotton, washing dishes and scrubbing floors, or in the mines. Some explained their failure to attend school by the long distances they had to walk, or by the early death of one or both parents. Some

Topic	*Field Site*		
	Spain *Civil War period 1930s*	**USA** *Baltimore illiterates 1930s*	**Germany** *death Camps 1940s*
Methodology	Statistics, cartography, bibliography, oral sources, 120 interviews*	Oral sources, bibliography, 24 interviews†	Oral sources, over 1200 collaborative interviews, bibliography‡
Illiterate groups identity	None	African American	No illiterates in sample
Role of religion	Catholic church opposes group	Support of local churches	Religion persecuted
Dominant ideology	Anarchism	Liberal democracy	Nazism
Democracy output	Failure of Spanish civil war leads to Franco dictatorship	Success of civil rights movement	Failure, death camps

* Some interviews published in Mercedes Vilanova, *Las Mayorías Invisibles* (Barcelona: Icaria Editorial, 1995).

† Some interviews published in Mercedes Vilanova, *The Fourth World, Baltimore Narratives 1990* (Istanbul: Bogazicci University Press, 2005).

‡ About 800 interviews belong to the Mauthausen Survivors Documentation Project, directed by Gerhard Botz, University of Vienna; and about 500 interviews belong to the Slave and Forced Labour during National Socialism in Germany Project directed by Alexander von Plato, Fern Universität Hagen, Germany.

say they did not wish to learn. Child labor was especially pronounced for girls, who had to take care of their siblings or their sick parents or grandparents.

In both Spain and the United States narrators had migrated at an early age in search of work, usually turning over the first money they earned to parents or relatives: "What money my father got (from my work) he put it in his pocket." "The money was for my brother-in-law." In Baltimore, narrators tended to have married twice and had four children, families were less structured, and relations among family members and bosses were more violent than in Spain. While interviewees in Baltimore and Barcelona came from large families with many siblings, in Barcelona they had adapted themselves to the demographic model of Catalonia and had only one or two children. As in Barcelona, when I asked Baltimore narrators what their parents taught them, the answer was very clear: "Not to steal." "To keep my hands off what don't belongs to me."

Illiterates: A Nonradical Group

The most obvious difference in our samples was that African Americans thought of themselves and acted as a group, regardless of their status as illiterates. In contrast, white illiterates in any location never form a visible or self-conscious group. Black illiterates' sense of collective identity was reinforced by a common history, itself signified by the term "African American." Africa and slavery gives them a geographic and social origin, and all remembered the era of segregation. Even those who were homeless were aware of who Lincoln, Roosevelt, Kennedy, and Martin Luther King were. This knowledge of historical figures, strikingly absent in the Barcelona interviews, was the result of African Americans' experience of spectacular social changes during their lifetime when they overcame legal and extralegal impediments to vote. As a result, they place a high value on elections and tend to believe a strong federal government will better protect them, even though as in Barcelona, they did not fully understand what a political party or a trade union was. Indeed, many did not know the word "democracy": "That is a race, ain't it?" "It is a worldly thing." "I can't explain that word."

African Americans' sense of history, was heightened by their experience of religion. It is well known that the church is a key to African Americans' sense of identity and a source of social support. In addition, the church offers a teleological vision of the world and provides an understanding of events in a temporal framework. Even though racial oppression was terrible, it had nonetheless been assuaged by church membership; by the late twentieth century, the church itself promoted a progressive view of social change and a hopeful sharing of experiences. In Baltimore I came to understand more deeply how Spanish workers—marginalized politically and socially—had also been defeated spiritually by a church that defined the Spanish civil war as a holy crusade.

Voting is an example where interviews with nonliterate persons show their nonradical behavior and introduce us quickly to worlds that challenge theories about illiteracy. In contrast with our findings, political and social theories have traditionally suggested illiterates are erratic, intolerant, and easily swayed in their voting behavior. We found that illiterates where quite moderate both in Baltimore and in Barcelona. In Baltimore the importance of the right to vote was recognized by all African Americans: "It made you feel that you was a part of something, you are a citizen of the United States of America." This attitude is different in Spain where in general people distrusted politics and admitted that they voted "To lose less" because politicians "all wear the same tie, they all dress in blue." In the United States all support the Democrats and tend to demonize Republicans: "I vote Democrat, Republicans take all the money from the poor and give to the rich." African Americans are firmer than European Americans in their commitments to the Democrats: "To my idea, the Republicans mostly brought slavery in." And when they do not vote they feel guilty. White illiterates exhibited more variation in their voting behavior, and some had never voted.

In Barcelona, during the 1930s, there was pressure on workers not to vote; traditionally this has been attributed to the influence of the anarchist slogan "Do not vote." One of the illiterate workers shared with me her experience: "When one did not go to vote, the owners appreciated you more you know; people with money, some of the people, do not like that the workers are rebels." Even though the charismatic leaders told them not to vote, and even though the owners did not want them to vote, the illiterates and functional literates persistently went to the polls to elect moderate candidates. These statements gave me a lucid explanation about the failure of their social revolution: "How could we do a revolution if we did not know the letter O was round?"

Like voting, union membership was not a means to radicalize an illiterate's position. Unions in Baltimore seemed to be exclusively for men who joined, like they did in Barcelona, to find a job and obtain job security. In both places, interviewees never considered the possibility of being a union activist, and when asked why, the answer was always the same: "Because I did not have an education." We have found that almost all Spanish Republican deportees to the Nazi camps where literate, further supporting the notion that radicalization is a literate phenomena.

Illiterates are moderate and want to appear so in the societies they live in. In Barcelona, when I asked to what social class they belonged, they quickly responded: "We are normal. We do what others do." In Baltimore, white illiterates responded similarly, they also want to pass as "normal." African Americans on the other hand, recognizing the dehumanization thrust upon those with dark skin, answered very quickly: "We are human, don't you believe it?" In Brazil, the illiterates told me: "we are beggars," recognizing the conditions of their misery. In France, one gets a different image, because the label *analphabète* (illiterate), sounds like "silly" or *bête* (animal), and since illiterates do not want to be called this, they refer to themselves as *handicapé* (handicapped). Perhaps the French Ministry of Culture introduced the word *illetré* to solve this semantic problem. Of course, illiterates do not view themselves as abnormal, inhuman, beggars, silly, or handicapped; these are descriptions that the literate assign to them.

It is unclear why illiterates show such a moderate behavior given their limitations. But interviews show that illiterates can reach certain levels of professional sophistication. Economic theories originating in the 1960s about development stressed that literacy was a condition of modernity. These theories promoted the myth that literacy was necessary to think, criticize, establish democratic governments, or maintain political stability, even to use birth control. The illiterate persons I have interviewed have worked in manufacturing for civil and military production, in mines and on the railroad; they have driven trucks and operated forklifts. Their illiteracy has not prevented them from working as foremen or overseers. "I worked on the painting line I told them I couldn't read that good, but I could do the work." And they have served in the military with honor: "Sure they knew I did not know how to read, but they were desperate for men, for soldiers. In Korea I was a truck driver." In other words, illiteracy per se is not a social problem.

What Illiterates Miss

In our study of Barcelona we concluded that illiterates experience a certain reduction in their perception of the world, and that their lives tend to be circumscribed by their paid work and their household. Those interviewees who were able to remember their salaries, nonetheless recalled little about the enterprises where they worked, including what happened in their collectivized factory during the war. In Barcelona and Baltimore, they usually had a passive attitude toward matters outside their immediate world, whether social revolution or the civil rights movement, and they also lacked chronological memory. They often did not know the year they were born, when and how long they had been married, or when their children had been born. Compared to mainstream discourse, their testimony generally is also briefer and more limited in vocabulary. It suggests greater difficulty in understanding and expressing some abstract concepts, such as democracy or socialism. In fact, illiterates rarely use these terms and, when specifically asked about them, claim not to understand them, a condition that also hampers political engagement.

One of the most striking discoveries I made was that even in small villages, their neighbors did not remember them. Is this lack of remembrance the greatest historical marginalization? Illiterates' personal memories did not extend beyond their parents; not knowing their grandparents, they were not able to tell us anything about them; they did not even remember the names of their closest family members. Had they forgotten them? Did they ever exist for them? Their memories were reduced to their immediate lives, as if they were trees without roots, beings without consciousness of their origins or of the forest that surrounded them. When they were not physically with someone they were literally alone, unable to communicate with themselves by keeping a diary, writing letters, or reading. Was this absence of memories, this lack of connection with others the greatest poverty?

Illiterates acknowledge feelings of shame and embarrassment, especially in their youth. "I felt bad...when you can't read the whole world is hidden from you." They hide the fact that they cannot read or write from friends, work mates, and even spouses. "When I don't know something, I always keep it to myself." To hide their illiteracy many have learned how to sign their name. "I learned how to sign later on in life....If you know how to sign your name, it comes in handy to you." But they also know how to accept their limitations: "They were silent movies, oh yeah. They would show you different things; it was nothing like it is today. You still could see the pictures, but the reading part you did not see. A lot of times somebody that I would go with would read it."

Four conjectures: Azaustre, Ant Followers, Mauthausen, and Galileo

Our field work led us to conclude that illiterates do not show a disruptive behavior and in turn show a moderate response, and thus they can not be held responsible for ideological support to conflict, or voluntary participation in civil wars or in mass-destruction atrocities. From these assumptions it follows that such atrocities can only result from literacy. Such conclusion is captured in what we call the *Azaustre conjecture*, in memory of Manuel Azaustre.[6] This conjecture states: "The loss of common sense and idealism that can produce mass-destruction atrocities are a result of literacy."

In resonance with the Azaustre conjecture, the *Galileo conjecture* states that to combat the power of linear texts in support of failures of democracy, the linear text has to be replaced by fragmented narrations and a view of history as a net of relationships. In other words, "the history-as-a-linear-text paradigm must be replaced by a history-as-a-network paradigm to prevent dictator-like abuse of historical texts." The disruptive behavior of certain democracies is a product of ideologies anchored in seminal texts. In our three samples, the main texts illustrated in very short quotations are:

> United States in 1868: Question to be asked of candidates to join the Ku Klux Klan: "Are you in favor of a white man's government in this country?"
>
> Germany in 1924: "Studying the history of the Jewish people I doubted whether destiny reserved to them the final triumph," from Adolf Hitler's *Mein Kampf.*
>
> Spain in 1933: "There is no other admissible dialectic than the dialectic of fists and pistols, when justice or the homeland is offended," by José Antonio Primo de Rivera, founder of La Falange, the official political party of Franco.

	Field Site		
Conjecture	**Spain** *Second Republic/Civil War period 1931–39*	**USA** *Baltimore new Deal – Civil Rights Movement 1930–1970s*	**Germany** *death Camps 1940–45*
Azaustre—*Failure of literacy*	No illiterates exiled	No confrontation of civil rights movement	No Spanish Republican illiterates in death camps
Ant followers—*Illusion of democracy*	Franco dictatorship	Slavery	Totalitarian Nazism
Mauthausen—*Latent camps*	Civil war repression	US civil war and segregation	Death camps
Galileo—*Failure of the linear text*	Combative memory: José Antonio Primo de Rivera	Official memory: Ku Klux Klan	Doctrinal text: Mein Kampf, Adolf Hitler

If we take a further leap in thought, we can conclude that the vast majority of voters are both nondisruptive and moderate. Probably the interrelationship between the democratic system and illiterates is representative of the whole electorate, since what is asked of most voters is to choose among a few candidates. The mechanisms that led to the emergence of leaders such as Hitler and the brutal consequences that followed, in many ways have not changed. In our three sites, democracies failed when they allowed the establishment of dictatorships, as in Spain with Franco and in Germany with Hitler, or they lead to adoption of segregation and discrimination, as in the United States. I capture these observations in the *Ant Followers conjecture* that reads: "Democracies are tacit dictatorships."

The testimony of illiterates, who were once a much greater percentage of the voting population particularly in the periods studied, has been replaced by younger people educated in the current public system. No one has demonstrated a significant difference between the former and the latter, which suggests that we remain at risk of experiencing another twentieth-century–like atrocity, even in the so-called developed world. I summarize this in a fourth and perhaps most worrying conjecture, the *Mauthausen conjecture* that reads: "The mechanisms that led to the atrocities of the twentieth century are still present in modern democracies and ready to act."

NOTES

1. This case study has been written with the help of Brian Subirana. A first version was written with the help of Linda Shopes and published as an introduction in Mercedes Vilanova, *The Fourth World: Baltimore Narratives, 1990* (Istanbul: Bogazicci University Press, 2005).

2. The major publications about this work are Mercedes Vilanova, "Anarchism, Political Participation, and Illiteracy in Barcelona, between 1934 and 1936," *American Historical Review* (February 1992). In Spanish, Mercedes Vilanova and Xavier Moreno, *Atlas of the Evolution of Illiteracy in Spain between 1887 and 1981* (Madrid, 1992); Mercedes Vilanova, *Las mayorías invisibles: Explotación fabril, revolución y represión* [*The Invisible Majorities: Industrial Exploitation, Revolution, and Repression*] (Barcelona: Icaria Editorial, 1995), which includes twenty-four interviews, translated into Catalan, Spanish, and Greek. In Catalan, Anna Monjo and Carme Vega, *The Workers and the Spanish Civil War: The History of a Collectivised Industry* (Barcelona, 1986). Using statistics, cartography, and oral sources published bilingually in Catalan and Spanish, Mercedes Vilanova, *Atlas Electoral de la II República en Cataluña*, 2 vols. (Barcelona: Enciclopedia Catalana, 2006).

3. Vilanova, *The Fourth World*, bilingual in English and Turkish; in Spanish with a different introduction; Vilanova, *Voces sin letras: Analfabetos en Baltimore* (Barcelona: Anthropos, 2005).

4. Vilanova, "Arbeit, Verfolgung und Tod nach dem spanischen Bürgerkrieg," in *Hitlers Sklaven und Zwangsarbeit Internationales lebensgeshichtliche Dokumentationsprojekt zur Sklaven und Zwangsarbeit*, ed. Alexander von Plato, Almut Leh, and Christoph Schlesinger (Vienna: Bohlau, 2008).

5. E. P. Thomson, *The Making of the English Working-Class* (London: Victor Gollancz, 1963).

6. The edited life history of Manuel Azaustre (1920–2002) in *Historia, Antropología y Fuentes Orales* (HAFO) 35 (2006).

BIBLIOGRAPHY

Vilanova, Mercedes. *Atlas Electoral de la II República en Cataluña.* Barcelona: Enciclopedia Catalana, 2006, 2 vols.

———. *The Fourth World: Baltimore Narratives, 1990.* Istanbul, Turkey: Boğaziçi University Press, 2005.

———. *Las Mayorías Invisibles: Explotación fabril, revolución y represión: 26 Entrevistas.* Barcelona: Icaria Editorial, 1996.

Von Plato, Alexander, Almut Leh, and Christoph Schlesinger, eds. *Hitlers Sklaven und Zwangsarbeit Internationales lebensgeshichtliche Dokumentationsprojekt zur Skalven und Zwangsarbeit.* Vienna: Bohlau, 2008.

PART II

MEMORY AND HISTORY

CHAPTER 5

MEMORY AND REMEMBERING IN ORAL HISTORY

ALISTAIR THOMSON

> But what is really important is that memory is not a passive depository of facts, but an active process of creation of meanings.
>
> —Alessandro Portelli

ALESSANDRO Portelli's reformulation of memory—written in 1979 as a riposte to critics of oral history who scorned the "unreliability" of memory as an historical source—helped to transform the ways in which oral historians work with people's memories.[1] For example, consider the following story from my own study of postwar British migration to Australia. In 1960, a twenty-six-year-old medical secretary by the name of Joan Pickett took a government-assisted passage for British migrants and traveled to Australia with her friend Jean. On the train from Manchester to the London docks Joan started a journal of her experience, which began:

> 6.9.60 Left Manchester, London Road, on the midnight (11.35 p.m.) train to St. Pancras, after a nightmare last day at home—was I doing the right thing, could I turn back even now? By sheer stubbornness and will-power, I kept going.... So we waited for the train to move off—the minutes dragged by—could we still turn back—no, there goes the whistle, the light is green and slowly we pull away, waving furiously out of the window until the platform disappears in puffs of steam and we enter the dark night outside. We're off!

Here is the same moment, recalled in our interview forty years later:

> And I always remember, those clouds of steam, it was something like *Brief Encounter*, it was quite late at night. My father was standing there with his raincoat and his trilby on, you know, and he sort of kissed us and he said, "Well, come back if you can, but if [pause] don't worry about us, you do what you want to do." And my mother was crying of course. And we were crying. (laughs) And the train pulled away, and my father sort of disappeared into this cloud of smoke, and I never saw him again.

These two accounts recount the same moment in very different ways. Most obviously, in the journal Joan and her friends are the central characters, but in the interview Joan's father takes center-stage. In 1960, writing within a few hours of departure, Joan expresses her anxiety and ambivalence about leaving, but also the start of an exciting adventure into the "dark night" of the unknown. Through her journal, Joan represents—and creates—herself as the hero of her own adventure story, and as she wrote what she imagined to be the first draft of a book about her travels, she had in mind the genre of women's travel stories and an imagined audience for her own account. Joan Pickett worked and traveled her way around Australia and New Zealand until her Australasian sojourn ended in 1968, somewhat reluctantly, when she returned to Manchester after the unexpected death of her beloved father. In our interview, the railway scene is now shaped by the loss of a father and by the grief and guilt of an absent daughter, powerfully expressed through the emotional register and increasing pace of her voice as she tells the story. As if to appease her own pain and provide a retrospective forgiveness, Joan includes her father's parting words, "don't worry about us, you do what you want to do." And, if the journal of 1960 was written in the contemporary genre of women's travel writing, the memory of 2000 recalls the popular British film *Brief Encounter* and the iconic resonance of emotional railway partings in the age of steam. At each point in time Joan Pickett is actively creating a meaningful story about the event, and as the time of the telling changes so too does the meaning and significance of the story.[2]

The literature about memory ranges across several academic disciplines and is daunting in size and scope. This chapter considers approaches to memory and remembering, which can enhance oral historians' understanding of the interview and its interpretation. I start by charting the history of oral historians' approaches to memory and then distill current research about memory and remembering—from neuroscience and psychology, cultural studies, and narrative theory—and signal its relevance to oral history.

Oral Historians and Memory

The genesis of contemporary oral history was the post–World War II renaissance in the use of memory as a source for historical research. Paul Thompson, among others, charts the prehistory of the modern oral history movement, explaining that historians from ancient times relied upon eyewitness accounts of significant events. The nineteenth-century development of an academic history discipline led to the primacy of archival research and documentary sources, and a marginalization of oral evidence, until the mid-twentieth century.[3] Gradual acceptance of the usefulness and validity of oral evidence, and the increasing availability of portable tape recorders, underpinned the development of oral history after World War II. Though the timing and pattern of this emergence differed markedly around the world, an increasing interest in "people's history" in the 1960s, and the parallel creation of regional and national oral history associations inspired a burgeoning oral history movement. The lived experience of working-class, women's, or black history was undocumented or ill-recorded, and oral history was an essential source for the "history from below" fostered by politically committed social historians in both community and academic contexts.

Paul Thompson's *The Voice of the Past: Oral History* became a standard textbook and a standard-bearer for oral historians when it was first published in 1978. Thompson sought to defend oral history against critics who claimed that memory was an unreliable historical source, and he determined to prove the legitimacy and value of the approach. As a socialist, he was committed to a history that drew upon the words and experiences of working-class people. He argued that oral history was transforming both the content of history—"by shifting the focus and opening new areas of inquiry, by challenging some of the assumptions and accepted judgements of historians, by bringing recognition to substantial groups of people who had been ignored"—and the processes of writing history, breaking "through the boundaries between the educational institution and the world, between the professional and the ordinary public."[4]

But the renaissance of oral history was shadowed by controversy. Positivist critics, who were mostly traditional documentary historians of a conservative political persuasion, feared the politics of people's history and targeted the "unreliability" of memory as its weakness.[5] At the core of criticisms of oral history in the early 1970s was the assertion that memory was distorted by physical deterioration and nostalgia in old age, by the personal bias of both interviewer and interviewee, and by the influence of collective and retrospective versions of the past. For example, the Australian historian Patrick O'Farrell wrote in 1979 that oral history was moving into "the world of image, selective memory, later overlays and utter subjectivity.... And where will it lead us? Not into history, but into myth."[6] Goaded by these critics, early oral historians developed their own handbook guidelines to assess the reliability of recorded memory (while shrewdly reminding the traditionalists that documentary sources—many of which were created as records of spoken events—were no less selective and biased). From social psychology and anthropology they showed how to determine the bias and fabulation of memory, the significance of retrospection, and the effects of the interviewer upon remembering. From sociology they adopted methods of representative sampling, and from documentary history they brought rules for checking the reliability and internal consistency of their sources. These guidelines provided useful signposts for reading oral history interviews and for combining them with other historical sources to find out what happened in the past.[7]

In the late 1970s, imaginative oral historians turned these criticisms on their head and argued that the so-called unreliability of memory was also its strength, and that the subjectivity of memory provided clues not only about the meanings of historical experience, but also about the relationships between past and present, between memory and personal identity, and between individual and collective memory. For example, Luisa Passerini's study of Italian memories of interwar fascism highlighted the role of subjectivity in history—the conscious and unconscious meanings of experience as lived and remembered—and showed how the influences of public culture and ideology upon individual memory and subjectivity might be revealed in the silences, discrepancies, and idiosyncrasies of personal testimony.[8] Also writing in the 1970s, the North American oral historian Michael Frisch argued against the attitude that oral history provided "a pure sense of how it 'really' was," and asserted that memory—"personal and historical, individual and generational"—should be moved to center stage "as the object, not merely the method, of oral history." Used in this way, oral history could be "a powerful tool for discovering, exploring, and evaluating the nature of the process of historical memory—how people make sense of their past, how they connect individual experience and its social context, how the past becomes part of the present, and how people use it to interpret their lives and the world around them."[9] Memory thus became the subject as well as the source of oral history, and oral historians began to use an exhilarating array of approaches–linguistic, narrative, cultural, psychoanalytic and ethnographic–in their analysis and use of oral history interviews.

The work of the Italian oral historian Alessandro Portelli exemplified this paradigm shift in approaches to memory and oral history. In "What Makes Oral History Different," first published in 1979, Portelli challenged the critics of "unreliable memory" head-on by arguing that "the peculiarities of oral history"—orality, narrative form, subjectivity, the "different credibility" of memory, and the relationship between interviewer and interviewee—should be considered as a strength rather than a weakness, a resource rather than a problem.[10]

Though conservative historians were the most vocal critics of oral history in the 1970s, oral historians' use of memory was also challenged from the Left. In the late 1970s and early 1980s some socialist historians were particularly critical of the notion that the method of oral history was necessarily radical and democratic. Luisa Passerini cautioned against the "facile democratization" and "complacent populism" of oral history projects that encouraged members of oppressed groups to "speak for themselves" but which did not see how memories might be influenced by dominant histories and thus require critical interpretation.[11] At the Centre for Contemporary Cultural Studies in Birmingham, UK, the Popular Memory Group developed a similar critique of British oral history in their writings about "popular memory." The Group situated academic and other historical practices within the much wider process of "the social production of memory," and argued that public struggles over the construction of the past are profoundly significant both in contemporary politics and for individual remembering. For example, oral history as used within the community and women's history movements could be a significant resource for making more democratic and transformative histories, and might in turn enable people to tell stories that had been silenced because they did not match the dominant cultural memory.[12] Yet the Popular Memory Group concluded that this radical potential was often undermined by superficial understandings of the connections in oral testimony between individual and social memory and between past and present, and by the unequal relationships between professional historians and other participants in oral history projects.

In the 1980s, a rather different consideration of the dialogic nature of the interview relationship also shifted our understanding of memory and remembering in oral history. One of the primary concerns of critics of oral history in the 1970s was that historians were creating, and thus unduly influencing, their sources. By the end of that decade oral historians like Portelli and Passerini in Europe, and Frisch and Ron Grele in North America, had begun to question the possibility of objectivity and to celebrate the subjectivity of the interview relationship. Throughout the 1980s positivist notions of researcher objectivity were increasingly questioned by feminist theorists, postmodern anthropologists and qualitative sociologists, and by oral history interviewers who were deeply reflective about the relationships they formed with their narrators. Oral historians were also influenced by developments in reminiscence work that highlighted the benefits of remembering for older people and reminded interviewers to consider the value of the exchange for both parties.[13] In an article published in the *Oral History Review* in 1997, Valerie Yow argued that from the late 1980s a new oral history paradigm permitted "awareness and use of the interactive process of interviewer and narrator, of interviewer and content."[14] Oral historians were increasingly alert to the ways that they were affected by their interviews and how the interviewer, in turn, affected the interview relationship, the memories it generated, and the interpretative process and product.

Yow's article exemplifies the interdisciplinarity that has been one of the most significant features of oral historians' approaches to memory since the 1980s. Though memory is now a respected historical source, history is just one of many academic disciplines and emergent intellectual fields that work with memories. Yow writes about the "trickle-over effect" from other disciplines such as qualitative sociology, anthropology, biographical and literary studies, and life review psychology. To this list we could add cultural studies, linguistics, communication and narrative studies, folklore studies and interdisciplinary work exploring the relationship between memory, narrative, and personal identity.[15] Taken together, this interdisciplinary work exemplifies the "ascent of 'memory' as an object of investigation by historians" in the last two decades of the twentieth century and into the new millenium.[16]

The growth of memory studies poses two significant issues for oral historians. First, oral historians can help to ensure that memory studies do not retreat into an arcane intellectual world of rarified debate, but rather are informed by our relationship with the men and women who tell us their memories and by our efforts to engage memory in political debate for social change. Second, oral historians need to keep abreast of a daunting interdisciplinary literature in the field, including new scientific research about the ways that memory works.

Memory Research

Recent memory research by neuroscientists and psychologists has confirmed Portelli's claim that memory is "not a passive depository of facts, but an active process of creation of meanings."[17] Ulric Neisser, among others, refutes the prevalent "hard-copy metaphors" about memory that assume that experience is simply recorded into the memory hard disc of the brain and then retrieved at the point of remembering. "Remembering," he argues, "is not like playing back a tape or looking at a picture; it is more like telling a story. The consistency and accuracy of memories is therefore an achievement, not a mechanical production."[18] The processes of that achievement are immensely complex, but awareness about some of its key features will help oral historians to understand what might be going on when they work with memories.

Scientists agree there is no single region of the brain that deals with memory. The neurobiologist Stephen Rose explains that "brains don't have a central processor, a super-manager controlling everything. Rather they are distributed networks of cellular ensembles, richly interconnected, which between them create the illusion of coherent experience that we all in our normally functioning moments share."[19] There are no discrete units that simply store and retrieve memory. Modern brain image scanning has confirmed that when we create or recall a memory we engage multiple sections of the brain, each of which deals with different aspects and tasks of remembering.[20]

Memory also works differently at different life stages. The British oral historian Paul Thompson has synthesized research that suggests that up to the age of about four, children create very little long-term memory, though they often have a photographic type of memory. As children grow up the development of cognitive processes enables them to perceive, sift, and articulate experience and create long-term memories, which in turn undermines the capacity for photographic or rote learning. From adolescence, and especially after about the age of thirty, although the "total memory store is increasing" our brains increasingly struggle to manage so much memory, and there is a progressive decline of "immediate memory." But "recent memory is affected first," and in later life the process of "life review"—involving the time and desire to remember one's life, and perhaps "a special candor"—may well compensate by enhancing long-term memory. The North American oral historian Donald Ritchie quotes an interviewer for New York's Ellis Island migration museum who noted that elderly interviewees "might not remember their daughter's phone number, but they do remember what it was like when they got off the boat." Like Ritchie, Thompson is impressed by the remarkable resilience of long-term memory in later life, and concludes—against critics of oral history who argue that memory is unreliable because it deteriorates with old age—that "interviewing the old...raises no fundamental methodological issues which do not also apply to interviewing in general."[21] Valerie Yow's recent synthesis of memory research extends this argument to encompass long-term autobiographical memory at whatever age and concludes "with a renewed respect for autobiographical or individual memory as evidence that oral historians can use."[22] Yow quotes the memory theorist Daniel Schacter's evolutionary explanation for the durability and reliability of autobiographical memory: "On balance our memory systems do a remarkably good job of preserving the general contours of our pasts and of recording correctly many of the important things that happened to us. We could not have evolved as a species otherwise."[23]

These studies all emphasize another important feature of memory research, the distinction between three different types of memory: short-term memory, long-term memory, and the "sensory memories" that are present in both short- and long-term memory.[24] We all have moments when a smell, taste, or image will trigger a powerful though not always clear or coherent memory of an earlier time in our life. The physical, sensory elements of the original experience have lingered in memory—not necessarily in the same regions of the brain that remember the event—and the sensory cue now elicits that associated memory. Sometimes the sensory memory survives without any associated memory story. Schacter argues that "memories that can be elicited only by specific tastes and smells are fragile: they can easily disappear because there are few opportunities for them to surface. [But] having remained dormant for long periods of time, the sudden appearance of seemingly lost experiences cued by tastes or smells is a startling event." Oral historians and reminiscence workers know that sensory triggers, such as interviewing in situ or the use of photos, can often enable rich and even unexpected remembering.[25]

The distinction between short-term and long-term memory is crucial. Much of our experience is not recorded in the first place because we are just not concentrating on that event or have no need to register the occurrence. Schacter labels this as the memory "sin of absentmindedness...a failure to properly attend to, encode, and store the memory."[26]

Furthermore, a vast proportion of experiences, which are initially registered in short-term memory, are not processed into long-term memory. In a memorable turn of phrase, Paul Thompson explains that this "initial discarding is by far the most drastic and violent" phase of forgetting.[27] The brain has an extraordinary capacity for memory, but it cannot record or retain all of our experiences; the overload would make life unmanageable. We forget so that we can manage our lives effectively by focusing on important tasks and memories. Mental good health requires us to forget much more than we remember. Researchers agree that most of what happens to us is lost to memory within a very short space of time, usually in the first few minutes or at most within a few days.

So how is short-term memory processed into long-term memory? In an introduction to a recent anthology about memory, the novelist A. S. Byatt translates the neuroscience. "Forests of dendrites [branchlike forms, from the Greek word for a tree], millions and millions of neurons connected into living and changing networks along axons that meet at synapses, arrange both our conscious and unconscious lives.... The image we have now [of memory]—which 'feels' to me like a good image—is one of constant communication and reinforcement and pruning of the network of cells in the brain, which is simultaneously a structure of molecules, and a system of electrical signals."[28] In that same anthology, the neurobiologist Stephen Rose explains that new learning (or remembering) generates physical changes in the brain and the activation of a memory trace. Central to this physical change is the "the remodeling of synaptic junctions" that communicate between nerve cells in the brain, with memory traces or "engrams" "encoded in terms of changed synaptic connectivities.... It is at the synapses that electrical signals travelling down one nerve axon trigger the release of chemical signals—neurotransmitters—that in turn carry the message across a small gap to an adjacent nerve cell, stimulating a response in the second cell." The "memory consolidation" process that underpins transition to long-term memory involves "a temporal sequence of molecular events—a biochemical cascade—occurring over the hours following training and which seem to culminate in the lasting modulation of synaptic strengths."[29]

Rose is careful to explain that these memory traces cannot be conceived as the storage units for a memory "hard copy." For one, during the "biochemical cascade" memory traces transfer across into different parts of the brain, and indeed different aspects of the long-term memory of any event (for example, sound, mood, story) may well be stored in several brain regions and are not necessarily remembered in precise combination. Rose also cautions that memory involves more than synapses, and that the consolidation of memory is dependent upon body state and emotion. "Alertness and attention depend on physiological processes such as blood flow and hormonal level. Memory involves emotion as well as cognition, and hormones produced outside the brain, notably adrenalin and its neurotransmitter relative noradrenaline, are engaged in determining what is remembered.... In this sense learning and remembering—memory—is a property not of individual synapses or nerve cells or brain, but of the entire organism, the person." Finally, Rose reminds us that when we recall and recount a memory—the process of remembering—we never simply reproduce the original memory traces. The pathways and processes of *re*-membering are different in subtle but important ways.[30]

Oral historians need to know how and why memories of certain experiences are consolidated in long-term memory while others are not. Here psychology and neuroscience combine with good effect. The short answer is that an experience is much more likely to be remembered if it is perceived to be significant (worth remembering) and is therefore articulated into a memorializing form, most typically a story. Valerie Yow explains, drawing upon Schacter's work on encoding and consolidation, that "the recording of a memory from the beginning preserves a *partial* record because we cannot take in every detail in a scene and therefore take in only what seems significant to us." Or, as Donald Ritchie succinctly concludes, "People remember what *they* think is important."[31] From the start, then, the creation of memory is, necessarily, a partial and subjective process.

What makes an episode significant, and thus memorable, in the first place? Here we need to attend to the specific circumstances of each remembered experience. Memorable events usually require direct personal involvement. They may well have had a dramatic impact or been subject to physical sensations or powerful emotion (neuroscientists point to biochemical processes through which emotion reinforces remembering—though they also explain that the biochemistry of the brain can block out traumatic experience).[32] Unless timing has a particular significance we are unlikely to have precise memories of chronology. Indeed, time is often remembered subjectively rather than chronologically. We may telescope the sequence of events in ways that emphasize periods of significance and diminish unmemorable times, or we may bring together temporally disconnected experiences that have a shared significance.[33] Paul Thompson argues that there is a "*general* tendency for recurrent processes to be better remembered than single incidents," and yet a single, unique incident may be particularly memorable—especially if it proves to have long-term significance.[34] For Joan Pickett, for example, leaving Manchester was always likely to be a memorable experience, and the powerful emotions of separation and the dramatic sensory impact of steam and sound ensured a potent memory. Over the years Joan commemorated her departure day in an annual anniversary letter to her parents, which reinforced the occasion in her memory, and after the death of her father the event assumed even greater significance.

Significant episodes are usually made into durable memories, and the creation and rehearsal of a memory story is fundamental to the consolidation of long-term memory. The cognitive psychologist Ulric Neisser studied memories of an earthquake among students living at different distances from its epicenter and impact, and concluded that "nowhere was there any correlation between reported arousal and later accuracy. Given this result, my colleagues and I prefer a different interpretation. What did happen, we think, is that people told their earthquake stories over and over again. Personal experience of a major earthquake is definitely worth talking about. Friends and relatives call to find out how you survived, acquaintances want to compare your story with their own. Once you realize that you have a story to tell, it's hard to stop."[35] In other words, significant experiences are created in long-term memory—the synaptic connections are consolidated—through the process of making story and sense. When Joan Pickett sat in the train after leaving Manchester and wrote in her journal about the departure scene, she was consolidating that significant episode into a first draft of memory.

Daniel Schacter characterizes the way that some memories refuse to fade as the virtue (and vice) of persistence. He explains that memories persist because of their significance, relevance, and usefulness because they are unique or charged with powerful emotion, and because they are rehearsed and consolidated through storytelling. Conversely, Schacter describes the "sin of transience" for memories that are not consolidated in this way. "But with the passing of time, the particulars fade and opportunities multiply for interference—generated by later, similar experiences—to blur our recollections. We thus rely ever more on our memories of the gist of what happened, or what usually happens, and attempts to reconstruct the rest by inference and even sheer guesswork. Transience involves a gradual switch from reproductive and specific recollections to reconstructive and more general descriptions."[36] Joan Pickett reflects with great insight about the factors that affected the persistence and transience of her memories of the eight-year sojourn. Toward the end of our first interview, I asked Joan about her Australian memories.

> Well they seem to be more vivid than other memories somehow. Because there were so many of them, and they were all such new experiences. And as I say, if I can't sleep at night, only occasionally, you know, I can go back to Ocean Island, and I can start walking round or driving round, and everything is still so vivid. Or I can go in Hobart, and I can climb up the road to Mount Wellington. I can see it all, it's still there. And I've got loads of lovely slides of course, I must get them collated one of these days. But, no, it's all so vivid, because it was, it was something so completely different. The other was sort of normal, and this was abnormal, and it stuck out in your memory. And it's still very—[pause] And of course, if anybody finds out, if I mention it occasionally, I don't bring it up in the conversation, but if anybody finds out, and they want to know all about it, so I have to keep bringing these memories out, so of course, I never get a chance to forget anything. And if I do, it's all written down there of course [in her letters]. But you know, things that I may have done in my earlier life, before that, those weren't documented. So I've probably forgotten a lot of things I did before that. But this was *so* different, and so out of the ordinary, that it stays fresh all the time. Mm.... Yes, it's something different that people keep asking you about. You don't get a chance to forget in other words. Yes.

Joan Pickett's thoughtful reflections highlight many of the factors that influence the persistence and durability of long-term autobiographical memory. Joan explains that the Australasian sojourn looms large in her memory because it was a special or "abnormal" time of vivid experiences. She shows how the eight years of travel are marked by clear signposts in her memory and thus readily recalled. She explains that the Australian slides and letters provide a source of reference that sustains her memory (and also created early drafts of memories), and she notes that she is often asked to tell the story about her years in Australia, "so I have to keep bringing these memories out." The memories help Joan to get to sleep, but they also serve as a profoundly significant record of a peak experience of a young woman's migration and contribute to Joan's very positive sense of identity and of a life well lived.

If consolidation through storytelling is an essential initial stage in the creation of long-term memory, then any subsequent remembering—"bringing the memories out"—is a complex and creative process of story reconstruction. Although elements of the original story will reappear, the remembered account is almost never the same as the original, or indeed of any previous recounting. Here we can return to recent work in memory science, which refutes the notion that when we remember we simply drag intact memory files out of "deep storage" and reopen them. Stephen Rose argues that "this mechanical model won't do," and his neuroscience echoes Portelli's formulation of memory. "Each act of recall is itself a new experience. Reactivated memories are subtly changed each time we recall them," Rose wrote.

> Far from passively recording the past, we in our memories actively reconstruct it. Very recently, neurobiology has begun to catch up with common sense and the psychologists. . . . Some researchers have begun to speak of this as "reconsolidation." However, the temporal dynamics of reconsolidation are rather different from those during consolidation; different brain regions are involved, and the biochemical changes do not exactly recapitulate those of consolidation. Of course, being reminded of a past experience is itself a novel experience. We don't step into the same stream twice, and memory depends on history. That neurobiologists have only so recently come to realize this shows just how blinkered and reductionist their—our—paradigms have been.[37]

Rose's recognition that memory depends on history alerts us to other, vital aspects of memory-making (consolidation) and remembering (reconsolidation). Both stages involve making sense of experience through story, and at each stage the memory process is both social and psychological as well as neurological. Here cultural studies and narrative psychology offer important and complementary perspectives on memory and remembering.

In the 1970s, the cultural studies pioneer Raymond Williams explained how we draw upon the lessons of prior personal experience and the language and meanings of our culture to bind and shape the initial, inarticulate consciousness or structure of feelings regarding an experience into a more fixed state. In the 1980s, members of the Popular Memory Group developed this notion into a theory about the relationship between cultural memory and personal memory. According to the Group, public representations of the past ("popular memory") are used as an aid in the constant process of making sense of personal experiences, "offering forms and general interpretative categories by means of which people can locate their own experience in terms of wider social patterns."[38] The Popular Memory Group was careful not to suggest a culturally determinist model for individual memory, explaining that the available public languages and forms never exactly fit experience and that novel experiences constantly stretch the old cultural forms and thus require and generate new ways of understanding, for individuals and in society.

The Popular Memory Group also introduced a useful distinction between the general and particular publics within which we articulate and remember experience. The general public includes the various media—newspapers, television, books and so on—that provide widely available representations and interpretative categories (the "public field of representations") in an indirect, impersonal relationship. We also make sense of experience within the active relationships and meaning systems of a particular public group, such as a family or voluntary association. This "particular public" is significant in a number of ways. First, a member of a social group may participate in and contribute to the development of its meanings. Second, because of the importance of social acceptance and affirmation the group is especially influential, and potentially repressive, in the construction of meaning and identity. Third, a particular public may provide an important site for the maintenance of alternative or oppositional meaning, a source of public strength for its members to filter or even reject and contest socially powerful narratives.[39]

The "narrative turn" in the humanities and social sciences has confirmed aspects of this popular memory approach and generated evermore sophisticated understandings of the social and psychological processes of memory and remembering. In a recent survey of narrative theory, the oral historian Mary Chamberlain explained that "We cannot look, imagine, remember, describe, or recount without first having the imaginative structures that enable this.... What is remembered, when, and why is molded by the culture in which [people] live, the language at their disposal, and the conventions and genre appropriate to the occasion."[40] Chamberlain reminds us that form as well as meaning is cultural, and that when we create and re-create stories about experience we adopt and adapt culturally available storytelling forms or genre.[41] In this manner, Joan Pickett first wrote about her departure using the genre of women's travel stories, and later recounted the same story through the *Brief Encounter* genre of emotional railway separations. Studies by Chamberlain and other oral historians have further shown that non-Western cultures have very different forms for storytelling and indeed very different approaches to autobiographical memory and storytelling.[42] While emphasizing the importance of cultural narratives and genre, Chamberlain cautioned that "this is not to suggest that all and every life story or oral history is culturally predetermined, or necessarily coherent or consistent." There are a variety of cultural forms and meanings—albeit some more powerful and influential than others—that we use to turn memory into a story, which is our own unique and distinctive creation.

Narrative theory also highlights the importance of social relationships and performance in remembering. Like Neisser's students recounting their earthquake experience to family and friends, or Joan Pickett "bringing out" her memories when people ask about her time in Australia, we most often relate memory stories in social relationships (the "particular publics" of popular memory theory). We perform our memories in ways that will communicate and appeal to a particular audience, and the expectations of the occasion and the audience will, in turn, influence the storytelling. Indeed, we seek recognition for our stories, and affirmation of ourselves, through performative remembering.[43]

The oral history interview is a distinctive type of performance and a particular genre of storytelling, though the stories that we record in an oral history interview have often been performed on previous social occasions. Michael Frisch coined the evocative phrase "shared authority" to describe remembering in the oral history relationship.[44] At its best, the interview is a dynamic, dialogic relationship that encourages active remembering and meaning-making. The interviewee may start by performing fixed or rehearsed stories, but in the process of remembering, and with the careful encouragement and gentle probing of the interviewer, more complex and unexpected memories may emerge.

When I first asked Joan Pickett why she went to Australia, she delivered an amusing and well-rehearsed anecdote about seeing a newsreel of sunny Australia at a Manchester movie theater on a "dark cold winter evening," and then joking to her friend Jean that they should go. The joke spiraled out of control, they were "swept along by events," and within six months were on their way. This was Joan's set-piece story about emigration, which concealed as much as it revealed about her motivations. In our interview, my questions about Joan's earlier life in Manchester triggered other memories and a much more complex, multilayered explanation. As the teenage daughter of a train driver, Joan had enjoyed the privilege of free train travel across Europe and developed a love of travel. Several Australian doctors at the hospital where Joan and Jean worked had "talked up" their homeland as a place of sun, space, and excitement, and offered places to stay. Perhaps most importantly, Joan remembered that her life in Manchester had reached an impasse. Her brother Harry married in 1958 and "obviously I was left at home with my mother and father, and I was at a bit of a loose end." The female cousins of her tight-knit extended family were now married and starting their own families, and Joan, still single at twenty-six, was beginning to feel "very very unusual.... I perhaps thought we were getting in a bit of a rut, and as you get older you want to do, and you know, most of my friends were getting married, perhaps I felt I was being left behind in some way. I don't know what it was." In the interview, Joan paused and pondered as she thought back to that period of her life. I asked if the sense of being "in a rut" influenced her decision, and she responded: "Well I suppose we mustn't have been completely happy in a way, but, perhaps we thought we were—[pause]I was–I was twenty-six. I—[pause]I don't really know. I've never tried to analyze it. It's just, it just seemed to happen at the time, and I just took advantage of it."

Joan said that she "never tried to analyze it," but between us, haltingly in the interview and then through correspondence and writing, we reached an explanation that situated Joan's personal decision in its wider historical context. The assisted passage scheme for migration to Australia offered an exciting alternative for two northern lasses who were in their mid-20s and not yet married. This was perhaps the only way (apart from marriage) that Joan could leave the family home and create her own independent life, and thus transcend social expectations for young working-class women in the early 1960s. At the time this was not an easy decision, and Joan felt conflicted by loyalty to her family and guilt about leaving home. Later, with the death of her father at the back of her mind, Joan found it difficult to assert her active agency in leaving home. But the dialogue of the interview facilitated rich and multilayered remembering and an expansion of her migration story.

In the interview Joan made new sense of her memories and herself. Narrative theory offers ways of understanding the place of subjectivity in memory and storytelling. Narrative is an attempt to create meaning for our lives and coherence in our self. As Ruthellen Josselson and Amia Lieblich argue in *The Narrative Study of Lives*, "Narratives are not records of facts, of how things actually were, but of a meaning-making system that makes sense out of the chaotic mass of perceptions and experiences of life."[45] Narrative psychologists like Jerome Bruner confirm that stories are pivotal to human subjectivity and that narrative is the way "we organize our experience and our memory of human happenings."[46] Memory narratives perform this meaning-making role at their point of creation and in any subsequent remembering of the experience.

Narrative theory posits a dynamic and dialectical relationship between memory and identity. Remembering is one of the vital ways in which we identify ourselves in storytelling. We construct our identities by telling stories about our lives, either to ourselves as inner stories or daydreams, or to other people in social situations. According to the neurologist Oliver Sacks, "It might be said that each of us constructs and lives 'a narrative,' and that this narrative *is* our identities."[47] Memory stories create identity and, in turn, our identities shape remembering. Who we think we are now and what we want to become affects what we think we have been. Our memory stories will be subtly influenced by our changed perspectives on that past, and by our current identities and aspirations. Memories are thus significant pasts that we compose to make a relatively coherent—though not necessarily comfortable or painless—sense of our life over time.[48]

Alessandro Portelli neatly juxtaposed the "narrated self" (at the time of the event) and the "narrating self" (at the time of the telling) and explained that every interview—and indeed all remembering—involves a dialectical relationship between these different selves at different times.[49] As oral historians, we are challenged by this dialectic between past and present, story and self, but we are also presented with a rich opportunity to explore the nature, meaning, and significance of subjectivity as it has changed over time. Joan Pickett looked back on her years in Australia from the perspective of a daughter who left and then lost her father, but also as a woman who "came of age" through travel and independence and who now, as an older single woman, remembers and explains these years as the "time of my life." Through Joan's memories we can begin to understand important aspects of the subjectivity of a young woman in the 1960s, and of Joan in later life.

Oral History and the Memory Paradox

There is a paradox in oral historians' approaches to memory. On the one hand, oral historians who have researched memory agree that long-term memory is remarkably robust and durable—in large part because it is consolidated and reconsolidated through storytelling—and is therefore a reasonably reliable historical source. On the other hand, precisely because we make and remake memory through storytelling, our memories are influenced by the neurological, psychological, and social processes of storytelling, at the time of the event and right through to the time of the telling.

As Portelli concluded, oral sources are "not *objective*. . . . they are *artificial, variable, and partial*."[50] At first sight, this conclusion sounds like surrender to the positivist historians who criticize unreliable memories. In fact, it offers a profound challenge to all historians and their other sources, both contemporary and retrospective. Every historical source that recounts human experience—the witness statement at a government inquiry or in a court of law, a newspaper report, the letter or diary, a memoir or interview—is an artificial, partial, and subjective representation, and all involve some degree of retrospectivity and thus variability over time. The retrospection of oral history is a matter of degree and not a difference in kind. Because of the contested nature of our sources, oral historians have been especially receptive to critical thinking about memory, and especially perceptive about the opportunities and challenges posed by working with memories. We have important lessons to teach other historians about their sources.

For oral historians, there is no easy way out of the memory paradox. One pragmatic response is to adopt a "double-take" approach to memory, and to use it to explore both the past (history) and the past in the present (memory). Oral testimony often illuminates (though never replicates) past experience and subjectivity. As historians we need to interrogate our interview sources critically, as we do any historical source, and to understand the ways in which memory stories have been shaped by the particular circumstances of the event and the complex processes of remembering. As Donald Ritchie concluded, "interviewers must be aware of the peculiarities of memory, adept in their methods of dealing with it, conscious of its limitations, and open to its treasures."[51] Oral historians are necessarily students of historical memory, and our interviews will illuminate the processes and relationships of remembering, and the ways in which the past is active in the present lives of individuals and society.

There are some questions we can ask of the oral histories we collect and interpret, which will help us to understand this challenging double role as student of both history and memory. Drawing upon research into the neurology and psychology of memory, Valerie Yow offered a helpful set of caveats: "Consider asking yourself: (1) What is the narrator's mood? (2) What emotional needs might impinge on the process of remembering? (3) What seems to be the narrator's purpose in recalling this particular memory this way? (4) How is gender showing up in remembering? (5) Is the gist of the memory recalled accurately? (6) What details does the narrator seem uncertain about? (7) How did I, as interviewer, interact with this narrator? (8) How does the environment in which the interview took place affect remembering? (9) What checks exist for corroboration or refutation of a particular memory?"[52] From narrative theory Mary Chamberlain adds to this list, and urges oral historians to "recognize that the interview is a multilayered document," which is both narrative and dialogue. She reminds us to consider how our interviewee has been engaged in "a continuous revision of self," and that "the individual voice contains a multiplicity of voices... it holds within it the shared meanings of languages and cultural narratives."[53]

To this list I would add: listen to how interviewees describe and explain their own memories and remembering. For if Joan Pickett teaches us anything, it is that memory work is not the exclusive preserve of the researcher. We all work with memory every day of our lives. Most people can offer profound insight about their own memories and remembering, and about their past experience and its meaning and significance in the present.

NOTES

1. Alessandro Portelli, "What Makes Oral History Different," in *The Oral History Reader*, ed. Robert Perks and Alistair Thomson, 37–38 (London: Routledge, 2006).

2. Joan Pickett, journal, Sept. 6, 1960; interview with Joan Pickett conducted by Alistair Thomson in Salford, England, Dec. 17, 2000. Joan Pickett's accounts are archived in Special Collections, University of Sussex Library, British Australia Migration Collection, P12. See A. James Hammerton and Alistair Thomson, *Ten Pound Poms: Australia's Invisible Migrants* (Manchester: Manchester University Press, 2005); Alistair Thomson, *Moving Stories, Women's Lives* (Manchester: Manchester University Press, 2010).

3. Paul Thompson, *The Voice of the Past: Oral History* (Oxford: Oxford University Press, 2000), 25–81.

4. Ibid, 8–12.

5. Among early critics were: William Cutler III, "Accuracy in Oral History Interviewing." *Historical Methods Newsletter* 3 (1970): 1–7; Barbara Tuchman, "Distinguishing the Significant from the Insignificant," *Radcliffe Quarterly* 56 (1972): 9–10; Enoch Powell, "Old Men Forget," *Times* (Nov. 5, 1981). For a critique from the Left of oral historians' naïve use of memory see: Eric Hobsbawm, "On History from Below," in *On History*, ed. Eric Hobsbawm, 266–86 (London: Weidenfeld and Nicolson, 1997) (written in 1985 and first published in 1988).

6. Patrick O'Farrell, "Oral History: Facts and Fiction," *Oral History Association of Australia Journal* 5 (1982–83): 3–9 (reprinted from *Quadrant*, Nov. 1979).

7. See, for example, the first edition of Thompson's *Voice of the Past* (1978) for a defense of oral history in these terms.

8. Luisa Passerini, *Fascism in Popular Memory: The Cultural Experience of the Turin Working Class* (Cambridge: Cambridge University Press, 1987); Passerini, "Work Ideology and Consensus Under Italian Fascism," *History Workshop* 8 (1979): 82–108.

9. Michael Frisch, *A Shared Authority: Essays on the Craft and Meaning of Oral and Public History* (Albany: State University of New York Press, 1990), 188. See also Alistair Thomson, Michael Frisch, and Paula Hamilton, "The Memory and History Debates: Some International Perspectives," *Oral History* 22, no. 2 (1994): 33–43. Ron Grele, another notable North American critic of oral history's theoretical naivety in the 1970s, suggested new ways of working with memory in *Envelopes of Sound: The Art of Oral History* (New York: Praeger, 1991).

10. Portelli's seminal work includes: *The Death of Luigi Trastulli and Other Stories: Form and Meaning in Oral History* (Albany: State University of New York Press, 1991); *The Battle of Valle Giulia: Oral History and the Art of Dialogue* (Madison: University of Wisconsin Press, 1997); and *The Order Has Been Carried Out: History, Memory, and Meaning of a Nazi Massacre in Rome* (New York: Palgrave Macmillan, 2003). See also the special section on "History, Memory, and the Work of Alessandro Portelli," *Oral History Review*.

11. Passerini, "Work Ideology and Consensus Under Italian Fascism," 84. Michael Frisch also criticized the populist "no history" approach to oral history in "Oral History and *Hard Times*: A Review Essay," *Journal of American Studies* 1, nos. 2/3 (1972): 217–31. Louise Tilly criticized oral historians' atheoretical and individualist tendencies, though from a more conventional academic standpoint, in her article, "People's History and Social Science History," *Social Science History* 7, no. 4 (1983): 457–74, reprinted with responses from leading oral historians in the *International Journal of Oral History* 6, no. 2 (1985):

5–46. For a comparable and contemporary Australian critique see J. Murphy, "The Voice of Memory: History, Autobiography and Oral Memory," *Historical Studies* 22 (1986): 157–75.

12. Popular Memory Group, "Popular Memory: Theory, Politics, Method," in Perks and Thomson, *Oral History Reader*. See also Anna Green, "Individual Remembering and 'Collective Memory': Theoretical Propositions and Contemporary Debates," *Oral History* 32 (2004): 35–44.

13. Joanna Bornat, "Oral History as a Social Movement," *Oral History* 17, no. 2 (1989): 16–20. Feminist oral historians have made especially important contributions in this regard, illuminating issues about oral history relationships and the interconnections between language, power, and meaning. The core texts for feminist oral history are Sherna Berger Gluck and Daphni Patai, eds., *Women's Words: The Feminist Practice of Oral History* (New York: Routledge, 1991); and Susan H. Armitage, ed., *Women's Oral History: The Frontiers Reader* (Lincoln: University of Nebraska Press, 2002).

14. Valerie Yow: "'Do I Like Them Too Much?' Effects of the Oral History Interview on the Interviewer and Vice-Versa," *Oral History Review* 24, no. 1 (1997): 55–79.

15. For an extensive set of references on memory studies in each of these fields, see "Interpreting Memories: Introduction," in Perks and Thomson, *Oral History Reader* (2006), 211–20. See also the new Sage journal, *Memory Studies*.

16. Omer Bartov, in a review of three books about the European memory of the Holocaust and World War II, in *American Historical Review* 106, no. 2 (2001): 660.

17. An excellent synthesis by an oral historian of recent memory research is in Valerie Raleigh Yow, *Recording Oral History: A Guide for the Humanities and Social Sciences* (Walnut Creek, Calif.: AltaMira Press, 2005), 35–67.

18. Ulric Neisser, "Memory with a Grain of Salt," in *Memory: An Anthology*, ed. Harriet Harvey Wood and A. S. Byatt, 88 (London: Chatto and Windus, 2008).

19. Steven Rose, "Memories Are Made of This," in Wood and Byatt, *Memory*, 67.

20. This dispersed geography of memory across different regions of the brain is one part of an explanation for so-called false memory. Valerie Yow explains that false memory is possible because the part of the brain that remembers what happens is proximate to the part of the brain that imagines what might have happened—and memory and imagination sometimes get entangled. Yow, *Recording Oral History*, 48–49.

21. Thompson, *Voice of the Past*, 136–37, 144; Donald A. Ritchie, *Doing Oral History: A Practical Guide* (New York, Oxford University Press, 2003), 31.

22. Yow, *Recording Oral History*, 52–53.

23. Daniel Schacter, *Searching for Memory: The Brain, the Mind, and the Past* (New York: Basic Books, 1996), 308.

24. A further research distinction contrasts procedural memory (how to do something) and declarative memory (remembering *that* something), with declarative memory further divided into semantic memory (details like numbers and dimensions) and episodic or autobiographical memory ("recall of episodes in one's own life") in Rose, "Memories Are Made of This," 56. Oral historians are, primarily, interested in episodic or autobiographical memory.

25. Schacter, *Searching for Memory*, 55.

26. Daniel Schacter, *The Seven Sins of Memory: How the Mind Forgets and Remembers* (Boston: Houghton Mifflin, 2001), 15–16.

27. Thompson, *Voice of the Past*, 130.

28. A. S. Byatt, introduction to Wood and Byatt, *Memory: An Anthology*, xiv–xvi.

29. Rose, "Memories Are Made of This," 60–64.

30. Ibid., 65.

31. Yow, *Recording Oral History*, 38; Ritchie, *Doing Oral History*, 32.

32. Yow, *Recording Oral History*, 44–47.

33. Alessandro Portelli, "'The Time of My Life': Functions of Time in Oral History," in *The Death of Luigi Trastulli and Other Stories* (Albany: State University of New York Press, 1991), 59–80.

34. Thompson, *Voice of the Past*, 158; cf. Yow, *Recording Oral History*, 41–43.

35. Neisser, "Memory with a Grain of Salt," 88.

36. Schacter, *Seven Sins of Memory*, 15–16, 206.

37. Rose, "Memories Are Made of This." 65–66.

38. Graham Dawson and Bob West, "'Our Finest Hour': The Popular Memory of World War Two and the Struggles over National Identity," in *National Fictions: World War Two in British Film and Television*, ed. Geoff Hurd, 10–11 (London, BFI Publishing, 1984).

39. Raymond Williams quoted in Dawson and West, "Our Finest Hour," 10–11. See also Popular Memory Group, "Popular Memory: Theory, Politics, Method."

40. Mary Chamberlain, "Narrative Theory," in *Handbook of Oral History*, ed. Thomas L. Charlton, Lois E. Myers, and Rebecca Sharpless, 389, 396, 399 (Lanham, Md: AltaMira Press, 2006).

41. See, for example, Elizabeth Lapovsky Kennedy, "Telling Tales: Oral History and the Construction of Pre-Stonewall Lesbian History," *Radical History Review* 62 (1995): 58–79. Christina Daley uses a similar approach to explain why brothers and sisters often remember their childhoods in different ways. As children they probably had different roles and experiences, but they also will have been socialized to remember their experience in different, gendered terms, for example in terms of relationships for girls or achievements for boys. Christina Daley, "'He Would Know, But I Just Have a Feeling': Gender and Oral History," *Women's History Review* 7, no. 3 (1998): 343–59. See also Yow, *Recording Oral History*, 51–52.

42. Mary Chamberlain, "The Global Self: Narratives of Caribbean Migrant Women," in *Feminism and Autobiography: Texts, Theories, Methods*, ed. Tess Cosslett, Celia Lurie, and Penny Summerfield, 154–66 (London: Routledge, 2000); Ann Laura Stoler with Karen Strassler, "Memory Work in Java: A Cautionary Tale," in *Carnal Knowledge and Imperial Power: Race and the Intimate in Colonial Rule* (Berkeley: University of California Press, 2002), 162–203.

43. See Della Pollock, ed., *Remembering: Oral History Performance* (New York: Palgrave Macmillan, 2005); Timothy G. Ashplant, "Anecdote as Narrative Resource in Working-Class Life Stories," in *Narrative and Genre*, ed. Mary Chamberlain and Paul Thompson, 9–113 (New Brunswick, N.J.: Transaction Publishers, 2004).

44. Frisch, *Shared Authority*.

45. Ruthellen Josselson and Amia Lieblich, eds., introduction to *The Narrative Study of Lives*, vol. 3 (London: Sage, 1995), 33.

46. Jerome Bruner, "The Narrative Construction of Reality," quoted in Chamberlain, "Narrative Theory," 391.

47. Oliver Sacks, *The Man Who Mistook His Wife for a Hat* (London: Picador, 1986), 105–6.

48. See Charlotte Linde, *Life Stories: The Creation of Coherence* (New York: Oxford University Press, 1993).

49. Portelli, *Battle of Valle Giulia: Oral History and the Art of Dialogue*, 185.

50. Portelli, "What Makes Oral History Different," 53. Italics in original.

51. Ritchie, *Doing Oral History*, 34.

52. Yow, "Do I Like Them Too Much?" 52–53.

53. Chamberlain, "Narrative Theory," 402–4.

BIBLIOGRAPHY

Chamberlain, Mary, and Paul Thompson, eds. *Narrative and Genre*. New Brunswick, N.J.: Transaction Publishers, 2004.

Gluck, Sherna Berger, and Daphne Patai, eds. *Women's Words: The Feminist Practice of Oral History*. New York: Routledge, 1991.

Frisch, Michael. *A Shared Authority: Essays on the Craft and Meaning of Oral and Public History*. Albany: State University of New York Press, 1990.

Perks, Robert, and Alistair Thomson, eds. *The Oral History Reader*. London: Routledge, 2006.

Pollock, Della, ed. *Remembering: Oral History Performance*. New York: Palgrave Macmillan, 2005.

Portelli, Alessandro. *The Death of Luigi Trastulli and Other Stories: Form and Meaning in Oral History*. Albany: State University of New York Press, 1991.

Schacter, Daniel. *Searching for Memory: The Brain, the Mind, and the Past*. New York: Basic Books, 1996.

Wood, Harriet Harvey, and A. S. Byatt, eds. *Memory: An Anthology*. London: Chatto and Windus, 2008.

CHAPTER 6

CAN MEMORY BE COLLECTIVE?

ANNA GREEN

MEMORY, in all its guises, has been at the heart of historical inquiry over the past three decades. Cultural and social historians, sociologists, social psychologists, and those working in cultural studies and literary criticism have generated a significant body of work exploring both individual autobiographical memory and collective, public memory. Intense interest in the subject of collective remembrance, initially focusing upon the social and cultural forms through which the violent and repressive history of the twentieth century were recalled and commemorated, has developed over time into a broader, interdisciplinary field focusing upon memory.[1] Over this period, however, research into autobiographical memory has often found itself relegated to the sidelines by the scholarly community's burgeoning interest in the social or cultural memory of the group.

The journal *History and Memory*, founded in the late 1980s with a particular focus upon the collective memories and legacies of Nazism, fascism, and the Holocaust, has recently been joined by the much newer journal *Memory Studies*, intended to facilitate interdisciplinary "dialogue and debate on the theoretical, empirical and methodological issues central to a collaborative understanding of memory today."[2] The first issue of the new journal of *Memory Studies* kicked off with an article by Henry L. Roediger and James V. Wertsch that sought to define the emerging interdisciplinary field of memory studies.[3] Within the landscape of memory studies the authors included empirical history, official national narratives, novels, memorials, case-based law, popular media, corporate memory, and religious ideas. Subsumed under the category of memory, therefore, were hugely divergent forms of historical evidence or representation that in other contexts would be identified by specific terms reflecting the different processes and purposes of creation, epistemological assumptions, and processes of dissemination/reception, including empirical history; discourse; oral tradition; historical representation or interpretation, performance; fiction; ideology; and myth.

The term "memory" has now expanded to encompass all these forms of historical consciousness, a development that received a less-than-enthusiastic response from those historians who define conventional history by its goals of objectivity and truth, as opposed to the subjectivity and partiality of memory. Whatever the merits of this argument, there is no doubt that the encompassing definition of memory studies above has many adherents across a wide range of disciplines, but even the authors acknowledge that the breadth of the field indicates the need for a much more precise terminology around memory.

Memory Studies and Oral History

This emerging interdisciplinary field sits alongside that of oral history, the collection and analysis of autobiographical memory, with its much earlier provenance. From the first written histories to the early nineteenth century and Jules Michelet on the French Revolution, the memories of those who participated in events were considered to be invaluable sources for the writing of history.[4] As historical research and writing became a professional, academic discipline with an emphasis upon written archival records in the mid-nineteenth century, autobiographical memory and oral sources lost favor. In Britain, one of the pioneering accounts of "spoken history" in the mid-twentieth century was George Ewart Evans's *Ask the Fellows Who Cut the Hay*, originally published in 1954. This collection of memories of rural labor and life in Suffolk in the late nineteenth and early twentieth centuries became part of the secondary school syllabus in the 1960s.[5] In the United States, the revival of oral history initially followed a different direction, beginning with the development of an oral history archive at Columbia University in 1948 for the memories of "significant lives."[6] Subsequently, in Britain and the United States, a new generation of postwar historians came to value oral history as an often unique source of information about the lives and perspectives of those outside political, social, or cultural elites. Two journals, *Oral History* (UK) and *Oral History Review* (U.S.), were founded in 1969 and 1973, the product of vibrant interdisciplinary oral history movements that brought together researchers working in the academic, public history, and community sectors.[7]

It might have been anticipated that those engaged in collective and individual remembrance would have a great deal to say to each other. Yet, despite the shared interest in the contexts, concepts, forms, and content of remembering, there has been relatively little interaction. Some scholars argue that autobiographical memories are irrelevant because they have no impact upon the public world. In Nancy Wood's study of memory in postwar Europe, individual and collective memories both avail themselves of "mechanisms like selection, narrativization, repression, displacement or denial." However, while the "emanation of individual memory is primarily subject to the laws of the unconscious," collective representations of the past represent the conscious purpose of social groups.[8] In this argument, collective action is permitted a high degree of intentionality, whereas individual memory (despite drawing upon the same cultural mechanisms) lacks a similar sense of purpose. Jay Winter and Emmanuel Sivan also differentiated between the active agency of collective remembrance, and "passive memory—understood as the personal recollections of a silent individual," or "*homo psychologicus*—the man of private memory."[9] In these definitions, individual memories were confined to the realm of psychology, presumed to lack conscious purpose and therefore irrelevant for the work of historians.

One of the reasons why there has been a lack of engagement between memory studies and oral history has been the deeply problematic relationship between the memory of the individual and that of the group.[10] As Katharine Hodgkin and Susannah Radstone have pointed out: "The concept of memory, in common use as well as in specialist writings, is now very generally taken to have purchase in domains beyond that of the individual; the idea of cultural or collective memory currently seems scarcely more contentious than the idea of individual memory. And yet the question of how, or indeed whether, memory might actually be considered salient at levels beyond the individual—of how we conceptualize memory in order to make such a move possible—remains... remarkably little investigated."[11] Despite this difficulty, and perhaps ironically, it is personal autobiographical memory that has vanished, collapsed into an all-encompassing concept of collective memory.

The difficulty originated with the original conceptual vocabulary around collective memory formulated by the sociologist Maurice Halbwachs in the 1920s. Halbwachs applied the idea of collective memory to the processes of remembering at every level of society, from the individual to the group, as well as to events directly experienced and those long in the past. Halbwach's understanding of collective memory is the place to start, followed by an exploration of the theoretical developments in both the humanities and social sciences that together created a receptive environment for the revival of his approach to memory from the 1980s on. One consequence of these developments in memory theory has been the complete assimilation of autobiographical or personal memory into that of the group, and the problems with this reductionist approach are explored in the second half of this chapter. The critique will revolve around the current conceptual utility of collective memory, the implications for interpretive theory of the very different social and cultural context—from that of Halbwachs's life—within which most remembering takes place in the early twenty-first century, and will conclude with alternative approaches that can provide a more nuanced and productive understanding of the relationship between the memory of the individual and that of the group.

Memories as Social Creations

What did Halbwachs originally intend when he formulated the idea of remembering as collective memory? First of all, he accepted that memory is a faculty of the individual brain. He wrote that "while the collective memory endures and draws strength from its base in a coherent body of people, it is individuals as group members who remember."[12] But he went on to suggest that memories are not individual but social creations. It was only through active discourse with others within the same social or cultural groups, such as the family or trade union, that the inchoate dreamlike impressions of individual recollection were turned into meaningful, durable memories. He rejected the idea of any purely individual conscious state, likening such a belief to assuming that "a heavy object, suspended in air by means of a number of very thin and interlaced wires, actually rests in the void where it holds itself up."[13] In some ways, this metaphor can convey the unfortunate image of the thinking, remembering individual as a marionette, rather than an active participant in conversational social relationships. This impression is reinforced when Halbwachs subsequently asserted that the process of sharing recollections of the past within the context of families and other small social groups harmonized individual memories, and contradictory memories faded away:

> It is not sufficient... to show that individuals always use social frameworks when they remember. It is necessary to place oneself in the perspective of the group or groups.... One may say that the individual remembers by placing himself in the perspective of the group, but one may also affirm that the memory of the group realizes and manifests itself in individual memories.[14]

Halbwachs included within these shared memories events beyond individual experience, describing the latter as "historical memory" through which individuals linked their own lives to the broader historical events and currents of their time. In a later essay he extended this to events beyond the human lifespan, drawing attention to the importance of both place and commemoration, reflected through the prism of contemporary needs and perspectives, in cementing collective memory for each generation. In "The Legendary Topography of the Gospels in the Holy Land," for example, Halbwachs explored the ways in which "the collective Christian memory adapts its recollections of the details of Christ's life and of the places where they occurred to the contemporary exigencies of Christianity, to its needs and aspirations."[15] These insights have generated extensive research, in particular, into the relationship between collective memory, ethnic conflict, and nationalism.[16]

Halbwachs's conceptualization of collective memory, therefore, should not be understood as the aggregation of individual memories. He believed that the deeply social process of remembering molds both personal and group memory into a cohesive whole, in accord "in each epoch, with the predominant thoughts of the society."[17] This dimension of Halbwachs's thought implied that some form of prior collective consciousness shared by all those in the group and into which individual memories are either incorporated or rejected. Halbwachs shared a close working relationship with the sociologist Émile Durkheim, and the latter's influence can be seen in Halbwachs's approach to the problem of memory. Durkheim was interested in the processes through which social cohesion is achieved, and in the *function* performed by cultural and social practices that integrated the individual into the group and created social harmony. Believing that memory performed a similar socially integrative function, Halbwachs's approach to memory was driven by a search for the mechanisms of social cohesion.

Halbwachs's ideas about collective memory lay dormant for fifty years, and until the end of the 1970s researchers were more interested in the experiential and evidential content of individual, or groups of individuals' memory. As the oral historian and sociologist Paul Thompson recalled, the first edition of his book *The Voice of the Past*, written in 1977, was "very much a positivistic work... the main argument is the positive value of these memories, and whether or not they're reliable, and how you decide whether or not they're reliable. That was the research tradition I was coming from, essentially a social scientific one."[18] By the time the second edition of the book was published ten years later it included a chapter on "Memory and the Self," reflecting the influence of new work by the Italian historians Luisa Passerini and Alessandro Portelli. Emphasizing the subjective and creative dimensions of remembering, including silences and distortions, Passerini and Portelli jointly transformed the analytical and interpretive approaches to oral history.[19]

The Subjective Dimensions of Oral History

In a pathbreaking article published in 1979, Luisa Passerini insisted that historians should recognize and value those subjective dimensions of oral history conventionally derided by historians. "The raw material of oral history," she wrote, "consists not just in factual statements, but is pre-eminently an expression and representation of culture, and therefore includes not only literal narrations but also the dimensions of memory, ideology and subconscious desires."[20] The role of female cultural norms, and subconscious resistance, were central to Passerini's analysis of women's self-representation in oral testimonies. Researchers from across the social science and humanities spectrum subsequently began to identify and explain the importance of understanding the subjective and cultural dimensions of autobiographical memory, including imagination, symbolism, myth and legend, narrative and genre.[21] These approaches to personal memory and subjectivity reflected quite a different approach to the positivism that informed the early work of Paul Thompson, and they paralleled theoretical trajectories emerging within the wider historical profession.[22]

In a subsequent seismic shift, one that led to acrimonious divisions among historians, the turn to cultural interpretation moved beyond its origins in literary theory, anthropology, and psychoanalysis to focus more exclusively upon language and discourse.[23] The linguistic turn in cultural theory, variously subsumed under the categories of postmodernism or poststructuralism, was based upon the understanding that language and discourse do not *reflect* the social and material world, they *construct* it. There was no accessible social or material reality separate from that constituted by language and discourse. Consequently, the idea of correspondence between language and reality, at the core of empirical history, was considerably reduced, for "language intervenes between human beings and their world," imposing a set of culturally established meanings.[24]

The implications for conventional approaches to history were profound. A raft of concepts long central to historical analysis, such as agency, intentionality, and experience, no longer appeared to drive human consciousness. At the most extreme end of the poststructuralist continuum, the thinking, reasoning, historical actor vanished, replaced by subject positions created through discourse.[25] Not all poststructuralists would agree that this approach to human subjectivity negated agency. Judith Butler, the feminist theorist, countered that "construction is not opposed to agency; it is the necessary scene of agency, the very terms in which agency is articulated and becomes culturally intelligible."[26] The goal for the historian working within the poststructuralist paradigm became one of disentangling the particular ways in which "subjects mediated or transformed discourses in specific historical settings."[27]

An example of a poststructuralist approach to oral histories may be found in Penny Summerfield's study of women's wartime recollections.[28] Summerfield compared women's oral histories with the dominant wartime discourses and slotted women's memories into a matrix of publicly available scripts, such as heroic or stoic narratives, or independent or obedient daughters. But it is impossible to understand, in this poststructuralist approach to oral history, why individuals adopt a particular discourse or how changes in individual perception could occur, without recourse to an external material reality. In many cases, oral history excerpts seem to suggest a more complex set of readings, with individual stories containing evidence of both discursive cultural templates and critical reflexivity. The capacity for reflexivity has the potential to give historians insights into the processes through which challenges to dominant discourses emerge.

Social Identity

Alongside the cultural, interpretive approaches to memory outlined above, and similarly highly influential among researchers in the field of memory studies, was the idea of social identity developed by social psychologists in 1979.[29] From that point on, the concept of the self came under increasingly critical scholarly scrutiny, eventually being displaced by the idea of social identity.[30] Definitions of selfhood are complex, but intellectual historians usually circle around three dimensions: "the material or bodily, the relational or social, and the reflexive or self-positing."[31] Social psychologists and social historians have largely focused upon the second dimension of self, the relational or social. Identities are created through relationships with other groups of people, and individuals may have multiple identities attached to different roles, groups, or organizations from the family to the nation. The volume of work on social identity is enormous, and as a concept it has been described as "vague, ambiguous, and enigmatic," resulting in a range of interpretive applications.[32]

As public and social, rather than private and personal, the concept of social identity provided historians with a means to connect human subjectivities with more abstract categories of political and social analysis.[33] This was particularly evident in the field of political history, where the concepts of identity and collective memory have led to a large body of work exploring the links between memory and national or ethnic identity, especially in contexts where either one or other is called into question through past or present conflict.[34] The use of reified memory extending far into the past, in such contexts, led some historians to define collective memory as ahistorical or anti-historical, the expression of "some eternal or essential truth" about a people or a nation state.[35]

Halbwachs's theory of collective memory therefore accorded with interdisciplinary developments in contemporary theorization around subjectivity that emphasized its relational, unconscious, and discursive dimensions. Its revival also owed a great deal to what has been described as a late-twentieth-century "memory boom" in societies across the Western world. This fascination with the past—variously described as an "obsession with memory," saturation with "creeping heritage," or more positively as "the historicist turn in national life"—was reflected in the expansion of museums, the building of new commemorative monuments, and the restoration of historic neighborhoods.[36] Historians began to think more deeply about social and cultural memory. In France, the historian Pierre Nora set out on an extended project to construct an alternative narrative of French history, one based upon a thematic approach to symbolic memory, the texts, sites, and symbols deemed to be central to French collective memory and French identity.[37]

Across a range of disciplines, cultural and social theory coalesced around the concept of collective memory, subsuming all forms of remembering, personal and group, experiential and learned, under one conceptual framework. As a consequence, human subjectivity came to be perceived as socially and culturally determined to the point where the idea of personal memory became irrelevant. The sociologist Michael Schudson, for example, argued that since memory can be expressed only through the "cultural construction of language in socially structured patterns of recall; in the most important sense all memory is collective cultural memory."[38] This emphasis upon the social and cultural structures of remembering, and upon form rather than content, undermined notions of human agency and, as a consequence, undermined the value of personal memory as a source of knowledge about the past. Was it possible, as James Fentress and Chris Wickham asked nearly twenty years ago, "to elaborate a conception of memory which, while doing full justice to the collective side of one's conscious life, does not render the individual a sort of automaton, passively obeying the interiorised collective will?" Turning the relationship around, how was collective memory created?[39]

The processes through which public or cultural memories are created and sustained are diverse and complex, emphasizing some aspects of the past while neglecting or repressing others. Some historians and sociologists have declined to use the vocabulary of collective memory for precisely these reasons. They prefer to use terms such as social, cultural, or public memory, or mnemonic practices.[40] Was it really possible to speak of a shared collective memory? Above all, has the idea of collective memory been extended beyond the point of conceptual utility?

Collective memory has, in the terms of Mieke Bal, become a "travelling concept."[41] It may be found across many academic disciplines, from sociology (where it began) to history, social psychology, marketing, and law among others.[42] As a result, there is no consistency concerning the object or meaning of collective memory. In practice, it may mean quite different things. The historical sociologist Jeffry Olick identified the major theoretical fault line running through collective memory theory. Collective memory, he suggested, may be either:

> the lowest common denominator or normal distribution of what individuals in a collectivity remember, or... "the collective memory" as a "social fact sui generis," a matter of collective representations that are the properties of the "collective unconscious" which is itself ontologically distinct from any aggregate of individual consciousness.[43]

The two sides can be described as the "distributed version" versus the "strong version" of collective memory. Halbwachs has generally been credited with the latter approach although his writings gave grounds for both positions.[44] While most contemporary scholarship adopted some form of the distributed version, it was not uncommon to find sweeping assertions about the degree of homogeneity within collectivities that invoked the existence of some form of external collective consciousness. In practice, many different forms of historical consciousness were included under the label of collective memory, for example memory as learned knowledge of the past alongside memory as recall of direct experience; and shared memories of recent events alongside knowledge of events beyond the human life span.

While agreeing with Bal that "travelling concepts" often lead to productive, interesting interdisciplinary cultural analysis, I also share her concern that the casual invocation of concepts as labels does not facilitate meaningful insights. In other words, the value of the concept lies in its capacity to help us "understand the object better *on its*—the object's—*own terms*."[45] The question that needs to be raised is whether the widespread and casual invocation of a single term, "collective memory," to cover virtually every aspect of historical consciousness assists the meaningful understanding of the object, that is, memory and remembering.

Another way of approaching this issue is to ask: What are the criteria for an effective and useful concept? The political scientist John Gerring began his study of this question with *Alice's Adventures in Wonderland and Through the Looking Glass*, when Humpty Dumpty insists that when he used a word, "it means just what I choose it to mean—neither more nor less." To this Alice responds, "The question is,... whether you *can* make words mean so many different things."[46] What are the criteria for evaluating whether a concept is providing an avenue for meaningful analysis, or has become a more or less generic label covering very different things? Gerring proposed a framework of eight criteria essential to what he describes as "conceptual goodness": coherence, operationalization, validity, field utility, resonance, contextual range, parsimony, and analytic/empirical utility. Let us look at how well the concept of collective memory fulfills Gerring's requirements for two of these criteria: coherence and validity.

All referential concepts, Gerring argued, "perform a grouping or sorting function. A concept gathers together things that are alike in some respect, distinguishing them from those things that are different."[47] Does the concept of collective memory, as currently applied, appropriately perform this sorting function? Closely allied to coherence is validity: to what extent is collective memory an accurate description of that it seeks to represent? As it stands, collective memory can be used to describe both remembered sense experience or learned information, two ways of knowing about the past. Autobiographical narratives, the shared oral traditions of groups such as the family, and the public myths of the nation state have all been described, at various times, as collective memory, as have films and novels. Are all these forms of thinking about the past sufficiently coherent? Is there a valid degree of alignment between term and object to justify the generic application of the conceptual term collective memory?

The Need for a More Precise Conceptual Vocabulary

The definition of memory most frequently accepted comes from psychology: the individual brain's ability to store, retain, and subsequently retrieve information, which encompasses both experiential and learned memory. It may be useful to draw a parallel here between episodic memory (personal, experiential) and semantic memory (collective, learned). These two forms of memory are closely intertwined. Cultural historians will rightly point to the importance of semantic memory—the norms and values of our social environment—in providing the structure and meaning for episodic memory.[48] Nonetheless, subsuming both forms of memory under the concept of "collective memory" has the effect of obliterating two obvious and major qualifications to this apparently seamless relationship.

First of all, each individual has an array of memories, which may not be shared by others. Such memories do not vanish, contrary to Halbwachs's assertions, in the absence of a social context through which they are constantly reinforced. While the frameworks for understanding past experience are derived from the social and cultural context, most individuals in contemporary societies are exposed to a cacophony of conflicting ideologies, values, and beliefs. Collective memory appears to operate on an understanding of semantic memory where remembering is reduced to a predetermined set of cultural norms. But in a culturally diverse and mobile world, to what extent are individuals able to select or choose from the alternatives open to them? There is also evidence that conceptual knowledge (semantic memory) differs in important ways between generations.[49] In searching for evidence of predetermined discourses and cultural identities within expressions of memory, are historians failing to hear or see the signs of critical reflection or contestation? Cultural history is frequently criticized for its failure to explain changing mentalities or subjectivities; could these be some of the reasons why?

A major problem for the field of memory studies lies in expanding the idea of memory beyond the individual. Scholars have argued that many ethnic and national identities in the contemporary world were constructed by memory, rather than the other way around. The basis for identification with the group, in Halbwachs's theory, is a moral and emotional desire for harmony.[50] In this case, identity, determined by collective consciousness, precedes memory: "Memory is determined by an identity (collective or individual) *that is already well established*.[51] However, contemporary conflicts suggest that insecurity around identity has also led different ethnic and national groups to create historical memories to stabilize and deepen group identification, to the extent that "a rule might be postulated: where identity is problematized, memory is valorized."[52]

This process became very clear during the breakup of Yugoslavia and the Soviet Union, at times with catastrophic consequences. In *Voices of Collective Remembering*, published in 2002, James Wertsch demonstrated the persistence of national cultural narratives in the context of the breakup of the Soviet state. Broad narrative templates continued into the present, even as detailed knowledge of specific events disappeared among the younger generations.[53] The point at issue here is whether this construction of historical consciousness is best conceptualized as a form of collective memory. The school students in Wertsch's study were too young to *remember* World War II. Their knowledge and understandings of the period were derived from a range of sources, including their grandparents' memories, state-sponsored textbooks, and popular film. Defining learned forms of historical consciousness as collective memory runs the risk of reifying national memory and obscuring the processes through which dominant political and cultural elites deploy cultural symbols and narratives in pursuit of ethnic or nationalist ends.

Any concept must surpass its rivals. If collective memory fails the test for "conceptual goodness," is there any other term that does a better job? First of all, the concept of collective memory does not adequately capture the complex cultural and social processes of personal or group remembering, subsuming these under a functionalist metaphor.[54] Secondly, its use has been stretched far beyond the boundaries of validity. Virtually all forms of thinking about the past—experiential and learned memory, history and fiction—have been dragooned into the collective memory compound. The old binary distinctions between individual and collective are clearly unsustainable, but neither is the collapse of personal memory into the collective. The memory of the group is not identical to that of the individual within it: "the emblems and articulations of memory in flags and films, memorials and museums, are in a different register of memory to that of the single individual's recollections of his or her own life, however, the two may connect."[55]

There is a desperate need for a more precise conceptual vocabulary around memory, not one generic label that forecloses on the analytical or interpretive process rather than opening it up. Many of these terms already exist but have been largely eschewed in favor of one label, that of collective memory. Public memory, cultural memory, social memory, autobiographical memory, mnemonic practices, mnemonic communities, among others, all have greater coherence and validity derived from stronger conceptual roots within established paradigms of intellectual inquiry.

In terms of autobiographical memory, is there a way forward that incorporates the social and relational dimensions of remembering, without the cultural reification implicit in much collective memory theorizing? At the core of Halbwachs's theory of collective memory was the exchange of memories within small familial or social groups, such as trade unions. While these exchanges undoubtedly still continue, the wider society of which they are a part has changed in fundamental ways. New communication technologies, such as the Internet, greater geographic mobility, and higher levels of education have all combined to create a very different context within which many people remember the past. The work of the anthropologist Daniel Miller is instructive in thinking about the implications of these changes.[56] Miller's research was based upon the diverse, multicultural, and relatively anonymous experience of living in urban London, in contrast to the small, stable, and more homogeneous communities of the early twentieth century upon which Halbwachs based his theory of collective memory.

Miller's analysis also brought together all three dimensions of the self: the material/bodily, the social/relationships, and the reflexive, and his conclusions fundamentally challenge much contemporary scholarly debate around human subjectivity. Taking thirty households in a randomly chosen London street, Miller undertook an ethnographic study exploring the role that objects from houses to pets to Christmas decorations play in human relationships. He predicated his approach on a belief that people find it easier to talk about their lives through their possessions than they do in response to direct questions. The modern state, Miller argued, provides a context in which material wealth and education, among other factors, permit individuals a much greater degree of "creative autonomy" than those from earlier human societies. In combination with a pluralist, multicultural society, he argued that identity and culture "increasingly look vestigial." Miller was struck by the "astonishing diversity and uniqueness" of those participating in his project, and he concluded:

> among the things once accomplished by religion or by the state but now increasingly delegated downwards, to individuals and households, is the responsibility for creating order and cosmology.... An order, moral or aesthetic, is still an authentic order even if one creates it for oneself and makes it up as one goes along, rather than just inheriting it as tradition or custom.[57]

Individual or household aesthetics, defined as the patterns or organizational principles, he concluded, are produced through reinforcing influences and networks of relationships, of interaction with other people, and with material culture. Miller's interactive model of human consciousness, grounded in the individual and his/her relationships and networks, contrasts with Halbwachs's static theatre metaphor, with its puppet connotations.

The capacity for self-fashioning, to borrow the term from Stephen Greenblatt's study of the Renaissance, may not be new. But while Miller rejected the vocabulary of "choice," there is surely an element of conscious personal selection among the potential relationships and networks available in modern, multicultural cities. There is, as some argue, "much leeway in what one can claim to be."[58] On the whole, theories based upon the idea of choice have been influential in the disciplines of economics and political science, where the possibility of conscious rational individual human choice and action has retained a stronger purchase upon intellectual enquiry and debate. Choice theory may have two dimensions, "an exploration of what it means to be rational or as a description of how people act in practice." The latter is not necessarily taken to imply a particular set of rational calculations, just that people "act as if they do."[59] This aspect of choice theory has potential links with emerging developments in cultural history. The linguistic determinism of the past two or more decades may be on the wane, moderated by cultural approaches that recognize the active nature of the engagement between culture and practice, and the creative role of human actors in this process. Although the vocabulary of choice remains restricted to the social sciences, interest in human intention and agency are re-emerging in cultural history through a focus upon the interplay between cultural systems and cultural practice.[60]

Personal and Collective Memory

The problem driving this analysis has been the conceptual incorporation of personal memory into collective memory, and it seems appropriate to end by reiterating the value of autobiographical memory to our understanding of both past and present. The specific content unique to personal memory and the choice (conscious or unconscious) of the frameworks through which personal experience is remembered and understood, provide the means through which historians can test grand narratives against personal memory or measure history from above against history from below. Personal memory can also tell us when, and sometimes why, ordinary people actively endorsed, acquiesced, or opposed inherited perspectives or dominant discourses. Oral historians need to remain alert to memories that do not fit the collective patterns, or those that are consciously reflexive and reveal the tensions between inheritance and critique in human consciousness. Contemporary theorizing around collective memory has paid too little attention to the capacity of individuals to reflect critically upon both their own experience and practice, and those of others. It is upon the latter, the capacity of individuals to recognize and critically reflect upon their experience and beliefs, that active human agency ultimately depends. Human subjectivity is more active, engaged, and critical than contemporary theory permits. We must keep space for the resistant, curious, rebellious, thoughtful, purposeful human subject.

NOTES

1. Henry L. Roediger III and James V. Wertsch, "Creating a New Discipline of Memory Studies," *Memory Studies* 1, no. 1 (2008): 9–22. This has been accompanied by anthologies, readers, and theoretical texts on the subject of memory. For recent examples, see Barbara A. Misztal, *Theories of Social Remembering* (Buckingham: Open University, 2003); two volumes in the Transaction Memory and Narrative series: Katharine Hodgkin and Susannah Radstone, eds., *Memory, History, Nation* (New Brunswick, N.J.: Transaction, 2006) and Susannah Radstone and Katharine Hodgkin, eds., *Memory Cultures* (New Brunswick, N.J.: Transaction, 2006); in the Stanford Cultural Memory in the Present series, Jan Assmann, *Religion and Cultural Memory* (Stanford, Calif.: Stanford University Press, 2006); Geoffrey Cubitt, *History and Memory* (Manchester: Manchester University Press, 2007; Michael Rossington and Anne Whitehead, eds., *Theories of Memory: A Reader* (Edinburgh: University of Edinburgh, 2007).

2. See Andrew Hoskins et al., "Editorial," *Memory Studies* 1, no. 1 (2008): 5.

3. Roediger and Wertsch, "Creating a New Discipline of Memory Studies," 9–22.

4. Jules Michelet, *The People*, trans. John P. McKay (Urbana: University of Illinois Press, 1973), xxvii, 4–5.

5. George Ewart Evans, *Ask the Fellows Who Cut the Hay* (London: Faber and Faber, 1956).

6. Donald A. Ritchie, *Doing Oral History* (New York: Oxford University Press, 2003), 22.

7. See the editorial, fortieth-anniversary issue of *Oral History* 37, no. 1 (2009): 2.

8. Nancy Wood, *Vectors of Memory: Legacies of Trauma in Postwar Europe* (Oxford: Berg, 1999), 2.

9. Jay Winter and Emmanuel Sivan, "Setting the Framework," in *War and Remembrance in the Twentieth Century* (Cambridge: Cambridge University Press, 1999), 6, 10.

10. For an early formulation of the conceptual difficulties attached to collective memory, see James Fentress and Chris Wickham, *Social Memory* (Oxford: Blackwell, 1992); see also the discussion in Assmann, *Religion and Cultural Memory*, 1–30.

11. Katharine Hodgkin and Susannah Radstone, "Rethinking Memory," *History Workshop Journal* 59 (2005): 130.

12. Maurice Halbwachs, *The Collective Memory*, trans. Francis J. Ditter Jr. and Vida Yazdi Ditter (New York: Harper and Row, 1980 [1950], 48.

13. Ibid., 49.

14. Maurice Halbwachs, *On Collective Memory*, ed. and trans. by Lewis A. Coser (Chicago: University of Chicago Press, 1992), 40.

15. Ibid., 234.

16. For contrasting perspectives on this relationship, see Patrick J. Geary, *The Myth of Nations: The Medieval Origins of Europe* (Princeton, N.J.: Princeton University Press, 2002) and Anthony Smith, *Myths and Memories of the Nation* (New York: Oxford University Press, 1999); see also Ed Cairns and Micheál D. Roe, eds., *The Role of Memory in Ethnic Conflict* (New York: Palgrave Macmillan, 2002); Jeffrey Olick, ed., *States of Memory: Continuities, Conflicts, and Transformations in National Retrospection* (Durham, N.C.: Duke University Press, 2003).

17. Halbwachs, *On Collective Memory*, 40.

18. Paul Thompson, interview by Karen Worcman, Sweden, 1996, 32. See Qualidata, University of Essex: http://www.esds.ac.uk/qualidata/online/data/edwardians/biography.asp.

19. Luisa Passerini, *Fascism in Popular Memory: The Cultural Experience of the Turin Working Class* (Cambridge: Cambridge University Press, 1987); "Women's Personal Narratives: Myths, Experiences, and Emotions," in *Interpreting Women's Lives*, The Personal Narratives Group, 189–97 (Bloomington: Indiana University Press, 1989); Alessandro Portelli, *The Death of Luigi Trastulli and Other Stories* (Albany: SUNY Press, 1991) and *The Battle of Valle Giulia* (Madison: University of Wisconsin Press, 1997).

20. Luisa Passerini, "Work Ideology and Consensus under Italian Fascism: Work in Progress," *History Workshop Journal* 8 (1979): 84.

21. Some examples from an extensive body of work are Raphael Samuel and Paul Thompson, *The Myths We Live By* (London: Routledge, 1990); Marie-Françoise Chanfrault-Duchet, "Narrative Structures, Social Models, and Symbolic Representation in the Life Story," in *Women's Words*, ed. Sherna Berger Gluck and Daphne Patai, 77–92 (London: Routledge, 1991); Graham Dawson, *Soldier Heroes: British Adventure, Empire and the Imagining of Masculinities* (London: Routledge, 1994); and Alistair Thomson, *Anzac Memories: Living with the Legend* (Oxford: Oxford University Press, 1994).

22. See Lynn Hunt, ed., *The New Cultural History* (Berkeley: University of California Press, 1989); Victoria E. Bonnell and Lynn Hunt, eds., *Beyond the Cultural Turn* (Berkeley: University of California Press, 1999); Peter Burke, *What Is Cultural History?* (Cambridge: Cambridge University Press, 2004); and Anna Green, *Cultural History* (London: Palgrave Macmillan, 2008), chap. 4.

23. Ron Grele was one of the first oral historians to draw explicitly upon theories from linguistics in the 1970s, using linguistic structuralism to identify the narrative frameworks of stories about past labor conflicts: "Listen to Their Voices," *Oral History* 7 (1979).

24. Catherine Belsey, *Poststructuralism* (Oxford: Oxford University Press, 2002), 6.

25. See J. W. Scott, "Experience," in *Feminists Theorize the Political*, ed. Judith Butler and Joan W. Scott (London: Routledge, 1992).

26. Judith Butler, *Gender Trouble: Feminism and the Subversion of Identity* (London: Routledge, 2006), 201.

27. Kathleen Canning "Feminist History after the Linguistic Turn: Historicizing Discourse and Experience," *Signs: Journal of Women in Culture and Society* 19, no. 2 (1994): 373–74.

28. Penny Summerfield, *Reconstructing Women's Wartime Lives* (Manchester: Manchester University Press, 1998).

29. H. Tajfel and J. C. Turner, "An Integrative Theory of Intergroup Conflict," in *The Social Psychology of Intergroup Relations*, ed. William G. Austin and Stephen Worchel (Monterey, Calif.: Brooks/Cole, 1979).

30. For a good discussion of self and identity in social psychology, see Martha Augoustinos, Iain Walker, and Ngaire Donaghue, *Social Cognitition*, 2nd ed. (London: Sage, 2006), chap. six.

31. Jerrold Seigel, "Problematizing the Self," in *Beyond the Cultural Turn: New Directions in the Study of Society and Culture*, ed. Victoria E. Bonnell and Lynn Hunt, 285 (Berkeley: University of California Press, 1999).

32. Fernando Aguiar and Andrés de Francisco, "Rational Choice, Social Identity, and Beliefs About Oneself," *Philosophy of the Social Sciences Online First*, doi:10.1177/0048393109333631 (Mar. 25, 2009):5. Economists have been more interested in the problematic relationship between social identity and rational choice theories; in history and historical sociology, the focus has been upon social identities and group cohesion.

33. See Charles Tilly, ed., *Citizenship, Identity and Social History* (Cambridge: Cambridge University Press, 1996), 7.

34. Jeffrey K. Olick, ed., *States of Memory: Continuities, Conflicts, and Transformations in National Retrospection* (Durham, N.C.: Duke University Press, 2003), 4; Allan Megill, "History, Memory, Identity," *History of the Human Sciences* 11, no. 3 (1998): 39–40.

35. Peter Novick, *The Holocaust and Collective Memory* (London: Bloomsbury, 2001 [1999]), 4.

36. Andreas Huyssen, *Twilight Memories: Marking Time in a Culture of Amnesia* (New York: Routledge, 1995), 5; David Lowenthal, *The Past is a Foreign Country* (Cambridge: Cambridge University Press, 1985), xv, xvi; and Raphael Samuel, *Theatres of Memory* (London: Verso, 1994), 169.

37. Pierre Nora, *Realms of Memory: Rethinking the French Past*, trans. Arthur Goldhammer (New York: Columbia University Press, 1996–98), 3 vols.; see also Green, *Cultural History*, chap. 6.

38. Michael Schudson, "Dynamics of Distortion in Collective Memory," in *Memory Distortion: How Minds, Brains and Societies Reconstruct the Past*, ed. Daniel Schacter, 346–47 (Cambridge, Mass: Harvard University Press, 1995).

39. Fentress and Wickham, *Social Memory*, ix.

40. See Green, *Cultural History*, 105–6.

41. Mieke Bal, *Travelling Concepts in the Humanities* (Toronto: University of Toronto Press, 2002).

42. Alon Confino, "Collective Memory and Cultural History: Problems of Method," *American Historical Review* 102, no. 5 (Dec. 1997): 1386–87; James W. Pennebaker, Dario Paez, and Bernard Rimé, eds., *Collective Memory of Political Events: Social Psychological Perspectives* (Mahwah, N.J.: Lawrence Erlbaum Associates, 1997); Judy Foster Davis, "'Aunt Jemima is Alive and Cookin?' An Advertiser's Dilemma of Competing Collective Memories," *Journal of Macromarketing* 27 (2007): 35; Mark Osiel, *Mass Atrocity, Collective Memory, and the Law* (New Brunswick, N.J.: Transaction, 1997).

43. Olick, *States of Memory*, 6.

44. James V. Wertsch, *Voices of Collective Remembering* (Cambridge: Cambridge University Press, 2002), 20–29.

45. Bal, *Travelling Concepts in the Humanities*, 8. Italics in original.

46. John Gerring, *Social Science Methodology: A Criterial Framework* (Cambridge: Cambridge University Press, 2001), 38–39.

47. Ibid., 41.

48. Assmann, *Religion and Cultural Memory*, 2–3.

49. Pennebaker, Paez, and Rimé, *Collective Memory of Political Events*, 40–43.

50. See Noa Gedi and Yigal Elam, "Collective Memory—What Is It?" *History and Memory* 8, no. 1 (1996): 30–50; and Osiel, *Mass Atrocity, Collective Memory, and the Law*, 213–14.

51. Megill, "History, Memory, Identity," 44. Italics in original.

52. Ibid., 40.

53. Wertsch, *Voices of Collective Remembering*, 176–77.

54. Gedi and Elam, "Collective Memory: What Is It?" 30–50.

55. Hodgkin and Radstone, *Memory, History, Nation*, 8.

56. Daniel Miller, *The Comfort of Things* (Cambridge: Polity Press, 2008).

57. Ibid., 293.

58. Megill, "History, Memory, Identity," 41.

59. Michael Allingham, *Choice Theory: A Very Short Introduction* (Oxford: Oxford University Press, 2002), 9.

60. See Gabrielle M. Spiegel, *Practicing History: New Directions in Historical Writing After the Linguistic Turn* (New York: Routledge, 2005), 18.

BIBLIOGRAPHY

Cubitt, Geoffrey. *History and Memory*. Manchester: Manchester University Press, 2007.

Hodgkin, Katharine, and Susannah Radstone, eds. *Memory, History, Nation*. New Brunswick, N.J.: Transaction, 2006.

Mistral, Barbara A. *Theories of Social Remembering*, Buckingham: Open University, 2003.

Radstone, Susannah, and Katharine Hodgkin, eds. *Memory Cultures*. New Brunswick, N.J.: Transaction, 2006.

Rossington, Michael, and Anne Whitehead, eds. *Theories of Memory: A Reader*. Edinburgh: University of Edinburgh, 2007.

Wertsch, James V. *Voices of Collective Remembering*. Cambridge: Cambridge University Press, 2002.

CHAPTER 7

CASE STUDY: ROME'S HOUSE OF MEMORY AND HISTORY: THE POLITICS OF MEMORY AND PUBLIC INSTITUTIONS

ALESSANDRO PORTELLI

THIS case study is about the organization and politics of public memory: the House of Memory and History (Casa della Memoria e della Storia), established by the city of Rome in 2006, in the framework of an ambitious program of cultural policy. Inaugurated by Mayor Walter Veltroni on March 24, 2006 (a symbolic date, being the anniversary of the Nazi massacre at the Fosse Ardeatine, the most dramatic event in the history of World War II and Resistance in Rome), the House has become a center for public events, a resource for research, and a memory community in itself.[1] Here, I will summarize the history of the House's conception and founding, describe its activities and the role of oral history in them, and discuss some of the problems it faces.

The Crisis of Anti-Fascism

At the start of the twenty-first century, Rome's city government realized that a number of historic anti-Fascist and Resistance-originated institutions were losing their leases and finding themselves without a space. These included ANPI (Associazione Nazionale Partigiani Italiani, the left-oriented National Association of Italian Partisans), FIAVL (Federazione Italiana Volontari della Libertà, the liberal-oriented Federation of Freedom Volunteers), ANED (Associazione Nazionale ex-Deportati [Italian Association of Former Deported Persons], which included Shoah survivors as well as political deportees), ANPPIA (Associazione Nazionale Perseguitati Politici Antifascisti [association of former victims of Fascist political persecution]), ANEI (Associazione Nazionale Ex Internati [association of Italian military prisons who refused to join the Nazi and Fascist military]). Most of these organizations, established after World War II, had originally served a role of assistance and support to their members, but had also been instrumental in reinforcing the anti-Fascist ethos of the new democratic republic. They were granted state funding by law and were housed free or for a nominal rent in public housing complexes or in state- or city-owned apartments. As their numbers dwindled with age, and the immediate assistance needs grew less urgent, all of these associations accentuated their role in public and cultural discourse and took on an increasingly necessary task of memory.

Two factors converged in making their continuation precarious in the 1990s: the crisis of anti-Fascism and the privatization of public-owned housing. The collapse of the Communist and Socialist parties, and crises in the New Left, deprived anti-Fascism of a dependable political representation.[2] At the same time, the new forces that rose in the government—from Silvio Berlusconi's Forza Italia to the (nominally) former Fascists of Alleanza Nazionale to the rabidly chauvinistic Northern League—all located themselves outside the anti-Fascist pact built in the Resistance that had originated Italy's democratic constitution. Even in the bankrupt former Left, a discourse of "reconciliation" (without "truth," indeed with a serious dose of historical revisionism and manipulation of memory) took hold and helped defuse the relevance of the Resistance and of its memory and meaning. While funding as provided by law to the veteran anti-Fascist organizations was reluctantly continued, many benefits were gradually lost and, most importantly, there grew around them a frustrating sense of isolation, of impotence, and irrelevance, accentuated, of course, by the aging and dwindling numbers of the survivors, which also meant the loss of some revenue from members' dues. Even more than in institutional terms, this process has become dominant in the media and much of public opinion. As I was writing these observations in February 2008, a bill was pending in the House to legally equate former partisans with veterans of the Fascist units that fought on the side of the Nazis.

The other (not unrelated) factor was the gradual process of alienating and privatizing state and public property. As the spaces used by these organizations—often located in the center of the city or in historic buildings—became the property of banks and other private concerns, the new owners expected a profit. Thus, some of them were evicted, and some saw their rents raised to levels that they could not afford. This was a serious risk for the preservation of important archives and libraries. Often, precious documents had to be temporarily housed in church cellars or other unfit spaces. But it was also a symbolic wound to the democratic memory of Rome and Italy.

At the time, the city government of Rome was run by a center-left majority, while all other institutions, from the national government to the provincial and regional administrations, were controlled by very right-wing coalitions, with strong revisionist and anti-intellectual ideological tendencies.[3] In his first term as mayor, Walter Veltroni placed culture and history at the very center of his vision of city government: the cultural heritage of the past and the contemporary cultural role of Rome as a major European capital were to be both the core of its identity and a major element in its economy. As opposed to the right-wing domination of the national, regional, and provincial governments, Rome was to some extent a space of resistance to the onslaught of the anti-cultural revisionist mentality propagated by the Right and by the TV channels that were nearly all owned or controlled by Berlusconi.

Cultural policy, therefore, was a major channel for the preservation and reconstruction of a different ethos and polity. Along with mass events and spaces: the "White Nights," in which all museums and cultural institutions stayed open from dusk to dawn and thousands of shows and cultural events were offered free of charge; free mass rock concerts in the historic spaces of the city; and the new auditorium, which offered all musical genres and hosted Veltroni's pet project, the Rome Film Festival. Under the mayor's impulse, the city government created institutions like the House of Cinema, the House of Theaters, the House of Jazz, the House of Literature. A most important project was the organization of students' visits to Auschwitz, accompanied by the mayor and by those survivors who felt they were up to the task. These visits were not just school trips; they were prepared by year-long projects in the participating schools and were followed by new projects and activities in which the students engaged on their return.

Memory, History, and Politics

The idea of a House of Memory and History grew in this cultural and political context. The city government was concerned with the material need to find spaces for the organizations of the veterans of the Resistance and the survivors of deportation, imprisonment, political discrimination. On the other hand, memory and history were a crucial part of Veltroni's overall political and cultural project. In fact, for the first time the city appointed a mayor's advisor for the preservation and development of the city's democratic memories. My book on the Fosse Ardeatine had just been published, and I was appointed to fill the role.[4] While there were serious operational and budget limits to the new position, it was itself an indication of a vision of the importance of the politics of memory. That the first advisor on memory was designated on the strength of an oral history book was a sign of the coming of age of an approach to history and memory that had been long marginalized in academic circles. My first project led to Rome's city government hosting the 2004 International Oral History Association conference on "Memory and Globalization."

When the House of Memory and History was first conceived, its function was primarily that of helping ANPI and the other veterans' organizations survive, by finding them a space. This was achieved by accepting a proposal from the Jewish community, to swap a city-owned building in the Jewish ghetto with the Jewish-community–owned building of the Jewish school in the old history-rich neighborhood of Trastevere, between the International Women's House and the old city jail at Regina Coeli.[5] This allowed the Jewish community to concentrate all its educational activities in one space, which they designated as the Palazzo della Cultura (Culture Building), while making a space available for the House of Memory project. As plans were being drawn, however, several people and groups, including myself and ANPI President Massimo Rendina, pointed out that—to put it bluntly—placing all these old veterans in one building and naming it "House of Memory" had a somewhat cemeterial connotation. Rather than making anti-Fascist memory central to the present life of the city, it relegated it to a marginal, fading past.

Indeed, it was clear that the memories of the veterans' organizations had a necessarily limited time horizon. Their younger members were by then in their late seventies. What would happen to their memories (and to the organizations themselves) once they were gone?[6] The question, in fact, was the meaning of the concept of "memory." While there was no doubt that these organizations and their members were precious first-person bearers of memories, many observers and participants insisted that if memory was to be part of a democratic social awareness, it should not remain the exclusive patrimony of its bearers, nor ought it be cherished uncritically per se, but should be researched, collected, and analyzed as a historical source and as the subject of critical historical inquiry, and shared as public cultural capital. As former president of the Republic, Oscar Luigi Scalfaro, said during the inauguration ceremony, "This House will be instrumental in forming human beings capable of saying no to war as is stated in our Constitution."[7] Mayor Walter Veltroni, in turn, explained that the House would be "dynamic and active, with a rich program of events, and it will not be only the space given to the associations that act in defense of memory, but a house to which all citizens may come to re-read history, to make sure that the tragedies of the past do not happen again."[8]

For these reasons, it was agreed that, in order to underline the project's proactive approach, the new space would be renamed House of Memory *and History*, and would host research organizations and resources as well as the veteran organizations. At the time, Rome's two most important research structures dealing with democratic and anti-Fascist memory also had a problem of space. The former Istituto Storico della Resistenza (Resistance Historical Institute), recently renamed as IRSIFAR (Istituto Romano per la storia d'Italia dal Fascismo alla Resistenza [Rome

Institute for Italian History from Fascism to Resistance]) was housed in prestigious but decaying and wholly inadequate spaces, also provided by the city. IRSIFAR is part of a national network of Resistance History Institutes. It possesses a unique library and archive of Resistance-related and contemporary-history books and papers, and along with historical research projects, it carries out a precious work of teacher-training and educational projects in the schools. Placing IRSIFAR alongside with the former partisans' own offices thus made a great deal of sense. They cold support the veterans' cultural presence in public discourse, and at the same time they could involve personally the former partisans and camp survivors in their teaching and training projects. Memory and history were, literally, side by side.

Public Events

The condition of the Circolo Gianni Bosio—an independent, movement-oriented cultural organization that has established Rome's most important sound archive of folk music and oral history—was even worse.[9] After years in which we had not been able to house our collections properly because of inadequate spaces, the Circolo was now literally squatting in an abandoned school building in the center of Rome. We had finally been able to put all our tapes and books in one space, but it was less than ideal because of temperature and dust. Yet, the fact that the archive existed, along with a specialized library and media collection, a folk music school, a series of public concerts, a number of publications of books and CDs, and a film series included in the Rome Film Festival, gave the Circolo a credibility that allowed us to play a visible role in Rome's cultural life. The proposal of moving the archive and library to the House of Memory and History meant that we would also be part of a broader design, make our resources more easily available to interested citizens and scholars, be able to use a space for public programs, and interview the former partisans, anti-Fascists, and camp survivors with whom we shared the House for our own archive as well as for their own organizations.

The inclusion of IRSIFAR and the Circolo Bosio derived also from another policy of memory consideration. In order to function as an alternative and resistance to the dominant right-wing discourse, democratic discourse must reach beyond the immediate sphere of its own bearers. In order to justify its own existence in a publicly owned space, the House of Memory and History needed to be more than a haven for living memories and a resource for specialists. It had to become an irradiator for critical social awareness and public sharing and discussion of democratic history and memory. IRSIFAR's work with schools, and the Circolo Bosio's use of music were seen as ways of reaching out to citizens, and especially to younger generations. Beyond their institutional tasks, then, the organizations that found a space in the House of Memory and History were to turn themselves into a public service through the organization of public events open to the community and especially to schools. The inclusion in the House of a specialized branch of the city library system, a multimedia space and Internet services, were also part of this vision.[10]

The architects who redesigned the building had conceived it mainly as office and archive space. The room set aside for public events was intended to seat no more than thirty-six people. It took a concerted effort of all organizations to get the city bureaucracy to change the chairs and add more rows so that occupancy could reach about one hundred. It is technically illegal, however, for more than one hundred twenty people to be in the building at the same time. From its very inception, however, the House of Memory and History went beyond this aspect to develop an additional purpose as the focus of public events including seminars, book panels, exhibitions, conferences, films, readings, and music.

Hardly a day has gone by since inauguration in which there was not some event going on. Some were promoted and organized by the individual organizations, others were joint projects coordinated by the city's Office of Cultural Policy. Among the more recent examples of the former type in the series of seminars organized by ANPI on "Ideologies of the Twentieth Century," which included round tables with contemporary political leaders; the IRSIFAR's series on "Women, Work, and Cinema"; and the Circolo Bosio two-day series on oral history and folk music in Umbria. Some of the coordinated projects were "Cinema, memory and—" a series of events featuring feature and documentary films, readings, music, each event organized by one of the House's organizations. Circolo Bosio, for instance, arranged a presentation of Elio Petri's *La Classe operaia va in paradiso*—"the working class goes to heaven"–followed by a documentary on steel workers and a concert by topical singer Paolo Pietrangeli. Or "Testi e testimony" (texts and testimony), a series alternating seminars and readings on works of literature with a memory theme (I presented one on Toni Morrison's *Beloved*), with public oral history interviews (I interviewed a former army internee on military resistance in World War II). A recent, very successful project, in terms of attendance, was the exhibition on "Ellis Island: The Italian's Gate to America," with images and memorabilia of Italian emigration to the United States. Running from December 2008 to the end of February 2009, the exhibition was accompanied by film showings, a conference with papers by scholars from different disciplines,[11] and a closing concert of Italian songs of emigration performed by the folk music icons Giovanna Marini and Sara Modigliani and American songs of immigration performed by Mariano De Simone.

One should not overestimate the impact of these activities. Even in standing-room-only concerts, the audience is never much more than one hundred, and the average age tends to be rather high, except when schools are brought in—not necessarily by the students' own choice, though. What makes up for the small audiences are the continuity of events and their consistently high quality. The continuity of activities means that over the years in which it has been in existence, the House has been visited by several thousand citizens; the fact that audiences are not massive means that participation in events is active and very intense. The inclusion of cinema and music, especially in the events organized by the Circolo Bosio has helped bring in more diverse age groups and create a basic core of regular participants that form a kind of community in themselves.

Oral history has played a key role in the shaping and growth of the House's activity and identity. The Circolo Gianni Bosio's "Franco Coggiola" sound archive is a major European collection of oral history and folk music, going back to the late 1960s.[12] Along with my own tapes and sound files from Rome, Lazio, Umbria, the United States, Bulgaria, Spain, Brazil, and Scotland, it houses a number of collections from Calabria, Puglia, Umbria, and Tuscany, and is constantly being enriched by new research and by new deposits. The aim is to create a "critical mass" that will make it impossible for historians and researchers to keep ignoring oral history as a source. Though it operates almost entirely with volunteer work, the archive has managed to digitalize most of the collections, to publish most of the catalog on the Web, and to publish some of its holdings in audio and video format.[13] The collections are now available and are being used by a growing number of musicians, historians, anthropologists, teachers, journalists, theater actors, and authors. On the basis a recently approved grant from the Ministry of Cultural Heritage, the archive will become the hub of an electronic resource linking oral history archives nationally. Being located in the House of Memory and History also allowed us to start interviewing the former partisans and anti-Fascists who share the building with us. Interviews such as those with ANPI's president Massimo Rendina, a former military partisan commander in Northern Italy, or with Guido Albertelli, son of one of the Resistance leaders killed at the Fosse Ardeatine, are very important additions not only to our collection but also to the self-awareness of the partisans' own organization. We have also taped most of the events held at the House, thus gathering the stories of Shoah survivors, partisans, anti-Fascist exiles, and other protagonists of our democratic history.

Thanks to the availability of the House and its logistic supports, the Circolo Bosio was also able to take the initiative of creating for the first time an Italian oral history association (AISO, Associazione Italiana di Storia Orale). The first AISO conference took place at the House of Memory in March 2008, with then IOHA president Alistair Thomson as the keynote speaker; another conference, on the use of video in oral history, was held there in November 2008. The Circolo Bosio still lends office space and a mailing address to AISO.

The "Franco Coggiola" archive is not the only oral history resource and activity available at the House of Memory and History. Over the years, IRSIFAR has also collected a number of recordings of interviews and events—for instance, the recording of the trial of the Fosse Ardeatine perpetrator, Erich Priebke. IRSIFAR and Circolo Bosio cooperated on oral history interviews with former partisans. ANED, the association of former camp inmates, has an excellent collection of video interviews with Shoah survivors, antedating the Shoah Foundation's initiative. ANPPIA (the former victims of Fascist persecution and discrimination) recruited the Circolo Bosio archive and expertise to carry out a project of interviews with former political exiles from the Roman hills area.[14]

Political Changes

The House of Memory and History can be considered a success, limited perhaps but not insignificant. Problems and difficulties remain, however, beyond the question of limited attendance and insufficient space (the library has already used all its allotted space, and there is no room for expansion). Most immediate are the questions of funding and management. The House of Memory and History is literally a *house*; that is, it does not exist as an institution in itself but is a cohabitation of separate organizations. This means, for one thing, that there is no funding for the House in itself and its entirety; rather, each organization depends on its own resources, which vary with membership and with political pull. This makes it also more difficult to coordinate initiatives. Although there is a coordinating committee composed of representatives of ANPI, IRSIFAR, and Circolo Bosio, each organization tends to go its own way and not get involved in projects and events promoted by the others. Many of the common projects, in fact, do not originate within the House itself but are promoted by the de facto coordinator, the staff of the city's Cultural Policy Office.

This might not be much of a problem in itself, or at least it wasn't with the previous administration. However, the problems of a cultural institution with a democratic and progressive orientation, depending on a political institution like a city government, came to light in the spring of 2008. At that time the center-left administration was replaced by a right-wing coalition, which was greeted by Roman salutes, shouts of "Duce Duce," and black shirts on the Capitol steps on election night. Ironically, the overall situation was partly reversed: the region and the province are now run by center-left coalitions, while the national government is still in the hands of Silvio Berlusconi and his other right-wing allies. Although the new mayor, Gianni Alemanno, paid lip service to the Fosse Ardeatine and other Resistance memorials, it was clear that the cultural horizons of the new majority would revolve around the axes of historical revisionism, surface reconciliation without truth, anti-anti-Fascism, and opportunistic Catholic fundamentalism.[15]

There were good reasons to worry about what would become of the House of Memory and History and its organizations. Would it survive? Would the new government force a right-wing memory agenda on us? Actually, it was all much more subtle. The new head of the city Office of Cultural Policy came to reassure us that the new majority accepted anti-Fascism as the foundation of the Republic, and therefore would do nothing against the partisans and their organizations. In fact, we soon realized that the new administration was aware that interfering with the partisans and the ex-deportees would not look very good even in the current cultural climate. They knew very well that the House of Memory and History and its organizations would be relatively innocuous as long as they remained in their niche and kept preaching mainly to their audiences of the converted while the new administration carried out its own politics of memory on a much larger scale and with much more media access.

Two examples: (1) the mediocre and rabidly antipartisan *Il sangue dei vinti* was forced upon the Rome Film Festival program,[16] and (2) while the visits to Auschwitz were continued as required by a unanimous city council ruling in 2007, the Holocaust was now equated with repression in Russia, and much emphasis was placed on school visits to a place dear to right-wing memory, the *foibe*, the gaping caves (*dolines*) on the Eastern border, where the Yugoslav army brutally killed at least 5,000 Italians during World War II. The *foibe* have thus been a pet cause of the Right, always evoked in order to minimize and balance the Holocaust and the Fosse Ardeatine.[17] On those visits the students were offered less historical knowledge than horror stories and vulgarly offensive propaganda. Nothing was told about the Italian concentration camps where thousand of Slovenes and Croats found their death, the burning of Yugoslav villages, the mass murders perpetrated by Italian troops, the Italian appropriation of much of Yugoslavia before the *foibe* massacres took place, which does not excuse any of the Yugoslav partisans' war crimes but helps put them in context.[18]

Another question that has arisen in the House's activity is: On what memories should we concentrate? The House was originally conceived to house organizations whose origins go back to World War II and, in the case of the former victims of fascist discrimination and repression, even earlier. The origins of IRSIFAR as a Resistance history institute also reinforce this orientation (as does the right-wing insistence on the *foibe*). Too often, then, memory is identified with those events and times. It is a fact that the way in which we understand those events and times is crucial to the way we understand the contemporary identity and nature of the state. Historical revisionism is not just an academic matter. It paves the way for constitutional revisions that erode the civil rights and the forms of citizens' participation provided for by the anti-Fascist constitution.[19] Those events of sixty years ago are very far from the experience and concerns of today's young people. The risk is that if memory is identified and discussed in the terms set at that time (and often by the same individuals), it will appear as boring and irrelevant to the experiences and concerns of today's young people.

IRSIFAR and the Circolo Bosio have insisted on carrying the work of memory and history up to the present time. While there has been a general agreement on this approach, some difficulties did arise. In fact, the postwar democratic experience and the continuation of anti-Fascism are part of a history in which the Communist and Socialist parties, the unions, and later, the student movements and the New Left—no matter what their grave errors and limitations—played a crucial role. This is a history that many at this time would either like to forget or demonize in the name of anti-Communism in all its forms and variants, from Berlusconi's ranting to the attempt of former Communists to gloss over their history or to make apologies for it. The same, to some extent, applies to the memory and history of the student movements and the New Left that are too often and too easily associated with terrorism and the Red Brigades. The postwar memory presented at the House has paid due attention to, for one, the women's liberation movement, but it has all but ignored the labor movement and the working class.

While the House remains dedicated to the cause of human rights and peace, the search for a common ground among its organizations, as well as the need not to overly antagonize the institutions on which the House ultimately depends, have marginalized certain controversial topics. For instance, while the House has held a number of events dealing with the memory of military repression and the *desaparecidos* in Argentina, the project of a photo exhibition on Attica and Abu Ghraib was turned down. Some of the House's success has been due to the important contribution of several progressive Jewish intellectuals and cultural organizers; on the other hand, this has made any mention of Palestine and Gaza, if not off-limits, certainly very problematic. While the Ellis Island exhibition and the related events drew attention to the plea of today's immigrants to Italy, and while we did organize a couple of well-attended events on Rwanda, there has been no concerted effort to involve the immigrant communities in the House's activities.

Building a Cultural Future

The House of Memory and History is a significant example of a social politics of memory in which bearers of memory and research organizations come together under the aegis of a public institution of local government. Although the advent of a right-wing administration has determined no overt or explicit interference in the activities of the House and its organizations, the position of the whole project vis-à-vis the cultural and historic context had indeed changed. The House was born as one element in a strategy of development and growth of a democratic culture elaborated by a progressive administration. It is now a tolerated small space of resistance and an alternative to a cultural politics and a dominant common sense that goes in the opposite direction. At the close of the Ellis Island concert, the singers Giovanna Marini and Sara Modigliani and the entire audience joined in singing a great, rousing song of revolutionary exile and emigration:

> Nostra patria è il mondo intero
> nostra legge è la libertà
> ed un pensiero
> ribelle in cor ci sta
>
> Our homeland is the world,
> our law is liberty,
> and a rebel idea
> is in our hearts.

We sang it in the past as a theme song of the cultural future that the House of Memory and History was working to build; it was sung this time as an act of defiance to the new power. Harmless defiance, perhaps—they don't care what we sing, as long as we do it within four walls of our House. But like the proverbial small farmer in the Western movie that won't give in to the railroad, we refuse to sell.

NOTES

1. Renata Mambelli, "Ardeatine: per non dimenticare. Inaugurata la 'Casa della memoria' a Trastevere," *Repubblica*, Rome ed., Mar. 25, 2006; Gabriele Santoro, "Storia e memoria hanno trovato Casa," *Il Tempo*, Mar. 25, 2006.

2. When the new Democratic Party (born of a merger of ex-Communists and ex-Christian Democrats) drew up its charter, they simply forgot to mention anti-Fascism and the Resistance among the values that inspired the new political organization. It was tacked on later, after rank-and-file complaints and protest.

3. The then president of the Regional Council, ex(?)-Fascist Francesco Storace, launched a campaign to cleanse history textbooks used in schools of "Marxist" and anti-Fascist contents. Groups of young Fascist activists broke into bookstores trying to destroy the books of which they did not approve. After debating them in a number of occasions, I realized that they had not even bothered to read them.

4. Alessandro Portelli, *L'ordine è già stato eseguito: Roma, le Fosse Ardeatine, la memoria* (Rome: Donzelli, 1999) [*The Order Has Been Carried Out: History, Memory, and Meaning of a Nazi Massacre in Rome*] (New York: Palgrave, 2003).

5. The address is via San Francesco di Sales 5, 00186 Rome. The house is open Monday to Saturday from 9 a.m. to 7 p.m.

6. With this problem in mind, ANPI is revising its membership eligibility rules. Until recently, only former partisans were entitled to join the association; with the recent changes, any citizen willing to participate in anti-Fascist cultural and political activity may join. While this has brought many young people into the organization, some of its original members have argued that it destroys its nature and reason of being.

7. "Una Casa della Memoria per imparare a dire no alla Guerra," *l'Unità*, Mar. 25, 2006.

8. R. Mambelli, "Ardeatine: per non dimenticare."

9. I am the Circolo's founder and current president.

10. "E' nata nella Casa della Memoria una nuova biblioteca con 5mila volumi," *l'Unità*, June 6, 2006.

11. Actually I presented two: a brief one on how Italian folk songs on emigration express the resentment and sense of betrayal of those who were left behind, and one on Italians in the coal mines of Appalachia.

12. The archive is dedicated to the memory of Franco Coggiola, who created and directed (for little and often no pay) the first Italian sound archive at the Istituto Ernesto de Martino, founded by Gianni Bosio in 1966.

13. A recent, very successful, video project is *Canti lontani dal centro* (2008), a film history of the role of music in the homeless movements of the 1970s, directed by Marco Marcotulli and Susanna Cerboni. We are now planning a fifteen-CD series combining selections from the music archives with chosen oral history documents.

14. Giusy Incalza, *La provincia al confino* (Rome: ANPPIA Provinciale, 2006).

15. Two examples: On the anniversary of Italy's Sept. 8, 1943, armistice with the Allies and the beginning of resistance in Rome, the new defense minister, Ignazio La Russa, at the

official ceremony paid homage not to the resistors but to the Fascist units who had fought with the Nazis. A few days later, Sept. 20, on the anniversary of the liberation of Rome from Pope Pius XII's temporal domain, the officially appointed "memory representative" of the mayor celebrated the event by commemorating the pope's soldiers who fought against Italian unity and independence.

16. The same head of the Office of Cultural Policy who had reassured us about the administrations "anti-Fascism" commented on this choice by telling the media that the festival's organizers "know very well who now has the power in this city."

17. After the Italian parliament established a Day of Memory on the anniversary of the liberation of Auschwitz (Jan. 27), the Right obtained the creation of a Day of Remembrance to commemorate, on Feb. 10, the massacres at the *foibe*—which were thus equated with the Holocaust.

18. Guido Crainz, *Il dolore e l'esilio: L'Istria e la memoria divisa d'Europa* (Rome: Donzelli, 2005); Marta Verginella, *Il confine degli altri: la questione giuliana e la memoria slovena* (Rome: Donzelli, 2008). The BBC series *Fascist Legacy*, which details many of the Italian war crimes on the Balkan front, was bought but never aired by the Italian state television.

19. Silvio Berlusconi is fond of saying that our constitution is Soviet-inspired.

BIBLIOGRAPHY

Luzzatto, Sergio. *La crisi dell'antifascismo*. Turin: Einaudi, 2004.

Portelli, Alessandro. *The Order Has Been Carried Out: History, Memory, and Meaning of a Nazi Massacre in Rome*. New York: Palgrave, 2003.

CHAPTER 8

HOW DOES ONE WIN A LOST WAR? ORAL HISTORY AND POLITICAL MEMORIES

FEDERICO GUILLERMO LORENZ

And have we done with War at last?

—Robert Graves, *Two Fusiliers*

How do memories of the Malvinas War fit with the memories of the Argentine military dictatorship? What revisions—in terms of the defeat and revelations of human rights violations—have those memories imposed on the republican patriotic cult that prevailed in Argentina even during the dictatorship? To what extent are those memories still functional for those sectors of society that uphold the role of the armed forces during the last military dictatorship? A system of values and beliefs, anchored in the idea of the nation and its symbols, was shared by dictatorial and democratic regimes alike, by revolutionary movements and established parties. Such ambiguity has allowed individuals responsible for crimes against humanity to remain unpunished, protected by the idea that they rendered services or fulfilled duties on behalf of the fatherland. Through oral history, an analysis of the memories of the Malvinas War, within the context of the military dictatorship and post-dictatorship in Argentina, provides a broader look at political memories as historical constructions, and a reflection on the place of historians in disputes over the past.

The Malvinas Islands, situated near the southernmost point of South America, were occupied by force by Great Britain in 1833, after which their recovery became one of the strongest and most constant symbolical elements in Argentine political culture. Between April 2 and June 14, 1982, Argentina went to war with Great Britain over the Malvinas Islands, which the British call the Falklands. Seizing the historical claim shared by thousands of Argentines, the military junta, which had been in power since a coup d'état in 1976, planned and ordered a deployment of troops to recover the islands for Argentine sovereignty. Having grown unpopular due to the economic crisis and accusations of human rights violations, military leaders received wide acclaim for their action in the Malvinas. However, the national consensus was as short-lived as the Argentine presence on the islands and lasted merely two-and-a-half-months, and it ended with their re-conquest by British troops after a brief yet bloody war.

Despite its short duration, the war had a profound impact on Argentina. It accelerated the fall of the bloodiest military regime in the nation's history, which had accounted for somewhere between 14,000 and 30,000 murders and disappearances in the years from 1976 to 1983. After ending in a catastrophic surrender, the war had wounded the national pride in a manner that determined the timing and particular features of the Argentine armed forces' withdrawal from power. This in turn had an impact on the historic narratives that were spun to explain not only the war but also the dictatorship and the return to democratic rule.

Like other collective catastrophes, wars give rise to a dialog between the state and its inhabitants regarding social identity and their idea of nationhood. Even when wars lead to victory, the costs can be traumatic, as in the case of World War I for France. Armed conflict redefines relationships among individuals and between them and their communities.

Defeat heightens this tension, and the failed Malvinas War left Argentine society at such a crossroads. Added to the defeat was the fact that the same armed forces that had failed at Malvinas were responsible for massacring their own people through state terrorism. The defeat brought significant discredit to the armed forces (for many people "they had failed in their specific function"). There was a loss of both the fear and respect they had instilled, encouraging more to come forward with accusations of their crimes. The atrocities committed during the so-called Process of National Reorganization came to light massively. In addition to news of clandestine mass graves and testimonies of human rights violations, the surviving draftees who had fought in the war returned as firsthand witnesses to the abrupt military failure in the South Atlantic. Thus began a period of acute political conflict in which oral testimony has played a role.[1]

Memory and Politics

All memories *are* political, but not all memories *affect* politics. In some cases, this is because they have been silenced, and in others because they remain in the individual sphere, and consequently are forgotten and disappear when their bearers die. Talking to others about their political memories can leads to conscious efforts to intervene in disputes over the past as a way of impacting upon the present. If we remember that memory, aside from being a subject of study, is essentially a recalling exercise; we can differentiate two core elements for understanding it as a historical phenomenon. First, memory directly connects the past and present. The questions we ask of the past derive from our present standpoint. That makes memory, secondly, a "dimension of political practice."[2] Exploring the political nature of memories requires us to reflect on the "operative nature of the relationship with the past."[3] That relationship—established by social players who sustain specific demands and projects—continually debates past memory of operations that sought to consolidate a given political circumstance and to lay the foundation for an imagined future. In this framework, the notion of political memory restores our responsibility for writing history in order to overturn present circumstances of domination, based on a criticism of accounts of past events, which reflect political struggles featuring vanquishers and vanquished. "While the relationship between the past and the present is based on silence, concealment, compartmentalization," writes Jean Chesneaux, "that which goes unsaid, the inverse relationship, between the present and the past, must be explicit, voiced in broad daylight, and, therefore, politicized."[4]

This politicization involves memory entrepreneurs, different social players who mobilize their energies toward a given cause, in this case anchored in memory.[5] Undoubtedly, the state apparatus, as well as nongovernmental organizations and social movements, is an agent of political ideas designed to manipulate the past. Dominique Schnapper calls them "political administrators of memory."[6] Historians and oral historians can also become memory entrepreneurs, in their role as makers of the great national narratives. Finally, the confrontations between memories of the past imply decisions to retain and forget historical processes and events, and in some extreme cases, even the human beings that embody those memories.

Memories of the Dictatorship

The first step in social processing of the reality of the Argentine massacre was the dissemination of facts about the crimes committed. It was imperative to find out and make known what had happened, and the forms the horror had taken on. These quandaries emerged forcefully in the public opinion in the latter half of 1982, and laid the groundwork for the accusations made by human rights organizations. The military's loss of prestige in the war encouraged the press, which until then had maintained a tombstone's silence on the subject, to publish increasing numbers of news items regarding the activities of human rights organizations. Especially those stories relating to the Mothers of Plaza de Mayo, who, with their head scarves and circular marches every Thursday, became the symbol of the fight against the perpetrators' impunity.

What had been whispered about as rumors for many years now materialized in the form of horrifying photographs of bones unearthed from cemeteries and personal accounts by witnesses. The strongest accusations came from the relatives of the missing victims, who in isolation had sustained the reports and claims made during the harshest years of the repression. Accounts circulated about the captivity of numerous Argentines, aberrant tales of abuse and torture, and testimonies of some of those who caused the repression, which intensified the ghastly images of the scene. This period was termed the "horror show." It established the permanent presence in public spheres of the victims and of the damage that had been inflicted upon them by their captors.

These accusations and revelations were incorporated into party platforms and programs, and became a key element in the transition to democracy. The magnitude of the exposed crimes generated a widespread repudiation and indignation that became deeply rooted in many social sectors. The crimes had been committed by a regime that had received wide public support when it took power, and that had recovered that consensus temporarily during the Malvinas War. The revulsion against those crimes now led to a change in the opinion regarding the military government and its actions. The "fight against subversion" began to be called an "illegal repression" and "human rights violations." The victims went from being "dangerous subversives" to "innocent human beings." The process of depicting the victims as innocent people aimed at heightening the criminal characteristics of the Argentine State, but it also diminished the possibility of doing any political analysis of these past events because it enlarged the proportions of the evil that had befallen Argentina.

The accounts of the repression consolidated a historical narrative regarding the social mobilization and political violence that had preceded the military coup. This process boiled down to the guerrilla violence prior to the Process of National Reorganization, which was in turn compared with the State terrorism within a framework of generalized contempt for violence. According to this reading, Argentine society had been a passive spectator, witnessing the confrontation of two forces equally violent in their methods, equally deserving contempt and rejection from a democratic society.

The emblematic model of this notion is the famous prologue to the *Nunca Más* (Never Again) report by the National Commission on the Disappearance of Peoples (CONADEP). It stated that "during the seventies decade Argentina was violently agitated by terror instilled in like measures by the extreme right and by the extreme left."[7] Known as the "two demon theory," this explanation fulfilled two key purposes for the transition to Argentine democracy: it offered the possibility of identifying the parties responsible for the tragedy (the guerrilla organizations and the armed forces) while simultaneously offering a route for proposing democracy as a new system that would be *foreign* to the two practices.

Consequently, the democratic system did not emerge as the heir of a historical process of unprecedented violence, but rather as the path for effecting basic change. To put it simply, this *theory* was effective because it explained the past period as aberrant and disruptive of a more *civilized* history. The identified responsible parties were alien to the majority of society and therefore enabled the commencement of a democratic phase by individuals belonging to the sector of innocent people who were alien to violence.

The construction of an image of the victims devoid of anything that could associate them with violence or assign any blame to them was a necessary complement of this historical vision. In contrast, the image of the armed forces as the personification of evil grew progressively larger and stronger. Youth played a key role in this process. During the dictatorship, the human rights movement—a minority group confronted by a repressive State—was attacked by dictatorial propaganda, which identified youth with subversion because of its propensity to fall under the influence of extremist ideologies. As a result, the claims made by the parents of missing persons as to the whereabouts of their children cautiously avoided the *political* causes that had led to their disappearance.[8]

In the mid 1990s, the accounts of the state terror were complemented by stories of the political militancy and struggle. Other survival accounts and experiences were added to the memory of horror in the form of stories by members of the revolutionary organizations, who vindicated their experiences during the years prior to the coup by pointing to the intense political and social unrest at the time. They no longer defined their personal experiences in the interpretive matrix of human rights violations as *victims*, but in their militant status as agents of change and social fighters. Documentaries and testimonial writings, analytical or fictional, constituted a significant publishing and journalistic boom, which has grown stronger with each anniversary of the coup. Needless to say, these accounts of the lives of political militants strongly contradict the earlier images of the victims of the dictatorship.

On March 24, 2004, the anniversary of the military coup, President Néstor Kirchner apologized on behalf of the State in a speech delivered at the ESMA (Higher School of Mechanics of the Navy), a huge building that had operated as a clandestine detention center during the military dictatorship.[9] Kirchner presented himself as a member of the generation persecuted by the repression. Only days earlier, he had entered the same site accompanied by former detainees, survivors of the clandestine detention camp, with whom he toured the premises.

The reactions to these events stirred up memories of political violence and repression, reviving debates that had been taken place two or three decades earlier. This has opened a new era in the political disputes over this memory, since the event held at the ESMA showed that the accounts of the past by firsthand victims now makes up the official policy of the Argentine State relating to human rights and memory.

For three decades, the keys to interpreting recent Argentine history lay with the image of the young victims of the military dictatorship, reinterpreted as revolutionary militants in the 1960s, then with the image of state terrorism and violence, and the with the image of democracy and respect for human rights "recovered" in 1983. The *Nunca Más* (Never Again) heading used for the report on state violence reflected the desire to lay a new foundation typical of the first half of the 1980s.

However, what place did memories of the Malvinas War, and of its protagonists, occupy within this framework?

Memories of Malvinas

Different players have gradually built aligned or directly opposed views of the Malvinas War. Although the Argentine defeat facilitated and expedited the departure from dictatorship, the experiences connected with Malvinas lost specificity within the more massive and shocking sphere of human rights violations.

When I began to interview former soldiers who had fought in the Malvinas War in the mid-1990s, one particularly notable fact came to light. During my interviews or when reading other testimonies, the soldiers' return to the "Continent" after the rendition emerged as a memory more painful than the war itself. The different "returns" had taken place quietly, invisibly, and acquired symbolic characteristics which to this day define their relationship with their co-nationals. Burdened with the logical component of a lost war (as in the case of the United States and Vietnam), these marks on their memories raised a question of the relationship between the public narratives of the years of dictatorship and the war, and the individual memories of the survivors of each.

Alejandro Cano fought in Darwin-Goose Green, while serving in an artillery component. What follows is his description of his reaction to the public memories during the war:

> In my opinion, they see us as..."Poor guys...what horrors they went through over there."...By degrading the Army, they degraded all the [war] veterans. They judged them all in the same manner and thus the courage displayed by the soldiers never came to light....If the weather had been warm, we would have died of heat. It was cold....We were freezing to death!...During a war one suffers hunger, one suffers the cold, one suffers the heat."[10]

Cano was confronting essentially two accounts with his testimony. One subordinated any account of the war to the story of the illegal repression ("by degrading the Army, they degraded all the [war] veterans"), which was the predominant position during the 1980s. The other was the reports that turned the soldiers who fought in the Malvinas into victims at the mercy of harsh conditions on the island and, in some cases, of their own officers. ("In a war one suffers hunger, one suffers cold.")[11]

Certain clearly identifiable forms emerged at the end of the war to refer to it and to its protagonists. These became consolidated during the first years of democracy and prevail to the present day in the literature on the period, and which are unlike the conceptual and thematic changes regarding other aspects of recent history. They all cross each other, and their ambiguity resides in the tension between the national identity, the patriotic cult, and the state terrorism experience.

THE PATRIOTIC WAR

Wars play a central part in the construction of collective national identities. In Argentina, the leaders and soldiers who fought for independence became the heroes and founding fathers featured in the school education of Argentine children. The nineteenth-century Argentine national mausoleum was built by a cultural and political elite, which arbitrarily selected elements with the aim of perpetuating a version of history and which was also a model of civilian virtues. In this national historical narrative, military institutions play a central part. Victorious officers and men killed in battle have subsequently joined the ranks of the revered heroes that lie in the national mausoleums. They are the models for those who come after them, who will render their sacrifice meaningful. If the first drive to uphold these values was anchored in the public education system, compulsory military service (an institution in Argentina that dates from 1904) constituted the second landmark in the lives of young Argentine men. At the age of eighteen, a drawing was held to decide which of them would be recruited into compulsory military service in one of the three armed forces. This draft was intended to give cohesion to the new republic, strengthen the role of the State, and instill national and social values in its young people.

From a symbolic standpoint, these citizen soldiers were the heirs to a civilian religion, which built its civilian values on military virtues and thus outlined the self-image of the nation. These "secular cults" fulfilled an educational function where "celebrating the citizens who had fulfilled their duty implied an exhortation for others to fulfill theirs."[12]

One of the ways of incorporating the experience of the former Malvinas combatants was through this patriotic discourse. This is where the initiatives of the armed forces and of the different civilian and military governments that alternated after 1982 converged, despite their divergent objectives. Seeing the war this way inscribes it in the official canonical history. It becomes a record similar to that of other warlike episodes in national history. It downplays the inherent political conflict: the fatherland is a sphere that has no place for domestic conflicts, inhabited only by the pure, including those who died for it. In this framework, the heroes from Malvinas include both civilians acting under allegiance to the flag and professional military people. When these two parties embodied the two symbolical sides of the political rhetoric, reference to the fatherland diminished any antagonism. Narrating the national history this way had been effective in building many national identities during the nineteenth and twentieth centuries, including the Argentine identity. It fed the imaginary of opposed conservative and revolutionary political forces, which, in a slow process of recovery, overcame the crushing weight of the armed forces to become the official voice of the state concerning the matter.

The soldiers who fought in the 1982 war against Great Britain were mobilized on the basis of that traditional cultural and historical matrix. After they died, despite having fallen into acute oblivion and marginality, they were remembered that way officially. But how were the soldiers killed during the Malvinas War be incorporated to the national mausoleum? On this issue, the war showed various thorny sides.

One of them was that the deployment of soldiers on the islands had received significant and diverse mass social support. This became a painful reminder of the civilian ties with the de facto government, the dictatorship responsible for human rights violations. During the two months and two days that the conflict lasted, civilians organized support networks throughout the country to send aid to the soldiers on the islands. Deliveries included food and warm clothes, donations, and letters written to the soldiers who were at the front. In addition to the young men summoned to the units, thousands of men who had completed their compulsory military service were sent to war as volunteers. The image of a dictatorship leading the fight against Great Britain faded before the idea of national vindication. In a country subjected to more than six years of severe censoring and self-censoring, the fact that isolated sectors flaunted slogans such as "the Malvinas Islands belong to the workers, not to the torturers" and "the Malvinas are Argentine, so are the missing people" was less than irrelevant.

Defeat brought to light a fact that had indeed been irrelevant during the war because it was practically unknown. A significant number of officers and senior enlisted personnel who had fought in a legitimate war had also participated in the so-called war against subversion, which was beginning to be considered a "dirty war." The public at large began to see the heroes of Malvinas as torturers and kidnappers. Doubts regarding the armed forces circulated, both because of the defeat before the British and because of the domestic repression. As far as the officers from the army, navy, and air force were concerned, these were two conflicts in which the institutions they belonged to had fought on behalf of the fatherland. From their professional military viewpoint, despite their different characteristics and endings, the two events were comparable. To Alfredo Astiz, a naval officer who had participated in the illegal repression, this only represented continuity in his career:

> I have been in four wars and over thirty battles. I was in a war against subversion, I was infiltrated in enemy lines with the Chileans, when people said there was no war, I was in the Malvinas and I took part as an observer in Algeria. This is my fifth war. Keeping quiet, having kept silent all this time without saying anything, this is my last war.[13]

Victims

The defeat fed a discourse of victimization. This was the exclusive terrain of the news media, the political parties, and first groups of war veterans. This discourse created a wide public consensus since it was aligned with the image that had been formed by young people during the transition to democracy. It fit their definition as victims of the dictatorship, which gained strength during this post-dictatorial era.

The idea of the *victim* was complemented by the idea of the *innocence* of the crimes attributed to these young people by the repressive forces–their participation in or support for guerrilla movements. They were shielded as far as possible from any association with political violence. This model of youth built around the accusations of human rights violations therefore became the archetype for the war veterans returning from the islands. Even though these were young men who had been exposed to violence and personal combat, and had wielded real weapons, they received endorsement from the same society that now hated violence in all its forms.

Consequently, the theme involving the war veterans emphasized the fact that they had received scarce instruction (since many had just begun their compulsory military service when they were shipped to the islands). If the term "war boys" used to refer to them during the conflict was an affectionate way of emphasizing their youth and symbolically making them the sons and brothers of the population at large, the same expression—"the boys," which was used after the defeat—referred to ill-prepared, defenseless youth in the face not only of their officers but also of the British.

The victimizing discourse depicted the soldiers as victims of their own officers and of the high command, in an analogy with the image that Argentine society had created of itself as a victim of its own armed forces. Both the soldiers and civilian society were therefore completely alien to the process that had generated political violence and state terrorism. This discourse accentuated the stories among the Malvinas veterans of misuse of authority, arbitrary decisions, and ill treatment, along with the suffering that resulted from poor planning, over and above the narrative relating to the actual battles with the British.

Who Are the Malvinas Heroes?

On December 10, 1983, Raúl Alfonsín took office as the first democratically elected president following the dictatorship. Among the issues he inherited was the commemoration of the Malvinas War. On April 2, 1984, in the city of Luján, seat of the basilica whose virgin is the patron of Argentina, Alfonsín presided over the central ceremony commemorating the "recovery of the Malvinas Islands."[14] What could a democratic president have to say about the Malvinas? How could he nurse the wounded national pride? How could he commemorate a defeat? He did that by replacing the notion of military glory for that of sacrifice, exercising the republican cult of the dead in the shaping of nations.[15] Death in battle was the highest surrender of the self to the national values, and it also represented a form of exercising civilian rights. This notion assigns a collective significance to death, beyond individual grief. In this framework, soldier-citizens die defending a community, which in turn adopts them as models. Alfonsín established this relationship in his emblematic speech:

> This 2nd of April I am here to commemorate with you, at the foot of this monument, our [nationals] fallen in battle, those brave Argentines who gave up their lives or generously exposed themselves on that southernmost portion of our nation. Although it is true that the government that made use of force did not consider the tremendous and tragic consequences of its action, it is equally true that the ideal that encouraged our soldiers was and is the ideal of every generation of Argentines: the definitive recovery of the Malvinas Islands, South Georgia and South Sandwich.... Countless uniformed citizens must have wanted to lay down their own lifeless bodies among the rocks, the peat and the snow after fighting strenuously and boldly. But God saw the virtuous, and among these the brave and the lively, from among the wounded and the heavy-hearted, He chose His heroes. He chose the ones that we commemorate today. Anointed by misfortune, devoid of the victory laurels, these dead that we honor today are a living lesson of sacrifice in the line of duty.... These tragic deaths strengthen further the conviction we have of the fairness of our rights.[16]

This reasoning was an attempt to deflect the focus of the war memories from the armed forces while allowing the new government to take possession, by democratic means, of symbols that had been associated with nationalism and which had been misused by the military.[17] Was it possible to maintain a nationalistic discourse and avoid its association with the memory of the bloodiest military dictatorship in history? Could the democracy contend with the armed forces and the right wing over such issues as "sovereignty" or "fatherland"?

These contradictions became evident during the first significant military crisis faced by the democracy. In December 1986, the National Congress enacted the Full Stop Law (*Ley de Punto Final*), which set a deadline for processing cases against illegal repression. In a little over two months, more than three hundred officers had lawsuits filed against them. Finally, in April, during Easter Week, Colonel Aldo Rico, who had been chief of Commandos during the Malvinas War, occupied the School of Sergeant Majors located in Campo de Mayo and demanded a "political solution." The military units led by Rico painted their faces with shoe polish, in a similar fashion to assault units, to differentiate themselves from forces loyal to the government. The *carapintada* uprising—or "*painted faces*"—revealed the symbolical weight of the Malvinas Islands and the lack of consensus over the meaning of that war.

Mass rallies were held throughout the country in support of the government, with a multitudinous gathering at the Plaza de Mayo to back democracy. There was fear that the crowds would march toward Campo de Mayo and cause a massacre. President Raúl Alfonsín announced from the balcony of the Government House that he was going to Campo de Mayo to demand the rendition of the rebels. Upon his return, he addressed the crowded square to announce:

> The seditious men have laid down their weapons. As it corresponds, they shall be detained and dealt with by the law courts. This is a group of men, some of them *heroes from the Malvinas War*, who took this mistaken stand.[18]

The president's reference to the Malvinas War was an unfortunate remilitarization of the war memories, and it downplayed the image of the mutineers. Should society show "understanding" toward them as victims of the consequences of the defeat? Or was the president resorting to deeper elements within Argentine political culture, those associated with the nationalism that nurtured the support for the recovery of the islands? Was this not an indication of the strong social commitment toward an unfortunate war and, therefore, toward the military leaders involved? The "painted faces" crisis had originally been seen as an attempt against democracy. Now the status of its perpetrators as veterans of a patriotic war provided an attenuating factor for the insurrectionists.

The ambiguity of the war had allowed Alfonsín to use the image of the military to define, through a reference to Malvinas, a political crisis that had been sparked by the policy of bringing the military to trial for human rights violations.

Memories of Former Soldiers

Through their war veteran groups, the young draftees who had fought on Malvinas presented a series of troublesome vindications of their actions and made demands in the context of the transition to democracy. Their claims emerged through a radical discourse that drew from national and popular political movements of the years prior to the dictatorship, and from revolutionary Marxist and Peronist left-wing discourse. They have defined the war as an episode in the Latin American anti-imperialist struggle. But this presented a twofold problem. The social rejection of violence as a manner of consolidating democracy left no room for the vindication of war or revolution, since both of these were associated with repressive state and the guerrilla organizations. These two demons had satisfied society's desire for self-exoneration while providing, at the same time, a historical view of the events that had occurred.

The fact that these young war veterans were using radical discourse short-circuited their public image as *innocent* people, and this generated a social desire to forget them. This came as a harsh blow for the war veterans. At the same time, the manner in which the first organizations of war veterans tried to vindicate their war experience separated them from the armed forces, which they accused of ill-treatment and inefficacy, and criticized for their surrender. Veteran draftees needed to establish a differentiation between themselves—the authentic soldiers—and the repressive army. Along these lines, a document issued in 1986 by the Center for Malvinas War Veterans states the following:

> Our generation shed their blood for the recovery of our islands and this gives us a moral right.... During the Malvinas War a new generation of Argentines expressed itself. After the war, it became aware of the atrocities the dictatorship had committed. We did not wear the uniform to vindicate that scourge, which can only be carried out by those that lack dignity. We wore the uniform because we are the living testimony of a generation that wore it to defend the fatherland, not to torture, to repress, and to murder.[19]

The attempt made by the Malvinas war veterans to insert themselves into a history full of popular strife that was deeply rooted in the ideology of national left-wing movements was not effective, and it did not earn them a place in the context of the movement to democratic institutions. As a result, of the three interpretative models for discussing the war from the point of view of its perpetuation, this one is the least used. It subsists to this day among some groups, but has generally succumbed to the reconfiguration of the political relationships of the 1980s and to the dispersion this produced among the war veterans.

Many war veteran groups continue to uphold their claim for *historical reparation*. Initially, this related to their economic claims, which have been met gradually over time. After that, reparation came to mean national public recognition for the sacrifice made on the islands. The traditional and patriotic symbolical route inherent in this recognition has become the most effective for the inclusion of those who lived through the war. This demand grew into a *movement*, and its influence on interviews about war experiences has grown progressively. Yet there is difficulty in reaching an agreement even on this point. During the "painted faces" uprising in 1987, some of the war veteran groups placed themselves at a distance from the mutineers: "We cannot fairly call [the *carapintadas*] 'Malvinas heroes,' as the nation's president referred to them on Easter Week," said one. "In our opinion, the only heroes are those who died fighting against imperialism on Malvinas."[20]

A law enacted by the national congress adopted a similar criterion, declaring the 649 soldiers who died on Malvinas to be national heroes.[21] What does the title of "hero" convey in this case? To define this, the law adopts this categorical criterion: to be a hero, one must have died. In relation to the Argentine past, however, this definition obliterates the ambiguity that a "national hero" according to this law may also have repressed his own people, acting in the name of the same values.

The Place of Historians

How can historians analyze these processes for the configuration of war memories? How can we incorporate them into other interpretations of the military dictatorship? A renewed treatment of the subject arose in the 1990s, with an abundance of publications on political violence and state terrorism, together with a turn to this field by historians and other scholars through "studies of memory." Yet similar new scholarship has been practically nonexistent in terms of the Malvinas War, which is why oral history must be conducted.

Many intellectuals, including historians, believe that the transition to democracy involved the rejection of old truths and the appropriation of new ones. The categories for studying society changed radically against those that guided research in the years prior to the dictatorship. Democracy and its institutions, together with the defense of human rights, became the guide for those who devoted themselves to the institutional reconstruction of Argentina.

During this process, the notion of "citizen" gradually replaced other more specific concepts such as Argentine, worker, or fellow partisan, political characterizations anchored in absolute such as those of nation, people, or revolution. Thus, the democracy-in-the-making movement forgot the populist classes and their political connotation.[22] This popular political maneuver is strongly linked to elements that relate to nationalism, and in particular to the Malvinas War.

For some intellectuals, this has created a dilemma in how to support the democracy-in-the-making. In an article that recalls the place of historians in the transition to democracy, the historian Luis Alberto Romero, one of the most influential writers in his field, explained his personal solution to this dilemma:

> As a person, a historian has two coexisting souls, be they in harmony or in conflict: he is as much a citizen as a historian. Sometimes he acts as one of them, others, like the other, and sometimes he seeks equilibrium, a balance between the two of them. This condition becomes clearly evident in the study of the "painful past": committed player and analyst; citizen who defends values, and performer of a knowledge that bestows relativity on them."[23]

Although it is now possible to criticize the accounts of the violence and the State terrorism constructed during the 1980s, at that time, he said, "professional historians who were identified with civility conducted themselves—ourselves—essentially as citizens, confirming this version and abstaining from raising any doubts. What could they have said in line with their professional preference for coloring and bestowing relativity on convictions? Only truths that would be uncomfortable and negative for the object of the time."[24]

Some Argentine historians made a choice not to debate certain historical views out of a political need. This shut the door on some issues regarded as potential tools for the vindicators of the dictatorship. The Malvinas War is one of those issues.

The predominant historical literature has treated the war as political. This thesis has reduced the war to the flailing hand of a drowning dictatorship faced with growing social discredit. It has turned a blind eye on the veterans' war experiences, reducing the war to a political event, which explains the motivations of the military junta but does not help us understand the reasons for the public support for the landing on the islands. And it says nothing about the role that the Malvinas War has played in the political imaginary of its participants. According to Rosana Guber, this is an *ex post*-reflection that fails to explain how the Argentines reached the war situation. On the other hand, it stands as a testimony of what we did with war memories afterwards.[25]

To recall the war and the support it received would have placed many people in an uncomfortable position. Many left-wing thinkers, most notably groups exiled in Mexico, supported the recovery of the islands while simultaneously condemning the dictatorship, without explaining the gap in this stand. Their endorsement of the military landing in 1982 has been attributed to an anti-imperialistic tradition, which had fostered armed conflict to achieve. In the context of the transition to democracy, any revision of this process and its ideological legitimacy would have been a complex task. It was all the more complicated for those who were trying to build the conceptual bases for democracy through criticism of these earlier forms of imagining social relationships and struggles.

Describing the war as a mere mechanism for upholding the legitimacy of the dictatorship enabled an evasion of these issues and strengthened the "two demon theory." This view put the Malvinas on the same interpretative plane: Argentine society was the victim of fear and of manipulation (in an understanding view), or an accessory of the dictatorship (from a condemning point of view), at the mercy of the decisions of the Military Junta. These analyses complemented the victimizing discourse regarding the war veterans (who were at the mercy of their commanders). This strengthened the possibility of eluding social responsibilities, and it remains effective to this day. The result is that looking back at the Malvinas War and its protagonists generally implies opinion-molding on the war and cannot avoid condemnation of the event to be analyzed and explained.

What has been written and produced about the Malvinas has come from other spheres than professional historians. This has produced gaps in the studies of recent history; mute spots that constitute dangerous argumentative mines, since they leave the vindicators of the dictatorship in the self-assigned role of the moral victors and guardians of an "unrevealed truth." This has enabled them to control identities and symbols of significant importance to a large part of society.

Why do historians find it so difficult to write about this war and its characteristics, and about those who died in the war? Perhaps this can be attributed to the trauma inherent to any war, and the inability of those who lived through it to emerge from the stupor caused by the horror of its forms. Perhaps it can be attributed to a lack of interest in it as an empirical subject. The reasons for the absence of historiography on the war can likely be found in the historical process of the 1980s, in patterns that were established to make sense of political and social change, and in some of the characteristics of the event under analysis.

As happened in other places, such as Spain, the end of a dictatorship generated a questioning and rejection of symbols and notions that were not the exclusive domain of the military, but which the military had used and abused, committing atrocities in their name. Ideas such as anti-imperialism, nation, or fatherland can be viewed as the spearhead of a resurgence of authoritarianism. Eager to leave behind a violent past, scholars discarded these symbols and notions in their conceptual destruction, but they overlooked some of their essential features: the fact that they exist throughout the whole republic; and the varying intensity with which the war was felt in the various regions of the country, such as Patagonia, or in provinces like Corrientes, and Chaco. Although not consistent with a vindication of the dictatorship, these symbolic elements enjoy a strong regional presence, which the defenders of authoritarianism view as their property.

The local dimensions of symbols and notions have been a largely overlooked facet of the political strife over memories. There is a saying in Argentina that "God is everywhere but he attends to Buenos Aires." With such attitudes, one frequently encounters generalizing explanations that disregard the cultural and regional differences at play in such a vast and diverse country. Its different hues have a direct impact on the manner in which people experienced the illegal repression and the war. In a large city like Buenos Aires, the war experience was diluted quantitatively and qualitatively vis-à-vis other political events. But in the less densely populated provinces, the phenomenon was exactly the opposite, as were the social appraisals of the war. The experience of state terrorism may also have had more significance in some regions of the country and for certain social players, but not for others. The repression of student activists and the ESMA form the axis of one type of memory, as do the blackouts, mobilizations, and red alerts in other parts of the country.

The military insurgents' use of such symbols as the flag, the nation, or the fatherland have caused them to be condemned per se, as Trojan horses of authoritarianism. In the process, the possibility offered by those symbols of launching a true symbolical battle against the years of dictatorship was lost. Similarly, this condemning attitude has permitted a reestablishment of the worst of the nationalistic ideology by the hand of the defenders of state terrorism to be seen in the Malvinas War.

This has been aggravated by the fact that many cadres of the armed forces, despite having fought on the islands, take credit for their involvement in what they term "another war"—on the illegal repression. It is therefore critical for researchers, instead of the abandonment of the field to automatic condemnation, to reexamine their assumptions. We must explore the idea that in many regions of Argentina, people regard the war against Great Britain as more significant than the State terrorism.

One conclusion is that the traumatic impact of the dictatorship has hindered historians' ability to consider certain processes outside the matrix of terror. This limitation can also be attributed to the ideological framework shaped by the intellectual political projects that sought to redefine social relationships in Argentina since the 1980s. Although the war took place during the dictatorship, and was actually triggered off by it, this undeniable event in our analysis must not dim the specificity of the conflict, especially considering that multiple elements that have converged to construct the diverse experiences and narratives of the war. The task, therefore, consists in our ability to divest our analysis of that conceptual and experiential confinement.

There is also an issue associated with the commitment toward life and the respect for pain, in a country that was faced with death far too much of the past fifty years. As pointed out at the beginning of this chapter, all memories are political, but not all of them are involved in politics or reach the realms of public discussion. Interviewers learn that certain memories prevail over others when people are discussing the past, and this generates hierarchies. Some historical experiences—losses, sacrifices, commitments, pride and debts—become less conspicuous than others.

This can lead to feelings of deep injustice. Seven out of ten Argentine Malvinas War veterans did not have the chance to decide whether to risk their lives: they were draftees, young men, the vast majority aged between 18 and 20. Some questions are uncomfortably simple and difficult: What is the difference between the family of a worker that was seized or murdered and that of a soldier that died on Malvinas? What separates these from other victims of the dictatorship, whose stories have more repercussion or resonance? The answers are also simple yet difficult: symbolical capitals, class status, and last but not least their exclusion from historiographical reflections of their own experience.

These oversights should lead to new research questions, and with them the injustice may diminish. The strength of political uses of memories may reside in this: More than a quarter of a century after the war and the commencement of democracy, we should be capable of dispelling certain conceptual ghosts by listening to other stories. We need to do this in order to acknowledge our fellow countrymen, the veterans, who have been pierced by a strong experience that shares many common elements with the Argentine massacre. We need to move beyond looking at them—in the best of cases—as the passive victims and—in the worst—as puppets of the murderers who, having completed the massacre of their own people, then turned their eyes upon the islands in the South Atlantic.

NOTES

1. According to Elizabeth Jelin, "Political openness, meltdowns, liberalizations and transitions enable a public sphere in which previously restrained and censored narratives and accounts can be incorporated. New ones can also be created. This aperture implies a scenario of struggles for the meaning of the past, featuring a plurality of players and agents that bring multiple demands and claims." Elizabeth Jelin, *Los trabajos de la memoria* (Madrid/Buenos Aires: Siglo XXI, 2002), 42.

2. Popular Memory Group, "Popular Memory. Theory, Politics, Method," in *The Oral History Reader*, ed. Robert Perks and Alistair Thomson, 75 (London: Routledge, 1998).

3. Jean Chesneaux, *¿Hacemos tabla rasa del pasado? A propósito de la historia y de los historiadores* (Buenos Aires: Siglo XXI, 1984), 67.

4. Ibid., 69.

5. Jelin, *Los trabajos de la memoria*, 48.

6. Dominique Schnapper, "La memoria en la política," in Françoise Barret, Ducrocq (director) *¿Por qué recordar?* (Barcelona: Gránica, 2002).

7. CONADEP, *Nunca Más: Informe de la Comisión Nacional Sobre la Desaparición de Personas* (Buenos Aires: Eudeba, 1997), 7.

8. This has a quantitative basis. According to 1984 data, 10.61 percent of the missing persons were between the ages of sixteen and twenty, 32.62 percent were twenty-one to twenty-five, and 25.90 percent were twenty-six to thirty CONADEP, *Nunca Más*, 294.

9. Located in the most expensive area of the city of Buenos Aires, an estimated five thousand detainees were held at the ESMA, most of whom are still missing. Currently, the premises of the ESMA, spanning almost forty-two acres, constitute the "Area for Remembering and Promoting and Defending Human Rights."

10. Interview with Alejandro Ramón Cano, Class 62, Airborne Artillery Group 4 (1994).

11. An investigation ordered by the armed forces established the serious logistic and organizational flaws of the Argentine war effort. These aggravated and worsened the deplorable conditions in which many of the Argentine soldiers fought. It should be noted that close to 70 percent of the Argentines deployed on the Malvinas were draftees, not regular soldiers. There are currently numerous lawsuits in process for the "Truth about Malvinas," filed on grounds of accusations of ill treatment by some Argentine officers inflicted on their subordinates in violation of human rights.

12. George Mosse, *Fallen Soldiers: Reshaping the Memory of the World Wars* (New York: Oxford University Press, 1990), 105.

13. *Trespuntos*, Jan. 1998, 9.

14. *Clarín*, Apr. 3, 1984.

15. Kristin Ann Hass, *Carried to the Wall: American Memory and the Vietnam Veterans Memorial* (Berkeley: University of California Press, 1998), 40.

16. *Clarín*, Apr. 3, 1984.

17. Paloma Aguilar Fernández and Carsten Humblebaek, "Collective Memory and National Identity in the Spanish Democracy," in *History and Memory* 1/2 (Autumn 2002). indicate that the "misuse" of nationalistic and patriotic symbols by totalitarian governments (they analyzed the case of Franco) prevented them from being appropriated and given re-significance by leftist groups. This is a key element in the struggle for memory considering the strong identity component inherent in these elements.

18. *Clarín*, Apr. 20, 1987. My italics.

19. Centro de Ex Soldados Combatientes de Malvinas, *Documentos de Post Guerra* 1, 1986, 23.

20. *Malvinizar*, Mar. 1988, 9.

21. Ley No. 24.950, "Héroes Nacionales," 1998.

22. Denis Merklen, *Pobres ciudadanos: Las clases populares en la era democrática (Argentina, 1983–2003)* (Buenos Aires: Gorla, 2005), 23.

23. Luis Alberto Romero, "Memorias de El Proceso y problemas de la democracia," *Lucha Armada en la Argentina* 4, no. 10 (2008): 5–6.

24. Ibid., 7–8.

25. Rosana Guber, *¿Por qué Malvinas? De la causa nacional a la guerra absurda* (Buenos Aires: FCE, 2001.

BIBLIOGRAPHY

Aguilar Fernández, Paloma, and Carsten Humblebaek. "Collective Memory and National Identity in the Spanish Democracy." In *History and Memory* 1/2 (Autumn 2002).

Chesneaux, Jean. *¿Hacemos tabla rasa del pasado? A propósito de la historia y de los historiadores*. Buenos Aires: Siglo XXI, 1984.

CONADEP. *Nunca Más: Informe de la Comisión Nacional Sobre la Desaparición de Personas*. Buenos Aires: Eudeba, 1997.

Jelin, Elizabeth. *Los Trabajos de la Memoria*. Madrid/Buenos Aires: Siglo XXI, 2002.

Lorenz, Federico. *Las guerras por Malvinas*. Buenos Aires, Edhasa, 2006.

———. *Malvinas: Una guerra argentina*. Buenos Aires, Sudamericana, 2009.

Guber, Rosanar. *¿Por qué Malvinas? De la Causa Nacional a la Guerra Absurda*. Buenos Aires, FCE, 2001.

Hass, Kristin Ann. *Carried to the Wall: American Memory and the Vietnam Veterans Memorial.* Berkeley: University of California Press, 1998.

Merklen, Denis. *Pobres Ciudadanos: Las Clases Populares en la Era Democrática (Argentina, 1983–2003).* Buenos Aires: Gorla, 2005.

Mosse, George. *Fallen Soldiers: Reshaping the Memory of the World Wars.* Oxford: Oxford University Press, 1990.

CHAPTER 9

DISAPPOINTED REMAINS: TRAUMA, TESTIMONY, AND RECONCILIATION IN POST-APARTHEID SOUTH AFRICA

SEAN FIELD

Do you remember where you were on the morning of February 2, 1990? On that morning, if people who took a global view of the various intractable historical conflicts such as Palestine and Israel, Northern Ireland, Apartheid South Africa, and others, were told that one of those conflicts would be resolved, and that a transition to democracy would occur, very few would have selected South Africa. On that day, however, President Frederick Willem de Klerk lifted the ban on the leading anti-apartheid organizations. Shortly thereafter, Nelson Mandela and other leaders of the fight against apartheid were released from prison. A dramatic transition began that day, and former enemies were soon locked into negotiations about the nature of post-apartheid governance. Death Squads attempted to destabilize this process, and fear of a right-wing coup was real. During the 1990 to 1994 period, the country underwent social and political fragmentation with sporadic violence, and the economy slid further into a deep recession. It was in this context that the negotiations brokered the "truth commission" idea, drawing on prior commissions in

Chile and Argentina. This became a key political compromise struck between former enemies. The first democratic elections held on April 27, 1994, were surprisingly free of violence. Then, in one of its first pieces of legislation, the new democratic parliament passed the Promotion of National Unity and Reconciliation Act of 1995, which created the Truth and Reconciliation Commission (TRC). It set up office in December 1995 and completed its public operations by 2000, submitting its final reports by 2003.

At the outset, the South African TRC promised to "uncover the truth" about past atrocities, forge reconciliation across a divided country, and provide "closure" and "heal the nation."[1] As oral historians, we should consider the oral testimonies that were given at the Human Rights Victim (HRV) hearings and reflect on the reconciliation process and what it means to ask trauma survivors to forgive and reconcile with perpetrators. While the TRC gave a boost to oral history work across South Africa[2] it became clear that there were differences between oral history interviews and the testimonies taken during the HRV hearings.

Since World War II, there had been sixteen "truth commissions" and another twenty-one "historical" type commissions, but the South African TRC in terms of its scope and budget allocated was the most ambitious truth commission in the world.[3] Since the TRC completed its work, other commissions have been established in East Timor, Sierra Leone, Liberia, and the Democratic Republic of the Congo (DRC). But truth commissions have become a fashionable human rights response in postconflict societies and have led some to argue that "the international community has become blindly besotted with truth commissions."[4] These processes raise questions about the meaning of bearing witness to violence and trauma.

The TRC: Reconciling the Irreconcilable?

The TRC's mission was to focus on "horrendous human rights abuses" committed during the years from 1960 to 1994, and it was intended to forge *social cohesion* in a post-apartheid context racked with sociopolitical divisions, violence, economic recession, and poverty. The TRC had the difficult task of encouraging conflicting audiences to participate in its proceedings. It received 21,298 written applications for assistance from survivors of human rights abuse. Of these written victim statements, 2,200 survivors gave oral testimony in the HRV hearings that became a public spectacle in South Africa and around the globe.

In stark contrast the amnesty hearings were more legally orientated and attracted much controversy, and the TRC offered neither pardons nor blanket amnesties. The opportunity for selective amnesty was to be granted if the applicant was regarded to have given "full disclosure" and to have shown that he or she acted under political orders and with political intent. Racist killing or abuses were to be excluded. The TRC received 7,115 perpetrator applications for amnesty of which 1,674 were successful. Bear in mind that the 21,298 victim-applicants referred to 37, 672 actual human rights violations. The amnesty applicants were therefore a small number of perpetrators and of those who applied, all were police and security personnel. No military officers applied for amnesty, even though the army was extensively involved in atrocities.[5] At the first HRV hearing in 1996, the head of the TRC, Archbishop Desmond Tutu, said:

> We have stared the beast of our dark past in the eye and we have survived the ordeal. And we are realizing that we can indeed transcend the conflict of the past, we can hold hands as we realize our common humanity.... Forgiveness will follow confession and healing will happen and so to contribute to national unity and reconciliation.[6]

These sentiments are compelling and expressed the TRC's laudable intention to help people who were suffering. There is no problem with trying to give people hope, but giving unrealistic hope is problematic. Where does one draw the line between appropriate support and misleading people? The historian Michael Ignatieff has argued that:

> Truth commissions can and do change the frame of public discourse and public memory. But they cannot be judged failures because they fail to change behaviour and institutions that is not their function. A truth commission can winnow out the facts upon which society's arguments with itself should be conducted. But it cannot bring these arguments to a conclusion.[7]

The TRC began with gusto, making grandiose claims about reconciliation, healing, and the recovery of truth. It was expected to change the social behavior of a large number of South Africans, moving them away from violence. Evaluated by its own initial high standards and goals, the TRC failed; but evaluated by the more pragmatic standard set by Ignatieff, the TRC was broadly successful. Since the TRC, it has been difficult for conservatives to question the widespread occurrence of apartheid atrocities. Many survivors experienced public recognition and established considerable "truth" about what happened to them and their loved-ones. The dramatic oral testimonies delivered at the hearings became the iconic public face of the TRC.

Consider some examples: On the June 27, 1985, four male South African anti-apartheid activists from Cradock disappeared. A few days later their bodies were discovered. Ten years later, on April 16, 1996, the wives of those men testified at the TRC. They described the events in the run-up to the killings, and how two prior inquests had failed. At times, like most TRC testimonies, their stories were harrowing. Nomonde Calata said:

> The man we as families asked to go and identify the bodies.... He said that he had seen the bodies but he discovered that the hair [of her husband] was pulled out, his tongue was very long. His fingers were cut off. He had many wounds in his body.[8]

Or as Nombuyiselo Mhlawuli read the postmortem documents:

> Reading them I was really worried, because it has to explain in detail what happened, I read through and came to understand that he had many wounds, in the upper abdomen were five wounds, these wounds indicated that different weapons were used to stab him or a group of people stabbed him. Now in the lower part he also had wounds but the wounds in total were forty-three. One other thing we understood, they poured acid on his face, after that they chopped off his right hand, I don't know what they did with that hand.... Even if I say those people should be given amnesty, it won't return my husband, but that hand which is said to be in a bottle in Port Elizabeth, we would like to get the hand.[9]

All four men had been brutally tortured prior to being stabbed and shot to death, and then their bodies were doused with gasoline and burned. The four women also testified about the various ways in which the death of their husbands had changed their lives and had impacted on people around them, particularly their families. Mhlawuli's father went to identify her husband's body:

> He said, "My daughter, they've killed my son bloodily," you know I felt very sorry, I was heartbroken. I went back home, that's the whole story. My father has never been the same since then. My mother was ill at the time became a real cripple because she had a stroke. My father was talking alone, saying, "The Boers killed my son, you Boers killed my son, my real right hand." My father and mother were on pension and many times would be up and down. My father was never a healthy person again.

And Sindiswa Mkhonto said:

> After the death of my husband my life never stabilized. My husband was everything to me, he did everything for me. His death was never a pleasant thing to me, today I don't have a husband, my child doesn't have a father, I have to answer many questions. Some questions I cannot answer. Today he asks me this question, tomorrow the next. Today, I don't have a husband, my son doesn't have a father, the family has lost.[10]

These testimonies are significant not just because of the bravery of the women in sustaining their lives but also by giving these testimonies in the public glare. During Calata's testimony she expressed a cry of anguish that was as one commissioner put it: "the primeval and spontaneous wail from the depths of her soul.... It was that cry from the soul that transformed the hearings from a litany of sufferings and pain to an even deeper level. It caught up in a single howl all the darkness and horror of the apartheid years."[11] In these testimonies we can sense their struggle to imagine what happened to their husbands in the final moments of their lives. And these testimonies are also striking in their repeated attempts to not only talk of their suffering but to also speak about the suffering of others. Nyameka Goniwe said:

> Yes, I've dealt with my own pain but obviously there are many people that have suffered out there... [her children] I guess I have to be stronger for them and they draw that strength from me. If necessary I try and protect them against exposure, against many other things, and I think they have coped very well... but as a mother, I think they are stronger and they will grew-up strong individuals as well, in spite of the fact that they don't have a father... with my son, its really good to

> have a family, good to have Cradock [their community] . . . and of course those are models, his models, so he insists to go to Cradock and he loves it.[12]

Their resilience shines through again, and with the support of others, how they have regenerated their lives after devastating events. While reading TRC transcripts I was struck by how very sensitive the commissioners were toward the survivors, but toward the end of each testimony the commissioners raise the reconciliation question, seemingly as a way of achieving closure. Analysts such as Richard Wilson have argued that there was a "systematic imposition" of forgiveness and reconciliation; in contrast Audrey Chapman argues that there is little evidence in the transcripts to support this claim.[13] Annelies Verdoolaege argues that survivors were "explicitly requested to reconcile could be seen as a subtle way of imposing the concept of reconciliation . . . survivors had to be decisive and strong-minded to refuse to reconcile with the perpetrator."[14] Only a small percentage of survivors raised the reconciliation issue themselves, and the TRC dialogs on the topic were frequently "characterized by a disjuncture, with commissioners and deponents speaking past one another."[15] Moreover, those who testified were praised if they displayed reconciliatory sentiments and showed some preparedness "to forgive." The commissioners kept emphasizing that reconciliation was the only way to "build a new South African society."[16] Given the media coverage around the TRC hearings, and the rhetoric enunciated by the TRC leadership, there is no doubt that the interconnected and frequently conflated notions of "forgiveness" and "reconciliation" saturated the public spaces that victims entered to testify. For example, in his closing statements to the Cradock widows, Archbishop Tutu said:

> We are proud to have people like you and your husbands and the reason why we won the struggle, is not because we had guns, we won the struggle because of people like you. People of incredible strength and this country is fortunate to have people like you, and I wanted to say to your daughter that her father where he is looking down, is proud of her, and you should feel you have done a tremendous job with her . . . and that she, your daughter should want to forgive, we want to forgive, after what she has experienced, and seen what happened to her mother and to her father, and she says, we want to forgive, but we want to know who to forgive. We give thanks to God for you, and thank you for your contribution to our struggle, and thank you, even if it was reluctant in a sense, rightly, thank you for sacrificing your husbands.[17]

The repeated articulation of "forgiveness" was overdone and softened by acknowledging the survivors' reluctance to forgive, but then Tutu says, "thank you for sacrificing your husbands." Was it a slip of the tongue, said in the midst of powerful emotions? Or was it a manifestation of Tutu's Christian theology? The intention to recognize what they endured is appropriate but "sacrificing your husbands," as in God sacrificed his "only son Jesus," was a crass intrusion of Christian thinking that Tutu repeated at the end of other victim testimonies. At times, this theology was married to notions of *ubuntu* (an African wisdom, that we are human through each other). For example, Cynthia Ngewu, mother of Christopher Piet [her murdered son] said:

> This thing called reconciliation... if it means the perpetrator, the man who killed Christopher Piet, if it means he becomes human again, this man. So that I, so that all of us, get our humanity back... then I agree, then I support it all.[18]

And when this mother forgave her son's killers, Tutu said, "You make me so proud Mama, to be a black person like you... what the world lacks, black people have."[19] The slide into cultural essentialism aside, the ideal type testifier was evident and fit with the logic of the TRC that the only way to stop violence was through the moral closure of forgiveness and reconciliation, which could then herald in the new nation-state. This teleology is "a redemptive narrative in that it offers the survivors of human rights violations the hope of deliverance from their traumatic experiences."[20]

While survivors of traumatic experiences crave the alleviation of their pain and other post-traumatic legacies, a central problem with the TRC's approach was its attempt to reconstruct these desires as seeking "redemption" (i.e., "salvation"), which is a Christian theological response to complex socio-psychological problems. Bearing in mind Ignatieff's comments, the theological proponents of the TRC tried to provide answers—at worst "absolutist" answers—to fundamental questions about the human condition, whereas researchers across academic disciplines argue that these questions remain unanswered. One such question revolves around survivors and whether it is possible for them to achieve "mastery" over their traumatic pasts.

Bearing Witness without Redemption

> I asked you not to ask too many questions, this history hurts me.[21]
> The inexpressibility of pain stops history in its tracks.[22]
> Witnessing is delicate, a deed that pushes against cultures' limits. It calls for action—a "not-turning-away" from seeing and hearing.[23]

Researchers are trained to delineate the "object" of their research. But what if the object is outside the limits of language, culture, and knowledge as currently understood? This intangible object is "traumatic experience." Dominic LaCapra argues that the violence of "limit events" and its human aftermath creates precisely this conceptual problem for survivors and researchers.[24] Moreover, the academic expectation that researchers be "on top of the material" sounds offensive when considered in light of the anguish experienced by survivors of wars and genocides. Survivors face enormous difficulties in constructing words and stories around the emotions contained within memories of their past experiences of violence. Yet many within the TRC adopted simple psychological notions that "truth-telling" confessions could help survivors to "master their painful pasts."[25]

What are implications for researchers? Personally, after more than ten years of working in this field, I still contend with feelings of self-doubt and leave many interviews feeling helpless. Every sentence I write about survivors feels as if I am doing them a disservice by analytically cutting into their shattered lives. We are left with two options: either to change research direction or to keep on working through these feelings by writing about our emotions and ideas evoked by experiences of "empathic unsettlement."[26] Achieving mastery over traumatic histories for both interviewees and interviewers is a fantasy.

What then is trauma? Traumatic experience has been described as rupturing "the membrane" that encases the individual self from exterior realities.[27] However, this membrane is not a dichotomy between the individual and the social world. Since self-boundaries are permeable, it is more useful to look at how traumatic experience impacts on the ways in which we internalize, mediate, and construct (or do not construct) meanings from these experiences. This means understanding the different ways in which the individual *in* society and *in* cultures were constructed prior to traumatic events, and not assuming a universal notion of "individuality" across societies, cultures, and time.[28] To add further complexity, psychologists note that while many people may experience the same event, only some may develop a trauma linked to it, and that some people may experience trauma over events that did not happen.[29] Other authors have criticized "trauma theories" for locating analysis in the crude search for "traumatic secrets," and for ignoring the significant function of childhood traumas and/or fantasies in shaping how people experience traumatic events later in life.[30] Still others argue that if the trauma debate involves a crisis in representation, "then this generates narrative *possibility* just as much *impossibility*."[31]

Since the emergence of Holocaust studies in the 1970s, testimony-based studies dealing with questions of trauma have proliferated, leading to the assertion that we are a "generation of memory."[32] We are living in an "era of the witness."[33] And we are caught up in a "witnessing fever."[34] These trends were given further impetus by the collapse of authoritarian regimes across Latin America, Africa, and Eastern Europe. In the South African context, the notion of trauma as a psychological term had been used in clinical settings but was not part of public discourse until 1985. During the political repression of 1985 to 1990, the term "trauma" gained relative currency among political detainees and their families. Trauma gained even wider public currency with the TRC after 1995.

What then does it mean to "bear witness to" what one remembers of traumatic experiences? "Bearing witness is an aggressive act," Kali Tal has written. "It is born out of a refusal to bow to outside pressure to revise or to repress experience, a decision to embrace conflict rather than conformity, to endure a lifetime of anger and pain rather than to submit to the seductive pull of revision and repression. Its goal is to change." It is doubtful that all acts of bearing witness are driven by aggression but when people narrate experiences of historical trauma inflicted through wars, genocides, torture, rape, sexual abuse, and other forms of violence then Tal's argument is correct. Her argument that bearing witness involves embracing conflict and enduring a lifetime of anger and pain contradicts the TRC's redemptive understanding of survivor testimonies.[35]

Ian Craib has argued that talking about feelings can create the illusion of solving emotional conflicts and is often bound up in a kind of "therapeutic evangelism," where people are encouraged to get things off their chest: "Talking can clarify, can replace impulsive and possibly destructive acting-out, it can be a forum for making decisions, but it cannot be an alternative to conflict and suffering." There is no doubt that some in the TRC, especially the religious advocates of forgiveness internalized this illusion, even though psychologists argue that "the best that psychotherapy can offer is the opportunity to be sadder but wiser, not some realization that the world is a wonderful and trustworthy place."[36]

While the oral history dialog can be a relatively safe space for interviewees to express their feelings, oral historians generally do not—and should not—have healing or therapeutic aims. However, some post-TRC organizations do conduct oral history with these aims.[37] Oral history research is usually defined by research and not by political functions. The TRC testimonies were motivated partly by research needs, but they were predominantly delivered within a setting driven by the grand political objectives of "reconciliation" and "nation-building." While oral historians have research agendas, their approach tends to be more open-ended, attempting to minimize the impact of the research agenda, to allow interviewees to speak as freely as possible. The TRC testimonies were to varying degrees circumscribed by the format of their prior written testimonies, and by the legal rules governing what could or could not be said in public forums.[38] Oral historians tend to do semistructured or, where possible, interviewee-led styles of interviews, which occur within an intimate one-on-one dialog, whereas TRC oral testimonies were delivered before TRC commissioners, lawyers, translators, media, and a crowded audience.

In contrasting the ways that TRC staff and journalists had interviewed them, one of the Cradock widows said in an oral history interview:

> you have come now in a different way, you are more interested in asking about me about myself, about my feelings... it seems as if I am telling differently now, with others I have been talking about my husband.[39]

During the initial stages of the TRC hearings in 1996, survivors were given some latitude to narrate their life stories, but this open-ended approach consumed too much time and would have caused the TRC to miss its deadlines. For example, Cynthia Ngewu, said in an interview:

> I didn't take it serious because my son left this morning and he was here last night, he was working at a bakery and I gave him money to go to work, I heard, I heard, I heard that my son is also in that group which was shot, I decided to go ask this to the police station, "They don't know, go check in Salt River" [the mortuary]... I went in and I find my son on a trolley, he was next to the door, and it was him.... I told my children, turn the TV on and I saw him, it was him.[40]

Imagine the impact of seeing the body of your child in a mortuary, seeing television images of the police dragging his body with ropes, and subsequently discovering that he and the other six men (know as "the Guguletu Seven") had been shot down with arms held high. Note the repetitions and enunciations in her speech, so typical to open-ended oral history interviewing. Initial TRC testimonies were, in part, similar to oral history interviews, but Mark Sanders has argued that "from the point of the law, testimony is *to be verified* it is, strictly speaking, *unverifiable* at the moment it is elicited."[41] While such ambiguities in oral testimonies could be validated through further research, the TRC changed its interviewing strategy. A TRC insider explained that by the end of 1997, they were using a short questionnaire to direct the interview instead of letting people talk for themselves. "The questionnaire distorted the whole story."[42] Critics pointed out that the new form of questioning represented "a shift in emphasis from the truths as seen by the survivors" to the TRC's production of an account commensurate with its overarching narrative of violence, forgiveness, and reconciliation.[43] If oral history methods had been made central to the TRC, it might have preserved, rather then stripped out, the "subjectivities of survivors" and retained the context and meanings of their narrative.[44] These arguments can be read as a call to oral historians to continue doing what the TRC was unable to complete.

There has been debate over the impact of the TRC's construction of a "master narrative" that involves the injustices and violence of apartheid counter-posed to the freedoms of the post-apartheid nation-state.[45] Lyn Graybill argued that it was Archbishop Tutu's statements that dominated, and "his disavowal of apartheid rests on twin doctrines: man as the image of God, and reconciliation through Christ's redemption."[46] Others saw that no one was immune from wanting a master narrative, "from wanting to be comforted by coherence."[47] But master narratives can comfort/contain or constrict/repress people—or both. Oral historians have argued that the process of "composing" one's life story has the potential to help the interview to feel a greater degree of "composure."[48] Whatever approach is adopted, the survivors' burden of living with post-traumatic legacies will frequently feel like "it is too much to bear." In the midst of many painful, potentially intolerable emotions linked to traumatic experiences, there are emotions that will remain in conscious and/or unconscious memory, and while pain alleviation is possible, no "healing truth" can redeem the past when torture and murder has been committed: "the memory of horror, the only experience unchanged by recollection, cannot be shared.... A debt that can be acknowledged yet remains impossible to settle."[49]

The promise of redemptive salvation as promoted by most religions is a theological premise, which people believe in as a matter of faith. It is precisely the "unbearable" aspects of traumatic testimonies that place truth commissioners, oral historians, and cognate researchers at a very delicate juncture. It is in these moments that it is easy to succumb to redemptive thinking, whether articulated through religious, political, cultural, or even psychological approaches. The promise of redemption is a myth, but if it helps people who are suffering to feel better, what does it matter that it is a myth? Oral historians have argued that myths are at times necessary for human survival.[50] My skeptical desire to critique redemptive myths remains, not when they are expressed by interviewees but when they are promoted by professionals as "solutions" to human miseries. The nonredemptive idea that salvation is *beyond experience* is in itself an intolerable thought for many. More critically, do redemptive beliefs, which have been developed within the domain of religious practices, belong in other spheres such as truth commissions and research?

A central problem with the TRC's reconciliatory discourses is that they took the theological discourse of redemption through forgiving and attempted to marry it with both clinical psychology ("healing") and political ideology ("nation-building"). This was then cast in an unbalanced setting, where the victim was expected to forgive the perpetrator while the perpetrator, applying for amnesty, was not expected to show remorse. Some survivors, who testified at the TRC, had their misgivings about the process, as Nyameka Goniwe, one of the Cradock widows tactfully put, in an oral history interview:

> It was a humbling experience for me, to hear people telling their stories... insofar as it helped people to verbalize their pain and to be recognized that worked... but the second phase, the forgiveness, this is a difficult process because it involves you.[51]

Was it ethical to place survivors in the God-like position of giving or refusing forgiveness? It was the TRC's intent to prevent conflict, to prevent the future scenario of "when victims become killers" that led them to ask survivors to forgive and reconcile with perpetrators.[52] For those survivors who refused to reconcile, did they feel ashamed or fear being called "unpatriotic"? And for survivors who forgave perpetrators, did this involve the suppression of their legitimate anger and rage? By blurring the responsibilities between individual and national reconciliation, the TRC placed unnecessary pressure on individual survivors. The TRC began a necessary national reconciliation process, but with what price for the survivors who had to reconcile on our collective behalf?

The level of reconciliation that the TRC achieved, or did not achieve, across culturally diverse communities has been vigorously debated.[53] Expecting direct reconciliation between victims and perpetrators was unrealistic, although that did occur in isolated cases.[54] What was emotionally less fraught, although not easy to implement on a societal scale, was reconciliation between the beneficiaries of apartheid and the victims of that system. In a multitude of episodes, there were acknowledgments, apologies, and expressions of guilt from many sections of the white community, but it is doubtful whether there was sufficient contrition. As an interviewee from the Cradock community put it: "We will see the change with our children, not with this generation and other generations back."[55]

After the TRC: Disappointed Remains

In what way should oral historians approach testimonies and histories of trauma? First, the fundamentally open-ended, empathic approach to oral history interviewing, with no promise of redemption or pressure to reconcile, is necessary. This means that oral history interviewers must reflect on their research motives, subject position, and post-interview feelings. In my experience, instead of avoiding unpleasant post-interview emotions, allowing time to think about the feelings the interviewee has expressed, and has evoked in us, can help us sharpen our intellectual contributions. Second, oral historians worldwide have been involved in post-interview social regenerative-type projects in communities.[56] Third, it is our intellectual responsibility to work through the intractable remains of traumatic memory, and how these "remains" of the past link to contemporary post-apartheid challenges.

The TRC emphasized restorative justice, but contrary to its claims the majority of survivors desired punitive justice.[57] Political compromise was central to the TRC's original formation, and an example of this was the granting of amnesty to perpetrators. In the post-TRC period, there have been signs that the National Prosecuting Authority will bring charges against particular individuals, but the vast majority of perpetrators will likely never face charges due to a lack of evidence. An estimated four tons of sensitive or incriminating documents were shredded by government departments between 1993 and April 1994.[58] Various limits placed on justice continue to be a source of disappointment to survivors.

In 2000, the TRC recommended that survivors receive annual payments for six years, amounting to an approximate grand total of 120,000 Rand per victim. Of the 21,298 victim-applications, 16,837 were identified as potential beneficiaries of reparation payments. The state controversially took four years to make a decision and then decided to give survivors once-only payments of 30,000 to 40,000 Rand, a decision that infuriated former TRC commissioners and staff members, and survivors.

In the run-up to the state's decision, Kulumani, a national network of survivors, held demonstrations protesting the state's lack of action. In Alexandria, a vast black working-class township near Johannesburg, a demonstration by the Kulumani group was confronted by African National Council (ANC) youth league members, who argued with them to not pressure the state to give them reparations but to let the state put its resources into job-creation and related programs.[59] While this was an isolated incident, it illustrated the difficult choices faced by communities and the state. It is also exposed the differing needs of an aging survivor generation in contrast to younger generations.

Consider the ongoing conditions of poverty that most survivors and their descendants continue to endure. The South African economy was in recession from 1982 to 2001. Since the late 1980s, using a broad definition of unemployment, the rate reached 40 percent of the economically active population. Using the narrower state definition, which excludes people who are in casual or seasonal labor, the rate was 24 percent. By 2003, 50 percent of the population was economically worse off than they had been under apartheid.[60] Since 2005 the economy gone beyond a 3 percent growth rate, which is the minimum for maintaining unemployment at current levels.[61] And the black working-class majority still live either in informal settlements or apartheid-built townships. They remain unemployed, or earn low levels of income through informal trading or casual labor. Not coincidentally, during the economic boom the protests against the state's lack of service delivery especially in relation to housing have been increasing.[62]

Moreover, during Nelson Mandela's presidency from 1994 to 1999, research evidence from the scientific community was showing that the HIV/AIDS pandemic would be catastrophic in South Africa. Instead of accepting these research findings and taking the lead in HIV/AIDS prevention and education programs, Mandela's successor, President Thabo Mbeki, chose to critique whether HIV caused AIDS, and questioned the efficacy of antiretroviral treatment. With these controversies, and the vacuum created by a lack of state support, the Treatment Action Campaign (TAC) emerged as the leading civil society voice representing people living with HIV/AIDS. The TAC pressed the state to develop a coherent national treatment plan, which the government belatedly agreed to in 2006.

South Africa has a total population of 47 million people of whom more than 5 million people are HIV positive. But fewer than 300,000 have access to antiretroviral medication. The pandemic has been politicized by a state reluctant to lead the fight against HIV/AIDS, that has instead supported "denialist" positions and unsubstantiated forms of medicine.[63] Thousands of those who are HIV positive or have already died from AIDS or secondary infections, survived the repressive apartheid regime only to be infected in the 1990s. Those most at risk are black working-class people between the ages of sixteen and thirty-five, with rural women being the most vulnerable. The tragedy for thousands of parents and grandparents is that they now take care of their children or grandchildren who must live with the physical, emotional, and social effects of the pandemic. When people voice their grievances around the pandemic and other issues, how does the state respond?

The ANC government under President Mbeki was easily wounded and attempted to silence critical voices by labeling them as "racist" or "ultra-leftist." Michael Ignatieff's argument that nationalism breeds narcissism is relevant here.[64] A narcissist finds it difficult to accept flaws in his or her self-image. Ian Craib argues that the denial of disappointment is double edged: "I might deny it first because I cannot stand the suffering of others, most probably because if I accepted the suffering of others, then I would have to accept my own suffering; and secondly because I cannot tolerate the thought of my own 'failure', my inability to achieve what I set out to do, which is to alleviate suffering."[65]

The Rainbow Nation of the 1990s has been replaced by the Narcissistic Nation. A small shocking example occurred in 2006 when President Mbeki, in response to a journalist's question about the pandemic, said, "I have never met someone who has HIV or AIDS." The anger from people living with the disease was widespread. Another tragedy is the xenophobic attacks on refugees that escalated into a national crisis in 2008. These primarily occurred within black working class communities, who feel threatened by the approximate 5 million African refugees who entered South Africa since 1994. President Mbeki's response was that there was "no xenophobia" in "our communities" and that the attacks were the work of a "few criminals."[66]

What is the intellectual responsibility of researchers in relation to the disappointing realities of post-apartheid South Africa? Jacqueline Rose believes that the

TRC experience compels intellectuals to reflect deeply on the miseries of others.[67] And David Lloyd argues that "melancholy survivals . . . rather than recovery, is what should guide our critique."[68] He means "recovery" in two senses: It is neither possible for survivors to recover to a prior mythical state of harmonious being nor should historians comfort themselves with recovering previously hidden stories. Researchers need to do more conceptual reflection on the effectiveness of our methodologies, and to evaluate the ways in which citizens are treated by modern democratic nation-states. Although it might have a limited impact, we also must play a role as critical public intellectuals. For oral historians and cognate researchers, it is crucial for us to continue witnessing peoples' stories of intractable past traumas and current melancholy survivals.

Another survivor, Nomonde Tyali testified to the TRC about her sixteen-year-old nephew, who was shot dead in September 1989. His death was made more painful because he had not been politically involved and was the victim of indiscriminate shooting by three policemen. They were acquitted on charges of culpable homicide. In an oral history interview she said:

> when he got there my brother asked him to go to the shop to buy bread just around the corner, he never came back. The police came to us and told us that he was shot dead. This has worried us, I phoned his mother and she got a heart-attack and died then. This worried my brother till he died because of Lubalo's death . . . there is no one who is not frustrated, everybody is disturbed. So is Lubalo, the killing of a child, an innocent child did nothing wrong . . . we testified to Boraine [the TRC] . . . we received a letter saying that it was all true what I have said. . . . But I don't want to lie we didn't do this because of money. We did this just to show that at least there is something that you did for your loved one.[69]

It is a profound experience for oral historians to listen to and recognize the mournful remains of survivor stories. Oral histories disseminated through such public forums as museums, memorials, and film documentaries can provide space for people to work-through their post-traumatic burdens, and to express their disappointments. But these activities are not ends in themselves.

Significant political freedoms have been won in South Africa and should be cherished. But feeling the disappointment of failed dreams and unfulfilled needs, while potentially painful, must also be acknowledged, and can be a turning point for trauma survivors. Recognizing that the nation-state is neither the perfect nor the "good-enough" symbolic parent opens space to reflect on the political implications of disappointing experiences. It releases people from the passivity that is induced by a government's narcissistic discourses on patriotism. The choices of the present are to act or not act, to participate or not participate, in movements to attain reparations, houses, jobs, health care, and the myriad other needs still to be fulfilled. Despite the Truth and Reconciliation Commission's promise to reconcile and heal the nation, there has not been redemptive closure. Working through the *disappointed remains* of the past-in-the-present frees people to reengage in political struggles. Sadly, while the survivors of apartheid traumas deserve a respite from a "life of struggle," the struggle continues and continues.

NOTES

1. Sean Field, "Beyond 'Healing': Trauma, Oral History, and Regeneration," *Oral History* 34, no. 1 (2006).

2. For an overview of oral history in South Africa, see Field, "Turning-up the Volume: Dialogues about Memory Create Oral Histories," *South African Historical Journal* 60, no. 2 (2008).

3. Priscilla Hayner, *Unspeakable Truths: Facing the Challenge of Truth Commissions* (New York: Routledge, 2002).

4. Teresa Godwin-Phelps, *Shattered Voices: Language, Violence, and the Work of Truth Commissions* (Philadelphia: University of Pennsylvania Press, 2004), 119.

5. Don Foster, Paul Haupt, and Marisa De Beer. *The Theatre of Violence: Narratives of Protagonists in the South African Conflict* (Cape Town: HSRC Press, 2005), 13.

6. Victim hearing, May 10, 1996, in *South Africa's Human Spirit, An Oral Memoir of the Truth and Reconciliation Commission*, Angie Kapelianis and Darren Taylor (co-producers), vol. 1, track 13 (Johannesburg: South African Broadcasting Corporation, 2000).

7. Michael Ignatieff, *The Warrior's Honor: Ethnic War and the Modern Conscience* (New York: Henry Holt and Co., 1998), 173.

8. Nomonde Calata, TRC transcripts, www.doj.za/trc/hrvtrans, 16.

9. Nombuyiselo Mhlawuli, TRC transcripts, www.doj.za/trc/hrvtrans, 41–43.

10. Sindiswa Mkhonto, TRC transcripts, www.doj.za/trc/hrvtrans, 29.

11. Alex Boraine, *A Country Unmasked* (Cape Town: Oxford University Press, 2000), 102.

12. Nyameka Goniwe, TRC transcripts, www.doj.za/trc/hrvtrans, 13.

13. Richard Wilson, *The Politics of Truth and Reconciliation in South Africa: Legitimatizing the Post-Apartheid State* (Cambridge: Cambridge University Press, 2001); Audrey Chapman, "Perspectives on the Role of Forgiveness in Human Rights Violations Hearings," in *Truth and Reconciliation in South Africa, Did the TRC Deliver?* ed. Audrey Chapman and Hugo van der Merwe (Philadelphia: University of Pennsylvania Press, 2008).

14. Annelies Verdooglaege, *Reconciliation Discourse: The Case of the Truth and Reconciliation Commission* (Philadelphia: John Benjamins, 2008), 64.

15. Chapman, *Perspectives on Forgiveness*, 63.

16. Verdoglaege, *Reconciliation Discourse*, 67.

17. Archbishop Desmond Tutu closing statement to Calata, Mkhonto, and Mhlawauli testimony, www.doj.za/trc/hrvtrans, 49.

18. Lyn Graybill, *Truth and Reconciliation in South Africa: Miracle or Model?* (Boulder: Lynne Riener, 2002), 34.

19. Claire Moon, *Narrating Political Reconciliation: South Africa's Truth and Reconciliation Commission* (Lanham: Lexington Books, 2008), 36.

20. Ibid., 61.

21. Sindiswa Mkhonto in "*We tell our stories the way we like*": *The Wives of the Cradock Four*, film documentary by Taryn da Canha, Gairoonisa Paleker, and Lauren van Vuuren (Cape Town: Historical Studies Department, University of Cape Town).

22. Boraine, *Country Unmasked*, 13.

23. Fiona Ross, "Linguistic Bearings and Testimonial Practices," in *Discourse and Human Rights Violations*, ed. Christine Anthonissen and Jan Blommaert (Amsterdam: John Benjamins Publishing, 2007).

24. Dominic LaCapra, *Writing Trauma, Writing History* (Baltimore, Md.: Johns Hopkins University Press, 2001).

25. Chris Colvin, "Shifting Geographies of Suffering and Recovery: Traumatic Storytelling after Apartheid," in *Borders and Healers: Brokering Therapeutic Resources in South East Africa*, ed. T. Luedke and H. West, 167–69 (Indianapolis: Indiana University Press, 2006).

26. LaCapra, *Writing Trauma*, 42–43.

27. Kim Lacy Rogers, Selma Leydesdorff, and Graham Dawson, eds., *Trauma and Life Stories: International Perspectives* (London: Routledge, 1999), 4.

28. Paul Antze and Michael Lambek, *Tense Past: Cultural Essays in Trauma and Memory* (New York: Routledge, 1996).

29. Thomas Douglass and Ana Vogler, *Witness and Memory: The Discourse of Trauma* (London: Routledge, 2003), 11.

30. Katherine Hodgkin and Susannah Radstone, eds., *Contested Pasts: The Politics of Memory* (London: Routledge, 2003).

31. Roger Luckhardt, *The Trauma Question* (London, Routledge, 2008), 83.

32. Jay Winter, "The Generation of Memory: Reflections on the 'Memory-boom' in Contemporary Historical Studies," *German Historical Bulletin* 27 (2000).

33. Annette Wievorka, *The Era of the Witness*, (Ithaca, N.Y.: Cornell University Press, 2006).

34. Fuyuki Kurasawa, "A Message in a Bottle: Bearing Witness as a Mode of Ethico-political Practice," http://research.yale.edu/ccs/papers/kurasawa_witnessing.pdf (2003).

35. Kali Tal, *Worlds of Hurt: Reading Literatures of Trauma* (Cambridge, Cambridge University Press, 1996), 7.

36. Ian Craib, *The Importance of Disappointment* (London: Routledge, 1994), 104, 117.

37. For example, the Institute for Healing Memories and the Institute for Justice and Reconciliation, both in Cape Town.

38. For example, Phil Bonner and Noor Nieftagodien, "The Truth and Reconciliation Commission and the Pursuit of 'Social Truth': The Case of Kathorus," in *Commissioning the Past, Understanding South Africa's Truth and Reconciliation Commission*, ed. Debbie Posel and Graeme Simpson (Johannesburg: Witwatersrand University Press, 2002).

39. Nomonde Calata in "*We tell our stories the way we like.*"

40. Interview by Andiswa Gidana, July 17, 2003, Centre for Popular Memory collections, University of Cape Town, www.popularmemory.org.za.

41. Mark Sanders, *Ambiguities of Witnessing: Law and Literature in the Time of a Truth Commission* (Johannesburg: Witwatersrand University Press, 2008), 6.

42. Quoted in Richard Wilson, *The Politics of Truth and Reconciliation in South Africa: Legitimising the Post-Apartheid State* (Cambridge: Cambridge University Press, 2001), 43.

43. Moon, *Narrating Political Reconciliation*, 82.

44. Wilson, *Politics of Truth*, 60.

45. Verdoolaege, *Reconciliation Discourse*, 52.

46. Graybill, *Miracle or Model?* 30.

47. Phelps, *Shattered Voices*, 126.

48. The Popular Memory Group, University of Birmingham pioneered this notion, and it was developed further in Alistair Thomson, *Anzac Memories: Living with the Legend* (Melbourne: Oxford University Press, 1994).

49. Emilios Christodoulis quoted in Erin Daly and Jeremy Sarkin, *Reconciliation in Divided Societies, Finding Common Ground* (Philadelphia: Pennsylvania Press, 2007), 131.

50. Paul Thompson and Raphael Samuel, eds., *The Myths We Live By* (London: Routledge, 1990).

51. Nyameka Goniwe in "*We tell our stories the way we like.*"

52. I have tended to maintain a binary between "victims" and "perpetrators," but more analytical work is required on the ways that victim/perpetrator roles and emotions are enmeshed in South Africa. See Ruth Leys, *From Guilt to Shame, Auschwitz and After* (Princeton, N.J.: Princeton University Press, 2007).

53. For critical approaches, see Wilson, *Politics of Truth*, and Moon, *Narrating Political Reconciliation*. For a defense of the TRC's contributions to reconciliation see Charles Villa-Vincencio and Wilhelm Verwoerd, eds., *Looking Back, Reaching Forward: Reflections on the Truth and Reconciliation Commission of South Africa* (London: Zed Books, 2000).

54. For example, Cynthia Ngewu and other family members of the Guguletu Seven, do forgive one of the killers in Lindi Wilson's film documentary *The Guguletu Seven*, (Cape Town: 2002).

55. Anonymous interviewee in "*We tell our stories the way we like*."

56. For examples see Field, "Beyond 'Healing.'"

57. Hugo Van der Merwe, "What Survivors say about Justice: An Analysis of the TRC's Victim Hearings," in *Truth and Reconciliation in South Africa*, 44.

58. Verne Harris in Charles Villa-Vicencio and Fanie Du Toit, eds., *Truth and Reconciliation in South Africa: Ten Years On* (Cape Town, David Philip, 2006).

59. The ANC government has opposed the Kulumani lawsuit against foreign companies that benefited from and supported the Apartheid regime. These cases are currently pending within the U.S. legal system. See Moon, *Narrating Political Reconciliation*, 154.

60. Steven L. Robins, *Limits to Liberation: Apartheid. Governance, and Culture* (Oxford: James Currey, 2005), 2.

61. Jeremy Seekings and Nicoli Nattrass, *Class, Race and Inequality in South Africa* (New Haven, Conn.: Yale University Press, 2005).

62. For an overview of service delivery protests, see *Mail and Guardian*, Sept. 14, 2007.

63. Nicoli Nattrass, *Mortal Combat: AIDS Denialism and the Struggle for Antiretroviral Treatment* (Cape Town: David Philip, 2007).

64. Michael Ignatieff, *Blood and Belonging: Journeys into the New Nationalism* (London: Vintage, 1994).

65. Craib, *Disappointment*, 11.

66. *Cape Times*, July 29, 2008.

67. Jacqueline Rose, "Apathy and Accountability: The Challenge of South Africa's Truth and Reconciliation Commission to the Intellectual in the Modern World," in *On Not Being Able to Sleep: Psychoanalysis and the Modern World* (Princeton, N.J.: Princeton University Press, 2003).

68. David Lloyd, "Colonial Trauma/PostColonial Recovery?" *Interventions* (2000): 212.

69. Interview by Andiswa Gidana, Nov. 7, 2003, Centre for Popular Memory collections, University of Cape Town, www.popularmemory.org.za.

BIBLIOGRAPHY

Chapman, Audrey, and Hugo van der Merwe, eds. *Truth and Reconciliation in South Africa: Did the TRC Deliver?* Philadelphia: University of Pennsylvania Press, 2008.

Foster, Don, Paul Haupt, and Marisa De Beer. *The Theatre of Violence: Narratives of Protagonists in the South African Conflict*. Cape Town: HSRC Press, 2005.

Gobodo-Madikizela, Pumla. *A Human Being Died That Night: A Story of Forgiveness*. Cape Town: David Philip, 2003.

Godwin-Phelps, Teresa. *Shattered Voices: Language, Violence and the Work of Truth Commissions*. Philadelphia: University of Pennsylvania Press, 2004.

Hayner, Priscilla. *Unspeakable Truths: Facing the Challenge of Truth Commissions*. New York: Routledge, 2002.

Moon, Claire. *Narrating Political Reconciliation: South Africa's Truth and Reconciliation Commission*. Lanham, Md.: Lexington Books, 2008.

Robins, Steven L. *Limits to Liberation: Apartheid. Governance, and Culture*. Oxford: James Currey, 2005.

Ross, Fiona. *Bearing Witness: Women and the Truth and Reconciliation Commission in South Africa*. London: Pluto Press, 2003.

Sanders, Mark. *Ambiguities of Witnessing: Law and Literature in the Time of a Truth Commission*. Johannesburg: Witwatersrand University Press, 2008.

Verdooglaege, Annelies. *Reconciliation Discourse: The Case of the Truth and Reconciliation Commission*. Philadelphia: John Benjamins Publishing, 2008.

Wilson, Richard. *The Politics of Truth and Reconciliation in South Africa: Legitimatizing the Post-Apartheid State*. Cambridge: Cambridge University Press, 2001.

CHAPTER 10

CASE STUDY: MEMORY WORK WITH CHILDREN AFFECTED BY HIV/AIDS IN SOUTH AFRICA

PHILIPPE DENIS

IN the early years of the AIDS epidemic, relief organizations focused their efforts on the material needs of children, but their psychological and emotional needs are no less important. Recognizing this, the Sinomlando Centre for Oral History and Memory Work in Africa, a research and community development center located at the University of KwaZulu-Natal, in Pietermaritzburg South Africa, has pioneered a model of psychosocial intervention for children in grief—particularly but not exclusively in the context of HIV/AIDS.[1] This model uses the methodology of oral history in a novel manner, combined with other techniques such as life story work and narrative therapy. Here, unlike conventional oral history methodology, the primary purpose of the interview is not to create knowledge about the past for the use of the public. Instead, its aim is to help families affected by HIV/AIDS to deal with their past.

As in any oral history project, an interviewer, in this case called a "memory facilitator," invites one or several persons to engage in a conversation about the past. Best described as memory work, these psychosocial interventions invite the families to share their stories in the presence of the children. Whenever possible, the memory facilitators also organize sessions for children of the same age, during which families stories are talked about and processed. The underlying assumption of this methodology is that children who have a positive recollection of their parents' illness or death will be better able to cope with the hardships of their condition. They will develop what psychologists call resilience: "the universal capacity which allows a person, a group or a community to prevent, reduce or surmount the negative effects of adversity."[2]

South Africa has the largest number of people living with HIV/AIDS in the world. Currently there are an estimated 1.2 million orphans in the country, and their number is expected to reach 2.3 million by the year 2020.[3] Such grim statistics inadequately express the hard reality of lives confronted day after day by death, poverty, and shame. The consequences of HIV/AIDS on children are dramatic. Nonattendance at school, ill health, and the need to care for sick parents deprive them of being able to learn and play. Due to the stigma that surrounds this disease, many live in isolation from their peers, with no support from family and community, and as a result, are unable to share their grief.

The Memory Box

Memory work is relevant in all cultural contexts.[4] Initially developed in Britain and in France for children placed in foster care or in institutions, it was introduced into Africa by the National Community of Women Living with HIV/AIDS (NACWOLA) in Kampala, Uganda. Trained by Carol Lindsay-Smith, a British social worker who specialized in memory work, the NACWOLA women have been producing "memory books" since the mid 1990s.[5] From Uganda, this methodology soon spread to other countries, including Zambia, Zimbabwe, and South Africa.

In 2001, Sinomlando jointly conducted a pilot study with Sinosizo, a home-based care service for AIDS patients initiated by the Catholic archdiocese of Durban, to determine how to conduct memory work in AIDS-affected households.[6] The practice of engaging the children in creating "memory boxes" in which the story of the family and various artifacts evoking the memories of the deceased parent would be stored, gave its name to the training unit established by Sinomlando. Since 2001, the Memory Box Program has organized training workshops for more than one hundred fifty AIDS-related organizations, in six South African provinces and several African countries.

During the early years of the project, the model followed for the family visits was the oral history interview. After the purpose of the exercise was explained to the caregivers, and their consent given, they were invited to answer questions about the history of the family. If possible a tape recorder was used during the interview. In this process, the children, who are the principal beneficiaries of the exercise, rarely participated in the conversation. The content of the tape was transcribed and edited with the cooperation of the family. At the end of the process, the memory facilitators solemnly presented, during a closure session, the tapes and a booklet containing the story of the family to the children and their caregivers. Family visits typically involved seven to twelve sessions, depending on how receptive the family was to memory work.

Later on, in an effort to increase the participation of the children in the project, Sinomlando and its partner organizations arranged for orphans aged six to thirteen to meet in sessions after school, on weekends, or during the holidays. The primary purpose of these sessions was to provide children affected by HIV/AIDS with life skills that would strengthen them. Special emphasis was placed on memory work, with modules on family trees, "rivers of life," and "hero books," a technique helping children to re-envisage their life stories in positive terms. The children would create their memory boxes during these sessions, placing into the boxes the various artifacts they produced under the supervision of the memory facilitators.

Over time, the methodology underwent further changes. The family visits no longer took the shape of a formal interview, with questions and answers about a certain topic, with a tape-recorder to capture the flow of the discussion. The memory facilitators describe the process through which the family members tell their story as a "conversation" rather than an interview. But, as explained by the program's coordinators, Nokhaya Makiwane and Cliford Madondo, it is a "guided conversation."[7] This terminology recalls Ronald Grele's definition of oral history interviews, in *Envelopes of Sound*, as "conversational narratives." Such narratives, he pointed out, not only constitute a record of what really happened in the past, they also contribute to how we understand ourselves today.[8] The Sinomlando memory facilitators use similar language. They freely engage with the family members, in the presence of the children who are old enough to understand, about the history of the family. But as the conversation moves along, they guarantee that the children have enough elements to make sense of their history in a positive manner. To help the family members overcome their reluctance to talk about death issues and open up, they use such techniques as the family tree or the "river of life," which are routinely practiced during the children's sessions. Several visits are usually needed for the story to unfold. In one case, a memory facilitator paid no less than twelve visits to a family.

The Caregiver as Narrator

In a typical family, the narrator will be the grandmother, sometimes accompanied by an aunt. The children's mother will have died at least a year before. Sometimes the narrator is the mother herself, who is already sick but still able to speak (this does not happen often since people with AIDS tend to approach AIDS organizations for assistance so late in their disease that they are not well enough to participate in memory work). Numerous children, grandchildren, members of the extended family, or neighbors, will be present. The children's ages range from one to thirteen or fourteen. Older children are often away when the intervention takes place. If the grandfather or an uncle is in the house, he rarely takes part in the conversation. In our experience, men are generally absent from African households. In the families in which Sinomlando has done memory work since 2001, single motherhood is the rule. A father, whether married or not, is the exception.[9]

When the memory facilitators visit the caregivers for the first time, usually in the company of a volunteer from a local organization, they explain that talking about the past may be painful but it will help the children to deal with their grief and facilitate their growth. This message is often met with resistance. In traditional societies, people are socialized to believe that children are "too small to understand" serious matters and that exposing them to the thought of death would cause more harm than good.[10]

At any point, the participants may withdraw. Sometimes they will insist that other family members whom they consider important take part in the conversation. Another meeting is then scheduled. When they are ready to talk, they start by evoking the hardships experienced as a result of the absence of the daughter or son who died recently. Problems such as the price of food, the difficult of finding a job, the quest for social grants, problems of health, or the children's unruliness dominate the conversation. Such issues may distract the family members from their task, which is to describe the life story of the sick or deceased person. The role of the memory facilitators is to guide them during the process. "Tell us about the life of our daughter. What do you remember of her?"

Interviewers have found that following a chronological order helps the participants to put the most painful part of the life story—the sickness and death of the children's parent—in perspective. It is important for a child to know when and where his or her mother fell sick and in what circumstances she died, but also to know how she grew up, where she went to school, in which context she met the father, what job she found, and how they came to live in the house they now occupy. When the grandmother is the main speaker, other family members, including children, may add details to the story. The whole family takes part in an exercise of collective memory. The memory facilitators are careful to maintain a form of balance in the story. The bad moments in the life of the deceased person are recognized but are not allowed to outweigh the good moments. Laughter has its place after the tears. The story that brings the family together is a story of life, not of death alone.

All families hold secrets. The biggest one in the case of families affected by HIV/AIDS is the name of the disease that took away some of their members. As trust starts to build up, it is not unusual for the family members to make explicit reference to HIV/AIDS in the conversation. The name of the disease does not need to be pronounced. They will say "that thing" or "the new disease." For the children, such a declaration does not necessarily constitute a disclosure, because typically they have understood implicitly that their mother died of AIDS. Yet the fact of speaking openly of the disease allows that knowledge to become concrete in the family context and gives the children the opportunity to move on. Memory work creates a space in which painful and controversial family issues can be addressed. The mere fact of talking freely about family matters is more important than what is actually said. Memory work allows the children to then grow in a climate of greater openness.

The use of the tape recorder is recommended because families in grief appreciate the possibility of accessing the story of the family at the push of a button. For practical reasons, however, most significantly the lack of resources in many AIDS-related organizations, tape recorders are not often used for memory work. Instead, family members, sometimes school-age children, are encouraged to take notes when the main storyteller, the grandmother, an aunt, or a neighbor gives the story. When that is not possible, one of the memory facilitators plays the scribe.

In parallel, the children are invited to create a memory box. If they are lucky, they have participated in one of the children's camps run by Sinomlando or one of its partner organizations and have received from them a wooden box specially designed as a memory box. Otherwise, the families construct, buy or find somewhere a box of cardboard, metal, wood, or plastic. That is where the notes taken during the conversation and the objects or artifacts evoking the memory of the deceased person are placed and preserved by the family.

Skills in Memory Work

Doing memory work with families in grief requires a wide range of skills. The first prerequisite is to have dealt with one's own experiences of grief. Only those who know how to process their painful memories are able to help others to remember in times of grief. Memory facilitators require good counseling skills, knowledge of gender and cultural norms, and empathy when deep emotions are expressed. They should also know at which point and to whom they should refer the children who are too traumatized to benefit from memory work. Ill-prepared interventions may heighten tensions in families and create confusion in the children's minds. At the same time, the amplitude of the epidemic and the lack of professional services in the areas most affected by HIV/AIDS warrant efforts to provide emotional support to the countless children who battle to overcome their grief. But the challenge of scaling up memory work without compromising the quality of the service offered is enormous. Innovative methods must be found to transfer memory-work skills to the people in regular contact with the children. These include the staff and volunteers of nongovernmental organizations, primary school teachers, health care personnel, and social welfare agency staff.

To scale up its work, the Sinomlando Centre designed a comprehensive, ever-expanding training and mentoring program. When an organization or group expresses interest in memory work, they first participate in an awareness workshop, usually for half a day. These are often community members working as volunteers, and they are later invited to take part in a four-day training workshop during which they learn basic bereavement counseling skills and are introduced to the methodology of the memory boxes. They are also shown how to facilitate children's sessions. In the following months, the memory facilitators accompany the trainees on family visits. Their work is evaluated during a follow-up workshop, held three to six months after the initial workshop.

In addition, the Memory Box Program runs an extensive course in memory work and psychosocial support to orphans and vulnerable children for members of partner organizations. After several months of formal instruction and supervised fieldwork, the trainees receive a certificate of competence awarded by the University of KwaZulu-Natal. The first participants were all from KwaZulu-Natal, but since 2008 the course has been open to community workers from other South African provinces. Sinomlando now offers exposure programs, usually for three weeks, for program coordinators and social workers from AIDS-related organizations in countries such as Zimbabwe, Tanzania, Rwanda, Ethiopia, and Cameroon. It also ran a series of training workshops in the Central African Republic, one of the most under-resourced countries in Africa. Evaluations of that program showed that the method initiated in South Africa could be applied with great success in other parts of the African continent despite significant cultural and socioeconomic differences.[11] To facilitate the transfer of skills in South Africa and beyond, the Sinomlando Centre has compiled two training manuals in English and French: one for the training of memory facilitators, and another one for the facilitation of children's sessions.[12]

Although a new practice, memory work as a psychosocial intervention for vulnerable children builds on century-old forms of family-based storytelling. Oral history is a key element of the methodology developed by the Sinomlando Centre. Memory work based on interviewing and guided conversations allows families in grief to cope with extraordinarily painful matters in a climate of dialogue and openness. This model offers an opportunity to enhance the resilience of the ever increasing cohorts of children orphaned by HIV/AIDS in Africa.

NOTES

1. Philippe Denis, ed., *Never Too Small to Remember: Memory Work and Resilience in Times of AIDS* (Pietermaritzburg: Cluster Publications, 2005). A revised and enlarged French edition of this book is also available: Philippe Denis, ed., *Les enfants aussi ont une histoire. Travail de mémoire et résilience au temps du si*da (Paris: Karthala, 2007). See also Philippe Denis and Nokhaya Makiwane, "Stories of Love, Pain and Courage: Aids Orphans and Memory Boxes," *Oral History* 31, no. 2 (Autumn 2003): 66–74. In isiZulu, *sinomlando* means "we have a history."

2. Edith H. Grotberg, *A Guide to Promoting Resilience in Children: Strengthening the Human Spirit* (The Hague: Bernard van Leer Foundation, 1995), 7.

3. Statistics provided by UNICEF. http://www.avert.org/aidsorphans.htm (accessed Sept. 2007). See also Jay Gow, Chris Desmond and Deborah Ewing, "Children and HIV/AIDS," in *Impacts and Interventions: The HIV/AIDS Epidemic and the Children of South Africa*, ed. Jay Gow and Chris Desmond (Pietermaritzburg: University of Natal Press, 2002). An orphan is defined here as a person under the age of eighteen whose mother has died.

4. Suzanna Radstone, "Working with Memory an Introduction," in *Memory and Methodology* (Oxford and New York: Berg, 2000), 1.

5. C. Lindsay Smith and R. O'Brien, *Memory Box in Africa* (London: TALC, 2000). See also C. Lindsay Smith, "The Memory Book—and Its Close Relations . . .", *Aids Bulletin* 13, no. 2 (July 2004): 23–26.

6. The pilot story is accessible online on the Sinomlando Centre's Web site: http://www.sinomlando.org.za.

7. Nokhaya Makiwane and Cliford Madondo, interview conducted in Pietermaritzburg on June 28, 2008.

8. Ronald J. Grele, ed., preface to the 2nd ed., *Envelopes of Sound: The Art of Oral History*, xv–xvi (New York: Praeger, 1991).

9. Philippe Denis and Radikobo Ntsimane, "The Absent Fathers: Why Do Men Not Feature in Stories of Families Affected by HIV/AIDS," in *Baba? Men and Fatherhood in South Africa*, ed. Linda Richter and Robert Morrell, 237–49 (Pretoria: HSRC Press, 2005).

10. Radikobo Ntsimane, "Memory Boxes and Zulu Culture," in Denis, *Never Too Small*, 35–40.

11. Vincent Sezibera, "Rapport de Mission 10–17 Avril 2008. Formation à la *Memory Box* des Médiateurs de Mémoire en République Centrafricaine," Secours Catholique–Caritas Centrafrique, Avril 2008.

12. Available online: www.sinomlando.org.za. See also Denis, *Never Too Small*, 74–102; *Les enfants aussi ont une histoire*, 127–211.

BIBLIOGRAPHY

Denis, Philippe, ed. *Never Too Small to Remember: Memory Work and Resilience in Times of AIDS*. Pietermaritzburg: Cluster Publications, 2005.

Denis, Philippe, and Radikobo Ntsimane, eds. *Oral History in a Wounded Country: Interactive Interviewing in South Africa*. Scottsville: University of KwaZulu-Natal, 2008.

Gow, Jeff, and Chris Desmond, eds. *Impacts and Interventions: The HIV/AIDS Epidemic and the Children of South Africa*. Pietermaritzburg: University of Natal Press, 2002.

Grele, Ronald J., ed. *Envelopes of Sound: The Art of Oral History*. New York: Praeger, 1991.

Grotberg, Edith H. *A Guide to Promoting Resilience in Children: Strengthening the Human Spirit*. The Hague: Bernard van Leer Foundation, 1995.

Radstone, Suzannna, ed. *Memory and Methodology*. Oxford and New York: Berg, 2000.

PART III

THEORY AND INTERPRETATION

CHAPTER 11

THE STAGES OF WOMEN'S ORAL HISTORY

SUE ARMITAGE

ORAL history was my door to women's history. Like many first-generation women's historians, I had been trained in another topic, and when I first taught a women's history course in 1974, I was desperate for resources. The available books were scanty, and awfully "Eastern" as well–for someone who was teaching in Colorado.[1] To compensate, I turned to local histories for information about local women, only to find... absolutely nothing. I was astounded and indignant: the published histories read as if women had never been there and had never done anything. You might say that my career as a western women's historian began right there. Like many feminist teachers in other communities across the country, I turned with enthusiasm to oral history to fill the gaps in the written histories. My "on the job training" and the assumptions I brought to women's oral history were, I think, characteristic of many others at the time, and those beginnings have certainly influenced my opinions about subsequent developments in the field. Equally characteristic was the way my opinions changed over time, as women's oral history developed. Hence my title, "The Stages of Women's Oral History."

Over the years, *Frontiers: A Journal of Women Studies* published four special issues on women's oral history, which serve as chronological markers for the development of women's oral history. Because I was involved in all four of the special issues, and edited the 2002 compilation, *Women's Oral History: The Frontiers Reader*, I will recount the story in a more personal way than I might otherwise.[2]

Discovery and Celebration

In the beginning, I lacked the tools to conduct the kinds of interviews with women that I wanted. The only oral history I knew was the interviews of the politically elite men that Allan Nevins had pioneered at Columbia University. Nevins's narrators were articulate, even verbose, while I faced the problem of getting women to talk at all. "I don't know why you want to interview me," my potential narrators kept saying. "I haven't done anything." Trained as a historian and faithful to its disciplinary boundaries, I knew nothing about the fieldwork techniques in folklore and in anthropology from which I might have learned. Several years later I finally read Sandy Ives's classic manual, *The Tape-Recorded Interview*, and was embarrassed to realize that several of the interview characteristics that I had confidently asserted to be female were in fact shared by other "ordinary" narrators.[3] In 1974, it seemed clear that if I was going to interview ordinary women about their lives, I was going to have to make the methodology up as I went along. Armed only with Willa Baum's *Oral History for the Local Historical Society*, I started in.[4]

The early days of doing women's oral history were exhilarating. I bought a tape recorder and some cassette tapes, and gathered together a group of women students in an experimental, off-campus class. Collectively, we drew up a questionnaire and fanned out into the community looking for interesting women to interview. Sometimes we struck gold: one of the students, Theresa Banfield, elicited from Dr. Ruth Flowers such a sharp-eyed and personal portrait of the segregation and discrimination endured by African Americans in a small western college town that I have returned to it repeatedly throughout my career. We interviewed miners' wives, farmers' wives who remembered the Dust Bowl, even a single woman homesteader (then thought to be quite a rarity). We were guilty of bias: we ignored middle-class town-dwelling women because they hadn't "done" anything; we sought out minority women; we really wanted to know about sex and birth control but were often afraid to ask. In short, we reflected the feminist ferment of our time. We were "women's libbers."[5]

Nothing more fully expressed our feelings than Sherna Gluck's rousing declaration of independence in the 1977 special issue of, *Frontiers*, A new feminist journal:

> Refusing to be rendered historically voiceless any longer, women are creating a new history—using our own voices and experiences. We are challenging the traditional concepts of history, of what is "historically important," and we are affirming that our everyday lives *are* history. Using an oral tradition, as old as human memory, we are reconstructing our own past.[6]

The entire 1977 *Frontiers* special issue was packed with articles reporting on women's oral history projects all over the country, "how to" suggestions, and detailed interview questions. It was invaluable. From it, I learned that many of the early women's oral history projects across the country were similar to mine. Usually collective projects, with several interviewers, they simultaneously documented women's activities while celebrating them. They usually targeted specific groups of women: rural women; female shipyard workers in World War II; union women; immigrant women. A common pattern was to use excerpts from completed interviews to create public programs, to bring back to their communities for presentation and discussion. One common structure for these early projects had an academic director whose scholarly qualifications looked good on grant applications, a mix of student and community interviewers, and a range of community contacts. Funding came from universities (sparsely), state Humanities Councils (which were quite generous, at least in the West), and private fundraising (garage sales, bake sales, and the like). These activities reflected the spirit of the times; many different groups, labor groups in particular, were actively involved in bridging the university-community gap.[7]

Women's oral historians developed a specific methodology. Following Gluck's article in the 1977 *Frontiers*, we used nondirective biographical interviews, deliberately giving control to the narrator, backstopped by topical questions about events in the female life cycle that the interviewer might use as necessary. The results of these early interviews were substantial. We *did* discover evidence of hardworking women everywhere, shattering the myths that women were "just housewives," or only working for "pin money," and chipping away at the worst of the racial and ethnic stereotypes about women. We *did* experience the pleasure of hearing women speak freely and fully about their lives, demonstrating that they were not "inarticulate" but overlooked. We *did* celebrate our discoveries, thereby raising feminist consciousness and pride among many women and fostering a general public awareness of women's history. Looking back, it seems clear to me that the impact of all of these women's oral histories was to establish the reality of gender difference. There really were distinct male and female versions of events, male and female life histories. Today this seems so basic as to be trivial, but it is important to remember that prior to the women's movement women had been defined not so much as different as deficient. They were considered to be lacking essential male intellectual attributes (not to mention the famous physiological one).[8]

We did not change the male bias in textbooks, however, because the quality of the evidence was deemed insufficient. In truth, few projects were systematic enough to be considered representative, as well as being more directed at community needs rather than academic analysis. In many cases, both the sound quality and the interview content were poor or superficial. In addition, many women's projects lacked the money to transcribe interviews, so the information remained difficult to access.

The picture was not entirely gloomy. There were some outstanding books, most notably Sherna Gluck's *From Parlor to Prison*, which revealed unsuspected layers to the woman suffrage movement; the Feminist Press volume *Las Mujeres: Conversations from a Hispanic Community*, edited by Nan Elsasser, Kyle MacKenzie, and Yvonne Tixier y Vigil; and more popular books such as Kathy Kahn's *Hillbilly Women*, Sherry Thomas's *We Didn't Have Much, but We Sure Had Plenty: Stories of Rural Women*, and Teresa Jordan's *Cowgirls*. Several important films, among them *With Babies and Banners* about the 1936 Flint, Michigan, strike, and *Union Maids*, were also based on oral histories with women.[9] They shared some common characteristics: they were compilations, not of raw transcripts but of edited accounts in which only the narrator's voice remained. Although the editors of these volumes explained their major purposes in the introductions, none included either their interview questions or a discussion of the ways in which the transcripts were edited. In other words, these early women's oral histories *appeared* more transparent than they really were.

As Columbus learned long ago, discovery does not take you very far. When the sheer enthusiasm of discovering women's voices wore off, a number of us began trying to think more seriously about methodological and analytic issues. This concern was evident in the second special issue on Women's Oral History that *Frontiers* published in 1983. Sherna Gluck described the care she had taken, in her *Rosie the Riveter Revisited* project, to select narrators who accurately reflected the composition of the labor force, even if it meant omitting some of the best storytellers. She was beginning, long before most of us, to be concerned about the racial, ethnic, and class differences among narrators. In my article, I concentrated on the ways in which project-design and interviewer-purpose shaped the interview and the outcome. While recognizing the individual diversity of interviews, I was acting like a good historian of the time and seeking ways to bundle all the variety together into grand generalizations.[10]

That aim did not last much longer, for the central unifying mantra of the women's movement—"sisterhood is powerful"—was on the verge of collapse. In many ways, that was regrettable. The feeling of common purpose had bonded the women's movement together, and it was that same sentiment that drove me to interview women as different from me as possible. Those early Colorado interviews remain the foundation of my understanding of the lives of western women.

As the enthusiastic unity of the women's movement splintered, the conservative mood of the early 1980s dried up the money that had been available for community and women's projects. In spite of that, the 1983 *Frontiers* issue listed more than fifty women's oral history projects nationwide, which was certainly an undercount. A few of the projects were very large and well-endowed. The "Voices of Women Homemakers" project was well enough funded by the National Endowment for the Humanities to allow for five interviews in each of forty states with farm women who were members of the agricultural extension Homemakers clubs, and to produce a series of books and copies of transcripts and tapes for each state. The Schlesinger Library at Radcliffe College (now Harvard University) launched the Black Women Oral History Project that interviewed more than seventy notable African American women about their lives and their contributions to black life, producing an estimated 25,000 hours of tapes and fifty-six bound volumes of transcripts. And academic work had substantially advanced. Three 1987 volumes based on extensive women's oral histories made an impact: Vicki Ruiz's *Cannery Women*, Sherna Gluck's *Rosie the Riveter Revisited: Women, The War and Social Change*, and the wide-ranging history of southern textile mills, *Like a Family*, by Jacquelyn Dowd Hall, James Leloudis, Robert Korstad, Mary Murphy, Lu Ann Jones, and Christopher B. Daly.[11]

Transition: Searching for Women's Culture

In the early years of women's history, many of us were focused on defining male/female difference, which meant identifying the distinctive aspects of the unitary entity we called "women's culture." In this search, women's oral history seemed a much more usable approach than combing archives for women's papers, many of which were still buried in the collections of their husbands or their fathers and not yet separately cataloged.[12] In 1987, an interdisciplinary article that attempted to develop such an approach to women's culture, "Beginning Where We Are: Feminist Methodology in Oral History," paired two historians (Kathryn Anderson and myself) with a practicing psychologist/counselor (Dana Jack) and a sociologist (Judith Wittner). The theoretical grounding for the article was provided by the writings of two feminist theorists, the sociologists Marcia Westkott and Dorothy Smith, both of whom tried to glimpse what one might call the "real woman" as distinct from ideologies that defined women's roles. Westcott argued that in a patriarchal society, women were constrained to conform to expected roles, but that they simultaneously contained the possibility of opposition (what we would now call resistance, not yet a word in common use). Smith grounded her "institutional ethnography" in the actual daily lives of women and moved from that basis to explain how many of the ways women actually operate in their institutional roles (for example, as mothers and teachers) remained invisible in patriarchal society. Thus the task for women's oral historians, the article argued, was to develop interview techniques that asked women to ascribe their own meaning—their own feelings—to their lives. The starting point for the article was Kathryn Anderson's realization that although she wanted to find out how women *felt* about their lives, she was asking standard historical questions that elicited answers about behavior, not about emotions. Dana Jack described the kinds of questions that elicited emotional rather than descriptive responses from her clients, and finally Judith Wittner and I discussed the ways in which individual interviews might be aggregated into larger generalizations. Taken as a whole, as a reviewer suggested, the article offered a view of oral history that was "neither a psychological interview nor secondary documentation...the oral historian walks a narrow line between the two."[13]

The high point of the "woman's culture" approach had occurred in 1982 when Carol Gilligan's *In a Different Voice*, with its emphasis on women's relationship skills, created a sensation. Subsequent books such as the 1986 publication by Mary Field Belenky et al., *Women's Ways of Knowing: The Development of Self, Voice and Mind* and Sara Ruddick's *Maternal Thinking* were similarly based on the identification of distinctive traits that all women shared. All of these books were based largely on interviews with women, although none of them claimed to be women's oral histories. As it turned out, the belief among feminist scholars in a sweeping, unitary women's culture was remarkably brief, and the methodological experimentation suggested in "Beginning Where We Are" was diverted into new directions.[14] I found that now that I had used oral history as a way to find out "the lay of the land"—the general contours of the lives of western, rural women—I could use archival sources with greater focus and insight than I had ten years previously. I believe that many other feminist scholars who shared my delight in the discovery phase turned, as I did, back to more conventional sources for much of our subsequent work.

Women's Words

In the late 1980s, the twin waves of postmodernism and postcolonial theory engulfed us all—historians, literary critics, anthropologists, sociologists, women's studies, and ethnic studies scholars—and changed the practices of our disciplines. The new ideas fundamentally altered the ways that practitioners of women's oral history went about our work. First, the destruction of the notion of objectivity undermined the confident interview methods used by historians and anthropologists, drawing attention to the difficulties inherent in the relationship between interviewer and narrator. Second, the reality of multiple (especially racial) differences ended notions of a unitary women's culture and created a much more complex world of individual intersections between gender, race, class, and culture.[15] Oral history remained a popular and democratic method, much used by local historical societies and groups, the beneficiaries of oral history workshops that were widespread in the 1970s. But with the postmodern turn, within the academy the design, execution, and analysis of women's oral histories became much more complex. Armed with new tools to analyze and describe difference, feminist historians abandoned generalizations in favor of specificity. There was considerable variation in the facility and ease with which we learned the new approaches, and some of us were never fully comfortable. Across the academy, scholars in many humanities and social science fields became similarly engrossed in learning the lessons of postmodernism. Eventually, the new theories and new realizations enriched us and our research, but they took time to learn and fostered the popular perception that in the 1990s academics had become even more self-absorbed and elite—especially in language—than ever before.

In 1991 Sherna Gluck and Daphne Patai published *Women's Words: The Feminist Practice of Oral History*, an anthology that reflected these changing currents.[16] The thirteen individual authors represented different disciplines and perspectives, but the volume as a whole moved beyond a simplistic approach to feminism and stressed the difficulty of interviewing across barriers of class, race, and culture. Reflecting postmodern thinking, problems in interviewing were described, not in the old "insider" and "outsider" terms but as questions of power inequality. Three articles in particular considered the intricacies of the interview process. Judith Stacey's "Can There Be a Feminist Ethnography?" was a painfully honest exploration of the ways in which her feminist ethnography based in empathy and commonality led her into situations of exploitation and betrayal of confidences with women workers in Silicon Valley. Two other authors, Sondra Hale and Daphne Patai, described interview situations where Stacey's problems were compounded by cultural (Sudan and Brazil) and class differences. These three articles were indeed sobering, and forced us—as the editors insisted—to leave our "innocent assumptions" about female commonality behind. In good postmodern fashion we became not only more self-conscious as interviewers, but we paid closer attention to class, race, and cultural differences between ourselves and our narrators. To use the language we were still learning: we learned reflexivity by becoming aware of our own subjectivity and learned to state clearly our own partiality and "positionality." One might more colloquially say, or hope, that we became more thoughtful and responsible interviewers.

One of the articles in the collection, Kathryn Anderson and Dana Jack's "Learning to Listen," dropped the outdated theoretical baggage that Judith Wittner and I had contributed to our original joint article. Anderson and Jack were able to focus on the interview process itself and to insist on a more nuanced approach based on much more skilled listening. They suggested that learning to listen "in stereo"—to both conventional and muted meanings—was not a matter of new questions but of a genuinely interactive process in which the language and the feelings that narrators expressed were constantly explored. In effect, the authors claimed that standard oral history interview techniques were inadequate, and suggested that the interactive techniques of therapeutic interviews would lead to better women's oral history interviews. Few took up this sharp challenge at the time, but it has remained a persistent question about the congruence of the purposes and methods of women's oral history.

In other respects as well, *Women's Words* broke new ground. Almost half the articles in the volume were concerned with the analysis of interviews, casting a postmodernist eye on questions of language, silences, and interpretation. Because so much earlier work on women's oral history had focused only on interview techniques, or on the narrator's unmediated words, this new attention to analysis was welcome. Four articles were devoted to issues of advocacy and representation, which had been key aspects of women's oral histories from the beginning, although, as with so much else, not initially regarded as problematic. Now in these articles the authors sought to analyze the tensions caused by diversity itself, by the different expectations of community and academy, and how one responsibly represents the opinions of others for the sake of a political cause. This last was the question that Sherna Gluck confronted in "Advocacy Oral History: Palestinian Women in Resistance." To get Palestinian women to talk to her at all was difficult, and she could not get the amount of personal detail about women's lives that she would have liked. On the other hand, she came away with powerful personal testimony to support her advocacy of Palestinian independence to audiences in the United States. This article, in its straightforward discussion of the compromises one makes in community interviewing, epitomized the honesty that characterized the entire volume.

In all, *Women's Words* covered a lot of new ground, topically and theoretically, with the frankness and honesty that has always characterized the best feminist work. It was the "state of the art" volume that allowed women's oral history to correct the enthusiasms of the early days of women's history and to chart a more reflective, analytic, and generally more limited future path. As I reviewed it at the time, however, I was taken aback by the intensely hortatory, not to say scolding, editorial tone and wondered whether, in spite of its wide adoption in the classroom, it would deter rather than encourage beginners in women's oral history.[17]

Life Histories and the Problem of Representation

Postmodernism affected feminist anthropologists as well as historians, casting doubt on the scholar's ability to first immerse herself in the participant observation technique of fieldwork and then to distance herself enough to provide a cultural context for the lives of the women with whom she had shared confidences. These strains were especially apparent in life histories. Because interviewers often spent hundreds of hours with their subjects, the questions raised by Judith Stacey about the conflicting pulls of friendship, power inequality, and exploitation were acute. Furthermore, the choices made in the process of editing large amounts of information for publication became "problematic" (another word in our new vocabulary). Finally, feminist anthropologists were obligated by the life-history model itself to challenge male bias directly as they sought to describe the cultural contexts in which their subjects were located. At least at first, women's historians had left their challenge to male historical bias implicit, expecting (unrealistically, as it turned out) the new material on women's lives to be self-evident reason for adjustment.

Given these multiple tasks, it was not surprising that the life-history process itself became a subject for concern. In 1986 Susan Geiger raised these and other issues in an outstanding review article for *Signs*: "Women's Life Histories: Method and Content."[18] She pointed out that traditionally, anthropologists have used the life-history method to illuminate the cultures of "tribal" and "primitive" peoples, the kinds of cultures that have been understood to be "vanishing." Life histories have been most successful when the culture under investigation is itself oral. Several important life histories with African women were published in the early 1980s, introducing many American historians to African women's voices for the first time. Among the best known were Margaret Strobel's *Muslim Women in Mombasa, 1890–1975* and Claire Robertson's *Sharing the Same Bowl: A Socio-Economic History of Women and Class in Accra, Ghana.*[19] Strobel discussed some of the problems of interviewing as an outsider (a white American in African and Muslim Kenya) in the first *Frontiers* women's oral history issue, and Robertson raised the question of bias in life histories in a later issue, but both articles were published before the full tidal wave of postmodernism hit.[20] After that, it was no longer acceptable, in life histories or elsewhere, for privileged First World women to "speak for" or claim to represent, poorer, illiterate women. All over the world, in fact, women were insisting that their voices and their perspectives be directly heard, a demand that at first surprised

American feminists greatly when it arose at the first World Women's conference held in Mexico City in 1975 and which was voiced even more loudly at subsequent conferences in Copenhagen, Nairobi, and Beijing. Not only did American activist feminists have to reconsider their claim to speak for "all women," but it followed that anthropologists could no longer invisibly create "as if" autobiographies from their interviews. Instead, the presence of the interviewer in life histories needed to be acknowledged.

Life histories were reconfigured in two main ways. The first was to present the life history as a fully cooperative enterprise from the beginning. In *Forged Under the Sun/Forjada Bajo el Sol: The Life of Maria Elena Lucas*, the historian Fran Leeper Buss, who called herself the editor of Lucas's autobiography, described the eleven-year relationship between the two women. Buss saw herself as providing the historical and economic context within which Lucas could tell her own personal and spiritual story. As Buss explained, one of the primary goals of the work for both of them was to bear witness to "the degradations of body and spirit suffered by Maria Elena and her people. To do so Maria Elena stretched deep into the recesses of her memory, and I traveled and searched through primary and secondary sources and field notes, preparing pages of new questions to ask her each time we met." Although Buss was trained as a historian, she was not an academic but an activist who found her role in this and other oral histories by writing in such a way as to "provide a forum through which poor women could speak about the conditions of their survival."[21] In short, Buss approached this life history project as an advocate rather than as a critic.

Similarly, Julie Cruikshank trained as an anthropologist but was not an academic. Cruikshank credited at least part of her success in recording the life histories of three Yukon Native women to that fact. Suffering no pressure to quickly record, analyze, and publish, she spent years interviewing Angela Sidney, Kitty Smith, and Annie Ned, eventually publishing *Life Lived Like a Story: Life Stories of Three Yukon Native Elders*. Cruikshank described the ways in which over the years the three women brought her to understand the importance of traditional stories in their lives and the reasons why not just their personal histories but the tribal stories were an integral part of their life histories. Cruikshank not only respected their judgment but came to believe that inclusion of the stories was an important way to make the reality of their cultures apparent to readers from other cultures.[22] Cruikshank's stance toward her narrators was that of a student. Like Buss, she stressed her subordinate role in the cooperative life history enterprise.

A far different approach toward women's life history was adopted by Ruth Behar, a professor of anthropology at the University of Michigan, who published *Translated Woman: Crossing the Border with Esperanza's Story* in 1993. What made this life history unusual was the vocal presence of Behar, and her own life story, in the text. Although the major subject was Esperanza, a poor woman in Mexquitic, Mexico, Behar did not remove herself from the narrative. She wrote openly about the uncertainties she felt as she interviewed Esperanza, and of the problems and academic pressures she experienced as she edited the interviews into book form. Behar thus went farther than the other two interviewers in acknowledging her own powerful role in the creation of the life history, and in so doing she triggered quite a controversy. By abandoning a modest and self-effacing role, was she inexcusably self-absorbed, or simply honest? Having removed the veil of scholarly objectivity and distance, how *do* you deal with the power inequities of the life history process? The best current answer seems to be the injunction to always be attentive to reflexivity. In other words, be there, be attentive, and be honest—simple to say, hard to do.[23]

Once the Dust Settled

By the late 1990s, between the postmodern storm and the new theoretical attention to memory, a lull developed, which allowed an assessment of the state of the art. In 1998 *Frontiers* published two issues on women's oral history, the first since the special issue in 1983. Because the response to the call for articles was so great, the planned single issue became two, the first devoted to varieties of women's oral history, and the second to postmodern theoretical issues and anxieties. Finally, in 2002, came *Women's Oral History: The Frontiers Reader*, an effort to combine the "best of" articles on women's oral history techniques and examples from the four *Frontiers* special issues from 1977 to 1998. This renewed attention to women's oral history by *Frontiers* occurred in part because I was the editor of the journal at the time. The response to the call for articles made me suspect that although women's oral history interest and practice were strong, it had become more difficult to publish articles because journals had moved on to newer approaches. I was particularly glad, therefore, to have the opportunity to provide a forum for a field that had meant so much to me.[24]

Taken together, the articles in the three volumes illustrate the most common current uses of women's oral history. At the top of the list would be classroom use. Interviews with (usually) older women are common in courses in women's history and women's studies as a way of reinforcing the notion of the historicity of "womanhood," and of personalizing the abstract lessons of the course. A second common usage is in family history, for the simple reason that women outlive men and are alive longer to do the reminiscing.[25] In both of these popular uses, the quality and value of the interview is likely to be low, no matter how much each interview may mean to individuals. This seems to me to be an acceptable price to pay for having such a versatile and democratizing tool, although not all oral historians would agree.

By far the most important use of women's oral history continues to be what it has been from the beginning: uncovering and documenting women's overlooked activities in history. Sometimes this is a matter of documenting the evidence, as in Dolores Delgado Bernal's re-incorporation of female students into a well-known episode of Chicano resistance, or Diane Sands's documentation of a not-very-hidden network of abortionists in Montana during the period when it was illegal. Bernal's research challenged a male-centered theory of grassroots organizing, and Sands laid bare the class divide—that family doctors safely provided abortions for middle-class girls, while working-class women and abortionists were arrested.[26] Another important use of women's oral history caught women in transition between old circumstances and new, as in Valerie Grim's interviews with African American women who migrated to Chicago from rural Mississippi or, as in Rosemary Sayigh's article on Palestinian women, in the grip of a nationalist ideology that incompletely fit their personal needs.[27] Finally, and probably forever, women's oral history is used to give voice to women who have not been heard. Still, it is relatively rare to publish straightforward transcripts, since narrative techniques borrowed from literature and/or skillful editing help to enhance understanding and readability.[28]

The classic oral history dilemmas remain, with new ones added. Questions of trust between interviewer and narrator remain central: Is she telling me the truth? Did I not really hear what she said? Am I imposing my interpretation or being culturally insensitive? What are my obligations to this woman? Painful as they often are, these questions will not go away. Not fully resolvable, they are the price of participating in a genuinely mutual oral history interview, and honesty about these dilemmas is one of the greatest contributions of women's oral history.[29]

Current Women's Oral History: A Quick Survey

What follows is a brief survey of recent books and projects, offered in an effort to convey some sense of the current range of work that is being conducted under the rough rubric of women's oral history. Each of these examples shows, in different ways, that women's oral history has spilled beyond the bounds of traditional publication.

Judy Yung's history of Chinese women in San Francisco, *Unbound Feet* and its companion volume, *Unbound Voices*, are exemplary illustrations of research that goes far beyond "insider" oral history. Beginning with her own personal knowledge and access to Chinatown women, Yung uses Chinese- and English-language newspapers, official documents, personal accounts, and earlier oral histories to produce an authoritative account of the stages in which Chinese women became Chinese American while remaining extraordinarily transnational. The decision to publish both volumes was brilliant: *Unbound Feet* is written as a conventional history in which oral history was clearly one source, but *Unbound Voices* allows all readers to share the exceptional richness of that source.[30]

The historian Claire Robertson, a veteran student of African women, published in 2000 *"We Only Come Here to Struggle": Stories from Berida's Life*. That this is a postmodern life history is evident in a number of ways. Robertson and Berida

Ndanbuki, a Kenyan market woman, are listed as co-authors, and the volume contains a postscript of Berida's questions about Robertson's personal life and about the United States. Robertson directly discusses the issue of exploitation in life history in the introduction. But the changes go deeper: The text contains pictures and sidebars with excerpts from the original tape transcriptions to compare to the text. An accompanying videotape (*Second Face*) allows one to see Berida and her family, her home, and market relationships. In all these various ways, Robertson responds to the challenges of collaboration and representation across cultures.[31]

Still another contemporary version of life history is provided by Daniel James in *Doña Maria's Story: Life History, Memory, and Political Identity*. His edited interviews with an Argentinian working-class Peronista are paired with interpretive essays that explore narrative style, gender, memory and oral history methodology.[32] While Robertson pushes the edges of representation by coupling visual elements to her book, James's choice to divide his book between testimony and analysis shows the increasing importance of theory. Each of the four interpretive essays is substantive, beginning with a prologue devoted to the description of a quintessential working-class location. For all of its virtues, it is not "an exemplary work of women's oral history" as Alistair Thomson commented in an influential article.[33] James is interested in Doña Maria's factory work and in her politics, not (except in passing) in her family work—housework, mothering, and the rest. Thus a good book, by failing to consider the entire woman, contributes less than it might have otherwise.

A final published example is Gail Hershatter's elegant essay, "The Gender of Memory: Rural Chinese Women and the 1950s," which appeared in *Signs* in 2002. Hershatter uses interviews with a rural Chinese woman, Cao Zhuxiang, to explore two different topics: shifting gender roles in rural China in the 1950s, and more recent shifts in popular thinking about Maoist politics in that decade. Cao Zhuxiang was designated by the Communist Party as a model laborer, which gave her both prestige and power. Hershatter, suggesting that Cao herself had become a "site of memory" for her village, reinterprets political history through her eyes and others. The article is a *tour de force* of the use of an obscure individual history to illuminate a much larger picture of how popular memory denies or "smooths out" difficult political and economic history in order to create a narrative of progress. This is a particularly clear example because, historically, Maoist China directly attacked traditional Chinese female gender roles. Thus, is there any reason to doubt that gender must surely always be a key element in memory studies?[34]

Taken together, such recent works clearly demonstrate ways in which academic women's oral historians have pushed the boundaries, using new theories and new modes of presentation to make their work relevant to wider audiences. This exciting work shows how fully women's oral history has become cutting-edge research. As I read it, current popular collective projects have a different goal in mind. They are determined to document women's activities to prevent them from being lost to history again. The Valley Women's History Collaborative of western Massachusetts and the New York Activist Women's Voices: Oral History Project are organized similarly, operating from a base in the university (University of Massachusetts and CUNY) with outreach into the community. Both are committed to preserving the histories of activist women, especially, as the CUNY project states, "unheralded activist women in community-based organizations." Both groups do oral histories and run community workshops in oral history. Following the long tradition of women's organizations, they are underfunded, they rely on volunteers, and they appear to be regarded as marginal by their home institutions. Both projects continue to actively interview, although more slowly than they would like.

A better-funded example illustrates some of the possibilities and pitfalls of projects of this kind. The Washington Women's History Consortium (WHC) was founded and funded by the Washington State legislature in 2005 to document the history of women in the state, especially their recent political history. Washington has a female governor, two female U.S. senators, and one of the nation's highest percentages of women members of the state legislature. Funding has supported an executive director of the WHC and an official oral historian to conduct interviews, as well as paying to have them transcribed. The first oral history project undertaken by the WHC was to document the 1977 International Women's Year conference in Ellensberg, Washington. (The interviews were limited in scope to a particular event, and were not full-scale biographical surveys.) Because of the unexpected last-minute participation of several hundred conservative women at the time, this conference remains contentious today. For interviewing, it was easier to find liberal women who had participated than conservative women. If the numbers were unequal, could the project be balanced? Because state funds were used for the project, this question had to be asked and satisfactorily answered.[35]

And Now, Digital

Two aspects of the still-unfolding digital revolution seem particularly important for women's oral history: the growth of online collections, and the "Do It Yourself" (DIY) interview movement. Online collections of all kinds are growing rapidly, offering unprecedented and easy access. At least fifty women's oral history projects came online via the Alexander Street Press, a commercial site, which charges for research use.[36] By far the most extensive women's oral history online site is the Virtual Oral/Aural History Archive compiled by Sherna Gluck and colleagues at California State University–Long Beach. It archives eleven separate collections, ranging from the Rosie the Riveter interviews to Asian American activists. Its drawback is that only the audio interviews are online, without transcripts, but it is still a remarkably diverse collection.[37] The precise usage of all of these online resources remains unclear. Will they mostly be used as a quick and easy source by students, or are they potential sites for serious research? What is clear is the sheer amount of information available—and it is growing fast.

The other trend worth watching is the DIY oral history movement, projects such as StoryCorps and new digital sites like the YourStory Project at the University of Utah. Here, participants record their own stories, usually assisted by a friend or family member. The trained interviewer disappears. What sort of interviews might this new method produce, and what are its implications for women's oral history? I have been inclined to dismiss StoryCorps as oral history "lite," incomplete, hitting emotional high spots and minimizing the mundane. But Kathryn Anderson, coauthor of the influential "Learning to Listen" article, disagrees. She believes that emotional honesty is enhanced by minimizing the distance between interviewer and narrator, and that the sheer accessibility of DIY projects will encourage wide use. Will ease and familiarity encourage women to bare their souls in the interview booth? Anderson acknowledges that "The concern that such a democratized process might result in shallow or romanticized versions of the past is one to consider carefully, though oral histories collected by trained interviewers with institutional backing may be subject to the same critique."[38] The potential for DIY projects to reach all kinds and classes of women is stunning to consider. All of a sudden an accessible but still limited interview method is expanded to Everywoman!

These potentially unlimited possibilities prompt me to take a quick look backwards. Forty years ago, we took up women's oral history in the face of emptiness. No women in the history books and strictly limited ways (we thought) to recover their lives. Sherna Gluck spoke for many of us when she refused to be "historically voiceless." In the intervening years, American women's historians *have* created a new history and *have* re-created our past. Women's oral history has been an indisputable component in that effort. Now, as the sources of women's oral history multiply, it is time to recognize the importance of that work—and to continue it.

NOTES

1. In fairness, though the books were few, they were classics, especially Eleanor Flexner's *Century of Struggle: The Women's Rights Movement in the United States* (Cambridge, Mass.: Belknap Press, 1959), Gerda Lerner's *Black Women in White America: A Documentary History* (New York: Pantheon, 1972), and Nancy Cott's *Root of Bitterness: Documents of the Social History of American Women* (Boston: Northeastern University Press, 1972).

2. The four special issues were *Frontiers: A Journal of Women Studies* 2, no. 2 (Summer 1977); 7, no. 1 (1983); 19, no. 2 (1998); 19, no. 3 (1998). Susan H. Armitage, Patricia Hart, and Karen Weathermon, eds., *Women's Oral History: The Frontiers Reader* (Lincoln: University of Nebraska Press, 2002).

3. Edward D. Ives, *The Tape-Recorded Interview: A Manual for Fieldworkers in Folklore and Oral History* (Knoxville: University of Tennessee Press, 1995 [1974]).

4. Willa Baum, *Oral History for the Local Historical Society* (Nashville, Tenn.: American Association for State and Local History, 1969).

5. Sue Armitage, Theresa Banfield, and Sarah Jacobus, "Black Women and Their Communities in Colorado," *Frontiers* 2, no. 2 (Summer 1977): 45–51; Sue Armitage, "The Mountains Were Free and We Loved Them," in *African American Women Confront the West*, ed. Quintard Taylor and Shirley Ann Wilson Moore, 165–77 (Norman: University of Oklahoma Press, 2003); Ruth Cave Flowers in www.blackpast.org.

6. Sherna Berger Gluck, "What's So Special About Women? Women's Oral History," *Frontiers* 2, no. 2 (Summer 1977).

7. See, for example, Amy Kesselman, Tina Tau, and Karen Wickre, "*Good Work, Sister!* The Making of an Oral History Production," and Corky Bush, "Telling Our Stories," *Frontiers* 7, no. 1 (1983).

8. Gluck, "What's So Special About Women?"; Naomi Weissstein, "Psychology Constructs the Female," in *Sisterhood Is Powerful*, ed. Robin Morgan (New York: Random House, 1970).

9. Sherna Gluck, ed., *From Parlor to Prison: Five American Suffragists Talk About Their Lives* (New York, Vintage Books, 1976); Nan Elsasser, Kyle MacKenzie, and Yvonne Tixier y Vigil, *Las Mujeres: Conversations from a Hispanic Community* (New York: The Feminist Press, 1980); Kathy Kahn, *Hillbilly Women: Mountain Women Speak of Struggle and Joy in Southern Appalachia* (New York: Doubleday, 1973); Sherry Thomas, *We Didn't Have Much, but We Sure Had Plenty: Stories of Rural Women* (New York: Anchor Books, 1981); Teresa Jordan, *Cowgirls: Women of the American West* (New York: Anchor Books, 1982); the films *With Babies and Banners* (1979) and *Union Maids* (1976).

10. Gluck, "Women's Oral History, the Second Decade," *Frontiers* 7, no. 1 (1983), 1–2; Sherna Gluck, *Rosie the Riveter Revisited: Women, the War and Social Change* (New York: Twayne Publishers, 1987); Sue Armitage, "The Next Step," *Frontiers* 7, no. 1, 3–8; "Women's Oral History Projects," *Frontiers* 7, no. 1, 114–21.

11. *Voices of American Homemakers*, RR 2, Box 48, Rushville, Ind., 46173, Eleanor Arnold, director. Sponsored by the National Extension Homemakers Council and funded by the National Endowment for the Humanities; *Black Women Oral History Project*, Schlesigner Library, Radcliffe College, 10 Garden St., Cambridge, MA, 02138, Ruth E. Hill, coordinator, Patricia M. King, director; Vicki L. Ruiz, *Cannery Women, Cannery Lives: Mexican Women, Unionization, and the California Food Processing Industry, 1939–1950* (Albuquerque: University of New Mexico Press, 1987); Gluck, *Rosie the Riveter Revisited*; Jacquelyn Dowd Hall, James Leloudis, Robert Korstad, Mary Murphy, Lu Ann Jones, and Christopher B. Daly, *Like a Family: The Making of a Southern Cotton Mill World* (Chapel Hill: University of North Carolina Press, 1987).

12. The cataloging problem began to be solved by the 1979 publication of Andrea Hinding et al., *Women's History Sources: A Guide to Archives and Manuscript Collections in the United States* (New York: Bowker, 1979).

13. Kathryn Anderson, Susan Armitage, Dana Jack, and Judith Wittner, "Beginning Where We Are," in *Feminist Research Methods: Exemplary Readings in the Social Sciences*, ed. Joyce McCarl Nielsen (Boulder: Westview Press, 1990), 94–112, comment by Nielsen, 94.

14. Carol Gilligan, *In a Different Voice* (Cambridge, Mass.: Harvard University Press, 1982); Mary Kay Belenkey et al., *Women's Ways of Knowing: The Development of Self, Voice, and Mind* (New York: Basic Publishing, 1986); Sara Ruddick, *Maternal Thinking: Toward a Politics of Peace* (Boston: Beacon Press, 1989).

15. For historians, the death of objectivity came in Peter Novick, *That Noble Dream: The "Objectivity Question" and the American Historical Profession* (Cambridge: Cambridge University Press, 1988). For anthropologists, the challenge came the same year in James

Clifford, *The Predicament of Culture: Twentieth Century Ethnography, Literature, and Art* (Cambridge, Mass.: Harvard University Press, 1988).

16. Sherna Berger Gluck and Daphne Patai, eds., *Women's Words: The Feminist Practice of Oral History* (New York: Routledge, 1991).

17. Susan Armitage, George Lipsitz, Gary Mormino, "Women's Words": A Review Symposium, *Oral History Review* 20, nos. 1/2 (Apr. 1, 1992): 105–11.

18. Susan Geiger, "Women's Life Histories: Method and Content," *Signs* 11, no. 2 (Winter, 1986): 334–51.

19. Margaret Strobel, *Muslim Women in Mombasa, 1890–1975* (New Haven, Conn.: Yale University Press, 1979); Claire Robertson *Sharing the Same Bowl: A Socio-economic History of Women and Class in Accra, Ghana* (Bloomington: Indiana University Press, 1983).

20. Margaret Strobel, "Doing Oral History as an Outsider," *Frontiers* 2, no. 2, 68–72; Claire Robertson, "In Pursuit of Life Histories: The Problem of Bias," *Frontiers* 7, no. 2 (1983), 64–69.

21. Fran Leeper Buss, ed., *Forged under the Sun/Forjada bajo el sol: The Life of Maria Elena Lucas* (Ann Arbor: University of Michigan Press, 1993), 3, 32.

22. Julie Cruikshank, in collaboration with Angela Sidney, Kitty Smith, and Annie Ned, *Life Lived Like a Story: Life Stories of Three Yukon Native Elders* (Lincoln: University of Nebraska Press, 1990).

23. Ruth Behar, *Translated Woman: Crossing the Border with Esperanza's Story* (Boston: Beacon Press, 1993); Maya Socolovsky, "Moving Beyond the Mint Green Walls: An Examination of (Auto)Biography and Border in Ruth Behar's *Translated Woman*," *Frontiers* 19, no. 3 (1998); Sherna Gluck in "Reflections on Oral History in the New Millennium: Roundtable Comments," *Oral History Review* 26, no. 2 (Summer–Autumn, 1999), 8.

24. *Frontiers* 19, no. 2 (1998); *Frontiers* 19, no. 3 (1998); Armitage, *Women's Oral History*.

25. Anne M. Butler and Gerri W. Sorenson, "Patching the Past: Students and Oral History," *Frontiers* 19, no. 3, 200–213, and *Frontiers Reader*, 196–210; Connie Broughton, "Filming Nana: Some Dilemmas of Oral History on Film," *Frontiers* 19, no. 3, 190–99, and *Frontiers Reader*, 173–82.

26. Dolores Delgado Bernal, "Grassroots Leadership Reconceptualized: Chicana Oral Histories and the 1968 East Los Angeles School Blowouts," *Frontiers* 19, no. 2, 113–42, and *Frontiers Reader*, 227–57; Diane Sands, "Using Oral History to Chart the Course of Illegal Abortions in Montana," *Frontiers* 7, no. 1 (1982), 32–37, and *Frontiers Reader*, 213–26.

27. Valerie Grim, "From the Yazoo Mississippi Delta to the Urban Communities of the Midwest: Conversations with Rural African Women," *Frontiers* 22, no. 1 (2001), 126–44, and *Frontiers Reader*, 272–92; Rosemary Sayigh, "Gender, Sexulaity, and Class in National Narrations: Palestinian Camp Women Tell Their Lives," *Frontiers* 19, no. 2 (1998), 166–85, and *Frontiers Reader*, 317–37.

28. See, for example, Malia Mulder-Wollan, "Harvest Stories: Interviews with Gladys Lillian Marke," *Frontiers* 19, no. 2 (1998) 1–15.

29. See, for example, Sandy Polishuk, "Secrets, Lies, and Misremembering: The Perils of Oral History Interviewing," and Gail Stearns, "Reflexivity and Moral Agency: Restoring Possibility to Life History Research," *Frontiers* 19, no. 3 (1998), 14–23 and 58–71; Judy Yung, "'A Bowlful of Tears' Revisited: the Full Story of Lee Puey You's Immigration Experience at Angel Island," *Frontiers* 25, no. 1 (2004), 1–22; and Debbie Storrs, "Like a Bamboo: Representations of a Japanese War Bride," *Frontiers* 21, no 1/2, Asian American Women (2000): 194–224.

30. Judy Yung, *Unbound Feet* (Berkeley: University of California Press, 1995), and Yung, *Unbound Voices: A Documentary History of Chinese Women in San Francisco* (Berkeley: University of California Press, 1999).

31. Berida Ndambuki and Claire C. Robertson, *"We Only Come Here to Struggle": Stories from Berida's Life* (Bloomington: Indiana University Press, 2000).

32. Daniel James, *Doña Maria's Story: Life History, Memory, and Political Identity* (Durham, N.C.: Duke University Press, 2000).

33. Alistair Thomson "Four Paradigm Transformations in Oral History," *Oral History Review* 34, no. 1, 64.

34. Gail Hershatter, "The Gender of Memory: Rural Chinese Women and the 1950s," *Signs* 28, no. 1, Gender and Cultural Memory (Autumn 2002): 43–70.

35. The Valley Women's Collaborative Web site is www.umass.edu/vwhc/; the Activist Women's Voices: Oral History Project is http://web.cuny.edu/Womenstudies/activism.html; the Washington Women's History Consortium is www.washingtonwomenshistory.org/. I am a member of the Advisory Board.

36. The Alexander Street Press Web site for oral history is alexanderstreet.com/products/orhi.htm.

37. The CSULB Virtual Oral/Aural History Archive is at csulb.edu/colleges/cla/departments/history/programs/oral.html.

38. The YourStory Project is at www.yourstory.utah.edu/about.html; StoryCorps at www.storycorps.net; Kathryn Anderson, personal communication with author, Oct. 10, 2008.

BIBLIOGRAPHY

Armitage, Susan H., Patricia Hart, and Karen Weathermon, eds. *Women's Oral History: The Frontiers Reader*. Lincoln: University of Nebraska Press, 2002.

Buss, Fran Leeper, ed. *Forged under the Sun/Forjada bajo el sol: The Life of Maria Elena Lucas*. Ann Arbor: University of Michigan Press, 1993.

Cruikshank, Julie. With Angela Sidney, Kitty Smith, and Annie Ned. *Life Lived Like a Story: Life Stories of Three Yukon Native Elders*. Lincoln: University of Nebraska Press, 1990.

Gluck, Sherna Berger, and Daphne Patai, eds. *Women's Words: The Feminist Practice of Oral History*. New York: Routledge, 1991.

Ndambuki, Berida, and Claire C. Robertson. *"We Only Come Here to Struggle": Stories from Berida's Life*. Bloomington: Indiana University Press, 2000.

Yung, Judy. *Unbound Feet*. Berkeley: University of California Press, 1995.

———. *Unbound Voices: A Documentary History of Chinese Women in San Francisco*. Berkeley: University of California Press, 1999.

CHAPTER 12

RACE AND ORAL HISTORY

ALBERT S. BROUSSARD

One of the most remarkable developments in the historical profession in the past forty years has been the explosion of African American history and its movement to the center of the American experience. No longer treated as an aside or relegated to the margins of U.S. history, black history, as it came to be known during the decades of the 1960s and 1970s, occupies a prominent place in the discussion and interpretation of numerous historical eras and controversies. Indeed, historians have reinterpreted a sizable slice of American history when African Americans and race are incorporated. Although scholars consult numerous sources in reconstructing and interpreting the past, oral history has played a critical role in shaping much of the broader discussion of race and African American history. Oral history evidence has illuminated the African American experience during slavery and Reconstruction and the modern civil rights movement. Additionally, scholars have utilized oral interviews effectively in writing black urban history, and the role of African Americans in the labor movement, politics, and family history.

Oral History and American Slavery

No field in U.S. history has been revised more dramatically by oral history than American slavery. The earliest studies of slavery were dominated by white southerners such as U. B. Phillips (1877–1934), who taught at Tulane, the University of Michigan, and Yale, where he trained an entire generation of southern historians.

Phillips's *American Negro Slavery*, published in 1918, argued that slavery was a benign, humane institution, which served primarily as a school of civilization for ignorant, barbaric, and unenterprising Africans. It remained the standard work in the field for almost fifty years.[1]

It was a folklorist, John Lomax (1867–1948), however, whose research in the South during the 1930s, began to reshape the way most scholars and students came to view slavery. Working for the Federal Writers' Project, a New Deal agency established in 1935 under the Works Progress Administration (WPA), Lomax and a team of researchers collected the oral testimonies of former slaves, talking about their life under the "peculiar institution." Some 2,300 interviews were conducted, and the notes and transcripts were deposited later in the Library of Congress.[2] In contrast to the histories of slavery recorded by Phillips and other southern historians, former slaves told a radically different story. Their collective voices confirmed what the one hundred printed slave narratives had maintained for nearly a century: that slavery was a brutal and dehumanizing institution. While earlier histories of slavery had argued that enslaved people had been well cared for, received sufficient food, clothing, health care, and adequate housing, the WPA's slave narratives (as they are commonly known) painted a picture of hardship, depravation, and cruelty. Slave families were separated frequently, and slave parents lacked the same parental controls over their offspring as white parents. Contrary to Phillips, slaves were poorly fed and scantily clothed, and the life span of enslaved people was considerably shorter than that of whites. Slaves from every region of the South experienced an array of health disparities, the result of excessive work, neglect, inadequate diets, and a reliance on folk remedies.

The WPA narratives revealed the brutality of slavery in a manner than few published histories had documented. Elderly former slave narrators told interviewers how their white overseers, masters, and mistresses had given little thought to beating or torturing men, women, and children for even the most minor offense. They remembered the brutalization of family members, as well as the sadistic punishments often meted out to runaways or slaves who openly and defiantly resisted their bondage. They also spoken freely about the sexual exploitation of women and children, and the casual sexual liaisons that masters had with enslaved women.[3]

The slave narratives also ran contrary to published histories of slavery by revealing that slaves enjoyed a rich, dynamic, and vibrant cultural life. As brutal as slavery developed on most southern plantations and small farms, enslaved people possessed the wherewithal to create a rich cultural life that served in part, as the cultural historian Lawrence Levine has written, as a buffer to ensure that physical slavery never became mental slavery.[4] The WPA narratives were replete with examples of slaves who continued to speak an African language, along with English, adopted an African name, practiced a hybrid of African and Christian worship, and engaged in African forms of prayer and dance. The linguist Lorenzo Turner (1890–1972) was one of many scholars who believed that enslaved people retained part of their African culture into the twentieth century. From 1929 to 1949 he conducted extensive research on the Gullah people on the Sea Islands, a group of barrier islands located off the coasts of South Carolina and Georgia. Turner discovered that as late as the 1940s, the Gullah all possessed African personal names and spoke more than 4,000 African words from twenty-one African tribes.[5]

Similarly, the slave narratives revealed that African music, dance, folk expressions, and religious practices, not only flourished in the American South but were constantly created and re-created as a direct response to the unique experiences of American slaves. Anthropologists such as Melville J. Herskovits (1895–1963) confirmed that African cultural retention existed in many slave societies throughout the Western Hemisphere.[6] Since the majority of enslaved people handed down their songs and cultural traditions orally from one generation to the next, there was seldom a fixed or final version of any song, whether religious or secular. Hence a variety of circumstances, including regional differences in diction and pronunciation, as well as faulty memories, might yield several versions of the same song. Slave culture, therefore, encouraged improvisation, and more than one observer, such as the New England abolitionist and writer Thomas Wentworth Higginson (1823–1911), who had commanded a regiment of black soldiers from South Carolina during the Civil War, noted the uncanny ability of African Americans to remake an old song to fit a new situation and to create a new song on a moment's notice.[7]

The oral narratives collected in the 1930s were consistent with the earlier slave narratives that revealed the African Americans' consistent longing for freedom and the many ingenious ways that the enslaved resisted their bondage. Contrary to the assumptions of their masters and mistresses, enslaved people knew and valued the meaning of freedom. They saw free people on a regular basis on their farms and plantations, and a small number of slaves possessed the independence to hire themselves out or to work for wages in factories and urban areas, where they came into contact with free men and women of all races. Frederick Douglass (1818–95), perhaps the most famous fugitive slave, wrote in the acclaimed narrative of his life that an urban slave was almost like a free man. Indeed, hundreds of slave narratives revealed that slaves thought about their freedom on a daily basis. "I saw no prospect that my condition would ever change," the ex-slave Lunsford Lane (1803–63) wrote in his published narrative. "But I used to plan in my mind from day-to-day, and from night-to-night, how I might be free." Solomon Northup (1808–63), who was kidnapped and spent twelve years in bondage illegally before his release, also wrote in his highly popular narrative that the thought of freedom occupied his consciousness almost every waking moment.[8] Frederick Douglass, was even more insistent that slaves, irrespective of their individual circumstances, valued their freedom. "If a slave has a bad master," Douglass wrote, "he desires to have a good master. And if he has a good master, he desires to be his own master."[9]

The frequency with which enslaved people resisted their bondage supports the claims of Lunsford Lane, Solomon Northup, and Frederick Douglass that slaves were not content with their bondage. The slave narratives confirm a multitude of ways that slaves struck out at their masters and mistresses, and rebelled against their condition—from faking illnesses and breaking farm tools to running away and setting fires. These day-to-day acts of resistance served as one way for enslaved people to retaliate against their masters and overseers and, from their point of view, to undermine the system. Some enslaved people learned to read and write, despite laws in the slave states that prevented any form of literacy among slaves as well as the threat of severe punishment from their masters. Other bondsmen routinely left the plantations without permission to visit family members and love ones, or to hunt and fish in order to supplement the meager rations that enslaved people were provided on a weekly basis. A small number of narratives also indicate that enslaved men and women killed masters, mistresses, and overseers who had crossed the line. Slave resistance collectively reveals not merely the disdain and contempt that many enslaved people had for the institution of slavery, but also that slaves felt, if only on a small level, that they could take ownership of some aspect of their lives and chart their destiny.

Freedom came to the majority of enslaved people in the South, not from slave resistance but from the advance of the Union army through the rebel states between 1861 and 1865. As the historian Leon Litwack wrote so beautifully in *Been in the Storm So Long: The Aftermath of Slavery*, the Union army represented an army of liberation for slaves, and it comprised black as well as white liberators. Here, the WPA narratives helped re-create the momentous feeling of exhilaration that millions of slaves felt on the Day of Jubilee.[10] Yet the oral narratives also revealed many of the hardships that former slaves faced as they made the transition from bondsmen to freedmen. Former slaves spoke eloquently of their desire to legalize marriages, reunite families, educate their children, and find work suitable to support their families. Others acknowledged the disappointment that they were not provided with land following emancipation, and their bitter dismay that the Freedmen's Bureau and the federal government did so little to protect their lives. But for the majority of African Americans, freedom represented the dawning of a new era and a new beginning, and whatever hardships that they might face as free people, they would pale in comparison with slavery.

This hope was predicated on the fact that African Americans were now free to chart their destiny, to plan for their future, to select their own leaders, to strengthen their communities, and to build secular and sacred community institutions. As black men and women moved around the South in the wake of emancipation, testing the limits of their new found freedom and attempting to ascertain what it *really* meant to be black and free after 1865, they acknowledged rather quickly that building strong communities and strengthening families would become major imperatives if African Americans were going to advance. As the slave narratives reveal, finding employment was the first priority. However, constructing schools and churches were nearly as important in the minds of many freedmen, for these two institutions would help to prepare African Americans for citizenship, as well as train a new generation of leaders for the future.

Students and scholars must use caution, however, when reading and interpreting the WPA narratives, for these elderly black interviewees took race and the delicate social etiquette of the South in the 1930s under consideration when they answered the queries of white interviewers. In one instance, Susan Hamlin, an ex-slave who lived in Charleston, South Carolina, gave two entirely different accounts of slavery—depending on the race of the interviewer. When the interviewer was white, Hamlin presented slavery as a benign institution and portrayed her fellow bondsmen as ignorant and barbaric, and therefore unfit for freedom. When an African American interviewer queried Hamlin, she painted the institution in much harsher terms, describing brutal whippings, the breakup of families, and the harsh work regimen. Hamlin also described the joy that she and other slaves felt when they learned of their freedom from the Union army.[11] The race of the interviewer clearly played an important role in the responses that this former slave gave as a narrator. Caution should also be exercised in using the WPA narratives because of the substantial gap between the end of slavery in 1865 and the years from 1936 to 1938 when these interviews were conducted. Seven decades had elapsed, and memories of specific details regarding one's childhood and adolescence might well have grown clouded with the passage of time. Yet despite these shortcomings, the WPA interviews remain one of the most important primary sources at the disposal of historians as they attempt to reconstruct the day-to-day realities of African American slaves in the South.

Family and Community

Historians have also made effective use of oral history in family history and local community studies. The writer Alex Haley (1921–92) did more than any single individual to stimulate interest in researching genealogy, black or white, with the publication of *Roots: The Saga of a Black Family* in 1976. Based on oral recollections of Haley's extended family, matched with archival research, *Roots* became a national bestseller. The six-part television series, *Roots: The Triumph of a Black Family*, which aired in 1977, became the highest rated mini-series ever produced in America. It inspired families by the ten of thousands to search in earnest for their own roots. Few historians followed Haley's bold lead, but a small number of important studies on African American families, which drew on oral history, began to appear. These studies have enriched our understanding of African American families across generations and provided new insights into family relations, gender, patriarchy, activism, and reform.

In my own case, I interviewed several descendants of T. McCants Stewart, a prominent nineteenth-century southern leader, in writing a three-generational history of the Stewart and Flippin families, *African American Odyssey: The Stewarts, 1853–1963*. Oral interviews permitted me to understand how this particular African American family rejected white society's negative image of blacks and worked tirelessly to improve themselves and to uplift their race. My interviews with Katherine Stewart Flippin and Beryl Keen, the patriarch's granddaughters, helped me understand how each generation of the family fulfilled a mission to provide service and leadership to its community and to develop effective strategies to cope with prejudice and racial exclusion.[12] Oral histories also revealed how Stewart women, such as Carlotta Stewart-Lai, an African American teacher and principal, coped with the isolation from the community of the black middle class while living and working in the Hawaiian Islands for more than four decades. I was also able to reconstruct Hawaii's small African American community prior to World War II by reading the oral history transcripts of African Americans in Hawaii at the University of Hawaii's Center for Oral History.[13]

Urban and labor historians have also supplemented their archival research with oral histories in reconstructing both white ethnic and African American communities in the twentieth century, and in many instances oral history has made a profound difference. Studies of black urban communities began to accelerate during the 1970s and 1980s with the explosion of social history, which called for studying American society from the bottom up. Ordinary people, Americans from working-class families, as well as the middle and upper classes, suddenly became of interest to historians, who asked a new set of questions about how these individuals organized their lives and functioned within their communities. The emergence of the new social history converged with the explosion of interest in African American studies, and black urban communities in all regions of the country were being examined by historians. Studies of African American migration, settlement, and adjustment to such cities as Chicago, Pittsburgh, Milwaukee, Detroit, Seattle, Phoenix, and San Francisco each used oral history creatively to hear the voices and aspirations of black southern migrants who had moved to the North or West.

These studies uncovered new community leaders and organizations that historians had overlooked, and oral histories helped reveal how they adapted to oppressive conditions in urban life. Matthew Whitaker, a historian at Arizona State University, conducted a study of African Americans in Phoenix, Arizona, that drew extensively upon the lives of two prominent NAACP officials, Lincoln and Eleanor Ragsdale. Whitaker's interviews illuminated the activism of these heretofore unknown community leaders, and they also showed how racial activists altered their strategies over time to face changing conditions.[14] The journalist Don Wallis interviewed twenty African American residents in the small Ohio River community of Madison, Indiana; his oral histories revealed not only a persistent pattern of discrimination and deprivation against blacks in this northern community, but also how black residents bonded together through an effective network of social, educational, political, and religious institutions.[15] Similarly, Gretchen Eick's history of the civil rights movement in Wichita, Kansas, used oral interviews to demonstrate how the NAACP reacted to the challenges of radical young leaders within the local branch. This important work also revealed that Wichita, Kansas, rather than Greensboro, North Carolina, was the scene of the earliest sit-in demonstrations by black students across the nation.[16] Gretchen Lemke-Santangelo and Shirley Ann Moore, both professors of history in California, interviewed African American migrant women who came to Richmond, California, and the San Francisco East Bay during World War II to work in defense industries and to better their lives. Their interviews also revealed how these black migrant women adapted to their new urban locales, and how southern traditions and folk culture helped ease the transition from the deep South to California.[17]

Urban historians have also used oral histories to document the role of women's clubs, interracial organizations, and a myriad of black social and fraternal organizations in northern and southern cities. The historian Darlene Clark Hine directed an extensive program documenting the history of African American women in the Midwest, and from that research she uncovered the history of the Indiana chapter of the National Council of Negro Women, a middle-class black women's organization.[18] Similarly, scholars such as Christina Greene and Alphine Jefferson have uncovered important community organizations that fought for the rights of working-class tenants in cities such as Chicago and Durham, North Carolina, by conducting oral interviews. Greene's study, which examined the black freedom movement in Durham, found that black women, rather than men, were the pivotal figures in the grassroots activism that brought a larger measure of social justice to that city after World War II. Her oral interviews also revealed that African American female activists worked with progressive southern white women, and they also brought a more radical voice into the civil rights movement than established black organizations such as the NAACP. These women, for example, believed that direct action, rather than cautious negotiation, was the most effective strategy to bring social change to their community.[19] The voices and commitment of these individuals, some of whom resided in public housing, labored as maids, factory workers, or domestics, are rarely captured by historians because they seldom leave written records. Talking with a trained oral historian, as Greene and Hine learned, may well have been the only opportunity to document the activities of these organizations and to learn about the multifaceted roles of unsung local female leaders.

Labor historians have interviewed local labor leaders in their effort to document interracial unionism and the struggle for racial equality within the labor movement. The historian Michael Honey interviewed many black and white labor leaders in Memphis, Tennessee, to connect the southern labor movement during the 1930s and 1940s to the modern civil rights movement. Honey's research uncovered a strong tradition of interracial industrial union organizing, and his oral interviews introduced his readers to many heretofore unknown black union leaders such as Thomas Watkins.[20] Robert Korstad, another historian, also interviewed many lesser-known black and white tobacco workers in Winston-Salem, North Carolina, who worked collectively to secure a measure of economic equality and justice for black workers after World War II in the CIO unions. Korstad's interviews reveal that African Americans viewed the war as a turning point and took the lead to demand not only racial justice but also a strong, racially unified labor movement.[21]

Oral Histories of the Civil Rights Movement

No subfield in African American history, save slavery, has benefited more from oral history than the study of civil rights. Recent biographies, organizational histories, and case studies of civil rights campaigns in local communities have all profited tremendously from documenting the role of individual civil rights leaders and organizations through oral interviews. Additionally, many prominent colleges and universities, local and state historical societies, state historical commissions, and research repositories have created programs to record the role of civil rights leaders and organizations. This commitment has resulted in an abundance of riches for scholars: literally thousands of taped interviews and transcripts are available for students and scholars to consult, and these interviews focus on the roles of both men and women and represent a cross-section of the country.

The Ralph J. Bunche Collection in the Moorland-Spingarn Research Collection at Howard University contains one of the largest collections of oral history interviews devoted to civil rights in the nation. Formerly known as the Civil Rights Documentation Project, it contains more than seven hundred oral history tapes and television transcripts that document the civil rights struggle during the 1960s. These interviews are particularly valuable because many are conducted with local community leaders who had gone largely unnoticed by scholars. The Ralph J. Bunche Collection also includes interviews with civil rights leaders of all races and nationalities, in addition to a representative number of black women. The project leaders even had the prescience to venture into several western states such as California.

Another central repository of oral histories on civil rights is the Bancroft Library Regional Oral History Program, located on the campus of the University of California–Berkeley. Although these interviews are scattered throughout the program's sizable collections, several dozen interviews of black and white Californians who worked for social and racial justice were conducted as part of the Earl Warren Oral History Program. The lengthy interview with C. L. Dellums (1900–1989), for example, covers topics that range from the early civil rights activities in California to the prodigious struggle of the Brotherhood of Sleeping Car Porters, of which Dellums served as president, to gain formal recognition by the Pullman union for black porters.

Flagship state universities are generally safe bets when inquiring about the availability of oral history programs. The University of California–Los Angeles, rivals the Bancroft Library in its collection of oral history relating to civil rights, African American political leadership, and contemporary race relations. Not only can students find informative interviews with political leaders such as Tom Bradley (1917–98), Los Angeles's first African American mayor, and Yvonne Braithwaite Burke (1932–), a congresswoman and co-chairperson of the Democratic National Convention in 1972, but also with hundreds of African American community leaders. Washington State University established a Black Oral History Collection, where a team of researchers interviewed African American pioneers and their descendants throughout Washington, Oregon, Idaho, and Montana between 1972 and 1974. This relatively modest program, nonetheless, reveals important information on early African American settlement in the Pacific Northwest, as well as material on African American employment patterns, social life, politics, and community institutions. In contrast, the University of Kentucky library contains one of the largest oral history programs in the nation, including considerable material on race relations, African American leadership, segregation, and civil rights. That oral history collection, however, is limited to Kentucky history. Far more germane is the extensive black oral history project launched by the Kentucky Oral History Commission. The Civil Rights Movement in Kentucky Oral History Project documented the struggle by African Americans and others to end legal segregation in Kentucky between 1930 and 1975. The collection, containing more than two hundred oral interviews, was used extensively in the award-winning film produced by the Kentucky Oral History Commission, "Living the Story: The Civil Rights Movement in Kentucky." Here, black men and women share their painful story of exclusion and their quest to gain citizenship and full equality in the Bluegrass state.

The University of North Carolina at Chapel Hill's Southern Historical Collection stands as one of the most respected and widely used oral history collections in the South. Its Southern Oral History Program contains over four thousand interviews, and although not limited to race relations in the South, encompasses considerable material about it. An ambitious oral history project to document civil rights was conducted by Duke University's Center for Documentary Studies. This project contains approximately 1,300 oral interviews and thousands of family photographs that document the civil rights movement in North Carolina and throughout the South. As a service to researchers, duplicate copies of the transcripts in many instances have been deposited in local repositories throughout the South.

Modern historians and journalists have made the most judicious use of oral histories in writing biographies of both significant and lesser known civil rights leaders. Taylor Branch, a journalist by training, interviewed hundreds of white and black leaders in the course of writing his three-volume history of Martin Luther King Jr. (1929–1968).[22] The interviews detail not only the public and private life of King, but Branch himself illuminates the role of many lesser known men and women in the civil rights struggle. Another biographer, David Garrow, interviewed more than seven hundred of King's closest associates as well as many of the white southerners who opposed him in the course of writing about Dr. King and the Southern Christian Leadership Conference (SCLC), providing new insights into King's life, the role of Coretta Scott King (1927–2006) and other African American female activists, and the inner workings of SCLC.[23] Historians writing about lesser-known civil rights figures have also used oral history imaginatively. Cynthia Griggs Fleming conducted interviews to reconstruct the important role that a little-known activist, Ruby Doris Smith-Robinson (1942–67), played within the Student Nonviolent Coordinating Committee (SNCC).[24] Kay Mills and Chana Kai Lee each used oral histories selectively in writing a biography of the important Mississippi grassroots leader Fannie Lou Hamer (1917–77).[25] The documentary film producer Henry Hampton interviewed a broad spectrum of African American leaders as well as white public officials in producing his epic six-part series on the civil rights movement, *Eyes on the Prize*. And the writer Constance Curry interviewed several generations of one African American family in the Mississippi Delta in producing her film, *The Intolerable Burden*, which examined in microcosm the impact that school integration had an individual black family and the lasting scars suffered by black children.

New Insights from Oral History

Recent studies of the black freedom struggle in southern, northern, and western cities have all used oral histories to introduce new leaders and to bring fresh new insights into the literature. John Dittmer's study of the black freedom struggle in Mississippi, *Local People: The Struggle for Civil Rights in Mississippi*, draws heavily upon oral history in reconstructing the early phases of the civil rights movement in Mississippi during the 1940s and 1950s. Dittmer's interviews are critical in demonstrating that ordinary black Mississippians, rather than national leaders or national organizations, were the backbone of this struggle. The historian William Chafe, in his notable study of the civil rights movement in Greensboro, North Carolina, interviewed black and white participants in order to elicit their point of view regarding the painfully slow process of desegregation in a racially moderate southern city.[26] Chafe's interviews displayed the conflicting expectations of blacks and whites, how social change occurred, and the generational conflict that went on within the African American community.

To understand the dynamics of race relations and civil rights in San Francisco between 1900 and 1954, I interviewed community leaders of all races. These interviews revealed the presence of civil rights activity prior to World War II, its continuity after the war, and the important role that interracial organizations played in that city's civil rights struggle.[27] Quintard Taylor did the same with community leaders and civil rights activists in reconstructing Seattle's African American freedom struggle, including its rich tradition of strong black labor leaders.[28] George C. Wright also incorporated oral interviews in his largely archival study of African Americans in Louisville, Kentucky, and their quest for racial justice.[29] Wright interviewed many of Kentucky's established middle-class African American leaders, as well as those in working-class occupations.[30] More than an important corrective to the previous historical record that African Americans were insignificant in Kentucky history, the interviews he conducted for his book, *Life Behind a Veil*, demonstrated that black leaders waged a long, protracted struggle to gain racial equality. They established parallel institutions such as churches, schools, community centers, and small businesses, each of which served as a bulwark against segregation.

As scholars have moved forward, they have continued to interview important subjects. David Hilliard, a former member of the Black Panther Party, interviewed many party members in his brief history of this radical organization.[31] The journalist Wallace Terry (1938–2003) relied exclusively on oral histories in his study of black Vietnam War veterans.[32] Terry's interviews with twenty black veterans suggested how oral history could expose the frustrations that black soldiers experienced, often at sharp odds with their white counterparts, and how African American soldiers could see the purpose and meaning of that war through a different lens. Contemporary studies of African American life, generally the purview of journalists, also illuminate how oral history, in the absence of archival sources, can be useful in understanding the struggles of blacks trapped in inner city ghettos. Two studies, in particular, are exemplary in using interviews. The journalist Ron Suskind followed the life of Cedric Jennings, a black inner-city Washington, D.C., student, as he completed his final two years in high school and enrolled at Brown University. Suskind's interviews provide a rare glimpse of the obstacles that many black students face in poorly performing inner-city schools, the below-par expectations of teachers, the ubiquitous gang violence in school and in their neighborhoods, the prevalence of drugs, and the low barriers that the majority of black students establish for themselves. Suskind's study was even more intriguing, for it also examined through numerous interviews the difficult and often painful transition that African American students like Cedric are required to make when they leave home and attend flagship colleges and private universities.[33]

The journalist Leon Dash used oral interviews almost exclusively to follow the day-to-day travails of Rosa Lee Cunningham to reveal the plight of the black underclass in the nation's capital.[34] Dash, a respected *Washington Post* investigative reporter, met with Rosa Lee and her extended family, who resided in one of Washington, D.C.'s drug-infested public housing projects, almost daily for four years in an attempt to understand the complex and often disturbing contours of her troubled life. Dash's articles in the *Washington Post* won a Pulitzer Prize and received more mail and phone calls than any previous subject, a testament, Dash believed, to the emotional volatility and significance of this subject matter. Members of the black underclass, or the white underclass, for that matter, seldom find their way into oral history collections, for scholars are more inclined to seek out individuals who shed a more positive light on African American progress and reflect the values of the black middle class.

The widespread use of oral interviews by Suskind and Dash, as well as the extensive interviewing conducted by the sociologist William Julius Wilson in his quest to explain the persistence of unemployment, underachievement, and poverty among African Americans in Chicago, in addition to what Wilson calls "ghetto-related behavior," reveals how contemporary social scientists and journalists have relied heavily on oral histories to supplement their quantitative data in analyzing contemporary social problems.[35] Interviewing these individuals has added an important dimension to our knowledge of African Americans whose voices, concerns, hopes, and frustrations are seldom recorded. The journalist Leon Bing, in trying to understand the evolution and significance of two African American gangs in inner-city Los Angeles, the Bloods and the Crips, felt compelled to interview gang members. Her interviews revealed not only the ubiquitous acts of violence and illegal activity that are widely reported, but also the sense of belonging, camaraderie, and security associated with gang membership. In many instances, Bing observed, gang affiliation filled a void left by absent fathers, dysfunctional families, failed schools, and poverty. Gang membership also provided respect and offered gang disciples the false hope that their aberrant behavior would provide the material comforts that were beyond the means of their parents.[36] This explained in part why so many African American children rejected the more traditional routes to the middle class, such as education, sacrifice, and hard work, and chose instead to peddle drugs and engage in a broad spectrum of criminal activity.

Contemporary scholars, journalists, and filmmakers have also sought to understand the importance of sport in the broader context of African American culture through oral history. Professional basketball, in light of such great players as Michael Jordan, Dwayne Wade, Kobe Bryant, Shaquille O'Neal, Allen Iverson, and Lebron James, has inspired children of all races and nationalities. These athletes have become cultural icons across the globe, and their popularity and glamorous lifestyles may explain why so many African Americans embraced basketball as the Holy Grail. Inner-city African American teenagers, rightly or wrongly, often see basketball as their ticket out of the ghetto and into the limelight, replete with all of the glitz, glitter, and approbation they can witness nightly on ESPN or numerous cable channels. *Hoop Dreams*, a widely acclaimed 1994 documentary by Steve James, Frederick Marx, and Peter Gilbert, captured this scenario of exalted expectations as well as the disappointment that basketball brought to the lives of William Gates and Arthur Agee, two black Chicago teenagers. Despite weak academic records, both students were recruited to play basketball for a predominantly white middle-class parochial high school. The three-hour documentary follows the lives of these students for six years, revealing the joy but also the countless frustration that they encountered as they pursued their dreams.

Reuben A. May developed a similar theme in his award-winning book, *Living Through the Hoop: High School Basketball, Race, and the American Dream*.[37] May played the role of a participant observer and assistant coach for seven years at Northeast High School in Northeast, Georgia, where he witnessed the disproportionate emphasis as well as the extraordinary commitment that African American students placed on basketball. As May gained the respect and confidence of these teenagers, the majority of whom lived in poverty and faced a grim future, he asked them to explain in their own words, why basketball played such an important role in their lives. His conversations and poignant observations reveal a great deal about the motivation of these young African American teenagers, the limited choices at their disposal, the stigma of urban poverty, and their lives at home—an environment that provided few role models and even fewer opportunities to excel. Rather than denigrate his subjects for their choices, May found much to praise as he examined the commitment and hard work that these students gave to improve their lives.

Living Through the Hoop, which included eighteen exit interviews, showed that playing basketball kept these young men away from the dangerous street life that had destroyed the lives of so many others. This singular activity also helped them focus on completing high school, and even offered the possibility of attending college to a gifted few. Playing basketball, May concluded, helped young black men to order their lives in a society that placed little value on the worth and achievements of young African American males.

In a more limited manner, oral interviews have shed light on how race and gender are perceived in the gay, bisexual, and transgender communities. Do gay African Americans face the same obstacles as gay men and women from other racial and ethnic groups? Do black gays face a unique set of problems because of race? Does the region where one lives or one's occupation and social status affect how African American gays are received? Do black gays have access to the same health care as white gays? How does one explain the disproportionately high rate of HIV infections in the black gay community? These are just some of the questions that oral historians are posing to black gay men and women.

The Emmy award–winning filmmaker Marlon T. Riggs (1957–94) combined personal testimony, poetry, rap, dance, and performance art to produce *Tongues Untied* in 1989. The controversial fifty-five-minute film focused on the unique challenges that black gay men face. Although partly autobiographical, Riggs felt that *Tongues Untied* accurately reflected the homophobia and racism that the majority of black gay men experienced in America, and he produced it "to celebrate the struggle, lives, and loves of gay black men in America." Riggs's film was groundbreaking in another important respect: it explored African American sexual identity more candidly than any previous documentary. The subject matter of *Tongues Untied* drew sharp criticism but aired, nonetheless, over public television stations and received numerous awards in the United States and abroad.

Riggs's pioneering work examined the experiences of gay men only and failed to explore the experiences of African American lesbians or transgendered persons. Since then, a number of oral history projects have broadened our understanding of these neglected groups. The Minnesota Historical Society established the Twin Cities Gay and Lesbian Community Oral History Project to interview gays and lesbians of all races, and has documented the gay experience in the Twin Cities from World War II to the early 1980s. The Bancroft Library's Sexual Orientation and Social Conflict Collection documents and preserves the history of sexual minorities in Berkeley and the Bay Area communities. The History Project in Boston also documents local gay African American, Latino, and GLBT residents and their communities. Embedded in the transcripts of numerous public and private oral history collections are interviews with or references to African American gay, lesbian, bisexual, and transgendered people and the multifaceted communities and support networks that they have created. *StoryCorps*, which documents the lives of ordinary people and whose transcripts are archived at the Library of Congress, contains interviews on such subjects as race relations, segregation, and sexual identity. The historian Nan Alamilla Boyd's excellent history of gay San Francisco, which drew upon forty-two oral histories of gay men and women who lived in San Francisco since the 1930s, also contains occasional references to gay African Americans.[38]

An Important Corrective

From the folklorist John Lomax's interviews with former slaves to filmmakers and historians such as Marlon Riggs and Nan Alamilla Boyd, who have attempted to explain gender identity, homophobia, and the significance of the gay bar subculture, oral histories have informed our knowledge of race and African American life. This work has also given many marginalized and neglected groups as factory workers, women, farmers, students, the elderly, and an array of activists an opportunity to explain—in their own voices—their contributions to their workplace or community. Oral history has broadened the scope of African American history and made its history far more inclusive. It has served as an important corrective, as George C. Wright learned when writing his history of Louisville's African American community during the era of segregation. Had he relied solely on the written record, he concluded, the black presence in Kentucky would have been rendered virtually invisible. The same may be said for many other historical inquiries. As the eminent labor historian Nick Salvatore wrote when he reconstructed the life of Amos Webber (1826–1904), a relatively unheralded black freeman in nineteenth-century Philadelphia, "we all got history."[39] In spite of the vagaries of memory and the impact of race and class differences between interviewers and interviewees in obtaining accurate testimonies, oral history has provided a richer, more complex, and more complete picture of the African American past.

NOTES

1. Ulrich Bonnell Phillips, *American Negro Slavery* (New York: D. Appleton and Co., 1918).

2. George P. Rawick, *From Sundown to Sunup: The Making of the Black Community* (Westport, Conn.: Greenwood Publishing Company, 1972); and Rawick, ed., *The American Slave: A Composite Autobiography* (Westport, Conn.: Greenwood Press, 1972–79). The University of Virginia has posted a sample of these at *American Slave Narratives: An Online Anthology*. at http://xroads.virginia.edu. See also the Library of Congress Web site on *Born in Slavery: Slave Narratives from the Federal Writers' Project, 1936–1938*, http://memory.loc.gov/ammem/snhtml/.

3. A notable exception was Kenneth Stampp, *The Peculiar Institution: Slavery in the Antebellum South* (New York: Knopf, 1956).

4. Lawrence Levine, *Black Culture and Black Consciousness: Afro-American Folk Thought from Slavery to Freedom* (New York: Oxford University Press, 1977).

5. Lorenzo D. Turner, *Africanisms in the Gullah Dialect* (Columbia: University of South Carolina Press, 2002 [1949]).

6. Melville J. Herskovits, *The Myth of the Negro Past* (Boston: Beacon Press, 1958 [1941]).

7. Thomas Wentworth Higginson, *Army Life in a Black Regiment* (Boston: Beacon Press, 1962).

8. Lunsford Lane, *The Narrative of Lunsford Lane* (Boston, n.p., 1848); Solomon Northup, *Twelve Years a Slave* (Baton Rouge: Louisiana State University Press, 1968 [1853]).

9. Frederick Douglass, *Narrative of the Life of Frederick Douglass, an American Slave: Written By Himself* (Boston: Bedford Books, 1993 [1845]).

10. Leon Litwack, *Been in the Storm so Long: The Aftermath of Slavery* (New York: Knopf, 1979).

11. James West Davidson and Mark Lytle, *After the Fact: The Art of Historical Detection* (New York: Knopf, 1981).

12. Albert S. Broussard, *African American Odyssey: The Stewarts, 1853–1963* (Lawrence: University Press of Kansas, 1998).

13. The Center for Oral History, under the direction of Dr. Warren S. Nishimoto, is located on the campus of the University of Hawaii at Manoa.

14. Matthew Whitaker, *Race Work: The Rise of Civil Rights in the West* (Lincoln: University of Nebraska Press, 2005).

15. Don Wallis, *All We Had Was Each Other: The Black Community in Madison, Indiana* (Bloomington: Indiana University Press, 1998).

16. Gretchen Eick, *Dissent in Wichita: The Civil Rights Movement in the Midwest, 1954–72* (Urbana: University of Illinois Press, 2001).

17. Gretchen Lemke-Santangelo, *Abiding Courage: African American Migrant Women and the East Bay* (Chapel Hill: University of North Carolina Press, 1996); Shirley Ann Wilson Moore, *To Place Our Deeds: The African American Community in Richmond, California, 1910–1963* (Berkeley: University of California Press, 2000).

18. Darlene Clark Hine, *When the Truth Is Told: Black Women's Culture and Community in Indiana, 1875–1950* (Indianapolis, Ind.: National Council of Negro Women [Indianapolis branch], 1981).

19. Christina Greene, *Our Separate Ways: Women and the Black Freedom Movement in Durham, North Carolina* (Chapel Hill: University of North Carolina Press, 2005).

20. Michael K. Honey, *Southern Labor and Black Civil Rights: Organizing Memphis Workers* (Urbana: University of Illinois Press, 1993).

21. Robert Rogers Korstad, *Civil Rights Unionism: Tobacco Workers and the Struggle for Democracy in the Mid-Twentieth-Century South* (Chapel Hill: University of North Carolina Press, 2003).

22. Taylor Branch, *Parting the Waters: America in the King Years, 1954–1963* (New York: Simon and Schuster, 1988).

23. David Garrow, *Bearing the Cross: Martin Luther King Jr. and the Southern Christian Leadership Conference* (New York: William Morrow, 1986).

24. Cynthia Griggs Fleming, *Soon We Will Not Cry: The Liberation of Ruby Doris Smith Robinson* (Lanham, Md.: Rowman and Littlefield, 2000).

25. Kay Mills, *This Little Light of Mine: The Life of Fannie Lou Hamer* (New York: Penguin Group, 1993); Chana Kai Lee, *For Freedom's Sake: The Life of Fannie Lou Hamer* (Urbana: University of Illinois Press, 1999).

26. William Chafe, *Civilities and Civil Rights: Greensboro, North Carolina, and the Black Freedom Struggle* (New York: Oxford University Press, 1980).

27. Albert S. Broussard, *Black San Francisco: The Struggle for Racial Equality in the West, 1900–54* (Lawrence: University Press of Kansas, 1998); also Broussard, "Oral Recollection and the Historical Reconstruction of Black San Francisco," *Oral History Review* 12 (1984).

28. Quintard Taylor, *The Forging of a Black Community: Seattle's Central District from 1870 Through the Civil Rights Era* (Seattle: University of Washington Press, 1994).

29. George C. Wright, *Life Behind a Veil: Blacks in Louisville, Kentucky, 1865–1930* (Baton Rouge: Louisiana State University Press, 1985).

30. Also useful is George C. Wright, "Oral History and the Search for the Black Past in Kentucky," *Oral History Review* 10 (1982): 73–91.

31. David Hilliard, *This Side of Glory: The Autobiography of David Hilliard and the Story of the Black Panther Party* (Boston: Little, Brown, 1992).

32. Wallace Terry, *Bloods: An Oral History of the Vietnam War by Black Veterans* (New York: Random House, 1984).

33. Ron Suskind, *A Hope in the Unseen: An American Odyssey from the Inner City to the Ivy League* (New York: Broadway Books, 1998).

34. Leon Dash, *Rosa Lee: A Mother and Her Family in Urban America* (New York: Basic Books, 1996).

35. William Julius Wilson, *When Work Disappears: The World of the New Urban Poor* (New York: Knopf, 1997).

36. Leon Bing, *Do or Die* (New York: HarperCollins, 1991).

37. Reuben A. May, *Living Through the Hoop: High School Basketball, Race, and the American Dream* (New York: New York University Press, 2008).

38. Nan Alamilla Boyd, *Wide-Open Town: A History of Queer San Francisco to 1965* (Berkeley: University of California Press, 2003).

39. Nick Salvatore, *We All Got History: The Memory Books of Amos Webber* (New York: Times Books, 1996).

BIBLIOGRAPHY

Broussard, Albert S. *Black San Francisco: The Struggle for Racial Equality in the West, 1900–54*. Lawrence: University Press of Kansas, 1993.

Chafe, William H. *Civilities and Civil Rights: Greensboro, North Carolina, and the Black Freedom Struggle*. New York: Oxford University Press, 1980.

Dash, Leon. *Rosa Lee: A Mother and Her Family in Urban America*. New York: Basic Books, 1996.

Dittmer, John. *Local People: The Struggle for Civil Rights in Mississippi*. Urbana: University of Illinois Press, 1994.

Honey, Michael Keith. *Black Workers Remember: An Oral History of Segregation, Unionism, and the Freedom Struggle*. Berkeley: University of California Press, 1999.

Litwack, Leon. *Been in the Storm So Long: The Aftermath of Slavery*. New York, Knopf, 1979.

Suskind, Ron. *A Hope in the Unseen: An American Odyssey from the Inner City to the Ivy League*. New York: Bantam, 1998.

CHAPTER 13

REMEMBERING IN LATER LIFE: GENERATING INDIVIDUAL AND SOCIAL CHANGE

JOANNA BORNAT

BOTH oral history and what has come to be known as "reminiscence work" acquired a public profile around the same time, during the 1970s and early 1980s, in Europe and North America. Though each only made rare references to the other as they developed, they shared a focus: older people's remembering.[1] For oral history, remembering is seen as a means to an end. By contrast, reminiscence work fixes on the process, the social interactions and changes brought about by engaging in remembering. This is not to say that oral historians have not also been aware of the impact of their activity on the older people, often remarking on how interviewees spontaneously reflect positively on the process or appear to be physically changed as they enjoy the recall. However, those responses are viewed as an interesting by-product, rather than the purpose or planned outcome of the interview.

In considering the emergence of reminiscence work, a case study from the United Kingdom will serve as a useful example to explore the origins of the turn to reminiscence and the debates concerning its role as an intervention in work with older people. Reminiscence work continues to be discovered and applied by practitioners and researchers without much awareness of its history and origins. Looking back with the UK experience may suggest why this particular intervention, which is sometimes described as a therapeutic approach, persists in inspiring succeeding generations of care workers and others involved in the lives of frail older people.

Reminiscence Emerges

The many manuals providing basic instruction for reminiscence work with older adults and training opportunities (Googling "reminiscence training" brings up copious examples) rarely include any kind of reflective investigation as to its contextual and theoretical origins.[2] With a focus on practical know-how, these publications are less interested in exploring the emergence of what is now an established intervention and activity. Applying a historical framework for reminiscence activity leads to the identification of when and how the practice first grabbed the attention of care workers, researchers, and scholars. Knowing something of those first and early developments may help to explain why reminiscence as an activity continues to provoke excitement and result in re-invention. It also helps to provide an understanding of how reminiscence work has persisted, how it has adapted, and been adapted, as provision and practice have changed in care work, and to what extent practice has responded to more recent research and writing.

No account of the origins of reminiscence work is complete without citing the American gerontologist Rose Dobrof's story of her experience of the impact of the recognition of life review as a basis for communicating with older people in the 1960s. Indeed most of the key texts debating the provenance and nature of reminiscence and life review include some or all of the quotation which follows as part of their discussion:[3]

> Perhaps tape recorders and word-processing machines are to the spoken word what the phonograph is to music: they make it possible for us to preserve the voices of our mothers and fathers telling us the history of their times.
>
> Technology expands the possibilities, and interest rises with the dawning recognition of the possibilities. In the field of aging, interest began with the publication in 1963 of a seminal paper by Dr. Robert Butler.... It is not often that one paper has so important and immediate an effect. I was then a very junior social worker on the staff of a home for the aged. I remember well being taught by our consulting psychiatrists and the senior social work staff about the tendency of our residents to talk about childhood in the shtetls of East Europe or arrival at Ellis Island or early years on the Lower East Side of New York.
>
> At best, this tendency was seen as an understandable, although not entirely healthy preoccupation with happier times, understandable because these old and infirm people walked daily in the shadow of death. At worst "living in the past" was viewed as pathology—regression to the dependency of the child, denial of the passage of time and the reality of the present, or evidence of organic impairment of the intellect.

> It was even said that "remembrance of things past" could cause or deepen depression among our residents, and God forgive us, we were to divert the old from reminiscing through activities like bingo and arts and crafts.
>
> And then the Butler paper came out and was read and talked about, and our world changed. The Life Review became not only a normal activity; it was seen as a therapeutic tool. In a profound sense, Butler's writings liberated both the old and the nurses, doctors and social workers; the old were free to remember, to regret, to look reflectively at the past and try to understand it. And we were free to listen and to treat rememberers and remembrances with the respect they deserved, instead of trivializing them by diversion to a bingo game.[4]

Rose Dobrof was writing twenty years after "'the Butler paper came out." At the time she was a junior member of staff in a very much hands-on care setting. In highlighting "the Butler paper," she contrasts it strikingly with existing thinking on old age. Given the context in which she was writing this was understandable but perhaps takes some explaining, now that time has created distance from what she describes with such drama. By 1984 when her account was published, she had been editor-in-chief of the *Journal of Gerontological Social Work* for five years and co-director of the Brookdale Center on Aging with Robert Butler. In 1984 she was therefore writing with experience and an established reputation as an innovator in teaching and learning about old age. Looking back, as an academic and as a former care worker she was highlighting the practical significance of what she signals as a minor scientific revolution.

"The Butler paper" was indeed seminal as a search through citation lists illustrates.[5] With five hundred academic journal references alone, by 2005 it was still being referred to and incorporated into discussions relating to life review and reminiscence. Its own early history shows that the article had become part of the literature of both psychiatry and gerontology within a very few years of first publication with its argument identified as having practical significance. For example, in 1970 it was being cited in an article on the implications of reminiscence for social work practice.[6] In the process, reminiscence had shifted from being studied by psychologists for its function, pattern and content in inner life, to becoming an activity that was deliberately encouraged and established as beneficial.

As a principal investigator into the mental health of older people living in the community in the late 1950s, Butler argued that he was challenging the received understanding among psychiatrists and psychologists that talk of the past—reminiscence—was a sign of pathology, of mental deterioration. During this research he describes encountering older people whose accounts of their past lives were "often fascinating and in no sense reflected pathology." From this he developed the idea that life review could have a positive role. As he later explained, he had no notion that a paper, published to a biomedical audience would be understood and taken up so widely across so many different professions and disciplines within such a short space of time.[7]

Butler was writing from the perspective of someone who had close experience with older people in clinical settings. He wrote with conviction and knowledge, and with the benefit of professional observation. Moreover, he was evenhanded. He could point to examples of "certain adaptive and defensive aspects" of life review, arguing that "Some of the aged have illusions of the 'good past'; some fantasy the past rather than the future in the service of avoiding the realities of the present; some maintain a characteristic detachment from others and themselves."[8]

In contrast with prevailing negative stereotypes of aging and old age, he suggests the need for a new focus, a positive psychology of old age, which recognizes that the benefits of reflection and moves away from a framework of solely negative thinking about late life. What was also new was his emphasis on listening to what older people were saying about their experience of aging:

> It is . . . of interest to notice the positive, affirmative changes reported by the aged themselves as part of their life experience, and to find constructive alterations in character, possibly as a consequence of the life review. . . . It is necessary to study the changes wrought in life by experience, eventful or uneventful, by brief or enduring relationships with other human beings, or even through images evoked by hearing or reading of the experiences or efforts of others.[9]

In his own study of reminiscence in community settings in the UK, Peter Coleman traced this period of change and acceptance farther back to an earlier period. Though he acknowledged the significance of Butler's paper, he pointed out that Charlotte Bühler, a Viennese developmental psychologist, had highlighted the role of reminiscence in ageing in 1933.[10] Nevertheless, it was to be Erik Erikson's work that provided the framework for much of the theorizing of reminiscence in the period following Butler's 1963 paper. Erikson's concept of eight life stages, including old age as a developmental stage, indicated changing perspectives toward late life among some psychologists like Butler.[11] With Erikson's framework there could be a role for life review and reminiscence, given his eighth stage of "integrity" in which the older person seeks a way to accept the life lived. Coleman found Erikson's model ideal, making no reference to the types of conflicting experience and generational dislocation that can threaten perceptions of past life in old age.[12] Still, the notion that in late life development and reflection are both positive and necessary was an encouraging counter to Freudian psychiatry in which older people appeared only as negative reference points for younger people in a developmental model that allowed for little change beyond early adulthood.

Revaluation of life review as an unavoidable activity that might contribute to successful aging was an aspect of Butler's argument, one that other research psychologists were also taking up around the time his paper was published. A study of Spanish American war veterans by A. W. McMahon and P. J. Rhudick found a well-adjusted group of men who reminisced freely.[13] They went on to argue, on the basis of what they observed among this particular group, that reminiscence could make a positive contribution in late life at a time when loss of identity and a sense of social value might be a common experience. This more positive construction of the role of recall in late life contrasted with the dominant gerontological discourse at this time: disengagement theory.[14] Disengagement theory had developed in the United

States during the late 1950s among sociologists who were seeking ways to explain what they saw as decline in late life, from having interviewed older people living in middle America. Central to the theory was the idea that as people age they withdraw from society to concentrate on their inner life, becoming more contemplative and less active.[15]

The theory was criticized for its convenient assumption that withdrawal from active participation in the labor market was an acceptable state for older people. It was challenged by older people themselves, as well as some gerontologists, who saw the theory as justifying marginalization and exclusion on grounds of age, and who took a more political, deliberately engaged position.[16]

The appeal of Butler's paper was amplified by his reputation as an outspoken critic of ageist policies in U.S. health care and social policy. His critique of government policies drew on evidence as to the social, political, and psychological determinants of late life marginalization, and indeed his *Why Survive? Being Old in America* won a Pulitzer Prize for nonfiction within a year of its publication in 1975. The chapter on "Growing Old Absurd" includes "the tendency toward life review" among ten "special characteristics of later life" that prevent "placing the old…in prescribed roles."[17]

The background to these developments suggests that a positive role for life review and reminiscence was supported theoretically and politically by changing perspectives of old age in American society. The late 1970s also saw the beginning of the popularization of remembering in late life, when Barbara Myerhoff completed a film (1977) and a book (1979) both titled *Number Our Days*, was later also adapted as a stage play. Drawing on the memories of a group of members of a Jewish older people's care center in Venice, California, the book was listed as one of the ten best social science texts in 1979. About this time, Myerhoff began teaching life history workshops at the Brookdale Center in New York, where Rose Dobrof was director. The appeal of Myerhoff's book lay in its engagement with memories of an earlier Jewish life of family and community in a context where everything seemed to be changing around them. Reminiscence and life review, as an active and popular form of intervention, had begun to interest a wider audience than psychologists and gerontologists.

The terms "life review" and "reminiscence" tend to be used interchangeably, and yet they have different meanings and uses. Life review involves the recall and evaluation of a life with the purpose of making sense, accepting, and "taking stock." Life review may be a deliberate undertaking at the end of a life or may follow some major change. By contrast, reminiscence is viewed more as a natural process, remembering and recall not being attached to any particular stage of life. Though reminiscence may be private, it can also arise in social settings, prompted by other people or by aspects of a particular context that evokes meanings and memories.[18]

As with oral history, life review is essentially a one-to-one process in which narratives, stories, and accounts are elicited for a purpose, perhaps to answer the questions of an interviewer, to construct a life story, or to engage with another in some kind of therapeutic exchange. By contrast, reminiscence may have less defined outcomes and is open to sharing of experience and to more social forms of engaging with the past. The distinction has significance for the ways in which reminiscence has developed as an intervention, with outcomes that are therapeutic in the broadest sense.

It might be tempting to assume that the dramatic elements in Rose Dobrof's account support a post hoc argument in defense of reminiscence, and that effective networking and positioning may also have played a part. This may be so, but a case study drawn from a different context, the U.K. Reminiscence Aids Project, provides illuminating corroboration for her claim about the theoretical and political underpinnings of the turn to reminiscence as an intervention in work with older people.

From Life Review to Reminiscence Aids

In the UK, reminiscence as an intervention emerged and developed rather differently. While between 1969 and 1972 the psychologist Peter Coleman had carried out his doctoral research into the adaptive function of reminiscence and had published work from it, the context for his findings was clinical and psychological, at least until he broadened his treatment of the topic in a book published in 1986. Here he developed themes that demonstrated the significance of paying attention to the social and historical aspects of older people's reminiscing. His study remains unique, not only because he combined psychological tests with taped interviews, a multimethod approach, but because he returned to a small surviving group of his original interviewees after an interval of ten years.[19] Time, in his study, therefore had many dimensions, and his data were better because of this.

Cohort experiences of wars and unemployment were given significance in Coleman's study, along with the fact that all his group lived in sheltered accommodations and were making a transition in late life in response to their changed personal circumstances. Reminiscence processes, as he explained them, were historically and socially shaped, and temporally constructed. In drawing up his four categories of high and low morale of those who reminisced and those who did not, he noted that people had different attitudes toward the past, and different uses of it as they reflected on their lives.[20] When he wrote up the different cases, he included details of those past lives within the context of a social history of the first half of the twentieth century, as experienced by a group of working-class Londoners. Coleman's shift from clinical and research psychology in 1974 to a broader social psychological perspective in 1986 was paralleled by the way in which reminiscence had emerged in the UK.

This more socially oriented role for reminiscence was to distinguish developments in the UK, where the breakthrough for reminiscence work came from a commitment to change contexts and provision for older people, and focused less on the rewards of one-to-one life review approaches. Readers of the UK's national press and radio in 1978 and 1979 would already have heard of a new idea, "Reminiscence Aids."[21] Images and recordings were being used to illustrate articles that pointed to the rewards of "an audio-visual method of stimulating reminiscence in elderly people including those with mental infirmity."

Reminiscence had also been given a start by an architect working in a government department, the Department of Health and Social Security (DHSS) in London, who persuaded his managers that they might fund a project to explore the possibility that aids to reminiscence might effectively help "elderly confused patients."[22] The initiator of this idea, Mick Kemp, was an "architect and adviser on accommodation for the Elderly Mentally Infirm." His job was to design and prescribe the layout and planning of environments provided by the state. As a result of his many visits to institutions such as hospitals and Local Authority old people's homes, Kemp had observed how many older people tended to talk about the past: "The need for a facility of this kind grew out of the increasing isolation of old people in various institutions, and in particular, their isolation from younger members of the community to whom, traditionally, old people would, for one reason or another, relate their memories. The process of talking about the past is a means of retaining memory and hence a sense of identity and status. It is also a very practical and pleasant means of mental exercise. Today, with so much changing around them, and the increasing nucleation of the family, the old person is deprived of both the stimuli to memory of familiar surroundings and younger people to talk to. Removal to an old people's home or a geriatric ward makes this deprivation total."[23]

As Kemp recalled in an interview with Pam Schweitzer in 1999, it was not only the bricks and mortar, the design of the accommodation that necessarily contributed to the depressing settings he encountered:

> I spent some time going round the country looking at these appalling old institutions and finding in some of them sweetness and light and quite an atmosphere of hope, and others, something out of Dante. I realised that you can have a ball going on in the worst of Victorian buildings.... I realised that it was the regime, it was the way people behaved towards people that mattered, and that started me thinking about how we behave towards elderly people and how our behaviour affects them.... However, there was a point at which I said to myself, "Well you're an architect first of all! Where's the architecture?" And it was one of those moments of truth.... I thought, "Well I wonder if there is a stimulus from the actual environment?"[24]

In the interview he described how the DHSS was then "a rather free-thinking, anarchical organisation."[25] That environment enabled him to carry out a study in a since-demolished hospital to find out what would happen if the environment was changed to look like something that patients might remember from their past lives. They bought "antique furniture" and decorated spaces to look like late Victorian and early-twentieth-century interiors. Patients with dementia were then left to walk freely while nurses observed how they used the space. Even though Kemp judged the experiment a failure, as it did not appear to change residents' preferences for sitting near to toilets, a comment by a senior nurse made him realize that the environment might not be everything. She commented:

> I know that it worked.... If for no better reason than that, for this period of time, the nurses have been coming in and seeing these people... in a nicer setting, and a setting that relates to their age and suddenly they've been talking to them like human beings.[26]

Awareness that the behavior and attitudes of staff might play a part in stimulating a more humanistic, individualized care environment was not to feature prominently in the subsequent development of what became known as "reminiscence work." However, that these were key factors is beyond dispute.

During his interview, Kemp mentioned "doing a bit of research" and coming across the work of Robert Butler, which provided him with the theory he needed to show that: "as elderly people came near to death, they would go through the business of reviewing their life and it seemed to him to be a very natural thing." The link with Butler's work was to be significant for further developments in the UK, but what was to provide the distinction between British and American work in the area of reminiscence and life review was the direction taken by Kemp, and those who further developed his developments.[27] The project that developed in the UK had two distinctive features: engagement with older people's memories, and a creative base in the arts. Kemp justified his approach by contrasting it with "the versions of history that photographers, reporters and historians considered important.... They weren't really picking up what ordinary people remembered. So what I wanted to do was go a level below that—what does this famous photograph which was created for spectacular purposes or for its newsworthiness, what did that remind you of, little old lady in East Cheam?"[28]

This key issue came to be, not so much the factual truth of sounds and images from the past, but what they enabled people to share among themselves. Presentation and the creation of the means to facilitate this process thus became a distinctive aspect of reminiscence work as it was to develop in the UK.

Alongside this creative approach was Kemp's other commitment: the involvement of older people themselves in the process. As he explained in the report he subsequently wrote for the DHSS:

> ...to rely totally on published material to evoke the personal past in old people would be to miss the central target of their true reminiscence. It was decided... to draw on the recollections of elderly people themselves for the subject matter of our presentations.[29]

Kemp employed a multimethod strategy for the collection and selection of material. Photographs from decades corresponding to the life spans of older people were shown in hospitals and care homes to groups of older people with mental infirmity. Radio broadcasts, both local (BBC Radio London) and national (Woman's Hour) and international (World Service), as well as articles in magazines and newspapers, included appeals for information and also helped to publicize the project. Books of photographic collections were searched for relevant images. Finally, and perhaps most critically, he created a multidisciplinary advisory committee comprising a geriatrician, a psychiatrist, a psychologist, print and radio journalists, an archivist and sound adviser from the BBC, a nurse, a hospital volunteer organizer and voluntary workers, and a pensioner, who joined the team after hearing a radio broadcast.

The project team included Mick Kemp, a psychologist, and a number of artists, including a musician and a photographer. Together, they assembled Reminiscence Aids, which they defined as "audio visual method of stimulating reminiscence in elderly people, including those with mental infirmity."[30] From the start they agreed to adopt a "ground level" approach to the past. Historical events would be included not for any epoch-making reason, "but because we were more concerned with the archaeology of human memory rather than an historical analysis of society."[31] For example, the royal abdication of 1937, still very much a point of reference and debate among older people in the 1970s and 1980s, was seen as important for what it evoked at a personal level, and not for reasons of the historical record. Indeed, in later evaluations the team questioned whether major events were always so salient in people's experiences as later generations might assume.

Showing sequences of sounds and images in London care homes demonstrated the success of the project. Staff reported to the team:

> In discussions held with residents following the first showing, a lady from one of the homes, talked at length and in great detail of her memories of that period and in particular of the air raids. Staff commented that she had never talked about this period in her life, until she saw the sequence. She continued to "reminisce" for about another twenty-four hours, before reverting to her "old self." A similar incident occurred in the other home where a lady chatted happily about war-time incidents, and what she would do to Hitler should she ever meet him in the street. It was discovered later that contrary to the impression given, this lady normally never spoke from the moment she got up to the time she went to bed.[32]

By 1979 several sequences had been assembled, and formal testing with the World War II program was carried out, attempting strict control conditions. The sequence was shown to people individually and to groups of older people in four care homes. Using various tools but principally questionnaires, which were administered during viewing of the sequences, attempts were made to measure the increase in reminiscing. However, statistical analysis of the results showed no definite causal link between showing the sequence and amount of reminiscing. Moreover, the environments for carrying out the tests were found not to be helpful, and practical difficulties made the results difficult to assess. Although this was disappointing, more anecdotal observation of foot-tapping, nodding, and smiling confirmed people's engagement and interest.[33]

The Reminiscence Aids project stirred up a great deal of interest, and as Mick Kemp explained, his manager at the time was beginning to express uneasiness explaining what an architect might be doing, "swanning around being a quack psychologist or a sociologist."[34] So even before the budget cuts in public services imposed by the Thatcher government, the project's future had become uncertain. By then, only two young artist researchers were still working on the sequences. In order to prevent the whole idea from being extinguished, Mick Kemp approached the charity Help the Aged for help with additional funding.

The national charity Help the Aged had an education department that was publishing materials on age and aging. The idea of reminiscence aids fitted well with the ideas of its director, Susanna Johnston, who persuaded the charity to fund the project. The charity took on the two researchers with a view to transforming the sequences into materials for care workers and groups of older people to use independently.[35] This was something of a gamble. Although the idea and the sequences themselves had captured the interest not just of the media but also care workers who had been involved in developing and testing the images and sounds, it was not yet obvious that "reminiscence aids," or *Recall* as the published version came to be called, were something that people might want to buy and use for themselves.

The simplicity and immediacy of the six tape/slide programs that made up *Recall* led to instant recognition of an activity that care workers and older people had wanted, even needed, to take part in. Rose Dobrof took Robert Butler's 1963 paper as the catalyst and inspiration of change in the United States, and that paper's influence had indeed spread to the UK, too. The Reminiscence Aids Project and *Recall* also played a more public role. *Recall's* tape/slide programs were produced in manageable packs, with each sequence timed to last twelve minutes, accompanied by an explanatory guide. It placed the doing of oral history in the hands of people who had neither expertise in history as a discipline, nor any experience as practicing psychologists. And it made expert witnesses out of the older people who took part. The six sequences covered the first eighty years of the twentieth century, more or less paralleling the lives of older people who took part in the 1980s. Illustrations of childhood were located in the pre–World War I years, and the final sequence covered the building of postwar Britain. The images were selected from personal and commercial archives, together with music of the times, the words of older people, and recordings from street life and newsreels. Showings of *Recall* broke down traditional boundaries and led to an enthusiastic new recognition of the value of past lives. At the time it, everyone felt like taking part in a social movement.[36]

How did *Recall* work and why was its success so immediate? In the first few years after 1981, hundreds of copies of the packs were sold. Although hardly anyone now will remember *Recall*, its spirit and form live on in the many other subsequent examples, versions and formats marketed over the years.[37] There were two reasons for *Recall's* immediate success. First, its format as a package of sounds and images meant that it could be presented in almost any setting and did not require presenters to be experts in modern history. Care staff, who might not be expected to have a background in historical research, were able to explore the past through technologically simple means. All that was required to show the six sequences was a cassette player, slide projector, and a white wall or screen. Now technologically superseded, tapes and slides still had advantages over video and DVD formats. They allowed for larger, clearer, images and could easily be interrupted to show a clear and still image if people wanted to linger over a particular picture.

The second reason for *Recall*'s success was that it offered legitimation of an activity that previously had been ignored or treated as a pathology, as Dobrof suggests. Her recollection of the impact of the original Butler paper was evident as care workers and family members learned more about the older people they dealt with. More than that, roles were reversed as older people became experts, eyewitnesses whose testimony care workers and others found themselves responding to. People who had been described in terms of their deficits came to be known by what they had experienced in life, the roles they had played, the jobs they had held, and the achievements they had accomplished. Without the encouragement for them to talk, none of this would have been known. This extended to people who were not so able to communicate their reactions verbally. Staff reported how they became intrigued at the responses of people with dementia, and they began following up with questions to relatives. In some cases, they even did research themselves into the life histories of people for whom they cared.[38]

Recall and similar programs developed around the assumption that the deliberate stimulation of reminiscence was a compensatory intervention, geared to deficits in the lives of older people living in institutions. There was a tendency to assume that such activities would have outcomes that would be positive for those so engaged.

Changing Practice

Rose Dobrof's recall of the original impact of "the Butler paper" accurately emphasized how care staff were changed by what they witnessed. Research evidence as well as anecdotal observations have subsequently illustrated how participation in reminiscence-based activities could influence attitudes and practice among staff working in residential, day care, domiciliary, and nursing home settings. Caregivers describe, and have been observed to adopt, a more personal and individualized style after they became aware of the biographical details of residents' and service users' lives.[39] Opportunities to talk about past lives and to include biographical details in care planning tend to be welcomed by care staff, older people, and their relatives and friends—admittedly at a fairly basic level—and have come to be included in assessments and care planning. Such approaches have helped to embed in care practice a more holistic and responsive approach to the assessment of need. They also prevent the exclusion in various service settings of older people, irrespective of frailty.[40] It had positive outcomes for carers too.[41] Yet this side of recall is rarely studied and, although the practice is encouraged and well embedded into activities programs, often routinized in the same way as bingo and dominoes, the skills associated with engaging and supporting people in remembering are still not part of any officially recognized training, at least in the UK.

This omission may be due to concerns as to unwanted or unexpected outcomes from interventions uncertainly positioned between therapy and diversion. Although Susanna Johnston wrote a guide to its use, *Recall*'s development was left very much in the hands of those who bought it. Early on, people began to point out how *Recall* could evoke painful emotions. This was known but was scarcely acknowledged or accounted for, since it had been associated with positive outcomes. Johnston's handbook for users made only a brief reference to sadness among *Recall* audience members:

> While in most cases people have come to terms with the sad episodes in their lives some may weep, perhaps for the first time, remembering a past grief which they have suppressed for years. One woman wrote of the "blessed relief" in releasing this emotion. She added however that the staff around her became very concerned when she cried.[42]

In the years since that was written, the debate about "trauma" in reminiscing has taken on greater dimensions. Staff and relatives have expressed concern, and it has become a key emphasis for trainers. The focus on protection from exposure to what might be uncontrollable emotion, both of the older people and of those caring for them, has resulted in more cautious use of reminiscence aids and renewed emphasis on what is positive and diversionary. This is not necessarily a development to be welcomed.[43] Indeed Johnston went on to point out in the original *Recall* handbook how younger people may misguidedly seek to shield people from emotional upset. There is strength to be gained from the sharing of emotions, she argued, and people "take a pride or sombre satisfaction in recalling the dangers and emotional upheavals which they have survived."[44]

While not disregarding the range of emotions that recall of the past may stimulate, Faith Gibson, in her "practical guide" helpfully selects "people who are depressed" for specific attention.[45] Her approach comes close to normalizing depression as a state of mind in many older people. Sometimes this may be in response to the loss of a partner or a home. She also points out that depression may be a quite understandable response to awareness of developing dementia. She argues that some mental health problems are "intractable," and in such cases specialist life review and reminiscence is probably most appropriate. Echoing Dobrof, she concludes that in general it is more cruel to exclude and protect people from remembering: "the greater risk is doing nothing, in leaving older, isolated people unstimulated and unsupported."[46] With others, she emphasizes the need for supervision and support for reminiscence workers.[47]

As in an oral history interview or any activity where memories are evoked, the process is never a one-way street. Outcomes may be unexpected on both sides. The oral historian and reminiscence theater director Pam Schweitzer gave an account of the effect of acting one woman's story through reminiscence drama, which she describes as a "medical miracle":

> This depressed, rather sickly woman just came to life when she saw her own memories being acted out before her. When she saw our representation of the

> story, she remembered the whole event much more clearly than when we interviewed her first, and added many details she had not recollected for fifty years... the interchange with the actors and the development of the story had an extraordinary physical effect on this woman. She sparked to life and became the "star" of the place.[48]

People's agency in their reminiscence is a reminder that it is quite a natural activity, and has a number of purposes. Researchers have identified six predominant types of reminiscence: "integrative, instrumental, transmissive, narrative, escapist, and obsessive."[49] This is not a definitive list; others have added "death preparation," "intimacy," and "problem solving."[50] Without entering into debates as to the salience of any one of these types it is worth noting that observations of reminiscence suggest that the agendas of those taking part may be varied, may conflict, and may or may not be social in intent or impulse. The significance in the findings lies in their ability to identify how reminiscence may be further used and developed, as well as in the extent to which they introduce awareness of the range and variety of subjectivities involved in a reminiscence session. As in oral history, there are many layers to what might appear to be an apparently simple act of recall.

Evaluations

Important as attitudinal change among staff may be, the pressure to demonstrate positive outcomes from participation in reminiscence, on either an individual or group basis, has persisted over the years. Barbara Haight and Shirley Hendricks's useful reviews of studies illustrate the range of types of discussion and of forms of measurement and intervention.[51] The review is divided under headings such as "Scholarly Discussion" and "Methods" and also includes forty-six papers under "Research." Thirteen report positive changes in participants, who vary from older people who are depressed and have been diagnosed with dementia living in care settings to older people living independently in a community. Of the thirteen, only one appears to have used a control group, and none adopted the type of longitudinal study used by Coleman, with the result that evidence for change tends to be limited to the period of the study or shortly afterwards. In the main, studies tend to be descriptive of small-scale interventions illustrating how people made sense of their recall or life review, often in relation to specific life events or change, such as parenting, in searches for sources of continuity or helpful processes. Although decreases in depression and increases in sociability were found among certain groups, changes were not dramatic, and the size of the groups and the generality of the qualities being investigated make the findings difficult to replicate.

Subsequently, a systematic review of the literature relating to reminiscence among people with dementia, carried out by Woods et al., found "promising indications." But the small number of random control studies they were able to track down, and the highly varied nature of the interventions and the variables they were measuring, meant that they could only conclude that more research was needed. A later study using controls pinned down some exact measures and positive outcomes for people with dementia and for their carers too.[52].

Conclusion

The search for an evidence base for interventions which have costs attached to them, such as staff time, resources, training, and the possibility of changes in practice and policy all of this has tended to take over the nature of evaluations and outcomes of reminiscence and life review. This is perhaps itself a measure of how public and professional attitudes and understandings of reminiscence have changed over the last half century. What was claimed as a normal activity, in danger of being disregarded and pathologized, much as older people may be distanced and problematized, is now looking for justifications that rest on the measurement of outcomes for specific groups. In a twenty-first century where value for money and quality measures seem to dominate many interpersonal activities, this may not be surprising. It would be a pity if such proofs and forms of evaluation were to determine the direction in which reminiscence-based activities develop in the future. Looking back, what was achieved by the pioneers in the United States and the UK, and their later followers, has been less about modifying aspects of the aging process and more about the humanizing of social care practices through the recognition and celebration of individuality and life experience in old age.

NOTES

1. Joanna Bornat, "Reminiscence and Oral History: Parallel Universes or Shared Endeavour?" *Ageing and Society* 21 (2001): 219, 241.

2. See for example, *Help the Aged, Recall—A Handbook* (London: Help the Aged Education Department, 1981); Andrew Norris, *Reminiscence with Elderly People* (Bicester: Winslow Press, 1986); James E. Birren and Donna E. Deutchman, *Guiding Autobiography Groups for Older People: Exploring the Fabric of Life* (Baltimore, Md.: Johns Hopkins University Press, 1991); Patricia Duffin, *Then and Now: A Training Pack for Reminiscence Work* (Manchester: Gatehouse Press, 1992); Irene Burnside and Mary Gwynne Schmidt, eds., *Working with the Elderly: Group Process and Techniques* (Boston: Jones and Bartlett Publishers, 1994); Caroline Osborn, *The Reminiscence Handbook* (London: Age Exchange, 1994); Valerie R. Yow, *Recording Oral History: A Practical Guide for the Social Sciences* (New York: Sage, 1994); Ruth Martin, *Oral History in Social Work* (New York: Sage, 1995); Roger Sim, *Reminiscence: Social and Creative Activities with Older People in Care* (Bicester:

Winslow Press, 1997); Michael P. Bender, Paulette Bauckham, and Andrew Norris, *The Therapeutic Purposes of Reminiscence* (London: Sage, 1999); Errolyn Bruce, Sarah Hodgson, and Pam Schweitzer, *Reminiscing with People with Dementia* (London: Age Exchange, 1999); Jeff Garland and Christina Garland, *Life Review in Health and Social Care: A Practitioner's Guide* (Hove: Brunner-Routledge, 2001); A. Burke and M. Corbett, *Looking at Life: Learning in Groups Through Oral History—A Toolkit* (Warboys: University of Hertfordshire, 2004); Pam Schweitzer, ed., *Mapping Memoires: Reminiscence with Ethnic Minority Elders* (London: Age Exchange, 2004); and Faith Gibson, *Reminiscence and Recall: A Practical Guide to Reminiscence Work* (London: Age Concern, 2006).

3. See for example Peter G. Coleman, *Ageing and Reminiscence Processes: Social and Clinical Implications* (Chichester: Wiley, 1986), 9; Jeff Garland, "What Splendour It All Coheres: Life Review Therapy with Older People," in *Reminiscence Reviewed: Perspectives, Evaluations, Achievements*, ed. Joanna Bornat, 21–31 (Buckingham: Open University Press, 1994); Bender, Bauckham, and Norris, *Therapeutic Purposes of Reminiscence*, 200; Garland and Garland, *Life Review in Health and Social Care*, 57–58; Gibson, *Reminiscence and Recall*, 43.

4. Rose Dobrof, "Introduction: A Time for Reclaiming the Past," in *The Uses of Reminiscence: New Ways of Working with Older Adults*, ed. Marc Kaminsky, xvii (New York: Haworth Press, 1984).

5. Robert N. Butler, "The Life Review: An Interpretation of Reminiscence in the Aged," *Psychiatry* 26 (1963): 65–76.

6. Allan Pincus, "Reminiscence in Aging and Its Implications for Social Work Practice," *Social Work* 15, no. 3 (1970): 47–53.

7. Robert N. Butler, "Foreword," in *The Art and Science of Reminiscing: Theory, Research, Methods and Applications*, ed. Barbara K. Haight and Jeffrey Dean Webster, xix (Washington, D.C.: Taylor and Francis, 1995).

8. Butler, "The Life Review," 69.

9. Ibid., 75.

10. Coleman, *Ageing and Reminiscence Processes*, 10.

11. Erik Erikson, *Childhood and Society* (New York: Norton 1950).

12. Coleman, *Ageing and Reminiscence Processes*, 8.

13. A. W. McMahon and P. J. Rhudick, "Reminiscencing: Adaptational Significance in the Aged," *Archives of General Psychiatry* 10 (964): 292–98.

14. Coleman, *Ageing and Reminiscence Processes*, 9–10.

15. Elaine Cumming and William Henry, *Growing Old: The Process of Disengagement* (New York: Basic Books, 1961), discussed in Chris Phillipson, *Reconstructing Old Age: New Agendas in Social Theory and Practice* (London: Sage. 1998).

16. Ibid, 16–17.

17. Robert N. Butler, *Why Survive?: Being Old in America* (New York: Harper and Row, 1975), 409.

18. Faith Gibson, *The Past in the Present: Using Reminiscence in Health and Social Care* (Baltimore: The Health Professions Press, 2004), 6.

19. Coleman, *Ageing and Reminiscence Processes*, 20–21.

20. Ibid., 37.

21. Articles and features appeared in *Community Care* 8 (1978); *Observer*, Nov. 12, 1978; *Daily Mail*, Mar. 29, 1978; *Woman's Hour*, Jan. 1979; and *Getting On* (ATV) July 8, 1979; as well as in the *Toronto Star*, Mar. 10, 1979; *Washington Post*, Mar. 1979; *Doctor Magazine*, Mar. 22, 1979; *London Police Pensioner*, Nov. 6, 1979; and *Radio London*, June 1978 (Help the Aged, *Recall—A Handbook*, 46). The author visited the project herself following the publication of an article in the *Observer*.

22. Department of Health and Social Security, *Reminiscence Aids: The Use of Audio-Visual Presentations to Stimulate Memories in Old People with Mental Infirmity* (London: DHSS, 1979), 3.

23. Ibid., 3–4.

24. Mick Kemp, interview by Pam Schweitzer, 1999, 3.

25. Ibid.

26. Ibid, 4.

27. Ibid, 4–5.

28. Ibid., 5.

29. DHSS, *Reminiscence Aids*, 5.

30. Ibid, 10.

31. Ibid, 19.

32. Ibid., 31.

33. Ibid.

34. Kemp interview, 1999, 6.

35. Help the Aged, *Recall—A Handbook.*

36. Joanna Bornat, "Oral History as a Social Movement; Reminiscence and Older People," *Oral History* 17, no. 2 (1989): 16–24.

37. See among many examples: "*The Memory Box's* guidebook and 120 discussion cards to facilitate general reminiscence, produce memory diaries, put together autobiographies or facilitate life reviews . . . divided into twelve themes . . . etc." (Milton Keynes: Speechmark Publishing Limited, 2006).

38. J. Adams, "Anamnesis in Dementia: Restoring a Personal History," *Geriatric Nursing* (Sept./Oct. 1986): 25–27.

39. R. G. Jones, "Experimental Study to Evaluate Nursing Staff Morale in High Stimulation Geriatric Psychiatry Setting," *Journal of Advanced Nursing* 13 (1988): 352–57; M. E. Pietrucowicz and M. M. S. Johnson, "Using Life Histories to Individualise Nursing Home Staff Attitudes Toward Residents," *Gerontologist* 31, no. 1 (1991): 102–6; S. McKenzie, "A Positive Force," *Nursing the Elderly* (May/June 1991); B. Arigho, "A Gift of the Past: An Exchange Theory Analysis of the Effects of Reminiscence Exchanges on the Relationships Between Student Nurses and Older Patients" (unpublished MSc thesis, University of London, 1992); A. Goldwasser and S. Auerbach, "Audience-based Reminiscence Therapy Intervention: Effects on the Morale and Attitudes of Nursing Residents and Staff, *Journal of Mental Health and Aging* 2, no. 2 (1996): 101–14; Joanna Bornat and P. Chamberlayne, "Reminiscence in Care Settings: Implications for Training," *Education and Ageing* 14, no. 3 (1999): 277–95; W. Puentes, "Using Social Reminiscence to Teach Therapeutic Communication Skills," *Geriatric Nursing* 12 (2000): 315–18; and A. Clarke, E. J. Hanson, and H. Ross, "Seeing the Person Behind the Patient: Enhancing the Care of Older People Using a Biographical Approach," *Journal of Clinical Nursing* 12 (2003): 697–706.

40. J. Adams, "A Fair Hearing: Life-Review in a Hospital Setting," in Bornat, *Reminiscence Reviewed.*

41. Pam Schweitzer and Errollyn Bruce, *Remembering Yesterday, Caring Today: Reminiscence in Dementia Care—A Guide to Good Practice* (London: Jessica Kingsley, 2008).

42. Help the Aged, *Recall—A Handbook*, 11.

43. Frank Furedi, *The Therapy Culture: Cultivating Vulnerability in an Uncertain Age* (London: Routledge, 2004).

44. Help the Aged, *Recall—A Handbook*, 12.

45. Gibson, *Reminiscence and Recall.*

46. Ibid., 203.

47. Garland and Garland, *Life Review in Health and Social Care.*

48. Pam Schweitzer, *Reminiscence Theatre: Making Theatre from Memories* (London: Jessica Kingsley, 2007), 31–32.

49. L. Watt and P. Wong, "A Taxonomy of Reminiscence and The Therapeutic Implications," *Journal of Mental Health Counseling* 12 (1991): 37.

50. Haight and Webster, *Art and Science of Reminiscing*, 148.

51. Barbara K. Haight, and Shirley Hendricks, "An Integrated Review of Reminiscence," in Haight and Webster, *Art and Science of Reminiscing*, 3–21; and S. Hendrix and Barbara K. Haight, "A Continued Review of Reminiscence," in *Critical Advances in Reminiscence Work: From Theory to Application*, ed. Jeffrey Dean Webster and Barbara K. Haight, 3–29 (New York: Springer, 2002).

52. Faith Gibson, Barbara K. Haight, and Y. Michel, "Evaluating Long-Stay Care Settings: A Study of a Life Review and Life Storybook Project," in *Evaluation in Dementia Care*, ed. A. Innes and L. McCabe, 124–43 (London: Jessica Kingsley, 2007).

BIBLIOGRAPHY

Butler, Robert N. *Why Survive?: Being Old in America.* New York, Harper and Row, 1975.

Coleman, Peter G. *Ageing and Reminiscence Processes: Social and Clinical Implications.* Chichester: Wiley, 1986.

Gibson, Faith. *The Past in the Present: Using Reminiscence in Health and Social Care.* Baltimore: The Health Professional Press, 2004.

Kaminsky, Marc, ed. *The Uses of Reminiscence: New Ways of Working with Older Adults.* New York: Haworth Press, 1984.

Schweitzer, Pam, Errollyn Bruce, and Faith Gibson. *Remembering Yesterday, Caring Today: Reminiscence in Dementia Care—A Guide to Good Practice.* London: Jessica Kingsley, 2008.

Webster, Jeffrey Dean, and Barbara K. Haight, eds. *Critical Advances in Reminiscence Work: From Theory to Application.* New York: Springer, 2002.

CHAPTER 14

THE PROUST EFFECT: ORAL HISTORY AND THE SENSES

PAULA HAMILTON

> Coming down the Spit hill you could smell the seaweed. This was the breath of home.
>
> —Dorothy Olsen

> And I found that of all the senses the eye was the most superficial, the ear the most haughty, smell the most voluptuous, taste the most superstitious and inconstant, touch the most profound and philosophical.
>
> —Diderot, *Letter on the Blind*, 1749

At least one of the five senses—sound, vision, touch, taste, and smell—is essential to all human experience. Yet oral historians who are concerned with the memory of those experiences have not yet engaged with the senses in their practice, beyond an obvious preoccupation with sound and listening in the production and communication process. The senses have been central to the literary imagination in poetry and prose over a long period, but it has taken new conceptual approaches to interpreting the nature of experience, first by anthropologists working with different cultures, then later cultural historians, before these ideas have become more widespread. It is time to explore some of the possibilities for oral historians to work with the "sensory revolution" in the humanities.[1]

It is well known that senses can act as a mnemonic device or a trigger to remembering. The smell and taste of tea and madeleines stimulated Proust's recollection of his past, in one of the most famous of all literary passages about memory. (It also reminds us along the way about the beautiful sensuousness of language itself):

> But when from a long-distant past nothing subsists, after the people are dead, after the things are broken and scattered, still, alone, more fragile, but with more vitality, more unsubstantial, more persistent, more faithful, the smell and taste of things remain poised a long time, like souls, ready to remind us, waiting and hoping for their moment, amid the ruins of all the rest; and bear unfaltering, in the tiny and almost impalpable drop of their essence, the vast structure of recollection.[2]

Proust called this suddenly emerging memory "involuntary memory," which seems to obliterate the passage of time between the original event and its re-experience in memory. Encapsulated by the expression often used in film to signify a flash back: "I remember it as if it happened yesterday." The senses have the capacity for bringing the past into the present at any time, but they can also be consciously foregrounded in the more formal setting of an oral history interview. Called by the scientists the "Proust effect" when smell associated with experience can recall the memory, it is nonetheless only socially meaningful when it is communicated to someone else.

For all the power of Proust's memories of smell, sensory experience is regarded traditionally as a physiological sensation shaped by psychology and personal history, and therefore not the domain of analysis and abstract thought. But Proust was not the only one in his time who understood the central role of memory in relation to the senses. The philosopher Henri Bergson also observed in 1909 that "there is no perception which is not full of memories. With the immediate and present data of our senses, we mingle a thousand details out of our past experience."[3] However, the respective insights of these men like those before them, seem to have fallen on deaf ears until the "sensory revolution" at the end of the twentieth century claimed the senses for study as part of the Humanities. The senses have now become what Douglas Howes calls: "the most fundamental domain of cultural expression, the medium through which all the values and practices of society are enacted."[4] For some years now, scholars have produced a growing body of work about both the history of individual senses, while emphasizing their integral relationships with each other.

All of those who have written as advocates for one or other of the senses refer to the hegemony of the visual sense in relation to understanding of experience. They argue that the unthinking dominance of the visual in accounts of the social limits our imagination and ignores the equally crucial role that other senses play in our experience and understanding of the world. Scholars have argued that to be aware of the senses is to see the world in a fundamentally different way. This has forced a rethinking about the nature of social experience, interpersonal as well as relationships to community, and even ideas about how we live and move through space.

Mark Smith, one of the foremost historians of sensory history, began his general study with the assertion that "the senses are historical; that they are not universal but, rather, a product of place, and especially time, so that how people perceived and understood smell, sound, touch, taste and sight, changed historically." Sensory history, he argued, has a very wide brief: it "takes the history of the everyday, the average, and the banal, as seriously as it takes the history of elites, the intellect, and the exceptional, in an effort to understand the full range of meanings people attributed to the sense in the past."[5] This sounds very much like the original "history from below" context in which the oral history movement first flowered to document the lives of those who had been "silenced," but it is significant that Smith believes it possible to use the senses in exploring the experience of those previously without sound, sight or smell, taste or smell. At its best this has proved to be the case, since there are already some fine studies of slavery and sound in the United States.[6] He also claimed that "At its most powerful sensory history is also explanative."

The anthropologist Constance Classen noted that the investigation of the sensory worlds of past eras should not merely describe the range of sounds and smells that existed at a particular time, as evocative as that might be, but should uncover the meaning that those smells and sounds had for people.[7] In other words, we should be engaged in not simply a description of many past experiences through the senses, but our work should be capable of interpreting the meaning of those experiences, particular those that make little sense if only known through the visual. For Mark Smith in summary, sensory history was less a "field" of inquiry and more a habit of thinking about the past, "a way of becoming more attuned to the past." When we think about the senses, we are exposed to "subliminal histories," which allow us to interpret the meaning of our previous interviews in a new light as well as rethinking the process and content raised in new ones.

The Senses in Memory

While the anthropologists have focused on how cultures differ in the social value accorded to one or other of the senses, the historians have concentrated on historical periods from the seventeenth century to the mid-twentieth century, and on various written texts, so the studies tend to be constituted as a dialogue in inventive ways with evidence generated from the time under study. There may be a variety of reasons why there is very little investigation to date in those periods within living memory that could utilize oral histories. The most important is the central problem of how the sense are remembered and then articulated *as* memory, thereby linking the physiological phenomena with the social and cultural. If, for example, visual stimuli remained longer in the memory in a physiological basis, then we would need to take account of this in our analysis of how it worked socially.

Precisely how the senses operate in relation to memory is as yet an imperfectly understood area by both researchers in psychology and science. In 2004, British neuroscientists claim to have found the physiological basis for why a smell or sound has the power to bring forth a flood of contextual memories. The key, they said, "is that memories relating of an event are scattered across the brain's sensory centres but marshalled by a region called the hippocampus. If one of the senses is stimulated to evoke a memory, other memories featuring other senses are also triggered."[8]

Smell, as Proust showed, has long been hailed as the memory sense, the one most likely to provoke reminiscence. "Odor seems to be the most resistant to forgetting," said Gottfried, one of the scientists, "previous research has found that memories of images begin to fade days or even hours after viewing whereas recall of smells remains unimpaired for as much as a year."[9] Nevertheless, a report from the Howard Hughes Medical Institute in 2008 identified smell as still largely a "neuroscientific mystery."[10]

Though all of the senses decline with age, in fact humans take far less information from our eyes than any other sighted organism. This seems odd given the overwhelming primacy we give to the visual in Western cultures in the form of technologies such as photography, film, and the circulation of mass images through television and the Internet. This is complemented by such technologies to enhance sound as radio and telephony, but as yet we know little about the critical importance of these new technologies on our senses and their transformation in memory. Mirko Zardini argues that in the new sensory revolution "the senses constitute not so much a new field of study as a fundamental shift in the mode and media we employ to observe and define our own fields of study."[11] He linked this sensory domain closely with new digital technologies and the enhanced possibilities for utilizing mobile communications to reach broader audiences. It seems that we can no longer detach the senses of sight or sound from the technologies that amplify them.

Psychologists, too, have made important advances in our understanding of memory and perception. Kurt Danziger has discussed the historical context of psychology's engagement with the senses and noted that "the experience of remembering itself involves not only a recall of he past, but a sense of the past in the present." He argued for a blurring of the lines between memory and perception, but crucially emphasized the way in which sensory memory is shaped by our personal past: "The way we take up any part of our sensory experience, the way we actually experience it, the meaning we give to it, is always affected by the rest of our experience, some of it current as background perception, some of it past as something retained from previous encounters with the world."[12]

Other than this, we know that each sense functions in various ways when it is recollected, though again it is as yet unclear how all their characteristics can be differentiated. Since they are essentially interrelated and governed by our feelings, this issue is one of great complexity. Nonetheless, scholars dealing with each sense individually have identified some features. Jim Drobnick, for instance, noted that "smells are inherently discontinuous, fragmentary and episodic" while the visual may be more intense and sustained. "Environmental and immersive smells are inhaled and thus become intimately bound with the body; they permeate the atmosphere and are inescapable."[13]

Paradoxically, the work on the senses has also shown the limits of our apprehending of past experience, particularly through oral histories. While there is no longer an assumption that human thought and experience is structured only through words, senses and the embodied experience are sometimes outside language, not just something one sees and hears but something one lives. Joy Parr refers to the writer Michael Polyani who noted succinctly in his *The Tacit Dimension* some years ago that "we know more than we can tell," that we all have embodied and situated knowledge, "which is implied, understood referentially." These are often things we have learned over a long period that we do habitually, ritually, without consciously thinking about it.[14] Nevertheless, oral histories do involve the reduction of the three-dimensional embodied experience into two-dimensional interviews, and then are frequently transformed again into writing.

Oral histories are, by their nature, articulating experience in speech, language, and gesture (if technical means have a visual dimension). Since oral histories are essentially about agency, or individuals as a central character in their life stories, it is important to make a distinction between the interviewee as a "consumer of the senses" and a "producer." As Peg Rawes noted, we all create our own landscape of the senses as we move through environments.[15] We are engaged in the active construction of our experience, but if we heard, saw, smelled, touched, or tasted in the past and this is articulated as a recollection, then we are discussing a context that cannot be reproduced in the present. How people heard or smelled in the past is not the same as we hear or smell today. It is critically important, therefore to "historicize" the senses. While re-creating and re-imagining the past in many forms, such as museum exhibits, has become fashionable, we cannot possibly really actually re-create the conditions of consumption and reception at the time. Some sensory experiences become even jarringly historical. Few can imagine today for example, the smell and taste of the first cigarette of the day as "pure joy." But, for two of the senses, the capacity for technical reproduction since the nineteenth century for vision and the twentieth century for sound has meant that we can retain them as sources of intangible heritage, frozen in time, kept in film and sound archives.

The Senses and Oral Histories

We would expect all kinds of references to the senses in interviews, both as part of the communication process and as an act of remembering. Here I draw on examples from different international archives as well as two community projects located in suburban areas of Sydney, Australia, with which I have been involved for several years. Although my research has thrown up a lot of material that relates to sight, sound and smell, I have uncovered very little on taste and touch. Taste seems to be a more circumscribed sense relating to food and is not much in evidence unless there are projects on that specific subject. Similarly, I have found touch in evidence as a mnemonic reminder for only one interviewee, Jean Hudson. When Jean walks around Manly, a suburb she has lived in for more than fifty years, she often puts her hand out and touches places like stairs or fences or buildings that remind her of people she loved now gone or events of importance that happened in her life. As Mark Paterson, who has written on touch observed, "touch seems more intimate, reassuring and proximal" but because it is "so much a part of ourselves, and is centrally a form of non-verbal communication" we are unlikely to speak about it, except in metaphor.[16] Yet it is through touch that we engage with the materiality of the world, and it can invoke powerful memories involving other senses, like those in Jean Hudson's life. Often people associate things they can touch with memories of particular people: feeling the smoothness of a father's pipe or the texture of a mother's taffeta dress.

There are several ways to consider the role of senses in oral histories. The first is to rethink the nature of the visual sense that has been taken for granted in so much of past practice. For example, a story told to me by Harley O'Regan about growing up in Mosman, a suburb of Sydney, took on greater significance once I thought more about his sense of the visual:

> It was a most beautiful swimming pool, blue and lovely, called Cavill's baths. The big attraction apart from the swimming was Rhoda Cavill. She was something unreal in terms of beauty. She had this beautiful figure and she used to dive like a swallow and it was fascinating just to watch her. She was a bit older than me and out of my class.[17]

Reading this story again, I was struck by O'Regan's description of what he can see in his mind's eye almost like a photograph. He also communicates a classical image of the Australian feminine modern, a sleek diving beauty, which he may have seen many times since, that now forms part of his memory. We can understand that the narrative of what he has *seen* is permeated with his wistful longing as a young man for the unattainable.

Second, the senses can be the central subject of a story told by an interviewee, or it might be a causal factor in explanation for action. Some of these have a physiological component and can function in a way like those of Oliver Sacks, the well-known neurologist who has explored conditions relating to perception through his published case studies.[18] These stories are rare, but this example from the San Francisco Oral History archive is an important case in point. Gloria Lyon was interviewed for the archive's memory of the Jewish Holocaust project in 2002. She was born in Czechoslovakia and was fourteen when, in May 1944, at Auschwitz, she lost her sense of smell:

> In 1944, sometime in May, 1944, I was assigned to work in the Canada work detail. And I just didn't feel good, I kept throwing up, I kept throwing up because of the smell of burnt human bodies, and bone, and hair. And the air was very, very bad. And I realize that that is why. And so I couldn't eat the little food we were given.
>
> This concerned my mother very much, and me too because I was losing weight rapidly. Even if I had not thrown up I would have been losing weight. Once one loses weight in Auschwitz, one doesn't live very long.... One day I no longer threw up. I heard others talk about it, but it no longer bothered me. I didn't know why I don't smell those things. Actually I didn't realize that I lost my sense of smell totally until I was liberated thirteen months later and taken to Sweden.

Gloria's is a remarkable story about traumatic experiences and their effect on the senses, but it is even more important when we hear how her sense of smell returned forty-seven years later. In 1991, Gloria went back to revisit the site of Auschwitz with her husband:

> Anyway after I went through the steps of revisiting Auschwitz—harmless touching of the electric wire fences, opened and shutting gates to make sure they were rendered harmless and talking a blue streak, oh my poor husband.
>
> We left and on the way out away from Auschwitz, we were still in Poland going through the serene countryside, I began to notice something. I said to Karl, "What's that I smelled? Is that manure?" Like I had my smell all along. He was driving at the time and he said, "you smell that?" I said, "I think so," just realizing, gee, I wasn't able to smell that before. He pulled over to the side and opened up the beauty box and pulled out his after-shave and he said, "smell this." For the first time in forty-seven years my sense of smell returned, just like that. But what I can't get over is how smoothly this went as if I had it along, what's the problem here? And thinking back now, it just seems very strange.[19]

This is clear evidence of what is known as "situated knowledge" and embodiment, that is, sensorial understanding related to a particular place and time. Gloria had to return to the place of trauma for her sense of smell to be turned back on like a switch.

In another context, a doctor's sense of smell saved Juliet Sheen's life. In the 1960s, living in suburban Sydney, she was very ill with a cervical abscess, but no one could figure out what was wrong. Old Dr. Barry, a fixture in the district, came to her house when she was dying. She recounted that "He stood by the bedside and sniffed [she sniffs] like that." He then said, "I've smelt that smell before in the trenches of World War I," and he gave her a large injection of penicillin, which dealt with the infection.[20] This story is a reminder of how much doctors rely on their sensory knowledge and the history of their sensory experiences for diagnosis, despite the technological enhancement provided by specific equipment for detecting illness.

Since oral histories depend for their existence on the technology of sound, it is little wonder that hearing the past features prominently in interviewing. Some oral historians feel that sound should be taken far more seriously as the central medium of communicating memory. Martin Thomas for example, commented that:

> too many historians still lazily mine oral histories (or preferably transcripts of them) for content alone—ignoring the ambience of the tape, the theatrics of the interview, and the particularities of the medium, all of which affect the evidential value.[21]

For Thomas, not just interviewing but also field recording and sound production "have always been part of his research practice." He makes an important point about the importance of sound not just for the content of interviews but also the process of oral history itself.

Another aspect of Juliet Sheen's narrative that concerns oral historians who work with the senses is the performative nature of sensory effects in interview. Juliet sniffs when emulating the doctor and people often act out or perform the senses on the interview tape. Without video, interviewees are limited in the use of their bodies to demonstrate or reproduce a sound, sight, or a smell, so they use speech in order to communicate either in metaphor or re-enactment. John Berry described what it was like to grow up adjacent to a suburban gasworks in Sydney, and it was important to specify the exact site of its location as well as performing the sound of it:

> The gasworks featured a lot in my life because we were very close to it, it was on the point between Quarantine and little Manly...and that sound of the wooompf, woomf woomp woomp, it was part of you, you were that close to the gasworks...and there was the whiff of gas.[22]

Berry was trying to demonstrate the way the sound became embodied and he clutches his chest as he makes the sound, but it is relational both in terms of place and with other senses, so he speaks of the "whiff of gas" as part of a joint association in his memory. These episodes do more than restore the sound dimension to experience of the past. They remind us how we move through the world utilizing senses in different frames, at different times. As Constance Classen asserted, "We not only think *about* our senses we think *through* them."[23] So too do various scholars remind us, that the relationship between sound and all the other senses is complex because they are always associated with emotions.[24]

Of course, there are various registers of listening and sound in interviews. Some of these relate to the notion of whispering an aside, confessions, eavesdropping, or secret listening. Marie Stanton referred to her childhood and the traditional Catholic confessional. The focus was on listening, not seeing:

> Old Father McDonald was there for years and years, you'd go to confession and he was deaf, he'd say "I can't hear you" so we'd all creep in and listen to him.[25]

For Marie and her friends "listening in" was a minor transgression of the church ritual and authority, but it is an instance of a story told about sound that was a louder volume, "out of place" than the occasion warranted and could be remembered as part of the younger risk-taking self.

Some experience of the senses can be historicized in a more exacting way, however. As Casey O'Callaghan said: "time is to audition what space is to vision."[26] For example, Jean Miles went to school in Sydney when they were building the Sydney

Harbour Bridge from the late 1920s to 1932. Her school was close on Observatory Hill overlooking the bridge site:

> We'd grown up with stones rattling on the roof of the building that my classroom was in from the blasting, you know…and the pneumatic drills going on….I spent so many years, my school years, listening to that noise.[27]

School is a place where extensive listening takes place in a formalized setting so it is no wonder that these sustained sounds across years become central to Jean's memory and understanding of girlhood. By other accounts too, we know the completion of the bridge was eagerly awaited by all those living on the north side of the city, as Jean was, who could not get easy access across the harbor, so this anticipation underpins her memory.

Place and the Senses/Sensory Urbanism

One of the community projects with which I have been involved is "Transforming the Local," in Balmain, Sydney. It charts the experience of gentrification since the 1960s of a former industrial working-class suburb, a phenomenon documented by urban historians in many cities of the world. Much of the research on gentrification tells the story of change through external measures such as house renovation and changing types of shops or income levels. Very little of it looks at the process from the point of view of the people who experienced them. Through this oral history project, I had the opportunity to test out new ideas about the senses by asking interviewees about what they remembered in terms of sensory experiences. With these questions I was seeking to create a more intimate scale, but also a more dynamic sense of how change is experienced over time. Michael Bull refers to the spatial nature of sound and experience that has been buried within the "largely visually inspired epistemology of experience that informs much contemporary social science investigation…our urban landscapes don't move easily."[28]

At first, these questions about smell and sounds proved fruitless, but I had better success if I alerted interviewees to my purpose and gave them time to reflect. The result is a rich portrait of a place and landscape that was moving from a suburb where working people lived and worked, to one where not only the kind of labor changed significantly, but also work and home became more separated.

We associate the modern city with a cacophony of sound, much of it defined as noise, which we screen out because it assaults our ears and, eyes, and nose. By contrast, we imagine the suburbs as "sleepy" and muted, if not silent. The inner-city suburbs of the id-twentieth century had a very different resonance. Smell and sound are deeply implicated in industrialization and Balmain, a harbor peninsular, attracted water-related heavy industry such as dockyards or drew on imported ingredients from overseas for chemicals or soap factories. Most of the people interviewed did not work in these industries but had moved there since the 1960s. One of the initial observations from the interviews was the way people oriented themselves in place according to smell. They were able to tell which way the wind was blowing by particular smells.

> I can remember if the wind blew from the west, you'd smell Monsanto chemicals, a very strong smell. The one I loved the most was the one from CSR across at Piermont (Colonial Sugar Refinery), that sugary, honey smell, I think it was more like treacle. It was in the southerly from memory [Interviewer "I didn't like it."] And in other winds you could smell the soapflakes from Palmolive, Lever, and kitchen—pears and sand soap, it was a clean smell.[29]

The sociologist George Simmel described smell as a "dissociative sense" for there is "something radical and non-negotiable about its emotional judgements." In this extract the interviewer also commented on the smell with a different judgment. This expressed a very localized sense of place, because in other parts of Balmain, where there were three power stations, you could, as another interviewee said, "smell coal dust from the coal loader, if the wind was blowing from the southwest."[30]

The rhythms of largely men's work also marked out time in everyone's lives who lived in the area. One of the islands off the Peninsular, Cockatoo Island, was used for ship-building. Joan Chapman remembered that you would know when work was finishing because "there was this strange haunting whistle." The men then caught the ferry a short distance from the island back to Balmain. Soon, "hundreds of them would come streaming up the street from the wharf" and there would be "an endless row of boys selling (afternoon edition) papers and yelling in competition."[31] These were the temporary but repeated sounds of the every day. They speak of the masculine world of work intruding but also operating alongside the changing domestic suburban landscape, where Joan had moved not long previously. Fran Tonkiss spoke of the senses, particularly sound as "capturing a larger urban tension between collective and subjective life" that would seem to be evident here.[32]

The story above also speaks of movement across landscape and our understanding of the city as a "sensorium"—a place where the senses are infused with each other and are strongly influenced by modes and styles of movement. Balmain was once a place where many walked from home to work and back. Few owned cars. A few years later another interviewee remembered doors slamming and cars revving up as the auditory signal of work's end. These evocatively reimagined soundscapes remind us of the diverse pitches, volumes, and tones in daily routines, and they help us orient the physical landscape in time. Moreover, some sounds of the modern were completely unwelcome: Diana Bryant married a doctor and moved into Balmain, living not far from the cargo wharves. To her "industry was peripheral because none of my friends worked there." Yet, she has a vivid memory of the advent of containerization in the late 1960s and the "clanging metal noise when they used to drop the containers on the ships...people who lived around that part of Balmain were definitely affected by that noise."[33] It is probable that there were different kinds of sound associated with loading and unloading cargo under the previous system such as the railroad shunting system and the sound of cranes and men shouting but people who had lived there for some time were acclimatized to those as part of their daily soundscape. What Bryant remembers here is the discordant, the new sound intruding in the newly claimed suburban domain.

Of course, some of factory workers interviewed remember the smells and sounds in very different ways: The Colgate Palmolive factory, for example, was established in 1923 on the waterside site of an old meatworks. At its peak in the 1960s, it employed 1,250 local workers. Peter Waterman came to work down at the "Olive," as it was known, being first employed there as an office boy:

> Well, when I walked down there was a multitude of aromas coming from this place. You know there was tallow which wasn't very nice and there was perfume, you could smell sweet perfumes and after about a week or so, when I used to walk down the street... I couldn't smell it anymore. It just became part of the area—if you worked in a place the smell was absorbed but you couldn't smell it.[34]

It may have been coincidence that sweet-smelling soap came to be built at an old meatworks, but that it was continued the tradition of things having a strong odor at that site. Waterman remembered that "the tallow—the animal fat—which was used in the soap, was delivered to the factory wharf. When it stood too long in the heat and started to melt then it smelled the worst."

It is commonplace that people speak of the habituation to particular smells and sound over time at their workplace, though there is a great deal of research yet to be done on the meaning of labor and work through the senses. Another side to this story is the smell of men's clothes when they were taken home. Wives or children remember the smell of their husband or father's work in their uniforms or overalls or jackets, which brought the unknown outside world into the intimacy of the domestic environment. These were not comforting but dissonant experiences of transporting senses "out of place."

These examples provided a very different understanding of the process of gentrification, one that was experienced from a variety of viewpoints. On the one hand, they revealed the complexity of the Balmain "community" and the layered histories and multiple meanings of place, despite the unity implied by the idea of the "local"; on the other, they gave some insight into the scale of the local and the way this is redefined across time and space in relation to extensive social change and different forms of mobility.

The senses is a field in its infancy for all those involved in writing, making or recording histories and there is still much to be worked out in terms of interpretive frameworks. But the historian Mark Smith is right when he claims that working on the senses becomes a "way of thinking about the past" or a habit of mind, since it involves a conceptual shift that brings new dimensions to the interview process and its outcome and provides evocative possibilities for the future study of memory.

NOTES

1. The phrase "sensorial revolution" is one used by Douglas Howes in "Architecture of the Senses," http://www.david-howes.com/DH&-research-sampler-arch-senses.htm. See also on memory and experience Kurt Danziger, *Marking the Mind: A History of Memory* (Cambridge: Cambridge University Press, 2008). On the current debates about the nature of experience, see the essay by Harold Mah, "The Predicament of Experience," *Modern Intellectual History* 5, no. 1 (2008): 97–119.

2. Marcel Proust, *A la recherche du temps perdu*, vol. 1, *Swann's Way*, 1913. Trans. D. J. Enright (New York: Vintage, 1992).

3. Henri Bergson, *Matter and Memory*, trans. Margaret Paul and W. Scott Palmer (1909) (London: Allen & Unwin, 1911).

4. Howes, "Architecture of the Senses."

5. Mark M. Smith, *Sensing the Past: Seeing, Hearing, Smelling, Tasting and Touching in History* (Berkeley: University of California Press, 2007), 3 and 5.

6. See Mark Smith, *Listening to Nineteenth Century America* (2001), and Shane White and Graham White, *The Sounds of Slavery* (2005). Smith also discusses touch in this context in "Getting in Touch with Slavery and Freedom," *Journal of American History* 95, no. 2 (Sept. 2008): 381–92.

7. Constance Classen, *Worlds of Sense: Exploring the Senses in History and Across Cultures* (New York: Routledge, 1993), 6.

8. BioEd Online, Biology Teacher resources from Baylor College of Medicine) May 31, 2004, http://www.bioedonline.org/news.

9. Ibid.

10. http:www.hhmi.org/senses/d140.html.

11. Mirko Zardini, "Towards a Sensorial Urbanism," in *Sense of the City: An Alternative Approach to Urbanism*, ed. Mirko Zardini, 22 (Montreal: Canadian Centre for Architecture, 2005).

12. Danziger, *Marking the Mind*, 253 and 257.

13. Jim Drobnick, ed., "Introduction to Olfactocentrism," in *The Smell Culture Reader* (London: Berg, 2006), 5.

14. Michael Polanyi *The Tacit Dimension* (1966), cited in Joy Parr, "Notes for a More Sensuous History of Twentieth Century Canada: The Timely, the Tacit and the Material Body," *Canadian Historical Review* Forum 82, no. 4 (Dec. 2001): 719–45.

15. Peg Rawes, "Sonic Envelopes," *Senses and Society* 3, no 1 (Mar. 2008): 65.

16. Mark Paterson, *The Senses of Touch: Haptics, Affects and Technologies* (Oxford: Berg, 2007), 8.

17. Harley O'Regan, interview by Paula Hamilton, Dec. 10, 2000, SHOROC Oral History Project and *Cracking Awaba: Stories of Mosman and Northern Beaches Communities* (NSW: SHOROC, 2005), 82.

18. See especially Oliver W. Sacks, *The Man Who Mistook His Wife for a Hat* (New York: Summit Books, 1985), and Sacks, *An Anthropologist on Mars: Seven Paradoxical Tales* (New York: Knopf, 1995).

19. The Urban School of San Francisco, Telling Their Stories Oral History Archives Project. www.tellingstories.org, Interview with Gloria Hollander Lyon, May 6, 2003. I am grateful to a member of the project who drew my attention to this wonderful archive at the OHA, in Pittsburgh, 2008.

20. Juliet Sheen, interview by Rose Pickard, Leichhardt Local History Project, Transforming the Local, Balmain, Feb. 27, 2009 (this and subsequent tapes currently in possession of author).

21. Martin Thomas, "The Rush to Record: Transmitting the Sound of Aboriginal Culture," *Journal of Australian Studies* 90 (January 2007): 107.

22. John Berry, interview by Paula Hamilton for SHOROC Council Project, Feb. 17, 2001 (interview available at libraries involved but see also Hamilton, *Cracking Awaba*, 45.

23. Classen, *Worlds of Sense*, 10.

24. See, for example, Steven Connor, "Edison's Teeth: Touching Hearing," in *Hearing Cultures: Essays on Sound: Listening and Modernity*, ed. Viet Erlmann, 154 (Oxford: Berg, 2004). The senses often work against each other. Connor refers to the way sight "often acts to interpret, fix, limit and complete the evidence of sound."

25. Marie Stanton, interview by Paula Hamilton, SHOROC Project, May 15, 2001, and also *Cracking Awaba*, 94.

26. Casey O'Callaghan, "The World of Sounds," *Philosopher's Magazine* 45 (2009): 66.

27. Jean Miles, interview by Paula Hamilton, SHOROC project, May 3, 2001, and also *Cracking Awaba*, 60.

28. Michael Bull, "Thinking about Sound, Proximity and Distance in Western Experience: The Case of Odysseus's Walkman," in Erlmann, *Hearing Cultures*, 173.

29. Bronwyn Monroe, interview by Annette Waterworth, Mar. 2, 2009, Leichhardt Local History Project.

30. John Williams, interview by Annette Waterworth, June 4, 2008, Leichhardt Local History Project.

31. Joan Chapman, interview by Annette Waterworth, June 30, 2008, Leichhardt Local History Project.

32. Fran Tonkiss, "Aural Postcards: Sound, Memory and the City," in *The Auditory Culture Reader*, ed. Michael Bull and Les Back, 303 (London: Berg, 2003).

33. Diana Bryant, interview by Annette Waterworth, Leichhardt Transforming the Local Project, Apr. 29, 2009.

34. Rosemary Block, "'Everybody Had a Cousin at Colgates': The Community of the Colgate-Palmolive Factory, Balmain, Sydney. The Colgate Palmolive Oral History Project," *OHAA [Oral History in Australia Association] Journal* 18 (1996): 69–78.

BIBLIOGRAPHY

Bandt, Ros, Michelle Duffy, and Dolly MacKinnon. *Hearing Places: Sound, Place, Time and Culture*. Newcastle, UK: Cambridge Scholars Publishing. 2007.

Bull, Michael, and Les Back, eds. *The Auditory Culture Reader*. Oxford: Berg Sensory Formation Series, 2003.

Classen, Constance. *Worlds of Sense: Exploring the Senses in History and Across Cultures*. New York: Routledge, 1993.

Classen, Constance, Davie Howes, and Anthony Synnott. *Aroma: The Cultural History of Smell*. New York: Routledge, 1994.

Collins, Diane. "Acoustic Journeys: Exploration and the Search for an Aural History of Australia." *Australian Historical Studies* 37, no. 128 (Oct. 2006): 1–17.

Connor, Steven. "The Menagerie of the Senses." *Senses and Society* 1, no 1 (2006): 9–26.
———. "The Modern Auditory I." In *Rewriting the Self: Histories from the Renaissance to the Present*, edited by Roy Porter, 203–23. London: Routledge, 1997.
Corbin, Alain. *The Foul and the Fragrant*. Cambridge, Mass.: Harvard University Press, 1986.
———. *Time, Desire and Horror: Towards a History of the Senses*. Cambridge, Mass.: Polity Press, 1995.
Cubitt, Geoffrey. *History and Memory*. Historical Approaches Series. Manchester: Manchester University Press, 2007.
Danziger, Kurt. *Marking the Mind: A History of Memory*. Cambridge: Cambridge University Press, 2008.
Deakin, Desley, and Joy Damousi, eds. *Talking and Listening in the Age of Modernity*. Canberra: ANU ePress, 2007.
Drobnick, James, ed. *The Smell Culture Reader*. Berg. Oxford: Berg, 2006.
Erlmann, Veit, ed. *Hearing Cultures: Essays on Sound, Listening and Modernity*. Oxford: Berg, 2004.
Jones, Caroline A., ed. *Sensorium. Embodied Experience, Technology and Contemporary Art*. Cambridge, Mass.: The MIT List Visual Arts Center, MIT Press, 2006.
Howes, David. "Can These Dry Bones live? An Anthropological Approach to the History of the Senses." *Journal of American History* 95, no. 2 (Sept. 2008).
———, ed. *Empire of the Senses: The Sensual Culture Reader*. London: Berg, 2005.
———. *Sensual Relations: Engaging the Senses in Culture and Social Theory*. Ann Arbor: University of Michigan Press, 2003.
Parr, Joy. "Smells Like? Sources of Uncertainty in the History of the Great Lakes Environment." *Environmental History* 11 (Apr. 2006): 282–312.
———. "Notes for a More Sensuous History of Twentieth-Century Canada: The Timely, the Tacit and the Material Body." *Canadian Historical Review Forum* 82, no. 4 (Dec. 2001): 719–45.
Paterson, Mark. *The Senses of Touch: Haptics, Affects and Technologies*. Oxford: Berg, 2007.
Rawes, Peg. "Sonic Envelopes." *Senses and Society* 3, no. 1 (Mar. 2008): 61–76.
Sacks, Oliver W. *An Anthropologist on Mars: Seven Paradoxical Tales*. New York: Knopf, 1995.
———. *The Man Who Mistook His Wife for a Hat*. New York: Summit Books, 1985.
Smith, Mark, ed. *Hearing History: A Reader*. Athens: University of Georgia Press, 2004.
———. "Producing Sense, Consuming Sense, Making Sense: Perils and Prospects for Sensory History." *Journal of Social History* (2007): 841–58.
———. *Sensing the Past: Seeing, Hearing, Smelling, Tasting and Touching in History*. Berkeley: University of California Press, 2007.
Thomas, Martin. "The Rush to Record: Transmitting the Sound of Aboriginal Culture." *Journal of Australian Studies* 90 (Jan. 2007): 107–18.
Zardini, Mirko, ed. *Sense of the City: An Alternative Approach to Urbanism*. Montreal: Canadian Centre for Architecture, 2005.

CHAPTER 15

AFTER ACTION: ORAL HISTORY AND WAR

MEGAN HUTCHING

How did they get the wounded off the beach?

> Good question. I've no idea. I'm afraid you didn't turn round to look back, you just kept on going. The impression I have is that you were expendable at that stage. Later on they became more organised with getting their wounded back in, but not in the initial assault wave. You were expendable, and you just kept your fingers crossed. I don't know whether there was a sense of relief. Initially, briefly, you were happy that you got there in one piece.[1]

Alan Roberts's memories of invading Peleliu in the Palau group of islands in 1944 reminds us what being in action is like for the individual in the front line. It is not straightforward; more often it is chaotic. There is danger, noise, death and injury, and often contact with those giving orders is lost. People must rely on their mates, their own sense of self-preservation, and their ability to adapt to circumstances beyond their control. As Roberto Rabel reminds us, wars are resolved collectively, but they are experienced individually.[2]

I use my own experiences of recording Second World War veterans over an eight-year period as a case study, while making more general points about oral history and war. Rather than discussing such things as the different ways in which emotion affects how people remember, or the ways in which people compose their memories during their lifetimes, which are all part of the larger study of oral history, I look at some of the reasons for studying war and at the different types of information that researchers have sought and found.

My own background is as a social historian, and while it was possible that the project I was involved with could have been done by a military historian,

I was eager to do it because I thought that I would approach it in a different way. I wanted to examine the effect of taking part in war on the individuals concerned, instead of concentrating on military strategy, accounts of battles, advances and retreats, and technical information about military materiel, which are the focus of standard accounts of war, intended as omniscient overviews of the military action.

Redefining War Experience

Oral history interviews illuminate the often-ignored experiences of ordinary people caught up in war and the range of reactions that different aspects of war evoked from them, while reminding us that combat—"the quintessential war experience"—is not the sole defining experience of war.[3] Interviews that concentrate on combat experiences reflect a very narrow concept of war. Most time in uniform is spent out of action. Most servicemen and women are not in front-line units. I was certainly interested in recording information about the military service of my interviewees and their reactions to their experiences, but also in the events that are usually unrecorded by conventional historians because they are so ordinary that they are taken for granted. Such activities included the domestic details of their service life, such as food preparation and keeping clothes and bodies clean.

The project I ran was state-sponsored through the New Zealand Ministry for Culture and Heritage. It began after Prime Minister Helen Clark returned from a state visit to Gallipoli in Turkey, which had commemorated the eighty-fifth anniversary of the landing of New Zealand troops there in 1915. During her visit, she read a book by the New Zealand writer Maurice Shadbolt, called *Voices of Gallipoli*.[4] The book was based on interviews he had recorded with Gallipoli veterans during the 1980s. Helen Clark had family connections with the Gallipoli campaign—one of her great-uncles was killed there—and so had an interest in the subject, but she was also struck by how vividly the men's experience was conveyed in the transcribed interviews in the book.

On her return to New Zealand, she asked the Ministry to consider doing a similar project for Second World War veterans because they were becoming very old and fewer in number. In 2000 I began the project by preparing to interview veterans of the Battle of Crete, fought in May 1941.

When I started, there was some discussion about who would be interviewed. There were people of the opinion that it would not be successful because all the officers and people "who knew what was going on" had already died. This was a reflection of the opinion that only those in charge can speak sensibly about the events they are experiencing. I disagreed strongly. I was interested in the experience of the ordinary serviceman or woman, those called "other ranks." It seemed to me that what happened to these people—and they were the vast majority—was very important to record if we were to gain a rounded picture of what it was like to have taken part in that war so long ago.

Since, initially, I was doing the project by myself, and since we wanted to record the interviews reasonably quickly because of the age of the people who had to be recorded, I needed to work out some way of making it manageable for one person.[5] I decided that I would encourage people to get in touch with me, after which I sent them a fairly lengthy questionnaire to fill in. This questionnaire covered basic biographical information, information about their Second World War service, and where they had served, and it also gave them the opportunity, if they wanted to take it, of writing at length about their experiences.

The project was divided into the campaigns that had been significant to New Zealanders. There were six themes altogether, including the experiences of prisoners of war, and of those who served in uniform at home.[6] For each of the themes, it was important that all of the significant parts of that particular experience were covered. For the interviews that dealt with their time in North Africa between 1941 and 1943, I had to make sure that subjects such as Operation Crusader, the New Zealanders' time in Syria, the breakout at Minqar Qa'im, and the battles at Ruweisat Ridge, El Alamein, and Takrouna, would be covered. The people I interviewed had to have been involved in at least one of those actions and thus have something to say about it.

There was a wonderful response. I was overwhelmed by the number of questionnaires that arrived, full of detailed information. I was only able to interview about fifteen people for each theme, which made the choice of interviewee very difficult. I was choosing them on the basis of their written contributions via the questionnaire, which meant that some who did not have well-developed written skills may have been overlooked; some who wrote well, but were not as articulate in speech, may have been interviewed. I was always aware of this shortcoming, but there was no way to overcome it with the limited resources and time.

While some projects may concentrate on a particular unit or event, in any series of interviews, it is useful to record a variety of viewpoints, even if the focus is narrow. I needed to be sure that the experiences of a range of units was included, and not just those which provided front-line troops. During the project, we interviewed an army dentist, a chaplain, a train engineer, nurses, clerks, and a conscientious objector as well as those who served in action.

I also wanted to make sure that I had good geographical coverage of the country. In New Zealand, a small country of four million people, this was easier to achieve than it might have been in other places. The geographical spread was important because I thought of these interviews as just as much a war memorial as the built ones that are present in every town around the country. This was a project being undertaken by the state, and it seemed to me that the interviews were another way of officially acknowledging and remembering the efforts and activities of those men and women who served during the Second World War.

This does not mean that I approached the interviews wearing my rose-colored glasses. While I wanted to acknowledge what these men and women had done, I was also interested in recording their opinions and so experience of the less savory aspects of war. The New Zealand Army Division (the "Div"), for example, was known as "Freyberg and his 40,000 Thieves" after the officer in command and because of the men's propensity for looting the bodies of dead enemy troops and keeping or selling the items they acquired. Tini Glover recalled:

> I've seen officers shot and lying with their Luger [pistol]. I always called a mate of mine, "Hey, there's some dollars here, lying on the ground." [My friend] used to go out looting, and he'd say, "I'll give you a few bob when I sell it." I didn't take things off a dead man.[7]

The men of the "Div" were also eager to acquire anything they felt they needed to make their lives more comfortable, whether they were supposed to have it or not. Ian Johnston, for example, recalled that his artillery unit had acquired many different things this way. "We even had a piano in one of our three-tonners [trucks]. We'd flogged that from some Italian crowd."[8] While they spoke about these activities in humorous tones, looting dead bodies was certainly against military law.

Typical Experiences

As oral historians, we are always conscious of the need to record both the "typical" experiences of ex-servicemen and women—things such as enlistment, training, and living in communities, for example—and the unique experiences of the individual we are interviewing. Often the two are intertwined. I was interested in discovering whether my interviewees would talk about being afraid while they were on active service. When I asked Roy Coates if he had felt frightened when he was waiting to be evacuated from Crete in 1941, he gave a much broader answer, which encapsulated his experience of war:

> I always found when you were in action, you didn't have an awful lot of time to think about being frightened. And although I would never have ever said it at any time, throughout the war I had a feeling that I was going to survive. I had no grounds for thinking that, but I suppose I've always had an optimistic outlook on life, and that does have an effect, if you think you're going to get through. But 90 percent of it is pure luck.[9]

I also felt it was important to record the participants' reactions to those they were fighting against and whether that had changed in the intervening years, along with their reactions to the people in the various countries they served. New Zealand troops based in Egypt found Cairo more alien than they had anticipated, and the behavior of the Egyptians was also difficult to come to terms with. Clifford Vause, who served in an infantry battalion, remarked that "Cairo's a very untidy place. You could argue over the price if you went to a shop. I don't think I ever took anything, but some of the jokers would just grab stuff and walk away. The locals couldn't do a thing. They'd just scream and yell."[10]

Those who served in the Pacific usually went with strong views about the Japanese they were fighting against, informed by a lack of familiarity with Japan and of Japanese culture. These negative views were consolidated as they came to learn of Japanese military behavior during the war. While some had changed their opinions in the years since the war ended, a number of the men explained that they still had difficulty buying Japanese goods or talking to Japanese people. It was therefore a surprise, and a reminder that while men fight wars, they do not necessarily hate the people they are fighting, when Ralph Williams recalled:

> I always remember, I think it was Vella Lavella and we were asked to go around where the Japanese had been and find out if any were left. A mopping-up exercise. We had to go through the jungle and we had stuff on us to make ourselves inconspicuous—burnt chalk to camouflage ourselves. A man felt a bit of a goat, in a way, but we went. We came through the jungle to a sort of bivouac where the Japanese had been, and it had one survivor. This poor emaciated little fellow, a Japanese soldier, the only one in the camp. And someone just shot him. I felt awful. To see a bloke shoot the Japanese. He had no weapon, nothing. And that really hit me hard. I said, "Look, no need to do that. He was defenceless, he had nothing."...I didn't like that one little bit. I wasn't the only one who felt that way.[11]

This extract also reminds us that one of the joys of oral history is that you always get so much more than you ask for. A simple question about attitudes toward the enemy, and the answer includes some information about jungle warfare, and reaction to being in camouflage, as well as the unexpected humanity of the reaction to what was perfectly acceptable behavior toward enemy troops.

Remembering that most time during wartime is spent out of action, I was interested in hearing how people spent their leave. Did the armed forces give them any advice about venereal disease and contraception? What was the punishment for contracting venereal disease? Was visiting brothels tacitly encouraged by the military authorities' provision of "clean" houses, which the men could visit without the risk of contacting sexually transmitted diseases? I wondered what the reaction would be to my questions about this sort of behavior. The interviewees were remarkably frank, although, like Tini Glover's remarks above about looting dead bodies, the experiences were sometimes presented as having happened to friends, or that they had experienced only as an interested bystander. They were much more prepared to speak of getting drunk and into fights with other servicemen. These incidents were often recounted in a humorous way, partly reflecting nostalgia about their activities as young men, and partly because they wished to have such incidents recorded but did not want to present their own activities in a bad light.

Most of the men interviewed did not spend their leave visiting brothels or getting drunk. Narratives of leave in Egypt and Italy were particularly interesting for the insight they gave into the role of servicemen and women as tourists. Most people at that time had some knowledge of the Bible and ancient history; many took the opportunity to make sightseeing trips to the pyramids and the Valley of the Kings, and Rome and Pompeii, as well as trips to what was then Palestine to visit the places mentioned in the Bible. For one interviewee, the chance attendance at an opera in a small town in Italy led to a lifelong interest in such music.

The domestic detail of war adds much to our understanding of the experience. Interviewees can be asked about what food they ate, and how they washed themselves and their clothes. Such questions will often elicit detailed information about interaction with, and attitudes to, the people of the country in which they are serving. Joseph Bacos recalled his tank unit's interaction with Italian people:

> We used to give sweets to the Italian children. They came clustering around. And salt. The salt! You got kissed on both cheeks. From the mothers—they kept their daughters away. There were some nice-looking young women in Italy. They'd say, "Sale! Sale!" They must have been desperately short of salt. We got to know the Italians and we gave them quite a bit of food—cheese and bully beef.... We used to talk to them in broken English and broken Italian.[12]

While recording the reactions of combatants to civilians is important, so is recording the experiences of the civilians themselves. As the twentieth century proceeded, wars were less often fought between countries but instead by different communities within countries. The effect of conflict on civilians has changed as wars have become less about set-piece battles and more guerrilla-like. Narratives from those who actively opposed war, such as conscientious objectors and partisans, illuminate another facet of the experience.

Interviews help us to unpick stereotypes. Prisoners of war, while still in uniform, are also permanently out of action. It was a life where the prisoners outwardly had little control over their lives and, if we grew up watching *Hogan's Heroes* on television, spent all their time organizing escapes. Jim Jackson, a rear gunner on a Lancaster bomber, was shot down over Berlin in 1941. For the rest of the war he was moved around many prisoner of war camps, including Stalag Luft VI at Heydekrug on the Lithuanian-Polish border:

> It was a well-organised camp. Through our whole time as prisoners...there was a chap called Dixie Deans. He was a great organizer, and he fought for us hard. He had a way of getting along with the [Germans] without giving in to them. The Red Cross used to send people round now and then, and the YMCA. He'd be the one who would deal with them. Dixie could always complain to the Red Cross people over treatment. He seemed to have a happy knack of getting on with them and saving us a little bit.
>
> We played a lot of sport [at Heydekrug], which was good. I used to play everything that was going. One school of thought was that you should save your energy and lie on your bed all day, but we thought we'd be better off playing. Even when we played a rugby match, we'd only play ten minutes each way. It kept us fit. I think it saved us, at the end of the day.[13]

Jim's interview tells us that there were checks on the behavior of those in charge of the prisoner of war camps, although others interviewed recounted the very different experiences of those taken prisoner by the Japanese, whose government had not signed the 1929 Geneva Convention Relative to the Treatment of Prisoners of War. Jim's information about playing sports reminds us of the continuation of everyday activities even in the most extraordinary circumstances.

As the extracts from Jim Jackson and Tini Glover show, interviews with veterans are an excellent way of inquiring about the myths and stereotypes that may have grown up around a particular unit or particular experience of war. The New Zealand Division had the reputation of being very egalitarian, where men and officers mingled, first names were frequently used, and saluting an officer was an exception rather than a rule. An almost certainly apocryphal story about Gen. Bernard Freyberg, the officer in command of the Second New Zealand Expeditionary Force during the Second World War, runs that he was in a jeep with a British officer in North Africa when they drove past a group of New Zealand soldiers. "Those men did not salute," remarked the British officer. "I find that if you wave at them, they generally wave back," Freyberg replied. This story was told to me many times but closer inquiry revealed, for example, that some officers were sticklers for proper respect, and that officers and men rarely spent time together when on leave. On the other hand, the fact that the story was told so many times reveals interesting insights into how the New Zealanders wanted to present their unit.

Oral history interviews allow us to gain personal insights into the behavior and character of those in command. Watt McEwan was the radio operator for the command vehicle tank of General Freyberg. Watt spent many hours in close contact with Freyberg and was able to offer insights not recorded in more traditional biographies of the man:

> From [Divisional] headquarters before we moved to the start line at Alamein, the general's batman arrived with a bottle of whisky, a bottle of brandy and a bottle of gin, which we very carefully tucked up in the ration box, very well protected. At one stage during the battle, just after quite a successful action, George [the tank driver] suggested to the general that it would be a good opportunity to sample one of these. The general explained to him that they were for emergencies only. George suggested that not only was this an emergency but this was a little celebration because we'd given the Jerries a good bloody nose at that stage. So the general agreed, but the first person that he said got the drink was me, because I was still in the tank. He was outside—you'd think he'd have forgotten all about me.

War is the most violent way of dealing with conflict, and interviews with those involved must reflect this facet of it. Tini Glover remembered fighting in Italy around Florence:

> We got a call that Tiger tanks were seen on the ridge and one of our platoons was in difficulty. They were pinned down and we had to go up and get them. I saw a lot of dead bodies on the way up. Our boys. Counted about six of them.
>
> We went up a long, winding hill, and when we got up there our 13 Platoon was there. There were many casualties. The Germans let us through. Three or four of us. Then our platoon sergeant was bringing up our main force and that's when the [Germans] attacked him with a machine gun. Smashed his arms. It was a

> bloody mess. He was lying on the ground, moaning and groaning, and his brother said to me, 'I'm going down to look at Charlie.' I said, 'He's all right. He's a bit over the ridge. He's lying down.' But he went down to pick him up. I thought, if it was my brother, I'd go. He went to pick Charlie up and the next minute a machine gun opened up. I said to Whiro Tibble, "I've got it in my sights, Red." He said, "What the hell are you waiting for?" And I peppered the [haystack] and got that joker. He threw his arms up, and then two jokers crawled out and went running up the hill. One was running as if he had a crook leg, and I shot them both. I'd wondered what it was like to shoot a man. You didn't get pleasure out of it, but satisfaction that you'd done a job.[14]

This is a rich and detailed narrative, which combines a recounting of Tini's role in the events that occurred along with his reflections on mateship, seeing comrades injured, and the archetypal war experience of killing another man.

The experience of war does not end when peace is declared. For some, the psychological effects of their experiences are a continuing blight on their life. Some suffer physical consequences, either long- or short-term. Others, such as Harry Spencer, initially find it very difficult to adapt to the ways of civilian life and the demands of family. Harry explained that he missed the Army life:

> I was one of the boys, and when I came out into civvy life it was completely different.... It took me a long time to put up with my family. I was used to a big crowd of men around me all the time, and then to come home to a quiet house with the family.... I was very easily upset.[15]

Others find something positive in their experiences. Ted Martin-Smith was lucky to be one of these:

> It was [exhausting]—but it was marvellous the way you got carried along on the excitement. I was in quite a lot of action, but I never worried going into action. I was worried after it. Jesus, what the hell did I do that for?! That was the biggest worry—after it had happened. Not while it was happening, because I'd do everything spontaneously. It was a wonderful education for me, to go to war. I found out that everybody wasn't the same, and I found out that a bloke working on the rubbish tins was as good as a doctor. I didn't have that same outlook before the war.[16]

The distance in time that separates the events being discussed and the interview must be acknowledged, and it presents challenges to the researcher. Some things will not be remembered; sometimes narrators will remember nothing other than that an event occurred; sometimes it is as if they are actually reliving the experience. Bill Flint's recollections of his feelings just after he was taken prisoner by German troops in Greece in 1941 are almost incoherent in their immediacy:

> And it was quite touch and go, I think. And the feelings—it was almost indescribable. The horror of it... I don't know what it was, it was just, sort of, angry, sort of, that it happened to—Why me?[17]

Strength of emotion experienced at the time of the event helps to instill vivid memories, and it is often times of extreme personal danger or despair that are remembered in such a way. The way in which other stories are told—their construction and narrative flow, for example—hints that they have been told many times before. They are often perfect anecdotes with a beginning, middle, and end. These are the types of stories told at unit reunions, returned servicemen's clubs, or to family members. Some stories are never told., perhaps because no one has never asked or because the events are too traumatic. The former are often those about day-to-day activities, which seem too mundane to be interesting to others. Great care must be taken when inquiring about the latter, and learning to recognize the behavior that signals distress is important. These signs include long silences, inability to tell a story, and changes in voice and body language, among other things. While it is important to record such memories, it is even more important to make sure that the interviewee is emotionally safe once the interview is completed. An oral history interview is not a therapy session, and unlike a counselor, you will not be available afterwards to console a distraught person.[18]

I have discussed some of the aspects of people's involvement in war that oral historians have sought. As a result, our understanding of the impact of war has become much richer and deeper. We discover that the "misery of war can paradoxically yield some positive outcomes, and how its sorrow can be lightened by certain ordinary, but humanly important, aspects of life."[19] People meet and fall in love during wartime, soldiers organize parties for children in areas that have seen fighting, lifelong friendships are made, and when the conflict has ended, men who have served join together to deliver aid to people in the places where they have fought.

The ongoing effects of war on the narrator's life are often marked. Sometimes these may be psychological or physical consequences, but often they are more subtle. Serving in a war is one of the extremes of experience that a person can undergo even if they have not taken part in front-line action. Settling back into civilian life is not always easy, particularly if the war has become unpopular with the general population or if the participant has been on the defeated side. It is not easy for those they return to, either. Families must resume life with a person they may not have had contact with for extended periods of time and who have often been through experiences, which they cannot or do not wish to share with their loved ones. Interviews that cover life after service, and with family members of servicemen or women, are particularly useful for recording another of the impacts of war on individuals and society.

Commemorating Collective Experience

Commemorating war is often a collective experience. Parades of former servicemen and women on national days that remember war, and memorials, such as tombs of unknown soldiers or national war cenotaphs, all provide a time or place when communities can acknowledge what their citizens have experienced. At such commemorations we tend to be reminded of the participants' sacrifice and of their honorable deeds.

There is nothing wrong with this sort of commemoration—it is a part of building the nation state—but it is a simplistic way of looking at times of conflict. By contextualizing the individual experience in the narrative of war, oral history adds texture to those collective narratives, and as researchers using oral history, we are able to add complexity and richness to people's understanding of the experience of war.

NOTES

1. Alan Roberts, in *Against the Rising Sun: New Zealanders Remember the Pacific War*, ed. Megan Hutching, 240 (Auckland, N.Z.: HarperCollins, 2006). All oral history quotes in this article are from published versions.

2. Roberto Rabel, introduction, in *A Fair Sort of Battering: New Zealanders Remember the Italian Campaign*, ed. Megan Hutching, 21 (Auckland, N.Z.: HarperCollins, 2004).

3. Ibid., 22.

4. Maurice Shadbolt, *Voices Of Gallipoli* (Auckland, N.Z., Hodder and Stoughton, 1988).

5. I later had help with recording the interviews and, for the books, used interviews recorded by other people.

6. The themes were: the Battle of Crete, North African campaign, Italian campaign, the war in the Pacific, the experiences of prisoners of war, and service in uniform at home. Each had an accompanying book, all edited by Megan Hutching: *A Unique Sort of Battle: New Zealanders Remember Crete* (Auckland, N.Z.: HarperCollins, 2001); *The Desert Road: New Zealanders Remember the North African Campaign* (Auckland, N.Z.: HarperCollins, 2005); *A Fair Sort of Battering*; *Against the Rising Sun*; *Inside Stories: New Zealand Prisoners of War Remember* (Auckland, N.Z.: HarperCollins, 2002); *Last Line of Defence: New Zealanders Remember the War at Home* (Auckland, N.Z.: HarperCollins, 2007).

7. Tini Glover, in Hutching, *Fair Sort of Battering*, 256.

8. Ian Johnston, in *The Desert Road: New Zealanders Remember the North African Campaign*, ed. Megan Hutching, 118 (Auckland, N.Z.: HarperCollins, 2005).

9. Roy Coates, in *A Unique Sort of Battle: New Zealanders Remember Crete*, ed. Megan Hutching, 70 (Auckland, N.Z.: HarperCollins, 2001).

10. Clifford Vause in Hutching, *Desert Road*, 83.

11. Ralph Williams, in Hutching, *Against the Rising Sun*, 205.

12. Joseph Bacos, in Hutching, *Fair Sort of Battering*, 76–77.

13. Jim Jackson, in Hutching, *Inside Stories*, 111.

14. Tini Glover, in Hutching, *Fair Sort of Battering*, 251–52.

15. Harry Spencer, in Hutching, *Last Line of Defence*, 68–69.

16. Ted Martin-Smith, in Hutching, *Unique Sort of Battle*, 187.

17. Bill Flint, in Hutching, *Inside Stories*, 69.

18. Alison Parr, "Breaking the Silence: Traumatised War Veterans and Oral History," *Oral History* 35, no. 1 (Spring 2007): 62. See also Parr's *Silent Casualties: New Zealand's Unspoken Legacy of the Second World War* (Auckland, N.Z.: Tandem Press, 1995).

19. Rabel, in Hutching, *Fair Sort of Battering*, 22.

BIBLIOGRAPHY

Hutching, Megan, ed. *Against the Rising Sun: New Zealanders Remember the Pacific War.* Auckland, N.Z.: HarperCollins, 2006.

———. *A Fair Sort of Battering: New Zealanders Remember the Italian Campaign.* Auckland, N.Z.: HarperCollins, 2004.

Parr, Allison. *Silent Casualties: New Zealand's Unspoken Legacy of the Second World War.* Auckland, N.Z.: Tandem Press, 1995.

Shadbolt, Maurice. *Voices of Gallipoli.* Auckland, N.Z.: Hodder and Stoughton, 1988.

CHAPTER 16

CASE STUDY: "ABOVE ALL, WE NEED THE WITNESS": THE ORAL HISTORY OF HOLOCAUST SURVIVORS

JESSICA WIEDERHORN

HOLOCAUST survivor and witness accounts began long before the Second World War ended. Diaries, journals, letters, notes hidden, buried, and stuffed into jars or between floorboards were mostly lost and destroyed, but those that have been recovered express a desperation to tell, to document, to bear witness, and to commemorate. Testimony collection also began throughout Europe during the war and continued in its immediate aftermath, gathered primarily by Jewish volunteers, Jewish institutions, and refugee organizations.[1] By 1948 many thousands of testimonies had been collected: the Committee of Liberated Jews (CHC) had amassed about 2,550 throughout Europe; and the Zydowski Instytut Historyczyny (ZIH) had taken more than 7,000 testimonies from Poland alone. By 1950 the YIVO Institute for Jewish Research in New York had collected more than 1,200 first-person accounts; and by the time it was formally established in 1953, Yad Vashem, the Holocaust Martyrs' and Heroes' Remembrance Authority in Israel, held 15,000 testimonies in its archives.

Together with the countless thousands of testimonies that would be recorded during the next sixty years, these eyewitness accounts would change the face of research and education, not only in the field of Holocaust studies but across academic boundaries.

Survivors needed to let the world know about the unspeakable devastation that had been wreaked upon them, their families, and their way of life; and because the many Jewish committees, commissions, and institutions were encouraging them to do so, thousands recorded their first-person accounts in the immediate postwar years. Although classified in various archives and repositories as "oral histories," they were not recorded on tape, but were either written responses to questionnaires or at best were conversations "transcribed" or summarized by the collecting institutions' staff.

The First Survivor Oral Histories

The first "true" oral histories of survivors and witnesses of the Holocaust were conducted and recorded on a wire recorder by the unlikely figure of David Boder, a psychologist on the faculty of the Illinois Institute of Technology in Chicago. An immigrant from Eastern Europe, Dr. Boder was born in Latvia and educated in Lithuania, Germany, and Russia, conversant in a number of languages that would serve him well. Boder conducted interviews in 1946 in Displaced Persons (DP) camps in France, Switzerland, Italy and Germany.[2] These interviews, ranging from twenty minutes to four hours in length, were deposited in the Library of Congress but not discovered until 1998.

Boder's interviewing methodologies preceded current practices and understanding of trauma and Post Traumatic Stress Disorder (PTSD) and are shocking to the twenty-first-century oral historian. In a 1946 interview with Alexander Gertner, nineteen years old, inarticulate, and not particularly forthcoming but imparting a horrific testimony, Boder thanked him abruptly and tried to conclude the interview. But Gertner said politely, "I would like a few more words..." and proceeded to add, "My Jewish name is Sholom... my mother was née Gonz." It is a heartbreaking moment and to his credit, Boder continued the interview, asking Gertner to spell his mother's maiden name and say more about his family.[3] Today we know, as Lawrence Langer observed, that every survivor's story is defined "not merely by its own survival; but by the destruction of others," and interviewers offer as much opportunity as interviewees need to commemorate those who perished.[4]

The Boder interviews are shocking in other ways as well. The atrocities of the Holocaust were new to the interviewer. He asked witnesses to spell and define *Musselman*, today a familiar concentration camp term for the walking dead who had lost the will to live.[5] He did not know the names of concentration camps that are now in the lexicon of the most inexpert student of the Holocaust. Boder was uninformed and appeared naïve. Yet the Boder interviews, together with the conversations recorded on paper by the volunteers and employees of the Jewish committees in Europe are today acknowledged for their special value, in part because the Nuremberg Trials (1945–49), which could have taken the opportunity to document the Holocaust through survivor testimony, bringing testimony to the foreground of Holocaust history and thus empowering testimony itself, did not do so.

Those who conducted the Nuremberg Trials made a deliberate choice not to use survivor testimony because they thought it did not provide the believability or the steadfast power of other documentation. "While eyewitness and survivor testimony might offer a human dimension to the suffering caused by Nazi atrocity, such testimony...would be vulnerable to charges of hyperbole," especially if the witnesses could be manipulated and confused by defense attorneys.[6]

Except for the testimony that was collected by attorneys for the persecution of war criminals in local trials, which took place throughout Germany, and for the early work of Boder and the Jewish committees, Holocaust survivors remained largely silent and marginalized during the 1950s. Societies and individuals wanted to forget the tragedies of the past and look to the future.

Renewed Interest in Survivor Narratives

Sixteen years after the end of the war, on April 11, 1961, Adolf Eichmann was put on trial in Israel. Unlike the Nuremberg tribunal, this trial was structured around eyewitness accounts. Survivor testimony brought the horrors of the Holocaust to the forefront of history and began the process of "de-marginalizing" their stories. Momentous for many reasons, the trial was particularly meaningful to advocates of personal narratives as legitimate historical and legal evidence. Ordinary people's emotional accounts of traumatic events that had taken place decades before were not dismissed as unreliable and biased in a court of law. "At the heart of this newly recognized identity as survivor was a new function, to be the bearer of history. With the Eichmann trial, the witness becomes an embodiment of memory (*un homme-mémoire*), attesting to the past and the continuing presence of the past."[7]

In the global economic upswing that characterized the 1960s, Holocaust survivors raised their children and were working hard to improve their circumstances and advance their lives, especially those who had emigrated to North America, Israel, and Australia, as well as those in Western Europe. This focus on family, occupation, and assimilation, coupled with the social turmoil of the '60s counterculture, antiwar, civil rights, and feminist movements, swept up and deeply engaged many of the Holocaust survivors. Despite the recognition that survivor testimony gained during the Eichmann trial, public interest in survivors' experiences remained low.

The Diary of Anne Frank, first published in the United States in 1952, had been adapted into a motion picture in 1959 and remade again for television in 1967. Along with films like *The Pawnbroker* (1964), *The Shop on Main Street* (1965), and *Garden of the Finzi-Continis* (1970)—the latter both winners of Best Foreign Film Academy Awards—*Anne Frank* kept the survivor story alive. Two of the most renowned Holocaust memoirs were published in English just as the 1960s began (*Night* by Elie Wiesel and *Survival in Auschwitz* by Primo Levi), but they were not widely read at the time.

Interest in Holocaust survivor narrative saw its beginnings in the late 1970s. It was then that the people who eventually formed the groundbreaking Fortunoff Video Archive for Holocaust Testimonies at Yale began conducting interviews. The television miniseries, *Holocaust*, broadcast in 1978 (on the heels of *Roots*, televised a year earlier to a spectacular response) was a huge success in both the United States and Germany. The *zeitgeist* of the times was such that the ideology of human rights had caught the public imagination, ethnicity was valued, and the politics of identity had arrived. "The idea has taken hold that all lives equally deserve to be told."[8]

Moreover, the survivors, whose average age at the end of the war was in the mid-twenties, had now reached their mid-to-late fifties. Many of them were struggling with children who were intermarrying and losing their Jewish identity. Distressed by these trends, some Jewish leaders invoked the Holocaust itself in an attempt to stem the tide.

> With a diminishing birth rate, an intermarriage rate exceeding 40 percent, Jewish illiteracy gaining ascendance daily—who says the Holocaust is over?...The monster has assumed a different and more benign form...but its evil goal remains unchanged: a *Judenrein* world.[9]

Despite loss of interest in "Jewishness," enrollment in courses on the Holocaust by Jewish students was growing. By 1978 courses were offered at more than seven hundred colleges.[10] The historian Peter Novick contended that in the age of identity politics, Jewish identity in America shifted from religious practice, identification with Israel, or even a sense of ethnic pride, to the Holocaust: "The Holocaust, as virtually the only common denominator of American Jewish identity in the late twentieth century, has filled a need for a consensual symbol."[11]

All of these cultural, political, and demographic forces continued to intensify in the 1980s. William Styron's highly acclaimed and best-selling novel *Sophie's Choice* was published in 1979 and adapted to film in 1982, starring Meryl Streep. In 1985 *Shoah*, the nine-hour documentary made exclusively from first-person testimony by Claude Lanzmann, was broadcast on American public television. It introduced a large portion of the American public to both the Holocaust and survivor testimony, and brought to the fore the issue of Holocaust representationality.[12] In 1986 Elie Wiesel, by now a Nobel laureate, would say in an interview for the new journal *Holocaust and Genocide Studies* that "any survivor has more to say than all historians combined about what happened."[13]

Survivors of the Shoah Visual History Foundation

The 1990s saw a worldwide proliferation of Holocaust centers and institutes for remembrance and research. Many of these institutions began collecting testimony from survivors living in their regions and used the testimonies for their educational and commemorative activities. By 1998, when the Swedish government initiated the Task Force for International Cooperation on Holocaust Education, Commemoration, and Research, and created an international directory, it listed more than one thousand such institutions. On this list of governmental and nongovernmental institutions was the United States Holocaust Memorial Museum in Washington, D.C., which opened its doors to much acclaim and public exposure in 1994.

One year earlier, Steven Spielberg's film *Schindler's List*, had been a spectacular international box office success, and the recipient of seven Academy Awards.[14] This film, along with the events and developments of the previous three decades, set the stage for an organization that would initiate an oral history project of enormously ambitious proportions. *Schindler's List* would inspire Spielberg into embarking on a project of such consequence and provide him with the credential for acceptance into the international community of Holocaust survivors. The film was credible to those who had lived through the atrocities depicted, and it let loose an avalanche of survivors who wanted to tell their stories.

Spielberg founded Survivors of the Shoah Visual History Foundation in Los Angeles in 1994. Tens of thousands of survivors worldwide would be given the chance to testify to their experiences, each story would be preserved on broadcast quality videotape, and a digitized archive of testimonies would be cataloged and made accessible for serious inquiry.[15] Although the response from both the survivor population and the general public was enthusiastic, it was not universally shared by the academic community. For many scholars, the size of the project alone made it suspect; and the speed with which it was launched made it dubious. They considered Spielberg's intent commendable but regarded the complexity of the subject to be beyond the capacity of an institution conceived by a Hollywood director. Geoffrey Hartman, project director of the Fortunoff Video Archive for Holocaust Testimonies at Yale, which at the time housed the largest collection of videotaped interviews (then about 3,000 interviews; now 4,300), said: "We are with a great university that has education and research value.... Until they demonstrate that they have those same values, it would be disastrous if we simply said, 'Let them do it.' "[16]

Nevertheless, the Shoah Foundation succeeded. With the guidance of Holocaust historians, psychologists, and oral historians experienced in interviewing survivors, it launched an outreach program and developed an infrastructure on an international scale. From the beginning, the goal of interviewing Holocaust survivors worldwide in massive numbers was a race against time. The survivor population was aging, and many had died or were deteriorating. A large workforce of interviewers was needed. Interviewer training sessions, three-to-four days in length, were held in twenty-four countries. Interviewers came from a wide range of backgrounds—most commonly educators, psychologists, journalists, graduate students, and historians. Many were children of survivors. I attended a training in Los Angeles in 1995 and worked on the staff until 2001. During the four years of the interviewing phase, this army of more than 2,300 trained interviewers conducted interviews in thirty-two languages, with interviewees in fifty-six different countries.

Perhaps most impressively, the Shoah Foundation did thousands of interviews in the former Soviet Union, where the fall of the Iron Curtain had made outreach to survivors possible for the first time since the war. Many of these survivors still lived in the towns where they had experienced the Holocaust, sometimes in close proximity to those who had been their persecutors. The Foundation worked with local Jewish and survivor groups wherever interviews were conducted, adjusting outreach procedures and interviewing methodology to respond to the cultural needs of specific populations. Since many Eastern European survivors had hidden their Jewish identity after the war, for instance, standard reflective questions about what it means to be Jewish today were omitted from those interviews.

The Shoah Foundation eventually won its struggle for legitimacy in the academy. Its collection of nearly 52,000 testimonies is housed at the University of Southern California in Los Angeles and is part of an interdisciplinary center, the USC Shoah Foundation Institute for Visual History and Education. The collection is distributed to university libraries and museums around the world, including the Fortunoff Video Archive at Yale. As part of Spielberg's original vision, the interviews were not transcribed, compelling researchers to go directly to the digitized video interviews themselves. Distinguished by sophisticated technology in every aspect of the undertaking, the Shoah Foundation's patented system for cataloging and indexing its 100,000 hours-plus of testimony is a twenty-first-century model research tool. Using a thesaurus of more than 50,000 keywords, indexers divided each testimony into segments, and assigned keywords to each segment.[17] This process of "bookmarking" important events and ideas enables scholars to more easily find specific information in the vast archive.

The Shoah Foundation's struggle for legitimacy, for a sense of identity as an institution, for acceptance of the historic worth of its collection of interviews, and even for its academic dignity, has not been uncommon in the field of oral history and can be seen as reflective of the very history of the field itself. The need and desire to rush to document the experiences of "those who were there" before it's too late is how many oral history projects begin. Their architects only stumble upon the theoretical issues inherent in the endeavor later, when those issues cannot be avoided and after it has become apparent that there is little that is self-evident, direct, or unmediated in the process of producing oral histories of "eyewitness" accounts. In her book *The Era of the Witness*, Annette Wieviorka wrote:

> In principle, testimonies demonstrate that every individual, every life, every experience of the Holocaust is irreducibly unique. But they demonstrate this

> uniqueness using the language of the time in which they are delivered and in response to questions and expectations motivated by political and ideological concerns.[18]

Personal, subjective memories—decades old and trauma-infused—are now finding legitimacy and acceptance even by the most objectively inclined historian. Inaccuracies and distortion of "fact" no longer invalidate survivors' accounts of Holocaust events. History and memory "are no longer considered rivals," Aleida Assmann has written.[19] "With the acknowledgment of personal voices and their inclusion in historiography, as, for instance, exemplified by the Holocaust survivor and historian Saul Friedländer in his book on Jews in Nazi Germany (1997), the clear-cut borderlines between 'factual history' and 'remembered past' becomes to some extent permeable."[20]

More than six decades have passed since the first survivors of the Holocaust told their stories. The Shoah Foundation's interviews with people reaching the end of their lives, for the most part in their seventies and eighties, constitute the great bulk of the last interviews with survivors of the Holocaust. These videotaped interviews, together with the oral and written testimony collected throughout the world since 1945, comprise the "largest collection of testimony ever gathered about one specific event in history."[21] In addition to the more than 100,000 testimonies collected by large projects, smaller local projects at historical societies, temples, and other community organizations have interviewed thousands more.[22]

This huge number of Holocaust survivor testimonies offers unique opportunities for understanding the many facets of the oral history enterprise. It is the largest collection of oral histories on a single subject, and because these interviews have been conducted over the course of six decades throughout changing times and over great distances, there is much we can learn. We can compare testimonies taken at different points in time, in different cultures, in different languages, and at different phases in the life cycle. Some survivors were interviewed more than once for different projects, enabling us to compare one individual's testimony given to different interviewers, sometimes separated by decades. In its early days, the Shoah Foundation was criticized for "redoing" what others had already done by interviewing survivors who wanted to be part of "Spielberg's Project." Now we can appreciate the extraordinary value of these "repeat performances." Rita Horváth, a Research Fellow at Yad Vashem in 2005–6, wrote:

> By comparing the guidelines and actual testimonies it is possible to analyze the different underlying historiographic assumptions, research methods and aims that govern the collection of testimonies. The novelty of this approach lies in the attempt to assess the dynamic interrelationship of the changes in the conception of history on the one hand, and the changes in the notions of witnessing on the other–all of which occurred as a consequence of the Holocaust.[23]

Researchers who study trauma and memory are finding a wealth of material in these interviews, which demonstrate how enduring trauma can be, and how it can be triggered by the commonplace, like an association with a smell, as well as singular and frightening events, like those of 9/11. The "most pervasive finding about memory for atrocity is its extraordinary persistence."[24] Scholars who study narrative structures can find patterns of narrative that illustrate the power of storytelling genres. Even in the telling of the Holocaust experience, "the interviews often strive to fit into the genre expected of them."[25] We can contrast Eastern European testimonies to American testimonies, which tend to follow the cultural standard of a happy ending: narratives that adhere "to a formula that begins in trauma, atrocity, and loss and that ends in healing, hope, and redemption."[26] Those studying issues related to witnessing can study all facets of the subject, from the victim as witness to the interviewer as witness.[27]

Documentation, Commemoration, and Pedagogy

Oral historians interested in the interaction between interviewer and interviewee will find tensions between documentation and commemoration from the earliest interviews to the most recent. While interviewers strive for precision, thoroughness, and historical relevance, survivors may value the interview as a memorial to family and friends. In fact, they may need *not* to remember certain experiences. What can the interviewer pursue and how can one know when to draw back?

> But can the historian, when face to face with a living person, act morally as a "memory critic"? The suffering conveyed by the story of a survivor–by one who may be the last repository of an entire procession of the dead whose memory he or she carries with him or her—paralyzes the historian. The historian knows that all life stories are constructions but also that these (re)constructions are the very armature, the vertebral column, of life in the present.[28]

Many of these interviewing issues are universal to the practice of oral history. All living primary sources require a sensitivity not needed for other modes of research. But testimony in all its forms has played a central and transformative role in the historiography of the Holocaust, and survivor testimonies have become a model for conducting the oral history of atrocity. Today, the Shoah Foundation is one of numerous Holocaust institutions involved in documenting genocide in Rwanda and Darfur through oral history.

Holocaust oral history continues to break new pedagogical ground. The teaching of Holocaust history has been infused with the oral histories of survivors and other witnesses, bringing deeper awareness and understanding to students worldwide through their contact with individual voices—and faces. Teachers and students have found that one way to understand immense events usually deemed "incomprehensible" is to study them through individual stories of loss and survival. These stories can be riveting and unforgettable and—in alliance with more traditional documentation—incomparable educational tools.

The borders of scholarship continue to broaden. Academia is learning to value emotional truth and to acknowledge the implicit subjectivity of "pure fact." The choice to videotape interviews with survivors of the Holocaust, along with the indexing technology developed by the Shoah Foundation for researching the videotaped interviews—not the transcripts—assures that a direct human encounter will be had by researchers. The more accustomed scholars and students grow to such encounters, the more the practice of oral history becomes an essential, expected component of learning, not just about the Holocaust but about a wide range of subjects, enriching historical scholarship and narrative with new depth and complexity.

NOTES

Title quotation: Yehuda Bauer, *Rethinking the Holocaust* (New Haven, Conn.: Yale University Press, 2002), 23.

1. Some of these organizations include the Weiner Library in London, the Centre de Documentation Juive Contemporaine, established in Grenoble in 1943; the volunteer-run Jewish Historical Commission founded in Lublin in 1944 (to become the Zydowski Instytut Historyczyny (ZIH) in 1947); the National Relief Committee for Deportees in Hungary (DEGOB), established in Budapest in 1945; and the Committee of Liberated Jews (CHC) founded in the American Occupation Zone in Munich of 1945. In Palestine, Vaad Hatzala and the Jewish Congress collected testimonies, as did the World Jewish Congress and the YIVO Institute for Jewish Research in New York.

2. Seventy of Boder's 109 interviews are translated and transcribed, and available to read online at: http://voices.iit.edu/index.html.

3. Alexander Gertner, interviewed by David Boder, Aug. 26, 1946, Geneva, Switzerland. Transcript of Spools 77, 78, and 79, http://voices.iit.edu/index.html.

4. Lawrence L. Langer, *Holocaust Testimonies: The Ruins of Memory* (New Haven, Conn.: Yale University Press, 1993), 16.

5. Adam Krakowski, interviewed by David Boder, July 30, 1946, Paris, France. Transcript of Spool 5A, http://voices.iit.edu/index.html.

6. Lawrence Douglas, *The Memory of Judgment: Making Law and History in the Trials of the Holocaust* (New Haven, Conn.: Yale University Press, 2005), 18.

7. Annette Wieviorka, "The Witness in History," *Poetics Today* 27, no. 2 (Summer 2006): 391.

8. Frédéric Gaussen, "Le goût pour les récits de vie," *Le Monde*, Feb. 14, 1982 (as quoted by Wieviorka in "Witness in History," 391).

9. Norman Lamm, president of Yeshiva University, quoted by Peter Novick, *The Holocaust in American Life* (New York: HoughtonMifflin Harcourt, 1999), 185.

10. Ibid., 188.

11. Ibid., 7.

12. See Shoshana Felman and Dori Laub, MD, *Testimony: Crises of Witnessing in Literature, Psychoanalysis and History* (New York: Routledge, 1992); Saul Friedländer, ed.,

Probing the Limits of Representation: Nazism and the "Final Solution" (Cambridge, Mass.: Harvard University Press, 1992); Geoffrey Hartman, ed., *Holocaust Remembrance: The Shapes of the Past* (Oxford: Blackwell, 1994); Geoffrey Hartman, *Scars of the Spirit: The Struggle Against Inauthenticity*. (New York: Palgrave Macmillan, 2002); Marianne Hirsch and Irene Kacandes, eds., *Teaching the Representation of the Holocaust* (New York: The Modern Language Association of America, 2004); and Dominick LaCapra, *History and Memory After Auschwitz* (Ithaca, N.Y.: Cornell University Press, 1998).

13. Harry J. Cargas, "An Interview with Elie Wiesel," *Holocaust and Genocide Studies* 1 (1986):5.

14. The film's television premiere was seen in 65 million homes in 1997, one of the largest audiences in the history of American television.

15. Although the vast majority (about 90 percent) of the Shoah Foundation's interviews are with Jewish survivors, the Foundation also interviewed homosexual survivors, Jehovah's Witness survivors, liberators and liberation witnesses, political prisoners, rescuers and aid providers, Sinti and Roma (Gypsy) survivors, survivors of eugenics policies, and war crimes trials participants.

16. Laura Shapiro, "Race Against Time: Holocaust Survivors Tell Their Own Stories," *Newsweek*, Nov. 21, 1994, 98.

17. "Indexing is the process of watching each testimony and digitally attaching keywords (people, places, events, ideas) to moments in the testimony. For example, when a survivor shares the story of a Passover celebration in Krakow in 1932, the keywords 'Passover,' 'Customs and Observances, Jewish,' 'Krakow (Poland),' 'Poland [1926–1935]' are all attached to the video's timecode for that story." Shoah Foundation Newsletter, *PastForward* (Summer 2003), 12.

18. Annette Wieviorka, *The Era of the Witness*, trans. Jared Stark (Ithaca, N.Y.: Cornell University Press 2006), xii.

19. Aleida Assmann, "History, Memory and the Genre of Testimony," *Poetics Today* 27, no. 2 (Summer 2006): 263.

20. Ibid., 263.

21. Tony Kushner, "Holocaust Testimony, Ethics, and the Problem of Representation," *Poetics Today* 27, no. 2 (Summer 2006): 275.

22. The USHMM collections contain more than 9,000 audio and video interviews; Yad Vashem's archive houses 44,000 audio, video, and written testimonies; the Shoah Foundation has 52,000; and Fortunoff has completed 4,300 interviews. The USHMM lists 139 local projects that have contributed testimonies to its archive.

23. Rita Horváth, "'On Comparing Jewish Survivors' Testimonies taken by the National Relief Committee for Deportees in Hungary and Other Large-Scale Historical-Memorial Projects of She'erit Hapletah in the Immediate Aftermath of the Holocaust (1945–1948)," *Institute News* (Yad Vashem International Institute for Holocaust Research) 8, no. 2 http://www1.yadvashem.org.il/about_yad/departments/institute/Dr_Ritahtml.html

24. Robert N. Kraft, "Archival Memory: Representations of the Holocaust in Oral Testimony," *Poetics Today* 27, no. 2 (Summer 2006): 315. I gratefully acknowledge the valuable resource of this special issue of *Poetics Today* focused on Holocaust oral history.

25. Kushner, "Holocaust Testimony," 285.

26. Walter Reich, "Unwelcome Narratives: Listening to Suppressed Themes in American Holocaust Testimonies," *Poetics Today* 27, no. 2 (Summer 2006): 466.

27. See Assmann, "History, Memory, and the Genre of Testimony": "Victim and witness are no longer separated but, rather, two aspects of the same person in the case of the Holocaust survivor" (267). Avishai Margalit, in *The Ethics of Memory* (Cambridge,

Mass.: Harvard University Press, 2002), "introduced the term 'moral witness' to distinguish the witness who actually suffered persecution from other witnesses who are bystanders or professional reporters. Suffering and secondary witnessing, so categorically divided in the case of the religious and secular witness, merge in the Holocaust witness" (Assmann, 269).

28. Wieviorka, *Era of the Witness*, 395.

BIBLIOGRAPHY

Douglas, Lawrence. *The Memory of Judgment: Making Law and History in the Trials of the Holocaust.* New Haven, Conn.: Yale University Press, 2005.

Hartmann, Geoffrey, ed. *Holocaust Remembrance: The Shapes of the Past.* Oxford: Blackwell, 1994.

LaCapra, Dominick. *History and Memory after Auschwitz.* Ithaca, N.Y.: Cornell University Press, 1998.

Langer, Lawrence L. *Holocaust Testimonies: The Ruins of Memory.* New Haven, Conn.: Yale University Press, 1993.

Novick, Peter. *The Holocaust in American Life.* New York: Houghton Mifflin Harcourt, 1999.

Wieviorka, Annette. *The Era of the Witness.* Translated by Jared Stark. Ithaca, N.Y.: Cornell University Press, 2006.

CHAPTER 17

CASE STUDY: FIELD NOTES ON CATASTROPHE: REFLECTIONS ON THE SEPTEMBER 11, 2001, ORAL HISTORY MEMORY AND NARRATIVE PROJECT

MARY MARSHALL CLARK

> My familiarity with oral history tells me that oral historians often engage persons or groups that have either been exposed to traumatic events or bear the marks of traumatization. Consequently, oral historians have already contributed much to addressing the traumas of political violence, even if it hasn't been specifically framed as such.
>
> —Stevan Weine, Psychiatrist

THE collection of nearly four hundred oral histories in New York City during the year following the terrorist attacks of September 11, 2001, gave interviewers at the Columbia Oral History Research Office opportunities to witness the process of meaning-making through the creation of stories of those who survived the events and their aftermaths. The purpose of this case study is twofold: to explore the natural capacity of oral history, an ethical practice, for supporting the active process of historical remembrance even in its most nascent stages; and to use the September 11, 2001, Oral History Narrative and Memory Project as a means of defining a possible approach to documenting historical trauma through oral history.

As we turn from one century to another, and reflect upon the rise of oral history in the public imagination and the popular media, it is important to remember that the serious purpose of oral history—to explore the boundaries of memory, trauma, and suffering—has also expanded with the development of oral history as an interdisciplinary field and professional practice. The growth of oral history along these lines coincides with a global question of how to interpret the catastrophic events we are exposed to on a daily basis through the mass media, but rarely have the opportunity to respond to directly. The place of oral history in documenting the political aftermath of traumatic events in the present is increasingly relevant to the task of understanding the collective experience of catastrophe in human terms, and preparing for a historical accounting that takes place later. But as the psychiatrist Stevan Weine has suggested, oral history's greatest value in the historical present may be that it supports the process of meaning-making for those who live through traumatic events, as well documenting that process for professionals who are responsible for understanding the multiple dimensions of crises in catastrophe's wake.

Weine called this a necessary contribution, suggesting that it is more necessary than oral historians recognize: "Necessary because trauma mental health, which has lots of experience working with those persons who might give oral histories, nonetheless has problems relating to survivor stories.... This is of concern because there are many who would agree that the very idea of trauma is that it can overwhelm, disrupt, distort our storytelling capacities, which is an essential part of our humaneness, and a necessary element in engaging history's nightmare."[1]

TRAUMA ORAL HISTORY

Psychologists who study the impact of massive catastrophic events, from genocide and war to natural catastrophes, define this range of work as "trauma mental health." The importance of making this definition clear is that psychological and physiological trauma events produce very specific emotional, mental, and psychological responses in people who have suffered through them as well as those who listen to their stories. Just as psychologists and human rights workers are trained to respond sensitively to people who have suffered trauma, oral historians working in the aftermath of traumatic events should be encouraged to refine their understanding of their work in the realm of trauma. This genre of oral history work, valuable not only to oral historians but to psychologists, social workers, historians, human rights workers, and others working in the aftermath of trauma, might be referred to as "trauma oral history," defined as a highly focused form of the natural capacity of oral history to support meaning-making on multiple levels of subjectivity in post-traumatic contexts.

Oral history has demonstrated its value in recording traumatic and catastrophic events, whether natural or human-made. As I wrote in 2005 while preparing a report on our activities to the *New York Times* Foundation, I believe that there is an emerging genre of oral history whose purpose is to document catastrophic and traumatic events for the sake of all concerned. This genre of telling and listening in cases where the media and government have a stake in defining public meaning is especially important. It investigates the "silences" that oral historians often write about decades later as they try to recover the conversations—from the vantage point of memory—that took place on street corners, in private places, in public protests, or in spontaneous memorials. The commemorative and historical value of oral history is that we have a chance to influence the development of public meaning both immediately and over time:

> Oral history is in its purest sense dialogue; and dialogue is the basis of all human relations and therefore the most ancient and precious art we possess. Storytellers who live to tell sometimes also tell to live. That is, they tell for a purpose, as they are conscious they have witnessed tremendously influential historical events. As interpreters of these events, they are the most reliable witnesses we can have, even where their testimony (centered on meaning and subjectivity) may differ from highly factual accounts. They are the first bearers of a social and potentially collective memory, those who can construct a narrative that will testify to the event's meaning over time. There is a long tradition of witnessing that involves the courage of some to speak publicly about the meaning of what they have lived through so that all might understand. In the wake of a catastrophe, when meaning itself seems to have been destroyed, to perform the act of witness is a courageous attempt to make sense of that which is incomprehensible.
>
> For witnesses to catastrophe to take up this task of speaking to the public is to become active in the process of defining the meaning of the event, in a process of commemorating experience that is communal in nature, constructive in form and permanent in essence. This process of telling for the sake of creating a collective memory leads to the concept of historic witness, which brings together the ancient traditions of testimony and the professional concerns of oral history in the task of preserving a memory that might otherwise be lost.[2]

This approach to oral history allows us to see that those who are traditionally portrayed as "victims" of catastrophe are, in fact, history's agents who define for the rest of us the multiple ways in which history is experienced and read. For oral historians—the second witnesses to historic and traumatic events—the challenge is to use the innately supportive and professional context of oral history to facilitate the active process of remembrance.

While we had many intellectual reasons for documenting the histories we did, we also acknowledged that our work was commemorative in nature, as reflected in these goals:

To honor the experiences of those who have been directly traumatized through listening and observing them in a way that gives them the full status of a historical witness

To support those who have lived through catastrophe to describe it for themselves

To support those who have lived through catastrophe to interpret it for themselves

To support those who have lived through catastrophe to participate in the shaping of public memory through commemoration as well as interpretation.

The September 11, 2001, Oral History Narrative and Memory Project

A week after the terrorist attacks, the sociologist Peter Bearman and I began to construct a large, longitudinal oral history of the September 11 events and their aftermath. Our purpose was to take life stories from a large, and diverse, range of individuals who lived in New York City and its environs, all of whom who had very different levels of proximity to the events, as well as to consider the aftermath of 9/11 in Muslim, Latino, and immigrant communities. We were interested in how this national and global event would be interpreted in diverse communities over time, and interviewed over 400 people in the first year of our work, which began within weeks after 9/11. We re-interviewed 202 people beginning eighteen months after the catastrophe.

Although we did not define trauma as a focus of our work, because of the broad diversity of our outreach, the immediate proximity to the events themselves and the anti-immigrant, anti-Muslim, and anti-Arab backlash after the events, we encountered trauma on multiple levels in many of those we interviewed. These included challenges to meaning-making on the collective sphere, the nation, or city; the cultural sphere, in relation to community identity; the institutional sphere, work, or religious affiliation; and the personal sphere, including family, friendship networks, and home. The project responded to the complex challenges posed by working during and after the catastrophe through relying on the implicit promise of oral history to document multiple levels of suffering through life-history interviewing.

Working in the Immediate Context of Trauma, 2001–2002: Phase One

Because we initially planned to interview three hundred to four hundred people during the first year of our work, and return to some of those in later phases of interviewing, we chose to work with thirty interviewers, thus reducing the number of interviews each person would have to complete. The interviewers were assigned to interview people in order to explore how the themes of nationalism and war, highlighted by the government and the mass media, entered their own life stories and accounts of the events as they affected their work, their families, their communities, and their friendship networks.

While trauma was itself not an explicit theme or category of our work in the first year, we were immediately confronted with the challenge of how to listen to stories of extreme trauma. It is important to note that while we did not focus on trauma and its meaning explicitly in the first year of our work, we did give those we interviewed lists of trauma service providers and offered to work with them to find free or low-cost services.

The stories we gathered from those in downtown Manhattan the morning of 9/11 were more often than not highly intimate, gruesome, and raw. Their graphic quality far exceeded any representation offered in the media, which was focused either on those who died or on reporter eyewitness accounts. The traumatic content of the interviews was deeply affecting. Many of those we interviewed, who were in a six-block radius of the towers, could not stop talking about people jumping from the buildings, stories that were muted in the media until much later.[3] Second, our work in immigrant, Muslim, Latino, and refugee communities revealed shocking accounts of government intrusion in the lives of ordinary people, as well as accounts of civilian violence. These levels of trauma were tragically combined in those who experienced both the terrorist attack itself and the backlash against the "other" in the aftermath.

A conversation with Stevan Weine in October 2001 confirmed what I had suspected by late September when we had been in the field for two weeks. The role that oral historians might play was tremendously important. Unlike psychologists, we were not there to diagnose or treat people, or tell them whether they would suffer from post-traumatic stress disorder (PTSD). As oral historians our primary agenda was to listen to the full scope of what they had lived through and witnessed, with no greater agenda than to hear their life story.[4] Giving permanence to this act of witness was our plan to archive their memories and make them available to generations of students, scholars, and the public at large. As a result, unlike psychologists, we had no trouble finding people to talk with us. In fact, the response was overwhelming.

Our decision to work with a cohort of thirty interviewers benefited the project in multiple ways. It reduced the amount of trauma exposure for any one individual, and provided a community structure through which the project could grow, intellectually and methodologically. Since it was unclear how the aftermath of 9/11 would play out, and since our knowledge of its impact was constantly unfolding, Peter and I held optional weekly meetings for the interviewers. We were surprised that all the interviewers regularly attended and that the meetings often lasted for three to four hours. While we thought of the meetings as a time for information sharing and strategic planning, we quickly realized that the meetings functioned on a much deeper level. For the interviewers it was a crucial opportunity to re-tell the stories they had heard, in a supportive context, and to work with each other to devise questions and strategies for handling the trauma they were experiencing in their narrators and in themselves.

Not having immediate funding for transcriptions of the interviews, while frustrating, turned out to benefit the group process. To understand what was happening in the field, Peter and I had to listen to at least fifteen hours of interview recordings each week prior to the meetings. This allowed us to experience the secondary effect of trauma on the interviewers far more effectively than if we had read transcriptions of the voice. In an indirect way, we gained an intimate exposure to the realities the interviewers were facing, and of the scope of the catastrophe itself.

Moreover, since we had no special training or expertise in trauma on how to run groups, Peter and I simply listened to the interviewers and spoke only when asked to make an intervention. In reaction to our admiration for the interviewers' work and personal courage, we conveyed our respect by staying silent while the group members retold the stories they had heard. In retrospect, we were mirroring the oral history process to the oral historians by acting as their witnesses.[5]

This "lack of structure," or perhaps, organic and nonhierarchical structure, was in fact the most important structure we could provide, as we later heard from the interviewers in the project.

Working in the Aftermath of Trauma, 2002–2003: Phase Two

By 2002, without being conscious of it we had created one of the largest archives in the United States on a mass disaster, and realized that trauma had become an intellectual category of our work. In the second phase of our work, we returned to 202 narrators we had interviewed in phase one. By then, fieldwork conditions, interviewer communication, and the sense of purpose about the project as a whole had changed. We were more distant from the catastrophe, less connected to the interviewers and the narrators, and the use of 9/11 as a political and moral rationale for instigating a war in Iraq had led to a political depression for many New Yorkers. It was also clear that our interviewers, many of whom had experienced the catastrophe themselves, needed more of an outlet for the trauma they were accumulating than the group could provide. While not trained in psychology, I could recognize the signs of what psychologists refer to as secondary trauma. Some of the interviewers were unable to sleep, took on the physical symptoms of those they interviewed, or showed other signs of acute stress.

For these reasons, I asked a close colleague at New York University to recommend a psychologist who understood trauma from a research perspective, but who was also clinically trained. Dr. Marylene Cloitre, who had just moved to New York University from the Cornell Medical Center, came highly recommended. In addition to being a trauma researcher, she had run a trauma unit at Cornell and had brought with her a team of talented clinicians. She found funding from the *New York Times* Foundation to work with us to provide up to sixteen free counseling sessions for the narrators as well as the interviewers. In addition, she was interested in the constructive potential of oral history to mitigate the pernicious effects of PTSD by facilitating the integration of the trauma story within the life story.

Marylene Cloitre was extremely helpful to the project, but some of the interviewers initially resisted having her and the other psychologists present twice a month at our weekly meetings.[6] While she was careful to play only a supportive role, and did not take part in defining the intellectual goals of the second phase, there was confusion about her presence, amplified by concerns about how the follow-up interviews should be conducted. While few questions had been needed in the first phase of our work, the interviewers were unclear about how to return to the narrators in the second round. This meant that I had to take a more authoritative role in directing the project, altering the organic way in which the group had previously functioned.

My decision to approach the second round of interviews by asking, "How have you been since we last met?" was frightening to some of the interviewers because of its purely subjective nature. On the other hand, those interviewers who could tolerate it quickly saw that it worked well as a strategy to re-enter the life history before approaching the trauma history. While the tensions in the group took some time to settle, the interviews in the second round were an evident success. While not as dramatic, compelling, or riveting to read as the first set of interviews, the second recordings are filled with nuanced accounts of how people struggled to re-enter their work lives, reconnect with their families, and the ways they negotiated: the tremendous pressures on them to account for the public meaning of 9/11 on purely political levels. The narrators felt free to traverse the personal, social, political, and collective spheres of meaning-making with leisure because we did not impose a structure, or an agenda, on the interviews.

The psychologists' presence, while not immediately visible, made us feel confident in exploring the subjective and subtle effects of 9/11 by opening the interviews up into a wider format. As Dr. Cloitre and others helped us see, giving the narrators the freedom to create their own ways of telling was appropriate for those who suffered multiple levels of violence in which the structuring of prior beliefs and personal understandings had been destroyed. Having the services of excellent clinicians we knew and trusted was critically valuable in the few instances when narrators reporting extreme suffering and requested professional support.

As many of the narrators told us as we compiled their reviewed and edited transcripts for submission into the Columbia archive, the opportunity to record their reminiscences for future generations gave them a sense that their reflections were a significant contribution to how the events and aftermath of September 11 would be remembered. This recognition, reinforced by the ways in which we recognized our narrators as agents rather than victims, mitigated against their often powerful fear that their experiences would be forgotten or misunderstood.

Reflections

The project convinced us that oral history methodology is a meaningful and effective tool for recording the myriad ways in which catastrophe and disaster disrupt meaning in personal, social, cultural, and institutional networks. Many of us who lived in New York City during and after the terrorist attacks of 2001 recognized the essential "humanness" of storytelling that Stevan Weine wrote about as part of the *natural* response to catastrophe. Oral history facilitates the accumulation of meaning by extending this natural process into the documentary realm. Catastrophe imposes silence and isolates its victims. Oral history invites those who have suffered catastrophe to explore the contours of silences that cannot be spoken, and to bring words to experiences that can be named and shared.

Trauma oral history relies, most of all, on the personal and interpersonal abilities of the interviewer to elicit, hold, and pass along the knowledge gained in the interview. This highly sophisticated form of communication requires special qualities among interviewers, the most important of which are:

1. the ability to connect viscerally and emotionally with the narrator;
2. the ability to create an environment of neutral and supportive listening in which any experience, no matter how graphic or harrowing, can be conveyed and absorbed without the interviewer demonstrating excess emotion;
3. the ability to convey concern without being intrusive or over-identifying with the narrator's experience of the event or life situation;
4. the ability to acknowledge the connections narrators make between their life experiences and the experiences of others, widening the circle of meaning beyond the interview;
5. the ability to engage in critical as well as constructive listening;
6. the ability to suspend the need to fit stories that are fragmented and partial into "coherent" narratives of the catastrophe offered by the media and government;
7. the capacity to convey to the narrator connections that they have made that are not yet visible to them, in the form of responsive questions, without causing an interruption in the narrative flow;

8. the ability to ask questions in a way that yields explanations and explanatory stories. Explanatory stories lead to theories about causes as well as to the process of interpreting the meaning of events and are extremely important for those who have experienced trauma.
9. the ability to shift back and forth within the interview between alternative and often contradictory explanations offered by narrators, as they often reflect the contradictions of experience as a byproduct of the experience of catastrophe.

This interplay between connection and analysis, ideally present in all oral history interviews, is vital for those who have lived through violent trauma as the balance between emotional, subjective, and communal memory and chronological, historical memory has been disrupted by the extreme impact of the event on the human mind. Evidence of this split was present in the fractured ways that stories were told, and also evoked by the almost universal use of the word "surreal" to describe what happened. Part of the task of trauma oral history is to recognize this imbalance and to support the narrator in restoring a sense of order in the *telling* of their life narrative, even when it is a story that is marked by fragments and distortions. As Wendy Rickard has written, "Oral history offers the possibility of affirming and destabilizing a personal narrative."[7] Through the exploration of the links between violence, suffering and memory, those who conducted interviews for the September 11, 2001, Oral History Narrative and Memory Project learned that through respecting the ethical and professional requirements of trauma oral history, the risks of destabilization can be minimized for both interviewers and narrators.

The goal of any contemporary oral history project that is focused on catastrophic trauma is to create permanent archive respecting both memory and history. A prism through which catastrophic events can be consumed and understood over time, the creation of living archives becomes the final objective of an oral history and its most precious act. For it is in this act of preserving memory, and commemorating suffering, that oral history helps individuals, communities, and cultures escape the silence and oblivion that catastrophe—particularly catastrophe caused by political violence—so often creates.

NOTES

1. This presentation, titled "Survivor's Testimonies, Bakhtin's Intuition and a Narrative Vision" was part of a panel, "Memories of Trauma and Resistance" at the 2001 meeting of the Oral History Association, held in St. Louis Missouri, Oct. 17–21, 2001.

2. The Columbia University Oral History Research Office Report to the *New York Times* Foundation, May, 2005, with the inclusion of CU-OHRO special report, "Documenting Catastrophe through Oral History: A Working Guide."

3. The *New York Times* did not print a story on the collective experience of watching people jump from the buildings until April 2002. The U.S. English-language broadcast

media made a decision not to repeat the images of the jumpers they showed immediately after the catastrophe.

4. Dr. Ghislaine Boulanger, a psychoanalyst I interviewed about 9/11 in 2005, talked about the experience of being interviewed by an oral historian in a paper she gave to the Psychoanalytic Division, Division 39, of the American Psychological Association in April 2008. In her paper, "The Continuing and Unfinished Present: Narratives in Psychoanalysis," Dr. Boulanger wrote about the greater degree of freedom she felt in the oral history interview to talk about the range of her life experiences in relation to 9/11 than she might have in a typically structured psychoanalytic session.

5. Dori Laub has described this witnessing to the witnesses as the third level of witnessing.

6. In the end, more of our interviewers accessed NYU's services than did the narrators.

7. Wendy Rickard, "Oral History—'More Dangerous than Therapy'? Interviewees' Reflections on Recording Traumatic or Taboo Issues," *Oral History* 26 (Autumn 1998): 34–43.

BIBLIOGRAPHY

Borradori, Giovanna. *Philosophy in a Time of Terror: Dialogues with Jurgen Habermas and Jacques Derrida*. Chicago: University of Chicago Press, 2003.

Bussey, Marian, and Judith Bula Wise, eds. *Trauma Transformed: An Empowerment Response*. New York: Columbia University Press, 2007.

Greenberg, Judith, ed. *Trauma at Home: After 9/11*. Lincoln: University of Nebraska Press, 2003.

Neal, Arthur G. *National Trauma and Collective Memory: Extraordinary Events in the American Experience*. Armonk, N.Y.: M. E. Sharpe, 2005.

Seeley, Karen. *Therapy after Terror: 9/11, Psychotherapists, and Mental Health*. New York: Cambridge University Press, 2008.

PART IV

THE TECHNOLOGICAL IMPACT

CHAPTER 18

DOING VIDEO ORAL HISTORY

BRIEN R. WILLIAMS

Oral historians once tended to regard the sound recording of interviews as only the *collecting* stage of their enterprise. They considered the transcript as the authoritative document of record. Later, however, aural recordings acquired more authority and began to be seen as a legitimate, if not co-equal, version of the interview. Now, oral historians are steadily adding video recording to their work. What circumstances drove this progression? What are the advantages of video? Does adding video change the nature and scope of interviewing? What practical and technical aspects should oral historians consider when adding video to their work? As an oral historian and video producer/director, I will admit at the outset to being a strong proponent of "videohistory," while acknowledging that the medium is not suited for everyone or for every oral history project.

In a media-driven world, information is increasingly conveyed through visual means rather than via the written word. While predictions of the demise of the written word are hyperbolic, it is clear that more and more information is being conveyed visually through broadcast television, cable channels, the Internet, cell phones, CDs, and DVDs, with the likelihood of even more inventive communication modes to come. If as oral historians we limit our work strictly to sound and transcripts, we also limit its potential dissemination. It seems incumbent on us to evaluate seriously the implications of *not* recording at least a video portion of these interviews in light of the growing demand for visually conveyed information. The advent of low-cost and simple-to-operate video equipment that produces surprisingly high-quality video recordings should make the evolution to video even more enticing.

Video's Advantages

Foremost among the advantages of using video is the increased information obtained even in a simple "talking head" interview. Whole new areas of exploration open with the visual component that aural recordings and text can convey only with difficulty or not at all.

There is more to an interview than spoken words. An interviewee's personality and emotions are conveyed in a transcript only by means of verbal stylistics and word choices. An aural recording conveys more expressiveness through intonation, volume, and audible nonverbal cues, laughter, sighing, and the like. Yet, these expressions are sometimes unclear and can be captured in a transcript only clumsily, and possibly with an editorial slant, by using italics or adding such phrases as "forcefully" or "with a quivering voice" and the like, within brackets. Videotaping reveals physical gestures and facial expressions that can greatly expand on the meaning of the spoken word. A smirk signaling irony accompanying a statement would pass unnoticed in an aural recording, unless noted by an attentive interviewer and indicated in the transcript.

Beyond providing nonverbal information and an indication of an interviewee's emotional being, video images almost inevitably cause viewers to form psychological and emotional responses to the speaker. When meeting people first on the telephone and then encountering them in person, we conjure up mental pictures of the person from the phone conversation, but the face-to-face meeting can cause definite and sometimes very different emotional responses based on a person's appearance and carriage. This phenomenon is universal, profound, and not without implications that we oral historians need to consider.

One might debate the relevance of this experience, especially if the goal is exclusively the accumulation of intellectual information. Then, personal demeanor and attractiveness would seem to have no relevance. If, however, an objective in conducting an oral history is to find out who that person is, then the visual expression of his or her personality will be an integral part of the individual gestalt that we wish to capture.

Video allows for the collection of whole new worlds of information. On the micro scale, a video can show an inventor as he handles an object he has created, pointing to and identifying its parts and explaining their functions. A World War II veteran can show photographs from his military service and identify comrades in arms. A dancer can demonstrate how a particular movement would be made in a classical ballet as opposed to modern dance. On the macro scale, video can show large equipment, whole laboratories, manufacturing plants, artists' studios, and other physical spaces and objects that are germane to the subject of inquiry, all accompanied by an interviewee's expert commentary.

When moving beyond merely shooting talking heads, video production becomes complex and forces changes in the way we normally conduct oral history. Even if our objective is strictly to accumulate information and create a historical record for use by researchers, we must capture visual information clearly (although not necessarily in a highly polished and aesthetically pleasing way). If the footage might be used in the media—in a news story, documentary, or Web site—shots must be of a higher technical and aesthetic order. Video also raises issues of narrativity. How do you structure shots that tell a story visually? Using video involves being aware of and following the principles of filmic language developed by professionals who tell stories visually in a seamless manner. While for the academic record, it might suffice to shoot a whole set of actions in one single shot, zooming in and out to catch details as appropriate, such ad hoc camera movements are not tolerable when shooting for a production. For narrative, the common practice is to shoot the whole process first in a wide "master shot" and then meticulously pick the action apart to record a series of detailed close-ups that will flow smoothly when edited together. "Neutral shots," such as a person looking on, are totally irrelevant for academic purposes, but they may be useful to cover the edit points and shorten time-consuming action.

Using the term "filmic language" reflects how much video production depends on the legacy of film. This does not excuse the frequent use of the term "filming an interview" when, in fact, it is being videotaped! But even the term "videotaping" can be misleading as the industry moves away from tape to other forms of recording media. The principles of filmic language require study to master. An easier and more reliable approach is to hire a professional videographer or director familiar with the language of film to direct the video production.[1]

Guidelines for Doing Videohistory

If you plan to start using video with simple one-on-one talking-head oral history interviews, here are some suggested guidelines:

Equipment

- The equipment needed will include a consumer-grade video camera (a "camcorder") with at least one external microphone input, a camera tripod, and one or more quality microphones.
- While today's cameras produce reasonable pictures using ambient light, projects may need to include some basic lighting equipment. Many videographers use a simple setup: one professional soft light as a "key light," to one side of the interviewee, a small spotlight behind and above the interviewee as a "backlight," and a simple reflecting board opposite the key as a "fill light." Lighting predominantly from one side with a key light will give contour and texture to a person's face. The back light produces a halo effect on the top of the head, which gives the picture a crisp look and separates a person's head from the background.

- Technical innovation and fiercely competitive industry marketing have made a wide range of camcorders available. Besides overall technical quality (usually reflected in price range), the main differences among these camcorders are the recording format and recording medium. At one time, all audio and video recording consisted of analog signals recorded on magnetic tape. Analog has now given way to different digital formats, recording media, and screen shapes. In the absence of universal standards for these new formats, we are forced to make choices, and we will need to convert recordings from older formats to newer ones as older equipment becomes obsolete. Due to the rate of technological change, it is not worthwhile to make equipment recommendations here. The best advice is to follow industry developments and rely on trusted retailers for advice.

Production techniques

- Always mount the camera on a tripod. It is impossible to record an oral history interview while holding a camera steady for any length of time.
- Do not use the camera's built-in microphone, whose sound quality will be poor. Use a lapel microphone (a "lavaliere") or a microphone on a stand that is connected to the camera's external microphone input to record the interviewee's voice. It will not be necessary to provide a microphone for the interviewer, since the interviewee's microphone will record the interviewer's voice well enough to be understood. Some oral historians record sound on both the camera and an audio recorder to insure having at least one audio recording. In my own work, I use two lavaliere microphones attached to an audio recorder. A cable connects the output of the audio recorder to the two microphone inputs on my camera so that the sound of both interviewee and interviewer is recorded on both pieces of equipment.
- Cameras may be equipped with features that are unnecessary for oral history work. If your camera is on a tripod, you will not need to activate a "steady shot" feature. Use the optical zoom on the camera but avoid digital zooming, which diminishes picture clarity. For the same reason, avoid any internal light-boosting features of the camera. Provide enough ambient light to get a good image. Most cameras have an "auto focus" feature, but this should be avoided because it focuses on whatever is in the central portion of the picture. If a person moves out of that central area, the camera will reset the focus on whatever now occupies that space, most commonly the background. Cameras may also have manual overrides of automatic iris settings, shutter speed, and "white balance" (setting the correct rendition of color), which only specialists should use. If the camera features different recording speeds, always chose the fastest speed, even though this means having to make recording media changes periodically. The faster the speed, the higher the recording quality.

- For the two-person interview, the camera should face the interviewee at a distance of about five feet and be placed at the interviewee's eye level. The interviewer should be unseen and sit right beside the camera. (If a project involves interviews with a number of different people, I alternate interviewers from one side to the other of the camera to avoid having all the interviewees looking in the same direction.) A useful way to think of an interview is as an exchange of energies between interviewee and interviewer with the main energy flow occurring along a line between them. Placing the interviewer right beside the camera means the camera will capture the maximum amount of the interviewee's energy and show facial expressions most clearly. The interviewee should talk directly to the interviewer and not to the camera. Making eye contact with the camera interferes with the dynamic between interviewee and interviewer, and breaks one of the conventions of the television interview: interviewees do not talk directly to the camera except under special circumstances.[2]
- I used to shoot interviewees in a tight close-up in order to capture the maximum amount of energy flow. Now I prefer a somewhat looser shot, known as a medium close-up (MCU) extending from the upper chest to just above the top of the head. If you chose this shot and your interviewee doesn't change position a lot, you will probably not have to move the camera at all during the interview.
- Often beginners want to put both interviewer and interviewee together on the screen. This works well when you have more than one camera and can shoot close-ups of both participants. Absent a second camera, however, shooting a "two-shot," as it is called, has two disadvantages. It puts the energy axis between the participants at right angles to the camera so that we see only one side of their faces, and the camera captures little of the energy that passes between them. A two-shot also shrinks them on the screen, and makes their nonverbal cues harder to detect. Although it is tempting to videotape group interviews, it should be avoided unless you are using more than one camera. Trying to shoot a group discussion with one camera is difficult unless you settle on just a static wide shot of the group, which has the same disadvantages as the two-shot.. (A static wide shot, however, is of great value to transcribers for identifying multiple speakers.) If a project has the luxury of more than one camera, standard procedure is to leave one camera on a wide shot covering the whole group, and use the additional camera or cameras to get close-ups of speakers as the discussion flows. Group interviews also present audio challenges. If each participant is miked, a submixer will be needed to combine the audio from multiple microphones for recording on one or two of the camera's audio tracks.
- With dual experience as a camera operator and oral historian, I am able to work the camera and conduct an interview at the same time. With practice this is not all that difficult to do, but without that experience it is safer to hire a cameraperson.

- When hiring professionals for the camera work, make them aware of the differences between doing videohistory and the video production practices they are likely accustomed to following. In standard television production, everything is geared to a specific final product—a program or news story. Videohistory interviews are end-products in themselves. They tend to explore topics at length and are covered in long, continuous shots. In standard production, there is an inclination to record short shots of various types, from extreme close-ups to wide shots, for pacing and dramatic effect. In videohistory, change for change's sake is unnecessary and should be avoided. The production process itself is transparent in standard production. Cameras, microphones, and crew are all hidden from view. In videohistory, there is no need to obscure the production process. At times, there are advantages to witnessing the production process and having people both off- and on-camera communicating with one another.[3]
- Video also has the advantage of placing people in physical environments that are expressive of their personality and interests. Consequently, it is preferable to interview people in their homes or offices where they are likely to be most comfortable. But the location must be quiet. Extraneous sounds that we easily block in real life become more pronounced in a recording and can seriously mar it. For that reason it is advisable to avoid doing interviews outdoors, or even indoor interviews near airports, schools, or fire and police stations. Try to schedule interviews on days when landscapers with their mowers and blowers are less likely to be in a neighborhood.
- Take care in placing interviewees. They should never be directly in front of a window, as daylight will cause them to appear as shadowy silhouettes. At night, reflections on the window will be distracting. Try to remember to cast a critical eye over the camera's picture for visual distractions before beginning an interview. Normally, we often do not see such details, but the picture screen will magnify them. In one interview, I missed seeing a grimy light switch immediately behind the speaker until I reviewed the recording. If not careful, a lampshade will morph into a ridiculous hat on the interviewee; a picture frame at a certain height will appear to pierce a person's head.
- As often happens during the course of an interview, an interviewee makes reference to and picks up an object, such as a photograph, to show the interviewer. It is virtually impossible to get a good shot of these handheld objects on the fly. Concentrate instead on the interviewees during the interview, regardless of what they might want to show. Then go back to shoot that object after the interview is completed. While reshooting, ask the interviewees to repeat their comments. A reliable method of shooting objects, particularly photographs, is to place them, in turn, on a desktop easel. The interviewee and interviewer can sit facing the easel with the camera behind them focusing on the objects. This way, the camera sees exactly what they are talking about as they point out details.

- Many oral historians have expressed concern about the possibly negative impact of video on an interview. They argue that equipment is intimidating, a camera operator is distracting, and that "being on television" makes people self-conscious. Based on my own years of experience, however, I have observed no serious negative effects. It is true that interviewees are aware of the equipment during the setup and are often nervous as the interview begins, but once underway they seem to be oblivious of the video components. Of course, it is essential that a camera operator and anyone else in the room other than the interviewer and interviewee remain quiet and unobtrusive. With a lifetime of watching television interviews, some people may assume a "TV interviewee" persona when being interviewed with cameras. The reality of the recording situation may therefore have bearing on the conduct of the interview, although this might be said of aural-only interviews as well.[4]

Following production, in the days of analog recordings, videohistorians made copies of the original recordings for use and tried to preserve the originals under optimum atmospheric conditions, reserving them for special uses only, such as in documentaries. The same practice should be employed for today's digital recordings: making multiple copies for use and restricting access to the primary copy stored under optimal conditions.

The Video Tour

Video production becomes more complicated when shooting demonstrations, processes, and tours of objects and work spaces. These are the situations that dramatically expand the parameters for doing oral history, but they require the use of television production values that go beyond the simple techniques needed for recording talking heads. The need for clear and informative shots becomes paramount, especially if one's objective is to produce footage of sufficient quality for use in media presentations. At times, this need forces us to deviate from some of oral history's normal practices.

Shooting a wide range of objects—everything from a single piece of equipment to something as large as a manufacturing plant—constitutes a "video tour." A typical first step is to have the interviewee point out and explain the parts of an object or a place with the camera covering in wide shots. Usually, but not always the interviewee will be included in the picture. After an initial tour, go back to reshoot details as clearly as possible. This will usually mean breaking the action up into a series of separate close-ups and moving the camera around to obtain the best angle on what's being shown. The interviewee again identifies and explains what we see and may enter the picture frame to point out components or demonstrate processes. Sometimes, when it is hard to include the interviewees in the picture, have them watch the output of the camera on a monitor and explain "voice-over' (heard but not seen) what the camera is showing. This works particularly well when dealing with large objects. On such a tour, the interviewee may even direct the camera moves.

This technique works well for accumulating visual information for the historical record. When contemplating future media presentations, however, other techniques need to come into play to guarantee high-quality pictures. Shots must be in focus, with no unsteady camera movement. They must convey the pertinent visual information in an unmistakably clear way without any visual distractions. The videohistorian must anticipate how the shots will flow together in an edited program where you are really telling a story. Shooting is still likely to consist of a balance of wide, establishing shots, and detailed close-ups. You must now pay attention to maintaining uniform screen direction among shots because viewers will be confused when a camera's point of view reverses direction. Find shots that will move action along from point to point smoothly since processes are often shortened in edited programming. Pay careful attention to the staging of the action and avoid distractions and unbecoming shots.

You may need to shoot "neutral" or "reaction" shots, such as the close-up of a worker, to cover edit points in a final program. In most cases, we want to record natural sound with these shots without interviewee commentary, although people will be shown going about their work or silently demonstrating actions. Finally, it is necessary to rehearse shots and actions when doing tours. Oral historians put a high value on spontaneity, but the complexity of shooting action accurately and aesthetically makes it is essential to discuss in detail and perhaps rehearse what actions are about to occur before the shooting begins. Expect to repeat actions and shots, too, to achieve perfect visualization.

By the time an oral history occurs, the appearance of a place and its contents have often changed. I found this especially true when recording scientists and inventors who, unlike historians and archivists, generally do not think about preserving objects and places intact, even if they involve important discoveries. It is in their nature to move to the next project, thinking nothing of purloining parts of a revolutionary piece of equipment to construct something new. As a result, we often asked people to re-create the look of a place, such as a scientific laboratory, or to reassemble parts that once made a whole. At times, this can be done only by showing pictures of how things once looked and fit together, and then eliciting reminiscences from interviewees. In projects tracing the history of medical instrumentation, we covered what few original items still existed and then conducted detailed tours showing the manufacture of current versions of the equipment.

On a few occasions, videohistorians have staged enactments. Once, we asked an astronomer to demonstrate his observational techniques in daylight, which he normally did in darkness. He proved to be a masterful actor. Re-creations and enactments, of course, challenge a basic assumption of oral history: that we are collecting historically accurate information. It is reasonable to argue, however, that the video recording itself often makes clear the extent and nature of the manipulation of reality taking place as it shows people being given cues and assuming roles. If there is likely to be any confusion, however, one should state the fact directly on the recording that a re-creation or enactment is taking place.

To sum up, while directing the Smithsonian Institution's Videohistory Program on early African American aviators, I witnessed a poignant exchange between the interviewer, Theodore Robinson, himself a former Tuskegee Airman, and interviewee Janet Harmon Bragg, a pioneer female pilot, who had been denied entrance into the Women's Airforce Service Pilots (WASPs) during World War II because of her race. After studying a video copy of this interview, I attempted to describe within square brackets as best I could the nonverbal expressions that accompanied the narrative in this sequence.

> TED ROBINSON: You made application to join the Women's Air Service Pilots organization. Tell me about that.
>
> JANET HARMON BRAGG: Oh [*pauses, with a resigned smile*], some of these things [*coughs*] really hurt. At the time I was [*smiles*] operating this little flight school, Mr. Johnson and myself. We had several girls, white girls [*raises eyebrows*], who flew my planes and sometimes I would go up with them, you know.
>
> ROBINSON: You, of course, by now had a pilot's license.
>
> BRAGG: Yes. And we would go up. And one day one came to me and said, [*raised eyebrows*] "Janet I brought an application for you for the WASPs." "Yes." She said, "Fill it out and let's see, maybe we can get in." "Fine." I filled it out and sure enough I got a telegram from a Mrs. Sheehy. Mrs. Sheehy roomed down at one of the hotels in Chicago. I went up to the suite of rooms and several of the girls were waiting for me to come in. And I walked in to Mrs. Sheehy's room and she looked up [*raises her eyes skyward imitating*] and said, "Ahhhh!" I told her who I was and she had my application and everything there. And she said, "Oh, no." [*furrows brow feigning consternation and with a strained voice*] She said, "I don't know what to do." I said, [*leaning forward*] "What do you mean you don't know what to do?" She said, "Well, I've never interviewed a colored girl for flying." I said, [*furrows brow*] "Oh, we have plenty of them." [*Laughs*] She said, "I just don't know what to do." And she didn't interview me [*drops head*] or anything. And she told me that I would hear from her.
>
> [*Ironic smile*] About two weeks after that, I did hear from her with the signature of Jacqueline Cochran who was head. And she said, "Whatever Mrs. Sheehy told me still stands." So I was not admitted [*raises eyebrows*] into the WASPs because I was black although I was qualified [*ironic/resigned smile and tilt of the head*].[5]

I strongly feel this excerpt demonstrates what is missing when we do not videotape our interviews and consequently fail to record the nonverbal language that adds such a large extra measure of meaning and humanity to our work.

NOTES

1. For an introduction to video production, the best textbooks are by Herbert Zettl: *Television Production Handbook* (Belmont, Calif.: Wadsworth Cengage Learning, 2009), and *Video Basics* (Belmont, Calif.: Thomson/Wadsworth, 2007).

2. Directly addressing the camera usually occurs only in live interviews when the participants are not in the same location. Under these circumstances, the convention is to have both speak to the camera. This means that they talk to each other through the viewer, a noteworthy psychological phenomenon. For a provocative discussion of television and energy fields, see Herbert Zettl, *Sight, Sound, Motion: Applied Media Aesthetics* (Belmont, Calif.: Thomson/Wadsworth, 2008).

3. For a further discussion of these differences, see Brien Williams, "Recording Videohistory: A Perspective," in *A Practical Introduction to Videohistory: The Smithsonian Institution and Alfred P. Sloan Foundation Experiment*, ed. Terri A. Schorzman (Malabar, Fla.: Krieger Publishing Co., 1993).

4. Ibid.

5. Oral history Record Unit No. 9545, "Black Aviators," Nov. 28, 1989, The Smithsonian Videohistory Collection, Smithsonian Institution Archives, Washington, D.C.

BIBLIOGRAPHY

Schorzman, Terri A., ed. *A Practical Introduction to Videohistory: The Smithsonian Institution and Alfred P. Sloan Foundation Experiment*. Malabar, Fla.: Krieger Publishing Co., 1993.

Zettl, Herbert. *Sight, Sound, Motion: Applied Media Aesthetics*. Belmont, Calif.: Thomson/Wadsworth, 2008.

———. *Television Production Handbook*. Belmont, Calif.: Wadsworth Cengage Learning, 2009.

———. *Video Basics*. Belmont, Calif.: Thomson/Wadsworth, 2007.

CHAPTER 19

CASE STUDY: OPENING UP MEMORY SPACE: THE CHALLENGES OF AUDIOVISUAL HISTORY

ALBERT LICHTBLAU

THE emergence of oral history was connected with a technical development—namely the possibility of recording human voices. The recording techniques developed rapidly. In the 1980s expensive filmmaking began to be replaced by more affordable video formats, which took the technical development of oral history to a new audiovisual level.

The paradigm shift generated by oral history in which historians began to generate their own primary sources announced another transformation of the way historians worked: taking leave of the written form and communicating scholarly results in audiovisual form. Resistance against this development is still enormous, but the everyday practice of oral historians has made this resistance absurd. For instance, exhibitions having to do with contemporary history can no longer dispense with film presentations. When our task is to use the most important audiovisual media as means of posing scholarly and political relevant questions, and if we are to be able to actively participate in designing this film presentation, then we should not be overwhelmed by the "power of the image" but rather learn to master it.[1]

The Camera's Eye

What I seek to achieve in this essay is to describe what the integration of the visual aspect means for oral historians in generating documents of remembrance. I hope to be able to communicate the sense of fascination with the audiovisual, because that considerably expands the range of oral historians' work. This is why I have titled this essay "Opening Up Memory Space" because I am convinced that the visual component enables us to place commemoration into a more complex context.

Here I elaborate on a few concrete examples of how integrating the camera's eye has changed my work as an oral historian. The challenge of the audiovisual is to perceive what is visual both before and during the interview, and to include this in our questions and the activities that we undertake with our interviewees. Oral historians know that a person's home is very often a private archive filled with treasures and commemorative artifacts that send signals in the direction of the past. Even when we used to conduct oral history interviews in private homes and looked around in them in search of objects from the past, this process did not occupy the focal point of our attention. Perhaps we took note of interior spaces, made our own observations, possibly even copied documents and took a couple of photos. The spatial arrangement, and the way the interviewees encountered and dealt with these objects that evoked memory, were hardly our prime consideration. Nevertheless, these are the things that can tell us so much about how certain periods of a person's life are represented in private spaces or how events that had previously had primary importance in a person's life have now been shifted into the background. Although they are seemingly hidden, they are still very much present.

Two examples that illustrate the process of observing the interior of an interviewee's home come from my experience as an audiovisual historian. My colleague Helga Embacher and I were working on a film about émigrés who had fled the Nazis and were working as writers in New York.[2] One was poet Mimi Grossberg. She was born in 1905 in Vienna and was trained as a hatmaker. When we met her in the 1990s, she was still living—and this alone was visually fascinating—in Washington Heights, a New York City neighborhood in which many Jewish immigrants from Europe had formerly lived but had become a predominantly Hispanic neighborhood. Entering Mimi Grossberg's apartment brought one into direct contact with the history of her life. Just to the right of the front door were shelves containing dozens of women's hats that she had made and still liked to wear when she went out. The very act of beholding these creations was to take a trip back into the fashions of the 1930s to the 1950s.

In the "hat scene" of our film, she took hats in hand and showed us how they were to be worn in the most flattering way. Thanks to these hats, this lady, who actually preferred to give her accounts in long-winded narratives, succeeded impressively in condensing the story of her life as a working girl. After she had finished school, a girlfriend had advised her to learn a trade so that she wouldn't be totally dependent on her husband. This was inconsistent with the bourgeois conception of the role of the wife that prevailed in those days. Her mother suggested that she become a hatmaker because she could pursue this profession anywhere in the world. And that proved to be good advice in that she had no trouble finding a job in her chosen profession in her country of exile, the United States.

The camera's eye can help us to show more clearly that remembrance is an interactive process that not only attempts to mobilize the memory but also uses the haptic sense and physicality. In the case of Mimi Grossberg, she used hats, facial expressions, gestures, and movements to portray her history, which went back to the 1930s. Because of their haptic quality, objects like these hats can make it possible to "grasp" the relationship between the present and the past. It also enables the people we work with to more easily approach their previous lives.

The next example is that of Gabriele Margules, whom we visited as part of the making of a film for a museum exhibition. She is the daughter of a rabbi whom the Nazis interned in the Dachau concentration camp in November 1938. Before the outbreak of the war, the rabbi and his wife and two daughters were able to flee to England.[3] Gabriele Margules took a rather unusual approach to dealing with her childhood memories: she described them from the point of view of her teddy bear, August. When we visited her and began filming, we asked her if she still had the teddy bear. She proceeded to fetch August. With him in her arms, she read his story aloud—how he came to England with the family and during the Blitz was always afraid that Hitler could come there too. But "Hitler Never Came to Tea," as the key line of one of her poems read. The physical contact with the teddy bear that had accompanied Gabriele Margules throughout her life made it possible for her to establish contact with her own childhood. Oral historians are familiar with this frequently observed phenomenon: the way the faces of elderly people can change when they think back to their own childhood. That is exactly the way it was in this case in which biographical authenticity came out strongly via the nonverbal level of facial expression.

In both examples the interviewees moved about, which is to say they were active. Thus, bodies have more latitude of movement compared to classic oral history whereby the interviewees normally remain seated. I am convinced that physically active remembering also influences the narration, especially when psychology and mentality can be brought into contact with the past.

Relics of the Past

I recognized very early in my career doing oral history interviews how important physical contact with relics from the past can be. In an interview with a woman whose family had emigrated from Czechoslovakia to Austria, her apparent loss of memory became a problem for our conversation. But it turned out that she was an enthusiastic photographer. It wasn't until she offered to show me old photos that her memory blockage dissolved. The act of standing up, looking for the photos, and then displaying them enabled her to go more deeply into her life. It was not necessary for a film camera to have been there, yet this is one of many examples in which physical objects from the past have come into use as an aid in order to break down memory blocks and to encourage recollection via concrete impulses. Letters, diaries, photos, or even drawings that the interviewee had made are like voices from the past. Working with them is a tried-and-true method of encouraging recollection. For audiovisual work, these are indispensable steps.

As an oral historian, I was mostly interested in factual aspects of photographs—that is to say what-when-who-where can be seen and who took the picture. But in working with film, it is also a matter of dimensions that go beyond the factual—namely, the associative-emotional quality of the photographs. Some images have meanings that go far beyond that which can be seen on the surface because they address levels that have to do with personal experiences, fears, or longings. And these, in turn, are related to real-life experiences and thus to a memory that has to be dealt with. It has been my observation that it doesn't necessarily just have to be privately archived photos; it can also be generally communicated images that trigger such reactions.

During the making of a film for an exhibition about the crimes of the German Wehrmacht, I asked the guides who conducted the tours through the exhibition which of the exhibited images had great significance for them. In light of the fact that many of the photos showed people who had been murdered, I correctly assumed that this would allow them to go deeper only into individual images, since going into all of these images of murder would have been an emotional overload. To my amazement, none of the guides selected any of the generally familiar images. Instead, each of them chose a different image from the many pictures on display. And none of these individuals, in explaining their selection, cited purely factual grounds. They all connected their own experiences to the picture they chose. Some of them even referred to their dreams. This was not a matter of the factual visual information communicated by these pictures, but rather a matter of personal points of contact that made it possible to bring the image into contact with the person's own current world of experience. Such feelings, emotions, fears, and hopes make tangibly clear the great extent to which the narratives of remembrance presented to us in biographical interviews reflect only the surface of a much more profound process.

Working with films opens up the possibility to incorporate photographs but also private footage when it is available.[4] The technical developments in this area have been moving forward very rapidly—in Web blogs, video podcasts, and cell phone videos—and these are sources that we have to learn to use in an appropriate way. I would like to give two examples of working with this private footage, because I am convinced that our interests are totally different from those of commercial media. When I was working on a film about the conductor Michael Gielen, I found out that his wife Helga Gielen had lots of Super-8 footage documenting the Gielen family's life over the years. I asked Helga and Michael if they would screen these films with us and tell us their thoughts while watching them. Since these Super-8 home movies had no soundtrack, the couple had to explain to us what we were seeing. Going about this, we discovered film material that did indeed have historical value. For instance, there was footage of Gielen's aunt, Salka Viertel, a screenwriter and friend of Greta Garbo, as well as footage showing the making of the 1974 filming of Arnold Schönberg's opera *Moses and Aaron* by Jean-Marie Straub and Danièle Huillet. Even beyond the historical value of this material documenting film history, this private footage provided a detailed description of the way he had conducted the music for this film as well as the biographical and political significance it had for the conductor. Gielen said, "Rarely was I so happy with the way the teamwork functioned as I was with this project even though it was one that I had to withdraw to such extent. And Danièle later published something about the film in which she said, "Gielen discovered collective work. I had, so to speak, finally absorbed something of Socialism. I didn't think that was very nice at all."[5]

This footage is also a good example of how culture and aesthetics are products of a particular historical time, and especially for the Super-8 film format with its specific preformatted color quality as well as for things like clothing and hair styles and peoples' body language in the process of intergender and intergenerational communication.

The Negotiation of Remembrance

Another possibility of working directly with films is to screen excerpts from our filmed interviews or other scenes with the interviewees themselves and to discuss it with them. Sometimes we are too impartial in analyzing and interpreting this material and use what the interviewees say as material that we can take advantage of. Particularly in the case of film footage, this is very tempting. since we now have in addition to the level of language also the level of body language. It is fascinating to watch as they go about the process of recollection, and this makes it clear that verbal language and body language are not always congruent. I find it useful to confront individuals with such observations and to tell them our interpretation, and simultaneously give them the opportunity to either confirm or correct this. This is another one of the possibilities to reach the level of reflective remembrance, but it's also one that shows the great extent to which remembering takes place in a negotiational process involving various different protagonists. The interpretations can differ widely.

In everyday life, the negotiation of remembrance takes place within the scope of intrafamily communication or in the context of a group of people who recollect some incidents jointly. Interactions are important for the formation for structures of remembrance, and as the work of Erving Goffman and others has shown, they are highly complex processes. Here, the camera's eye can help us to observe nonverbal information as elements that communicate parallel to what is being said.[6] A final example to illustrate this: For a film about survivors of the Mauthausen concentration camp, we intentionally selected individuals who attended the opening of the new Mauthausen Visitor's Center in the company of their children. Previously conducted interviews with them were part of the new exhibition, and they were guests of honor on this day, which was also the annual celebration of the liberation of the camp. What we definitely wanted to capture on film was how these survivors communicated their pasts to their children at this traumatic site. The location alone triggered recollections, but at the same time these people were somehow put off by what they saw. "This didn't look the way it is now" is a key statement by concentration camp survivor Solomon J. Salat, one that clearly brings out the sense of estrangement of this beautified place of commemoration in the contrast between his recollection and what he could see before him.[7]

In such a situation, complexity achieves an intensity that encompasses several layers: the traumatic location with its codes and signs, the ritual of the commemoration ceremony taking place in the background, and the intergenerational interaction between the survivors and their children, as well the process of communication with the interviewer. Furthermore, we were in a follow-up interview situation, because we had already conducted interviews with the survivors in their homes. In the case of the Salat family, the survivor's daughters had brought a small camera with them to document their visit to the concentration camp memorial. Their film was an important document that served as a basis for our ongoing work, because it showed what choices they made. This is a good example that audiovisual work can help in depicting the extraordinary intensification of complex processes of remembrance.

Sometimes I use the camera exclusively as an accompanying instrument of observation, and my footage serves only as the basis of scholarly analysis. There is no substitute for the eye of the camera when the unity of remembrance consists of several persons and the remembrance takes place at several locations—as in the case of commemoration rituals. The visual messages are so numerous that these processes can only partially be captured even using photography. Film helps to encompass and bring together language, sound, interaction, and imagery. I use the camera to observe festivals of immigrants, which are often efforts to assure the cultural survival of the group and to stage an event displaying a virtual culture of the place of their ethnic origins.

New Methods and New Issues

"Opening Up Memory Space" with the help of audiovisuality means to opening ourselves up to new working methods and to new issues. This has methodological and theoretical implications, and raises the fundamental question of how we as historians go about communicating our insights and findings. Presenting them in film means having to learn a cinematic language, one that differs from the scholarly language that we are used to. It's astounding how the complex interrelatedness of the process of remembrance is able to be depicted on film. This has been illustrated by such outstanding films as *Shoah* (1985) by Claude Lanzmann and *The Thin Blue Line* (1988) by Errol Morris. But I want to strongly advise against orienting our efforts on commercial filmmaking, thus creating pressure to succeed in a medium that is almost impossible to fulfill. A much more important consideration would be how scholarly approaches can be integrated into work with film, such as the work we are familiar with from anthropological or ethnological films.

Furthermore, using film footage as source material for our written analysis can also open up new horizons for us, but we have not gotten that far yet. The new way of working already begins when we decide to use an audiovisual medium—in the selection of the protagonists or the development of the issues we want to investigate, in our preliminary considerations of what kind of memory triggers can be used in staged or accompanied interactions, the intensive consideration of private spaces in their function as places that represent people's life stories, the confrontation with documents, the actual process of going to places that were relevant in a person's biography, or the joint screening of private footage. As a source, visual material can provide us with important information as we go about considering the process of remembrance using the method of discourse analysis as well as embedding it in multimodal interactions.[8] This applies to "embodied modes"—the expressive possibilities of the body—as well as "disembodied modes" such as the influence of spatial conditions on the interaction or the effect of signs. How do we deal with this? What relevance does this have for us? What new insights can we derive from this? There are still many questions left to discuss.

NOTES

1. Dan Sipe, "The Future of Oral History and Moving Images," in *The Oral History Reader*, ed. Robert Perks and Alistair Thomson, 406–16 (London: Routledge, 2006).

2. Helga Embacher and Albert Lichtblau, *Wien–New York: Rückkehr in Büchern*, documentary film, 1992; 87 min. (www.unitv.org).

3. Helga Embacher and Albert Lichtblau, *Hitler Never Came to Tea*, documentary film, 2002; 9 min. (www.unitv.org).

4. James M. Moran, *There's No Place Like Home Video* (Minneapolis: University of Minnesota Press, 2002).

5. Albert Lichtblau and Alois Pluschkowitz, *Wer ist Michael Gielen?* documentary film, 2001, 45 min. (http://www.unitv.org).

6. Erving Goffman, *Interaction Ritual: Essays on Face-to-Face Behavior* (New York: Doubleday Anchor, 1967).

7. Albert Lichtblau, *Erinnerungsbilanz Mauthausen*, documentary film, 45 min., 2005 (www.unitv.org). Albert Lichtblau, "Recapitulation of Memory," in *Beyond Camps and*

Forced Labour: Current International Research on Survivors of Nazi Persecution. Proceedings of the International Conference, London, 11–13 January 2006, ed. Johannes-Dieter Steinert and Inge Weber-Newth (London 2008, CD-Rom).

8. Sigrid Norris, *Analyzing Multimodal Interaction: A Methodological Framework* (New York: Routledge, 2004); Gunther Kress and Theo van Leeuwen, *Multimodal Discourse: The Modes and Media of Contemporary Communication* (London: Hodder Arnold, 2001); Ron Scollon and Suzie Wong Scollon, *Discourses in Place: Language in the Material World* (London: Routledge, 2003).

BIBLIOGRAPHY

Kress, Gunther, and Theo van Leeuwen. *Multimodal Discourse: The Modes and Media of Contemporary Communication*. London: Hodder Arnold, 2001.

Norris, Sigrid. *Analyzing Multimodal Interaction: A Methodological Framework*. New York/London: Routledge, 2004.

Scollon, Ron, and Suzie Wong Scollon. *Discourses in Place: Language in the Material World*. London/New York: Routledge, 2003.

CHAPTER 20

ACHIEVING THE PROMISE OF ORAL HISTORY IN A DIGITAL AGE

DOUG BOYD

> In a revolution, as in a novel, the most difficult part to invent is the end.
>
> —Alexis de Tocqueville

THE phrase "digital revolution" is frequently used in both popular and academic discourse to describe the multiple contexts of our increasingly electronically enriched and computer-dependent society. In oral history and other academic areas utilizing the interview as a central methodological element, the "digital revolution" specifically refers to the mainstream integration of digital technologies into all facets of the oral history process—in the field, in the archive, and in the distribution of the interview content. This chapter will explore how digital technologies have significantly impacted and have become integral to the recording of oral history, as well as to the dual archival imperatives of access and preservation.

First and foremost, digital technology does not make us better interviewers, better project directors, or better oral history archivists. Digital technology does not change the multitudes of stories that can be documented, studied, archived, and preserved. Dramatic changes in technology often frustrate practitioners who must learn new methods: however, when one considers the core practice of oral history, digital recording alone changes very little. There is still a microphone connected to a recorder that converts sound into data on some form of media, which eventually needs to be archived and preserved properly. The recorders are smaller and can record a much higher quality signal. The media is no longer tape, and the data is no longer preserved in the form of magnetic particles. Although the essential addition of the computer in the workflow has changed the process dramatically, merely utilizing digital technologies to conduct oral history interviews does not constitute a revolutionary change.

The digital revolution will fulfill its promise to oral history more completely when digital technologies are utilized to change the ways in which oral history is organized, accessed, utilized, and preserved as an information package. Oral history collections have always been a complex resource to navigate. For the field of oral history, the true digital revolution has only just begun, and it entails more than the economic or technological changes that make recorders cheaper, smaller, and faster with better resultant sound. The real revolution will be a change in consciousness about how oral history, as a historical resource, can be engaged and discovered more easily, more widely and effectively distributed, and ultimately, more responsibly preserved.

Digital Recording

Since the late nineteenth and early twentieth centuries, interviewers in the professional practices of oral history, folklore, anthropology, ethnology, ethnomusicology, linguistics, sociology, and other related disciplines have relied on technology, specifically audio recording technologies, to record their data in the field. In 1890, the folklorist and anthropologist J. Walter Fewkes proclaimed that the study of folklore "cannot reach its highest scientific value until some method is adopted by means of which an accurate record of the stories can be obtained and preserved."[1] Over the course of the twentieth century, analog recording technologies improved greatly in regard to portability and fidelity. In a 1937 article for the *Southern Folklore Quarterly*, the folklorist John Lomax described his first "electrically driven" recording machine used in 1933 to record folk songs:

> Improvements have come slowly. . . . The amplifier weighed more than one hundred pounds; the turntable case weighed another one hundred; two Edison batteries weighed seventy-five pounds each. The microphone, cable, the tools, etc., accounted for sufficient weight to make the total five hundred pounds.

Lomax later described tearing out the back seat of his car to install the recorder, which, on one field trip, overturned. He recalled, "As a result my son got acid burns and lost a suit of clothes."[2]

In 1954, the anthropologist Alan Merriam wrote, "At present . . . the ethnographer is not so much interested in whether a recorder should be used, as in what type of recorder will give the best results." By then the acoustic cylinder recorder was obsolete. However, according to Merriam, "The choice among disc, wire and tape machines... still faces the ethnographer."[3] Cylinders, discs, and wire were soon replaced with magnetic tape. Open reel recorders maintained a dominant position for decades, eventually giving way to the portable and commercially popular, and at one time ubiquitous, audiocassette.

The reliance of professional and amateur interviewers on increasingly portable audio recorders to gather field data represented a revolutionary shift in both the purpose and practice of ethnographically oriented disciplines, heightening the centrality of the text as it was originally performed. Portable recorders created a radical change in methodology, in theory, and in the consciousness of the practitioners. As the oral historian Dale Treleven noted in 1984, "the mechanical recorder freed the new breed of historian-interviewers from scrawling interviewee responses on paper."[4]

I have been recording with digital audio and video field recorders since 1996. In recent years, I have interacted with many folklorists and oral historians in the context of facilitating their transition to digital recording technologies. I have observed that analog users display a distinct sense of comfort and security in pressing the mechanical play and record buttons together on the professional analog cassette recorders and feeling the recording process begin. The transition to digital audio and video technologies is no longer a blind nod to technological determinism or early adoption. Both digital audio and video provide numerous advantages over their analog counterparts, including, most importantly, quality.

In addition to capturing a wider dynamic range, digital audio is a much lower-noise recording. When comparing professional quality recorders, the sonic quality of the signal being recorded digitally can be far superior to the analog counterpart. The advantages digital audio provides, with regard to data migration, are significant as well. High quality copies of a field recording no longer need to be compromises in quality or in time. This listing of technological advantages does not mean that digital technology does not bring with it numerous challenges. The impending obsolescence of analog recording does, however, foster in many practitioners a sense of urgency, and hence frustration.

All technologies change. As improvements are made and then marketed to consumers, these technologies become commercially mainstream. Innovations are discovered, the technologies adapt, they are re-marketed as improvements the general consumer cannot live without, and the mainstream changes again. Each instance of change has had an impact on oral history methodology, but it did not revolutionize the profession. The methodological shift from interviewers "scrawling" on paper to utilizing portable recording technologies in the field was, indeed, a revolutionary shift in our field.

Magnetic tape recording technologies dominated our practice for decades. For almost twenty years, the major equipment decision an interviewer had to make was whether to purchase the Marantz or Sony cassette recorder. The Philips Company invented the audiocassette in 1963. Later that decade, 4-track and 8-track cartridge technologies competed for market share in the commercial music marketplace. The 8-track tape player gained a major foothold with its presence in automobiles, but from a commercial recording perspective, the cassette emerged as the dominant format. In the early 1980s the compact disc appeared as an alternative distribution media for commercial music. Despite the rise of the CD, digital recording technologies did not immediately filter down to mainstream, affordable portable field recording solutions until the early 1990s. In fact, audiocassette technologies continued to dominate fieldwork recording solutions at this time, while maintaining a strong foothold in the commercial music market. According to the Recording Industry Association of America (RIAA), commercial music cassettes continued to outsell compact discs until 1992. Surprisingly, the audiocassette held its ground through the 1990s. In 1997, the full-length audiocassette still made up 18.2 percent of musical sales. But by 2007, that number was down to .3 percent. Presently we face rapidly declining CD sales as rates of legal and illegal downloadable music increase dramatically.

The commercial music transition from cassette tape to CD changed very little about the music industry. Yes, the consumer had to purchase new equipment, but the basic paradigms and business models remained the same. It is the transition from CD to digital downloadable music that has completely revolutionized the music industry. Portable recording and preservation options for archivists, folklorists, and oral historians will always be subject to the dynamic trends of the consumer music marketplace whose interests are not always aligned with the needs of field recording and archival preservation. Oral historians, folklorists, ethnographers, and archivists do not, nor will they ever, drive consumer market trends for recording technologies and media.

Although the use of digital recording technologies in portable field recorders is a relatively new phenomenon, digital recording of audio had been conducted since the 1980s. Recorded sound has always been preserved as data in one form or another. Analog recording devices reproduce sound using transducers, in this case, microphones, which convert analog sound vibrations into an electric signal. In the case of magnetic tape, this electrical signal is represented by the arrangement of magnetic particles on the tape. To hear the recorded sound on the magnetic tape, this process is reversed. Computers do not read magnetic particles or electrical signals. Digital recording of audio adds, through the use of an analog to digital (A/D) converter, the conversion of electrical signals into discreet code that is readable by a computer. In order to play back digital audio, the digital data is converted, through the digital to analog (D/A) converters, from binary code to electrical signals resulting in sound vibrations projected from a speaker. Now, a digital audio file, from a data perspective, more closely resembles a Microsoft Word document than an analog recording on magnetic tape.

Digital audio recording uses time sampling and quantization in order to represent analog signals as data. Discreet time sampling, "the essence of all digital audio systems," involves sampling the sound wave at various intervals. An increased sampling rate yields a higher quality representation of the sound wave. If sampling represents time in the measurement of digital audio, "quantization represents the value of the measurement, or... the amplitude of the waveform at sample time."[5]

Because of the dominance of the compact disc, an early standard for digital audio quality was established. "CD quality" recording meant 16-bit/44,100KHz. A standard audio CD contained seventy-four minutes, or 650 megabytes of uncompressed, audio information. This standard is already beginning to change as storage media becomes dramatically less expensive and recording capabilities improve. As the capabilities of recording increased, data footprints of audio recording technologies have also increased. To counter the increasing size of audio data files and an increasingly limited amount of bandwidth available, compression algorithms (lossy and lossless) were employed for certain digital audio technologies enabling the network mobility of these files. Lossy compression algorithms utilize psycho-acoustics and noise shaping technologies in order to decrease the file size, also resulting in a reduction in recording sonic quality; lossless compression algorithms yield decreases in files size but retain the originally recorded sonic quality.

As with computer technologies, the digital audio marketplace has been a rapidly changing and dynamic environment. Formats and technologies that once held great promise have, in a very short time, become obsolete. Digital Audio Tape (DAT), one of the early portable digital recording formats, recorded on only one side of the tape and utilized a technically elaborate rotary recording head, which employed a helical scan method of encoding data on to the tape. Over time, DAT proved to be technically unstable, disastrously fragile from a preservation perspective, and was abruptly abandoned by recording studios and fieldworkers alike.

The Minidisc proved to be another fleeting format briefly popular among oral historians and folklorists. The primary market for this technology was the lucrative portable music market previously dominated by the lingering audiocassette. However, Minidisc failed in the commercial music marketplace losing market share to the less proprietary and more flexible MP3 compression technologies.

Despite the fact that the CD finally overcame the audiocassette in the commercial music market, early recordable CD technology was not affordable and thus not easily accessible. The cassette maintained its place in the marketplace in the face of the compact disc mainly because of the cassette's familiarity and its onetime ubiquity. Early into the twenty-first century, recordable CD technology (CD-R/RW) grew more common. Almost every computer sold came with a CD-R drive, yet the CD-R portable field recorder still did not catch on as a mainstream field recording option. Given the dominance of the audio CD in the commercial marketplace, I expected, at the time, for this format to take off. It had two important advantages: one could purchase recordable CDs almost anywhere, and one could be completely independent from the computer. However, one could record only seventy-four minutes on a CD-R and the format was limited to 16-bit/44.1khz, and most importantly, users in the commercial marketplace were getting away from the CD-R as their primary means of storing music.

By the time that portable CD-R recorders emerged on the scene, computers were fast becoming the primary means of managing individual music collections. Flash memory recording, a process that mirrored digital photography, emerged as the dominant portable, digital field-recording format. Flash memory recording involves very few moveable parts and is inexpensive, and one can record as long as one can afford additional memory. Once again, the dominant portable field-recording format of choice mirrors the commercial marketplace, a convergence resulting in greater market and format stability. Napster and Apple's iPod have revolutionized the digital music industry and the technology has matured. In June 2008, Apple announced "music fans have purchased and downloaded over five billion songs from the iTunes store." The paradigm of recorded sound as data files managed by a computer now dominates both the commercial music and the archival communities.

Digital Video

Digital video recording by consumers is wildly popular. Again, emerging technologies have made it possible to capture high quality digital signals on affordable cameras, edit video on home computers, create and distribute DVDs, or upload compressed files to YouTube—again, from the home computer. Affordable digital video cameras can capture extremely high quality digital audio in addition to a video signal that exceeds previous "broadcast quality" standards. Despite these capabilities, the usage of digital video field-recording equipment has not yet become standard practice. Archivists and oral historians have debated for years the pros and cons of video oral history. The high cost for the preservation of high-resolution, broadcast-quality video has deterred mainstream integration of video into standard fieldwork practice. From an access perspective, digital video will indeed challenge the dominant paradigms of oral history, especially as video transitions from standard definition to high definition. The prevalence of digital video on the Internet, the ability to record video with Web cameras and on low-cost cell phones, and the widespread use of oral history methodology in documentary films are just a few factors that have encouraged a societal expectation for video. Oral history will not be immune to this expectation, so oral history archives should prepare for a major influx of digital video. User expectations for video are increasing, however the archival challenges to preserve and provide access to digital video involve a much greater investment in resources. One high definition videotaped interview (recorded with a certain high-resolution codec) can equal the size of a standard computer hard drive. Ten of these interviews can equal the data footprint of many file servers currently deployed in archival settings. The current state of preservation technologies falls short compared with the current state of our ability to record high-resolution interviews. Once again, high-resolution video has become less expensive to record and simultaneously, more expensive to maintain and preserve. However, with the popularization of video sharing Websites such as YouTube, users' expectations for quality have actually diminished. The tolerance for highly compressed video has greatly increased and is even acceptable when broadcast on network and cable news television channels. The Internet delivers a dramatically increasing percentage of video content, enabling public access to videotaped oral histories from all over the world, sometimes within just a few moments of completion of the recorded interviews.

Access: Accommodating the Oral History User

Oral history professionals appreciate the historical and cultural richness embedded in oral history interviews. Oral history is gaining in popularity as a historical resource, but remains an underutilized resource for historical research. This may be due partly to the difficulty researchers have had in gaining access to oral history collections. The oral history information package may contain multiple recorded copies of an interview in a variety of formats: reel-to-reel tape, cassette tape, audio CD, multiple forms of digital data files. If the interview is transcribed, an archive could possess a typescript and an electronic transcript that may or may not exist in a variety of stages of completion (first draft, audited, edited etc.). Additionally, the information package should contain relevant descriptive and technical metadata at either the collection or the interview level that intellectually tie these multiple components together.

Digital technologies, specifically the Internet, have dramatically changed the archival profession and the practice of information seeking and retrieval. Between the 1970s and the 1990s, many oral history collections published printed collection guides. The conversion of these guides into an online environment meant repositories could integrate the processes of efficiently and remotely searching and browsing bibliographic records contained in large or small oral history collections, all in an online context. Simply using the Internet to distribute metadata records, however, meant that the user still had to physically come to the archive to interact with the interview materials, unless, of course, the repository's collections circulated.

Archival finding aids have traditionally been important tools for discovery and detailed description of archival materials. Yet, the "digital revolution" has dramatically altered users' expectations regarding what the Internet can provide. The physicality of the archive is no longer the preferred public access point for the typical user. What archivist has not heard in the past few years, "When will your collections be accessible online?" When users ask about collections being mounted online, they are not limiting their expectations to remote access to bibliographic records about the interview. Typically, users want access to digital surrogates of the interview itself. They want—even demand—access to archival materials of all kinds from their computer, while at home, in an airport, or sitting in Starbucks. Archives and digital programs have been rapidly initiating and dramatically increasing their digitization efforts during the last decade to address the demand. However, great strides made in providing digital content in the commercial marketplace decrease the general public's tolerance for the slower pace made by archival institutions placing their archival materials online.

Consider the older model of research methodology. Typically, researchers would discover the presence of an oral history collection or interview they needed for their research. This initial discovery was often made through a catalog, a printed guide, or word of mouth. The researchers would physically travel to the archive where they would be confronted with a large stack of tapes and transcripts (if the collection had even been transcribed). Information seeking and retrieval in a text-based, paper environment involves scanning text for keywords and concepts congruent to the information seekers' intentions. Browsing audio in an analog, mechanical environment is a comparatively inefficient way to seek out specific information in a textually oriented society. Compared to visually scanning text, cognitively scanning the analog audio is a much less efficient and slower process. If researchers were short on time or impatient, they would likely scan through a collection containing over ten thousand pages of transcript and choose to listen only to the audio that coincides with the relevant text, rather than making the commitment to listen to the entire audio collection, which could amount to more than two hundred hours of audio recording. For now, a transcript, if accurately generated, is still the most efficient tool for locating specific information in a collection. Navigating an analog audio collection, in the absence of a transcript, is greatly facilitated by the existence of a sequential, subject-based index. Less efficient is a finding aid that gives a brief item-level description and a listing of subject headings representing the interviews in the collection, but a collection level description with an inventory list would have been the more likely archival option. Ultimately, collection level description does very little for seekers of specific information embedded within interviews contained in large oral history collections.

Interview-level description has traditionally been the metadata ideal. Brief descriptive metadata enables the user of the physical collection to efficiently target specific interview content, browse, or discover serendipitously individual interviews not previously considered. The problem with generating item-level description has always been time and money. Archivists of large oral history collections often have difficulty committing to anything other than collection-level description. The typical user would be given a collection-level description, transcripts, and tapes, and would then begin the daunting task of manually seeking information.

As the Internet matured, repositories began to place full text transcripts and audio excerpts or interviews on static Web pages. Although some archivists resisted posting interviews online because of control issues, the practice dramatically changed the mode of distribution of oral history interviews making the interview accessible to a wider audience. This in no way changed the way in which the user interacted with the interview. The past decade has witnessed decreasing costs of both bandwidth and digital storage yielding numerous initiatives involving more innovative and effective ways of publishing oral history collections on the Internet.

In my own career, I moved from an oral history archival position to directing the Kentucky Oral History Commission. With an increasing focus on digitization and digital projects, I left the commission to direct the digital program for the University of Alabama Libraries. Having gained perspective working in the world of academic digital programs, I became director of the University of Kentucky's Louie B. Nunn Center for Oral History. During this same period, oral history was undergoing a transformation of presentation in a digital, online environment.

In 1998, the Kentucky Oral History Commission, a program of the Kentucky Historical Society, launched an initiative to document the struggle to end legal segregation in Kentucky. A project director conducted more than one hundred analog interviews. These interviews were accessioned and processed the same way other new collections had been processed, and the oral histories were described at the collection level. As the Civil Rights Project gained momentum, in 2000, the program launched production of a video documentary *Living the Story: The Civil Rights Movement in Kentucky*. Well received, the documentary continues to run on Kentucky Educational Television. As the archivist for the oral history collection at the time, I faced a demand for usage of the Civil Rights collection that we had not experienced with other collections. In the face of demands for specific and precise information, I found the collection-level system for archival description inadequate for this particular project in the physical archival context.

To better meet users' needs, I sought to develop an online interface to effectively deliver oral history materials as a total information package. The platform for our customized collection management database was a customized Microsoft SQL database which simultaneously controlled the *Statewide Guide to Oral Histories*. I felt the logical solution would be to integrate a content delivery system into the architecture of our preexisting collection management database. The integration of these databases ensured that the records would not have to be imported or exported into another interface for online distribution. Records were keyed just once, and with a single command and the addition of a link to the corresponding filename for the digital surrogates (i.e., digital audio file and transcript text file on the SQL server), the interview would be made public.

My overarching goal for the new interface was to allow users to quickly and easily browse and search both records and interviews, and listen to and view interview segments from the collection. The entire audio and video interviews were not delivered by the *Civil Rights in Kentucky Oral History Project Digital Media Database*, as the Kentucky Historical Society did not have ready access to streaming technologies. The goal for this digital initiative was to create multiple access points for this collection based on usage patterns of the collection I had observed thus far. Most users were seeking to browse the collection based on subject—subjects primarily based on the categories that structured the documentary. I observed that users seemed to want to interact with interviews on these particular topics: desegregation of education, life under segregation, public accommodations, open housing, and protests and demonstrations.

It became evident that users preferred to interact with "local" materials, so we constructed a drop-down menu that instantly isolated items from pre-selected Kentucky counties. In addition to providing the user the traditional, searchable metadata record, which included descriptive metadata including an interview synopsis and keywords, we enabled users to browse by subject, by county, and by decade.

Merely browsing metadata records containing descriptive metadata linking to audio and video excerpts and nearly ten thousand pages of text would be of little use to the serious researcher without powerful search capabilities. The *Civil Rights in Kentucky Oral History Project Digital Media Database* enabled users to search metadata records as well as to perform global and item-level keyword searches of full, oral history transcripts. In order to make the audio and video excerpts searchable, the transcript of each excerpt was dropped into an additional text field in the database and linked to the digital surrogate. In order to make the audio and video excerpts discoverable, each excerpt contained its own level of descriptive metadata. For this project, metadata needed to be generated at the collection-level, the interview-level, as well as the individual excerpt-level—a labor-intensive and ultimately expensive process.

The Digital Media Database for the Civil Rights in Kentucky Oral History Project was designed to enhance the user's experience when using oral history. This solution attempted to integrate the various modules: search, browse, and metadata. A reviewer, Mary Larson, stated:

> This site has just about everything that modern Internet users have come to expect in terms of searchability, ease of use, and good design. At the same time, it presents information in a number of different formats and for a number of varied audiences—from the general public to serious researchers to high school students—while making it relevant to all of them... this is a model oral history Web site and perhaps it will inspire other programs to look to this type of approach to projects in the future.[6]

The online database developed for the Kentucky Oral History Commission's Civil Rights Movement in Kentucky Oral History Project was a customized solution that required a tremendous amount of resources, effort, and maintenance—a model not easily replicated or realistically afforded for other collections. A more scalable model was needed for delivering the majority of our digital assets in a less labor intensive and less expensive fashion. One positive aspect of designing the database was that it was customized to work only with oral history materials. The text of the transcript worked well with the oral and visual dimensions of oral history. The downside of a customized solution built from the bottom up is providing ongoing support and maintenance. The programmer on the project, although extremely talented, utilized techniques not easily discernable by others. Additionally, Kentucky's state government Information Technology (IT) department consolidated and removed IT managers from the Kentucky Historical Society. When I left the position at the Kentucky Historical Society in 2006, the customized solution had virtually no support. A database that was originally designed for dynamism and rapid updates ultimately became a static exhibition.

Relatively inexpensive commercial platforms such as OCLC's CONTENTdm have enabled smaller institutions, public libraries, state historical societies, colleges and universities to construct a sophisticated, and relatively easy to manage digital archive. When I accepted the position as the director of University of Alabama's digital program, the library had already invested in CONTENTdm. I was comfortable with this interface in that I had been a member of the team that initially implemented the system at the Kentucky Historical Society. Like many other digital archive platforms, CONTENTdm originally was designed for delivering digital surrogates for photographic and manuscript materials. For these formats, the interfaces have greatly matured. The complexities of the oral history information package add a degree of difficulty for more generalized online interfaces. If the digital oral history collection is singularly dimensional and contains only audio files, or only transcripts, the complexity is minimal, and the collection and the interface are usually quite easily made compatible. However, if the object contains multiple dimensions, metadata, transcript, and audio or video, the effectiveness of interacting with oral history materials can prove awkward. CONTENTdm, out of the box, excels at presenting digital photograph collections online. The interface was designed for simplicity and efficiency. It is also fairly customizable if your institution has ready access to a good PHP programmer. Few institutions do. In the case of delivering oral history content, CONTENTdm, as originally designed, struggled.

Administrators of the local system can create "compound objects," associating multiple objects for the users to experience together. Theoretically, in the case of oral history, this enables the user to access the transcript and the audio together. In practice, this is not completely the case. Although the audio and the transcript are merged into a single record, the user must still use each component of the oral history package separately. At the University of Alabama we committed to putting online the *Working Lives Oral History Project*, an oral history project focusing on African American industrial workers in the central Alabama region. This collection, fortunately, was transcribed, which we possessed as typescript. After scanning the transcripts and digitizing the audio, we uploaded the materials into our CONTENTdm interface. The University of Alabama Libraries uploaded the interviews as compound objects, placing the scans of the transcripts under the same record as the digital audio files. Without a PHP programmer on staff, I struggled to make the presentation of the oral history interview work in a more integrated fashion. Clicking "access this item" opened the audio file, but it opened the audio file in a separate browser tab, taking the user away from the interview record. The user had to open the audio file, then reverse back to the interview record on the original browser tab, open the transcript, move the audio tab out of the way, and only then could the user follow along in the transcript.

The major challenge facing oral history collections in a digital archival environment is making the individual components of the collections all work together in a user-friendly, efficient, useful, and intuitive manner. There are countless examples of repositories mounting digitized oral history collections onto platforms that do not complement the potentially multidimensional, complex nature of oral history materials. Researchers can read and search the transcript, and one can listen to, or watch, an oral history interview. Researchers usually cannot do both in a user-friendly and intuitive manner, though. If they search on a single word in a transcript, they should be simultaneously linked directly to that moment in the audio or video file as well. If a digital collection is placed online and the interface for accessing the interviews is not usable, the responsible repository may have increased the potential audience for those archival materials; functionally, access will more closely resemble the access models represented by boxes of tapes and stacks of printed transcripts. The only difference between the two approaches is a change in venue. Technologies exist to make textual and audio materials work together online, and it is our responsibility as curators of oral history materials to make them easy and efficient to use.

Since becoming the director of the Louie B. Nunn Center for Oral History at the University of Kentucky Libraries, I have worked closely with the Kentuckiana Digital Library (KDL), the principle distributor of digital collections for the University of Kentucky Libraries Special Collections and Digital Programs and the Nunn Center, in order to refine their online oral history interface. The digital program had developed an innovative search and retrieval interface, but the interface was constructed in a way that made it very difficult to use. Very little collection-level metadata and no item-level metadata were presented to the user, resulting in a context in which users had to initially guess, or previously know, the contents of the collections in order to know what effective search terms to use. The search interface was indeed incredibly powerful and innovative, targeting the whole interview rather than pre-selected interview excerpts. Eric Weig, director of the Kentuckiana Digital Library and co-designer of the original interface articulated his intentions:

> Rather than trying to identify key moments in the audio or breaking it up into logical segments, we store landmarks in its metadata: the line numbers in the transcript associated with five-minute intervals in the audio.[7]

By embedding time-code into the transcript, we enabled time correlation between the transcript and the audio or video, yielding an integrated final product where the components work together. The search results were highlighted and contextualized by the inclusion of surrounding text in the transcript. Weig notes that the "line number that each search hit appears on is indicated.... The line number range for each five-minute segment of audio is also displayed, so the user can select the segment they want, and even estimate where in the segment they can hear their search term."[8] The connection between the transcript and the audio was rooted in the five-minute audio chunks that were automatically created and the corresponding time-code markers that were manually embedded in the transcript. The connection between transcript and audio was what other oral history online interfaces lacked at the time. As represented in the first incarnation of the KDL oral history interface, this connection was awkward, but we have worked together, at the University of Kentucky, to refine it. While closely scrutinizing the initial interface we determined that a major area of weakness was in the line numbering system. Line numbering functioned to inform the user of the location of search hits in the text and inform the user as to which corresponding audio segment to click on in order to listen to their search result. The user would click on the corresponding link and be delivered five minutes of audio to navigate. Neither line numbers or time-code appeared in the text of the transcript, though, and therefore had little meaning when navigating away from the search results and into the transcript. The user linked to the audio segment containing the specific information they sought, but they had to browse the entire transcript in order to locate the corresponding text. Navigating away from the search results page and into the PDF transcript/audio interface removed you from the "keywords in context" that were so useful in discerning the appropriate search result.

We have worked to embed the search engine and the resulting keywords in context into the same interface users navigated in order to view the transcript (see figure below). Additionally, we created a customized software solution to more easily (albeit still manually) embed time-code markers into the transcript. The decision was made to embed these markers at one-minute intervals throughout the transcript. The five-minute interval proved to be, still, too much text to scan while trying to determine the specific location of the information being sought in the audio file.

The new KDL oral history interface allows users to search text, contextualize search results, link search results to their corresponding place in the text, and finally, take the user within one minute of the search result in the audio file. As soon as the user decides to refine their initial search, they are able to quickly move around the audio and the transcript, and both discover *and* pinpoint the textual or conceptual information they sought. The layout of the component of the interface is a simple four-quadrant interface—the interview metadata and media player filling the upper quadrants with the transcript text and the search and retrieval interface filling the lower quadrants.

The time code just to the left of the transcript text appears as links, which corresponded to the time code in the audio file. Clicking on the time-code-link activates that particular audio chunk. Additionally, users are able to use the interface to download custom audio segments, or to print a formatted version of the transcript.

At the University of Kentucky, we are exploring ways that we can implement user-generated tags as a part of the metadata structure of the oral history interviews and collections. Modeling tagging methods used by Flickr and other online digital photograph-sharing sites, users can tag the content of oral history interviews, combining user-generated tags with the subject headings created by the archivist, empowering users to markup subjects important to them. The resultant record represents both user and archivist generated metadata enhancing the overall user experiences of both search and discovery. Additionally, we are exploring ways that the oral history collection could more efficiently and automatically integrate with the rest of the digital collection. Of course, the oral history interviews are included

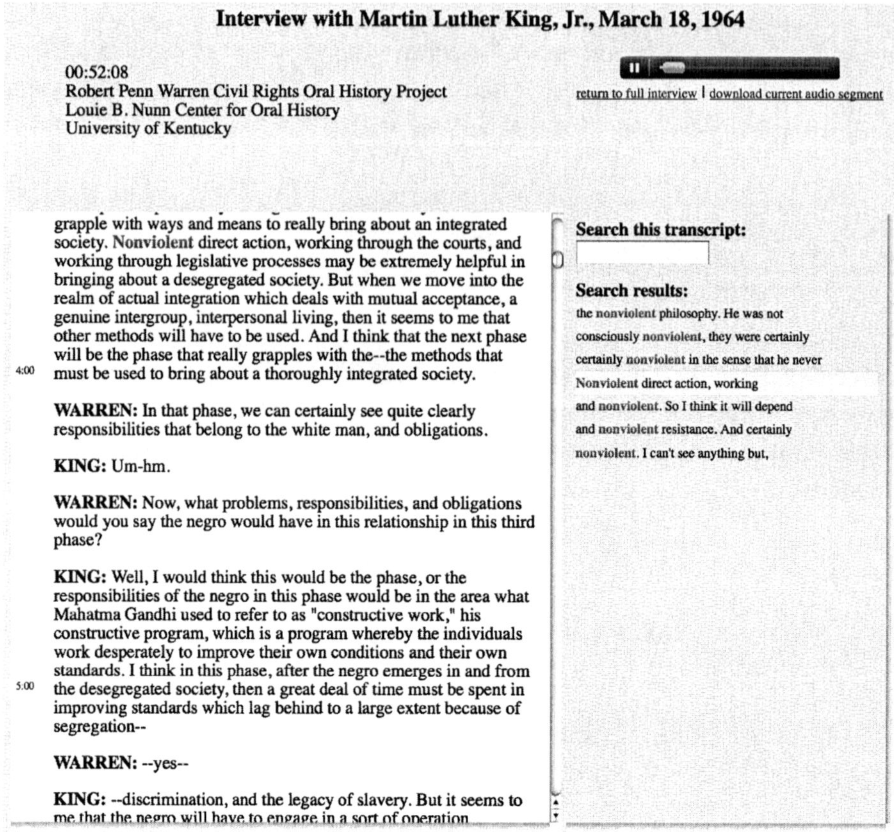

Figure 20.1. The new KDL oral history interface in September 2008.

in global searches of the KDL interface, yet I envision concepts and terms within the interview itself automatically linking to other related materials in the digital environment. If the name of a racehorse is mentioned in the oral history transcript, and the digital library contains digital photographs from the farm that bred the racehorse, we should offer the user the option to access these related materials, while interacting with the oral history interview.

The digital revolution has enabled sophisticated search, data mining, and query techniques that enable users to interact and engage with the large quantities of oral history material in a comprehensive and integrated fashion. As voice recognition technologies mature, nontextual searching is, no doubt, on the horizon, again enhancing the discovery capabilities of the information seeker. The digital environment can bring together the different digital surrogates in the oral history information package for the user or researcher to experience in user-customizable ways, a digital environment where the user decides how to navigate the oral history collections. In many cases, online archival delivery systems seem to be designed by archivists and librarians for other archivists and librarians. Designers of digital archival systems need to balance the needs of users and the content, and create a user-centered system of information architecture. These same designers need to study the ways that users of oral history collections use our collections, then design our discovery, retrieval, and delivery tools that serve up our material. Users want search and retrieval systems that are as simple to use and as effective as Google. Users want intuitive browsing interfaces such as those found at Amazon.com, or Apple's iTunes. Social networking provides great opportunities for users to instantaneously share oral history resources with much wider audiences outside of the traditional archival context. More creative, user-friendly, and intuitive ways of presenting oral history materials can transform the ways in which oral history materials are used today, and it is our job to continuously refine the process of enhancing access to our oral history collections.

Digital Preservation

A tangible result of the "digital revolution" has been the economic accessibility and affordability of professional-level audio digitization and recording equipment. I offer assistance to numerous institutions and individuals in making the digital transition with regard to recording and both analog and digital preservation. Most major oral history programs with an archival focus have been digitizing their recorded materials for preservation purposes. Audiocassettes and reel-to-reel tapes that were recorded on in the 1970s are reaching a critical time in their lifecycles. Because of rapid analog obsolescence, digitization has become the de facto means of audio preservation. However, oral history archivists face an impending preservation crisis, not related to the preservation of degrading analog tape. As digital recording technologies have improved over the years, very little attention has been paid, until recently, to the long-term preservation of this digital content.

In the early stages of digitization efforts, oral history repositories were storing their digital content on recordable CDs, as we were told that this technology would last more than one hundred years. Although testing has demonstrated that gold CD-Rs manufactured with phthalocyanine dye have proven more stable, CD-R methods of preservation are no longer considered long-term with some studies estimating end-of-life to be just ten years, much shorter than the analog tape-based medium housing the original analog recording. In addition to problems with life expectancy, digital audio preservation efforts have the added problem of media and format obsolescence. In the face of analog obsolescence we are given little choice for preservation measures; yet, as we generate massive amounts of digital content, too little attention has been paid in the archive, until just recently, to adopting precise, scalable strategies for responsibly preserving the digital content we generate.

Since hard drives are relatively inexpensive, we often hear recommendations to use them to back up materials. Those with institutional support are encouraged to place their materials onto a server-based, networked environment, which is also regularly backed up. Merely creating a backup copy of the interview is not responsible digital preservation. Although making backup copies of interviews is critical for short-term protection of the interview, long-term preservation of recorded audio demands protections to ensure that the digital files will remain uncorrupted and be accessible in the future, from both the hardware and software perspectives. Technological innovation is exciting, and improvements to applications and formats often make our lives easier. Change, however, is not without consequence.

Format obsolescence is often difficult to imagine in the context of the present. The current standard formats such as .wav, .MP3 or .pdf are so entrenched in the commercial marketplace that it seems difficult to imagine a scenario wherein these formats would become unusable. Inevitably they will. It is vitally important that archivists and practitioners continue the dialog to refine strategies and standards. Nonproprietary formats often do not equate to popular formats, yet popular formats are not immune to dramatic change or eventual abandonment. Nevertheless, it is critical for keepers of digital formats to continue to monitor current "best practices" in the archival and preservation communities, for these communities have a great stake in the matter.

It is also important to store digital files in an environment where future migration can be an efficient and automated practice. Placing large amounts of data on hard drives or in a networked environment enables future users to "batch convert" formats. The user simply sets up and runs a simple conversion script that migrates the file to another format according to the parameters set up in the script. Individually uploading hundreds or thousands of interviews that were recorded onto individual CD-DA discs or stored as data files on individual CD-Rom discs will prove to be time consuming and expensive. Automated format migration is much more efficient with large quantities of data files and is technology that is, now, quite affordable.

Another very real and difficult variable in the digital preservation equation is maintaining data integrity. Digital files corrupt, and there is little use in inadvertently making a backup copy of a corrupt file. Still, as our hard drives begin to fill with greater and greater amounts of data, workflows and procedures where archival staff must, each year, critically listen to each recording in the collection in order to ensure continued data integrity are unrealistic. Automated methods are available for conducting such a daunting manual task, but again, these methods are usually employed in large, server-based digital archival environments. I cannot underscore enough the importance, now more than ever, of working closely with well-funded archival institutions that have implemented a responsible digital preservation plan.

Although digital video technologies have matured from a recording/capture standpoint, digital video still poses a seemingly insurmountable challenge from a preservation perspective. Like its analog predecessor, tape-based digital video is a fragile medium. Hard drive storage of large quantities of high-resolution digital video continues to be prohibitively expensive for most individuals and institutions. But this is rapidly changing. As compression algorithms improve for video, and data storage options get increasingly inexpensive, we will see a surge in the usage of digital video in the field and in the archive. Digital video cameras are opting to record straight to onboard hard drives or removable flash drives rather than on optical or tape-based media. Because of the combination of the large data footprint of high-resolution digital video and limited bandwidth availability, digital video is only now emerging as a potential factor in the access-oriented component of the digital revolution. Technologies on the horizon will enable more affordable and automated approaches to long-term storage of high quality digital video.

Following Hurricane Katrina, several universities in Alabama received a grant from the Institute of Museum and Library Services (IMLS) to set up a statewide digital preservation network. This network was server based and implemented a simple software package known as LOCKSS, a platform that was developed by a group out of Stanford University. LOCKSS literally stands for "Lots of Copies Keep Stuff Safe." In this context the server application harvests digital items from one location and places exact copies of the item on five additional nodes. In our case, the "dark archive," the highly restricted, preservation-oriented digital repository, involved the University of Alabama, University of Alabama–Birmingham, Troy University, Spring Hill College, and the University of North Alabama, and the project was directed by Auburn University. Copies of University of Alabama's digital objects would be harvested by all of the other nodes in the network, as would the digital objects of other institutions be harvested by the University of Alabama's node. LOCKSS then employs a voting system that continuously monitors data integrity. If one of the files begins to demonstrate corruption, the other five files replace the corrupt file with a fresh copy. Distributed digital preservation is an excellent model for the future with regard to large archival institutions with adequate financial investment. Unfortunately, it is not as scalable for the smaller institution. More than ever, it is important to partner with a capable oral history archive, thus placing the burden of digital preservation on those institutions that demonstrate a level of commitment to both analog and digital preservation. In the case of smaller institutions, collaborative partnerships should be set up to address preservation needs.

The digital revolution has only just begun. Digital technologies have opened new and exciting opportunities for recording, preserving, and disseminating oral history interviews, potentially changing, in dramatic fashion, the entire field of oral history. At the same time, migration to digital technologies poses challenges that oral historians and archivists must overcome. Oral history has always been bound to technology, and technologies will forever change. That puts us in the position of depending on technology to save us from technology. Too many historical resources have disappeared because of format degradation or technologic obsolescence. The preservation of oral history materials demands our utmost attention in order to honor the stories that we have been so privileged to record.

NOTES

1. J. Walter Fewkes, "A Contribution to Passamaquoddy Folk-Lore," *Journal of American Folklore* 3, no. 11 (1890): 257–80.

2. John A. Lomax, "Field Experiences with Recording Machines," *Southern Folklore Quarterly* 1, no. 2 (1937): 58–59.

3. Alan Merriam, "The Selection of Recording Equipment for Field Use," *Kroeber Anthropological Society Papers* 10 (1954): 5–9.

4. Dale E. Trelevan, "Oral Historians: Masters of or Slaves to Technology?" *Oral History Review* 12 (1984): 101–4.

5. Bit depth is a measurement of the number of bits used to encode the dynamic range of each sample: the greater the bit depth, the higher the resolution of the sample. Ken C. Pohlmann, *Principles of Digital Audio* (New York: McGraw-Hill, 2005).

6. Mary Larson, "Review of the Civil Rights Movement in Kentucky Oral History Project Digital Media Database," *Oral History Review* 34, no. 1 (2007): 145–46.

7. Eric Weig, "Large Scale Digitization of Oral History: A Case Study," *D-Lib Magazine* 13, no. 5/6 (2007): 1–9.

8. Ibid.

BIBLIOGRAPHY

Pohlmann, Ken C. *Principles of Digital Audio*. New York: McGraw-Hill, 2005.

CHAPTER 21

ORAL HISTORY: MEDIA, MESSAGE, AND MEANING

CLIFFORD M. KUHN

An immense transformation in oral history and media has taken place over the past several decades. Reflecting on my own experiences, in the fall of 1978, I began work with Atlanta community radio WRFG's *Living Atlanta* project, an National Endowment for the Humanities (NEH)-funded series of fifty half-hour programs depicting life in the city between the World Wars. *Living Atlanta* was very much a product of its times, a direct outgrowth of the mission of WRFG, or "Radio Free Georgia," founded in the early 1970s by veterans of the civil rights and antiwar movements to provide a broadcast voice for those traditionally denied access to the media. More specifically, the series was designed to counter the prevailing triumphalist narrative of local history. Sociologist and WRFG co-founder Harlon Joye directed the project, while Bernard West and I were the principal historian-interviewers.

None of us had any experience in radio production beforehand. Equipped with fifty-pound, reel-to-reel tape recorders and cumbersome mike stands, eventually we interviewed a broad cross-section of some two hundred older Atlantans for the series. We quickly realized that conducting interviews for radio was quite different from scholarly endeavors for which we had trained. Attention had to be paid to background noise and mike placement. Interviewers could not interject as quickly as they might in normal conversation, and had to elicit stories rather than short bits of information. With radio in mind rather than television or film, interviewers could not rely on body language, facial expression, or the interview setting to help make a point, but rather had to try to get the narrators to paint an audio "picture" for the listeners.

After the tapes were dubbed and logged, material identified as potentially usable was copied by volunteers onto additional reels, and we created a mock-up of the interview portions of a given program, using a razor blade to cut and splice tape. We lacked the money to produce transcriptions. In addition to historical content, considerations of what would make good radio—timing, pacing, sound quality—informed the process. After the entire project staff reviewed and amended the mock-up, a final version was put together, including narration along with music from the historical period, and usually mixed on a four-track, reel-to-reel recorder.

Despite its seat-of-the-pants quality, *Living Atlanta* was considered a pioneer in the genre of radio oral history. Programs won national broadcast awards and were aired over National Public Radio, hailed by author Studs Terkel, highlighted by the NEH, and purchased by numerous schools and libraries. The series also spawned subsequent oral history–based documentaries at WRFG well into the next decade. In addition, both the programs and the *Living Atlanta* interviews, housed at the Atlanta History Center, were and continue to be frequently consulted by scholars and other researchers.

In 1985, the University of Georgia Press approved our proposal for a book drawing from the interviews. The reasons for such a work were numerous. Some 95 percent of the original interview material had never been made public, including much as rich as that actually aired, but never broadcast due to time and technical considerations. For the radio series, each program had to stand more or less on its own; we felt that a book would treat the subject matter in a more systematic, comprehensive manner as well as in a less ephemeral medium.

We also had to make decisions about *how* the oral history excerpts appeared in the book. For instance, the quick cuts that often made such compelling radio, and which we used in particular to juxtapose the memories of white and black Atlantans, simply did not work as well in print; accordingly, the interview excerpts in the book tend to be longer. We chose a format that was both oral and historical, with most of the book's chapters arranged topically, and the oral history excerpts woven into, rather than separated from, the narrative text. To convey something of the orality and subjectivity of the radio series, we also interspersed thirteen longer "profiles," extended interview excerpts with people we found especially informative and illuminating, and whose stories did not always fit neatly within the larger narrative. We also included eighty photographs throughout the book, which in various ways reinforced, complemented, and diverged from the interviews. *Living Atlanta: An Oral History of the City, 1914–1948* was published in 1990.

The advent of the digital revolution by the early 1990s helped spur a resurgence of interest in the *Living Atlanta* interviews, especially in nonprint formats. *Living Atlanta* narrators were interviewed for the film *Uprising of '34*, while a remark by another narrator led to the discovery of a film on the World War II B-29 bomber, which in turn was used in a public television documentary, *State of War*, on the home front in Georgia. Excerpts of programs and interviews were included in the *Will the Circle Be Unbroken* radio series on the civil rights movement in five southern capitals (by this time mixed digitally rather than on reel-to-reel recorders), winner of the 1997 Oral History Association nonprint media award. The pathbreaking *Who Built America?: From the Centennial Celebration of 1876 to the Great War* CD-Rom (which included film, song, speeches, and other audio-visual elements in addition to oral history, along with numerous other documents), as well as its sequel, featured *Living Atlanta* narrators, as did an Internet site sponsored by the Center for History and New Media on the 1919 flu pandemic. Most recently, interviews were utilized in conjunction with the centennial remembrance of the 1906 Atlanta Race Riot, in a dramatic performance by local high school students, and in the exhibit *Red Was the Midnight* at the Martin Luther King National Historic Site.

I relate the story of *Living Atlanta* not as an exercise in nostalgia but rather to illustrate the enormous transformations in oral history and media over the past several decades, as well as to point out the versatility of oral history in a wide variety of media and formats. Oral history interviews are particularly likely to be fruitfully employed in multiple applications when the interviews are grounded in historical scholarship, conducted with storytelling and a broad audience in mind rather than a comparatively narrow scholarly agenda, properly deposited to maximize usage, and recorded well. The greatly increased availability over the past two decades of good quality, increasingly affordable recording, editing, and playback equipment has enormously enhanced the possibility of high sound-quality oral history interviews being presented in a multiplicity of locations. In its immediacy and capacity to combine various sorts of information, including sound and moving images, the digital revolution has also rekindled an appreciation of the aural dimension of oral history and furthered the veritable explosion of oral history presentations in innumerable online and offline environments.

Oral History in Museums

The plethora of oral history–based media initiatives is astounding. In museums, for example, oral history has mushroomed. In 2002 Ron Chew, executive director of Seattle's Wing Luke Asian Museum, wrote that "Oral history has begun to permeate the museum," and a recent Google search of "oral history" and "museums" drew well over two million hits.[1] Just twenty-five years ago, oral history in a museum format, outside of flat text, had been a comparative rarity. With such technological developments as the computer-driven laser disc and the touch screen, oral history proved crucial to such seminal exhibits of the 1980s as the National Museum of American History's *A More Perfect Union* on the Japanese-American internment camps during World War II, and the restored Great Hall at Ellis Island.[2] Over the past two decades, such additional technological advances as sound cones, interactive computers, audio guides, and MP3 players, I-phones and other interactive devices have greatly expanded the possibilities of oral history in a museum setting.

These technological developments did not occur in a vacuum. The 1970s and 1980s also witnessed a reconsideration of the mission and meaning of museums, with distinct implications for oral history. Museum professionals reflected the broader movement within the history profession away from elites and toward so-called ordinary people. They sought to reinvigorate the museum-going experience to be more accessible for a broader audience, more contemporary and engaging, more interactive. Audience research showed that visitors often connected most fully with museums at a personal level, frequently through the means of first-person narratives. According to one major survey of the relationship between Americans and the past, people tend to trust museums more than other modes of historical presentation because museums represent authenticity and at the same time encourage what Michael Frisch calls "a shared authority" with visitors. They enable visitors to go at their own pace and to commonly share the experience with a family member of another generation.[3]

All of which means fertile ground for oral history to flourish in a wide variety of museum environments. In settings ranging from large municipal museums (Chicago Historical Society) to ethnic museums (Japanese-American National Museum) to neighborhood museums (Chinatown History Museum or Capetown's District Six Museum), oral history interviews are central in bringing to life the vibrancy and dynamism of often-neglected or marginalized communities.[4] Similarly, national museums such as New Zealand's Te Papa Tongarewa and the Museum of the American Indian feature personal narratives in conveying the experiences of indigenous people. Science, children's, and other museums comparatively open to sound and motion are among the leaders in incorporating oral history interviews.

At the Rock 'n' Soul Museum, in Memphis, Tennessee, visitors can select on an audio guide hundreds of oral history excerpts and musical selections that complement the exhibits. To engage visitors at multiple levels, museums documenting human atrocity (along with resistance) such as the U.S. Holocaust Memorial Museum and Poland's Warsaw Uprising Museum have simultaneously employed oral history interviews in a variety of locations, from personal, even intimate, spaces to highly public arenas. Oral history interviews have been effectively employed to complement artifacts in house museums like the Jimmy Carter Boyhood Home National Historic Site and museums of work and technology like Mystic Seaport. They also have supplanted artifacts as the core of exhibitions, on occasion providing the impetus for an entire exhibit, as in the railroad community of Frankton Junction, New Zealand. In addition, interviews increasingly have been gathered by museums as an integral part of their collecting policy.[5]

Perhaps because museums demand consideration of space, time, and audience, as well as sound, museum professionals have paid significant attention to oral historical issues in a museum setting. For instance, the specific constraints of a given gallery—area, height, color, wiring, traffic flow—impact how people experience either sound or moving images. The limited average length of time a visitor spends in a museum or any given exhibit also has obvious ramifications for the presentation of oral history, as does the relationship between oral history interviews and other artifacts in a museum, and the fact that often fully half of a museum's visitors are school-age children. Of course, equipment and cost concerns are always present as well.

There are other questions at all stages of the process that are imperative for museum personnel to address in order to most fruitfully use oral history. If a museum is generating its own interviews, where and how should the interviews be conducted? What should be the scope and range of the interviews themselves? What should the relationship be among historians, archivists, and curators? What considerations inform the editing process? In particular, while there has been a lot of talk within the museum world about shared authority and collaboration, what are the implications of removing the interviewers and the questions from the interview excerpts presented in public? What effect do high-tech exhibits have on how people receive information, on the nature and meaning of the message? How do we interrogate the subject of memory itself in a museum setting? How are the interviews going to be used in conjunction with a museum's programmatic elements? What are the issues concerning storage, access, and distribution? Will an institution allow visitors to download oral history interviews on portable devices? Will visitors be able to add their own stories to a museum's collection?

Oral History on the Internet

Since the 1990s, the explosion of oral history on the Internet has been as great as that in museum settings. The Web's immediacy, accessibility, dynamism, democratic quality, nonlinearity, interactivity, and ability to combine diverse forms of communication and information offer immense possibilities to move beyond conventional boundaries of space and time, with enormous ramifications for oral history. At the same time, however, oral history practitioners have only begun to consider and appreciate the attributes and implications of oral history in an online environment. For a while, oral history repositories resisted putting interviews on the Web, out of legal and ethical concerns. What would be the consequences of effectively losing control over the interviews? What were the obligations to narrators who had signed release forms before the Internet was even imagined? The dam broke in the mid-1990s, however, with the Billy Graham Center Archives at Wheaton College being one of the first places to put interviews online. Since then, interviews—both transcripts and audiovisual files—have become commonplace on the Web.[6]

Repositories have presented online oral history interviews in a variety of increasingly lengthy and sophisticated ways. Originally, transcripts alone were displayed, with modest supportive material supplying biographical information about the narrator and perhaps the circumstances of the interview's creation. By the late 1990s, entities such as the University of Southern Mississippi's Civil Rights Documentation Project provided online subject indexes to the transcripts.

Reflecting newly available technologies, by the early 2000s repositories had begun to mount audio files of interview segments (and very occasionally full interviews) on the Web. One of the leaders in this practice was the Virtual Oral/Aural History Archive of California State University, Long Beach, which, in an attempt to get users to actually *listen* to the interview segments, featured only audio excerpts (no transcripts) along with accompanying descriptive material. In recent years, a growing number of institutions have placed video as well as audio segments and full interviews online, often with the transcript also available for those users who wish to read while they listen or watch, along with more elaborate descriptive aids and indexes tied to audio cues as well as to transcripts. Among the more successful Web sites in terms of overall design and the integration of sound/moving images with other elements are those of the Regional Oral History Office of the University of California–Berkeley; Densho, documenting the experience of Japanese-Americans in the internment camps; and two sites on quilters developed in conjunction with the MATRIX Center of Michigan State University.

Of particular note is the recent initiative of the University of Alaska–Fairbanks's Project Jukebox. Project Jukebox originated in the late 1980s as a pioneering initiative in the digital integration of oral history interviews—many conducted with Native Alaskans—with photographs, maps, and other documents, along with contextual information about the interviews and the settings in which they took place. Project Jukebox was distinctive in other ways, too; the interactive CD-ROM-based "jukeboxes" often featured audio/video of entire interviews and were commonly located in or near the communities where the interviews originated, often in remote parts of the state. After conducting a survey in 2000 of Web sites using oral history and consulting with some of the narrators about Internet usage, the project has put dozens of jukeboxes online. In 2006 the Project Jukebox staff began working with personnel from the Australian Centre for Oral History, who had begun to utilize software that simultaneously delivered digital audio, video, images, and text to a user's browser, with linkages among the various modes of communication. The two institutions have subsequently developed an online demonstration project for the Community of Memories jukebox.

While publishing oral history interviews remains perhaps the most common usage of oral history on the Web, the Internet contains many other applications as well. (A glance at the mushrooming number of "oral history" entries on YouTube only begins to suggest the diversity, complexity, and possibilities of online oral history.) The Oral History Association's revamped Web site offers perhaps the greatest single clearinghouse to the field. The University of North Carolina's Southern Oral History Program and other institutions have put up oral history "how-to" aids, while the *History Matters* Web site now includes *Oral History Online* with a guide to evaluating online oral history sites. The Web site *Talking History* at the State University of New York–Albany features a course syllabus on "Aural History and Historical Audio Documentary Production," along with links to prominent radio-audio producers and the *Talking History* radio programs. Interviews have been included in online museum exhibitions, as materials complementing audio, film, and television documentaries, in publications such as the *Journal of Multimedia History*, and as part of audio "installations" such as the *Sonic Memorial Project*, a collaborative effort by leading documentarians collecting and presenting sounds of the World Trade Center in the aftermath of the events of September 11, 2001.

One site that ably demonstrates the range of oral history applications on the Web is *London's Voices*, sponsored by the Museum of London. *London's Voices* was originally a three-year initiative designed to engage diverse audiences through innovative oral history projects. The Web site contains links to online exhibitions featuring short oral history excerpts about a particular topic, for instance, cinema and theater-going in London. It offers a downloadable booklet for others interested in community-based oral history efforts. It includes links to full transcripts of oral history interviews as well as short audio and print excerpts arranged thematically. It documents an oral history and photograph collecting project in the borough of Lewisham. And it introduces other nontraditional oral history–based initiatives, including a performance piece based on a review of the interviews conducted with new immigrants to London.

The site also links to the Web site of artist Graeme Miller, describing the aptly named Linked project, an installation in a neighborhood in London's East End where some 350 houses were demolished in the 1990s to make way for the M11 link road. Described as "a landmark in sound, an invisible artwork, a walk," Linked is an audio trail, broadcast from hidden transmitters to audio headsets, and creatively interspersing fragments of oral history interviews along with music and other sounds. It represents the outer edge of another mushrooming arena of oral history, the guided tour, a medium facilitated by the advent of podcasts, MP3 players, and advances in cell phone technology. One person who has developed model audio walks and thoughtfully considered the attributes of the medium, is Miller's occasional collaborator, the cultural geographer Toby Butler, who has his own distinctive Web site, *Memoryscape*.[7]

Personal Narratives and Digital Storytelling

In addition to "conventional" oral history, involving a two-party, face-to-face encounter, the Web contains a great deal of first-person narratives. In the late 1990s, George Mason University pioneering Center for History and New Media began gathering online personal accounts—in print—about the recent history of science and technology, including recollections about the early pregnancy test kit and the computer scientist Claude Shannon. These efforts helped pave the way for the CHNM's extensive collection of personal narratives about the events of September 11, 2001, part of the groundbreaking 9/11 Digital Archive. As of late 2004, over 35,000 individuals had submitted their stories online.

At a conference surrounding the launch of the 9/11 Digital Archive, the oral historian Linda Shopes questioned whether such methods of collecting narratives could substitute for "the cultivation of rapport and... lengthy in-depth narratives through intense face-to-face contact; the use of subtle paralinguistic cues as an aid to moving the conversation along; the talent of responding to a particular comment, in the moment, with the breakthrough question, the probe that gets underneath a narrator's words." While not discounting such concerns at all, CHNM members Roy Rosenzweig and Daniel Cohen have argued that online collections of personal narratives are likely to be more diverse and inclusive than those of conventional archives. Moreover, since respondents do their own typing, these narratives are substantially less expensive than transcribed oral history interviews.[8]

In any event, there is no doubt that first-person narratives have exploded on the Web, a central component of a wide range of sites. They figure especially prominently in Web sites of particular constituencies or interest groups dedicated to revisiting, expanding, and challenging the received historical wisdom about particular events and developments with which they have had first-hand experience. Though rudimentary in design (and therefore a model of what can be done with limited resources), one interesting site is that of the Civil Rights Movement Veterans, which as of December 2008 was receiving hundreds of thousands of hits a month. The site's introduction clearly states its intention: "The Civil Rights Movement was above all a mass peoples' movement—people coming together to change their lives for themselves. But all too often that central fact has been quietly dropped out of history in favor of a 'benevolent' court ruling, a few charismatic leaders, a handful of famous protests in a few well-known places, some tragic martyrs, and the gracious largess of magnanimous legislators. Our purpose is to make sure that there is at least one place where the Movement story is told by those who actually lived it." The site contains a wealth of easily located information, including transcripts of oral history interviews and a model release form, FAQs about the civil rights movement (which could be asked in an interview) along with posted answers from movement veterans, as well as memoirs, photos and other primary documents, a timeline, discussion sections (including one called *Telling Our Stories*), and numerous other features.

In addition to print-based personal narratives, the Web contains a burgeoning number of digital storytelling sites, where individuals relate short personal stories, often related to a particular theme, and usually with a montage of photographs and other images, narration, and perhaps music accompanying the video clip. There are centers for digital storytelling both within and outside academia, and digital storytelling has also been proven to be an effective device in pedagogy.[9] One of the most ambitious digital storytelling sites is the BBC's *Capture Wales*, which arranges stories by category, provides an index to the stories collected, and offers a guide on how to create and submit one's own story.

A close cousin to the digital storytelling movement is StoryCorps, the brainchild of David Isay. Along with The Kitchen Sisters (Davia Nelson and Nikki Silva). Jay Allison, Steve Rowland, Joe Richman, Dmae Roberts, and others, Isay belongs to a new generation of audio documentarians who have moved light years beyond the radio documentaries of the 1970s and 1980s in their technical sophistication, integration of numerous elements in addition to oral history excerpts, challenges to the conventional documentary format, and presentation of their work in a variety of formats and media, including the Web, to encourage the greatest possible accessibility and usage.[10] In 1994 Isay founded the production company Sound Portraits, "dedicated to telling stories that bring neglected American voices to a national audience." In addition to radio broadcast, Sound Portraits productions characteristically have an associated Web site with audio, transcripts, and related documents; some have spawned books, CDs, and even classroom guides in an exemplary usage of multiple media.

Inspired by the WPA life histories project of the 1930s, in 2003 StoryCorps opened as a booth in New York's Grand Central Terminal. With the assistance of an on-site facilitator, visitors conducted a forty-five-minute interview, usually with a family member or friend. They were given a CD version of the interview, while another copy was deposited with the American Folklife Center of the Library of Congress. Excerpts of selected interviews were also broadcast over National Public Radio. In 2005 StoryCorps inaugurated two traveling booths, which since have traveled extensively across the United States, and in 2007 launched StoryCorps Griot, gathering stories of African Americans, in collaboration with the forthcoming National Museum of African American History and Culture. In addition to regular NPR broadcasts and the multifaceted StoryCorps Web site, interviews have been featured in group listening events in numerous communities and in the book *Listening Is an Act of Love: A Celebration of American Life from the StoryCorps Project*, which, more than the radio excerpts, arranges interviews in a thematic fashion. Indeed, StoryCorps has become a phenomenon far beyond what Isay ever originally imagined.

While StoryCorps certainly dovetails with the democratic impulse, interactivity, and aural quality of oral history, and has greatly enhanced popular appreciation of storytelling, not all within the oral history community feel comfortable with the initiative. When Isay addressed the 2008 meeting of the Oral History Association, and in subsequent issues of the OHA newsletter, critics claimed that in its fragmentary, nonstructured quality StoryCorps really did not constitute oral history as oral historians knew it. Others asserted that in its popularity and success, StoryCorps had siphoned funds away from other deserving, more serious endeavors.

There exist other facets of the digital environment, beyond technological issues alone, with which "conventional" oral history practitioners often feel uneasy. Online digital stories or solicited personal narratives, and no doubt many other modes of presentation, frequently feel strange or even a bit threatening. I can attest to how jarring the new universe can seem when I recently listened from my computer to an interview I had conducted in 1977 with a retired textile worker, now part of the University of North Carolina's Documenting the American South digital publishing project. Yet rather than reject digital storytelling or other online personal narratives out of hand, oral historians need to critically consider their attributes from creation to editing to dissemination: what they do and how they function, both by themselves and in relationship to other developments. Alexander Freund of the University of Winnipeg has queried whether the attributes of the digital storytelling movement reinforce or diverge from either master narratives or the "broadcast yourself" sensibility of our times, privileging individual stories of persistence and success over those of failure or collective action.[11]

There have been other criticisms of oral history online. Even some enthusiasts of oral history in the digital environment have raised questions about decontextualization. If the majority of users arrive at interview transcripts through Google, for instance, they bypass institutional disclaimers or any material situating the interview within the circumstances of its creation, the body of interviews to which it belongs, other documents, and the pertinent historiography. The instant access nature of the Internet also raises a number of potential legal and ethical matters. What about the issue of third-party damage claimed by individuals who were not the narrator in an interview that has been published? Will the knowledge that one's interview could be broadcast over the Internet have a chilling effect on the candor of narrators?

A Multimedia Future

There exist countless examples of increasingly well-conceived and well-carried-out digital oral history applications, in a myriad of formats and environments. Indeed, the catchword of the day is multimedia, and the most successful practitioners have ably combined and navigated across disparate media, providing portals for people from diverse vantage points. Yet there also are at least as many examples of mediocre projects, where just because one *can* mount online streaming video, for example, one does it, without really interrogating the nature of the medium itself or of its composite parts, with regard to oral history.

A critical assessment of oral history in the digital environment also demands revisiting recorded sound and moving images—along with photographs, other documents, and, yes, the printed word—on their own terms as well as in contrast and combination with each other. How does the nature and setting of a videotaped interview, for instance, influence how it is presented and received on a Web site? What are the considerations in editing audio interviews compared to video? What are the strengths as well as the problematic aspects of oral history in various media and formats? How can we best draw attention to the sources themselves in a digital environment, to the relationship between history and memory, the past and the present, to the two parties jointly creating an oral history interview? How do we think about audience on the Web, about interactivity, about authenticity? When and how does the sophisticated use of technology detract from or enhance communication? What is the relationship between medium and message? As we encounter a sometimes dizzying array of technological options, we need to ask such fundamental questions if we are to make the most fruitful use of oral history in diverse media.

NOTES

1. Ron Chew, "Collected Stories: The Rise of Oral History in Museum Exhibitions," *Museum News* (Nov./Dec. 2002).

2. On "A More Perfect Union," Selma Thomas, "Private Memory in a Public Space: Oral History and Museums," in *Oral History and Public Memories*, ed. Paula Hamilton and Linda Shopes, 90–95 (Philadelphia: Temple University Press, 2008); on Ellis Island, Michael Frisch, "Audience Expectations as a Resource and Challenge: Ellis Island as a Case Study," in *A Shared Authority: Essays on the Craft and Meaning of Oral and Public History* (Albany: SUNY Press, 1990), 99, 215–24.

3. Chew, "Collected Stories"; Roy Rosenzweig and David Thelen, *The Presence of the Past: Popular Uses of History in American Life* (New York, 1998), 31–32, 105–8, 181–85.

4. Catherine Lewis, *The Changing Face Of Public History: The Chicago Historical Society and The Transformation of an American Museum* (DeKalb, Ill.: Northern Illinois Press, 2005); Ciraj Rassool and Sandra Prosalendis, eds., *Recalling Community in Cape Town: Creating and Curating the District Six Museum* (Capetown: District Six Foundation, 2001); John Kuo Wei Tchen, "Creating a Dialogic Museum: The Chinatown History Museum Experiment," in *Museums and Communities: The Politics of Public Culture*, ed. Ivan Karp et al. (Washington, D.C.: Smithsonian Institution Press, 1992). The Chinatown History Museum has been renamed the Museum of Chinese in America.

5. On the Warsaw Uprising Museum, Marta Kuekowska-Budzan, "Oral History in Public Space, a Report from Poland," unpublished paper delivered at the Oral History Association annual meeting, Oct. 2008; Anna Green, "The Exhibition that Speaks for Itself: Oral History and Museums," in *The Oral History Reader*, 2nd ed., ed. Robert Perks and Alistair Thomson, 416–24 (London/New York: Routledge, 2006); Chew, "Collected Stories."

6. It is beyond the scope of this essay to include a detailed discussion of the legal issues surrounding publication of oral history interviews on the Internet. One good introduction, written in 2000 by Karen Brewster, is "Internet Access to Oral Recordings: Finding the Issues," http://www.uaf.edu/library/oralhistory/brewster1/research.html. See also the latest edition of the Oral History Association pamphlet "Oral History and the Law" by John A. Neuenschwander, available through the OHA, and John A. Neuenschwander, *A Guide to Oral History and the Law* (New York: Oxford University Press, 2009).

7. Toby Butler and Graeme Miller, "Linked: A Landmark in Sound, a Public Work of Art," in Perks and Thomson, *Oral History Reader*, 425–33; Toby Butler, "Memoryscape: How Audio Walks Can Deepen Our Sense of Place by Integrating Art, Oral History and Cultural Geography," *Geography Compass* 1 (2007): 360–72.

8. Linda Shopes, "The Internet and Collecting the History of the Present," paper delivered on Sept. 11 as "History: Collecting Today for Tomorrow Symposium," Library of Congress, Sept. 10, 2003; Daniel I. Cohen and Roy Rosenzweig, *Digital History: A Guide to Gathering, Preserving, and Presenting the Past on the Web* (Philadelphia: University of Pennsylvania Press, 2005), esp. 161–64, 175, 181, 184–87.

9. Rina Benmayor, "Cyber-teaching in the Oral History Classroom," in Perks and Thomson, *Oral History Reader*, 434–45.

10. To learn more about the history of audio documentaries, see Charles Hardy III, "Authoring in Sound: Aural History, Radio and the Digital Revolution," in Perks and Thomson, *Oral History Reader*, 393–405; Hardy and Pamela Dean, "Oral History in Sound and Moving Image Documentaries," in *Thinking About Oral History*, ed. Thomas L. Charlton, Lois E. Myers, and Rebecca Sharpless, 268–319 (Lanham, Md.: Altamira Press,

2008). Among the Web sites featuring audio documentaries are Stories1st.org, Hearingvoices.com, and RadioDiaries.org, in addition to the sites of individual producers.

11. Alexander Freund, "On the Respectability of Oral History," Canadian Oral History Blog, Apr. 24, 2009, http://blog.uwinnipeg.ca/ohc/2009/04/; Alexander Freund, letter to the editor, *OHA Newsletter* (Spring 2009).

BIBLIOGRAPHY

Cohen, Daniel I., and Roy Rosenzweig. *Digital History: A Guide to Gathering, Preserving, and Presenting the Past on the Web*. Philadelphia: University of Pennsylvania Press, 2005.

Hamilton, Paula, and Linda Shopes, eds. *Oral History and Public Memories*. Philadelphia: Temple University Press, 2008.

Kuhn, Clifford M., Harlon E. Joye, and E. Bernard West. *Living Atlanta: An Oral History of the City, 1914–1948*. Athens: University of Georgia Press, 1990.

Neuenschwander, John A. *A Guide to Oral History and the Law*. New York: Oxford University Press, 2009.

Perks, Robert, and Alistair Thomson, eds. *The Oral History Reader*. London/New York: Routledge, 2003.

Rassool, Ciraj, and Sandra Prosalendis, eds. *Recalling Community in Cape Town: Creating and Curating the District Six Museum*. Capetown: District Six Foundation, 2001.

CHAPTER 22

MESSIAH WITH THE MICROPHONE? ORAL HISTORIANS, TECHNOLOGY, AND SOUND ARCHIVES

ROBERT B. PERKS

For decades, oral historians and their tape recorders have been inseparable, but it has also been an uneasy marriage of convenience. The recorder is both our "tool of trade" and also that part of the interview with which we are least comfortable. We rely on technology to create and preserve the data source that we place at the heart of our historical analysis, yet we retain an ambivalent attitude toward that technology and struggle to understand it. For the post–World War II generation of pioneering oral historians, there was an initial aversion to using any form of audio technology at all. When they did use it, some were reluctant to take audio quality seriously, preferring to work from transcriptions of the audio documents, not the sound itself. Until recently, the more innovative uses of audio technology for spoken history have been left to radio broadcasters, museums, and sound artists.[1]

Oral historians' relationship with archivists has been an uneasy one. From the very beginnings of the modern oral history movement in the 1940s, archivists have played an important role. By the early 1980s, although oral history remained the object of suspicion among traditional archivists and librarians, particularly in Britain, a technical and archival consensus about interview practice had emerged, which has only recently been unsettled by the digital revolution. The arrival of "artifact-free" digital audio recorders and mass access via the Internet have transformed the relationship between the historian and the source. Accomplished twenty-first-century oral history practitioners (usually among arts, humanities, and social science researchers) are now expected to acquire advanced technological skills to capture, preserve, analyze, edit, and present their data to ever larger audiences. Ironically, the roles of data creator and data archivist have converged at a time when the complex underlying technology is increasingly unknowable. High fidelity interviews are easier than ever to gather, and the "oral" in oral history is increasingly accessible, but the ethics of the interplay between technology, sound archives, oral historians, their interviewees, and wider public users have never been more debated.

Oral Historians and Recording Technology

Thomas Edison invented recorded sound—the phonograph—in 1877, but for many years collecting and storing audio was extremely difficult. The phonograph had the major disadvantage that recordings could not be duplicated. Although in the 1890s Emile Berliner invented a way of recording onto a flat disc, which could be copied, the equipment was cumbersome, sound quality was relatively poor, and the costs involved were beyond the means of most people. Recordings, initially on wax cylinders, were extraordinarily fragile, and only a small number of original spoken word recordings have survived from before World War I.[2]

When recordings ventured out beyond the controlled environment of the studio, they remained extremely challenging. Anthropologists were the first to use the new apparatus for what they termed "field recordings." The American Jesse Walter Fewkes was using a phonograph to collect Native American stories as early as 1890 and recommended "those magic cylinders of wax where they are indelibly fixed forever" to the Cambridge professor Alfred Cort Haddon, who led the first British field recording expedition to the Torres Straits in 1898.[3] Folklorists quickly followed, and in Britain the musicians Percy Grainger, Cecil Sharp, and composer Ralph Vaughan Williams were collecting English folk song before 1914.[4] By the interwar period the arrival of microphones (around 1925) and instantaneous (so-called "acetate") disc recorders allowed longer and better quality recordings to be made, but outside the growing music industry, radio broadcasters, and a handful of enthusiasts and specialists, sound recording remained an esoteric pursuit. Until the BBC, which, from its formation in 1922, tended to broadcast live and not record, accidentally set up its own sound archive in 1936, no significant sound archive existed in Britain.[5] The British Museum had grudgingly accepted a batch of metal master recordings from the Gramophone Company as early as 1906, but by 1925 held only several dozen of the 100,000 records it was estimated had been issued throughout the world.[6]

In the United States in the 1930s, the folklorist Alan Lomax was extensively recording songs and stories in the American South. But the many thousands of interviews collected by the New Deal Federal Writers' Project, regarded by some as the beginning of modern oral history, were largely written down, not recorded. Some of the better-known oral history pioneers began by not using recorders at all. Allan Nevins, who founded the Oral History Research Office at Columbia University in 1948, started out without a recorder, using a student to take notes as the interview progressed. Nevins estimated that he could gather about 60 percent of what he was told using pen and paper.[7] Very soon, however, he was using the first kind of magnetic recorder—the wire recorder—and later open-reel recorders. It was the advent of these portable and cheaper magnetic recorders from the 1950s that made it possible for a new breed of historians to carry out recordings in any numbers. The University of California at Berkeley created its Regional Oral History Office in 1954, utilizing the new technology. In Britain, the pathbreaking Survey of English Dialects at Leeds University collected recordings of both linguistic and social history interest over a ten-year period in more than three hundred locations.[8] Other centers such as the Irish Folklore Commission,[9] the Welsh Folk Museum in Cardiff, and the School of Scottish Studies in Edinburgh were also active, very much in the anthropological, folklore, and linguistic tradition, though all contributed to the emerging oral history movement.

Most influential to the pioneers of the British oral history movement was the work of the folklorist George Ewart Evans, whose innovative agricultural history, *Ask the Fellows Who Cut the Hay*, based on conversations with his neighbors in rural Suffolk, appeared in 1956. The same year he was loaned a new EMI "Midget" open-reel tape recorder by the BBC:

> This portable tape-recorder caused a revolution in outside broadcasting. Previously, to record someone outside the studio was an expensive exercise requiring a special van and two or three personnel. A Midget was a very good machine, comparatively simple to operate and with its own batteries so that one could record anywhere.[10]

Evans quickly recognized that he could use the new technology to capture not merely the words (to save him writing them down) but ways of speaking. He called this "the unadorned purity" of language, which was "a proper and more durable clothing" to the information conveyed.[11] At a time when many rural homes still lacked electricity, the portable Midget, with its innovative integrated circuits and small electric motor, liberated recordists and broadcasters, among them another pioneer of British oral history, Charles Parker. In the 1950s, Parker and the folk singer Ewan MacColl pioneered a new kind of radio oral history at the BBC, leading to *Radio Ballads*, which aired between 1958 and 1964. These shows were based on the unmediated, largely unheard, personal testimonies of "ordinary" people like miners and railway staff.[12]

By the time that social historians Paul and Thea Thompson had met Evans, and also Allan Nevins in the United States (where an Oral History Association had been formed in 1967), a British oral history movement was getting underway. Other portable tape recorders were coming onto the market. Philips had developed the audio compact cassette in 1963, although it was not regarded as "professional" quality, and many interviewers continued to use open-reel technology. The Uher Report Monitor became the standard recorder used by many oral historians in the 1970s. It had its challenges, however, as Paul Thompson, who used it himself for his first major oral history project, reflected in 1996:

> We got advice from the BBC. We used the Uher machine, very heavy... semi-portable, really. And it's clumsy also, in that every time you turned the tape, you had to re-thread it. And also, it has a really very awkward microphone, a big microphone, so in many ways, it's quite difficult to use. But it does produce beautiful quality recordings, and it's good for radio work, because you can cut up the tapes, it's an open reel, you see. So it does have some advantages. And, for a long time, it was thought to be the only kind of tape which had a long-term archival quality. It's only in the last ten years that cassettes have been regarded as okay for archives. But I think, on the other hand, we had a real problem with the quality of the recording, because it is extraordinarily difficult to train people to use the machines properly.[13]

The Uher survived, increasingly used with lapel or "lavalier" microphones rather than handheld microphones, until better, so-called broadcast-quality, cassette recorders like the Marantz Superscope (later renamed the CP-range), came onto the market. The analog audiocassettes made possible the explosion of community-based oral history in Britain at that time. Before long, virtually all oral historians were using audiocassettes.[14]

Thompson had put his finger on one of the continuing challenges for oral historians: how to master the technology sufficiently to produce audible recordings without impinging unduly on the interview relationship. In the early days, it was clear that very few researchers had come across tape recorders or knew how to operate them, and they treated recording devices with suspicion. Charles Morrissey thought there was "a danger of too much reliance on tools and not relying sufficiently on old-fashioned intuition," but he noted that interviewers were more scared of the equipment than their interviewees: "They didn't know whether they were doing the right thing, whether the volume was high enough, whether the mike was close enough, and this sort of thing. It bothered and affected the quality of the interview."[15]

Opinions varied about how technically skilled and adept an interviewer should be, and the iconic U.S. oral historian Studs Terkel made a virtue of an extreme, almost Luddite position:

> I don't know how a tape recorder works. Not even the simplest one that's ever been invented...I don't know how to open it, I don't know how to put in the cassette, which way up it goes, how to close the lid when it's in, which button to press to get it to start recording, which is the button to press to make it stop. None of it, I don't know any of it....What am I describing? I'm describing one of my biggest assets. Its name is ineptitude. Why's it an asset? Well, would you be

> frightened of a little old guy who wants to tape-record a conversation with you—*and he can't even work his tape recorder?*... I'm not the Messiah with the microphone, I'm just another human being.[16]

Minimizing the presence of the technology became a key concern, and oral history handbooks devoted considerable attention to the problem: "When using a tape recorder it is important to avoid drawing attention to the machine, and diverting one's own attention, by fussing about it," one recommended.[17] "Develop a rapport... particularly with older people because they are often suspicious of strangers and nervous about tape recorders."[18] "Shaking hands breaks down an important psychological barrier at an early stage."[19] Some of the manuals advised playing back a few minutes of the tape to reassure the interviewee.[20]

Gradually, as oral historians became more confident with recording equipment, a technical consensus began to emerge, which defined the "best" oral history practice worldwide. By the mid-1980s, although opinion varied about which model of recorder to use (for both open-reel and cassette formats), there was broad agreement that one-to-one interviews were best; that interviewees tended to forget about the recorder if it was discreetly placed; that using lapel rather than handheld microphones helped; that extraneous "noises off" should be minimized to improve overall audibility; that active listening without making audible interjections made for better recordings, which could be more easily transcribed and edited later; and that time was well spent learning how to set recording levels for optimum audio quality. This mantra of fundamental techniques, which now seem self-evident, actually emerged over a thirty-year period. For the second generation of oral historians that had grown up with recording technology, and had lost their sense of technological awe, the equipment became a less intimidating aspect of doing interviews. With the arrival of smaller, less intrusive cassette recorders and the first digital recorders, consideration of the interview relationship moved away from concerns about the technology to interpersonal issues such as subjectivity and co-construction.

Sound Archivists and Oral Historians

The development of oral history in many parts of the world was influenced by the involvement of sound archivists and librarians.[21] In the United States, after a period when tapes were routinely destroyed once they had been transcribed,[22] archivists and librarians eventually won an important debate in the 1960s about the primacy of the tape over the transcript, and the need to save the original tape "for replaying to later researchers, and for the possibility that some new truth may be discovered from the oral original not revealed by the typescript."[23] Martha Jane Zachert's 1968 article, "The Implications of Oral History for Librarians," marked one of the first published attempts to survey and assess the likely impact of the new discipline for information professionals.[24] Ron Grele has argued that archivists and librarians retained a pervasive guiding influence on the development of U.S. oral history, although, at least initially, "most projects were elitist to the core."[25]

Oral history in Britain had its origins in folklore, linguistics, and ethnography, so the archival imperative emerged quite early on, and there have never been any serious suggestions that original recordings should be abandoned in favor of only transcripts, as Paul Thompson recalled:

> I think we fairly quickly realised that we had, really, fallen on an extraordinarily rich material, and we couldn't possibly exhaust it with one book [*The Edwardians*]. And that was how the idea of creating the Archive came. And this was a completely independent decision. We knew of nobody who was doing anything in that way, creating an archive like that.[26]

Others shared Thompson's essentially radical purpose for oral history, notably Raphael Samuel and the socialist-feminist History Workshop movement, who saw oral history as a means not merely of collecting the "hidden histories" of marginalized groups but giving these voices a permanent presence in archives and libraries. As Samuel remarked:

> The collector of the spoke word—of oral memory and tradition—is in a privileged position. He is the creator, in some sort, of his own archives, and he ought to interpret his duties accordingly. His role, properly conceived, is that of archivist, as well as historian, retrieving and storing priceless information which would otherwise be lost. At present the archive in which his material could be copied or stored does not exist.... Historians in the future will bring fresh interests to bear upon the materials we collect; they will be asking different questions and seeking different answers.[27]

Several British archives were already collecting linguistic and folkloric recordings, notably the School of Scottish Studies at Edinburgh University, set up in 1951,[28] and the Welsh Folk Museum at St. Fagans (which had begun collecting field recordings of oral traditions and dialects in 1957).[29] But it was certainly true that the collection of audiovisual records lay outside the purview of most local libraries, archives, and record offices, a situation that remained unchanged for several decades. Significantly, the founding meeting of what would become the British Oral History Society took place in 1969 at the British Institute of Recorded Sound (BIRS, now the British Library Sound Archive). It would be another twenty years before it appointed an oral history curator, although it did archive copies of both Thompson's and Evans's recordings.[30]

Gradually, during the 1970s and 1980s, a fragile infrastructure of sound archives blossomed regionally in England with the emergence of such archives as the North West Sound Archive (which later became part of the Lancashire Record Office), the Wessex Sound and Film Archive (part of the Hampshire County Record Office), and collections at the Norfolk, Suffolk, and Essex County Record Offices. Other major oral history collections began to be assembled in national museums like the Imperial War Museum (IWM) in London. The 1978 booklet *An Archives Approach to Oral History*, penned by the IWM's keeper of sound records, David Lance, was probably the first substantial publication of its kind in the UK up to that point,[31] although it is clear that he was uneasy with the "pioneering zeal" of the social history approach to oral history led by Thompson, Samuel, and others. Lance became a founding committee member of the Oral History Society, but he grew disillusioned with the "dominance of sociologists," always felt "at arm's length," never "part of the in-crowd," and eventually parted company.[32] His unease was shared by other influential sound archivists, such as Ken Howarth, who founded the North West Sound Archive in 1979 and was involved in oral history but never took an active role in the Oral History Society.[33] Both Lance and Howarth built a close relationship with the BBC, which, although it had shifted somewhat away from speech radio, easing out Charles Parker,[34] continued to play a role as de facto the UK's largest sound archive with an important "trickle down" influence on thinking about the recording formats that oral history practitioners utilized.

This period was also one of significant growth in oral history activity in local museums all over Britain, partly due to government funding for community-based projects aimed at reducing unemployment.[35] The major museum collections in Bradford, Newcastle, Southampton, Beamish, and Birmingham all started in this way. In the UK, museums took the lead in creating oral history archives rather than library, archive, and record office networks. This contrasted with the United States and South Africa, where university and college libraries and archives played a more crucial role. By 1980, the Oral History Society's *Directory of British Oral History Collections* reported at least fifty museum-based oral history archives, some with many thousands of tapes, and this figure grew through the decade.[36]

Worldwide among archivists and librarians, audiovisual records brought new challenges to the basic concepts of the profession. The response to this new challenge, and a readiness to embrace change, has varied considerably between Britain and North America. For many years what might be called the "supplementary model" was the prevailing approach favored by archivists in both locations: the view that oral history, as memory, was inherently unreliable and might therefore (at best) supplement the "real" archives of paper-based documentation. As late as 1991, the UK Business Archives Council's professional manual relegated oral history to a chapter, "Supplementing the Collection," located at the end of the manual, as something to be considered after "the essential work of the archive... is well in hand."[37] Oral history represented a key challenge to notions prevalent in Western cultures of archivists as *passive and neutral* collectors of historical materials that had naturally accrued from the ferment of time. Traditional approaches firmly eschewed archivists taking any active role in *creating* archives.[38] The active creation of records, it was argued, threatened to undermine the concept of a document's organic spontaneity and impartiality. Furthermore, archivists did not have the expertise, funding, or time to indulge in "creating records of marginal value" when document backlogs needed attention.[39]

In Britain, unlike the United States and Canada where oral history was greeted rather more enthusiastically by archivists, this was a significant stumbling block to archivists' active involvement in oral history, and arguably in audiovisual records more generally. While the Society of American Archivists (SAA) had established an oral history committee as early as 1969, and published many engaging pieces in *American Archivist*, its British counterpart remained aloof. The *Journal of the Society of Archivists*, in more than fifty years of publication, has published no more than a handful of articles, only recently engaging with oral historians.[40]

Nonetheless by the early 1980s, through pressure from an emerging breed of audiovisual information professionals, a second model for oral history's role in archives was emerging. This was the "activist archivist" or "filling the gap" model—influenced by James Fogerty's 1983 article of the same name in the *American Archivist*, which highlighted the intrinsic limitations of personal papers, diaries, and organizational records, and oral history's ability to illuminate key life events, such as childhood; to uncover the experiences of the "inarticulate [and] the uneducated...who have no personal papers or records to donate"; and to plug gaps in the documentation with "candid opinion." Fogerty claimed that oral history was "a necessity rather than a luxury," and he argued for *active* involvement by archive staff in creating and collecting personal testimonies.[41] In the same year, oral history figured for the first time in discussions at the International Association of Sound and Audiovisual Archives (IASA), itself regarded by many within the mainstream archival profession as an outsider special interest group. The Canadian audiovisual archivist Richard Lochead led several contributions in favor of archivists' active involvement in oral history.[42]

IASA's various national branches and membership proved to be crucial in setting technical standards for oral history fieldwork and sought to better inform paper-based information professionals about preservation standards for audiovisual records. At that time, those subjects were rarely discussed and poorly served by taught courses on records management in the university sector worldwide.[43] IASA, together with an emerging international network of oral historians,[44] also disseminated best practice to emerging oral historians and sound archivists in the developing world. There, archivists have more readily embraced oral testimony as a substitute for the lack of written archives.[45] Similarly, the former Communist countries of Eastern Europe and the former dictatorships of Latin America have adopted oral history as a corrective to state-manipulated archives. They have played a key public role in rescuing and preserving memories of repression and state terrorism, which would otherwise be lost.[46] In South Africa, Australia, and New Zealand, new testimony-led archives featured prominently in reconciliation processes and land-rights cases.[47] The UK branch of IASA, the British Association of Sound Collections (BASC), had many oral history projects among its membership. Its meetings aired live issues such as the reel-to-reel/cassette debate. It monitored new developments, offered advice on cataloging and new digital formats as they emerged, and generally provided a crucial expert technical underpinning of much oral history activity in Britain from the late 1980s.[48] The symbiosis of IASA/BASC, led by the British Library's National Sound Archive, and the British oral history movement, was completed when the British Library appointed the Oral History Society's secretary as its first Curator of Oral History in 1988.[49]

A third model for archivist and librarian engagement with oral history emerged during the 1990s—what might be called the "postmodern model." This was put forward most cogently by Canadian archivists Jean-Pierre Wallot and Normand Fortier. They dismissed the cautious view of the archivist as an impartial collector of items in favor of a postmodern vision of active collection: activist archivists self-conscious about their own personal and political views and abilities to shape their collections.[50] This keyed into the debates taking place in the United States among those interested in "deconstructing" archives. They argued that both archivists and their users are active agents in creating their own values and meanings, finally putting to rest the concept of archiving as a neutral and objective process.[51]

This archival turn to postmodernism coincided with a lively academic debate around the *re-use* of archives for the secondary analysis of interview data. Joanna Bornat wrote that "Recognizing that data is produced within a social and historical context, and that our revisiting is itself a social act, should be part of the repertoire of skills and understanding of the researcher."[52] She posed questions about the ethics of archivists granting public access for the re-use of oral histories for reasons entirely different from the original purpose of the interview. Is it acceptable, she asked, for users to reinterpret archived data in endlessly different ways, decontextualized and perhaps unacceptable to the interviewees themselves? Although this debate has been led by sociologists concerned with qualitative data, rather than with oral history collections per se, it is nonetheless one that has resonances for oral history archivists.

As more oral history and sound archives have become accessible via the Web and can be browsed and cherry-picked at will, so the context of their creation and moral ownership has become both less evident and more important.[53] As recently as 2006 James Fogerty remarked that "The lasting value of oral history interviews can be realized only if they are carefully preserved, made available for wide and easy use, and supported by records that faithfully document the context within which they were created," but already in the intervening period the model of the gatekeeper archivist has been eroded by digitization for remote offsite and virtual access over which less direct control can be exercised.[54]

It is clear that the pace of change in archives and libraries has varied greatly around the globe. If the new postmodern thinking was impacting on North American archival practice and on international audiovisual archivists, one British archivist noted that "all this debate and re-evaluation within the USA has had little impact upon the way in which the archive profession in the UK operates.... UK archives, both in terms of the kind of material which is held, and the nature of its users, appear to be far from representative of British society."[55] Nonetheless the beginning of the twenty-first century saw major changes as politically driven policy initiatives forced archivists to operate in a different environment and with new external pressures to their predecessors, based around "customer-facing" services, community involvement, and cross-sectoral partnerships, where anticipating user needs often had greater currency than passive collecting.[56] As new strategic organizations have been set up to bring museums, libraries, and archives more closely together, oral history projects appear to deliver many of the expectations of local and national government paymasters for social inclusion and social relevance. Many county and local record offices have begun to take more active roles in oral history and sound archiving.[57] Simultaneously, new funding streams, particularly the Heritage Lottery Fund (HLF), have led to hundreds of new community projects, all of them seeking permanent repositories for their audio (and increasingly video) oral histories.[58]

It used to be argued that archivists and librarians are not naturally interdisciplinary and are by temperament introverts, happier "caring for papers and books rather than mingling with people," while oral historians are rather the opposite: outward looking and collaborative.[59] There is growing evidence worldwide that these stereotypes are shifting and blurring. Certainly those British archivists and librarians previously reluctant to embrace oral history have been forced to respond to the pressure of events. The question looking forward is the degree to which the archives of the future will be even more subject to the vagaries of political trends than they have ever been before. If we accept archivists (and oral historians) as active agents of change, with their own beliefs, passions, and prejudices, what reliable archival yardsticks remain with which to protect the very notion of archives? If new Web 2.0 user-led models of acquisition become dominant, and as oral historians' and archivists' respective roles merge, where does this leave professional archival concepts of selection, authority, permanence, and provenance?[60]

The Digital Revolution

A climate of uncertainty and role insecurity has emerged from the gathering pace of the digital technological revolution that started with the advent of digital compact discs (CD) in 1982, followed by the arrival of portable digital audio tape (R-DAT) recorders in 1989. These new formats enabled the collection of hiss-free digital interviews, which could be duplicated without degradation or loss of quality, and which could be time-coded and easily edited. Most sound archivists urged caution about early-adoption and among oral historians analog audiocassettes prevailed in terms of cost, longer battery-life for portable machines and the archival longevity of ferric audiocassettes over the metal tape used by DAT.[61] In 1992, however, DAT was succeeded by another portable format, MiniDisc (MD), which promised hi-fidelity, long-play digital recordings from a recorder the size of a cigarette package, and at a price well within the budget of private individuals and small projects. Initially, at least, MD heralded a liberating new dawn. Entering an affordable digital domain promised an end to real-time archival copying times and the arrival of automatic indexing.

The initial euphoria quickly began to wear thin as it became clear that MiniDisc recorders were tricky to use in the field, and some of the digital carriers, particularly recordable CDs but also DAT, were not as robust and indestructible as had been first claimed. Some digital formats, such as MiniDisc, relied on proprietary means of compressing the data (fivefold in the case of MD) that were not universally shared and that relied on computer software supported (and copyrighted) by only one manufacturer. This made them potentially unreliable and unsustainable into the future.[62] As Peter Copeland observed in 1997, the objectives of sound archivists and manufacturers were diverging fast:

> Long-term preservation implies thought-processes which are almost the antithesis of thought-processes elsewhere in the audio-visual industry. There, developments are taking place rapidly, but neither sound nor pictures are being recorded with significantly greater fidelity than twenty years ago. Instead the word "developments" implies the equipment is cheaper, lighter, and easier to use; and in turn this means that the media (upon which sound and images are stored) keeps changing. Which is exactly what archivists do not want.[63]

The new digital formats also prompted debate about their long-term viability and archival reliability. The worldwide consensus that had evolved around the correct storage and preservation conditions for analog recordings[64] was ruffled by considerable disagreement among audiovisual archivists about the new digital formats, which, some twenty years later, has only recently settled into something approaching a digital consensus. Even this shifts at the pace of audiovisual technological innovation and is heavily resource-reliant.[65]

This crisis of confidence about digital initially encouraged many sound archivists to be extremely cautious, with the result that analog audiocassettes remained the format of choice by many oral historians until the arrival of the next generation of digital recorders. Solid-state compact flashcard (and hard-drive) recorders became available around 2005.[66] Once again the new format seemed at first to offer unbeatable advantages for oral history interviewers: it was cheap, compact, could record three hours of high-quality stereo sound to a nonproprietary international standard (.wav, and many hours more of compressed poorer quality MP3 audio), was time-coded and indexable. But importantly solid-state marked a watershed from *artifact-based* recording—where an audio object is created, which needs to be labeled, shelved, and physically preserved—to *artifact-free* recording where an audio file is created on a temporary memory device, which must then be transferred to a computer for permanent preservation. Aside from normal anxieties about new formats and new recording equipment, this shift has also demanded a completely new way of working for oral historians, which has eroded the separation between creation and curation.

Entire high-fidelity sound archives can now be created, stored, cloned, and digitally edited on personal computers and external hard drives, using free software downloadable from the Web. Without recourse to a physical artifact, or to the interviewee, or to an archivist, these recordings can then be shared with a worldwide audience of millions via the Web in any number of forms. An exhilarating democratization of the process of creation and dissemination has led to an explosion, not only of oral history activity but of sharing personal and life history audiovisual data. In its most extreme form—so-called "life caching"—ever-cheaper and ever-larger memory storage allows every waking sound and image to be digitally captured and stored.[67]

New ways of creating and processing data pose a number of issues for oral historians and archivists. On a practical level, archives now need to acquire large amounts of sustainable computer memory capacity and develop new systems for identifying and retrieving audio files held within those computers. Robust new life-cycle preservation strategies are required for backing up and migrating data that might otherwise disappear or become inaccessible. Digital audio data might be easier than ever to acquire, but arguably it is also even more fragile than its analog predecessors. A recent report warned that "Digital documents may disappear without pre-warning at any time. Consequently the most important principle of all is that at least two copies of each document must be available at any time…and held in different places…in the case of disaster."[68]

At the British Library the transition of fieldwork and preservation practice from analog to digital capture and storage has been painful and protracted, requiring significant funding, staff retraining, and confidence-building. Not only do the oral history interviewers carry out the recording, they now also upload, accession, and clone their data, encompassing some of the traditional tasks of the archivist. Some of them remain uncomfortable with the "intangibility" of an artifact-free procedure and they have all had to adapt their interview practice to allow for longer continuous recording, rather than the natural thirty-minute breaks that using audiocassettes (and open reels) demanded. This has subtly changed the intellectual ebb and flow of the interview. A library-wide digital object management (mass storage) system has been acquired and tested, and an entirely new accessioning system developed. As each individual audio track needs a unique number and descriptor, an early policy of automatically segmenting recordings into thirty-minute tracks was abandoned as it was taking too long to number and document each individual track (much longer than writing a shelf number on an audiocassette).

As digital tracks can be accidentally erased and edited without trace at the point that they are downloaded from the temporary flashcard storage to hard drive, there has been a need for scrupulous training and data management. The speed and ease with which digital files can be cloned is a clear advantage over analog, but with so many competing data and audio file formats, care is needed to use only recognized international standards and to avoid proprietary data compression as much as possible. Even then, not all remote users have access to the right technology to access the files. There is no doubt that a cultural chasm exists between the early-adopters of new technology and an older age-group without access to computers. In short, oral history interviewers, whether they like it or not, are becoming data managers.

The huge benefit that digital recording brings is enhanced access for remote users, who are increasingly reluctant to travel to archives. They expect online access to archival collections from their desktops and on the move.[69] In fact, the Web is particularly appropriate for those people who are more comfortable with oral and visual, rather than written, forms of memory and narrative, as projects with Aboriginal peoples have found.[70]

After years in which oral historians have grappled with different documentation strategies, debated transcription methodologies, and agonized over cataloging protocols, the Web's global reach has brought a paradigm shift in thinking.[71] Still, the old debates remain relevant. Although voice-recognition and automated audio-indexing software are improving, it is clear that we will require text-based finding aids for large oral history archives for some years yet. Content summaries and transcripts are enormously time-consuming and expensive to produce, and it is likely that only organizations such as archives will have the resources to carry out this work in a sustainable manner. In other words, the blizzard of personally generated audiovisual data on the Web may simply be inaccessible in the future.

What is emerging is a new model of partnership working between oral historians—both in the community and in higher education—and archivists, where both can create and document contemporary culture in a collaborative relationship. This model sees archives not merely as "places of deposit" but pro-active partners in creating, preserving, and sharing data with new global audiences. It believes that archives must be representative of, and sensitive toward, their own communities. And it sees oral historians as archival data managers, utilizing new technologies not merely to capture personal memory but analyze and disseminate it in new ways. With the correct safeguards in place to respect personal moral rights, recognize cultural ownership, and contextualize individual recordings, new creative uses can be made of oral history data, through powerful search engines, linkages such as the semantic Web,[72] Web 2.0 user interactivity, and the blending of related images and textual sources. We have only just begun to imagine their potentials.[73]

NOTES

1. Charles Hardy, "Authoring in Sound: Aural History, Radio and the Digital Revolution," in *The Oral History Reader*, ed. Robert Perks and Alistair Thomson, 393–405 (New York/London: Routledge, 2006). See Toby Butler and Graeme Miller, "Linked: A Landmark in Sound, a Public Walk of Art," in ibid., 424–33, for an example of oral history–based sound art.

2. Peter Copeland, *Sound Recordings* (London: The British Library, 1991).

3. Martin Clayton, "Ethnographic Wax Cylinders at the British Library National Sound Archive: A Brief History and Description of the Collection," *British Journal of Ethnomusicology* 5 (1996): 67–92.

4. Andrew King, "Bright golden store: a background to English traditional music recording," at http://www.bl.uk/collections/sound-archive/traditional_music.html.

5. Sean Street's BBC Radio 4 *Archive Hour*, "Saving the Sounds of History," Sept. 1, 2007, tells the story of temporary secretary Marie Slocombe's mission to create an archive:

http://news.bbc.co.uk/1/hi/magazine/6968321.stm. On the shortcomings of the BBC Sound Archive, see also Paul Thompson, "The BBC Archives," *Oral History* 1, no. 2 (1971).

6. Timothy Day, "The National Sound Archive: The First Fifty Years," in *Aural History: Essays on Recorded Sound*, ed. Andy Linehan, 42 (London: British Library, 2001).

7. Allan Nevins, interview by Columbia University, 1963, 238; Louis Starr, "Oral History," in *Oral History: An Interdisciplinary Anthology*, ed. David Dunaway and Willa Baum, 8–9 (Nashville: American Association for State and Local History, 1984).

8. Harold Orton, *Survey of English Dialects: An Introduction* (Leeds: E. J. Arnold, 1962); Rob Perks and Jonnie Robinson, "'The Way We Speak': Web-based Representations of Changing Communities in England," *Oral History* 33 (Autumn 2005): 79–90.

9. Sean O'Sullivan, "The Work of the Irish Folklore Commission," *Oral History* 2 (Autumn 1974).

10. George Ewart Evans, *Spoken History* (London: Faber and Faber, 1987), 4, 141–42. See also his "Flesh and Blood Archives" *Oral History* 1 (1973).

11. Evans, *Spoken History*, xv.

12. http://www.birmingham.gov.uk/charlesparkerarchive.bcc.

13. Paul Thompson, interview by Karen Worcman, June 1996, 29–30, http://www.esds.ac.uk/qualidata/online/data/edwardians/biography.asp. "Family Life and Work Experience before 1918," carried out between 1970 and 1973, was the first national oral history interview study to be carried out in Britain. Thompson cited both the sociologist Peter Townsend and his interview-based study *The Family Life of Old People: An Inquiry in East London* (London: Routledge/Kegan Paul, 1957) and George Ewart Evans as key influences in developing oral history in Britain (*Spoken History*, 15, 24).

14. Ronda Jamieson, "Aspects of Oral History Projects and Archives: New Zealand, the United States of America and the United Kingdom," *Oral History* 20 (Autumn 1992): 53–60.

15. Charles T. Morrissey, "On Oral History Interviewing," in *Elite and Specialized Interviewing*, ed. L. A. Dexter (Evanston: Northwestern University Press, 1970).

16. Tony Parker, *Studs Terkel: A Life in Words* (London: HarperCollins, 1997), 163–64.

17. Paul Thompson, *The Voice of the Past: Oral History* (Oxford: Oxford University Press, 1978), 173.

18. Stephen Humphries, *The Handbook of Oral History* (London: Inter-Action Imprint, 1984), 19.

19. Ken Howarth, *Remember, Remember: Tape Recording Oral History* (Hebden Bridge: Pennine Heritage Network, 1984), 34.

20. Evans, *Spoken History* 1987, 27; Valerie Raleigh Yow, *Recording Oral History: A Practical Guide for Social Scientists* (London: Sage, 1994), 59.

21. Wilma MacDonald, "Origins: Oral History Programmes in Canada, Britain and the United States," *Canadian Oral History Association Journal* 10 (1991): 12–24.

22. In 1962, Louis Starr, director of the Columbia Oral History Research Office, noted that "We erase most of our tapes for re-use," quoted in Donald A. Ritchie, *Doing Oral History: A Practical Guide* (New York: Oxford University Press, 2003), 165–86.

23. Allan Nevins, "The Uses of Oral History" in *Oral History at Arrowhead: The Proceedings of the First National Colloquium on Oral History*, ed. Elizabeth Dixon and James Mink, 40 (Los Angeles: Oral History Association, 1967).

24. Martha Jane Zachert, "The Implications of Oral History for Librarians," *College and Research Libraries* 29 (1968); also Willa K. Baum, "Building Community Identity Through Oral History: A New Role for the Local Library," *California Librarian* 31 (Oct. 1970): 271–84.

25. Ronald J. Grele. "Oral History as Evidence" in *Handbook of Oral History*, ed. Thomas L. Charlton, Lois E. Myers, and Rebecca Sharpless, 47 (Lanham/Oxford: Altamira Press, 2006).

26. Paul Thompson, interview by Karen Worcman, June 1996, 24; also see his "BBC Archives" in *Oral History* 1 (Autumn 1971).

27. Raphael Samuel, "Perils of the Transcript," *Oral History* (Autumn 1971): 22.

28. http://www.celtscot.ed.ac.uk/archives.htm; Eric Cregeen, "Oral History," *IASA Phonographic Bulletin* 29 (Mar. 1981); Alan Bruford, "The Archive of the School of Scottish Studies," *Oral History* 2 (Autumn 1974).

29. Beth Thomas, "A Special Responsibility: Folk Life Archives at the Museum of Welsh Life," http://www.leeds.ac.uk/english/activities/lavc/Conference%20Paper%20PDFs/BethThomas.pdf.

30. BIRS was set up in 1955, joining the British Library in April 1983 when it was renamed the National Sound Archive (NSA). It is now Britain's national center for oral history with the largest archive in the UK: http://www.bl.uk/collections/sound-archive/history.html. See Timothy Day, "National Sound Archive," in Linehan for a history of BIRS/BLNSA.

31. David Lance, *An Archives Approach to Oral History* (London: Imperial War Museum/International Association of Sound Archives, 1978); also his "Oral History Archives: Perceptions and Practices," *Oral History* 8 (Autumn 1980).

32. David Lance, interview by Michelle Winslow, June 20, 2003, British Library Sound Archive ref. C1149/01/01–02.

33. Ken Howarth, *Oral History* (Stroud, Glos: Sutton, 1998). Also: http://www.lancscc.gov.uk/education/record_office/about/archive.asp.

34. See one account in Evans, *Spoken History*, 141–50.

35. Alistair Thomson, "Oral History and Community History in Britain: Personal and Critical Reflections on Twenty-Five Years of Continuity and Change," *Oral History* 36 (Spring 2008).

36. Anne McNulty and Hilary Troop, eds., *Directory of British Oral History Collections* (Colchester: Oral History Society, 1981). For reflections on museum-based oral history in the UK, see Stuart Davies, "Falling on Deaf Ears? Oral History and Strategy in Museums," *Oral History* 22 (Autumn 1994): 74–84; Annette Day, "Listening Galleries: Putting Oral History on Display," *Oral History* 27 (Spring 1999): 91–96. For a listing of some five hundred UK sound archives and collections at the end of the 1980s, see Lali Weerasinghe and Jeremy Silver, eds., *Directory of Recorded Sound Resources in the United Kingdom* (London: British Library, 1989).

37. Alison Turton, ed., *Managing Business Archives* (Oxford: Butterworth-Heinemann, 1991), 395.

38. Ellen D Swain, "Oral History in the Archives: Its Documentary Role in the Twenty-First Century," *American Archivist* 66 (Spring/Summer, 2003): 139–58.

39. Jean Dryden, "Oral History and Archives: The Case Against," *Canadian Oral History Association Journal* 5 (1981/2): 34–37; and Derek Reimer, "Oral History and Archives: the Case in Favour," *Canadian Oral History Association Journal* 5 (1981/2): 30–33. Also F. Miller, "Social History and Archival Practice," *American Archivist* 44 (1981): 119, and T. Abraham, "Collection Policy or Documentation Strategy: Theory and Practice," *American Archivist* 54 (1991).

40. See: http://www.archives.org.uk/thesociety/specialinterestgroups/filmsoundandphotographygroup/celebratingmemoryanoralhistoryofthesocietyofarchivists.html (accessed May 2008). An exception to the paucity of published articles is Graham

Eeles and Jill Kinnear, "Archivists and Oral Historians: Friends, Strangers or Enemies?" *Journal of the Society of Archivists* 9 (1988).

41. James E. Fogerty, "Filling the Gap: Oral History in the Archives," *American Archivist* 46 (Spring 1983): 148–57.

42. Richard Lochead and Rolf Schuursma, "Oral History: The Role of the Archivist," *Phonographic Bulletin* 37 (1983): 3–12. For IASA, see http://www.iasa-web.org/pages/oohomepage.htm. See MacDonald, "Origins," for an overview of the development of oral history in Canada.

43. Dale Treleven, "Oral History and the Archival Community: Common Concerns about Documenting Twentieth Century Life," *International Journal of Oral History* 10 (1989): 50–58; Helen Harrison, ed., *Audiovisual Archives: a Practical Reader* (Paris: UNESCO, 1997), online at: http://unesdoc.unesco.org/images/0010/001096/109612eo.pdf.

44. The first international oral history conference was held at Essex University in March 1979: Paul Thompson, ed., *Our Common History* (London: Pluto, 1982).

45. W. W. Moss and P. C.Mazikana, *Archives, Oral History and Oral Tradition: A RAMP Study* (Paris: UNESCO, 1986); see also C. Hamilton, "'Living by Fluidity': Oral Histories, Material Custodies and the Politics of Archiving," in *Refiguring the Archive*, ed. C. Hamilton, V. Harris, J. Taylor, M. Pickover, G. Reid. and R. Saleh, 209–27 (Dordrecht: Kluwer Academic Publishers, 2002); S. Peet and K. Manungo, "'We Have a Tradition of Story–Telling': Oral History in Zimbabwe," *Oral History* 16 (Autumn 1988): 67–72.

46. See for example: M. de Moraes Ferreira and J. Amado, eds., *Usos & Abusos da História Oral* (Rio de Janeiro: Fundação Getulio Vargas, 1996); Ann Applebaum, *Gulag: A History of the Soviet Camps* (London: Allen Lane, 2003); Catherine Merridale, *Night of Stone: Death and Memory in Russia* (London: Granta, 2000); introduction to M. Loskoutova, *Oral History Reader* (St. Petersburg: European University at St. Petersburg, 2003); Orlando Figes, *The Whisperers: Private Life in Stalin's Russia* (London: Allen Lane, 2007); G. Kozák, Z. K. Rösi, and A. Molnár, eds., *Oral History Archive, Budapest* (Budapest: Institute of the History of the 1956 Hungarian Revolution), 1996; Robert Perks, "Ukraine's Forbidden History: Memory and Nationalism," *Oral History* 21 (Spring 1993): 43–53.

47. Rosanne Kennedy, "Stolen Generations Testimony: Trauma, Historiography, and the Question of 'Truth,'" in Perks and Thomson, *Oral History Reader*, 2006, 506–20; Kenneth Christie, *The South African Truth Commission* (London: Macmillan Press, 2000).

48. BASC folded in the late 1990s and was succeeded in 2006 by British and Irish Sound Archives (BISA): http://www.bisa-web.org.

49. Robert Perks, "The National Sound Archive," *Oral History* 17, no. 2 (Autumn 1989): 52, 58–59.

50. Jean-Pierre Wallot and Normand Fortier, "Archival Science and Oral Sources" from *Janus* 2 (1996): 7–22, repr. in Perks and Thomson, *Oral History Reader*, 1998, 365–78.

51. See for example Tom Nesmith, "Seeing Archives: Postmodernism and the Changing Intellectual Place of Archives," and Mark A. Greene, " The Power of Meaning: The Archival Mission in the Postmodern Age," in *American Archivist* 65 (Spring/Summer, 2002): 24–41 and 42–55. See Ian Johnston, "Whose History Is It Anyway?" *Journal of the Society of Archivists* 22, no. 2 (2001): 213–29, for the British take on this.

52. Joanna Bornat, "A Second Take: Revisiting Interviews With a Different Purpose," *Oral History* 31, no. 1 (Spring 2003): 50. See also N. Mauthner, O. Parry, and K. Milburn, "The Data Are Out There, Or Are They? Implications for Archiving Qualitative Data," *Sociology* 32, no. 4 (1998): 733–45; O. Parry and N. Mauthner, "Whose Data Are They Anyway? Practical, Legal and Ethical Issues in Archiving Qualitative Data," *Sociology* 38, no. 1 (2004): 139–52; L. Bishop, "Protecting Respondents and Enabling Data Sharing: Reply

to Parry and Mauthner," *Sociology* 39, no. 2 (2005): 333–36; O. Parry and N. Mauthner, "Back to Basics: Who Re-uses Qualitative Data and Why?" *Sociology* 39, no. 2 (2005): 337–42; Niamh Moore, "(Re)using Qualitative Data?" *Sociological Research Online* 12, no. 3 (May 2007) at http://www.socresonline.org.uk/12/3/1.html is a good summary.

53. Karen Brewster, "Internet access to oral history recordings: finding the issues," 2000, "Research Results" at www.uaf.edu/library/oralhistory/brewster1/index.html (accessed May 2008).

54. James E. Fogerty, "Oral History and Archives: Documenting Context," in Charlton and Sharpless, *Handbook of Oral History*, 235.

55. Ian Johnston, "Whose History Is It Anyway?" *Journal of the Society of Archivists* 22, no. 2 (2001): 213–29. One of only a handful of articles in this journal addressing this issue and the role of oral history.

56. Andrew Flinn, "Community Histories, Community Archives: Some Opportunities and Challenges," *Journal of the Society of Archivists* 28, no. 2 (Oct. 2007): 151–76. Flinn notes that Johnston's 2001 critique of the "top-down custodial view of professional activity" aroused no response whatsoever from the profession (163). Museums, Libraries, and Archives Council (MLA), *Listening to the Past, Speaking to the Future*, Archives Task Force Report (London: MLA, 2004), also at http://www.mla.gov.uk/programmes/action_for_archives/background.

57. Helen Forde, "Access and Preservation in the 21st Century: What Has Changed?" *Journal of the Society of Archivists* 26, no. 2 (Oct. 2005): 193 200.

58. Between 1999 and 2007 Heritage Lottery Fund contributed in excess of an estimated £49 million to oral history, mainly community-based (Thomson, "Oral History and Community History in Britain," 103, from internal HLF sources). By 2009 this had risen to £72 million for some 2,600 projects. HLF and other funders such as the Wellcome Trust and some research bodies make archival deposit a condition of their funding.

59. Swain, "Oral History in the Archives," 355–56.

60. A concern shared by David Lowenthal, "Archival Perils: An Historian's Plaint," *Archives* 114 (2006): 49–75.

61. Peter Copeland, interview by Paul Thompson, "Why DAT Matters to Oral Historians," *Oral History* 17, no. 1 (Spring 1989): 56–61; Peter Copeland, "Technical Notes," *Oral History* 20, no. 2 (Autumn 1992): 66.

62. Kevin Bradley, "Risks Associated with the Use of Recordable CDs and DVDs as Reliable Storage Media in Archival Collections—Strategies and Alternatives," UNESCO, online at: http://unesdoc.unesco.org/images/0014/001477/147782E.pdf (accessed Dec. 2007).

63. Peter Copeland, "New Recording Media," *Oral History* 25, no. 2 (Autumn 1997): 93–94. On MD see also Alan Ward, Rob Perks and Peter Copeland, "Technical Update: Minidisc Versus Cassette," *Oral History* 27, no. 2 (Autumn 1999): 90–92. Peter Copeland and Barry Fox with Robert Perks, "'All or Nothing?': Current and Future Recording Technologies for Oral History," *Oral History* 30, no. 2 (Autumn 2002): 101–9.

64. For a recent summary see Dietrich Schuller, *Audio and Video Carriers: Recording Principles, Storage and Handling, Maintenance of Equipment, Format and Equipment Obsolescence*, TAPE, 2008, online at http://www.tape-online.net/docs/audio_and_video_carriers.pdf (accessed June 2008). In the UK there is a British Standard for audiovisual archives (BS5454 June 2000): http://www.bsi-global.com/en/. See also Alan Ward, *A Manual of Sound Archive Administration* (Aldershot: Gower, 1990).

65. Kevin Bradley's *Guidelines on the Production and Preservation of Digital Audio Objects* (2004), published by the International Association of Sound and Audiovisual Archives (IASA TC-04), and *The Safeguarding of the Audio Heritage: Ethics, Principles and*

Preservation Strategy (IASA, 3rd ed. 2006, TC-03) are essential reading: details at http://www.iasa-web.org.

66. A U.S. survey in 2000 found that 90 percent of sound recordings in archives were audiocassettes: quoted in Nancy Mackay, *Curating Oral Histories: From Interview to Archive* (Walnut Creek, Calif.: Left Coast Press, 2007).

67. http://trendwatching.com/trends/LIFE_CACHING.htm (accessed June 2008).

68. Schuller *Audio and Video Carriers*, 14.

69. Robert Perks, "Web Access to Archival Oral History in Britain," paper presented to the International Oral History Association conference in Sydney, July 2006.

70. K. Flick and Heather Goodall, "Angledool Stories: Aboriginal History in Hypermedia," in Perks and Thomson, *Oral History Reader*, 1997; also Robert Perks, "Bringing New Life to Archives: Oral History, Sound Archives and Accessibility," *International Association of Sound Archives Journal* 12 (1999).

71. Marion Matters, *Oral History Cataloging Manual* (Chicago: Society of American Archivists, 1995), l; see also C. Clark, "The National Sound Archive IT Project: Documentation of Sound Recordings Using the Unicorn Collections Management System," *IASA Journal* 5 (1995): 7–25; and B. H. Bruemmer, "Access to Oral History: A National Agenda," *American Archivist* 54, no. 4 (1991): 494–501. Among the huge literature about transcription see Ritchie, *Doing Oral History*, 64–75; and Yow, *Recording Oral History*, 227–36.

72. http://semanticweb.org.

73. Michael Frisch, "Oral History and the Digital Revolution: Toward a Post-Documentary Sensibility," in Perks and Thomson, *Oral History Reader*, 2006, 102–14.

BIBLIOGRAPHY

Bradley, Kevin. *The Safeguarding of the Audio Heritage: Ethics, Principles and Preservation Strategy*. IASA, 3rd ed., 2006.

Copeland, Peter. *Sound Recordings*. London: The British Library, 1991.

Evans, George Ewart. *Spoken History*. London: Faber and Faber, 1987.

Hamilton, C., V. Harris, J. Taylor, M. Pickover, G. Reid, and R. Saleh. *Refiguring the Archive*. Dordrecht: Kluwer Academic Publishers, 2002.

Harrison, Helen, ed. *Audiovisual Archives: a Practical Reader*. Paris: UNESCO, 1997.

Mackay, Nancy. *Curating Oral Histories: From Interview to Archive*. Walnut Creek, Calif.: Left Coast Press, 2007.

Matters, Marion. *Oral History Cataloging Manual*. Chicago: Society of American Archivists, 1995.

Perks, Robert, and Alistair Thomson, eds. *The Oral History Reader*. New York/London: Routledge, 2006.

Yow, Valerie Raleigh. *Recording Oral History: A Practical Guide for Social Scientists*. London: Sage, 1994.

CHAPTER 23

CASE STUDY: BETWEEN THE RAW AND THE COOKED IN ORAL HISTORY: NOTES FROM THE KITCHEN

MICHAEL FRISCH
DOUGLAS LAMBERT

The Paradox of Method in Oral History

Our work with new audio and video digital indexing technologies in oral history—conducted through a consulting office, the Randforce Associates, in the University at Buffalo Technology Incubator—has led us to reflect more generally on the challenge of turning oral histories into more broadly usable resources. We have come to understand that identifying, understanding, and responding to these challenges has little necessarily to do with technology, digitization, or the restoration of the oral as primary source via audio or video, though these have been the focus of our specific project work and of some extensive comments developed in other publications. By tracing the story of this work with particular reference to one project that serves as a case study, we hope to underscore the centrality of making the rich complexity of oral history documents more legible and navigable, in whatever mode and for an unbounded range of potential uses, from research to public engagement.

For a long time, oral history documents have been encountered and understood in two polar dimensions, not inaccurately described as "raw" and "cooked." Considering oral (small-h) history as primary source material, many discussions focus on the conducting, collecting, preserving, transcribing, and organizing of interviews as the basic "stuff" of work in the field. Alternatively, oral history has been often been approached from the vantage of its use—as selectively "cooked" and presented as (capital-H) History—in or as an exhibit, a film, a book, an article, a Web site, a text sidebar, and so on. These dimensions are each vitally important, of course, and much of the discourse of the field has been oriented to one or the other of these poles.

This prevailing "h/H" or raw/cooked dichotomy suggests a broader paradox in conventional understandings of oral history. Simply put, most training programs, workshops, manuals, and methodological guides in oral history focus predominantly and in some cases exclusively on interviewing: organizing projects, planning and designing interviews, equipment and techniques for using it, interview skills and protocols, and all the related issues surrounding the generation and production of small-h oral history documentation, and its preparation, usually through transcription, for whatever placement or use is to follow.

It may seem that this interview-production profile has been rapidly changing of late. Certainly recent primers, guides, and handbooks have a very a different feel than the narrower "how-to" manuals and workshops of earlier years. They now routinely include complex discussions of memory, narrativity, subjectivity, and dialogic complexity in the interview process itself—in its generalized dynamics, and in the social and political relationships that construct these in particular ways. But these matters are generally presented as interpretive and theoretical, commentaries that inform what we do, how we do it, and what we do with it, but not really part of basic oral history "method" as such. Organizing, describing, and referencing interviews are all seen as important, but these are conventionally imagined as something really "done," in terms of methodology, by librarians and archivists. And while oral history guides now often deal with construction of oral-history representations, from documentaries to Web interfaces to teaching modules to digital storytelling, these discussions have a "next-step" feel and generally take the basic oral history material and the methodology producing it as a given. In sum, neither theoretical readings nor information architecture nor output production are generally seen, or engaged, as fundamental elements of oral history methodology.

All this seems perfectly appropriate and straightforward, until we realize how unusual these assumptions are in the context of historical methodology more generally. Methods courses and books in history, for instance, pay some attention to generating a documentary base—to searching, locating, and approaching source materials. But their center of gravity, the center of methodological concern, is in tools, concerns, protocols, caveats, and techniques for how historians approach, organize, and work with documents. "Doing" capital-H History, in methodological terms, has revolved around doing something with the primary and secondary sources brought into view. But "doing oral history" has had a converse center of gravity in the generation of primary sources, or drawing them into output forms, each a very different point in the process.

This distinction is now rapidly collapsing, a process driven in large part by new technologies of organization and access. What is emerging is a more unitary and inclusive definition that makes work with interview collections—that ground in between raw and cooked—a fascinating destination in its own right. The work of mapping content and meaning within and across interviews for more fluid and meaningful exploration in even large collections is becoming an increasingly central, exciting, and fast-moving dimension of method, a development with significant transformative implications for the field.

Cataloging, Indexing, and the History Makers Childhood Stories Project

Let us turn to tracing how our own audio-video digital indexing work led us to this relatively unexplored terrain of method. Though informed by a number of projects, our discussion focuses on our collaboration with the History Makers, Inc., a Chicago organization building an unprecedented, highly significant collection of extensive video life history interviews—more than two thousand to date amounting to nearly ten thousand hours richly documenting every dimension of African American life in the twentieth century—and, in the process, the broader story of American history.

We began our practice with exploring applications of InterClipper, an off-the-shelf software tool from the market-research field that holds enormous promise for oral history. It places digital audio and video files within a database environment in which passages of recording (from whole interviews to segments to specific passages of interest) can, on review without prior transcription, be framed, annotated, and richly cross-referenced. With this indexing in place, the media can be searched, browsed, and explored as easily as any well- organized and cross-referenced text.

Relatively early on, we were given an opportunity to develop a prototype database, via InterClipper, of portions of some fifteen History Makers interviews, dealing with family background, childhood, and growing up, about twenty-five hours of interviewing in all. Working closely with the History Makers, we developed an indexed, annotated database featuring numerous dimensions of metadata and thematic coding to support the locating, sorting, gathering, display, and export of passages across the collection sharing particular content, qualities, or themes. We subsequently used this interactive video database, and others, in a number of Teaching American History (TAH) projects, wherein teachers and students identify passages for use in lesson plans, multimedia productions, and the like, all proceeding from the ability to fluidly explore more than one hundred hours of material, in many different collections or data sets, from a wide variety of angles of inquiry, and for a wide variety of possible pedagogic uses. These TAH workshops provided an exciting "proof of concept," showing the power of a fine-grained content map, like a rich book index or other metadata scheme, for exploring efficiently good-sized audio or video collections.

In the improvisation and experimentation that this work involved, we found ourselves navigating tricky channels new to us. These gradually revealed themselves to be tributaries flowing into some major rivers of discussion in evolving approaches to historical content management. Two of these are particularly important here, and are worth careful attention.

The first involves a seemingly simple dimension revolving around an axis with cataloging at one end and indexing at the other. In traditional libraries, the catalog helps you find a needed or relevant book, and the index locates content of interest within that book once you have found it. Modern information tools narrow the distance between these very different functions, opening up an intriguing but sometimes confusing middle ground. No longer limited, as were old card catalogs, to the author and title plus one or two subject headings, digital catalogs can reach more deeply into the content of books, identifying sources through multiple subject heading tags and varied combinations among tags. That said, such descriptors still necessarily tend to be relatively general subject headings, and do not identify or connect to specific passages.

Indexes have always been different in this respect. For hundreds of years, indexing has offered flexible tools for identifying very precise content, and dimensions of meaning or abstract theme as well, with no privileging or narrowing of engagement in the process. When the index of a book directs readers to page 312, they have access to the full text surrounding the identified point or passage. The index, in effect, is a nonlinear, hypertext mode for navigating the text. Digitization transforms the power of a traditional index as significantly as it is transforming subject-heading cataloging, in that various terms and dimensions of terms can be easily combined in any combination or order to filter and search the contents at the level of specific passages in texts or, in our oral history work, within audio or video interview recordings. Additionally, in digital realms there is no inherent barrier to extending the concept of indexing from one book to a shelf of related books, from one interview to entire collection, or across similar collections for that matter.

Our small pilot project with the History Makers Childhood Interviews was an early effort to develop such passage-level indexing for a specific oral history collection. In the process, we discovered some of the power and pitfalls of a convergence of cataloging and indexing sensibilities in contemporary approaches to information. The richness of the History Makers collection made it possible to develop an indexing frame that reached deep into and across interviews for specific themes or content. We could easily draw together passages from across the twenty-five hours sharing a precise thematic tag, export them from the database, and place the video clips in a PowerPoint slide. For example, four different people commented on how, in their childhood communities, any adult would step in to discipline a child acting inappropriately in public space. This "a village raises a child" point is presented with both theme and subtle variations dramatically visible when the passages are displayed and played side by side, available for immediate, focused exploration.

In producing the indexed interview database, the broader ambitions of the History Makers collection argued strongly for using standardized and consistent metadata terms to encourage legibility and connectivity across information sources and search environments. We did this wherever possible, but in the process we encountered a dilemma rooted in the indexing/catalog distinction noted here: most term lists, thesauri, and control vocabularies derive essentially from cataloging subject-heading frameworks, whether of the broader Library of Congress variety or the more field-specific sort such as Brown's Subject Headings for African American History. They made perfect sense, but rarely could provide the granularity needed for generating useful indexing power within a reasonably consistent body of content. There simply is little purchase gained by coding stories or passages for "education, primary school" when everyone in the collection spends a good bit of time describing their childhood experiences in school. The particularity of those discussions almost necessarily flies "under the radar" of the subject heading.

In this prototype project, we were able to make use of available term frameworks as far as they could carry us, and we built onto these with more specific taxonomies more responsive to the nuances in the content—terms that users find helpful in quickly locating a more particular story or subset of stories in a range of interviews.

A second broad dimension of practice that emerged in the History Makers work and other of our early projects flows from the capacity of any database to define distinct fields of reference. InterClipper offers three major control-vocabulary fields, and more than five additional fields for nominal information, numerical information or codes, and a range of special qualities. In the real-time. live-recording. market-research setting for which it was initially developed, the software did not treat its major fields as independent (i.e., each with its own taxonomy of codes and focus) because it was more important to provide multiple fields for coders to quickly tag items of interest as they flowed by.

We quickly determined that for working with oral histories there was much to be gained by crafting these fields as independent variables, each with its own reference taxonomy. We ended up defining three of these for the major fields of the History Makers life history/childhood stories database: a primary field that mapped the explicit content as closely as possible; a second field that located that content in a spectrum of biographical story types, independent of specific content; and a third field that sought to map broad contexts of historical reference—categories of curiosity and relevance from the outside in, so to speak, imagined as "an historian or student interested in . . . ," within which the story or anecdote or statement being referenced, whatever its literal content or biographical dimension, might be usefully placed.

A given anecdote might be located by searching in the typology of biographical stories (say, conflict with parents), or by a searching the typology of historical or cultural contexts (say, the civil rights movement). Unlike random searches that might combine explicit terms, in these modes richer exploration is possible. Selecting all stories about conflict with parents subsorted by historical topic, or, alternatively, all stories about the civil rights movement subsorted by biographical theme, would lead different users to the hypothetical combination of interest—say, conflict with parents during the era of the civil rights movement. But in getting there, these users would discover and explore a wide range of combinations for which they might never have thought to look.

In addition to permitting more coherent multivariable searches at the level of content, this approach also helped us to realize that other dimensions beyond explicit content may be germane to exploring historical sources, especially affect-rich oral history interviews. We came to think of this as meaning-mapping in contrast to content-mapping. Though major challenges of consistency and subjectivity are inherent in defining and assigning tags for qualities, there is a common-sense value to such capacities, especially in a public history project like the History Makers, where interest in searching particular domains of content or context may be matched or exceeded by more general interest in finding stories of courage, or discrimination, or any number of historically relevant affective dimensions as they are located, across those seemingly more objective categories of content or context.

Four Dimensions of Ferment

While we were completing the pilot History Makers project, the History Makers received a major grant from the Institute of Museum and Library Services (IMLS) to build the comprehensively indexed video database it had been developing for some time in conjunction with Carnegie Mellon University computer scientists Howard Wachtler and Michael Christel, and their Informedia Digital Video Library. Linking powerful transcript searches and a series of powerful search and cross-referencing tools to video documentation, the CMU software was particularly well suited to such a large and diverse video collection. Under the IMLS grant, CMU and the History Makers have produced a truly extraordinary resource for American history—a richly searchable four-hundred-interview, twelve-hundred-hour collection of History Maker African American life stories. We were privileged to help beta-test the first iteration of this pathbreaking tool. That, in turn, led to another project, a next-level collaborative refinement and addition to the History Makers/CMU resource, for which our indexing insights and experience proved germane.

It may be helpful to summarize what we learned as our practice on other projects broadened beyond the initial small History Makers pilot and brought us into the ferment of new developments and approaches bearing on oral history content management in general, and on evolving information technologies in particular. Our understanding of some of the more important contemporary trends can be presented under four broad and significantly inter-connected headings:

Intra-Interview Passage Referencing

The first discovery has been that the cataloging/indexing tension encountered in our own work turns out to mark a much broader and currently quite exciting challenge in the field, a challenge whose significance is magnified considerably as access to large digitized oral history collections expands dramatically, online and within institutional holdings as well. The basic dilemma is that powerful library science and archival tools for describing, identifying, organizing, and mapping content within and across large collections turn out to be designed primarily for core reference units: they identify aspects of a book, article, artifact, object, document, or, in oral history, an interview. Most efforts to fashion and concentrate cross-collection use around shared, consistent metadata standards, such as Dublin Core, necessarily focus on such broader, object or unit-level descriptors. These can be pushed to open access to particular themes or aspects or sections within, but the fundamental item of reference remains the unit, in most prevailing systems, and it remains more closely bound by the assumptions and contours of unit cataloging than of content indexing as such.

This presents some real obstacles for oral histories, especially where the unit is large, the time demands of review and exploration are considerable, and the range of content, theme, or dimension of potential interest within the material is expansive. Such obstacles are magnified when collections offer users access within and across very large collections, and especially when they offer access to the primary source—the audio or video recording—since unlike text transcripts that can be skimmed, recordings have got to be listened to and watched in real time. In practical terms, referencing that cannot lead users pretty directly to the sections or even specific passages of interest within larger units is not likely to prove very satisfying or useful. How to provide this, within library or collection management database systems that are necessarily unit based, like CONTENTdm, is at present the object of considerable attention and experimentation. In short, finding ways to bring the intra-unit power of close indexing and the cross-unit and large-scale collection power of complex digital cataloging—this is very much a front-burner issue in the field as a whole.

The most common response to this dilemma has been to combine unit-level descriptors and categories with text or transcript-based keyword searches that bring the user to a precise point within a document. This might be sufficient were full text and transcripts always available, and were locating specific words or explicit terms or even identifiable keywords the fundamental objective. But these assumptions are too restrictive and inconsistent with the promise of wide-scale access to large oral history collections, including those that may not have been reduced or are not reducible to text, as is the case with so much video documentation. This point leads directly to a second dimension of the current ferment.

"CVS" or Multidimensional Referencing

Another characteristic of the cataloging/indexing tension is the degree to which the former is restricted to content. The revealing term "subject heading" is usually given a literal, descriptive, denotative meaning applied only to content. Indexers, on the other hand, have always felt free to reference all sorts of things in addition to content, such as abstract ideas, themes, and categories of meaning and experience.

We encountered the tension between these notions early in our work, in large part because the InterClipper database system does not rely on keywords or text-string searches, but rather on easily customized assigned metadata values. It also offers, like any database, diverse fields and tables for such values that, while independent of each other, can be brought together relationally through the assignments that each contributes to the profile of an individual item of reference.

The more we worked with these database notions, the more we observed how unusual they seem to historians, and in archives and libraries for that matter, and yet how commonplace they are in social science fields more accustomed to qualitative analysis. To social scientists, significance in data is not necessarily or even usually explicit or nominal, something to be navigated via the transcript. Rather, it is meaning identified in response to an inquiry, and then coded for sorting and analysis as such. Social scientists are also comfortable with the notion that there may be wholly different fields through which every unit of data in a study needs to be described and categorized. A social psychologist documenting and studying conflict in a playground, for instance, may not need or want to know whether the kids began fighting over a pail or a ball. The project is more likely to be concerned with applying a complex typology to conflict-initiating behaviors and settings, and its coders are trained to apply these consistently to a body of documentation so patterns and associations can be studied.

In applying such approaches to historical and archival projects where they seemed less readily understood, we adopted a common-sense cookbook metaphor that has served nicely to convey the sensibility. For us, it became the "CVS" approach to cross-referencing, with our CVS standing for "Chinese," "Vegetable," and "Spicy." This is very close to what, elsewhere, is coming to be called faceted referencing, and the idea is quite simple: In a cookbook, or in a database with ten thousand recipes, a given recipe might be Chinese or Italian, made of vegetables or meat, and very spicy or not. Everyone instantly recognizes that it is nonsensical to ask: "Is this recipe Chinese or is it made of broccoli?" These are not either/or choices of descriptor, but rather choices within distinct dimensions of the recipe, which represent aspects or facets of the same thing. There could be many additional independent dimensions (cooking time, nutritional value, presence or absence of nuts or other allergens) with which any individual recipe could be described and categorized. And in any dimension, any number of levels of subdivision and granularity are possible: Is Chinese sufficient, or should Chinese be broken down to Mandarin, Hunan, Cantonese?

However obvious when applied to recipes, it is not so easily understood how such notions could be applied to the anecdotes or stories or specific passages in an interview. If interviews can be mapped in many possible domains of reference, what *are* those domains? What are the independent dimensions of historical meaning and reference, for the project or set of stories, equivalent to our cookbook's ethnicity (item: Chinese), composition (item: vegetable, sub-item broccoli), and spiciness (item: very hot)? For each dimension identified, what is the project-specific optimal granularity for mapping that dimension?

What began for us as an applied interest in particular tools for working with audio and video oral histories directly has thus evolved through practice into a fascination with the intellectual implications of this altered relationship to content. We have discovered widespread interest in such ideas, especially in relation to digital tools and Internet access. In electronic form, such approaches become more powerful, as if the entire book or group of books were being re-indexed on demand, with content displayed and organized through the lenses of any combination of index terms. The ease of manipulation and navigation, and the analytic capacity these confer, is one reason why information tools have so dramatically advanced the power of fluid, relational approaches to information. It means the same content can easily be explored from a variety of contrasting directions. These directions are hardly limited to formal research. The push to develop and deploy them is coming from a very different dimension, from the more casual but yet more powerful search and exploration tools that digital and Internet modalities are generating to match the unlimited accessibility to information that these modes provide. This point informs our last two categories of analysis.

Referencing as Sorting the Laundry, or, Exploring, not Searching

In our early InterClipper oral history databases, including but not limited to the History Makers pilot, we were discovering and applying many of the insights discussed earlier, approaches very well supported by the software architecture and the way we were learning to customize and apply it to rich oral history content. Gradually, however, we came to realize that the power to mark and cross-reference particular passages at a very precise level could exact a curious price for the capacity it conferred.

In response to subtle variations and nuances of content or meaning, the coding frameworks we developed, in collaboration with clients interested in accessing and cross-referencing that complexity, initially tended to become increasingly elaborate and granular. As in indexing a book, the natural pull in coding was to notice distinctions, and to adjust terms so that these could be caught in the cross-referencing, and thus rendered accessible by the searches operating on it. In effect, the mark-up process exerted a kind of nominalist, "splitting, not lumping" pull, with any given next passage often seeming so interestingly particular as to call for yet another variant coding term of its own.

This worked well for marking very well-focused interview sets, like the History Makers childhood stories, which could then be searched at the passage level effectively using the precise coding frameworks developed for them. But it risked becoming overwhelming in collections where the content had a broader, more inclusive reach, or where users had broader curiosities and less precise research questions. As our practice evolved, we came to think about how the same cross-referencing capacities might be deployed more fluidly and variably in calibrating frameworks to the specific material, needs, and interests of particular collections.

One of the most helpful adjustments came from a straightforward shift in how we understood what we were doing in the code assignment process. We shifted from asking "How do we name this passage, and what is it *really* about?" to asking "Where can we put it so that it can be found?" Instead of the "nail it" objective in indexing and coding, we came to think of this as a more informal "sorting the laundry" approach, which had the advantage of being adjustable to the laundry being sorted as this varied in composition and scale. For a first pass, "socks, shirts, underwear, linens" might be sufficient for the baskets into which items were sorted. Then, on a need-driven basis, as any basket filled to an overflowing point of diminishing returns, meaningful subcategories for the collected items in any basket would be easier to define and provide. Increasingly, this has proven a more practical and effective way to develop cross-referencing scheme for many projects, permitting a first-level pass that can be done more quickly, and more elaborated referencing that can be built out as the collection is engaged in sustained practice.

Working in this mode helped us, and our collaborators, to realize that the objective was not only, and sometimes not primarily, to support precise searches for precise items. We began to regard as somewhat misplaced and unhelpfully restrictive the whole orientation around searching that has dominated the digital information world, especially online. Simply put, users are not necessarily or primarily searching for something particular, or for that matter searching for anything. They can more accurately be understood as exploring, looking to see what is there and what might be of interest or use. This can be through very informal browsing, or through the intuitive, alert-to-resonance way students and scholars research large bodies of material, in whatever form or format. To make this as meaningful and productive as possible, they are less in need of search engines to move them down tracks of curiosity, and more in need of better overall maps of the material, to guide them in deciding where to lay those tracks and in what direction to have them go. Exploration can help identify more particular destinations or demarked areas of more focused interest, at which point a different kind of search tool—MapQuest or Google Map directions from a precise here to a precise there—can be of real use.

The notion of exploration is also more appropriate and helpful for the multidimensional referencing described above, since it provides a wealth of potential paths to a destination: Instead of having to drill down from the broad catchment to the specific target with ever more restrictive and refined searches, exploration through a multiple array of dimensional lenses can filter the contents in different ways, permitting different arrays of results. In our metaphor, an ethnic group banquet might approach recipe selection by filtering for ethnicity and subsorting that by ingredient subsorted by spiciness. This would be different than if an international event or a Hot Pepper and Garlic Festival dinner were being planned, where the variables would be filtered in a different order, to permit a different array from which choices could be made.

In the information world, there is growing interest in such approaches, notwithstanding the genuflection to the awesome power of Google and other engines to produce huge catchment through linear searches instantly arrayed in priority order for manageable examination. Quick-and-dirty searching, however assisted by such immensely powerful tools, can still reduce to hit or miss casts. These are not at all the same as directed yet intuitive and curiosity-driven exploration of a landscape. To shift from the horizontal to the vertical, if search-engine data mining assumes a clear difference in value between that which is being drilled to and that which is being drilled through, exploration is more like the capacity to sift efficiently through loose soil or sand, alert to whatever may be found that has value for whatever reason or purpose.

That metaphor, in turn, begs the question "Who is sifting that soil, and why?" And this question leads to a final dimension of the current ferment in digital information and Internet circles, one with very substantial implications for the domain of method we have been discussing.

User-generated and Vernacular Referencing

As we moved out from the initial History Makers childhood stories and other small pilot projects, we found ourselves challenged by collections so large or diverse in potential uses as to make a complete and anticipatory thematic indexing at the micro passage level inadvisable and impractical.

Beyond the "sorting the laundry" approach to coding, we and our client collaborators have improvised another general way to deploy the same software architecture to respond to this challenge constructively. The choice has often been to build a somewhat more general indexing and cross-referencing frame at a somewhat larger unit level—segments generally five–twelve minutes long—which can serve to get explorers reasonably close to material of interest. On the basis of these segment summaries, users themselves can then identify, frame, annotate, and code particular passages or stories within the segment, adding these to the database for others to use.

Instead of designing paths through the forest of material, such maps bring visitors to a forest zone of interest, within which they themselves wear paths that represent how curiosity, interests, and needs have led users to particular material. This produces a more articulated map of the content, in which collaborative and interactive input has played a significant role.

Here again, what began for us as improvisation in practice has come to converge with a deepening fascination in the world of digital information. Vernacular "folksonomy" or user-community information management has become widely familiar through Wikipedia, and through the tag-clouds used to represent user-generated maps of interest on many sites. In computer science, where computer processing by artificial intelligence was once considered a way of moving beyond the limited and limiting capacities of human intelligence, there is now greater interest in human-computer interactions, through which systems can learn from and respond to the input of human users, in a dialectic back and forth. As museum and library users have become more attuned to the simple, intuitive, own-language searches so effective on Internet search engines, it is not sufficient to expect them to put all that aside and operate only with the control vocabulary and search syntax of formal professional referencing systems.

There will always be those who approach such junctures with sour jeremiads about declining standards, or with utopian enthusiasms about the transformative power of every new capacity. But reliance on conventional either/or conceptions is giving way to an interest in elaborating creative both/and systems that can mobilize the strengths of all these approaches to finding content, meaning, and use in rich information.

Such developments can be thought of as anticipating a kind of digital extension of the reference librarian, always the core of a good library. The reference librarian or archivist stands by definition between the formal, professional organization mapping the holdings, and the queries presented, however imprecisely or unprofessionally, by those coming to the reference desk for help. The successful librarian is the one who can make the connection, respecting and attending to the user's curiosity and interest, while helping that user to access the power of a more richly informed system of organization to satisfy that curiosity and explore that interest. In oral history, it is intriguing to reflect on how emerging approaches to mapping the content of interview collections may be headed in a similar direction. This thought returns us to the History Makers, and a project the organization has recently undertaken to add additional dimension to what was already the strikingly successful digital resource it had built in collaboration with Carnegie Mellon University's Informedia Digital Video Library.

The History Makers Thematic Coding Project

The richly indexed and searchable History Makers prototype video oral history collection is immensely powerful. It was built by combining highly innovative information processing from CMU's computer scientists and exacting content knowledge and insight from the History Makers staff. The result is a system with a wealth of sophisticated features through which users can explore the collection with an ease, depth, power, and precision unprecedented in any African American oral history project, and in any general American history collection of this scale.

Each interview is divided into segments—generally an average of ten minutes long, based on the contours of the content and interview flow—which are identified by a wealth of temporal, topical, and geographic variables. These can easily be deployed to produce subsets of video selections for review from within and across interviews, scaled by likely relevance to queries ranging from simple to elaborate. More exacting searches operate directly on full interview transcripts seamlessly linked to the video stream. These searches draw on powerful and sophisticated content-analysis tools, rather than simple word searches, and thus are able to produce meaningful results for efficient review in even broad searches in a huge database.

We were among a group of institutional participants in a focused beta-test project working with the system and database. This aimed to improve the functionality of the interface and its tools, and to refine its capacity to work effectively with the particular content of this collection in relation to the needs of students, researchers, and the public. The test results have been encouraging, validating many of the strengths of the system while helping to identify numerous refinements to make the interface more comfortable and productive to work with. As is common in such work, the beta-testers also generated free-form "wish lists" of additional features or capacities worth developing at some point.

One of the most prominent features testers asked for had in fact been seen as significant from the start, but for various reasons could not be developed in the initial phase of the project: a system of thematic coding tags for interview content, complementing what could be achieved through even sophisticated transcript searches. Even before the beta-test was complete, the History Makers' executive director Julieanna Richardson had determined that the time had come to build this dimension into the system.

Because this need was broadly resonant with our experience developing non-transcript-based coding schemes in InterClipper, including our work with the small subset of History Makers childhood stories, we were invited to be part of a small team including archivists from the History Makers, faculty and doctoral students in African American history from the University of Illinois, other graduate students from the University at Buffalo, and our own Randforce office, all in close collaboration with the Informedia computer scientists at Carnegie Mellon. The thematic coding framework was built in a frantic few months of work in the first half of 2009, and implemented in the summer of the same year.

We were fortunate in that the CMU system had already built intra-interview units, broadly content- and interview-defined rather than arbitrary or mechanical, that could be the basic units for thematic coding: over eighteen thousand segments of the four hundred interviews. It was determined early on that we needed to be able to make multiple assignments for any segment, since even these small units might have range of topics, themes, and meanings within them. It was also clear from the start that some multidimensional referencing power was needed to catch meaning important to the project that the CMU system was not able to reach at all—meanings grounded in yet basically independent of explicit historical content, such as examples of leadership, inspiration, character, courage, or other particular affective and spiritual qualities.

As the work proceeded, everyone came to see the need to design a framework of broader categories in which content could be categorized. Something akin to our "sorting the laundry" approach would be necessary if the thematic framework were not to become overwhelmingly and hence counterproductively elaborate and complex given the sheer scale of material and its density of meaning. In trying to reach this, each of the threads presented turned out to be central to the process, and visible in the weave this project has produced. In effecting this weave, we encountered two fundamental obstacles that blocked progress until they could be resolved.

The first dilemma was how to understand the complementarity between the new thematic coding and the existing power of the search-based organization and interface. Should coding aim only at things not already reachable in the text-based system? Or should it attempt as well to "map" in broadly thematic ways historical content and meaning that the system was already good at reaching through more directed, specific searches?

The second dilemma flowed from the first. To the extent that a coding frame was attempting to reach such broad categories or elusive qualities not easily reducible to specific content, how could the pitfalls of subjectivity be avoided? How could something even roughly approximating the inter-coder reliability prized by social scientists be achieved? If consistency could not be guaranteed, how useful could the results prove to be in guiding users through the collection?

What we came up with responded to these dilemmas less by solving them than by seeing that they represented opportunities more than problems. Our group decided that it would *not* be redundant to provide broad historical coding, since this could be used for fluid exploring from the outside in. It could constitute an alternative modality, an added-value filtering mode for moving in toward material of interest, arguably preferable for many users or situations when search queries were either uncomfortable or difficult to frame productively. In addition, potential breakthrough advantages could arise from this pairing: powerful text search and broad thematic code assignments might at some later point be associated analytically and modeled, to permit the former to generate the latter. That is, analysis of text transcription that had been thematically coded might identify linguistic and language usage patterns predictive of particular code assignments, opening a path to automated thematic indexing of transcriptions or even, ultimately, of sound recordings themselves.

The danger of subjectivity also receded as a problem, once it was clear that the purpose of much of the coding was to facilitate informal exploration and browsing, which complemented the system's already existing ground in formal content search capacity. We reduced inconsistency as much as possible—a goal probably achievable more through careful protocols, examples, definitions, and instructions than through the coding architecture itself. But in the final analysis, we realized that for the fields involving more subjective and conceptual assignments, it might be better to think of our coders as proxies for the general user, rather than as social scientists producing consistent data for analysis. Ultimately, this might become part of the general interface itself instead of an organizational taxonomy produced for using the system. The result may be a system that could at least in some areas accumulate user responses and make them available as vernacular maps of how the material spoke to those exploring it. These are exactly the kinds of cloud mechanisms proving so compelling and exciting in guiding people through exploration of vast Internet collections.

The result of all this was a set of rich initial coding menus, simplified considerably in practice in the interest of efficiently coding a massive amount of material with limited human resources at hand. The framework had three very broad "families" of categories, an elaboration that is evocative of, but reaches far beyond, the "CVS" dimensional framework of our earlier InterClipper projects. The first family focuses on a series of categories mapping African American historical topics. The second views the collection through the lens of biography, with menu choices tracing life-course arc, dimensions of personal growth, and connections between personal experience and historical themes. The third broad family of categories offers opportunities to code story and narration types, to tag particular affective qualities, and to flag personal stories that are particular apt examples of specific general themes. On review of each of the eighteen thousand segments, coders are making as many assignments as possible in each of these families of terms, and they have had the opportunity as well to suggest new terms or to flag particular highlight moments nominally.

With the coding still in process at this writing, it is too early to say how all this will work out, although we are reasonably confident the approach will be productive. This confidence is built on the degree to which the challenge, the process, and the response all seem to be at the very center of a significant, open-ended "moment" in approaches to working with historical content in general, and oral history documentation in particular. This returns us to the point about method in oral history with which our essay began, and with which we wish to conclude.

Making Oral Histories Accessible on a Vast Scale

It is clear that digitization, the explosion of digital tools and capacities, and the Internet are combining to make oral histories instantly accessible on a vast scale. The process can only accelerate. But what does accessible mean, as scale increases? If we are not sure how to meaningfully explore the content of ten interviews, or fifty, how meaningful can it be to make 150,000 accessible?

Such considerations up the ante considerably, and they underscore the value and usefulness of bringing hands-on work with the materials of oral history into the core methodology in our field. We have sought to suggest, through this case study essay, the need to get beyond a traditional emphasis in oral history on generating the raw source material, and beyond our fondness for regarding the cooked versions produced in exhibits, films, and Web sites as the main locus for instruction, appreciation, and criticism, which is to say the place where the discourse of meaning and value is grounded. Instead, we encourage practitioners and students alike to engage more actively the challenge of mapping what interviews say and mean, and how that meaning can be explored for an expanding range of users and purposes. Tools and techniques for doing that ought to be as much in the center of our discourse as are digital recorders and instructions for how to operate them.

By way of a conclusion, here is the chorus of "Papa on the Housetop," a wonderful 1930s song by Leroy Carr, an Indianapolis bluesman. Each of the characters mentioned could be given some sort of coded relevance to our discussion, but to strike a chord that resonates with our argument we comment on only one:

> Baby's in the cradle, Brother's gone to town,
> Sister's in the parlor, trying on a gown
> Mama's in the kitchen, messin' all around
> Papa's on the housetop and he won't come down.

The kitchen is the in-between space where the raw and the cooked come together. In our applied practice, we certainly have learned a great deal about oral history in the broadest sense from the messin' around we have been doing in project kitchens over these past few years, and that is where we think a good deal more work in oral history might usefully be centered.

BIBLIOGRAPHY

The History Makers, Inc: http://www.thehistorymakers.com/

The Randforce Associates: http://www.randforce.com

Carnegie Mellon University, Informedia Digital Video Library Project: http://www.informedia.cs.cmu.edu/.

Christel, Michael, and Michael Frisch. "Evaluating the Contributions of Video Representation for a Life Oral History Collection." Proc. ACM/IEEE-CS Joint Conference on Digital Libraries. Pittsburgh, Penn., June 2008.

Cohen, Daniel, Michael Frisch, Patrick Gallagher, Steve Mintz, Kirsten Sword, Amy Morrell Taylor, William G. Thomas III, and William J. Turkel. "Interchange Forum: The Promise of Digital History." *Journal of American History* 95, no. 2 (Sept. 2008).

Frisch, Michael. "Three Dimensions and More: Oral History Beyond the Paradoxes of Method." In *Handbook of Emergent Methods*, edited by Sharlene Nagy Hesse-Biber and Patricia Leavy. New York: Guilford Press, 2008.

———. "Oral History and the Digital Revolution: Towards a Post-Documentary Sensibility." In *The Oral History Reader*, 2nd ed., edited by Robert B. Perks and Alistair Thomson. London: Routledge, 2006.

PART V

LEGAL, ETHICAL, AND ARCHIVAL IMPERATIVES

CHAPTER 24

THE LEGAL RAMIFICATIONS OF ORAL HISTORY

JOHN A. NEUENSCHWANDER

At each of the biennial meetings of the International Oral History Association, which shift from continent to continent, an average of forty nations are represented. This number merely underscores the obvious: oral history has become a research tool in virtually every country in the world. In the United States, the Veteran's History Project, StoryCorps, and thousands of other community and academic projects, publications, and media presentations demonstrate its enormous reach. But like any other form of human inquiry, oral history is not immune from legal challenges and lawsuits.

While the vast majority of oral history programs have not and likely never will be confronted with a lawsuit, the implementation of legally and ethically sound procedures are the best ways to insure that this does not happen. All oral historians should make themselves familiar with the legal issues that relate to the practice of oral history, such as legal release agreements, challenges to interview restrictions, defamation, the privacy torts, copyright, the Internet, and institutional review board (IRB) review of human subjects research. The focus of this article is American law, but the issues discussed should be relevant to oral historians from other nations and encourage practitioners to consider how their own legal systems address them.

Legal Release Agreements

The memories that an interviewer records begin as the intellectual property of the interviewee. People own the copyright to their words. The standard method by which oral historians transfer ownership of this property right, as well as the recording itself, to themselves or their program is by a legal release agreement. To be legally binding, such agreements must be drafted in accordance with the legal mandates of the state in which the program is located. While most states agree on the basic elements that are required for such agreements, there are enough subtle variations among the states that one should never assume that the terminology of an agreement adopted by an oral history program in another state can be safely applied elsewhere by simply changing the names of the parties.

A controversy surrounding the opening of the papers of former Supreme Court Justice Thurgood Marshall provides a good illustration of what can happen when the parties have a significant disagreement about the terms of a transfer agreement. When Justice Marshall, a noted civil rights attorney and the first African American to sit on the U.S. Supreme Court, donated his papers to the Library of Congress, including several oral histories, he insisted that after his death there should be immediate public access. When he died in 1993, that is exactly what happened. Marshall's candid observations about his colleagues and how the court decided certain key decisions proved upsetting to some of the Justices who were still on the bench. Before the furor subsided, a U.S. Senate subcommittee looked into the matter and the Librarian of Congress was forced to publicly defend the transfer agreement with Marshall. The subcommittee's inquiry focused on whether the Library of Congress had abided by the terms of the agreement. After Marshall made the decision to deposit his papers, the Library of Congress drafted a deed of gift agreement for his approval. The clause that reflected his stated wish that there be immediate and unrestricted access to his papers after his death read: "Thereafter the collection shall be made available to the public at the discretion of the Library."[1] The Librarian of Congress maintained that the extent of the library's discretion was purely technical in nature. All that it involved was the time period that library staff needed to prepare the papers for public access. Critics of this position, including Chief Justice William Rehnquist, believed that the meaning of the word "discretion" was far more expansive and encompassed the right of the Library of Congress to delay access for an extended period of time.

The most common type of transfer agreement is a deed of gift. This reflects a lengthy philanthropic tradition of using such transfer agreements to convey memorabilia and papers. A gift, or *inter vivos* donation, is the voluntary transfer of any property other than real estate. Three elements are required: (1) the intent to donate, (2) actual delivery, and (3) the acceptance of the gift.[2] In the context of an oral history interview, the intent would be satisfied by the individual's willingness to be interviewed and then to gift the resulting recording and transcript. The elements of delivery and acceptance are easily met where the recording of the interview and transcript are retained by the interviewer or archive. Two sample deeds of gift transfer agreements are included at the end of this article.

Contract-style transfer agreements are used to a lesser extent. To qualify as a legally binding contract, such an agreement must contain four elements: (1) agreement, (2) consideration, (3) competent parties, and (4) a lawful objective.[3] A signed agreement that identifies the respective parties and the interview to be transferred would satisfy the agreement requirement. Consideration requires that each party gives something up in the bargain. In a typical oral history interview situation, the bargain is the sharing of memories by the interviewee in exchange for the interviewing, recording, editing, and archiving of these memories. The competency element should really never come into play. If a prospective interviewee is thought to be mentally incompetent, the interview should never be conducted. Similarly, an oral historian who knowingly or somehow is duped into conducting an interview that will aid some illegal purpose, such as fraud or misrepresentation, is the type of unlikely scenario that would clearly not meet the lawful objective element. A sample contract style transfer agreement can be found at the end of his article.

Beyond the importance of using a legally binding deed of gift or contract type of transfer agreement, two other essential drafting issues should always be carefully considered. The first is the future-use clause. Given the ever-expanding uses being made of recordings and transcripts, clauses that are overly narrow or excessively vague should be avoided. The most effectively drafted future-use clauses articulate the necessary specifics while also providing reasonable anticipation of all possible future uses. The following clause exemplifies this balance: "Future uses of my interview/s may include quotation from and publication/broadcast in any media including the Internet."

The second essential drafting consideration is to make sure that the legal release agreement obtains the transfer of copyright from the interviewee. Physical possession of an interview is meaningless without the copyright. There are currently thousands of oral history histories that many oral history programs have that are closed; they cannot be safely utilized for research or publication because the original creators neglected to secure a transfer of copyright. The U.S. Copyright Act, which is in accord with international standards, specifically requires that any transfer of copyright be in writing to be legally binding. The act prescribes no particular form, only a simple recital. According to one court, "It doesn't have to be the Magna Charta, a one line *pro forma* statement will do."[4]

The best legal release agreements contain precise but not overly legalistic language, document the full meeting of the minds between the parties on all relevant issues, and provide a roadmap for future use and administration. In other words, agreement should be readily explainable to lay persons and defensible in court should such a challenge ever come to pass. Courts do not go out of their way to interpret contested agreements but when forced to do so generally apply fairly standard rules of construction. Although the deed of gift that Justice Marshall signed did not end up in court, if it had the court would have treated it just like any other agreement that required judicial interpretation to settle a dispute. To reach a definitive interpretation of the meaning of the "discretion" afforded the Library of Congress to make his papers available, a court would have considered evidence regarding Marshall's intent, the generally accepted meaning of the word in previous donor agreements, and the custom of the industry (i.e., preparation time for cataloging collections). At the very least there would have been a lot of time and money spent on discovery and lawyers fees. The resulting decision in turn might not have supported the limited interpretation of "discretion" that the Library of Congress invoked.

Challenges to Interview Restrictions

Since the modern oral history movement emerged in the 1940s, some narrators have refused to be interviewed unless they could control access to their interviews or were allowed to seal them for an extended period of time. At first, such individuals were usually politicians or government officials like Edward F. Prichard Jr., a Kentuckian who was considered to be one of the most brilliant political minds of his generation, but who was convicted of tampering with ballot boxes in an election. After his imprisonment, he rehabilitated himself by leading a major reform of his state's educational system. Two years before his death in 1984, Pritchard did a series of interviews focusing on his long and checkered political career. It was not until his wife died in 2006, however, that his "cooling off" period officially ended and his interviews were opened to the public. As might be expected, members of the media and the curious were waiting outside the door on the first day of access.[5]

Today, limiting access to interviews has become far more widespread. This development largely reflects the increasingly sensitive topics that oral historians are exploring, including prostitution, illegal immigration, drug use, AIDS, and government-sponsored torture. Although restricting access to interviews involving sensitive topics may seem to be more about protecting the interviewees from prosecution and/or retribution, the responsibility of the oral historian is still the same. He or she must make sure that such restrictions are not only carefully spelled out but that they are vigorously defended if challenged.

Such challenges usually fall into two categories. In the United States, federal, state, and local governments are all subject to the Freedom of Information Act (FOIA). The purpose of this act is to insure that official records are accessible to the media and the general public. History-related programs sponsored by state institutions are usually not exempt from freedom of information requests absent some special statutory exemption, so an FOIA request would likely supersede any restriction or seal placed on an interview held by a public institution. Oral historians in the federal government, however, have long operated under the assumption that interviews given voluntarily, and not as a requirement of government service, can have restrictions placed on them by the interviewee. Since gifted materials, such as manuscript collections, are exempt from the FOIA, federal oral historians claim similar immunity.

Another challenge to access restrictions can come from court subpoenas. The fundamental assumption of American jurisprudence is that courts are entitled to examine every person's evidence. The adversarial nature of the legal system places the primary responsibility of discovering and accessing such evidence on the parties to a lawsuit. In recent years subpoenas have been issued to access academic research and even the researchers themselves. This trend has occasionally led to a clash between the access restrictions placed on an interview and a court-ordered subpoena. In virtually all of these contests thus far, the attorney bearing the subpoena has prevailed. Attempts to create an evidentiary privilege to protect scholars and/or collections from having to honor a subpoena have not been successful.

A 1998 murder trial in Mississippi involving an Imperial Wizard of the White Knights of the Ku Klux Klan, a violent offshoot of the KKK, provided a dramatic example of how a subpoena trumped an interviewee's access restriction. Samuel H. Bowers was charged with the murder of Vernon Dahmer, a black civil rights leader. Prior to his trial, the district attorney discovered that three oral history interviews with Bowers were housed in the Mississippi Department of Archives and History. At Bowers's request they had been sealed until after his death. Believing that these interviews might be useful at trial, the district attorney subpoenaed them. Attorneys for the Department of Archives and History sought a protective order claiming that the subpoena amounted to third party interference with a binding contract, but their efforts failed. Although the interviews were not ultimately used in the trial, the district attorney planned to use them for impeachment purposes had Bowers testified in his own behalf.[6]

There are, therefore, real legal limits to access restrictions. Interviewees who ask for, or who are encouraged to seek, such access restrictions should be alerted to these limits. Even though the prospect that a FOIA request or a subpoena may someday challenge restriction placed on an interview is very remote, serious thought should also be given to how a defense of the restrictions would be mounted and by whom.

Defamation

The pervasiveness of defamation was something that Samuel Johnson, the great English essayist, poet, and lexicographer, observed in his own eighteenth century: "Defamation is sufficiently copious. The general lampooner of mankind may find long exercise for his zeal or wit, in the defects of nature, the vexations of life, the follies of opinion, and the corruptions of practice."[7] Johnson's observation about the copiousness of defamation is perhaps even truer today. Defamation is an omnibus term that covers both libel and slander. Libel involves written statements, and slander oral ones. A defamatory statement from the audio portion of an interview would be considered slander; if the offending statement was contained in a transcript, it would be libel. While defamation lawsuits involving celebrities like Jerry Seinfeld and Roger Clemens have been closely followed by the media, hundreds of other lawsuits are filed annually by far less famous individuals.

For example, the filmmaker Michael Moore was recently sued by an army reservist who objected to a short clip of his interview being included in the documentary *Fahrenheit 9/11*. The reservist had originally been interviewed by NBC's Brian Williams regarding the effectiveness of a new pain blocker drug. A sixteen-second segment of this interview was used by Moore to illustrate the shortfall in medical support for soldiers wounded in Iraq. Because the documentary attacked the leadership of President George W. Bush and called the war itself into question, the reservist maintained that the mere appearance of his brief interview segment in the film defamed him because it falsely portrayed him as holding the same views.[8] Although his lawsuit was ultimately dismissed, it effectively demonstrates that defamation lawsuits are not solely the tool of the rich and famous.

To be defamed, five elements usually have to be established:

1. The words were in fact defamatory;
2. The person crying foul was clearly the object of the words;
3. The person who is being sued published the words to a third party;
4. The words were damaging to the reputation of the person suing;
5. The person publishing or uttering the words was at fault.[9]

Translated, the first element focuses on the question of whether the words are true or false. Truth is an absolute defense, so if the charge or accusation is actually a true statement, then there can be no defamation. Unfortunately, such a finding does not usually occur until a lawsuit is well advanced. The second element comes into play when a group of individuals are the object of the allegedly defamatory words. The individual claiming to be harmed must be able to show that he or she was readily identified by the defamatory words. The publication element is quite straightforward, but has special importance for oral historians because it does not just apply to the first person who utters the defamatory statements; anyone who republishes is also liable. When an oral history program makes the recording and/or transcript of an interview available to the public, it is considered to be a republisher. If a person named in an interview were to cry foul and sue for defamation, both the interviewee and the oral history program would doubtless be named as defendants.

The fourth element, damage to reputation, is best understood by considering the five major categories of injury: committing a crime, acting immorally, associating with unsavory people or otherwise acting disgracefully, demonstrating financial irresponsibility, and exhibiting professional incompetence.[10] The first three categories are patently obvious. An interviewee who claims another person is a criminal, is morally challenged, or associates with "the wrong" people should immediately raise a caution flag. The last two categories of reputation damage are the ones that are more likely to slip through a defamation safety net. Many oral history interviews focus on work or business experience, and having an interviewee criticize a fellow employee or business associate is not an uncommon occurrence in these types of interviews. Since such criticism does not automatically set off the same alarm bells like accusing someone of a crime, potentially defamatory statements about someone's poor work ethic, limited abilities, or bad business decisions might be overlooked. To avoid making such a mistake, individual interviewers and programs should see to it that categories four and five are given special emphasis when it comes to watching out for potentially defamatory statements by interviewees.

The Regional Oral History Program (ROHO) at the University of California–Berkeley had to defend against just such a lawsuit in 2003. The allegedly defamatory statements by an interviewee sharply criticized the head of a school for his endless funding requests, leadership style, and overall lack of professionalism. Although

ROHO was able to win a dismissal of this lawsuit in 2005, the interviewee who originally uttered the statements about the school leader was not able to secure a dismissal until the California Supreme Court finally ruled in his favor.[11]

Element number five, fault, is a very crucial element. Many defamation claimants who have managed to establish the first four elements have foundered on this element. The reason for this can be found in the 1964 Supreme Court decision, *New York Times Co. v. Sullivan*. To protect the First Amendment right to criticize public figures, the high court held that such individuals have a higher "fault" burden. To satisfy this, a public figure must be able to prove that the publisher of the defamation did so with "actual malice." Such malice is defined as, "knowledge of falsity or reckless disregard of whether the statements are true or false."[12] By contrast, a private figure need only prove that a publisher was negligent. This is a much lighter burden. Naturally, some of the fiercest legal battles have been fought over the classification of the person who is suing for defamation.

A related issue involves the question of whether the passage of time ever changes the classification of a person. In other words, can a public figure who has been out of the public eye for many years return to private figure status? According to three Federal Circuit Courts of Appeal, the answer is no: once a public figure, always a public figure. The most illustrative case on this issue involved Victoria Price, the chief witness in the infamous trials of the Scottsboro Boys that occurred in Alabama during the 1930s. Some forty years later, NBC produced a television dramatization of one these trials, *Judge Horton and the Scottsboro Boys*. In this production, Victoria Price was presented "as a woman attempting to send nine innocent blacks to the electric chair for a rape they did not commit."[13] Because more than forty years had passed since she had been in the national spotlight, Price claimed in her lawsuit for defamation that she was now a private figure and thus should only have to prove that NBC was negligent. Fortunately, the court rejected her claim of a change in status. In doing so it recognized that the ability of the press and historians to comment on and interpret past events would be severely crippled if public figures like Price were allowed to become private figures simply because they passed out of the public eye for a lengthy period of time.

The best way to minimize the possibility of a lawsuit for defamation is to establish a comprehensive prevention system. Such a system should include:

1. *Staff Training*: Everyone who has a role in the creation, processing, editing, and archiving of interviews should receive training. This should also be a continuous process in which potentially defamatory statements are discussed and reviewed whether they come from in-house interviews or other sources.
2. *Checklists*: Creating a series of questions to assess potential defamation is a good way to facilitate staff training. For example, is the subject of the remarks living, would it change a hearer or reader's opinion or estimate of the individual, is the negative statement supported by facts, and finally, is there other evidence to prove the truth of the interviewee's statements?

3. *Verify/Edit/Seal/Delete?* Not every shocking statement is defamatory. There may well be other evidence that points to the truthfulness of the statement. The historical record is not something that should be sanitized by its creators and keepers. If the claim or statement cannot be corroborated then start your damage control with the least invasive procedure. The last and least desirable option is deletion of the material.

The Privacy Torts

Defamation is not the only type of lawsuit that oral historians need to guard against. Two others, false light and public disclosure of private facts, could also arise from an interview or from a publication/documentary based on oral histories. False light is the privacy tort (a civil wrong to a person's reputation or commercial interests) most similar to defamation. Lawsuits alleging defamation almost always include a false light claim as a back-up cause of action. Three elements must be proven for a false light lawsuit to be successful:

1. The matter must be highly offensive to a reasonable person;
2. The author or publisher must have the necessary degree of fault, actual malice in most cases;
3. The publicity must be fairly widespread.[14]

Unlike a defamation claim, the word or images at issue do not have to be false; they only have to cast a person in a false light. The resulting injury is to a person's emotional well-being and not his or her reputation. The audience that hears such false light statements must also be substantially larger than is required for a defamation claim. Distortions or embellishment of factual situations are the most common sources of false light claims. In a 1997 case, Bobby Seale, a former leader of the Black Panther party, claimed that a docudrama had place him in a false light by implying that he had armed his followers by purchasing guns from a shady gun dealer. In point of fact, he had bought the weapons from a sporting goods store. Despite this clearly unfavorable embellishment of the historical record, Seale's false light claim was unsuccessful.[15] Another common source of such claims is false associations. This may be as minor as the publication of one's photograph in close proximity to a known criminal or a person with an unsavory reputation. A case of this type was filed in 2005 by the former sister-in-law of a Chicago mob boss. The sole basis of her lawsuit was the inclusion of her photograph in tell-all book about him and his ties to the mob.[16]

Fortunately, most courts have not viewed this very confusing and slippery privacy tort favorably. In some states it is not even recognized as a viable lawsuit. Where it is recognized, courts generally hold those who bring the lawsuits to the highest standard of proof, actual malice, because the injury is so hard to define and the safeguards that govern defamation law are not usually applicable.

The second privacy tort, public disclosure of private facts, is a much rarer type of lawsuit than false light, but nevertheless oral historians need to be aware of it. Four elements are required to successfully establish this privacy tort:

1. The disclosure of embarrassing private facts;
2. The publication must be to a fairly sizable group of people;
3. The facts must be highly offensive to a reasonable person;
4. The facts must relate to matters that are not of public concern.[17]

Unlike false light and defamation, this cause of action essentially allows someone to receive monetary damages for the truthful disclosure of private or intimate facts that are not newsworthy. The newsworthy element is the one that often determines the outcome of such lawsuits. This is especially true when the private facts involve something that is not contemporaneous but occurred a long time ago. In 1995 the *Idaho Statesman* ran a front page story, "The Boys Most Likely," which revisited a controversial incident in the mid 1950s involving homosexual men propositioning boys at the YMCA in Boise, Idaho. Based on a court record that was reproduced in the story, a respected member of the community who had never been linked to the scandal was implicated.[18] Because almost forty years had passed, the man sued for private disclosure of public facts claiming that the incident was no longer newsworthy. His lawsuit was ultimately dismissed because the private facts that the newspaper published had been contained in a public record, even though the court recognized that the disclosure caused him great pain and embarrassment so many years after the fact.

For those who publish oral history material in any form, it is important to stress that this tort does not require any falsity. Private facts that embarrass a person are all that is required. So when deciding whether to include extremely personal details in a book, anthology, or media production, one should step back and ask whether publicizing this information could be offensive to the person in the community where he or she lives. If the answer is yes or maybe, then consider a different approach.

Copyright

The late-night comedian David Letterman's "top ten" lists have become cultural icons and have spawned many other lists of humorous or odd types of human behavior. The list most pertinent to oral historians are the "Ten Common Copyright Permission Myths." Several of these myths underscore why oral historians need to be concerned about copyright protection for their interviews, publications, and productions:

1. If I give credit I don't need permission;
2. Since I am only using a small portion of the work, I don't need permission;

3. I can always obtain permission later;
4. Since I'm planning to use my work for nonprofit educational purposes, I don't need permission.[19]

The best way to counter such misconceptions is to develop a sound understanding of copyright law, the protections that it offers to authors, and how such protections can be defended. Copyright is a form of legal protection afforded to most creative works. It is a type of intellectual property like a patent or trademark. The owner of a copyright may sell, lease, divide, or bequeath his or her interest. The framers of the U.S. Constitution relied upon an economic rationale for copyright "To promote the Progress of Science and Useful Arts by Securing for Limited Times to Authors and Inventors the Exclusive Right to Their Respective Writings and Discoveries."[20]

Under the 1976 Copyright Act, "original works of authorship fixed in any tangible medium of expression, now known or later developed" may obtain copyright protection.[21] It is now well established that an oral history interview is an original work that can be copyrighted. The Copyright Act in turn categorizes oral histories as nonfiction "literary works." The nonfiction designation is especially important because creators of such works receive considerably less protection than do creators of fiction. One of the basic premises of copyright law is that facts cannot be copyrighted, and are considered to be in the public domain. Were it otherwise, researchers who uncovered facts would be able to prevent others from using them, in effect imposing a monopoly on those facts to the detriment of society.

The reach of the public domain also extends to the interpretations that writers attach to their factual discoveries. For example, if a historian develops a novel interpretation, it also becomes a fact and is considered to be in the public domain.[22] On occasion, this basic premise has been challenged in court. An author of two books on John Dillinger, a Depression-era bank robber, sued the CBS television network after it incorporated his unique interpretation into one of its crime shows. The author claimed copyright infringement for this unauthorized use of his historical interpretation. The court, however, dismissed his lawsuit, explaining that "The inventor of Sherlock Homes controls that character's fate while the copyright lasts; the first person to conclude that Dillinger survived does not get dibs on history."[23]

Oral historians and other creators of nonfiction works can only claim copyright in "(1) the author's original narration and original expression of facts, ideas, theories, and research and (2) the author's original selection, coordination, and arrangement of material."[24] This is called "thin" copyright. Had CBS taken a substantial amount of the author's actual words and his selection or arrangement of material, then he might have had a viable claim for infringement. Since his unique interpretation was itself a fact, however, it was in the public domain and not protected by copyright.

Copyright protection begins at the moment of creation. In a typical oral history interview, this would be when the recorder is turned off. The next step is usually the transfer of the interviewee's copyright interest via a legal release agreement.

From then on, the oral historian or program is the entity that holds the copyright. There is, however, an additional consideration to be addressed, namely whether an interviewer has any copyright interest in the interview that he or she conducts? Copyright law recognizes that there may be more than one author of a work. It defines a joint work as something that is "prepared by two or more authors with the intention that their contributions be merged into inseparable or inter-dependent parts of the unitary whole."[25]

While no court has yet established any binding precedent that an interview qualifies as a joint work, a strong case can be made that when such a decision is reached, it will be in the affirmative. The strongest support for this position comes from the U.S. Copyright Office itself. Whenever an application is received to register an interview, if only the name of one of the parties to the interview is on the registration form, the staff is instructed to seek further clarification as to ownership before proceeding. This position is predicated on the presumption that "A work consisting of an interview often contains copyrightable authorship by the person interviewed and the interviewer. Each owns the expression in the absence of an agreement to the contrary."[26] Additional support for the interviewer being a joint author comes from a 2007 trial court decision involving a documentary film, *Your Mommy Kills Animals*. One of the parties claiming to be a joint author of the film had conducted a series of interviews that were incorporated into the documentary. She wrote all of the questions for these interviews and did background research. Her interviewing was enough to satisfy the jury that she had made independently copyrightable contributions to the film. Because they also found that the parties fully intended to be joint authors from the onset, she was declared to be a joint author.[27]

The best course of action is to assume that unless an interviewer is a full-time employee, any other interviewer whether he or she is an independent contractor, part-time employee, or volunteer, is a joint author of the interviews that he or she conducts. The "work-made-for-hire" doctrine is the reason that the copyright in interviews done "by an employee within the scope of his or her employment." automatically passes to the employer.[28] This doctrine rarely applies to interviewers who are independent contractors or part-timers.The best practice is to have all nonemployee interviewers relinquish their putative copyright interests by means of a legal release agreement.

Having such interviewer's sign a legal release is especially important because of the considerable legal authority that each joint author has over the utilization of the copyright. The Copyright Act of 1976 gives each joint author an undivided interest in the copyright. This means that one author is free to use the work without obtaining the approval of the other author. The only obligation that one joint author has to another is to account for and share any profits that the copyrighted work earns. While most oral history interviews are not moneymakers, projects still should make singular and not joint authorship of interviews and transcripts their primary goal.

The joint work doctrine does have one special benefit. This comes into play when someone offers to donate a collection of interviews for which no legal releases were ever secured. If efforts to locate the interviewees or their heirs are unsuccessful, the best fallback position is to turn to the interviewer if he or she is known and available. Treating an interviewer as a joint author would permit them to sign over their copyright interest. The program or archive could then make the interviews available to researchers. In the event that such an interview ever earned a profit, the only legal obligation would be to share such profits with the interviewee of his/her heirs.

As intellectual property, a copyright conveys six rights to the holder: (1) reproduction, (2) the preparation of derivative works, (3) the distribution of copies, (4) public performance, (5) public display, and (6) public performance of sound recordings by means of digital audio transmission. All of these rights may be licensed or transferred to another party individually or as a whole—which occurs routinely whenever an interviewee and interviewer sign a legal release.

Copyright is not an unlimited monopoly that allows the holder unfettered discretion for many decades to decide who can or cannot use the work. One important limitation is the fair use privilege. Fair use tries to balance the intellectual property rights of the holder with the public's need to have at least limited access to creative works without having to secure permission or pay the copyright holder. Fair use exists for purposes such as "criticism, commentary, news reporting, teaching, scholarship, or research, so long as it does not infringe on copyright."[29]

Finding the boundary line between copyright protection and fair use is not an easy task. When courts are called upon to make such a determination, the Copyright Act of 1976 sets forth a four-part test for them to apply. This test requires close examination of the parallel relationship between the infringing publication and the copyrighted work. The first part of the test focuses on the purpose and character of the usage by the alleged infringer, particularly whether it is commercial in nature or for nonprofit educational purposes. Part two takes into consideration the nature of the copyrighted work. If for example, it is unpublished, this usually is beneficial to the copyright holder because the infringing work may have damaged the future publication prospects. Part three delves into the amount and substantiality of the usage in relation to the totality of the copyrighted work. Part four is usually the most important one, namely, the effect of the usage upon the potential market for or value of the copyrighted work.

Since the copyrights to the vast majority of interviews are held by oral historians, the question that naturally arises is: What types of usages might be deemed to go beyond fair use? Wholesale appropriation of interviews would certainly go beyond fair use. But what about an unauthorized quotation that involves only a small portion of an interview? The best answer is that given the "thin" copyright protection that oral history interviews have, the unauthorized use would need to be quite substantial in order to lose the fair use privilege. In one case where a writer took about 5 percent of his material from a collection of published interviews, his unauthorized use was deemed to be protected by the fair use privilege.[30]

Oral historians can do a number of things to protect against the unauthorized use of interviews. The first defense is to make sure that a copyright notice appears on all interviews. This should be supported by clear instructions on the fair use of interviews for noncommercial purposes and how to go about securing permission whether for more extensive usage or for commercial purposes. The last defense, short of filing a lawsuit, is to send a warning letter when someone's unauthorized use appears to exceed fair use. Since lawsuits for copyright infringement tend to be very expensive and are often unsuccessful when the copyrighted work is nonfiction, taking this step should be the last course of action.

One way to avoid copyright altogether is to renounce it. This can be done by inserting a clause into a legal release agreement that places the interview into the public domain. The public domain is the vast storehouse of knowledge that contains both facts and creative works for which the copyrights have expired. Taking such a step is something that oral historians should seriously consider if they have no desire to police their interviews for possible infringement and wish to encourage the most unfettered access.

This discussion has focused solely on copyright law in the United States. Protecting interviews against copyright infringement by individuals from other nations is a much more involved undertaking. While most nations have signed international treaties that give legal standing to the copyrights of foreign nationals, exactly how much legal standing varies greatly from country to country? There is also considerable variance among nations as to the rights of copyright owners. Canada, for example, extends copyright protection to works created by the national government, while the U.S. government is not permitted to claim copyright for works created by its various agencies. Thus, a work that has been legally copyrighted in one country may or may not receive the same level of protection in another.[31]

The Internet

The World Wide Web has not only democratized access to oral histories but serves as a development opportunity for archivists and librarians to demonstrate to their institutions that they are expanding the visibility and availability of their collections. At the same time, ease of access and instant portability of materials raise the possibility of far greater misuse than traditional on-site research. Although the uniqueness of the information superhighway has forced some modifications in the way that the law is applied, for the most part the same legal principles that apply at ground level are also applicable in cyberspace. The same protective measures discussed earlier are thus readily applicable. The future use clauses in a legal release agreement should demonstrate that interviewees clearly agreed to online display of their voices and words. The same screening measures advocated earlier to detect and manage potentially defamatory language are even more crucial since the potential readership of interviews online is so much greater. It is especially important to put a notice of copyright ownership on all uploaded interviews and set forth a well-defined procedure for fair use (limited quotes and paraphrasing) and when and how to secure permission for more extensive utilization.

Institutional Review Boards

Practitioners of oral history affiliated with colleges and universities may need to address an additional administrative hurdle that comes to them courtesy of the campus institutional review board (IRB). These committees of faculty members, researchers, and public representatives not only have the authority to decide whether an oral history project can proceed, but all too often impose restrictions that are at odds with accepted oral history practices.

Institutional review boards have the responsibility of preventing the abuse or mistreatment of human beings who are the subjects of research studies. The impetus behind such boards was the public outrage over the sadistic medical experiments performed on Jews and other minorities by the Nazis and the shameful Tuskegee Syphilis Study sponsored by the U.S. Public Health Service (in which African Americans with syphilis were treated only with placebos). These travesties, coupled with the certainty that continuing biomedical research on human subjects was essential to improving the health of all people, led to the creation of a national monitoring program. Initially, this program was established to review only federally funded research, but over the years risk-adverse college administrators have required IRBs to review virtually all on-campus research, including undergraduate projects. Because biomedical research is most likely to inflict the greatest harm, the protective regulations contained in the so-called Common Rule naturally emphasize the natural sciences.[32] This emphasis unfortunately works to the detriment of qualitative researchers who do oral history research. Because of the biomedical focus of the Common Rule and the overwhelming hard science orientation of most IRB members, oral history projects have often been sidetracked or saddled with excessively restrictive confidentiality requirements, unrealistic security provisions, and dire warnings in legal release agreements.

Although the Common Rule allows IRBs to exempt certain types of research from review, including oral history, qualitative researchers have had little success in securing exempt status. The American Historical Association and the Oral History Association sought to free most oral history research from IRB control by working through the federal Office for Human Research Protection (OHRP), which oversees all human subjects research protection programs. Their effort resulted in an OHRP policy statement in 2003 to the effect that oral history interviews do not contribute to "generalizable knowledge" as defined in the Common Rule, they therefore can be "excluded from institutional review board (IRB) because they do not involve research as defined by HHS regulations."[33] Despite this definitive policy statement, a survey conducted by the AHA in 2006, revealed that only a small number of IRBs had implemented the OHRP policy statement and thus no longer included oral history among reviewable research. Although campus IRBs are legally empowered to review and approve all federally funded research, the task of lifting their heavy hand from oral history research is actually an administrative issue and not a legal one. The intent of the Common Rule is to make sure that IRBs are truly independent. As a result, while all campuses include some form of appeal and review process, challenges to the authority and decisions of an IRB are rarely successful.

The best path to securing IRB acceptance of the OHRP policy statement excluding oral history research from review, or at least having oral history research classified as exempt, is a combination of lobbying and education. There is often a huge intellectual gulf between the scientifically trained IRB members and qualitative researchers from the humanities and social sciences. Attempts to educate or re-educate an IRB to the nonintrusive and usually harmless properties of oral history research should include the following:

1. Preparing a guide that thoroughly explains oral history methodology as a research tool;
2. Developing a bibliography of oral history sources including examples of similar oral history research that has been published or is housed in libraries or archives;
3. Explaining how the research project follows the the Oral History Association's *Best Practices for Oral History* particularly in regard to the informed consent of the interviewees;
4. Detailing your own training and work in oral history;
5. If there is enough oral history research being conducted, have your department create a committee to review all proposed oral history projects;
6. Present the IRB with examples of policies at other universities that either implement the OHRP policy statement or generally consider oral history research to be in the exempt category. The University of Michigan, University of Texas, and Columbia University are three of the leading research institutions where the IRBs either follow the OHRP policy statement on oral history or routinely grant oral history research exempt status.

Sound Legal Safeguards

There is an old saying that "ignorance of the law is no excuse unless you can afford to hire a good lawyer." The fallacy of this notion should be readily apparent. Modern litigation is expensive and time consuming, and the publicity surrounding a lawsuit could damage the reputation of an oral history program, even if the final decision is favorable. The wiser approach is to incorporate sound legal safeguards into all areas of the program to lessen the likelihood of legal challenges: have an attorney review your legal release agreements, initiate a staff training program to inform interviewers and others connected with the project of the potential areas of liability (educate yourself if you work alone), and keep as up to date with new legal developments as you do with new scholarship and equipment.

DEED OF GIFT WITH RESTRICTIONS

The mission of the Longview Historical Center is to document the history of Northern Wisconsin. An important part of this effort is the collection of oral history interviews with knowledgeable individuals from all walks of life. In order for your interview/s to be placed in the Center's archive for future historical use, it will be necessary for you to sign this agreement. Before doing so you should read it carefully and ask any questions you may have regarding its terms and conditions.

I,________________[interviewee], of__________________[address, city, state, zip code] herein permanently donate and convey to the Longview Historical Center my oral history interview/s. In making this gift, I understand that I am conveying all right, title and interest in copyright to the Longview Historical Center. In return, the Center grants to me a nonexclusive license to utilize my interview/s during my lifetime. I also grant to the Center the right to use my name and likeness in any promotional materials for publications or projects.

I further understand that I will have an opportunity to review/edit my interview/s before it is/they are made available for historical research whether in audio/video and/or transcript form. The Center will then make my interview/s available to researchers subject to the following restriction/s. Future uses may include quotation from and publication or broadcast in any media including the Internet.

Restrictions

_____I wish to close my interviews until___________________________

_____I wish to close specific portions of my interview/s until _________

_____I wish to restrict access to on-site users until__________________

_____No researcher may quote from my interview/s without my permission until____________________________________

_____I wish to be identified by a pseudonym and have all references from which my identity could be known redacted until____________________

The Center agrees to take all reasonable steps to honor my restrictions. I understand, however, that the Center may not be able uphold my restriction/s against either a freedom of information request or a subpoena.

____________________	____________________
Interviewee	Interviewer or Agent
____________________	____________________
Date	Date

DEED OF GIFT: VOLUNTEER INTERVIEWER

The Milwaukee Neighborhoods Project is dedicated to the preservation of historic neighborhoods. To help achieve this goal, oral history interviews are being conducted with elderly Milwaukeeans throughout the City. This Project is partially funded by a grant from the Wisconsin Humanities Council and sustained for the most part by the work of volunteers. To insure that the interview/s that you conduct as a volunteer interviewer can be archived and used for research, you are asked to sign the following agreement. Before doing so you should carefully read it and ask any questions regarding its terms and conditions.

I________________[interviewer] of________________[address, city state, zip code] do herein permanently donate and convey all interviews that I conducted for the Milwaukee Neighborhoods Project to the Milwaukee Historical Society. In making this gift I understand that I am conveying all right, title and interest in copyright that I might hold as a joint author to the Society.

I understand that I will have the opportunity to review the interview/s before it is/they are made available for historical research whether in audio/video and/or transcript form. The Society will then make the interview/s available to researchers without restrictions. Future uses may include quotation from and publication or broadcast in any media including the Internet.

____________________	____________________
Project Director	Interviewer
____________________	____________________
Date	Date

CONTRACTUAL AGREEMENT

The mission of the U.S. Army History Center is to document and preserve the individual histories of U.S. Army personnel in recent wars and conflicts. The goal of the Desert Storm Oral History Project is to record the experiences of participants in this War. To deposit your interview/s with the Center it will be necessary for you to sign this agreement. Before doing so you should carefully read it and ask any questions regarding its terms and conditions.

In consideration for the audio and/or video recording, editing, processing and archiving of my interview/s by the Desert Storm Oral History Project, I_______________[interviewee], of_______________[address, city, state & zip code] herein permanently transfer to the U.S. Army History Center my interview/s. In doing so I understand that I am conveying all right, title and interest in copyright to the Center. In return, the Center grants to me a nonexclusive license to utilize my interview/s during my lifetime. I also grant the Center the right to use my name and likeness in any promotional materials for publications/ projects.

I understand that I will have the opportunity to review/edit my interview/s before it is/they are made available for historical research whether in audio/video and/or transcript form. The Center will then make my interview/s available for research without restriction. Future uses may include quotation from and publication or broadcast in any media including the Internet.

______________________	______________________
Interviewee	Interviewer or Agent
______________________	______________________
Date	Date

NOTES

1. Barbara Bryant, "Thurgood Marshall Collection Press Stories Stir Furor Over LC's Opening of Papers," *Library of Congress Information Bulletin* (June 13, 1993). http://www.loc.gov//lcib/93/9312/marshall.html.

2. 38A C.J.S. *Gifts Inter Vivos* § 5 (2007).

3. John R. Allison and Robert A. Prentice, *The Legal Environment of Business*, 5th ed. (Chicago: Dryden Press, 1990), 181.

4. *Effects Associates, Inc. v. Cohen*, 908 F. 2d 555, 557 (2d Cir. 1990).

5. Kenneth H. Williams, "'I'm sure there were some that thought I was too smart for my own good': The Ed Prichard Oral History Interviews," *Register of the Kentucky Historical Society* 104 (Summer/Autumn, 2006): 395–97.

6. Sam H. Bowers, "Contract of Gift" (Oct. 24, 1973), Mississippi Department of Archives and History.

7. Samuel Johnson, Idler 45, Feb. 24, 1759.

8. *Damon v. Moore*, 520 F. 3d 98 (C.A. 1, 2008).

9. Lloyd J. Jassin and Steven C. Schecter, *The Copyright Permission and Libel Handbook* (New York: Wiley, 1998), 109.

10. Bruce W. Sanford, *Libel and Privacy*, § 4.12, 130, 2nd ed. (New York: Aspen Publishers 2002).

11. *Hebrew Academy of San Francisco v. Goldman*, 42 Cal. 4th 883 (2007).

12. *New York Times Co. v. Sullivan*, 376 U.S. 254 (1964).

13. Ibid.

14. John L. Diamond, Lawrence C. Levine, and M. Stuart Madden, *Understanding Torts*, 3rd ed. (Newark, N.J.: LexisNexisMathewBender, 2007), 391.

15. *Seale v. Gramercy Pictures*, 964 F. Supp. 918 (E.D. Pa. 1997).

16. *Raveling v. HarperCollins Publishers Inc.*, 33 Media L. Rep. 1417 (NO-04–2693 (C.A. 7 (Ill), 2005).

17. Diamond, *Understanding Torts*, 392.

18. *Uranga v. Federated Publications, Inc.* 138 Idaho 550 (2003).

19. Loyd J. Jassin, "Ten Common Copyright Permission Myths," http://www.copylaw.com/new_articles/copy_myths.html.

20. U.S Constitution, article 1 § 8.

21. 17 U.S.C.A. §102 (2005).

22. Marshall Leaffer, *Understanding Copyright Law*, 4th ed. (Newark, N.J.: LexisNexis, 2005), 93.

23. *Nash v. CBS*, 899 F. 2d 1537, 1541 (7th Cir. 1990).

24. William F. Patry, *Patry on Copyright*, vol. 2 (St. Paul, Minn.: Thomson/West, 2007), 3–176.

25. 17 U.S.C.A. §101 (2005).

26. U.S. Copyright Office, *Compendium II, Copyright Office Practices*, § 317 (1984).

27. *Berman v. Johnson*, 518 F. Supp. 2d 791, 796–97 (E.D. VA, 2007).

28. 17 U.S.C.A § 101 (1) (2005).

29. Id. §105 (2005).

30. *Maxtone-Graham v. Burtchaell*, 803 F. 2d 1253 (2d Cir. 1986).

31. Ellen M. Kozak, *Every Writer's Guide To Copyright And Publishing Law*, 3rd ed. (New York: Henry Holt, 2004), 94.

32. 45 C.F.R. § 46 (2005).

33. Linda Shopes, "Negotiating Institutional Review Boards," *Perspectives* 45 (Mar. 2007), 38–39.

BIBLIOGRAPHY

Copyright

Copyright and Fair Use Center, Stanford University Libraries, http://fairuse.stanford.edu. Provides articles, news, featured cases blogs and links to other useful Web sites.

Creative Commons, http://creativecommons.org. A nonprofit organization that encourages copyright holders to take a less restrictive view of how their works may be utilized by others. They provide tools like Creative Commons licenses that allow copyright holders to reserve certain rights but waive others for the benefit of future creators.

Fishman, Stephen. *Copyright Handbook: What Every Writer Needs to Know*. 10th ed. Berkeley, Calif.: Nolo, 2008.

Kozak, Ellen M. *Every Writer's Guide to Copyright and Publishing Law*. 3rd ed. New York: Henry Holt, 2004.

Leaffer, Marshall. *Understanding Copyright Law*. 4th ed. Newark, N.J.: LexisNexis, 2005.

United States Copyright Office, www.copyright.gov. Information on filing for registration, enforcement and laws, including more than seventy-five brochures on key copyright issues: *Copyright Basics, Work-Made-For-Hire Under 1976 Copyright Act*, and *Copyright Registration for Online Works.*

Defamation/Privacy

Diamond, John L., Lawrence C. Levine, and M. Stuart Madden, *Understanding Torts*. 3rd ed. Newark, N.J.: LexisNexisMathewBender, 2007.

Jassin, Lloyd J., and Steven C. Shechter. *The Copyright Permission and Libel Handbook*. New York: Wiley, 1998.

Sanford, Bruce W. *Libel and Privacy*. 2nd ed. New York: Aspen, 2002.

CHAPTER 25

ETHICAL CHALLENGES IN THE ORAL HISTORY OF MEDICINE

MICHELLE WINSLOW

GRAHAM SMITH

It is a mark of the contribution of oral history to the history of medicine that studies located within living memory are open to criticism if they fail to include oral history. Paula Michaels, in a review of a history of modern Chinese medicine, noted that

> an oral history component to this project would no doubt have yielded a less passive, more vivid picture of what it meant as a lived, everyday experience to study and practice medicine in early Communist China.[1]

However, oral history's contribution to the history of medicine is a complex one, and we will highlight this in an exploration of the history of professionals in medicine and medical professions, and in the emergence of the patient's story. We subsequently consider the problems of "shared authority": working with professionals when interviewee "power" is a factor and, conversely, our relationships with "patients" who may be viewed as "vulnerable" oral history subjects. Interwoven throughout this discussion is the question of ethics, and we raise some of the ethical challenges that arise within the history of medicine.

The History of Professionals in Medicine and the Medical Profession

Part of the reason for the popularity for oral history among modern historians of medicine is the long-established use of biography and life history material in the subdiscipline. Before the 1970s, most medical histories were written from the perspective of men of importance—and the occasional woman—discovering new treatments and cures. In the mid-1950s, for example, Ralph Major published *A History of Medicine*, in which he described how "great" men "found" medical knowledge in a history that was an unrelenting intellectual progress from superstition through enlightenment to technological discovery.[2] While Major acknowledged the broader historical contexts in which his heroes operated, he presented historical change as a result of individual endeavors, rather than as a result of wider social history. In such a context it is unsurprising that oral history, even as early as 1960, had been adopted as a method of producing autobiographies of those great men.[3] By the early 1970s, though, Saul Benison, a pioneer oral historian and longtime member of the Association of American Historians of Medicine, was suggesting that the use of oral history in making hagiographies had its problems, since the focus remained firmly on the individual contribution to the progress of medicine.

The belief that the history of medicine was simply one of individual clinicians and scientists making medical discoveries became challenged with the rise of social history. In Britain, members of the *Society for the Social History of Medicine*, established in the late 1960s, combined an interest in the history of public health with social science methods, including social history. In a series of articles, Thomas McKeown argued, in what became known as his "thesis," that medicine makes no significant contribution to reducing the death rate when compared to the impact on the death rate of improvements in economic and social conditions.[4] It was a startling claim that has been subsequently the subject of periodic debate, but importantly it directed the attention of historians of medicine outwards toward broader historical change.

By the mid-1960s, historians of medicine were beginning to be influenced by the development of social history. While medical professionals like McKeown continued to dominate the subject area, often claiming that their clinical knowledge provided particular insights, it was academic historians and social scientists that set the intellectual pace. They were beginning to explore how social historical contexts shaped medicine, arguing for example over the significance of the French revolution in the rise of hospital medicine, which also marked a change in doctor-patient relationships.[5]

The study of individual contributions was giving way to examinations of the social forces that produced change in medicine. For many historians, this meant studying the rise of specialization and emergence of professions. As John C. Burnham later noted, "the idea of profession changed the writing of medical history."[6] It also prompted many contributions to the growing critique of medicine and medical professionals that arose, at least in part, from the women's movement and as a backlash against medicalization; the turning of the conditions of everyday life into medical issues, and some have claimed a corresponding social control by health professionals.[7]

For oral historians, including Saul Benison, subjectivity was becoming increasingly important. An advisor on oral history for the U.S. National Library of Medicine, Benison in 1967 published an oral history memoir of Tom Rivers, a pioneering virologist.[8] In praising the book, a reviewer in the *American Historical Review* proclaimed that Benison "has clearly produced a new kind of historical document that is at once the memoir of an important scientific figure and the creation of a historian-interviewer who has framed all the questions and set the historical problems." Within a few years, Benison was noting:

> Actually, the collection of half-truths, myths, and prejudices is as valuable for history as pristine truth if they are appreciated and evaluated adequately. Often they lead to contradictions. In fact it is the contradictions that emerge from such material which pose the nicest historical problems.[9]

Understanding the significance of subjectivity would not only lead to identifying half-truths, but also contribute to understandings of how medical knowledge was historically and culturally made. By the 1980s, the construction of medical knowledge had become a central concern to historians of medicine. It was increasingly noted how the various medical professions and specialties differed in their views of the patient's body, of diseases, and of medicine itself.[10] By the early 1990s, for example, Lindsay Granshaw was writing about the differing perspectives of surgeons, anatomists, and the rise of the specialty of rectal surgery.[11]

Among the theories of knowledge that have proved important to historians of medicine was social constructionism, in its many varieties. For Ludmilla Jordanova, social constructionism in the history of medicine had a particular character: a sympathetic understanding of the "actors" whose beliefs and actions were shaped by professional interests, power, technology, and the content and contexts of their lived experiences. In this manner she identified the significance of the way language was used in medicine. For Jordanova, the prize was "A historiography capable of explaining the imaginative reach of ideas of health, healing, and sickness." Such a historiography was set to produce an antimodernist or antiprogressivist narrative that would be shared with other historians.[12]

Social constructionism was used to counteract what its advocates saw as scientism and Whig-like historical practices in existing accounts. But adopting an explicit position that privileged society as an explanatory category (rather than medicine or technology) signaled a particular disciplinary orientation. The history of medicine has always consisted of constituencies that are somewhat similar to those that have existed within oral history, what Dorothy Porter called "An eclectic mix of amateur and professional historians."[13] Adopting theories that emphasized the social was in the interests of academic historians of medicine, at the expense of those clinicians who could now be shown as amateur dabblers in medical history.

An example of the approach in action can be found in Roger Cooter's application of a Weberian analysis to war and medicine:[14]

> If the relationship between war and modernity has been subjected to at least a measure of thoughtful and theoretically sophisticated sociological and historical analysis, the same cannot be said of the interaction between war and medicine...until very recently, this literature has been overwhelmingly dominated by practitioner-centred accounts of how medicine has benefited from and been advanced by war. Such triumphalist reckonings are as implicitly militaristic as they are naively positivist and partial.[15]

Cooter's explicit argument was that medicine did not simply service modernity. Instead, it was a midwife of modernity, helping to bring modernity into being. He was also implicitly arguing that the history of medicine cannot be left to clinicians, working or retired.

Why this should be important to oral historians of medicine is partially opportunistic. The way we collect and analyze subjective narratives lends itself in many ways to an approach that emphasizes the social. It also provides a number of challenges to the oral historian working in this area. These include locating the biographical narratives we collect within wider social historical contexts. As oral historians, our insights into the making of memory and consciousness equips us to undertake this task. We are practiced at gathering and using conflicting accounts; as well as how we relate to those we interview.

In the mid-1990s two major reviews of oral history in the history of medicine were undertaken: one in Britain by Paul Thompson, and the other in the United States by Nancy Tomes.[16] Thompson identified a range of different approaches being adopted, although he found that a great deal of oral history was being utilized in a supplementary manner. That is, oral history was simply an additional source used to illustrate or support existing documentary evidence. Thompson could identify few examples of oral history being collected to challenge existing documentary-based accounts. Instead, he found that oral histories were being collected to explore specific issues in the history of medicine, and included in-depth systematic autobiographical approaches, mainly of doctors, as well as whole life history interviews. Such an approach was also beginning to be adopted in social science-type surveys.

In the United States, Tomes identified a similar pattern and added that oral histories exploring the histories of particular organizations, including hospitals, were much in evidence, as were projects documenting events and innovations, including the development of antibiotics in the 1950s. Somewhat inevitably, there were studies of the lives and works of leading medical scientists and clinicians. But she also noted attempts by some of those who were using oral history to demystify structure and bureaucracy, and so challenge ideas of "progress." While such histories continued to place emphases on human agency, there were also attempts at correctives, such as investigating the relationship between individuals and the informal "colleges" that had been thus far hidden from history. There were even attempts to highlight the problems of particular developments, including the perils of medical specialization. In Tomes's survey we can see the growing convergence around subjectivity between the projects of oral historians and those of historians of medicine—a movement to include histories of the professions as well as medical professionals.

Repeating the surveys by Tomes and Thompson would now be an enormous task. Since 1995 there has been an explosion in the oral history of medicine throughout the world. Yet it is worth identifying a few examples of how the approaches identified by Thompson and Tomes have continued and developed. It is also worth noting that there have been a number of new developments.

In spite of leading historians of medicine being ever more critical of hagiographic projects, "greatness" and "progress" continued to be celebrated, especially in North America where testimony-based accounts about individuals abound.[17] It is particularly ironic that oral history continues to lionize the individual lives of medical grandees, when so many oral historians remain committed to history from below, and providing a voice to those who are too often hidden from, or by, historians. There are also publications that have attempted to go beyond this approach by concentrating on specialties, such as Allen Weisse's *Heart to Heart: The Twentieth-Century Battle against Cardiac Disease: An Oral History*.[18] There are also signs of unease among some of the biographers, such as Shelley McKeller, who brought a fine sense of irony to her portrait of the late Donald Walter Gordon Murray. Based on testimonies from his colleagues, the picture that emerged was of an audacious, dazzling, accomplished, flawed, and grumpy Canadian surgeon. She expressed her disquiet memorably in her introduction by describing her work as "dead white guy history."[19]

Ronald Bayer and Gerald Oppenheimer carried out an oral history study with doctors in the United States whose lives and careers were dominated by the AIDS epidemic, from the 1980s to 2000. They amassed important perspectives but came to understand that stories were multidimensional reflections on the epidemic's history. As interviewees spoke of events, they divulged personal meaning that changed over time as individuals gained experience, knowledge, and authority. In relating their personal interpretations of the significance of their experience of AIDS, contributors bore witness to horrors, not only in relation to patients and doctors but to societal stigma and taboo—including from within their own profession.[20]

Using oral history to supplement and inform documentary evidence has remained important, especially in the underresearched area of medical and health policy. Yet testimonies have been increasingly used with greater sophistication, most notably in Virginia Berridge's *AIDS in the UK: The Making of Policy, 1981–1994*.[21] In the historiography of AIDS/HIV, the study upon which this book is based may be unique. The AIDS Social History Programme charted a national health crisis over time, remained unaffiliated from policy and pressure groups, and used oral history in the absence of government documentation. Berridge explored the challenges that the study faced, which included questions of relevance. Between 1987 and 1989 the collection of oral histories about policy decisions could have been seen as a frivolous diversion from alleviating suffering and searching for treatments.

Mainstream medical sociology was attacked for "lacking in practical application, more concerned to develop general sociological theory than to have an impact on the course of the virus spread." One way around this was for social scientists to claim their research as immediately policy-relevant. As a result, as Berridge has noted, there was a more general "revival of positivist social science."[22]

Other research further has reinforced the significance of understanding policy through oral history without adopting a positivist position. This has included exposing the reasons for policy failure. An excellent example of this can be found in a history of the 1964 typhoid outbreak in Aberdeen, Scotland, by David Smith, H. Leslie Diack, T. Hugh Pennington, and Elizabeth M. Russell.[23] They described the complex relations between the health professionals, the media, local authorities, and central government, and their different responses to the event. They convincingly argued that the outbreak reinforced regulatory approaches to the education of consumers and diverted attention from policy-making processes, as well as reinforcing the position of civil servants and their experts rather than politicians. Their conclusion is especially significant in understanding why subsequent large-scale food poisoning incidents occurred and why they were dealt with in the ways they were.

Oral history also continues to be used as correctives. Even when there is a vast amount of archival data, oral historians have shown how testimonies can provide alternative accounts. Anne Perez Hattori, for example, used evidence from Chamorro-speakers to provide a cross-cultural description of the U.S. Navy's health policies in Guam that was missing from the administrators' extensive archives of sanitation and hygiene.[24] Similarly, oral history has offered insights into how different communities made use of popular preparations and used pharmaceuticals and technologies in ways that manufacturers had never intended, including the self-treatment and "medicine" of isolated communities, such as those in Newfoundland.[25]Similarly, in examining the affect of birth control on women's lives, Kate Fisher has demonstrated the importance of oral history in understanding contraception in cultural and social contexts, particularly the interrelationship of gender and social class in the provision of contraception services.[26]

The Patient's Story

In addition to the impact of medicine and medical science on sections of the population, oral historians and historians of medicine have increasingly become interested in the patient's story., Roy Porter, one of those who set out to rectify a perceived imbalance in the history of medicine, observed that "We have histories of disease, but not of health, biographies of doctors, but not of the sick."[27] It was a complaint that oral historians were already familiar with. The number of oral histories of patients prior to 1985 was small and likely to be found in "health" in a broad sense rather than in medicine. For example, the journal *Oral History* has carried articles on birth control and on opium use, but there was precious little else in the way of patient accounts and testimony.[28]

The delayed arrival of the patient in the historiography of medicine was not simply a matter of forgetfulness or ignorance. Not only had Roy Porter needed to locate new sources of information pertinent to the story, but he had to reject at least in part the idea that the "patient" was a construction of medical power. Porter's call for patient history was taken up by Flurin Condrau who commented that "how to write the patient's history, how to deal with subjectivity, experience and perhaps even choice, is still very much unchartered territory for historians of medicine."[29]

Oral history studies increasingly began to address the invisibility of recipients of medicine in the history of medicine, and oral histories of patients have rapidly grown in number. These include the stories of people who experienced particular diseases and treatments. A fine example is Sanjiv Kakar's history of leprosy sufferers and missionary medicine in British colonial India.[30] Other studies have involved patients in palliative care, documenting memories with people aware of their incurable medical conditions.[31]

While these approaches tend to display sensitivity to wider social historical contexts, they have not challenged medical constructions of "the patient" in the same way as those oral historians who have identified inappropriate medicalization and oppressive uses of medicine. Some of these counternarratives have even been published in clinical journals. Most notable is an article in the *British Medical Journal* that recounted the medical treatments of homosexuality in Britain from the 1950s on, drawn from testimonies of former patients.[32]

As well as people whose sexuality was diagnosed as unhealthy, oral historians have collected the life stories of those who suffered less from their disabilities and more from medical interventions (iatrogenesis). For example, Claudia Malacrida recorded the memories of survivors of a total institution for "mental defectives" in the province of Alberta, Canada.[33] She has noted how difficult that project turned out to be, and how barriers confronted her at every turn. She was initially denied contact with the survivors, and then refused access to the institution and its archive. Despite such barriers, Malacrida was able to record "rich and powerful testimony to the brutality of institutionalization" and to produce "an emancipatory history from the perspectives of those most oppressed by disability policies and practices." Kerry Davies's history of mental illness described how patients have been silenced by institutionalized systems but nevertheless found a way to express an "acceptable" voice via frameworks of loss. This loss was not solely through the effects of illness but also through a curtailment of liberty and their objectification as "the patient." In such narratives, there is a development of the self as a patient, survival, self-discovery, and a regaining of personal agency.[34]

Since the mid-1990s, oral historians have recorded testimonies with those who have suffered at the hands of medicine, and have also sought to promote changes in care. The Open University's pioneering Social History of Learning Disability Group has been especially active in making change. Their publications focused on the memories of people with learning difficulties, such as *Good Times, Bad Times:*

Women with Learning Difficulties Telling Their Stories, and later included those of families and careers, including *Witnesses to Change: Families, Learning Difficulties and History*.[35] Both family members and those with learning difficulties were shown as active agents of change who challenged inadequate and poorly conceived health and social care. The result provided new ways of understanding disability in the past and new ways of influencing future policy. This has been reinforced by the group's use of oral evidence to argue that people with learning disabilities are able to direct their own lives as fully active members of their communities. The group has extended its work and collected accounts of self-advocacy from Australia, Britain Canada, and Iceland, which have been subsequently published as "testimonies of resistance."[36]

Oral history as a form of empowerment and advocacy has been taken up by other groups. Scope, a British national disability organization, has completed a pioneering oral history of people with cerebral palsy. Its monthly podcasts, *Speaking for Ourselves*, have drawn upon 230 hours of recorded testimonies by people with cerebral palsy over the age of fifty, interviews that have been deposited for public access with the British Library Sound Archive and the Wellcome Library.[37] The photographer Karen Hitchlock combined portrait images with oral testimony to give people living with multiple sclerosis an opportunity to express their own unique experience of living with MS, and of being a participant in research trials. She has cited the well-known expression that "science knows no boundaries," and stated that

> in fact scientists are very good at setting boundaries, obeying protocols and focusing on results. It is this type of knowledge that seems to matter to the scientific community. It is impersonal, public, productive and verifiable. But there is a weakness in this approach as it allows scientists to become more and more abstracted from their clients and their client's reality. It also encourages a dispassionate and detached approach, which is in conflict with the clinician's dual role as the objective researcher and the caring clinician.[38]

In their narratives of MS, participants raised issues important to them, finding common ground and mutual understanding of the impact of disease on their lives. Presenting stories in photographs and narrative encourages a reappraisal of the relationship between the research scientist and research volunteer, producing a shift of values that draws away from the analytical and impersonal method and moves toward personal experience.

The Nurse's Story

Oral history has long been used to document not only the lives of leading clinicians but also rank-and-file practitioners, especially those belonging to the "Cinderella" professions, including general practice and gerontology.[39] However, it is the history of nursing that has attracted the greatest use of oral history work. There are now oral histories of numerous nursing specialties and many different aspects of nursing experience have been collected. In the United States, Jacqueline Zalumas used oral history for a history of critical nursing.[40] David Russell carried out a study of mental health nurses.[41] Duncan Mitchell and Anne-Marie Rafferty considered the work of learning disability nurses after the Second World War in the UK.[42] Sheryl Brennan described the "contradictory stories" that a cohort of nurses in Australia told when they recalled their 1960s training.[43] Helen Sweet and Rona McDougal detailed the role of community nursing in primary healthcare in Britain.[44] Challenging the assumption that nursing is an exclusively female occupation, Carolyn Mackintosh drew on oral history sources to present a history of men in nursing in Britain.[45] Other projects have established such archives as Nursing Voices in England and the Royal College of Nursing Archive in Scotland.

The Heritage Lottery Fund, a major funder of oral history projects in the UK, has supported a number of hospital-based projects, which combined testimony of nurses with patients, doctors, and other staff. Some of these include a project on Muckamore Abbey Hospital, Northern Ireland (2002); a community initiative to tell stories surrounding groundbreaking medical developments in Liverpool's Aintree Hospital (2005); the Royal Albert Hospital Archive recording the heritage of a long-stay hospital for people with learning difficulties (2005); the All Saints Heritage Project on the contribution to the Health Service in Wolverhampton of Black and Minority Ethnic communities working at the Royal Hospital (2007); Hospital Histories on Dartford isolation and mental hospitals (2007); and the Doncaster Gate Hospital Heritage Project, recording the history of a Rotherham hospital as it approached closure (2008).[46]

The Problems of "Shared Authority"

Oral history in medicine has raised a number of ethical issues. Until recent years, as the South African oral historian Philippe Denis has highlighted, the tendency for the humanities in most universities and research institutions was to view the ethical conduct of research as a matter for the conscience of the individual researcher. This has changed, and there is a growing movement to regulate researchers' use of private material and their relationships with the researched, as well as to develop ethical guidelines to reduce the risk of harm to participants in an interview situation.[47] Issues such as whether oral history is always good, whether interviewees always want to participate, why people tell their stories, what stories are told, what tensions exist around professional interest and patient autonomy, and the nature of the relationship between interviewer and interviewee are familiar to oral historians in any discipline but are discussed here in the context of medicine. Oral historians are increasingly required to be accountable to medical ethics committees about their research and their relationships with medical practitioners and patients.

Where oral historians seem to be at their most comfortable in the history of medicine is confronting challenges of working with the disempowered, the marginalized, and those with very little presence in the historiography. "Shared authority," to use Michael Frisch's phrase, sees interviewer and interviewee working together reflexively to produce understandings of the past.[48] We have provided examples of projects—and there are many more—in which testifying has facilitated including those with learning difficulties, mental health problems as well as people who have been stigmatized by medicine. Great care has been taken to create partnerships and alliances with the less powerful. Such projects are often reflexive, as for example in the research of AIDS/HIV survivors by Wendy Rickard.[49]

In 1997, a notable development in the study of the history of medicine in the UK occurred with the commencement of the Wellcome Witness seminars. The seminars invited significant figures in twentieth-century medicine to gather together and discuss specific discoveries or events in recent medical history. Under the guidance of Tilli Tansey, they have covered a range of subjects including drugs in psychiatric practice, the development of cancer pain relief, and "Superbugs and Superdrugs: A History of MRSA."[50] Irvine Loudon, a historian of medicine, called these "oral history at its best":

> Regardless of your own areas of interest, all the volumes make compulsive reading because the participants tended to 'let their hair down' and talk more freely than they would have at a scientific meeting. They discussed openly the hidden realities of the evolution of medical practice and medical research. But the Witness Seminars are more than just fun to read. They are, primarily, important historical records.[51]

The immediacy of working with people whose histories we seek to (re)present has its own challenges in the history of medicine. Oral histories of policy, patients, and practitioners can produce particular difficulties in terms of "shared authority," which oral historians working elsewhere are perhaps less familiar with. This has been largely because medicine is a powerful social force in which practitioners, policy makers, and patients exercise differing degrees of power dependent on time and place. The relationship between historians of medicine and medical power or authority has also changed over time, moving toward more critical approaches that have attempted to place medicine within broader social and historical contexts. Oral historians have to make difficult choices about not only *whose* story should be told but *how* that story should be told.

Projects seeking to interview medical and health professionals during their career life will often come up against such sensibilities, particularly when their words will be read by an audience of their peers and possibly future employers. A project documenting the history of a London hospice encountered a number of concerns among professional interviewees, not least relating to representation of themselves and the organization.[52] Interviewees carefully checked their transcripts for information that might cast themselves or the hospice in a negative light, in addition to correcting "bad" grammar. The latter was negotiated with interviewees to retain verbatim speech as far as possible, but preserving candid extracts of speech for publication was more problematic. A number of reservations could be allayed through reflexive communication with interviewees, but not all.

There may be a broader problem here in terms of differences in the way oral historians might see the history of medicine in contrast to the views of those they interview. The interests of historians can conflict with the ways in which men and women steeped in a particular view of medical history want to be remembered. In working with former clinicians or medical scientists, it is often difficult to contextualize their individual contributions to their professions, especially when such accounts neglect to mention broader structural and cultural changes. Prompting for details of such changes in interviews can lead to a sense of frustration, even insult, among interviewees.

Even when conducting an oral history with rank-and-file practitioners, it is sometimes difficult to produce a question or an account that satisfies participants. Graham Smith in his interviews with family doctors in a Scottish town noted how some participants were reluctant to discuss family and home life, or indeed to even be interviewed at home. Robert Perks highlighted a similar problem arising from interviews with business professionals, explaining that an unwillingness to reveal the real self behind the work persona was perhaps a survival mechanism in a competitive working environment. This should be an equal consideration in interviews with medical professionals.[53]

The general practitioners in Smith's study were also eager to keep the focus on their individual contribution to the profession and to keep "hidden colleges" hidden. During the interviews it became clear that some practices were able to access different secondary care for their patients with differing degrees of success. This was dependent on a variety of social networks, but exploring these networks was problematic. One doctor was extremely reluctant, even hostile, about talking about her social life, which included a Highland dance society. As it turned out, she was able to have older patients seen by the local gerontological service, when other family doctors struggled to do so. The service was widely perceived to have been overstretched at the time and difficult to access. That the local gerontologists were also enthusiastic Highland dancers proved an important factor: membership in the dance society was in short more important than clinical reputation in the successful onward referral of patients.[54] Drafts of the story of the social networks that shaped the way medicine was practiced, along with all other potential publications, were sent to all general practitioners who participated in the study. This encouraged additional information but also led to some puzzlement. Even when the interviewees saw the impact of the social, including family and friendships, in the ecology of practice, theirs was a grudging acceptance. While the tension could be creative and agreement could be reached, at times it felt less like "shared authority" than a mutual standoff.[55]

The lack of recognition of social factors in the history of medicine has a particular significance when medical ethics committees operate a governance policy, as they do in Britain. Under governance rules, researchers can be denied access to medical professionals if it is deemed that the research is not a good use of professionals' time.

In a sphere in which such power can determine the significance of knowledge, it is important that clinicians are reminded of the social contexts in which they operate.

John Crellin, in a review of *History of Hospital Infection*, argued that oral history has the potential to raise important ethical concerns. He noted that oral history may point up ethical issues "such as hospitals wanting to keep infection data confidential amid the need for informed consent for patients.[56] It is easy to underestimate medical authority, and all too often medical ethics in different countries can silence voices. As mentioned earlier, access to mental health survivors in Claudia Malacrida's Canadian study was initially denied through legal guardianship orders.[57] The very powers intended to protect patients can be used to protect abusers and their institutions.

Interviewing those in receipt of medical care also brings the broader implications of using oral history in medicine into sharp perspective. In end-of-life care, oral history has benefits beyond recording histories, including sense of worth, finding meaning in life stories, and the projection of an identity as a legacy for family. Oral historians have also found remembering in a health care setting as having the capacity to build social relationships among patients and care providers, and to maintain identities where people are faced with loss and change.[58]

There are times when interviews can be potentially harmful, even dangerous. Farhat Manzoor, Greta Jones, and James McKenna explored ethical and professional dilemmas that typified nursing practice in Northern Ireland during the "Troubles." They based their work primarily on testimonies during the conflict relating to moral questions, choices and problems.[59] Moral and ethical issues include concerns about anonymity and permission to use material in published research. A less definable and more complicated issue is the potential harmfulness of an interview caused by recall of painful and distressing events. No oral history interview on any topic is free of such harmful possibilities since sharing both good and bad times in personal stories can bring traumatic memories to the fore. However, the potential to uncover painful stories that do harm is likely to be greater in the history of medicine.

There are circumstances in interviews in medicine when it is clear that an interviewee is in an emotionally vulnerable situation due to the nature of the topic, such as the palliative care project interviewing people with life-limiting diagnosis.[60] Obviously, a number of ethical considerations are part of working with the extremely ill, with an overriding question being whether oral history is ever therapy. Recall in interviews can have a therapeutic impact, but there is a difference between "therapeutic" and "therapy." Therapeutic reflects the beneficial process of talking at length with an empathetic listener, while therapy is an intervention that intends a health outcome. Leslie Lowes and Paul Gill have observed the cathartic outcomes that result from providing a nonjudgmental and confidential environment in which patients can talk in an open and unhurried manner with someone who is genuinely interested in what they have to say.[61] Since the interviews take place in a hospital ward, patients might also harbor concerns that nonparticipation could have negative consequences for their care and relationships with health professionals. Hence, oral historians make efforts to dissociate themselves from the clinical team and informed potential interviewees that there no care-related relationship existed between the two.

Interviews carried out in a palliative care setting remind us that oral histories have focused on lived lives rather than dying. Interviewees talk of themselves prior to the disruption of their lives by serious illness, before disease irrevocably altered their lifestyles and how they are viewed by others. There have been exceptions, particularly when interviewees have negative experiences of health care. Narratives with people facing death from cancer contain consistent themes as the moment of diagnosis, subsequent treatment and sufferings, and the experience of medical interaction.[62]

In end-of-life interviewing there is an imperative to consider the bereaved and to have discussions with the interviewee about including oral material that could be potentially distressing for a listener. Such information might include accounts of extramarital relationships and children not knowing their adopted status. The notion of sensitivity is as subjective as the interview itself; hence it is desirable that interviewees listen to their interview as soon as possible after it has been recorded, to make sure that they are comfortable with their account. In circumstances where an interviewee is uncomfortable with their recording, interviewers must heed their instincts and suggest editing of problematic material, an ethically sound approach although it violates the oral history principle of retaining an unedited copy.

Nigel Hunt and Ian Robbins have reasoned that in developing a life story narrative the teller is more likely to be able to come to terms with traumatic life events. They view narrative as a critical component in attempting to find ways of dealing with traumatic information. Narrative development is an effective way of reducing the emotional stress of traumatic memories that flood into a traumatized person's mind in an uncontrolled fashion.[63] Those who want to tell their stories are often those who believe that talking about the past is therapeutic. People who are not prepared to be interviewed will often make the judgment that talking would be harmful; and oral historians must respect their decision.

The motives for taking part in an oral history are not always obvious. Memories and perspectives of events may be communicated in interviews with motivations that are not always apparent at the outset. Personal reflections convey how the narrator perceives the significance and impact of events and actions, and can reveal their attempts to make sense of the past. Reflective processes during an interview can add to the interviewee's original motivations for taking part in it, but it is good practice, in line with most medical research ethics, to advise participants that they can end an interview or a series of interviews at any time, without having to explain their decision to the interviewer.

As with oral history interviewing in general, patients have a variety of reasons for telling their life histories. Oral histories with patients can raise their self-esteem and sense of worth, attach meaning to their life experiences, create a personal family record, give recognition, and validate experiences. They also provide gains for clinical practice and health research: better understanding of day-to-day living with life-threatening disease; raised awareness of patient perspectives of hospice, hospital, and home treatment; greater appreciation of the impact of life-threatening disease on identity and lifestyle; and insight into interrelationships between patient, family, and professionals.[64]

The relationship of narrative to medical ethics has been considered by Anne Hudson Jones, who sees the contribution through the content of stories (what people say) and through the analysis of their form (how they are told and why it matters). She advocates the study of both fictional and factual stories as aids to understanding in medical ethics, and believes that the techniques of literary criticism can be applied to the analysis of ethical texts and practices, shedding light on the different perspectives in an ethical dilemma. Listening to patients' stories, she asserts, can also help clinicians accept a patient's moral choices.[65] Such claims are, however, more easily made than they are proven.

The illness narrative has many potential interpretations, but the patients are the ultimate authors of their own text. Oral history offers them opportunities to produce a narrative with greater autonomy and input than is possible with other approaches. Participants become involved in the process of producing their own life histories. They recall personal experience in a whole life context, shaping their identity with a narrative that is comfortable for them. Oral history as a form of autobiography has advantages over written forms of narrative, such as diary writing and published illness stories, since it provides an opportunity for participation across a range of abilities, to people who may not wish to write but who can verbally tell their stories.[66]

The process of interviewing patients needs to be handled thoughtfully. An oral history usually involves, on one side, a healthy interviewer in paid employment who has a lifestyle independent of clinical needs, and on the other side, an interviewee with an illness that may be life-limiting, whose lifestyle has departed significantly from pre-illness circumstances, and who is encountering various degrees of uncertainty. This makes for a particularly unequal situation. It helps if there is time is available to form a relationship in advance of the interview, but that may not be the case if the interviewee is in poor health. Some who begin an interview talkative and outgoing can grow tired, withdrawn, and uncomfortable. With seriously ill people, interviews must be arranged and conducted on a short timetable and in short bursts, which can affect the quality of the interview. At worst, such interviews can err toward superficiality as the interviewer tries to draw out detail while the interviewee considers how comfortable he or she is engaging in a one-sided sharing of personal information.[67]

Can Oral History Make a Difference in Medicine?

In considering the role of oral history in the history of medicine, we can ask whether oral historians have made an impact on the practice of medicine. Some health professionals have recognized that oral history has a place in medicine.

Where patients are suffering loss, or attrition, of their sense of self, life history is a restorative intervention. In a textbook aimed at health professionals, Kathryn Boog and Claire Tester recommend life history as a nontherapeutic intervention in clinical settings:

> Where patients have very limited resources, making any form of physical activity unachievable, we need to help them change the emphasis of their view of themselves from that of a "doing" person to one of a "being." ... To help in this process, relating narratives of significant events in their life should be considered as a positive and meaningful exercise ... allowing patients to make choices about which stories to tell and how to tell them, and so encouraging the promotion of controlled self-expression.... The rediscovery of accomplishments and pleasures that may have been masked by subsequent negative episodes in that life leads to positive self-validation and improved self esteem.[68]

Writing about developing the profession of radiography with oral history, Sola Decker and Ron Iphofen have asked if lessons can be learned from the narrative of the career experiences of radiographer. They found that career experiences of radiographers can identify their unique strategies for coping with day-to-day work activities; that oral histories can act as a springboard for the socialization of entrants into the profession; and that interviews may inform policy making in education and practice. Narratives derived from the use of oral history create "an opportunity for reflection on professional activities."[69]

Oral history can make a critical contribution to articulating and understanding the meaning and transformations of mental health care from the point of view of families dealing with illness. Carlee Lehna's recordings with the twenty-two-year-old sibling of an eight-year-old diagnosed with leukemia highlighted the effects of a sister's childhood cancer on the sibling's life and home life at diagnosis, during, and after treatment. Fourteen years later, she observed that the themes of activity, closeness, anger, fear, worry, and spirituality that she had written about were "derived from the sibling's narrative." This suggested that health care professionals should take the emotions of the siblings of other children with cancer into account.[70]

Oral histories are also useful in resisting medical power including the power to shape the patient's story. Geertje Boschma's oral history accounts by family members in Alberta, Canada, demonstrated ambivalence toward the dominant biomedical explanation of mental illness. The stories illustrated mental illness as a culturally negotiated event, with agreements, for example, whether to frame a family member's behavior as mental illness. Boschma concluded that dominant cultural discourse affected how people enacted, accommodated, appropriated, and resisted particular ways of living with mental illness.[71]

We should also be clear that oral historians can contribute toward a critique of medicine and medical practice. Oral historians might be making a more significant contribution to well-being through helping to explore the history of medicine, than simply by offering medical professionals another tool in their encounters with the ill. There are those who claim that "oral history either on its own or combined with other interpretative research methods has the potential to guide the profession into the future," but oral history's first task is to critically examine medicine's past.[72]

Oral history in the history of medicine gives insight into past actions that allows their consideration in their contemporary circumstances. How were decisions taken? What were the options? What influences were at play? What actions ensued? Understandings of the successes and failures associated with these issues can enlighten present-day problems and further debate. A history of the hospice and palliative care movement in the UK found that accounts by health professionals and others involved in establishing services reflected what they perceived as personal achievements, what they still hoped to carry out, and what was left unfinished. Their contributions contained critical thought about the role of hospices within the spectrum of health and social care services, and offered reflections on future directions for hospice provision.[73]

Oral history has become established in the history of medicine, developing from "elite" histories of distinguished practitioners to explorations of what it is like to be "a patient." There is much room left for continuing the expansion of the oral history of medicine into new areas, such as contributing to a better understanding of embodied narratives, materiality, and social constructionism, as well as exploring everyday practice or ecologies of practice and their relationships to policy ideals. There remains much to do in appreciating the ethical challenges of working with both those in positions of power and those whose illnesses have brought a troubling realization of how little power they have over their own illnesses and their own lives. There is also the issue of how we generalize from our oral history research. Currently, oral historians of medicine are often engaged in small-scale local projects, which are very good for identifying local contingencies but less helpful for drawing generally applicable conclusions. The linking together of small studies through the reuse of testimonies will be one way of addressing this question. National and international studies in which the experiences of recipients and professionals of medical care can be compared and contrasted would also help, although the approaches required to do this are as yet underdeveloped.

We have deliberately chosen not to address legal, ethical, and governance oversight in this chapter. The differences in the ways in which ethics boards and committees, especially those in medicine and health, operate across the globe would have made the task difficult. In addition, a bewildering and growing myriad of laws, regulations, and guidelines that differ from country to country would have meant that any advice provided would have become quickly outdated. Instead we have tried to contextualize more broadly the ethical challenges faced by oral historians working in health and medicine.

There is a continuing need to be aware of the issues and debates faced by historians of medicine more generally. Such issues offer oral historians opportunities to recast our ethical concerns. So, for example, "giving voice" and "shared authority" have an added complexity in working with current and former professionals, patients, and carers. Partly this is because relationships in health and medicine have long been imbued with power and belief. Interviewing in this area therefore requires additional understanding and sensitivity. However, oral history is now established as an important method and source in studying the recent history of medicine and health care.

NOTES

1. Paula Michaels, "Chinese Medicine in Early Communist China, 1945–1963: A Medicine of Revolution," review of *Chinese Medicine in Early Communist China, 1945–1963: A Medicine of Revolution* by Kim Taylor (London: Routledge/Curzon, 2005), *Social History of Medicine* 19, no. 2: 338–40.

2. Ralph H. Major, *A History of Medicine* (Springfield, Ill.: Thomas, 1954).

3. George Sarton, "Notes on the Reviewing of Learned Books," *Science* 22 (Apr. 1960): 1182–87.

4. Thomas McKeown, and R. G. Brown, "Medical Evidence Related to English Population Changes in the Eighteenth Century," *Population Studies* 19 (1955): 119–41; McKeown and R. G. Record, "Reasons for the Decline of Mortality in England and Wales During the Nineteenth Century," *Population Studies* 16 (1962): 94–122; Mc Keown, R. G. Record, and R. D. Turner, "An Interpretation of the Decline of Mortality in England and Wales during the Twentieth Century," *Population Studies* 29 (1975): 391–421; McKeown, *The Modern Rise of Population* (London: Edward Arnold, 1976).

5. See Erwin H. Ackernecht, *Medicine at the Paris Hospital: 1794–1848* (Baltimore: Johns Hopkins University Press, 1967); and Ivan Waddington, "The Role of the Hospital in the Development of Modern Medicine: A Sociological Analysis," *Sociology* 7 (1973): 211–24.

6. John C. Burnham, *What Is Medical History?* (Malden, Mass.: Polity Press, 2005).

7. Including R. D. Laing, *The Self and Others* (London: Tavistock Publications, 1961); Ivan Illich, *Limits to Medicine: Medical Nemesis: The Expropriation of Health* (London: Boyars, 1976); and Graham Smith, "The Rise of the New Consumerism," in *Consumers' Perspectives on Health Care: Critical Approaches to Research Methods*, ed. Jennifer Burr and Paula Nicolson, 13–38 (London: Palgrave Macmillan, 2004).

8. Saul Benison and Tom Rivers, *Tom Rivers: Reflections on a Life in Medicine and Science: An Oral History Memoir* (Cambridge, Mass.: MIT Press, 1967).

9. Saul Benison, "Oral History: A Personal View," in *Modern Methods in the History of Medicine*, ed. Edwin Clarke, 286-306 (London: Athlone Press of the University of London, 1971).

10. Peter Wright and Andrew Treacher, eds., *The Problem of Medical Knowledge* (Edinburgh: Edinburgh University Press, 1982); Claudine Herzlich and Janine Pierret, "The Social Construction of the Patient: Patients and Illnesses in Other Ages," *Social Science and Medicine* 20, no. 2 (1985): 145–51.

11. Lindsay Granshaw. "Knowledge of Bodies or Bodies of Knowledge? Surgeons, Anatomists and Rectal Surgery, 1830–1985," in *Medical Theory, Surgical Practice*, ed. Christopher Lawrence, 232–62 (New York: Routledge, 1992).

12. Ludmilla Jordanova, "The Social Constriction of Medical Knowledge," *Social History of Medicine* 8, no. 3 (1995): 361–81.

13. Dorothy Porter, "The Mission of Social History of Medicine: An Historical View," *Social History of Medicine* 8 (1995): 345–59.

14. Roger Cooter, *Surgery and Society in Peace and War: Orthopaedics and the Organization of Modern Medicine, 1880–1948* (London: Macmillan, 1993); and Roger Cooter, Mark Harrison, and Steve Sturdy, eds., *Medicine and Modern Warfare* (Amsterdam/Atlanta: Editions Rodopi B.V, 1999).

15. Roger Cooter, Mark Harrison, and Steve Sturdy, eds., *War, Medicine and Modernity* (Stroud: Sutton Publishing Ltd., 1998).

16. Paul Thompson, "The Voice of the Past: Oral History," reprinted in *The Oral History Reader*, ed. Robert N. Perks and Alistair Thomson (New York: Routledge, 2001); Nancy Tomes, "Oral History in the History of Medicine," *Journal of American History* 78, no. 2 (1991).

17. For instance, Richard L. Rapport, *Physician: The Life of Paul Beeson* (Fort Lee, N.J.: Barricade Books, 2001); and Jay Schulkin, *Curt Richter: A Life in the Laboratory* (Baltimore: Johns Hopkins University Press, 2005).

18. Allen Weisse, *Heart to Heart: The Twentieth-Century Battle against Cardiac Disease—An Oral History* (New Brunswick, N.J.: Rutgers University Press, 2002).

19. Shelly McKellar, *Surgical Limits: The Life of Gordon Murray* (Toronto: University of Toronto Press, 2003), vii.

20. Ronald Bayer and Gerald Oppenheimer, *AIDS Doctors: Voices from the Epidemic—An Oral History* (New York: Oxford University Press, 2000).

21. Virginia Berridge, *AIDS in the UK: The Making of a Policy, 1981–1994* (Oxford: Oxford University Press, 1996).

22. Ibid., 181. A more complete survey of oral history and health and medical policy was given in a keynote lecture by Virginia Berridge, "Who Cared? Oral History, Caring, Health and Illness: Marking 60 Years of the National Health Service," (Oral History Society [UK] Annual Conference, in association with the Centre for the History of Medicine, University of Birmingham, 2008).

23. David F. Smith et al., *Food Poisoning, Policy, and Politics: Corned Beef and Typhoid in Britain in the 1960s* (Woodbridge: Boydell Press, 2005).

24. Anne Perez Hattori, *Colonial Dis-Ease: US Navy Health Policies and the Chamorros of Guam, 1898–1941* (Honolulu: University of Hawai'i Press, 2004); Raphael Samuel, "The Perils of the Transcript," *Oral History* 1, no. 2 (1971): 19–22.

25. John K. Crellin, *Home Medicine: The Newfoundland Experience* (Montreal: McGill-Queen's University Press, 2004).

26. Kate Fisher, *Birth Control, Sex and Marriage in Britain 1918–1960* (Oxford: Oxford University Press, 2006).

27. Roy Porter, "The Patient's View: Doing Medicine from Below," *Theory and Society* 14 (1985): 175–98.

28. Diana Gittins, "Married Life and Birth Control Between the Wars," *Oral History* 3, no. 2 (1975); Gittins, "Women's Work and Family Size Between the Wars," *Oral History* 5, no. 2 (1977); and Virginia Berridge, "Opium and Oral History," *Oral History* 7, no. 1 (1979).

29. Flurin Condrau, "The Patient's View Meets the Clinical Gaze," *Social History of Medicine* 20, no. 3 (2007): 525–40.

30. Sanjiv Kakar, "Medical Developments and Patient Unrest in the Leprosy Asylum, 1860 to 1940," *Social Scientist* 24, no. 6 (1996): 62–81.

31. Michelle Winslow, Karen Hitchlock, and Bill Noble, "Recording Lives: The Benefits of an Oral History Service," *European Journal of Palliative Care* 16, no. 3 (2009): 128–30.

32. Glenn Smith, Annie Bartlett, and Michael King, "Treatments of Homosexuality in Britain since the 1950s—An Oral History: The Experience of Patients," *British Medical Journal* 328 (2004): 427.

33. Claudia Malacrida, "Contested Memories: Efforts of the Powerful to Silence Former Inmates' Histories of Life in an Institution for 'Mental Defectives,'" *Disability and Society* 21, no. 5 (2006): 397–410.

34. Kerry Davies, "'Silent and Censured Travellers'? Patients' Narratives and Patients' Voices: Perspectives on the History of Mental Illness since 1948," *Social History of Medicine* 14, no. 2 (2001): 267–92.

35. Dorothy Atkinson et al., eds., *Good Times, Bad Times: Women with Learning Difficulties Telling their Stories* (Kidderminster: BILD, 2000); Sheena Rolph et al., eds., *Witnesses to Change: Families, Learning Difficulties and History* ((Kidderminster: BILD, 2005).

36. Duncan Mitchell et al., eds., *Exploring Experiences of Advocacy by People with Learning Disabilities: Testimonies of Resistance* (London: Jessica Kingsley, 2006).

37. *Speaking for Ourselves* podcasts: http://www.speakingforourselves.org.uk/index.php/home/scope_podcast.

38. Karen Hitchlock, *Face to Face* (Bridport, UK: Canterton Books, 2005).

39. See Graham Smith and Malcolm Nicolson, "Re-expressing the Division of British Medicine under the NHS: The Importance of Locality in General Practitioners' Oral Histories," *Social Science and Medicine* 68 (2007): 938–48; and Joana Bornat, Leroi Henry, and Parvati Raghuram, "'Don't Mix Race with the Specialty': Interviewing South Asian Over-Seas Trained Geriatricians," *Oral History* 37, no. 1 (2009): 74–84.

40. Jacqueline Zalumas, *Caring in Crisis: An Oral History of Critical Care Nursing* (Philadelphia: University of Pennsylvania Press, 1995).

41. David Russell, "An Oral History Project in Mental Health Nursing," *Journal of Advanced Nursing* 26 (1997): 489–95.

42. Duncan Mitchell and Anne-Marie M. Rafferty, "I Don't Think They Ever Really Wanted to Know Anything About Us: Oral History Interviews with Learning Disability Nurses," *Oral History* 33, no. 1 (2005): 77–87.

43. Sheryl Brennan, *Contradictory Stories: An Oral History of a Group of 1960s Nursing Students* (Launceston: School of Nursing and Midwifery, University of Tasmania, 2006).

44. Helen M. Sweet and Rona Dougall, *Community Nursing and Primary Healthcare and Primary Healthcare in Twentieth-Century Britain* (New York/Abingdon: Routledge, 2007).

45. Caroline Mackintosh, "Historical Study of Men in Nursing," *Journal of Advanced Nursing* 26 (1997): 232–36.

46. For details of projects see The Heritage Lottery Fund: http://www.hlf.org.uk.

47. Philippe Denis, "The Ethics of Oral History," in *Oral History in a Wounded Country: Interactive Interviewing in South Africa*, ed. Denis and Radikobo Ntsimane, 63–84 (Scottsville: University of KwaZulu-Natal Press, 2008).

48. Michael Frisch, *A Shared Authority on the Draft and Meaning of Oral and Public History*. (Albany, N.Y: SUNY Press, 1990).

49. Wendy Rickard, "Oral History—'More Dangerous than Therapy'? Interviewees' Reflections on Recording Traumatic or Taboo Issues," *Oral History* 26, no. 2 (Autumn 1998): 34–48.

50. L.A. Reynolds and E. M. Tansey, *Innovations in Pain Management* (London: The Wellcome Trust Centre for the History of Medicine, 2004), http://www.ucl.ac.uk/histmed/publications/wellcome-witnesses/witness-seminars.html.

51. Irvine Loudon, review of Wellcome Witnesses to Twentieth Century Medicine, *British Medical Journal* MJ 325 (2002): 1119.

52. Michelle Winslow and David Clark, *St. Joseph's Hospice, Hackney: A Century of Caring in the East End of London* (Lancaster: Observatory Publications, 2005).

53. Robert Perks, "'Corporations Are People Too!' Corporate and Business Oral History in Britain," unpublished paper presented at the 15th International Oral History Association Conference, Guadalajara, Mexico, 2008.

54. Smith and Nicolson, "Re-expressing the Division of British Medicine Under the NHS," 938–48.

55. Graham Smith, "An Oral History of Everyday General Practice 12: Reflections and the History of Disappointment," *British Journal of General Practice* 53 (2003): 490, 420–21.

56. John Crellin, review of *History of Hospital Infection* in *Bulletin of the History of Medicine* 79, no. 1 (2005): 167–68.

57. Malacrida, "Contested Memories," 297–410.

58. J. B. Wallace, "Reconsidering the Life Review: The Social Construction of Talk About the Past," *Gerontologist* 32 (1992): 120–25; K. Buchanan and D Middleton, "Voices of Experience: Talk, Identity and Membership in Reminiscence Groups," *Ageing and Society* 15, no. 4 (1995): 457–91.

59. Farhat Manzoor, Greta Jones, and James McKenna, "'How Could These People Do This Sort of Stuff and Then We Have to Look After Them?' Ethical Dilemmas of Nursing in the Northern Ireland Conflict," *Oral History* 35, no. 2 (2007): 36–44.

60. Winslow, Walsh, and Noble, "Life Stories in End of Life Care."

61. Leslie Lowes and Paul Gill, "Participants' Experiences of Being Interviewed About an Emotive Topic," *Journal of Advanced Nursing* 55, no. 5 (2005): 587–95.

62. Amanda Bingley et al., "Making Sense of Dying: A Review of Narratives Written since 1950 by People Facing Death from Cancer and Other Diseases," *Palliative Medicine* 20 (2006): 183–95.

63. Nigel Hunt and Ian Robbins, "Telling Stories of the War: Ageing Veterans Coping With Their Memories Through Narrative," *Oral History* 26, no. 2 (1998): 57–64.

64. Winslow, Walsh, and Noble, "Life Stories in End of Life Care."

65. Anne Hudson Jones, "Narrative Based Medicine: Narrative in Medical Ethics," *British Medical Journal* 318 (1999): 253–56.

66. Michelle Winslow and Bill Noble, "Life Stories in Supportive and Palliative Care: An Oral History Service for Patients," unpublished report for the Sheffield Macmillan Unit for Palliative Care, Academic Unit of Supportive Care, University of Sheffield, 2008.

67. Winslow, Walsh, and Noble, "Life Stories in End of Life Care."

68. Kathryn Boog and Claire Tester, *A Practical Guide to Working in Palliative Care: Finding Meaning and Purpose in Life and Death* (Edinburgh: Elsevier, 2008), 140.

69. Sola Decker and Ron Iphofen, "Developing the Profession of Radiography: Making Use of Oral History," *Radiography* 11 (2005): 262–71.

70. Carlee Lehna, "A Childhood Cancer Sibling's Oral History," *Journal of Pediatric Oncology Nursing* 15 (1998): 163.

71. Geertje Boschma, "Accommodation and Resistance to the Dominant Cultural Discourse on Psychiatric Mental Health: Oral History Accounts of Family Members," *Nursing Inquiry* 14, no. 4 (2007): 266–78.

72. Decker and Iphofen, "Developing the Profession of Radiography," 262–71.

73. David Clark et al., *A Bit of Heaven for the Few? An Oral History of the Modern Hospice Movement in the United Kingdom* (Lancaster: Observatory Publications, 2005).

BIBLIOGRAPHY

Atkinson, Dorothy, Michelle McCarthy, Jan Walmsley, Mabel Cooper, Sheena Rolph, Simone Aspis, Pam Barette, Mary Coventry, and Gloria Ferris, eds. *Good Times, Bad Times: Women with Learning Difficulties Telling Their Stories*. Kidderminster: BILD, 2000.

Bayer, Ronald, and Gerald Oppenheimer. *AIDS Doctors: Voices from the Epidemic: An Oral History*. New York: Oxford University Press, 2000.

Berridge, Virginia. *AIDS in the UK: The Making of a Policy, 1981–1994*. Oxford: Oxford University Press, 1996.

Clark, David, Neil Small, Michael Wright, Michelle Winslow, and Nic Hughes. *A Bit of Heaven for the Few? An Oral History of the Modern Hospice Movement in the United Kingdom*. Lancaster: Observatory Publications, 2005.

Mitchell, Duncan, Rannveig Traustadóttir, Rohhss Chapman, Louise Townson, Nigel Ingham, and Sue Ledger, eds. *Exploring Experiences of Advocacy by People with Learning Disabilities: Testimonies of Resistance*. London: Jessica Kingsley, 2006.

Weisse, Allen. *Heart to Heart: The Twentieth-Century Battle against Cardiac Disease—An Oral History*. New Brunswick, N.J.: Rutgers University Press, 2002.

CHAPTER 26

THE ARCHIVAL IMPERATIVE: CAN ORAL HISTORY SURVIVE THE FUNDING CRISIS IN ARCHIVAL INSTITUTIONS?

BETH M. ROBERTSON

The cost and complexity of managing archival collections in libraries and archives are increasing at unprecedented rates.[1] Collecting institutions are expected to do more with less, a common experience for most publicly funded repositories since the 1980s. Archival institutions already struggling with massive backlogs of unprocessed physical collections are now responsible for electronic collections that grow exponentially and require new formats with astonishing frequency. Archives must provide online as well as on-site services to satisfy researchers, and those who allocate funding. The need to find more space for swelling physical collections while coping with the cost of achieving large-scale digitization and managing electronic storage becomes more daunting every day.

Yet, these demands are gratifying because they confirm an abiding need for archival institutions and the continued relevance of their collections. It is also exciting to be able to present physical collections to the world online and to investigate the technological solutions being developed for managing digital collections. Funding seldom keeps pace, however, and is never guaranteed. Come budget time, managers sit down to decide how available resources will be allocated. Each year they ask: "Is there anything we can stop doing?" The aim is to balance the budget and reallocate funds to more pressing needs.

In some ways, oral history is well adapted to survive in this tumultuous environment. Many archival institutions have been educating local practitioners since the 1970s about the standards required by their repositories. Willa Baum, one of the first to write on the topic, called this "vicarious creating"—by which she meant archives have accepted donated interviews that were conducted independently of the institutions' own oral history programs while conforming to their standards. The way in which libraries and archives have embraced this role has been a mainstay of the growth of oral history worldwide.[2] Oral histories resulting from this model of collection development are "archive ready." Most archival institutions support oral history from the conviction that it makes their collections more complete, and going online has strengthened this belief. Publicly funded institutions are also expected to represent all sections of their constituency. The sound, images, and texts of oral histories enable this to occur, and can be very attractive to sponsors.[3]

In others ways, oral history is particularly vulnerable. The traditional tools of the trade—the analog cassette and semiprofessional cassette recorder—have become obsolete. So too is the preservation practice of copying cassettes to open-reel tape. Analog recordings can be stored indefinitely, but they require a cooler, dryer environment than paper to slow their deterioration, and replay machines and the parts to maintain them are no longer being manufactured. Archivists are in a race against time to digitize analog tape recordings, and since the initial transfer must be done in "real time," it is expensive.[4] Preservation-standard audio files are also large and expensive to store digitally. It is a common fallacy that electronic storage is growing cheaper. The unit cost of storage space such as hard drives is indeed falling, but the costs associated with managing stored files, including software systems and salaries, have been rising steeply as the number of files held increases.[5]

The key to survival is adaptability. When managers of archival institutions deliberate on how to save money, they also ask: "What can we do more efficiently?" They examine major functions including acquisition, cataloging, and preservation to determine which procedural changes might bring savings. They implement strategies such as risk management, mainstreaming, and outsourcing, and consider the transfer of collections to other institutions. There are no easy solutions. Just as voice-recognition technology is not an effortless substitute for the painstaking process of transcription, the likelihood of sustained funding increases to manage oral history programs remains remote. The chances of oral history surviving as an integral part of archival collections can be maximized if practitioners, librarians, and archivists can demonstrate not only the research value of recorded interviews but also the cost effectiveness of their management.

Appraising for Acquisition

Vicarious creating is a cost-effective form of acquisition. The State Library of South Australia's oral history collection, which was established in 1987, represents a population of 1.5 million spread over one million square kilometers (380,000 sq. m.). It collects about 350 hours of oral history recordings each year, of which over 75 percent are the fruits of the oral history curator supporting community-based projects. The curator provides training sessions in conjunction with the local oral history association, advises on budgets and funding applications, and lends digital field-recording kits to eligible projects. The recordings received in return are "archive ready" in terms of content, file format, and documentation, including conditions of use agreements with narrators and interview summaries if not transcripts. The curator alone could produce no more than one-quarter of the interviews herself in any given year if she was devoted to the task, and the cost of commissioning interviews would halve the intake again.[6] Of course, quantity is no measure of research value, and donated interviews tend to focus on particular locations, organizations, and events at the expense of in-depth life histories. However, in conjunction with a modest commissioned interview program, vicarious creating can result in oral history collections that truly represent the constituent population as well as serving research needs.

It is the balance of donations that are expensive to acquire, particularly those received from interviewers whose work predated, or were unaware of, or disdained the archival institution's oral history advisory services. Some of these donors are the stuff of legend! Consider, for example, a man of advancing years who lived overseas. He maintained his house in Australia and returned home from time to time to conduct personal business. On these occasions he took the opportunity to sort through papers he had accumulated during a lifetime of teaching and writing. On one visit he decided to dispose of twenty hours of tape-recorded interviews he conducted in the 1970s and '80s on topics of considerable controversy. Knowing that his next-door neighbor worked at an archival institution, he deposited the recordings in a tub in her laundry on his way to the airport. He had not told his neighbor of his intentions, and she was not home at the time. The tapes had labels but no other documentation.

What compelled this worthy gentleman's behavior? At its root is the expectation that a repository will assume responsibility for whatever it is given. This expectation is not necessarily ill founded. In their past efforts to establish collections, many archival institutions accepted oral histories without much discrimination. Today, they are more selective, but presented with a donation that appears to meet selection criteria repositories will invariably accept it. Some curators will conscientiously begin what they expect will be a protracted correspondence with the donor in an attempt to tie up myriad loose ends involved in such a legacy to posterity. They will allocate scarce resources to trace the narrators, listen to the recordings, write summaries, and create use copies. Other curators will put the donation in the "too-hard" basket along with more of its kind. The first response is costly and often inconclusive. The second defers the cost to another day and guarantees that the recordings remain unavailable to researchers.

No publicly funded archival institution can afford either to respond with such generosity or to procrastinate for much longer. There is a third way, which makes the same demands of the donors of unsolicited oral history as vicarious creating has always made of current community-based projects. Educating donors has been standard practice in government archives for many years. Government departments are given training and support, but they must prepare non-current records for transfer to the repository in accordance with stringent guidelines. Archives collecting private records are beginning to follow the same practice, requiring organizations, businesses, and individuals to list and box their papers *prior* to offering them for appraisal. The National Library of Australia's Manuscripts Branch introduced this procedure in 2006. Two years later the senior archivist reported:

> Frankly, we were a bit embarrassed about asking this to start with. What we have found is that not only are most donors happy to do this, they are also much more engaged with describing their records—including context that we would never be able to glean—and are becoming more thoughtful about their own record-keeping practices for paper and digital records. . . . We are absolutely sure that our donors feel more engaged in their relations with us, and that they understand that the information they produce about their own records may well stand as the permanent record or at minimum will greatly inform the work of the archivist working on their papers or records.[7]

When this approach is applied to oral history, unsolicited donations should be returned to sender (or the long-suffering next-door neighbor) with a package of information that explains what the donor will need to do before the archival institution will accept the recordings. First, the prospective donor completes an appraisal questionnaire, which allows the repository to determine whether to pursue the donation. The questionnaire should be based explicitly on the institution's oral history acquisition or collection development policy. The University of Alaska–Fairbanks Oral History Program's collection development policy begins conventionally:

Criteria for the acceptance of audiovisual materials into the collection include the following:

1. Materials should be Alaska and/or Northern Regions related;
2. Materials should have substantial content and/or provide unique insights into particular events or time periods;
3. Materials should be of the highest possible listening/viewing quality. Materials so poorly recorded or degraded as to be difficult and/or impossible for the user to access will not be accepted;
4. Materials should be accessible to users. Any restrictions put on the materials should not place undue burden upon the users and/or the library staff.[8]

Converted into an appraisal questionnaire, and with additional questions inserted to provide further information for donor education and the repository's appraisal process, the criteria could read:

1. Are the interviews related to [this] region?
2. Do the interviews have substantial content and/or provide unique insights into particular events or time periods? Please summarize;
3. How many interviews are in the collection? Please estimate how many hours in total;
4. Over what time period were they recorded?
5. What is your relationship to the collection (e.g., interviewer, radio producer, commissioning body)?
6. What was the original purpose of the interviewing program (e.g., community project, research for a book, radio program, university thesis)?
7. Was the interviewing program associated with a particular organization (e.g., university, radio station, commissioning body, publisher)? Please provide details about the people in the organization who were involved;
8. Does every interview have a release form signed by the narrator? Please provide a copy as a sample;
9. What kinds of restrictions have the narrators placed on their interviews?
10. What restrictions do you intend to place on the interviews?
11. If there are no releases or your sample form is unacceptable to [this institution], will you negotiate new releases with the narrators?
12. Do any of the interviews contain sensitive information? Please summarize;
13. What is the technical quality of the recordings (i.e., very poor, poor, good, excellent listening quality)?
14. What format/s are the recordings?
15. What were the brand names and model numbers of the recorder/s and microphones used?
16. How many plug-in microphones were used for recording (i.e., none, one, two)?
17. Does the collection include any of the obsolete formats listed in the Collection Development Policy (attached) that [this institution] is unable to accept?
18. Does every interview have a summary? Please provide a copy as a sample;
19. If there are no summaries or your sample is unacceptable to [this institution], will you create new ones?
20. Do any of the interviews have transcripts?
21. Is every recording labeled with the name of the narrator, interviewer, date and location of the interview?

A few prospective donors will react with dismay or even hostility to such requirements, and if complaints arise it is important that senior management support curatorial staff and the collection development policy. Should a collection be rejected on the basis of the appraisal questionnaire, staff can explain the outcome in terms of the criteria that could not be met and, if appropriate, suggest an alternative repository. The unsuccessful donor will at least have his or her collection in order for offering elsewhere.

The second stage of retrospective vicarious creating requires further effort on the part of the prospective donor. The curator provides the donor with electronic templates and forms that will enable him to provide an inventory of the collection and finalize the documentation for each interview. Practical support can be offered, such as lending the donor a well-maintained replay machine with foot-pedal control and headphones to assist the production of summaries, and supplying spare cassette cases and labels if the collection has fallen into disarray.

The process puts demands on curators as well. The relationship with donors of unsolicited oral histories is likely to be as intense as that with current community-based projects. But with prospective donors required to maintain responsibility for their recordings, the curator is freed from the much more time-consuming and frustrating task of piecing together the unfinished oral history projects of others. And one never knows: some newly educated donors might volunteer to investigate the orphaned donations still lurking in the "too-hard" basket!

Cataloging for Access

In libraries, the cost-effectiveness of different models of cataloging published material has been scrutinized and refined for decades. By definition, publishing involves the production of more than one instance of an item. If a new book, journal, map, DVD, or Web site has already been cataloged online by another agency, other libraries simply copy the record. Major libraries still engaged in original cataloging know the unit costs of the activity. Most will have been through the exercise of comparing in-house costs with those of commercial agencies. *Resource Description and Access* (RDA) is replacing the English-language cataloging standard *Anglo-American Cataloging Rules*, 2nd edition (AACR2). The new standard is intended to reduce the complexity of catalog records by minimizing library jargon and the number of mandatory elements in each record.[9]

Archival material is predominantly unique, and the traditional processing practices, which include arrangement and re-housing as well as description, or cataloging, have generally escaped critical attention from outside the profession. However, backlogs of unprocessed material have increased dramatically in the last few decades as the voluminous records created by governments, organizations, businesses, and individuals from the late twentieth-century have entered repositories. In a groundbreaking study published in 2005, American archivists Mark Greene and Dennis Meissner revealed that while it is now common for unprocessed backlogs to exceed one-third of a repository's holdings, the archival profession has continued to practice an ideal standard of processing in which archivists examine each collection at the item (or page) level. They provide alternative standards, which reduce processing times by a factor of four or five, and conclude with the exhortation to their profession:

> We have to start doing things differently if we hope to begin reducing our backlogs and serving our patrons, resource allocators, and donors better than we have done. If we need to comfort ourselves with the fiction that gearing our processing programs to a norm of 500 feet per processor per year rather than 50 or 150 feet is only a temporary expediency, and that "one day" we will go back and reprocess all those collections to the item level, it is a harmless fantasy. We would suggest, however, that it would be a sign of professional maturity for us to own up to the limitations we work under, and accept that the golden minimum we recommend here (or doing "good enough" rather than insisting on perfection) is all we can realistically accomplish. Instead of comforting ourselves with a fantasy, we could instead take comfort from the fact that we will be revolutionizing access to our holdings.[10]

The impetus behind the new cataloging movements in both libraries and archives is not merely cost saving; it is the conviction that material should be accessible to researchers within weeks or months of entering a repository, not years or decades. Both movements are also responding to the digital era. They acknowledge that the data created for catalog records will not only be generated by professional catalogers or archivists, but "whether we like it or not...by support staff, nonlibrary staff, and also publishers" during various stages of an electronically based workflow.[11]

It is simple to apply this approach to recordings produced by standard oral history methodology since this material has relatively uniform characteristics. Oral history curators engaged in vicarious creating are accustomed to assigning unique numbers to recordings as soon as they enter the repository so that subsequent processes, such as copying and transcription, can be properly controlled. Current practitioners and prospective donors are readily taught the labeling elements required from which a basic catalog record will be formed. Brief records can be expanded with technical data added by the audio engineer, a summary created by the donor, and subject headings entered by a professional cataloger.

A persistent phobia exists among librarians and archivists about working with audiovisual material. In fairness, few are provided with the right tools for the job. A librarian or archivist expected to work routinely on audiovisual material should have a compact rack of players for the most common formats on their desk, right next to the computer. Other staff should have access to another rack at a central location or on a trolley. If an institution includes facilities for the preservation transfer of sound recordings, processing needs should not interrupt preservation work flows or vice versa.

The unprocessed backlog—the contents of the conceptual "too-hard" basket—can be transformed by the new principle of cataloging for access. Both libraries and archives embracing the access revolution are revealing their processing backlogs by creating summary collection-level records in their catalogs. These may refer to a collection of 2,500 uncataloged posters or almost five hundred feet of unprocessed company records. Every part of an oral history backlog should also be described at a summary level so that it is visible in the repository's primary public catalog. For instance, the State Library of South Australia accepted about 1,000 hours of recordings from a local university's community radio station in 2000, which represented three years' normal rate of accessions in one fell swoop. It had to be consigned to the backlog, but the following record was added to the library's online catalog:

MARC tag[i]	*OPAC field label*[ii]	*Catalog record text*
090	Number	OH -
245	Title	Radio 5UV Tape Archive : TEMPORARY SUMMARY RECORD [sound recording].
260lc	Date/s	1974–1999.
300	Quantity	1,000 hours (approx.)
340	Format	Sound cassette; sound tape reel; Digital Audio Tape.
520	Summary	In 1999 it was decided that the State Library of South Australia's J. D. Somerville Oral History Collection would share with the University of Adelaide the responsibility of archiving Radio 5UV program material. The radio station's tape archive, selected over the years by 5UV staff, was transferred to the State Library. In November 2000, the Library selected South Australian material of research value for processing. The remainder of the tape archive was returned to the University of Adelaide Archives for storage.
505	Contents	The State Library's holdings of the tape archive are from the General section, with only minor representation from the Fine Music and Jazz sections. The Folk Cooperative collection was transferred to the State Library in 1994. Major program series include: Adelaide Festival Forums; Commemoration Ceremonies; Craft in South Australia; Driving with the Fringe; Foundation Lectures; Global Rhythm; Heritage Walks; Inaugural and Valedictory Lectures; Musical Brunch; Musical Instrument Making in South Australia; On Campus; Profiles in South Australian History; Profiles in South Australian Writing; Scholars of Distinction; State of the Arts; Stirling Memorial Lectures; The Technology of Music; Women and the Law; Writers' Week (1992, 1994, 1996); Writers' Radio/Authors' Proof.
506	Access	No access until processing is completed.
555	Finding Aids	'5UV Tape Archive Library Catalog as at 29/3/99', marked to show titles transferred to the State Library (184 pages).
530	Use Copies	Not currently available.
610	Subject	5UV (Radio station : Adelaide, S. Aust.)
710	Added Author	5UV (Radio station : Adelaide, S. Aust.)

[i] MARC stands for MAchine Readable Cataloging. It is an exchange format for bibliographic data between library catalogue systems.
[ii] OPAC stands for Online Public Access Catalog.

The title, contents, and summary fields are indexed for keyword searching. To date, one-fifth of the collection has been assigned unique numbers and processed, in response to researchers' requests for access and whenever resources are available. The scope of the temporary summary record is being whittled away accordingly.

The emphasis on providing access to collections does not mean that recordings from projects still in progress, or embargoed, are exposed to use. It does mean that researchers (and donors) can discover their existence. There should be very few exceptions to this principle. Researchers can apply for access to unprocessed recordings, which may or may not be granted according to a repository's policy governing the use of unprocessed material. Some archival institutions allow researchers to use unprocessed archival papers following a risk-management process in which staff quickly assess the contents and then supervise the handling of the material. Few archival institutions will risk providing access to original audiovisual material, which must be assessed by listening in real time and may be damaged during replay. The controversial topics included in the Australian expatriate's collection, for instance, would certainly require careful attention before the recordings were released. There may be circumstances, though, in which a researcher can assist the processes of cataloging and selection for preservation by being given supervised access to original oral history recordings.

Selecting for Preservation

Time is running out for prevarication. While the affordability of acquiring and cataloging oral history can be demonstrated, there is no denying the high cost of audio preservation. Most analog recording formats are subject to deterioration over time, and all are dependent on replay equipment that is rapidly becoming obsolete. The same critical factors also apply to most physical format digital recordings, including Digital Audio Tape (DAT) and MiniDisc that were widely adopted for oral history in the mid-1990s.

Worldwide, major audio archives are in the midst of transferring their collections to digital mass storage systems. The National Library of Australia has already digitized half of its oral history and folklore collections, amounting to more than 20,000 hours, and plans to complete the other half before 2020. The library is stockpiling spare parts necessary to maintain the replay machines, but acknowledges that "keeping the obsolete machines operational for the next decade or so will remain a challenge."[12] The United States' Library of Congress and the great audiovisual archives of Europe, which measure their collections by the millions of recordings, are working to the same time frame. They too are amassing replay equipment and parts, well aware that the machine-hours left may fall short of the hours of audio needing transfer. Meanwhile, most conventional archival institutions are unaware of the urgency, or maintain the pleasant fiction that while their current analog equipment, such as cassette field recorders, duplicators, and transcribing units are in working order, the future can wait.

The State Library of South Australia's oral history collection is more than 7,000 hours in size, and is one of several audiovisual collections in the library that comprise almost 30,000 sound, film, and video recordings. The greater proportion is analog. However, this audiovisual material represents only about 1 percent of the published and archival collections that the library is entrusted both legally and ethically to preserve for public use. South Australian newspapers alone represent 10 percent of the collections. A comprehensive plan will be needed to set out the priorities, goals, costs, and strategies to digitize the library's South Australian collections for preservation and access. Preliminary work has found that no more than a quarter of 1 percent of the entire collection has been reformatted over the fifteen years that digitizing technologies have been available. While no sizable archival institution aims to digitize all its holdings, preservation imperatives—as well as the growing expectations of users and funding allocators—require that the rate of digitizing be accelerated.[13]

Analog audiovisual material is the most at-risk of all collections due to the inherent instability of its formats and their absolute dependency on obsolete equipment. Ideally, while an archival institution may aim to digitize only 5 or 10 percent of its collections over time, that figure will include 100 percent of its analog audiovisual holdings. This goal will be achievable for a few well-funded institutions, but in reality significant amounts of audiovisual material will never cross the digital divide and will be lost. This could amount to a tragedy of missed opportunity, but in well-managed collections, pragmatic decisions will make sure that the most significant materials are preserved in time.

Applying preservation selection criteria to an oral history collection can be done in four stages, and is usefully represented as a decision tree:

1. Does this institution have preservation responsibility for the recording?
   If No:
   Determine the recording's future status in the collection.
   Consider transfer, repatriation or destruction.
   If Yes:
2. Is the interview and its recording of sufficient quality to justify preservation?
   If excellent interview + excellent recording → high-preservation priority.
   If excellent interview + poor recording → medium preservation priority → preserve as transcript.
   If poor interview + excellent recording → low preservation priority.
   If poor interview + poor recording → no preservation priority → benign neglect.
   If high-preservation priority:
3. Is the recording format actively deteriorating or at risk of deteriorating?
   If No:

Maintain high-preservation priority.
If Yes:
4. Is the recording format's replay equipment obsolete?
If No:
Maintain high-preservation priority → digitize as soon as possible.
If Yes:
Digitize immediately.

Some of the recordings that oral history collections hold may be the preservation responsibility of other institutions. The most common examples are radio programs and recordings of lectures, speeches, and public events. They include ethnographers' recordings of indigenous culture, which were frequently distributed as copies among colleagues and collecting institutions. Some folklorists of the mid-twentieth century did the same. Nor are all conventional oral history recordings unique. Australia's pioneer oral historian Hazel de Berg conducted more than 1,300 interviews between 1957 and 1984. The National Library of Australia supported her for most of her recording career and rightly considered her collection a national treasure. The State Library of South Australia arranged to purchase copies of her open-reel recordings, which resulted in a duplicate set of almost half of her collection.

Duplicate material may amount to hundreds or even thousands of hours of recordings in a collection, representing significant cost for preservation. Determining whether another institution—the originating broadcaster, a university, or a national archival institution—has accepted responsibility for its long-term preservation means that the savings can be applied to unique material instead. Oral history collections can also be the refuge of unique recordings of no intrinsic value whatsoever. When portable open-reel recorders became available in the 1960s, the novelty of the new technology resulted in all kinds of redundant recordings being formally accessioned. At the State Library of South Australia, these included test recordings, book readings (by some other than the authors), and administrative ephemera such as "Mrs. Fitzpatrick explaining our telex procedures."

The future status of duplicate and redundant material should be determined during a preservation selection process. Some duplicate recordings will be retained for local access. Others may be transferred or repatriated to the institution with preservation responsibility for the originals. Some, especially redundant recordings, should be deaccessioned and destroyed rather than put aside for a subsequent generation of curators to puzzle over. Such decisions must be appropriately authorized and documented in the institution's catalog and permanent files.

The greatest savings are likely to be made in the second stage of a preservation selection process. Most oral history collections will include sequences of donated interviews of poor recording standards. The sound quality means that the audio form of these interviews is unlikely to be used in the future. If these interviews have high research value and the content is captured in well-produced transcripts, preservation of the recordings can be deferred. If interviews are of marginal research value and have poor recording standards, they can be consigned to the realm of "benign neglect." They will be reformatted only if a research inquiry predates their eventual, but inevitable, deterioration beyond the critical point at which restoration will be impossible.

Having identified recordings that have a high-preservation priority, the order of preservation can be refined further by examining the condition of the recordings and the obsolescence status of their replay equipment. Most oral history collections contain open-reel recordings, standard cassettes, DAT, and MiniDiscs, with perhaps the odd micro-cassette format represented as well. Some collections include voice recordings, if not conventional oral history interviews, on wax cylinders, instantaneous discs (known as acetates or lacquers), and various other broadcasting formats such as 16-inch transcription discs and carts. Publications of the International Association of Sound and Audiovisual Archives and several authoritative Web sites provide detailed information about these audiovisual formats and their replay requirements.[14]

The State Library of South Australia applied these selection criteria to oral history acquisitions and preexisting library holdings between 1987 and 2003 to determine which recordings would be transferred to the particular formulation of open-reel tape that was the international preservation standard in the analog era. During that time 3,300 hours of original recordings from a potential 5,300 hours of acquisitions were reformatted. The preservation open-reels, representing original recordings of "high-preservation priority," have maintained that ranking in the library's current digitization plan.

Having established preservation priorities, an archival institution must determine how to implement the digitizing process and how to maintain the resulting digital objects in the future. None of the sustainable options is cheap. As the only cultural institution already engaged in audio preservation in its region, the State Library of South Australia decided to develop in-house facilities, requiring an initial investment of $A100,000 in 2004 to establish a digital audio archiving system. It spent an additional $A150,000 in stages over the following four years to enhance the original setup and establish a second workstation. Salaries and server storage space were additional costs.[15]

Outsourcing will likely play a role even for institutions that have in-house facilities. The 3,300 hours of high-preservation priority open-reels at the State Library of South Australia represent a uniform set of recordings that a commercial agency will digitize if additional funding in the order of $A500,000 can be secured. Outsourcing this work frees the in-house facilities to keep pace with current accessions, which will continue to include older analog recordings. Storage facilities must also be developed, since every hour of spoken audio captured at the preservation standard of 24-bit, 48 kHz is 1.02 gigabytes (GB) in size. The 3,300 hours of open-reel transfers will require 3.37 terabytes (TB) of managed storage.

Digitizing analog recordings in time will be daunting enough without adding to the backlog. Any archival institution still using analog field recording equipment should change to a digital system capable of recording at 24-bit, 48 kHz, such as a solid state Compact Flash card recorder. Since making this change, the State Library of South Australia has been under great pressure from community groups and professional historians to sell the trusty Marantz CP430 cassette recorders that had been lent to local practitioners for almost thirty years. Such a gesture, however, would do nothing to stem the tide of analog recordings requiring transfer, so the field recorders have been consigned to storage in case they are needed as replay units at some stage in the future.

Ensuring the Survival of Oral History Collections

The pragmatism required for appraisal, cataloging, and preservation strategies will be anathema to some passionate oral history curators, just as the underlying principles have been to some other librarians and archivists in recent years. To the budget-time questions, "Is there anything we can stop doing?" and "What can we do more efficiently?" they reply, "Nothing! Why can't we just be given the extra resources we need to do our jobs properly?" The managers may be sympathetic, but faced with finding "efficiency savings" as well as funding new online services each year, that answer does not suffice.

Even if a funding miracle occurs for oral history, collections with unmanaged backlogs and no identifiable preservation priorities except "everything" will not be in a position to capitalize on the opportunity. Those curators who have grappled with the need to change practices to meet changed circumstances are much more likely to benefit. The senior staff in the National Library of Australia's manuscripts branch are convinced of the ultimate rewards of such a stance:

> We've taken the risk that by really engaging with the wider library's ways of recording performance, and by shoe-horning our needs into a system that's designed for processing books and serials, we may have reduced our chances of eventually getting what we need for end to end archival processing. These risks may have consequences but we feel that taking these risks has paid off. We've demystified because frankly, the mystique just wasn't working for us, our readers, our donors or ultimately our employer.
>
> We are now firmly included in processing performance measures, and that raises the distinct possibility that our resourcing needs will be taken into account when our senior managers are making the near-impossible choices between competing needs in a low-resource environment.
>
> Our issues are firmly on the agenda in discussions about improving discovery of collections, and especially in improving management of collections. We have been key stakeholders in our newly developed Rights Management and Digital Preservation toolset. It is very sweet indeed to hear our own mantra, "If you can get this to work for Manuscripts, you'll get it right for everything" echoing from others' lips.[16]

To make certain that oral history can survive future funding crises in archival institutions, oral history curators must strive to be recognized as an integral part of their parent organizations. This does not mean that curators should be silent about the urgency and expense of digitizing analog recordings for preservation. They must speak out while demonstrating the unique contribution of oral history to the historic record, its potentials on the Web, and how readily the management of oral history collections can adjust to the resource realities of the digital era.

NOTES

1. Original oral history recordings and transcripts constitute archival, not published, material but are held in libraries as well as archives. Whenever the terms "archives" and "archival institution" are used in this chapter they are meant to stand for libraries as well.

2. Willa K. Baum, "The Expanding Role of the Librarian in Oral History," in *Oral History: An Interdisciplinary Anthology*, ed. David K. Dunaway and Willa K. Baum, 398 (Nashville, Tenn.: American Association for State and Local History, 1984). Ellen D. Swain provides an excellent analysis of the challenging but productive relationship between archival institutions and oral history in "Oral History in the Archives: Its Documentary Role in the Twenty-first Century," *American Archivist* 66 (Spring/Summer 2003): 139–58.

3. This chapter does not address video recordings, as the vast majority of oral histories produced in the analog era were sound recordings. The same principles apply to managing video oral histories, but the costs are even higher due to the greater complexity of producing excellent video. The interviewer usually needs the assistance of a camera operator and the setup includes lighting equipment. Cost are also higher due to the greater electronic storage requirements of high-resolution video (surpassing audio by a factor of about 100).

4. Major audiovisual archives are investigating ways of digitizing analog recordings at high speed. The Statens Ljud och Bild Arkiv (Swedish National Archive of Recorded Sound and Moving Images), which holds 7 million hours of audiovisual recordings, has developed a system for digitizing one of the one-quarter-inch open reel audio formats at four times the original speed. However, these specialized systems require a dedicated IT infrastructure. Martin Jacobin, "Migration of 1.5 Million Hours of Audio-visual Material," *International Association of Sound and Audiovisual Archives Journal* 31 (July 2008): 9.

5. Jonas Palm demonstrates the long-term financial commitment that is required to preserve access to information once it has been digitized in "The Digital Black Hole" (2006) by analyzing the costs of digitizing and managing electronic storage at the Riksarkivet (the National Archives of Sweden): "The more information is converted, the more the costs for accessing it go up. The digital black hole has got its firm grip on the [digitizing] project. It will go on swallowing either money or information: the funding must be continued or the input will have been wasted." He concludes that while there is no other choice but digitizing to preserve audiovisual material, microfilm produced from temporary digital files with the use of Computer Output Microfilm (COM) is likely to be a much more cost-effective way of preserving scans of paper-based materials. URL: www.tape-online.net/docs/Palm_Black_Hole.pdf.

6. The cost-effectiveness of vicarious creating at the State Library of South Australia is apparent even when the calculations include the original cost of the field recording kits

and the digital audio archiving system, amortized over ten years, and the audio engineers' salaries.

7. Dr. Marie-Louise Ayres and Emma Jolley, "Silk Purse or Sow's Ear? 'Good Enough' Collection Control at the National Library of Australia," paper presented at Australian Society of Archivists conference, Aug. 8, 2008. I am grateful to the National Library for allowing me to quote from this paper prior to its preparation for publication.

8. The University of Alaska Fairbanks Oral History Programs' Collection Development Policy is published in Nancy MacKay's *Curating Oral Histories: From Interview to Archive* (Walnut Creek, Calif.: Left Coast Press, 2007), 100, with other sample documents and forms that can be used or adapted by oral history collections.

9. See the Joint Steering Committee for Development of RDA, *Strategic Plan for RDA 2005–2009*, Nov. 1, 2007. URL: http://www.collectionscanada.gc.ca/jsc/stratplan.html.

10. Mark A. Greene and Dennis Meissner, *More Product, Less Process: Pragmatically Revamping Traditional Processing Approaches to Deal with Late Twentieth-Century Collections*, 31. URL: http://ahc.uwyo.edu/documents/faculty/greene/papers/Greene-Meissner.pdf. Originally published in *American Archivist* 68 (Fall/Winter 2005): 208–64.

11. Jennifer Bowen and John Attig, "RDA: Resource Description and Access: A New Cataloguing Standard for a Digital Future," paper presented to the Music Library Association, Mar. 7, 2007, 4. URL: www.musiclibraryassoc.org/BCC/Presentations/RDA_MLA_2007.pdf.

12. National Library of Australia, *Oral History and Folklore Collection—Preservation and Access Digitisation of Audio Recordings*, [2008]. URL: www.nla.gov.au/digicoll/audioprogress.html.

13. It is difficult to locate digitizing plans of collecting institutions that set goals in terms of the proportion of collections. The United States' National Archives and Records Administration (NARA) plans to digitize one percent of its collections by 2012. The National Library of Australia is aiming to digitize 5 percent of its Australian holdings. At the Library of Congress "despite its continuing and ambitious digitization efforts, perhaps only 10 percent of its 132 million objects held will be digitized in the foreseeable future." NARA, Draft for public comment of *Plan for Digitizing Archival Materials for Public Access, 2007–2016*, Sept. 10, 2007, 11, URL: http://www.archives.gov/comment/nara-digitizing-plan.pdf (the target is not repeated in the final version of the plan at www.archives.gov/digitization/strategy.pdf); Pamela Gatenby, Assistant Director-General, National Library of Australia, personal communication with the author, Aug. 2008; Kate Hafner, "History, digitized (and abridged)," in www.nytimes.com, Mar. 10, 2007.

14. See Kevin Bradley, ed., *Guidelines on the Production and Preservation of Digital Audio Objects: Standards, Recommended Practices and Strategies* (Aahus, Denmark: International Association of Sound and Audiovisual Archives [IASA], 2004); Majella Breen et al., eds., *Task Force to Establish Selection Criteria of Analogue and Digital Audio Contents for Transfer to Data Formats for Preservation Purposes* (Aahus, Denmark: IASA, 2004), URL: www.iasa-web.org/special_publications.asp; the European Union's PrestoSpace project to develop standardized practices for preserving European audiovisual content, URL: www.prestospace.org/; and *Sound Directions: Digital Preservation and Access for Global Audio Heritage*, established by Harvard University and Indiana University, which includes FACET, the Field Audio Collection Evaluation Tool, URL: www.dlib.indiana.edu/projects/sounddirections/index.shtml.

15. The State Library of South Australia uses Cube-Tec International's AudioCube and Quadriga systems to digitize sound recordings and transfer them into a digital object storage system. The library bypassed the burn-to-CD stage of audio preservation implemented by many archival institutions in the 1990s.

16. Ayres and Jolley, "Silk Purse or Sow's Ear?" 9.

BIBLIOGRAPHY

Baum, Willa K. "The Expanding Role of the Librarian in Oral History." In *Oral History: An Interdisciplinary Anthology*, edited by David K. Dunaway and Willa K. Baum. Nashville, Tenn.: American Association for State and Local History, 1984.

Bradley, Kevin, ed. *Guidelines on the Production and Preservation of Digital Audio Objects: Standards, Recommended Practices and Strategies*. Aahus, Denmark: International Association of Sound and Audiovisual Archives, 2004.

Breen, Majella, Gila Flam, Isabelle Giannattasio, Per Holst, Pio Pellizzari, and Dietrich Schüüller, eds. *Task Force to Establish Selection Criteria of Analogue and Digital Audio Contents for Transfer to Data Formats for Preservation Purposes*. Aahus: Denmark: International Association of Sound and Audiovisual Archives, 2004.

CHAPTER 27

CASE STUDY: THE SOUTHERN ORAL HISTORY PROGRAM

JACQUELYN DOWD HALL, INTERVIEWED BY KATHRYN NASSTROM

FROM its start in 1973 until 1999, the Southern Oral History Program (SOHP) was housed the history department at the University of North Carolina at Chapel Hill (UNC), rather than in the library or archives, where so many other oral history programs emerged. The SOHP is now part of UNC's Center for the Study of the American South, but it continues to play an integral role in the department of history. Concentrating on U.S. southern racial, labor, and gender issues, the program offers oral history courses, works with local communities, and uses interviews to produce works of scholarship, such as the prize-winning book *Like a Family: The Making of a Southern Cotton Mill World* (Chapel Hill: University of North Carolina Press, 1987 and 2000). Jacquelyn Dowd Hall has directed the program since its founding. This case study was condensed from two interviews conducted with her in 2008 by Kathryn Nasstrom, a graduate of the program and currently associate professor at the University of San Francisco.

Kathryn Nasstrom: It would be hard to talk about the history of the program without talking about your life and career. If I'm right about that, then it seems to make sense to talk about how those stories are intertwined.

Jacquelyn Dowd Hall: I first got involved in oral history when I moved to Atlanta from New York, where I was in graduate school in the late 1960s. After I took my qualifying exams, I got married, and my husband and I decided to move back to the

South. We knew people in Atlanta who were involved in the civil rights, anti-war, and women's liberation movements, and we were reading Atlanta's underground newspaper, so we just threw our meager belongings in the back of our red truck and moved. Three civil rights activists, Julian Bond, Howard Romaine, and Sue Thrasher, were starting something called the Institute for Southern Studies, which is still going in Durham, North Carolina. My then husband, Bob Hall, worked at the Institute while I got a job with Paul Gaston at the Southern Regional Council, organizing the council's papers for deposit. By sheer luck, those papers led me to the women's anti-lynching movement that became the subject of my dissertation and my first book.[1]

The folks at the Institute for Southern Studies were trying to combine activism with analysis, trying to figure out how to take the spirit of the movement into a new era. But they also wanted to understand the past. I was doing interviews for my dissertation, and Sue Thrasher, Leah Wise, and I started an oral history project on the southern radicals of the 1930s and 1940s. We tried (unsuccessfully) to raise money and just charged ahead, interviewing people. Some of those interviews eventually came to Chapel Hill, and I still consider them to be jewels of the SOHP collection. We were in the midst of putting out a special oral history issue of the institute's journal, *Southern Exposure*, when I took a job as the founding director of the Southern Oral History Program at UNC.[2]

Nasstrom: Coming up through the SOHP I always had a sense that it was unique for an oral history program to be part of a history department as opposed to a library or an archive. Is there a story to why it was done that way?

Hall: Yes, that was and is highly unusual, if not unique. I suspect that at the time the library was not particularly interested in housing the SOHP, but then neither was the history department, which made the whole thing pretty precarious.

The Southern Historical Collection in the University Library, where our interviews are deposited, has become one of our closest partners. It's that link between a major archive and a history department that has made this whole thing work. But when I first came here in 1973, there was a very different atmosphere, a different attitude toward these new kinds of sources and the kind of care they demand. Plantation records made up the heart of the Southern Historical Collection. Now our interviews are among its most heavily used sources, and it has vigorously collected twentieth-century manuscripts as well.

The history department has changed as well. Many of the students who apply to our graduate program in U.S. history cite the SOHP as one of the things that draws them here. Faculty members are using oral history to study everything from the history of fascism to rape in Bangladesh to the baby boom generation in Russia, with no sense of being part of a righteous but beleaguered movement (which is more or less how we saw ourselves in 1970). Those changes reflect the larger trajectory of how oral history is seen and used.

But in 1973, the department was a contentious and difficult place. A group of newcomers who saw themselves as modernizers in a backward institution were pitted against what they saw as an old guard of Southerners, which included George Tindall, who had secured a grant from the Z. Smith Reynolds Foundation to start the SOHP.[3] On top of that, the first real cohort of women faculty was just arriving at the university, and battles were raging over affirmative action, pay equity, tenure, and the like. I and the SOHP were caught in the middle of all this conflict. On the one hand, I was brought into the department by the supposed old guard. On the other hand, I was a woman doing oral history, women's history, and other new fangled things. The problem was not so much outright hostility as mutual incomprehension. I didn't identify with either of the department's factions: their issues were not my issues. And, with some important exceptions, neither side particularly got nor cared about what the SOHP was trying to do.

One sign of the precariousness of the situation was that, although I had been hired in a tenure track position, my salary was coming out of start-up grant money that would run out after five years. In 1975, two years after I arrived, the department brought in some of the major oral history leaders—Willa Baum, Ron Grele, and Charles Morrissey—to do a full-scale review of the SOHP. In the end, the department decided to keep me and the program. It also said in no uncertain terms that it saw me, and would judge me, first as a historian and only secondarily as the director of an oral history program.

So that's an important dimension of what it meant for the SOHP to be in a history department. It meant that the SOHP has never had the benefit of a full-time director. But it has had the benefit of being deeply involved in the teaching and research mission of a strong history department and in close communication with the larger world of historical research.

Nasstrom: Rewinding back to that moment in 1973 when you arrived, did you come with a certain vision in mind?

Hall: I did come with what you might call a vision. I know because I recently ran across an article I wrote for *South Today* in 1973, the spring before I came to Chapel Hill. The title pretty much says it all: "Oral History Movement: Seeking Out the Voices of Women, Blacks, Radicals, and Workers for a Better-Balanced Story." I mentioned the new program at UNC and quoted George Tindall as saying that it would "focus initially on interviews with prominent individuals," but that, once established, it might launch projects on the "inarticulate."[4] So there was a built-in tension between the kind of program the folks who started the SOHP had in mind and my orientation, which was a "history from the bottom up" approach that traced back to the Federal Writers' Project and the documentary tradition of the 1930s. Still, a "better balanced history" was the operative phrase. That was the core of my vision for the SOHP. I wanted it to focus on what Studs Terkel called the "uncelebrated," but also on the movers and shakers. One didn't preclude the other; a cross section seemed right to me. That seemed like what an oral history program at a public university should do. So there was a tension, but it was a creative tension, a refusal to think in either/ors.

Another tension was between creating sources for an archive, which is clearly what UNC had in mind, and the use of oral history in forwarding social change. The SOHP has always tried to take oral history to the public, engaging citizens in documenting their own histories and bringing a historical perspective to bear on contemporary issues. That mission has become stronger and stronger over the years, primarily because of the students and staff members who have taken on the job of creating a major archive and, at the same time, keeping our face turned to the outside world. Beth Millwood, our chief administrator and outreach coordinator, stands out in that regard.

There was a third "creative tension" as well: between creating archival sources and moving directly to scholarship ourselves. Most oral history programs see themselves mainly as the creators of primary sources for other people to use. I see that as our job too. A huge amount of our time and money goes into laboriously creating and processing those sources. But, again, in part because we were in a history department, our job was not just to create sources. We were also teaching young scholars to use those sources, to ask, "What does all this mean? How can we make historical meaning out of these individual stories?"

Nasstrom: That brings me to the question of how teaching fit in.

Hall: At its best, I think the SOHP has created an environment where students could resist some of the competitive, narrowing pressures of graduate training, bond with one another, and hold on to ideals of collaboration and civic engagement. A lot of my teaching has involved learning-through-doing and by example. But I've also been heavily involved in graduate student advising, and I've always taught an oral history seminar that's been absolutely central to our work. Those seminars have been the seedbeds for some of our best projects, and they've produced some of our great fieldworkers.

Nasstrom: How did you first take the vision we've been talking about and carry it forward?

Hall: We immediately got a grant from the Rockefeller Foundation to do two projects. One focused on the transformation of southern politics since World War II and included interviews with newcomers such as Bill Clinton, in his first campaign, and the young Al Gore, along with more established politicians.[5] The other project focused on women in the South who had been activists and intellectuals in the decades after 1920, when women won the right to vote. So right from the start, we were interviewing men who wielded power and women who didn't, albeit women who were remarkable in their own right.

Nasstrom: Can you talk about the evolution of the SOHP over time?

Hall: I'd say a new era started in 1978, which is when we got a grant from the National Endowment for the Humanities (NEH) for a project on the industrial revolution in the South. That project led to the writing of the book, *Like a Family*. Among the people who laid the groundwork for that project were Brent Glass, then a UNC graduate student and the first assistant director of the SOHP and now director of the National Museum of American History. We had a keen sense that the new working-class history of the 1960s and 1970s was ignoring the South and that historians of the South were ignoring workers. Our plan was to take advantage of the fact that in the South, unlike in much-studied New England, the industrial revolution had occurred within living memory. We wanted to interview members of the first generation to move from farm to factory and explore both the region's hidden history of labor conflict and the story of family, work, and everyday life.

My first step was to teach what turned out to be an especially memorable oral history seminar. I focused on Bynum, a mill town south of Chapel Hill, where the company still owned the houses and the same families had lived there for generations. We built the industrialization project out from those student interviews, stretching the NEH money out for years and interviewing more than five hundred people.

Nasstrom: Where did *Like a Family* come in?

Hall: I wanted a publication to come out of the project eventually, but just getting so many interviews done and into the archives was such a huge effort that I figured we'd have to stop there, at least for awhile. But as has so often happened, a next step emerged out of the creative energy of a group of graduate students who happened to be drawn together by the SOHP: Christopher Daly, Lu Ann Jones, Robert Korstad, James Leloudis, and Mary Murphy, all of whom have gone on to become distinguished scholars in their own right. As we finally got the interviews processed, we took a deep breath and said, in essence, "We did these interviews, we met these people, we're invested in their stories, and the stories are so touching, so rich with meaning. They're there to be used by other scholars, but we should take the first crack at saying what they mean, at least what they mean to us." So we decided to write a book, which UNC Press published in 1987 and then republished in 2000 with a self-reflective afterword.[6]

Of all the good things that came out of that project, one has given me special pleasure. Della Pollock, a new faculty member in performance studies, fashioned a student performance project based on the book. We authors traveled with the performance to mill communities around the state. Della and I have gone on to collaborate on other performance projects and to teach oral history and performance courses together. I've learned so much from her, and she has brought a whole different dimension to the SOHP's work.[7]

Nasstrom: Where did the program go over after that?

Hall: We spent a lot of time on outreach projects based on *Like a Family* and the industrialization project. As that wound down, I felt that we needed to be a bit less absorbed in thematic projects for a while. We needed to raise our profile as a program that also interviews notable individuals. I also thought it was important *and* politic to increase our attention to the history of the university. As our contribution to UNC's bicentennial in 1989, we completed three hundred interviews and an exhibit featuring everyone from service workers to students to chancellors. We have an especially rich collection on the food workers' strike of 1968-1969, a major event at UNC. We've continued to build the university history project ever since.

I hate to use money as the yardstick, but I'd say that the next era began in 1994, when Walter Royal Davis, a major benefactor of the university, created a fund to support oral history research. These were expendable funds, and with them we did a whole series of projects focused on the post-World War II transformation of North Carolina, concentrating on politics, business, women's leadership, Latino immigration, the impact of the military on coastal North Carolina, and the North Carolina Fund, a precursor to the War on Poverty.[8] We were also able to award student stipends for independent oral history research for the first time.

That period culminated in one of the SOHP's high points: our twentieth-fifth anniversary celebration and the 1999 National Humanities Medal, awarded by President Bill Clinton for work that has "deepened the understanding and broadened the public's engagement and access to important resources in the humanities." People came or wrote from far and wide.[9] The medal went to me, but it was really a tribute to the collective work of the SOHP.

Also in 1999 we got a sizable grant from the Z. Smith Reynolds Foundation for a project we called "Listening for a Change" to indicate that our aim was to use oral history to affect how people in North Carolina understood the past and made choices in the present based on that understanding. "Listening for a Change" was different in that the individual projects were led mostly by independent scholars, and each project had a strong civic engagement component. For instance, we did a community-based project on tensions between blacks and new Latino immigrants and created a documentary based on those interviews. We worked with prisoners, led teachers' institutes, and did a project on school desegregation and resegregation.

The project on the public schools led to our major focus today, a study of "The Long Civil Rights Movement: The South Since the 1960s."[10] For me personally this effort is something of a return to the question we were asking during those Atlanta years: "Where do we go after the fall of Jim Crow?" Barack Obama's election makes this project all the more poignant and important. He stands on the shoulders of the movement generation, of course, but he and his election also exemplify what happened next, as people pushed through the doors the movement opened, took advantage of new economic opportunities, forged new, integrated institutions, and confronted reaction from the Right.

We're taking long-time concerns in brand new directions in other ways as well. From the beginning, we wanted to make oral history accessible and useful beyond the academy. Now digital technologies are making that possible in ways I could not have imagined forty years ago. In collaboration with the UNC Library we have digitized almost six hundred oral histories originally recorded on cassette tapes, synchronizing sound with transcripts in a new way; providing commentary that situates interviews in historical context; and making them more easily searchable than ever before. This effort continues as we make interviews that are "born digital" available on line and work to bring more and more of our analog tapes on line as well. We're also in the midst of a collaboration with the Library, UNC Press, and the Center for Civil Rights at the UNC Law School, funded by the Andrew W. Mellon Foundation, aimed at experimenting with digital technologies to document and publish new work on the long civil rights movement.[11]

We've also made another big move: from being part of the history department to being part of a relatively new Center for the Study of the American South, and from two cramped rooms in one of the ugliest buildings on campus to offices in a beautiful renovated house on the main street through town. Definitely the start of a new era.

Nasstrom: How do you feel about where the SOHP stands today?

Hall: First of all, never in my wildest dreams did I think that oral history would blossom in the way that it has. And so my main feelings are surprise and gratitude:

that oral history has flourished and the SOHP has flourished with it. I'm also grateful that, although the SOHP is still dependent on gifts and grants for all its major projects, it finally has the base of financial security and predictability that we've struggled toward for so long. Yet, when I look back, I have to admit to a tiny undertow of nostalgia for the old days, hard as they were. We've accomplished what we have because of people who had a passion for this work. As we scratched and crawled our way to having some money and some stability, I'm sure there's been a certain routinization of the program such that we're more like other centers and programs in the university than we used to be. Also my role has evolved. I mainly provide intellectual leadership, raise money, mediate between the program and the university, and keep us plugged into the historical profession and the main currents of scholarly thought. I'm less intimately involved than I was in the early years.

Nasstrom: When I hear that, my instinct is to say that I presume for better and worse. What is the better, and what's the worse?

Hall: The better is that we *should* have decent institutional support by now. It would be ridiculous for so many people to have worked so hard for so many years and to have accomplished so much and for the SOHP to still be crammed into a couple of rooms and relying so heavily on soft money. But what has been lost? Well, I worry that it's harder for the graduate students who work for the SOHP to have a feeling of ownership, to be able to put their stamp on the program.

That's a critical point because the program's creativity has come from the generations of smart people who have passed through our doors. I wish I had the space to name them all. They have become outstanding scholars. Just as important, they've left here with a broad vision of what it means to practice history, and a striking number of them are leading oral history and public history programs and working as historians outside academe. More than anything else, it's what those people have done that makes me feel very lucky that a cascade of contingencies led me to land and stay in this place.

NOTES

1. http://www.southernstudies.org/; Paul Gaston, *Coming of Age in Utopia: The Odyssey of an Idea* (Montgomery, Ala.: New South Books, 2010); *Revolt against Chivalry: Jessie Daniel Ames and the Women's Campaign Against Lynching* (New York: Columbia University Press, 1983 [1979]).

2. Sue Thrasher, "Circle of Trust," in *Deep in Our Hearts: Nine White Women in the Freedom Movement*, edited by Constance Curry et al. (Athens: University of Georgia Press, 2000), 207–52; and Sue Thrasher and Leah Wise, eds., *Southern Exposure: No More Moanin', Voices of Southern Struggle* 1, nos. 2/3 (Winter 1974).

3. George B. Tindall, 1921–2006, served on the history faculty at the University of North Carolina at Chapel Hill from 1958 to 1985. He was president of the Southern Historical Association and a distinguished historian of the American South.

4. *South Today* 4 (April 1973): 2–3.

5. Jack Bass and Walter DeVries, *The Transformation of Southern Politics: Social Change and Political Consequence since 1945* (Athens: University of Georgia Press, 1995 [1977]).

6. Jacquelyn Dowd Hall, James Leloudis, Robert Korstad, Mary Murphy, Lu Ann Jones, and Christopher B. Daly, *Like a Family: The Making of a Southern Cotton Mill World* (Chapel Hill: University of North Carolina Press, 1987); reissued with an afterword by the authors and a foreword by Michael Frisch (Chapel Hill: University of North Carolina Press, 2000). For another prize-winning book by an SOHP staff member based on these interviews, see Allen Tullos, *Habits of Industry: White Culture and the Transformation of the Carolina Piedmont* (Chapel Hill: University of North Carolina Press, 1989).

7. Della Pollock, ed., *Remembering: Oral History Performance, with an Afterword by Jacquelyn Hall* (New York: Palgrave Macmillan, 2005).

8. This project has recently culminated in a book by two SOHP alumni: Robert R. Korstad and James L. Leloudis, *To Win These Rights: The Battle to End Poverty and Inequality in 1960s America* (Chapel Hill: University of North Carolina Press, 2010).

9. This event was spearheaded by then assistant director Spencie Love.

10. Jacquelyn Dowd Hall, "The Long Civil Rights Movement and the Political Uses of the Past," *Journal of American History* 91, no. 4 (March 2005): 1233–63.

11. http://www.sohp.org/; http://docsouth.unc.edu/sohp/; http://lcrm.unc.edu. The SOHP's assistant director, Joe Mosnier deserves credit for leading us into the digital age.

BIBLIOGRAPHY

Hall, Jacquelyn Dowd, James Leloudis, Robert Korstad, Mary Murphy, Lu Ann Jones, and Christopher B. Daly. *Like a Family: The Making of a Southern Cotton Mill World.* Chapel Hill: University of North Carolina Press, 2000 [1987].

CHAPTER 28

CASE STUDY: WHAT IS IT THAT UNIVERSITY-BASED ORAL HISTORY CAN DO? THE BERKELEY EXPERIENCE

RICHARD CÁNDIDA SMITH

UNIVERSITY-BASED oral history needs to undergo a transformation. The process of going out and interviewing people for firsthand knowledge of historical events is as old as the historical discipline itself. Both Herodotus and Thucydides based their histories on interviews, though all that remains are the paraphrases presented in their books. Interviews continued to be one of the most important tools for historians studying recent topics, but oral history as practiced today had its beginnings in the early nineteenth century when researchers began compiling and preserving stenographic records of the interviews they did. Modern oral history has centered on making the words of the historical informants accessible, so that narrators can continue to speak of their experiences to subsequent generations. Equally important, the historical interpretations of the researcher who conducted the interview can be checked and rechecked against the original source.

The tape recorder simplified the challenge of getting an informant's exact words. As the tape recorder was introduced, a number of universities in the United States established oral history programs to expand the interviews produced and to deepen methodological consideration. The Regional Oral History Office (ROHO) at the University of California—Berkeley, founded in 1954, is the second-oldest program at a research university in the United States. The mission of ROHO has been "to secure and preserve for history significant accounts of the development of California and the West."[1] It has collected more than 3,000 interviews on a broad variety of topics related to California history. ROHO's regional focus has been interpreted broadly so that given the centrality of California individuals and institutions to many international developments, ROHO interviews often have global relevance. In addition, scholars have donated more than 7,000 interviews produced in the course of their research.

Impressions on Being Interviewed

In the late 1990s, well before I had imagined that I might become ROHO's director, Lisa Rubens interviewed me for a series ROHO had organized on the free speech movement that shook the campus in 1964. I had been a first-year student at Berkeley in 1964, a supporter of the movement and of the strike protesting efforts by campus administration to limit distribution of political materials on campus. In no way, however, had I held a leadership position, nor was I privy to internal debates that shaped decisions student leaders made. Rubens interviewed me because I was a rank-and-file student whose experiences might illuminate how the student body responded to the contest between the administration and political activists. I had also participated in a "shop-in" at a local supermarket that had refused to hire African American checkers, an action that generated intense pressure from the local business community on campus administrators to stop the university from being used as a base for agitation.[2]

By the time Rubens interviewed me, I had been working in the oral history field for nearly thirty years. I had considerable experience as an interviewer, but I had never been the subject of an oral history. The experience of sitting on the other side of the tape recorder was an emotionally intense experience, which challenged some of my preconceptions about how the process unfolds. I had plenty to say, but every question generated confusion about how to respond, a reaction that I expect is widespread. The experience played an important role in my subsequent thinking about how ROHO could contribute more effectively to the work of a research university.

Rubens's questions were incisive. She was deeply familiar with both primary and secondary sources related to the topic, but she was equally attentive to what I wanted to say—or perhaps more accurately was *trying* to say. The first shock was how little I had to relate for some questions while having far too much for others. Specific events where I remembered clearly having been present proved particularly difficult and indeed painful to discuss. I simply could not go beyond the summary sentence or two I had formed over the years to describe what had happened.

Despite Rubens's careful probing, I was unable to move beyond the formulas lodged in my mind. Language had erased and completely replaced memory. Even when my answers were longer, I still had no recall beyond the words, and was totally unable to augment my descriptions. This limitation felt particularly frustrating because these were by far the easiest answers for me to provide.

For many other questions, fortunately, I experienced an intense flood of images and feelings. These answers were harder for me to put into words because I was unsure where to begin. I had so much I could potentially say that I desperately needed to know the larger themes guiding Rubens's specific questions if I were to select details that *might* be pertinent. This made me realize that to say that an oral historian provides an opportunity for a narrator to tell his or her own story could not possibly be accurate. I had many stories to tell, only some of them relevant to Rubens's interest. I could not begin to tell one account of many without listening carefully and trying to figure out her goals for the interview, unstated as well as explicit. In some instances, I felt a strong need to push beyond her goals. In particular, I insisted on telling the story of how in the middle of the fall 1964 term, at ten o'clock in the evening the Berkeley police department came knocking on the door of the apartment where I lived. A neighbor had apparently complained that my roommates and I were entertaining women. At the time, Berkeley had a local ordinance that made it a misdemeanor for unmarried people of the opposite sex to be in the same dwelling unit after 9:00 p.m., a law about which we knew absolutely nothing until the police informed us of their right to search our closets for hidden female guests. I had not thought about this event nor talked about it since 1964, but Rubens's interest in the reputation of Berkeley as a "liberal" community prompted both recall of a long-vanished memory and need to relay it and the deeply personal sense of attack each of us present felt.

As a historian I can now easily (probably too easily) explain the relevance of the anecdote for the campus climate in 1964, as well as the importance of local authorities as they invoked fears of unrestrained student sexuality in order to disparage a movement understood at the time as essentially about how a public university could most responsibly serve the broader public. At the time of the interview, however, I was not thinking as a historian. I just knew that I had to tell the anecdote, even though I could not explain why. In effect, the tension between personal experience as a form of vernacular history and professional historical analysis was playing itself within me.[3]

As I reflected on what I had learned about the dynamics of the interview experience, I became convinced that these moments—in which the dialogs of historians and narrators take deeper turns than anyone had anticipated—were what made oral history such an important and exciting form of research. Oral history thrives when it goes beyond collecting people's stories and prompts an engagement with the past that stimulates new interpretations. Every interview ought to be a link in a chain of dialogs that remained lively as long as new people continued joining the discussion and taking it in new directions.[4]

Setting Goals for ROHO

When I joined the Department of History at Berkeley in 2001 and became director of the Regional Oral History Office, my generalizing from this admittedly personal experience guided the goals I set for ROHO: (1) developing a research agenda for our interviewing to replace the older collections agenda; (2) engaging undergraduate and graduate students in all ROHO projects whenever possible and encouraging them to develop their own projects with official ROHO sponsorship; and (3) disseminating project findings to the broadest possible set of students, researchers, and public, beginning with but never limited to interview transcripts, through publication of the entire collection on the World Wide Web. Each of these directions challenged the archival assumptions that had shaped most university-based oral history practice in the United States since Allan Nevins founded the Oral History Research Office within the Butler Library at Columbia University in 1948. ROHO too has been a unit within the Bancroft Library, the campus's special collections and rare books library.

Library-based programs have focused on the archival aspect of oral history work: the collection of interviews that have been treated as functionally equivalent to other special collection materials such as diaries, letters, or manuscripts. In my view, the archival model for oral history was fundamentally flawed. Unlike letters, diaries, ephemera, or manuscripts, oral histories are not collected. The words and observations recorded in oral histories are not stored away somewhere awaiting retrieval. They have no physical existence prior to the interviewer and interviewee sitting down together over a tape recorder, nor do these words have immaterial existence. The shape of discussion flows out of the unique relationship of the specific individuals involved, out of the questions posed, and out of how the process stimulates both the expression of well-rehearsed formulas and the re-emergence of long-forgotten impressions, such as my recollection of the police visiting my home in 1964. The emphases of another interviewer on the free speech movement may likely have led me to select other stories to tell and perhaps another long-forgotten incident would have reemerged in response to an alternative lines of questioning. Oral history conversations may seem like first-draft memoirs, but they are remarkably different because we say things in conversation that we might never think to write down. If the interviewer does not understand what an informant is saying, he or she can ask questions in order to clear up confusions. If the interviewer knows that there are contrasting or contrary accounts, questions can help determine how strong the basis is for the informant's version and get the narrator to consider other interpretations.

In short, oral history interviews must be *produced*, and thus interviewers are *always* engaged in original research using a methodology that generates audio or video recordings and, often though not always, paper transcripts. Recordings and transcripts can, and should be, stored in libraries, but the administrative home that oral history programs typically have had in special collections libraries in the United

States (though less so abroad) generated an inverted understanding of oral history practice, which placed highest value on a secondary aspect of the work performed. Success was measured quantitatively—literally by the *number* of hours recorded, the *number* of pages transcribed, and the *number* of titles added to the oral history interview shelf list each and every academic year. The relevance of the materials produced could be assessed by the *number* of publications that cited the material. Records of requests for quotation were kept religiously, but there was no assessment of *how* scholars or journalists used oral history materials in the construction of their arguments or *how* what they had learned from oral history work challenged existing understandings.[5]

With this in mind, I wanted project organizers and lead interviewers on ROHO projects to be subject specialists who had completed advanced training, usually PhD's in history, having worked on and written about topics related to the subject areas they would develop at ROHO. They would know the historiography and current scholarly debates in the areas where they were interviewing. They were as well to have academic instead of staff appointments, providing recognition of their work as scholars and allowing them to teach as a regular part of their job. I wanted project organizers who had a strong personal need to maintain an active scholarly life, in which oral history work would be central to the arguments they were developing. I do not think that every oral history project, much less each interview, needs or ought to result in articles or a book. Regular writing, however, on the part of interviewers trying to understand how the work they are doing fits into the broader scholarly picture stimulates a deeper analytic process, which makes interviewers more alert to whether the material they are recording in fact augments the historical record and, if so, in what specific ways.

Active engagement with contemporary scholarship is essential for bridging the divide with those faculty who, in the history discipline at least, assess work by the explanatory power in scholarship and the new interpretations put forward based on the new bodies of evidence. Historians' suspicion of oral evidence is only in part based on their distrust of subjective sources. Most contemporary historians are well aware of the biases inherent in traditional archives and seek innovative sources that require a fresh look at old topics.[6] A deeper source of their suspicion of oral history lies in a relative lack of innovative, challenging interpretations based on oral sources. As one colleague said to me shortly after I joined the faculty at Berkeley, oral history was useful primarily for "local color" details. University-based oral history programs have an opportunity to demonstrate how important oral sources can be for developing new perspectives on the past. In truth, the status of oral history in the U.S. research university has suffered deeply because the dominant collections-development model gave little or no priority to intensive evaluation of project content. The research payoffs of the unit's work remained underexamined, as was its potential for developing interviews that might address the toughest debates in current scholarship.

The focus I gave to scholarly credentials challenged the parameters of library work. Given that oral history interviewers had been classified as editors, a staff position with no inherent research requirements, the question of whether a terminal degree ought be a requirement for a senior position in oral history became a topic for heated debate within the library at Berkeley. I had the support of the head of the campus library and of the director of the Bancroft Library, both of whom understood the long-range potential that ROHO had for changing how libraries participated in the university's research and teaching mission, so the switch of interviewers from staff to academic appointments was successful. This model will strike some as being at odds with the inherently democratic thrust of oral history as a movement to bring a broader variety of voices into discussion of the past. Yet what is appropriate for community-based oral history projects has not been a good foundation for university-based programs, with their distinct, specialized place in the field at large.

The volume of interviewing being conducted at all levels of society over the last half-century challenges oral history programs based in research universities to reflect more deeply on the unique aspects of their work. The number of interviews and interview projects has expanded into literally the hundreds of thousands, much of it underutilized and difficult to access. In 1989, while I served as executive secretary of the U.S. Oral History Association, Chadwyck Healey, a firm that reproduces archival resources, told me that they estimated there were over a *million* oral history interviews deposited in libraries and archives in the United States. They were trying to figure out, prior to the Internet, how to make these resources more available, but the sheer quantity of material stumped them. There have likely been hundreds of thousands of interviews added to collections during the intervening two decades. Chadwyck Healey's estimate also did not include those tapes still in researchers' possession—many of which will ultimately wind up in a repository.

The very success of oral documentation has been a shortcoming. The more interviews collected, the less likely the information they contain will be used beyond the immediate goals motivating the researcher. Oral history's ability to shape an understanding of the past remains more potential than realized, despite the fact that within existing collections lies material that likely challenges *every* major assumption in modern historiography. Oral history programs in universities have produced only a tiny fraction of the oral history research that is being done, and thus the deepest transformation of historical understanding will come from the work done elsewhere. Yet, the work that university-based oral history programs produce is relatively easy to find. The 3,000-plus interviews in the ROHO collection cover large segments of the history of the American West, but the collection is neither comprehensive nor complete. Compared to the ever-growing body of interviews available from individual scholars or from community-based institutions, interviews collected by a university research unit, however well funded, cannot provide *the* definitive set of texts documenting the various types of experience formed through the historical development of the state and the region. What they offer the academic world, where the most important work goes on, are controlled experiments in how to deepen interview content, how to introduce oral documentation into contemporary scholarly debates so their importance can be recognized, and how to make interview findings more meaningfully accessible to potential users.

Since its origins, oral documentation has undergone a twofold, contradictory trajectory. Oral history practice has expanded exponentially as it has professionalized. University programs have been the linchpin in this process. They have provided a body of practice in establishing standards for project design, interviewing, transcription, preservation, and accessibility. Not everyone can or will follow standards set by Berkeley, Columbia, UCLA, Chapel Hill, or the other important university programs, but these programs provide a persistent challenge to everyone else to think more deeply both about what they actually do and what they could do.

The role of oral history research in the contemporary university is not to duplicate collecting activities now occurring throughout society at large, whether in well-funded, commercial oral documentation projects that businesses commission or in the thousands of community-based projects that rely on committed volunteers. The staff of a university-based program has more opportunity to reflect on how to make oral resources more relevant to research, education, and public culture, how to make oral history an integral part of the way contemporary society debates the past, and the meanings that can be derived from what we know. Oral historians at the research university serve the democratic and enlarging spirit of the movement as a whole whenever their work contributes to the complex, interweaving conversations and debates that constitute academic life, especially when they convince their academic peers to ponder more deeply how individuals and communities have formed their own understanding of the past and then to integrate vernacular interpretations of the past into the warp and woof of professional historical practice.

Oral sources have been an important part of scholarly life for the past two centuries because they have made visible forms of collective life that are difficult (although not impossible) to document in other ways. Today just as in the past, people create and sustain a shared imaginative life wherever they gather and converse, at the kitchen table, the tavern counter, or in university hallways. These informal collective understandings permeate every decision that groups make—now matter how text-based they may be—and they form the background of every interview. At once both personal and social, these accounts provide evidence for reconstructing communities, their past concerns and past conflicts. Oral history allows the recuperation of ideas that were once important but might not be well documented in print or literary sources. My recollection of the police coming to determine whether my roommates and I were entertaining members of the opposite sex faded from my memory because—in very little time—the idea that the police could monitor the sex lives of college students became an absurdity. The event had no continuing relevance to everyday life.

In 1964, however, the occurrence was a shocking reminder that despite the social imperative for young adults to strive for personal autonomy, we faced a collective authority that sought to control purely personal behavior. A visit from the police department to look for girls was an event my roommates and I talked about endlessly with our friends, a factor contributing to my ability thirty-five years later to rediscover the event when asked the right questions. The anecdote had nothing to do directly with the free speech movement. It never led to a formal complaint, despite the disbelief of one roommate, an English exchange student, who protested as the police conducted their search, "But officer, there has been *no* fornication!" The shock of the event resonated with the anger many of my fellow students felt over new campus policies limiting advocacy. In a way, it strengthened militancy and an ongoing determination not to let them (any of them) get away with it (any of it).

While I do not want to overestimate the importance of a single personal experience, the account I provided for ROHO's oral history project on the free speech movement (FSM) is evidence for how oral sources reveal usually hidden modes of collective life and consciousness, and invite new interpretations that put people, their concerns, their beliefs, their fears, and their choices back into historical processes without romanticizing them. A more obvious linkage between personal reality and scholarly models of historical change is one of the features that attracts students to oral history research, where, working with subject specialists, they can explore the topics of interest with a greater level of sophistication than they would on their own.

Benefitting Students

Oral history has three immediate practical benefits for students. The first is a sharper understanding of the connections between everyday life, including their own, and larger social processes of transformation and conservation. Second, it provides a practical hands-on methodology, which authorizes students to produce original historical sources themselves. They learn that scholarship is not just a matter of summarizing what can be found in a library. Scholarship includes that, but too often students never get past this beginning point. Finally, oral history encourages students to think creatively about how to integrate their own backgrounds, interests, and experiences into what they are learning about the world at large. ROHO's classes, like those at other universities, challenge students to design research projects that describe the world as they have understood it, but then to relate what they learn to the larger images of the globe that the university has been so good at propounding. Rather than being asked to complete transcripts, students write analytic papers assessing what they learned from interviews and how their narrators' accounts fit into existing literature.

The most important questions facing everyone in education today are grounded in the everyday practices of oral historians: How do we teach students to read sources for their biases, in particular to become aware that much has been silenced? How do we teach students to think through the foundations of arguments they encounter and to assess how logic, evidence, *and* emotion have combined into a conviction? How does one develop common languages for areas of shared need and interest without losing sight of continuing differences in experience and standpoint? What is the relation of knowledge and conviction? As students place their work on a project's Web page, their attitude toward scholarship evolves. They are no longer writing papers just for a professor to read.[7] Their conversations with interviewees extend to a broader public that has encountered their work because of an interest in the topic. Their writing develops out of a new need to explain to a broader range of possible readers why what they learned from their interviewing is important. The essence of what university-based oral history programs can contribute to the democratization of history, as promoted by the oral history movement, is opening conversations about the past to all who have a need to join the discussion and keep it alive.

NOTES

1. Quoted in Regional Oral History Office brochure and other descriptive materials. See ROHO website at http://bancroft.berkeley.edu/ROHO.

2. For histories of the free speech movement and analysis of the background leading to the conflict over campus policies, see William J. Rorabaugh, *Berkeley at War: The 1960s* (New York: Oxford University Press, 1989), and Robert Cohen and Reginald E. Zelnik, eds., *The Free Speech Movement: Reflections on Berkeley in the 1960s* (Berkeley: University of California Press, 2002). Some of the FSM Oral History Project interviews are available on line, with other interviews related to the history of Berkeley. See the ROHO Web site http://bancroft.berkeley.edu/ROHO. My interview is sealed until my retirement from Berkeley.

3. The relationship of vernacular and academic oral history put into play by oral history work is a theme I developed in the essay "Analytic Strategies for Oral History Interviews," written not long after Rubens's interview with me. The essay was published in Jaber F. Gubrium and James A. Holstein, eds., *Handbook of Interview Research* (Beverly Hills, Calif.: Sage Publications, 2001), 711–32.

4. This type of development in the oral history exchange is an important element in what I believe Alessandro Portelli means by "story-telling" turning into "history-telling." See Alessandro Portelli, *The Battle of Valle Giulia: Oral History and the Art of Dialogue* (Madison: University of Wisconsin Press, 1997), 6ff.

5. I worked in the Oral History Program at UCLA from 1984 to 1993, and a good portion of our activities involved maintaining our "stats," which formed the sole content of our annual reports. Similar measurements had been the rule at ROHO. I abolished this kind of report when I arrived, and today, ROHO's Web site provides an ongoing "annual report" that gives priority to content and scholarly engagement over numbers, though any casual user will see that the numbers are indeed impressive.

6. Excellent discussions of oral history and its place in newer historiographical trends can be found in Peter Burke, ed., *New Perspectives on Historical Writing* (University Park: Pennsylvania State University Press, 2001) and Anna Green, *Cultural History* (London: Palgrave Macmillan, 2008).

7. Examples of student work from Berkeley, including both interviews and analytic essays, can be found on the education section of the ROHO Web site.

BIBLIOGRAPHY

Burke, Peter, ed. *New Perspectives on Historical Writing*. University Park: Pennsylvania State University Press, 2001.

Green, Anna. *Cultural History*. London: Palgrave Macmillan, 2008.

Smith, Richard Cándida. "Analytic Strategies for Oral History Interviews." In *Handbook of Interview Research*, edited by Jaber F. Gubrium and James A. Holstein, 711–32. Beverly Hills, Calif.: Sage Publications, 2001.

PART VI

PRESENTING ORAL HISTORY

CHAPTER 29

TOWARD A PUBLIC ORAL HISTORY

GRAHAM SMITH

PUBLIC history is a "slippery concept."[1] Perhaps the simplest definition of public history is that it describes a set of procedures undertaken by historians who are not employed in academic institutions.[2] Within this definition, at least for some, funding is an important element that distinguishes public from academic history. Public history, Valerie Yow has argued, is "commissioned research in special communities," so that "the targeted audience is the commissioner or the commissioner's chosen readers–not necessarily other scholars."[3] On the other hand, Donald Ritchie, a leading practitioner in both oral history and public history, has noted that definitions of public history have shifted from an association with the spaces and places in which historians work, in public agencies or as private consultants, to include the "publics" that such historians purport to serve or attempt to reach. As Ritchie observed, "Other professional historians, for whom the bulk of historical literature is intended, account for only a small portion of the public historians' audience."

> Public history is the organized effort to bring accurate, meaningful history to a public audience, and oral history is a natural tool for reaching that goal. The oral history and public history movements share a natural affinity, both having attracted practitioners and audiences different from those for more traditional history writing. Both oral and public history have experimented with videotape, slide-tape, and even interactive videos, in museum exhibits, dramatic performances, and other applications outside the classroom and in publications.[4]

Public history might therefore describe the production of historical interpretations that are intended for consumption by particular audiences. It has been argued that this is an important difference: while academic historians write for one another, public historians are interpreting the past for a wider audience.[5] However, practitioners have been careful to emphasize that despite differences of audiences and funding sources, both public and academic historians share common ground in practicing the "craft of history." "As historians," wrote Philip V. Scarpino, "we all do research, we all analyze and interpret our findings, and we all communicate the results."[6] Or, according to Charles Morrissey, who worked for many years as a self-employed oral historian, public history is history undertaken by professionally trained historians in nonacademic environments to academic standards.[7]

The challenges and opportunities for oral historians who engage in public history are exciting and potentially inspiring. Indeed, by bringing together a variety of activities in which oral historians are already engaged, along with a set of shared sensibilities, a new public oral history could be created. Such a public oral history would be based on participatory practices that have been developed as part of a shared aim of democratizing the interpretation of the past. Before arriving at this conclusion, the ways in which oral historians have engaged in public history will be discussed, beginning with the sensibilities that oral historians have brought to public history practices, followed by a consideration of the differences that have emerged—differences that have added to the ambiguity of the term "public history."

Oral History and Public History—Common Sensibilities

Understanding why oral history has been so close to the center of the explosion of public historical activity is easy. As an activity and a program production tool, it is accessible and familiar. Its products are generally interesting and hardly exclusive in their appeal. It thus contributes readily to the three dimensions mentioned above: the broadening of the audience, of the subject matter and issue of concern, and of the participatory base in history making. It is helping to refashion our sense of what history is, who does it, under what auspices, and to what end.[8] Public history is a political activity, whether practiced in the name of the people, or in the service of charities, religious organizations, governments, or capitalist corporations. Ludmilla Jordanova has argued that public history "weaves moral discourses," creating or sustaining historical narratives and that these moral and political dimensions are inseparable.[9]

Such discourses change over time, and arguably oral history has contributed to that change. In the mid-1980s, it could be claimed with confidence that the majority of past lives attracted little interest from academic historians. Oral historians at the time responded with projects that sought to include the stories of people whose histories have been marginalized or even excluded from the existing historical record.

Drawing on this legacy, oral historians continue to ask themselves who might be missing from the story. Given that public history has been too often the history of the powerful and the victorious, the tradition of oral historians questioning who might be hidden from history remains potentially a corrective to existing accounts of the past.

Oral historians have also been interested in exploring a variety of ways of representing the interviews they collect. This has been the case especially for those engaged in community oral histories who often reach out to new audiences through local independent publishing groups, exhibitions, television, and radio. For many oral historians, the point is not simply to describe or even analyze the past, but rather to (re)present recollections in ways that engage people in discussing the meaning of their own recollections along with the recollections of others.

As a part of recording memories, oral historians form relationships with interviewees that are most often based on mutual trust. It is therefore unsurprising that oral historians are concerned with the implications of collecting, using, and archiving testimonies. Ethical considerations involving both the public preservation and representation of narrated memories have therefore long been a concern of individuals and organizations involved in oral history. For oral historians, the practice of public history has often involved adopting the position described by Michael Frisch as "shared authority":

> What is most compelling about oral and public history is a capacity to redefine and redistribute intellectual authority, so that this might be shared more broadly in historical research and communication rather than continuing to serve as an instrument of power and hierarchy.[10]

Although subject to differing interpretations, "shared authority" has provided the basis for a variety of approaches to working with individuals and groups. This includes Daniel Kerr's "dialogue in the streets among the homeless," which resulted in the production of videos and radio shows based on the oral histories of Cleveland, Ohio's "homeless experts." He put the emphasis on the ability of people who might seem powerless to make social change. Through combining oral history and public history "the nexus between experience and social structure" could be explored, which for Kerr was "the root of agency."[11]

While there have been a number of critiques of "shared authority," it has remained an ideal that most oral historians aim at. It has also provided a means of exploring the impact of the interview relationship on testimonies.[12] But, as Frisch would later comment, sharing authority was a beginning, not a destination, and the challenge of sharing authority was "hardly uni-directional."[13]

In sum, oral historians have a number of shared practices and sensibilities when engaging in public history flowing from theoretical insights and ethical understanding. Yet oral historians also operate in specific contexts. Most obviously, the public histories of the specific geographic spaces in which they are located will exert influences resulting in local varieties of practice and understanding.

Public History and Oral History Internationally

Across the globe there are differences in the ways that public history is understood and the past imagined. There are also differences in both the products and practices of public history. At least in part such differences are shaped by the histories of the communities or audiences being served.

In Britain, public history has also long been associated with "people's history," with social conflict often seen as a driving force for historical change.[14] This might be contrasted with the search for social cohesion that marks much of the public history activity in the United States. (The difference should not be exaggerated, however. There are many local oral history projects in Britain that while committed to uncovering "history from below" often emphasize the significance of community cohesion and, in the process, neglect conflict.) There has also been an attempt in Britain by oral historians to maintain a commitment to the past as public property, and to avoid professionalizing oral history and public history. Instead, through handbooks, open training, and case studies, oral historians have disseminated examples of good practice, ethical approaches, and theories that can inform interpretation.

While it might be argued that public history as *product* has attracted less attention among oral historians who are often more interested in *process*, from the late 1990s the *Oral History* journal in Britain has carried regular features on public history that discuss the role of oral history in the products of public history. These have included oral history in public history installations, museum exhibitions, home movies, audio montage presentations, and Internet presentations as well as radio and television programs.[15]

Public history itself is subject to change. Such changes can be heard in eyewitness accounts of the past that are often influenced by the historical interpretations and reconstructions of existing public histories. The extent of these influences has been the subject of much debate and for some oral historians this aspect of the relationship between present and past has provided inspiration. For example, Alistair Thomson has explored how Australian servicemen's recollections of the First World War changed over time.[16] Such changes in memories reflects in part Australia's historical and shifting association with Britain, but more importantly—in terms of acting as a case study—Thomson showed the ways in which wider public history contexts shaped the former Anzacs' recollections of their soldiering.

In Australia and the United States a plethora of public history courses and degree programs have emerged, with both countries boasting more public historians than academic historians. Both have also experienced controversy as a result public history activity. However, there are also differences between the two countries. As well as providing a means for a relatively recent former colony to develop a historical identity independent of Britain's, Australia's history as a settler society has also informed its public history. This can be seen most notably arising from the campaigns of indigenous peoples for social and political restitution. In such circumstances, interpretations of the past have resulted in sharp exchanges. When, for example, the newly elected prime minister of Australia, John Howard, spoke in the aftermath of his electoral triumph in 1996, he attacked what he saw as attempts to "rewrite Australian history in the service of a partisan political cause."[17] For some, this marked the opening of "the history wars" in Australia.[18]

The term "history wars" had been adopted from the title of a book about an earlier controversy in the United States. In 1994 an exhibition at Smithsonian Institution's National Air and Space, marking the fiftieth anniversary of the end of the war in the Pacific, invited museum visitors to consider the moral implications of using nuclear weapons against Japan. This proved too much for some conservatives, including Newt Gingrich, the then Speaker of the House of Representatives and an "alternate" historian.[19]

While the result of this controversy may have meant a more cautious turn in public history in the United States, this has not been the case in Australia where there has been a vigorous response. The idea that there can be multiple and changing historical interpretations has been stoutly defended. Stuart Macintyre in particular has been critical of the charge that generating new knowledge of the past and reinterpreting history in light of changing concerns in the present is somehow a sinister attempt to undermine a "fixed, fully disclosed and final" history.[20]

Along with reinterpretations of the past, postmodernism, and the political Left, oral history has also drawn the ire of Australia's right-wing historians. So Keith Windschuttle, for example, has resurrected the criticisms of his former mentor Patrick O'Farrell:

> Pat made a very effective critique of the then emerging field of oral history showing just how unreliable it could be. Since then, however, oral history has grown to become a highly fashionable pursuit, especially in Aboriginal history—there are now journals and courses in the subject—but some of us still remember and can apply the critique that Pat originated.[21]

One way Windschuttle applies O'Farrell's critique is in statements such as: "Aboriginal oral history, when uncorroborated by original documents, is completely unreliable, just like the oral history of white people."[22] This is a fine example of a central tenet in the thinking of the new right in history: the past can never be re-interpreted; it is sufficient to replay the views of past historians regardless of whether new historical tools or sources are utilized or discovered. In a single sweep the history of oral historical methods post-O'Farrell is ignored, historical understandings of the fallibility of documentary sources are forgotten, and the significance and sophistication of orality and memory to a people who have little or no written records is shoved to one side.

Many of the arguments that oral sources are different from documentary sources have been well rehearsed and convincingly argued,[23] but Windschuttle not only neglects the arguments from within oral history but also from within a large section of the history profession itself. This includes discussions of the problems of confusing history with historiography.[24] More specifically there has been a failure to appreciate the significance of the complex historical processes, including the huge amount of organized effort and labor required in preserving, sorting, and making accessible the materials (including documents) that historians make use of in archives and record offices.[25]

To this we might add some of the insights from those with an in-depth understanding of oral tradition. Winona Wheeler has argued that indigenous people's oral histories should not be plundered for the bits that fit a Western sense of history. '"Facts," she noted, are extracted and the remaining "superfluous data set aside." As Wheeler so succinctly summed up: "The bundle is plundered, the voice silenced."[26] Yet just among the Cree, one of the largest group of indigenous peoples in North America to which Wheeler belongs, so among other peoples, conquerors, or survivors of conquest, oral history is more than an abstraction; rather it is a rich, complex, multiple faceted, and dialogical conception of time (past/present), space (private/public), and representation (memory/history).

Fortunately, others have not replicated Windschuttle's lack of understanding of the complexity or oral sources, and the oral evidence of indigenous peoples continues to be used not only in Australia but elsewhere. In New Zealand, for example, the Waitangi Tribunal in Aotearoa collected evidence of contemporary and historical breaches of the 1840 Treaty, which had placed New Zealand under British sovereignty. In doing so, the tribunal generated a rich resource through public history-making sessions with Maori claimants speaking, writing, and singing their histories.[27]

There have been skirmishes—if not wars—over how the past should be interpreted in other countries as well. This includes Canada, where similar debates occurred, to those experienced in the United States and Australia, with a retired historian attacking new ways of exploring and thinking about the past as both confusing and boring students.[28]

Elsewhere, controversies have taken a different shape. Peoples emerging from totalitarian regimes, including South Africa, Chile, Argentina, and the countries of the former Soviet Union and Eastern Bloc, have all engaged in processes of revisionism, attempting to understand their pasts in new ways. Oral history has become a key method in making new interpretations, especially where memories have been suppressed, with the resultant public history often claiming oral histories as eyewitness accounts of the inequities of the former regime. In Cambodia, the Cham Muslim Oral History Project, for example, uncovered the atrocities committed by the state during the period of Democratic Kampuchea (1975–79), when the Khmer Rouge were in power and an estimated two million people were murdered. In collecting testimonies, the project also engaged in educating young Cambodians about the genocide and attempted to foster closer relationships between a generation of parents, who experienced the destruction of their country and lives, and their children who find such experiences difficult to comprehend.[29]

In such settings the collection and presentation of oral histories in museums, exhibitions, and archives become a part of the processes of collective remembering, and this is often accomplished with the aims of either retribution or reconciliation. Such processes and aims can be problematic, however, and are seldom as straightforward as they first might appear. Challenges include the difficulty of understanding and representing the memories of oppressed peoples. For instance, Lindsay DuBois's account of the lives of working-class residents on the outskirts of Buenos Aires uncovered "the difficulties people face when trying to communicate stories and memories that are out of place and out of step." The memories of a squatter occupation that she collected were not simply oppositional, they did not even relate to existing oppositional accounts, such as those of people who belonged to human rights organizations. However, they could be explained according to DuBois as "subaltern"—narratives that are the product of powerlessness.[30]

Globally there have emerged a number of initiatives dedicated to uncovering the abuse of human rights, including state terrorism, genocide, and mass systematic torture. Collecting, interpreting, and publicly displaying these histories are especially problematic. As Federico Guillermo Lorenz has noted:

> Social memory is essentially dynamic. It grows and changes, constantly recovering or burying facts and meanings. Historians are part of this process: our work provides elements to allow individuals to feel part of a larger, collective whole. When the past to be told has elements of a tragedy of enormous moral implications, as in this case in Argentina, this task is more difficult to perform.[31]

Such work has demonstrated how different cultural experiences shape testimonies and silences. For example, Cuban women, speaking at the end of the twentieth century, publicly applauded the revolution and then privately stated their reservations after recording ended. In contrast, female survivors of Pinochet's Chilean dictatorship testify to their disappointment that despite becoming political activists, they still felt that they continued to be the victims of institutional and cultural sexism—even after living through a period of democracy.[32]

In South Africa, as part of "truth and reconciliation," the history of apartheid has been examined through the use of oral history. In recent years, an increasingly diverse range of topics have been explored, including recollections of shebeens and the alcohol trade between 1930 and 1980. What unites much of this work is a commitment to present oral history to a wider public. Their concern, noted Renate Meyer from the Centre for Popular Memory,

> is that the research [should] not just sit in our archives and get indexed into our digital repository. If we are to have a social purpose, the stories that we record need to go out into the world.[33]

As already noted, this is not a straightforward process. It is worth reflecting on Peter Read's note of caution with respect to reconciliation inspired activity. In his keynote address to the International Oral History Association meeting in 2006, exploring reconciliation and oral history in Australia and Chile, Read stated:

> If we oral historians don't continue to investigate and record and archive and transcribe and publish the darkest corners of our nations' histories, then when the consensus is taken to reveal all, or some, or just a bit, of what happened, then we won't be able to do it. What is denied cannot be reconciled.[34]

Doing public history involves making political decisions. At the simplest level, this means answering the question of whether to take sides or attempt to step back to take a wider view. Both are political decisions. Taking the wider view still means taking a position, but the danger in putting effort into retribution, of attributing guilt or innocence, is that more nuanced understandings of the past may be neglected. For example, a touring exhibition of Ukrainians in Britain proved to be a challenging project because it told a story that included the testimonies of older men who had fought alongside the Germans in the Fourteenth Waffen SS "Galicia" Division during the Second World War, as well as the women who had been slave laborers in Nazi munitions factories and on German farms. The exhibition, in spite of objections from some older interviewees, also included photographs of atrocities with which Ukrainians had been involved. There were also memories of the older generation's postwar dislocation, migration, and settlement, and the recollections of the children who had been raised as Ukrainians in exile, some of whom expressed concern about their fathers' wartime actions and inactions. By presenting a more complete picture of the community, a better understanding of changing ideological beliefs was reached.[35] In addition, the significance of people with very different experiences uniting around an "imagined identity," which included the creation of an alternative and nostalgic public history, was also made evident.[36]

Donald Ritchie has argued that "By dint of their positions in the public sphere, which lacks tenure and require nonpartisanship, public historians usually refrain from publicly expressing personal opinions about political issues."[37] The ideas of objectivity and of impartiality in working with oral history in public history are even trickier than this argument suggests. For example, oral historians in Hong Kong, in discussing the reuse of oral histories in a state-sponsored program, have had to address questions involving freedom of expression. Specifically, a debate has emerged about how much contentious material should be censored by the team in order to avoid the possible displeasure of the mainland government. Whatever decisions are made in such circumstances will seem, to some, partisan and even dangerous. While nonpartisanship may be easier in matters where there is accord, as David Glassberg has put it, "it is nearly impossible to reach a consensus on the public interpretation of a historical event that anyone still cares about."[38] And the most interesting public history that oral historians are engaged in involves a past that people still care about.

Academic historians in contrast to public historians, at least in the West, not only have tenure but most importantly academic freedom. This is a license for academic historians to take up unpopular cases and arguments, in part because it is recognized that in the past, claims of nonpartisanship and objectivity prevented the dissemination of new ideas. Indeed, public history itself could at least in part be a means of examining changing belief systems that would have seemed to be "objective," because objectivity itself is historically contingent.

In Poland and Ukraine there have been major public history projects to produce new views of the past, especially in response to the periods of Nazi and Stalinist dictatorships. In undertaking this revisionism, however, public historians need to be aware of a wide range of potential silences and absences. Annette Day, in her survey of Polish museums, was struck by the observation of a director of a regional museum about how local people did not remember—"or did not want to remember"—the Jewish community that had existed there prior to the Second World War.[39]

Oral historians working in the aftermath of political upheaval, when societies witness the making of new public histories, face particular challenges. In the Czech Republic Adam Hradilek, of the Institute for the Study of Totalitarian Regimes (USTR) in the Department of Memory and History, has collected oral testimonies of the Stalinist era. In doing so Hradilek claimed to have found evidence that Milan Kundera, the internationally celebrated Czech author and anti-Communist, had in his youth not only collaborated with the regime but had actively denounced an army deserter turned spy.[40] The revelation generated a great deal of media interest and sparked the beginnings of a debate about living under tyrannical rule. Such discussions of resistance, complicity, and accommodation have occurred in other countries, including Germany.[41] Commenting on "invented tradition," Yael Zerubavel noted that

> when a society undergoes rapid developments that shatter its social and political order, its need to restructure the past is as great as its desire to set its future agenda.... These "invented traditions" are particularly significant for the legitimation of the emergent social and political order, and their success depends, to a large measure, on their ability to reconstruct an acceptable view of the past.[42]

While restructuring the past may well emerge as a core project during turbulent times, the maintenance of invented traditions occurs in all societies, including those who are living through periods of historical stability. It is not difficult to see how invented tradition is an intimate of public history even if the activities and processes involved differ from locality to locality.

Memory, Narrative, History

Any discussion of public history and oral history would be incomplete without considering memory. Before outlining the work that oral historians and public historians have contributed in this area, it is worth recognizing that different types of memory exist. One way of thinking about this is in terms of individual, social, and public remembering.[43] Individual remembering includes both the unique and particular recollection of direct experience and the result of being reminded of such experiences through engaging with other people's recollections. Individual remembering also includes habitual body memory, which might be called "embodied memory." Social remembering broadly describes both the processes involved in individuals communicating their memories of a shared past and the knowledge that results from the act of reminiscing.[44] These are useful definitions in understanding how social and individual remembering operate.[45] In contrast, public memory includes the common narratives, public memorials, and commemorations of particular historical events, crises, or circumstances.

The relationships between public memory and social and individual remembering is not straightforward, and is the subject of much debate. Before exploring this further, the existence of a public history of oral history requires acknowledgment. This need has emerged from a growing number of publications that seek to delineate the recent history of oral history. Almost all of these histories claim that there was a significant shift at the end of the 1970s in the thinking of oral historians, when the study of memory began to be asserted as a central concern.[46] Alessandro Portelli, Luisa Passerini, Michael Frisch, and Ronald Grele are among those cited as making significant contributions to this change in perception. Portelli's chapter, "What Makes Oral History Different?" first published in 1979, argued that oral histories could provide historians with new ways of understanding the past, not just in what was recalled but also with regard to continuity and change in the *meaning* given to events.[47] In the same year, Passerini was counterpoising the populism of some oral history approaches with recognition of "a subjective reality which enables us to write history from a novel dimension undiscovered by traditional historiography."[48]

Leaving aside for the moment some of the difficulties that this version of oral history creates, it is worth thinking a little more about how oral historians have positioned themselves in relation to public historians' use of memory. Such consideration is even more important given that for some oral historians, there is a stated sense of disappointment that public historians have not engaged more fully with the insights into memory that oral historians have made. In common with much of the public history of oral history, Paula Hamilton and Linda Shopes have argued this lack of acknowledgment exists even though there has been a general growth of interest in memory beyond oral history. Hamilton and Shopes complained that many of those who have been engaged in the "memory turn" have ignored oral historians' contribution to understanding

> the dynamic nature of remembering, gaps and silences in the transmission of memory, the collapsing of past and present in individual recall, and people's sense of "living in time" or historical consciousness.[49]

In an attempt to explain why this might be the case, Hamilton and Shopes suggested that oral historians are much more engaged with lived experience than others whom they describe as critics of modernity. Postmodernism has certainly been viewed with suspicion and distaste by some oral historians, being seen as abstract and overly theoretical in reinventing earlier reflective insights about memory. It could therefore also be considered that the lack of engagement has been as much on the side of oral historians as on the side of those they seek to "other." In this regard, Michael Frisch's statement in *The Public Historian* can hardly be thought of as an attempt at building interdisciplinary understanding or partnership:

> we [oral historians] have "been there" for quite a while, regularly engaged in highly concrete and unmystified ways with issues supposedly discovered with so much huffing and puffing by explorers venturing aggressively into meta-history from bases in comparative literature and cultural theory.[50]

Hamilton and Shopes, however, have also usefully identified a number of additional reasons why there has been a lack of dialog in this area. They suggested that there are differences of scale in the studies in which the two groups are engaged—that oral historians have tended to study the local, while public memory work tends to be conducted at national, even international levels.[51]

Issues of scale are more complex than they first appear and are connected to the different ways in which oral historians and public historians approach the relationship between social memory and public memory. For David Glassberg, what distinguished the new scholarship on memory that had emerged by the mid-1990s among public historians was not subject matter but "approach." Instead of examining a single social group's understanding of its own past, the new approach was to understand "how various versions of the past are communicated in society through a multiplicity of institutions and media." In doing so he also suggested that a "problem of scale", so while autobiographical memory and reminiscence operates at "the most intimate of scales", public memory at the other.[52] Thus we have individual and public memory presented as opposites. Thinking about memory in this way is, however, problematic.

The chief conceit behind this binary construction is that public history frames, determined in some way or another, the way individuals and groups remember their pasts. Such an explanation offers a way of thinking about why some memories are more widely shared than others. It can explain what is remembered and why. Yet, as a number of oral historians have pointed out, individuals' understandings of the past are not simply constructed or constituted by public memory, public history, institutions, and media. Rather, by remembering in small social groups—such as families, work colleagues, and friends—individuals actively produce historical interpretations.[53] The process of remembering is influenced not only by public remembering but is also patterned by social structures, gender, generation, ethnicity, and ideological beliefs.

Accounts that contradict dominant public history narratives exist not only at an individual level but also within small social groups. Take, for example, the case of Winston Churchill. In both Britain and the United States, Churchill is normally portrayed in institutional and media histories as the pugnacious wartime leader who rallied a nation against Hitler's Germany.[54] And yet he has been remembered rather differently by various groups. Some people, such as those who lived in mining communities, presented him in recollection as a vicious opponent of workers' rights, especially in relation to the General Strike of 1926. Women in Dundee, where he had been an MP in the 1920s, portrayed him in memory as a drunkard and warmonger. And Polish émigrés in Britain remembered him as betraying Poland's interests during the Second World War in his appeasement of Stalin.[55]

It is also too easy to overstate the power of public discourse to silence individual or social recollections. Even when there are difficulties in recall as a result of recollections failing to fit accepted ways of remembering, these difficulties can be identified. Accounts that are uncertain, incomplete, unstable, faltering, and subsequently prove difficult to turn into neat transcription are some of the indications that an interview partner is having difficulty in recalling a past that does not have an existing narrative frame. We might see this as memory not only having difficulty in finding narrative expression but it may also be memory work in progress. After all, faltering recollection between people can lead to new discourses or "alternative frameworks," which in turn offer the possibility of oppositional accounts that challenge "official memory."[56]

Indeed, it could be argued that it remains one of the purposes of oral history to collect, consider, and understand alternative views of the past, and thereby challenge existing historical accounts. That such counterinterpretations exist is evidence that the influences of public history have limits even when associated with powerful forces. While Ludmilla Jordanova has noted that the state "lies at the heart of public history," Paul Ashton and Paula Hamilton have responded that the state is not monolithic: "Permissible pasts evolve over time given shifts in power and social and cultural change."[57] It might be argued that even before change, even prior to permission, oppositional accounts can be present.

While remembering might be often hidden from historians, the processes by which people recall the past together is a part of everyday life. As Kendall Phillips noted in *Framing Public Memory*, groups of individuals through remembering produce a memory of publics.[58] If the intimate or individual memory is simply juxtaposed with the influences of the public histories created by institutions and media, then the significance of the ways in which the past is interpreted and used within and between social groups can end up being understated. Even more importantly, the agency and ability to make new interpretations of the past by both individuals and the groups they belong to is likely to be ignored simply because they fail to be recognized as important by public historians who are attempting to fit individual memories into recognized public frames.

Toward a Public Oral History?

While oral historians are often eager to engage with their interviewees, even to the extent of sharing authority, what is less clear is the extent to which oral historians are willing to engage more broadly with the communities where interview partners and audiences are located. Public oral history could simply be an approach that uses oral history techniques. Or it could be something more. It could encompass not only the methods of oral history, but also its sensibilities and its connectivity to wider publics.

During the "turn toward memory," a critique of popular or community-based oral history developed that portrayed prevailing approaches as naïve or even mistaken. Both Luisa Passerini and the Popular Memory Group were rightly critical of oral historians who failed to connect their practice or methods to theoretical understandings of memory. Without such understandings, oral history was in danger of collapsing into nostalgia with recollections treated as self-evident, empirical truths, rather than socially constructed representations of the past that were being made in the present.[59]

While providing an important stimulus to oral history work, especially in relation to public history, such an evaluation may have had a less desirable impact on initiatives intended to extend oral history as a popular activity. It may have unintentionally supported the elitist view that only the qualified could interpret the past—the view that oral historians had originally set out to challenge. In any case, by the 1990s the drive to enable individuals and groups, especially those traditionally marginalized from the construction of knowledge, to create their own histories, was stalling.

It is worth recalling how significant community oral history was as a basis of activity. In the United States, a number of oral historians began their careers on community projects. This included Charles Hardy, a radio producer, oral historian, and author. The significance of the connection between oral history and community history becomes clear in his observation (speaking about coordinating a project in the late 1970s) that he "learned more about how people make sense of the history of their own communities—and about the range of their purposes."[60] In Britain, many oral historians experienced their first large projects on unemployment relief schemes during the recession of the 1980s. Government-sponsored projects also provided the material conditions that would promote oral history as a method that could be adopted in the wider community. This was especially important at a time when university history departments viewed oral history with suspicion and even hostility.

Community oral history has made significant contributions to how oral historians work in the public history sphere. But community-based practitioners have also influenced the theory and practice of oral history more broadly, including in academic settings. They did this in some instances through local museums. In South Africa, for example, social historians' rather limited use of oral history was challenged and transformed by the District Six Museum's expertise "in the cultural politics of oral memory."[61] A similar process can be identified in Britain with those oral historians who had gained experience in community-based projects later moving into heading up archives and teaching university-based programs. Additionally new partnerships have emerged between academics and nonacademics. One such joint venture between the Museum of London, London Metropolitan University, and fifteen different refugee organizations resulted in the Refugee Stories project.[62]

While the influence of community activity remains evident internationally, the training of wider publics in the use of oral history is less widespread. David Dunaway argued that:

> If historical understanding is to move beyond the library stacks, we must return it to those who created it. If history is to be more than a subject in classrooms and a few fine books, then those who practice history must find a way to share their enthusiasm with the public at large. That practice I'll call "public oral history."

But establishing such a program in the United States has proved challenging. In 2003, Dunaway was asked to find four oral historians who train members of the public at large. The task, he reported, "proved nearly impossible."[63]

In contrast, such programs have begun to emerge in other countries. In South Africa, the Centre for Popular Memory has developed a range of training courses.[64] But it is in Britain that the most systematic attempts can be found at establishing training programs intended to promote the use of oral histories at a community level. The Oral History Society has played a key role there by developing popular courses that introduce members of the public to the use of basic methods and practice, as well as theory, in community projects, turning oral history into theater, undertaking video interviews, and digitizing recordings.[65]

Interest in oral history training in Britain increased from 1994 on as a result of an increasingly large number of projects being funded by the Heritage Lottery Fund (HLF).[66] By 2007 the HLF claimed to have granted £49 million (approx. $75.5 million) to oral history projects.[67] By 2009 estimates suggested that this figure had risen to more than £60 million (approx. $92.5 million). Stuart Davies, a policy adviser to HLF, has pointed out that oral history projects "have an almost uniquely flexible ability to hit many HLF priorities and targets." This includes making strong community links and encouraging voluntary participation across a diverse range of people. In addition, HLF continues to celebrate oral history as a means of facilitating cross-cultural understanding as well as intergenerational communication. Davies has argued, "Oral history is generally a collaborative, socially interactive tool, particularly pertinent and accessible to village, community or neighborhood history or heritage groups."[68] All this remains especially important to a funding body sensitive to the variety of communities with which it is charged to engage.

Heritage Lottery Fund projects have included neighborhood oral histories, oral histories of disability (including sight loss and amputation), the state (including policing in Northern Ireland, by the Royal Ulster Constabulary George Cross Foundation), ethnicity, (including projects by Black History Consortium and the Bangladesh Women's Association), and sexuality (including queer histories from Birmingham, Nottingham, and Edinburgh). Projects involve volunteers, and most aim for a product that is accessible to interviewees and other community members. The outputs take a variety of forms: publications, exhibitions, plays, and audio, video, and Web-based presentations.[69]

Still, there are a number of challenges that arise from this activity. Above all else there needs to be a greater engagement in the key debates in oral history, especially around memory and narrative. A great deal of community oral history seems too ready to celebrate the past, rather than to think more critically about the ways in which interviewers and interviewees are constructing that past.

An associated problem is the way that the models of historical reconstruction that the public are offered by the media. High production values, which are challenging in themselves, are often matched by a rather simplistic view of history. Or as Jill Liddington noted:

> Yes, "the past is a foreign country"; they still "do things differently there." But increasingly... the popular past is presented as if it is just down the road, merely round the corner, just a finger tip away. No need for a passport or troublesome travel; you can just flick the TV switch, click on your mouse, browse on the History Channel, and you are instantly—frequently, pleasurably—*there*.[70]

In addition to these, there are strong arguments why a public oral history should include in its aims the development of training in collecting, interpreting, and presenting of oral testimonies in historical contexts. By doing so we would encourage critical thinking about how the past is understood and even challenge a type of public history that portrays audiences as essentially passive recipients, drifting through museums and galleries, absorbing media messages, quietly listening in classrooms.[71]

Because of its potential to democratize history, many were initially drawn to oral history in the 1970s.[72] Such an ideal is even more important in the twenty-first century. It is worth noting that some sociologists have come to a similar conclusion. Michael Burawoy, for one, has pointed out that large numbers of sociologists are working in community and local government settings outside of academic institutions.[73] Burawoy has also identified two types of public sociologist: traditionalist, and organic. While the traditional public sociologist *addresses* a broad, anonymous and often passive public, the organic public sociologist directly *engages* with more local publics that are active and are often engaged in activities that are contrary to the mainstream. Burawoy argues that both types must venture into the wider community to defend society against what he describes as "third-wave marketization." In this current historical period not only is labor bought and sold, and the volatility of financial markets protected by the state, as happened in the first and second waves of marketization, but, as Burawoy noted, nature—including land, other resources, environment, and our very bodies—has also become commodified in a more systematic way. This process is so widespread that it can be described as global. He argues that the lived experience of this third wave favors an organic public sociology. If Burawoy is right, it is also time for a public oral history—a public oral history best done with historical consciousness informed by an understanding of the relationship between public history and oral history.

NOTES

1. Jill Liddington, "What Is Public History? Publics and Their Pasts, Meanings and Practices," *Oral History* 30, no. 1 (2002): 83–93. In part this ambiguity arises from the ways in which "public history" has been used to describe both concepts and practices.

2. See, for example, the introduction to Public History Course by Michael Gordon at the University of Wisconsin, Milwaukee; http://www.uwm.edu/People/mgordon/hist700.html.

3. Valerie Yow, *Recording Oral History: A Guide for the Humanities and Social Sciences*, (Walnut Creek, Calif.: AltaMira Press, 2005), 144; Yow has also usefully explored in some detail the challenges faced in undertaking commissioned work (98–105).

4. Donald A. Ritchie, *Doing Oral History: A Practical Guide* (New York: Oxford University Press, 2003), 42. The English historian Arthur Marwick, in *The New Nature of History: Knowledge, Evidence, Language* (Basingstoke: Palgrave, 2001), defined public history in terms of audience although he questioned whether we need the term, of "American coinage," when "history is a social necessity" and preferred "applied history" to public history.

5. See Stephen L. Reckon, "Doing Public History: A Look at the How, But Especially the Why," *American Quarterly* 45, no. 1 (Mar. 1993): 188. Similarly Robert Kelley has claimed, "Public history refers to the employment of historians and historical method outside of academia," in Robert Kelley, "Public History: Its Origins, Nature, and Prospects," *Public Historian* 1 (1978): 16–28.

6. Philip V. Scarpino, "Some Thoughts on Defining, Evaluating, and Rewarding Public Scholarship," *Public Historian* 15, no. 2 (1993): 55–61.

7. As reported by Yow, *Recording Oral History*, 144.

8. Michael Frisch, A *Shared Authority: Essays on the Craft and Meaning of Oral and Public History* (Albany: State University of New York Press, 1990), 185.

9. Ludmilla Jordanova, *History in Practice* (London: Arnold, 2000), 156–62.

10. Frisch, *Shared Authority*, xx.

11. Daniel Kerr, "'We Know What the Problem Is': Using Video and Radio Oral History to Develop Collaborative Analysis of Homelessness," in *The Oral History Reader*, ed. Robert Perks and Alistair Thomson, 488 (London: Routledge, 2006).

12. See, for example, the issue of *Oral History Review* 30, no. 1 (2003).

13. Michael Frisch, "Sharing Authority: Oral History and the Collaborative Process," *Oral History Review* 30, no. 1 (2003): 111–13.

14. See, for example, Hilda Kean and Paul Ashton, eds., *People and Their Pasts: Public History Today* (Basingstoke: Palgrave Macmillan, 2009).

15. For example the journal has eclectically published Al Johnson, "Land of Laundries: An Oral History Installation," *Oral History* 26, no. 2 (1998); Annette Day, "Listening Galleries: Putting Oral History on Display," *Oral History* 27, no. 1 (1999); Stefan Szczelkun, "The Value of Home Movies," *Oral History* 28, no. 2 (2000); Charles Hardy, "Prodigal Sons and Painted Women: Some Reflections on Urban Folklore, Life Stories and Aural History," *Oral History* 29, no. 1 (2001); Rob Perks and Jonnie Robinson, "The Way We Speak: Web-based Representations of Changing Communities in England," *Oral History* 33, no. 2 (2005); Jill Liddington with Alan Dein and Mark Whitaker, "Listening to the Past on Radio," *Oral History* 35, no. 1 (2007); Sarah Housden and Jenny Zmroczek, "Exploring Identity in Later Life Through BBC People's War Interviews," *Oral History* 35, no. 2 (2007); and Steve Humphries, "Oral History on Television: A Retrospective, *Oral History* 36, no. 1 (2008).

16. Alistair Thomson, *Anzac Memories: Living With the Legend* (Oxford: Oxford University Press, 1994).

17. Cited in Melissa Nobles, *The Politics of Official Apologies* (Cambridge: Cambridge University Press, 2008), 103.

18. Stuart Macintyre, Anna Clark, and Anthony Mason, *The History Wars* (Melbourne: University Publishing, 2004).

19. Edward Tabor Linenthal and Tom Engelhardt, *History Wars: The Enola Gay and Other Battles for the American Past* (New York: Metropolitan Books, 1996). See also Jornanova, *History in Practice*, 156–59. Alternate historians write fictional "histories" and are similar, although usually less rigorously researched than counterfactual history. Known in France as *uchronie*, these "what if" histories explore such propositions as "what if the Japanese had pressed home their attack at Pearl Harbor," as in Newt Gingrich and William R. Forstchen, *Pearl Harbor: A Novel of December 8th* (New York: St. Martin's, 2007).

20. Macintyre, Clark, and Mason, *The History Wars*, 13.

21. Windschuttle speaking at the launch of his book *The Fabrication of Aboriginal History* in 2002 at the Tattersalls Club, Sydney. See http://www.sydneyline.com/Launch%20 speech.htm

22. Cited in Macintyre, Clark, and Mason, *The History Wars*, 45.

23. See, for example, Alessandro Portelli, "What Makes Oral History Different?" in Perks and Thomson, *Oral History Reader*, 32–53.

24. See, for example, Keith Jenkins, *On "What Is History?" From Carr and Elton to Rorty and White* (Oxon: Routledge, 1995), 16–21.

25. See Tony Bennett, *Outside Literature* (London: Routledge, 1991).

26. Winona Wheeler, "Reflections on the Social Relations of Indigenous Oral Histories," in *Walking a Tightrope: Aboriginal People and Their Representations*, ed. Ute Lischke and David T. McNab, 189–213 (Ontario: Wilfrid Laurier University Press, 2005).

27. Rachel Buchanan, "Decolonizing the Archives: The Work of New Zealand's Waitangi Tribunal," *Public History Review* 14 (2007). Michael Belgrave and Judith Binney have both been involved with the tribunal over a long period and both have experience of working in oral history. Michael Belgrave was the tribunal's former research manager and was the author of a hospital history, which was substantially based on oral histories, *The Mater: A History of Auckland's Mercy Hospital, 1900–2000* (Palmerston North: The Dunmore Publishing Company Ltd., 2000). Judith Binney was a member of the tribunal and has published on New Zealand's colonial past and on the experience of Maori individuals and communities. Her publications include "Bringing the Stories Back Home: Dialogues over 25 Years," in *Remembering: Writing Oral History*, ed. Anna Green and Megan Hutchin (Auckland: Auckland University Press, 2004).

28. J. L. Granatstein particularly objected to feminist and multicultural history in his *Who Killed Canadian History?* (Toronto: Harper Collins, 1998).

29. See Cham Muslim Students, *The 47 Essays About Their Parents' Experiences Under Democratic Kampuchea* (Documentation Center of Cambodia, 2007).

30. Lindsay DuBois, "Memories Out of Place: Dissonance and Silence in Historical Accounts of Working Class Argentines," *Oral History* 28, no. 1 (2000): 75–82. DuBois is drawing upon the Popular Memory Group's use of "subaltern" memory. The Group noted, "If this is history, it is history under extreme pressure and privations. Usually this history is held to the measure of private remembrance. It is not only unrecorded it is silenced. It is not offered the occasion to speak," in Popular Memory Group, "Popular Memory: Theory, Politics and Practice," in *Making Histories: Studies in History-Writing and Politics*, ed. Richard Johnson et al., 210 (Minneapolis: University of Minnesota Press, 1982).

31. Federico Guillermo Lorenz, "Argentina's Coup: Social Myth, Memory and History," *History Today* 54, no. 1 (January 2004).

32. See Janet Worrall's review of Rita Arditti's *Searching for Life: The Grandmothers of the Plaza De Mayo and the Disappeared Children of Argentina*, and Judy Maloof's *Voices of Resistance: Testimonies of Cuban and Chilean Women* in *Oral History Review* 28, no. 1 (2001): 153–57.

33. Renate Meyer, "Digitising African Oral Narratives in a Global Arena," in *Museums and the Web 2004: Proceedings*, ed. David Bearman and Jennifer Trant (Toronto: Archives and Museum Informatics, 2004) at http://www.archimuse.com/mw2004/papers/meyer/meyer.html.

34. Peter Read, international conference keynote address, "The Truth Which Will Set Us All Free: National Reconciliation, Oral History and the Conspiracy of Silence," *Oral History* 35, no. 1 (2007): 106.

35. The exhibition resulted in the publication of the book by Tim Smith, Rob Perks, and Graham Smith, *Ukraine's Forbidden History* (Manchester: Dewi Lewis Publishing, 1998).

36. See Graham Smith and Peter Jackson, "Narrating the Nation: The 'Imagined Community' of Ukrainians in Bradford," *Journal of Historical Geography* 25, no. 3 (1999): 367–87.

37. Donald A. Ritchie, "When History Goes Public," *Oral History* 29, no. 1 (2001): 92.

38. David Glassberg, "Public History and the Study of Memory," *Public Historian* 18, no. 2 (1996): 13.

39. Annette Day, "Displaying the Twentieth Century in Polish Museums, *Oral History* 32, no. 1 (2004): 92–93.

40. See Aviezer Tucker, *Czech History: The Coming Catharsis* (Transitions Online, Issue: 02/24/2009; http://www.ceeol.com/aspx/issuedetails.aspx?issueid=47dc3ae5-9234-4750-936a-65464031c0b8&articleId=0c4d5fe2-6c11-424c-b20c-74dc0dfde4bc).

41. See, for example, Molly Andrews, "One Hundred Miles of Lives: The Stasi Files as a People's History of East Germany, *Oral History* 26, no. 1 (1998): 24–31.

42. Yael Zerubavel, "Invented Tradition and Memory," in John R Gillis, *Commemoration: The Politics of National Identity* (Princeton, N.J.: Princeton University Press, 1994), 105–6.

43. The following description in part is inspired by Edward S. Casey, "Public Memory in Place and Time," in *Framing Public Memory*, ed. Kendall R. Phillips, 17–44 (Tuscaloosa: University of Alabama Press, 2004).

44. See, for example, Daniel M. Wegner, Toni Giuliano, and Puala T. Hertel, "Cognitive Interdependence in Close Relationships," in *Compatible and Incompatible Relationships*, ed. William J. Ickes (New York: Springer-Verlag, 1985). Within social remembering there are subprocesses such as transactive remembering.

45. See Graham Smith, "Beyond Individual/Collective Memory: Women's Transactive Memories of Food, Family and Conflict," *Oral History* 35, no. 2 (2007): 67–76.

46. See, for example, Alistair Thomson, Michael Frisch, and Paula Hamilton, "The Memory and History Debates: Some International Perspectives," *Oral History* 22, no. 2 (1994): 33–43; Alistair Thomson, "Four Paradigm Transformations in Oral History," *Oral History Review* 34, no. 1 (2007): 49–70.

47. Portelli, "What Makes Oral History Different?"

48. Luisa Passerini, "Work Ideology and Consensus under Italian Fascism," *History Workshop Journal* 8, no. 1 (1979): 82–108.

49. Paula Hamilton and Linda Shopes, eds., "Building Partnerships Between Oral History and Memory Studies," in *Oral History and Public Memories* (Philadelphia, Penn.: Temple University Press, 2008), vii.

50. Michael Frisch, "What Public History Offers, And Why It Matters," *Public Historian* 19, no. 2 (1997): 42.

51. While in recent years oral historians, especially those engaged in studying memory, have orientated toward the local, this has not always been the case. For

example, in the 1970s there were attempts at national oral histories, such as Ronald Fraser's *Blood of Spain: An Oral History of the Spanish Civil War* (London: Allen Lane, 1979) and Paul Thompson's *The Edwardians: The Remaking of British Society* (London: Weidenfield and Nicolson, 1975). Of course, neither book was discussing memory in the same depth as later oral histories would, but there are attempts at scaling up individual testimonies. In Fraser's case, Perks and Thomson comment on the attempt at composite autobiography "as remembered feeling and thought," Perks and Thomson, *Oral History Reader*, 82.

52. Glassberg, "Public History and the Study of Memory," 9–11.

53. Smith, "Beyond Individual/Collective Memory," 77–86.

54. See Stephen Mansfield's *The Character and Greatness of Winston Churchill: Hero in a Time of Crisis* (Nashville, Tenn.: Cumberland House Publishing, 2004).

55. See, for example, Alfred F. Havighurst, *Britain in Transition* (Chicago: University of Chicago Press, 1985); Smith, "Beyond Individual/Collective Memory," 77–86; and Fraser J. Harbutt, *The Iron Curtain: Churchill, America, and the Origins of the Cold War* (New York: Oxford University Press, 1988).

56. See Timothy G. Ashplant, Graham Dawson, and Michael Roper, eds., "The Politics of War Memory and Commemoration: Contexts, Structures and Dynamics," in *Commemorating War: The Politics of Memory* (London: Piscataway, 2004).

57. Paul Ashton and Paula Hamilton, "Places of the Heart: Memorials, Public History and the State in Australia since 1960," *Public History Review* 15 (2008).

58. Phillips, introduction to *Framing Public Memory*. Phillips contrasts this with what he calls the "publicness of memory," when groups are subjected to memories that are presented to them by institutions or the media.

59. Passerini, "Work Ideology and Consensus under Italian Fascism," Popular Memory Group, "Popular Memory: Theory, Politics and Practice," 205–52.

60. Charles Hardy, A People's History of Industrial Philadelphia: Reflections on Community Oral History and the Uses of the Past," *Oral History Review* 33, no. 1 (2006): 9. See also http://www.talkinghistory.org/hardy.html.

61. Ciraj Rassool, "Community Museums, Memory Politics and Social Transformation: Histories, Possibilities and Limits," in *Museum Frictions: Public Cultures/Global Transformations*, ed. Kratz Karp et al., 305 (Durham, N.C.: Duke University Press, 2007).

62. See Annette Day, "'They Listened to My Voice': The Refugee Communities History Project and Belonging: Voices of London's Refugees, *Oral History* 37, no. 1 (2009): 95–106 and http://www.refugeestories.org/

63. David K. Dunaway, "Public Oral History: Reflections on Educating Citizen-Historians, in *Preparing the Next Generation of Oral Historians: An Anthology of Oral History Education*, ed. Barry Lanman and Laura M. Wendling, 123 (Lanham, Md.: AltaMira Press. 2006).

64. See http://www.popularmemory.org.za/index.php?option=com_content&task=view&id=4&Itemid=3

65. Stephen Humphries commented on the use of video recordings by local groups in "Unseen Stories: Video History in Museums," *Oral History* 31, no. 2 (2003): 78. The training program was shaped in part by an earlier Oral History Society initiative of establishing regional representatives who were responsible for responding to inquiries from members of the public in localities across Britain and Northern Ireland. Almost all of these networkers are engaged in different types of public history. More details can be found on http://www.ohs.org.uk/index.php

66. See Stuart Davies, "A Million Before the Millennium: Oral History and the Lottery," *Oral History* 28, no. 1 (2000): 103–8; Stephen Hussey, "Bountiful Harvest? Oral History and the Local Heritage Initiative," *Oral History* 28, no. 2 (2000).

67. See http://www.hlf.org.uk/NR/rdonlyres/8AF513FD-A258-4114-A689-20D12199281D/0/OralHistoryFactsheetWEB.pdf

68. Davies, "A Million Before the Millennium," 107.

69. The HLF has produced a database of all funded projects in England that can be searched by key terms on their Web site: http://search.hlf.org.uk/English/GrantsDatabase/

70. Liddington, "What Is Public History?" 83–93.

71. George Lipsitz has usefully argued that audiences may neither be passive nor actively challenging, but might rather "negotiate" between what they are shown and their own beliefs, in *Time Passages: Collective Memory and American Popular Culture* (Minneapolis: University of Minnesota Press, 2001).

72. As Jordanova notes: "Although potentially a highly sophisticated technique, oral history can nonetheless be widely practised, and is, in a number of senses, a democratising approach to history." Jordanova, *History in Practice*, 53.

73. Michael Burawoy, "What Is To Be Done? Theses on the Degradation of Social Existence in a Globalizing World," *Current Sociology* 56, no. 3 (2008): 351–59.

BIBLIOGRAPHY

Frisch, Michael. *A Shared Authority: Essays on the Craft and Meaning of Oral and Public History*. Albany: State University of New York Press, 1990.

Hamilton, Paula, and Linda Shopes, eds. *Oral History and Public Memories*. Philadelphia, Penn.: Temple University Press, 2008.

Jordanova, Ludmilla. *History in Practice*. London: Arnold, 2000.

Kean, Hilda, and Paul Ashton, eds. *People and Their Pasts: Public History Today*. Basingstoke: Palgrave Macmillan, 2009.

Macintyre, Stuart, Anna Clark, and Anthony Mason. *The History Wars*. Melbourne: University Publishing, 2004.

Phillips, Kendall R., ed. *Framing Public Memory*. Tuscaloosa: University of Alabama Press, 2004.

CHAPTER 30

MOTIVATING THE TWENTY-FIRST-CENTURY STUDENT WITH ORAL HISTORY

GLENN WHITMAN

My evolution into an oral history educator began in a freshman historical methods course at Dickinson College, in Carlisle, Pennsylvania. One of the class projects required students to conduct an oral history interview, a historical process that I had known nothing about up to that point. My pre-collegiate history classes had been textbook-centered and lecture-oriented. They intrigued me but never fully allowed me to appreciate the value of what I was studying.

Like most inexperienced student oral historians, my first interview—with three Vietnam veterans at the Carlisle VFW Hall—was fraught with errors: moving through my questions too fast, failing to ask enough follow-up questions, not listening closely to each response, and struggling with the recording equipment. But I cannot overemphasize the extended significance of this experience for my career as an educator, and for the students I teach. What became clear to me since that first introduction to oral history was the unique ability of oral history to motivate and transform the learning experience. Educators can bring into the classrooms and programs of the twenty-first century a historical process once used by Thucydides to chronicle the Peloponnesian Wars, and use that process to challenge students with complex, real-world learning opportunities. When I went into pre-collegiate teaching, therefore, I hoped to empower my students to act and think like historians by introducing them to the most authentic, enduring, and meaningful work

I had done as a student, to give them the opportunity to become practicing oral historians.

Oral History in the Classroom

With the goal of making students think and act like historians, I devised a curriculum that included readings and discussions about what the job of a historian entails and what challenges they face the chronicling of the past. Such philosophical discussions of historical methodology should be apart of every history class, since they prepare students for their subsequent work as oral historians and signal that this class will be about more than covering factual content to be recalled in a test.

I start by asking the students to list the first ten names that come to their minds from U.S. history. Invariably, their lists are dominated by white men with names like Washington, Lincoln, and Kennedy. After we discuss these results, I ask students to consider who is missing from this list, to stretch their historical mindedness to include those uncelebrated persons and groups that were often excluded, or modestly covered in their textbooks. Each student-historian is then challenged to consider ways they can help balance what Clifford Kuhn has called, the "master narrative of history."[1]

This exercise is followed with a class reading and discussion of a portion of Barbara Tuchman's seminal book, *Practicing History*. Her chapter on "The Historian's Opportunity" discusses two types of historians: the professional "who has had graduate training leading to a professional degree and who practices within a university," and the amateur who is "outside the university without a graduate degree."[2] Since each brings a different perspective to the historical narrative, if recording history were left solely to the professional historian, far too many stories would be lost. To create the most inclusive history, the professionals and amateurs need each other. In this regard, oral history is unique in its ability to democratize the historical process. Oral history demands much more than pushing the record button and asking an interviewee to "Tell me your life story." With proper training, across disciplines from grade school to graduate school, and an array of individual experiences and abilities, students can conduct usable interviews. By training and then deploying student oral historians into the field, teachers give them the ability to encounter and uncover what Studs Terkel once called "the living repositories of our past." As historians in training, students can also play important roles in the research of professionals, as James Loewen has pointed out about his own work as a sociologist:

> Every passing year, sources die and events are forgotten, making important topics harder to research via oral history...so [educators] don't introduce your students to oral history only because it will make your courses more interesting—although it will. Don't do so only because it will be one of the most important learning experiences of their entire education—although it will. Also do it for me and for

> the legion of other social scientists and historians who will come upon your students' work ages hence—perhaps after you and they are gone—and will learn important things abut your community and how it was to live in what we, from our limited perspective, call modern times.[3]

The student-oral historian has many roles to play in the collection, preservation, and publication of the past and present for future generations, a revelation that emerges as they consider the variety of oral history projects being conducted at all levels. The Veterans History Project of the American Folklife Center of the Library of Congress actively seeks out students from middle school to graduate school to achieve its ambitious mission of "collecting the memories, accounts, and documents of war veterans and of those who served in support of them during World War I, World War II, and the Korean, Vietnam, and Persian Gulf wars." The only possible means to achieve this project's mission of preserving the experiences of 19 million American war veterans, of whom some1,500 die each day, has been to enlist the service of students.[4]

Before considering how an oral history project motivates students differently than other learning experiences, teachers must be convinced of its value as an educational methodology. The extent to which educators are willing and able to integrate oral history sources and projects into their classrooms or programs is largely dependent on time, scheduling, money, and the growing emphasis on national and state standardized testing. At minimum, all educators should be integrating passive, or ready-made, oral history sources into their curriculum "that expose students to oral history as a historical methodology as well as provide content for the curricular area of study."[5] Students are engaged by reading interviews because the historical actors become more real as opposed to the processed heroes students often encounter in their textbooks. Such sources provide another perspective when evaluating the past and are often more engaging because scholars have noted that the narrative form is the best medium "in which to contain, transmit, and remember important information."[6]

I introduce high school history students to "passive" oral history through a required summer reading of Studs Terkel's *My American Century*. Students are exposed to a broad representation of oral histories conducted by America's most prominent oral historian, a self-proclaimed "guerilla-journalist." Consequently, when we begin our study of the twentieth century, students often use Terkel's interviews to support their interpretations of events in the Great Depression, World War II, or the civil rights movement in America. Terkel's admission of his errors as an oral historian also humanizes the process for students because they will make mistakes similar to those of a prolific oral historian. Having students read and interpret oral histories such as Terkel's provides them with a standard of excellence in the field and a model for their own work, transforming the student learning experience and outlook on the past. In addition to Terkel's work, my students have read books such as *Bloods*, on the Vietnam War, or *The Fifties: A Women's Oral History*. Invariably, students find these sources as a refreshing as well as an engaging break from the textbook. What they begin to realize is that they can be Studs Terkel too.

Passive or ready-made oral history sources are the first step toward students becoming "active" oral historians through defined projects that could last a day, a semester, or an academic year. Active oral history involves questioning and listening to the "history makers" themselves. A check of Google or attendance at one of the Oral History Association's annual conferences (http://alpha.dickinson.edu/oha/) will highlight the growing number of "active" oral history projects at schools across the country and throughout the world. For example, Michael Brooks, a teacher at Suva Intermediate School in Bell, California, argues that his students' oral history interviews have "transformed his classroom." According to Brooks,

> My students learn to do research and to ask penetrating questions. They learn to listen, to transcribe, to edit, and to lay out a publication. They learn composition skills and some familiarity with tone, form, and audience. They are able to meet new people with ease and to make their way with confidence in communities, libraries, and other settings far from Bell Gardens. They gain recognition within the community, and they learn to respect the diversity of Bell Gardens as well as the story of their heritage as it is woven into the community history.[7]

Another school project, "Telling Their Stories: Oral History Archives Project," is an elective history class at the Urban School of San Francisco, where students conduct digital video-taped interviews with Holocaust survivors and Japanese American internees during World War II from the Bay area. The project's Web site—http://www.tellingstories.org—includes more than twenty hours of full-text and video. It serves as a model program for the collaboration between school and community as well as in the use of technology in the classroom. The program coordinator, Howard Levin, commented that "The program does not simply teach kids to make movies using computers. Rather, it seeks to empower youth leaders to develop digital literacy, workplace skills, creativity and positive civic values by promoting and honoring the contributions of older generations."

The North Coast California Rural Challenge Network Oral History Project—http://www.ncrn/org/projects/av/av_vov.html—evolved accidently because eight seventh-graders had a free period in their schedule. Their teacher, Mitch Mendosa, challenged them to turn the time into a meaningful project that could contribute to the school and community. After debating the possibilities, they created an Anderson Valley Oral History Project. In order to preserve the voices of the people they talked to, they learned how to use digital audio technology. Two years later they had completed *Voices of the Valley: Volume I*, a book and audio compact disc set. Similarly, in one of the poorest counties in Maryland, Dan Whetzel's students each year chronicle a specific period in the past and produce such books as *Reflections of the Silver Screen: A History of Allegany County Movie Theatres*. The teachers Judy Gulledge and her colleague Christine Capaci created an interdisciplinary oral history project with eighth-grade science and English students. They turned the interviews of residents of Smith and Tangier Islands in the Chesapeake Bay into a book, *Pennywinkle: Oral Histories from Tylerton, Smith Island in the Chesapeake Bay*. At Hampton High School, students in the After School Writers Club conducted interviews with longtime residents of Pittsburgh's Polish Hill community. Their work led to the publication of *Polish Hill Remembered.* Ken Woodard's high school students' oral history interviews have been combined with other historical sources and transformed into video documentaries shown on local public television. Daniel Kelin connects Hawaiian elementary and middle school students to their community through "an inquiry-driven project that uses oral history as its foundation and as an exciting way to explore and present them."[8]

Kerry McKibbin, a history and English teacher, was curious about how her eighth-grade students might "connect literature to the world around them" by using Harper Lee's *To Kill a Mockingbird* as an entry point into her teaching of oral history.[9] In the Shenandoah Valley Oral History Project, college students document the histories, stories, and perspectives of the marginalized populations of Virginia's Shenandoah Valley. This variety of projects represents the diverse opportunities available for students to engage directly with the living past and make their own meaningful contributions to the preservation of history.

Educators refer to this as "Project Based Learning" because it engages students in "learning knowledge and skills through an extended inquiry process structured around complex, authentic questions and carefully designed products and tasks."[10] Project Based Learning provides students a sense of ownership of their knowledge and skill acquisition as well as of their own confusion. It alters the often one-directional flow of information in the traditional classroom setting, with students collecting information on their own. The motivation for educators to bring an oral history project into their classroom or program is twofold: it allows them to invigorate their teaching and alters how students acquire critical content and skills; and, with the growing expectation that pre-collegiate students meet national and state standards of learning, an oral history project can exceed those standards because of the higher cognitive thinking it requires. While the research on the cognitive benefits of an oral history project in comparison to more traditional methods of teaching is limited, a study at an urban high school in Baltimore County, Maryland, concluded that "oral history did prove to be a legitimate method of teaching the course content of immigration and black history. This finding refutes critics who have made substantial and off-the-record comments that oral history is inferior, when compared to traditional instruction, for developing the cognitive domain of United States History."[11]

Oral history was an effective motivator when compared with traditional educational methodologies. The study pointed out that the strength of oral history was the way in which "students believed the method increased their participation and involvement in history," so that the increased affective attitude, acquired through oral history, assisted cognitive performance.[12]

Two educational theories particularly reinforced the value of an oral history project and helped define the essential knowledge, skills, and understanding students can gain from such work. Howard Gardner's identification of the "multiple intelligences" of students, and Benjamin Bloom's taxonomy, a systematic approach to studying the cognitive processes for the purpose of assessing learning outcomes,

Applying Gardner's Multiple Intelligences and Bloom's Taxonomy to An Oral History Project

	Interviewee Selection	Pre-Interview	Research/Content Background	Interview Questions	Interview Release Form Legal/ Ethical Issues	Interview	Transcription	Analysis/Interpretation	Products/Public Presentation	Archiving/Preservation	Oral History Method Training
Gardner's Multiple Intelligences											
Linguistic (syntax, phonology, semantics, pragmatics)	x	x				x	x		x		x
Musical (pitch, rhythm, timbre)	x	x	x			x	x		x		
Logical-Mathematical (number, categorization, relations)			x	x					x	x	x
Spatial (accurate mental visualization, mental transformation of images)			x	x		x			x		
Bodily-Kinesthetic (control of one's own body, control in handling objects)						x			x		x
Interpersonal (awareness of others' feelings, emotions, goals, motivations)		x		x	x	x	x	x	x	x	x
Interpersonal (awareness of one's own feelings, emotions, goals, motivations)	x	x	x	x		x	x	x	x		x
Naturalist (recognition and classification of objects in the environment)	x										
Bloom's Taxonomy											
Knowledge (of terminology; specific facts; ways and means of dealing with specifics. Is defined as the rememberings (recalling) of appropriate, previously learned information.)	x	x	x	x	x	x	x	x	x		x

Comprehension (Grasping (understanding) the meaning of informational materials.)	x	x	x	x	x	x	x	x		x
Application (The use of previously learned information in new and concrete situations to solve problems that have single or best answers.)			x		x			x	x	x
Analysis (The breaking down of informational materials into their component parts, examining (and trying to understand the organizational structure of) such information to develop divergent conclusions by identifying motives or causes, making inferences, and/or finding evidence to support generalizations.)	x	x	x		x	x	x	x		x
Synthesis (Creatively or divergently applying prior knowledge and skilvvtls to produce a new or original whole.)						x		x	x	x
Evaluation (Judging the value of material based on personal values/opinions, resulting in an end product, with a given purpose, without real right or wrong answers.)							x	x		x

both highlighted the value of an oral history project regardless of the ability levels or learning styles that exist in each classroom.[13] Few educational methods can match oral history, which requires a wide range of skills, in meeting each of the eight "multiple intelligences" identified by Gardner's *Multiple Intelligences: The Theory in Practice*. The chart on pages 454–455 measures how Gardner and Bloom's ideas fit into every potential phase of a student's work as an oral historian.

Through each phase of the oral history process, students develop and refine valuable primary- and secondary-source research skills. They work on their writing, editing, interviewing, active listening and questioning techniques, and their ability to analyze, interpret, and evaluate information. The oral history project encourages students to probe deeper into a topic that interests them while meeting, and often exceeding, state standards of learning. In the light of the sometime stifling nature standardized testing has in motivating educators to include an alternative assessment, such as an oral history project in their classroom, educators have to remind themselves "not to fall into the old trap that tells you that these guidelines and these skills can only be acquired by the use of the state-mandated workbooks and tests."[14]

What We Do: The American Century Oral History Project

Classroom oral history projects generally fall into one of two categories: those that focus on individual biographical/life review interviews, and those that deal with a particular theme, event, period, topic, or place. The American Century Oral History Project (ACP), conducted at St. Andrew's Episcopal School in Potomac, Maryland, since 1997, is unique in that it is perpetual. Each class of students adds to the rich collection of interviews archived in the school's library. The school places equal emphasis on the oral history process and product, two complementary educational goals. The decision to focus upon an expansive period—the twentieth century—as opposed to a specific event or narrower time frame, which most school oral history projects adopt, allows students greater flexibility to pursue their own areas of interest. As one student once commented, "I think that the Oral History Project was one of the first times that I was ever challenged with the freedom of selecting a topic, actively pursuing that interest, then individually refining the results into a manageable product that could be handed in. Because the project was self-driven from start to end, we had a chance to truly own the project." As students' research, they become "experts" in their topic. When the class arrives at that point of our study of U.S. history, the students become, in essence, co-teachers for that segment. Although each interview provides only a snapshot of a particular period or event from one individual's perspective, when combined with the collection of interviews generated over the years, a very broad and deep history of the American Century emerges.

The project is integrated into a U.S. history survey course in which national themes of race, war, culture, and politics have led students to interview some prominent individuals, given the school's close proximity to Washington, D.C. However, many of the students look beyond their initial desire to secure an interview with the most famous person possible by conducting interviews on events and with persons of local rather than national interest. This decision often emerges out of a student's realization—with a small push from their teacher—that they can contribute more to the records of state and local historical institutions if their interviews complement, supplement, or fill in the missing gaps of an institution's collection that might lack orally communicated historical sources.[15] This collection of interviews serves as an important reminder to them of how people shape their community and the relationship between individual lives and dominant, sometimes impersonal, historical narratives.

The following outline highlights each phase of "The American Century Oral History Project" and illustrates how each part contributes to a historically reliable and valid interview. Throughout the process students not only develop all of the skills required of a historian but advance toward preparing a bound copy of their work for public presentation, an institutional archive, and publication on the Internet.

Oral History Method Training

This method allows students to understand the challenges associated with oral history as a historical methodology. This training begins when students discuss their summer reading of Studs Terkel's *My American Century* at the beginning of the school year and continues after reading portions of Donald A. Ritchie's manual on *Doing Oral History* just prior to the project's introduction in early November. Method workshops for interviewee selection, interview preparation, transcription techniques, and legal requirements take place during the course of the project, which lasts for four months. Students apply their evolving understanding of the oral history process in a mini-interview and transcription, which takes place over two nights and are titled "Days of Infamy" and focuses on one individual's remembrances of December 7, 1941, November 22, 1963, and September 11, 2001.

Interviewee Selection

Students are responsible for selecting an individual of no relation to interview about a particular period or event in American history, a formidable, yet enriching, task for most students. The objective is to take students out of their comfort zone by requiring them to interview a non-family member. While students are initially eager to conduct an interview with prominent individuals living in the area, these people have usually been interviewed before. However, students are strongly encouraged to conduct interviews with those uncelebrated persons who will never make it into the headlines or the textbook. Interviewees must be willing to sign a release form that allows access to recordings, transcripts, electronic publications, and additional materials, though restrictions can be attached. Over the years, permission to publish transcripts on the Internet has been an important addition to the release. Without a release, interviews would be inaccessible.

Biography

Students develop a one-page biography (with photograph) that provides a sense of the interviewee's background and a biographical context to more deeply understand the interview.

Historical Contextualization

After securing an interviewee, students are responsible for a research paper, approximately seven to ten pages in length, that examines primary- and secondary-source documents related to their topic. This paper establishes a context for better understanding the interview. Students are expected to include in their source selection "newspapers of the day" as well as what leading historians say about the period, event, or person the interview covers. Requiring students to conduct in-depth research into their subject allows them to become "experts" on a particular period or event and provides them with a context for developing interview questions. Throughout the project, students are constantly reminded that they can never do enough research in preparation for their interviews, but they also need to be able to decide when to stop. As the historian Barbara Tuchman once said: "One must stop *before* one has finished; otherwise, one will never stop and finish."[16]

Interview and Transcription

Each interview is expected to last approximately one hour, which usually takes about six hours to transcribe—often the most dreaded part of the project for students. Prior to the interview, students use their research to formulate a logically ordered set of questions that are refined during a conference with the teacher. Even with a list of prepared questions, the unpredictability of an oral history interview challenges students to think on their feet by developing follow-up questions for clarification or further exploration. An important skill developed in this phase is listening, which allows students to ask what Donald Ritchie once explained to my students was one of the most important follow-up questions: "I didn't know that, can you tell me more?" Students are required to transcribe the entire interview as well as to provide an audio/video time indexing log.

Historical Analysis

A student's ability to determine the historical value of their interview is an essential skill in training them to think like historians. It also teaches students to analyze the strengths and weaknesses of oral history as a historical methodology. Students are required to determine where their interview fits into the existing history that they uncovered in their historical context and how it might add or detract from an overall understanding of the American past. Students examine questions as to whether their interview was biased, if it shed new light on a particular period or event, and whether it complements or contradicts the research they collected prior to conducting their interview. Students are also expected to examine their own biases and how their place in time, and what historian Arthur Schlesinger Jr. called "unconscious preconceptions," might have fostered certain questions and responses.[17] They begin the analysis of their interview by completing the "Written Document Analysis Worksheets" from the National Archives (http://www.archives.gov).

Final Product

Each student submits two bound copies of his or her project as well as the interview recordings. One copy is archived, the other is graded and returned. An additional copy is also made and given to the interviewee. Each bound copy includes: A Statement of Purpose, Biography (with photograph), Historical Contextualization, Transcription, Historical Analysis, and Works Consulted.

Public Presentation

At the end of the project students must present their interview to a general audience that includes their parents and their interviewees at an annual Oral History Coffeehouse. This evening event celebrates the work of the student oral historians and celebrates the lives of those they interviewed. Over the years, students have transformed their interviews into poster exhibits, one-act plays, PowerPoint presentations, and even interpretive dance, which they share with the community at the Coffee House. Their interviews are also posted on a Web site (http://www.mdch.org)—with written permission from the interviewees–giving them a world-wide audience.

The time committed to this project is a deterrent for most educators. By matching all phases of the ACP with the California academic standards, one can see how such an alternative assessment can meet, and exceed, state standards of learning.

Matching California Historical and Social Science Skills (Grade Nine Through Twelve) to an Oral History Project*

	Interviewee Selection	Pre-Interview	Research/Content Background	Interview Questions	Interview Release Form Legal/ Ethical Issues	Interview	Transcription	Analysis/Interpretation	Products/ Public Presentation	Archiving/ Preservation/ Publication	Oral History Method Training
Chronological and Spatial Thinking											
1. Students compare the present with the past, evaluating the consequences of past events and decisions and determining the lessons that were learned.	x	x	x	x		x	x	x	x		
2. Students analyze how change happens at different rates at different times; understand that some aspects can change while others remain the same; and understand that change is complicated and affects not only technology and politics but also values and beliefs.			x	x		x	x	x	x		
3. Students use a variety of maps and documents to interpret human movement, including major patterns of domestic and international migration, changing environmental preferences and settlement patterns, the frictions that develop between population groups, and the diffusion of ideas, technological innovations, and goods.			x	x		x	x	x	x		
4. Students relate current events to the physical and human characteristics of places and regions			x								
Historical Research, Evidence, and Point of View											
1. Students distinguish valid arguments from fallacious arguments in historical interpretations.			x	x		x	x	x			x
2. Students identify bias and prejudice in historical interpretations.	x	x	x	x		x	x	x			x
3. Students evaluate major debates among historians concerning alternative interpretations of the past, including an analysis of author's use of evidence and the distinctions between sound generalizations and misleading oversimplifications.			x	x		x		x			

4. Students construct and test hypotheses; collect, evaluate, and employ information from multiple primary and secondary sources; and apply it in oral and written expression.			x	x	x	x	x	x	x		
Historical Interpretation											
1. Students show the connections, casual and otherwise, between particular historical events and larger social, economic, and political trends and developments.			x	x		x		x	x		
2. Students recognize the complexity of historical causes and effects, including the limitations on determining cause and effect.		x	x	x		x		x	x		x
3. Students interpret past events and issues within the context in which an event unfolded rather than solely in terms of present day norms and values.			x	x		x		x	x		x
4. Students understand the meaning, implication, and impact of historical events and recognize that events could have taken other directions.			x	x		x		x			
5. Students analyze human modifications of landscapes and examine the resulting environmental policy issues.	x		x	x		x	x	x	x		
6. Students conduct cost-benefit analyses and apply basic economic indicators to analyze the aggregate economic behavior of the U.S. economy.			x					x			

[1] *History-Social Science Standards for California Public Schools: Kindergarten Through Grade Twelve.* Adopted by the California State Board of Education, October 2000.

The Twenty-first-Century Student

The most challenging questions facing educators today are what skills and knowledge will students need to compete in the twenty-first-century world, and how should they reshape the curriculum to support those critical skills? Within the first decade of this century, three books—Daniel Pink's *A Whole New Mind,* Tony Wagner's *The Global Achievement Gap,* and Howard Gardner's *Five Minds for the Future*—have challenged educators and schools to develop curricula that prepare students for the world they will inherit. They rightfully ask schools to rethink how to teach a generation that has grown up with a vastly different outlook on the world, work, and their abilities.

The twenty-first-century student is restless and eager to utilize the latest technological tools, from iPods to digital recorders, to advance their learning. They are "digital babies," and when asked to apply this knowledge and skills to their learning, their curiosity, commitment, and initiative are enhanced. Unfortunately, their creativity and ingenuity are too often stifled in the classroom. The first word many students associate with history classes is "boring." Such characterizations leave educators perplexed, since few disciplines can match history in the richness of material and utility for living in the present.

The twenty-first-century student arrives in our classes with a shorter attention span, an uncanny ability to multitask, and a need to find meaning in his or her academic requirements. While they are consumers of information, they are equally comfortable as producers, using YouTube and Facebook to "publish" their own work. As Rob Fried, a former teacher, has pointed out, "They are motivated by what interests them and are craving opportunities to do more intellectually challenging and creative work."[18] For too long they have experienced only teacher-directed learning while the world around them promotes a greater exchange of ideas, along with personal and virtual collaboration. They are the most connected generation in history. Along with their teachers, they also face a higher level of accountability than previous generations for what they learn through national and state assessments of learning.

Ironically, oral history, possibly the oldest method of recording the past, is well suited for the twenty-first-century classroom and its students. Educators have examined "Senses" (Daniel Pink), "Survival Skills" (Tony Wagner), and "Minds" (Howard Gardner), all of which are critical for a twenty-first-century student's future success. An oral history project is unique in its ability to meet all of these twenty-first century mind-sets (see table 3). When one employer was asked what qualities he most wanted in a potential employee, he declared, "I look for someone who asks good questions…I want people who can engage in good discussion—who can look me in the eye and have a give and take."[19] The ability to ask good questions and engage in discussion are central to the oral history process and highlight an oral history project's value as a twenty-first-century educational methodology, particularly in an age where computer networking has replaced the face-to-face conversation that remain critical in the work environment.

The twenty-first-century student brings new strengths and weaknesses to an oral history project. While members of the "Net Generation" are virtually "connected," they lack experience making the in-person, face-to-face connections that are the essence of an oral history interview. They struggle with listening skills and have difficulty asking probing questions. An oral history project allows students to develop exactly those skills. Daniel Goleman's work on emotional intelligence indicates how an oral history project can develop much more than a student's cognitive ability. Emotional intelligence is essential for the oral historian as it is a social skill that features quite prominently throughout each phase of the oral history project process. According to Goleman, emotional intelligence includes self-awareness, self-regulation, motivation, empathy, and social skills. Because one's emotional intelligence is not fixed at birth, an oral history project provides an important opportunity for students to acquire these skills, which have been identified as equally important in determining future success as IQ.[20]

For all the value that twenty-first-century students find in the material they collect through oral history interviews, far too many pre-collegiate oral history projects end with a completed transcript. They are rarely archived for future research.

Skills for the 21st Century

A Whole New Mind: Why Right-Brainers Will Rule the Future by Daniel Pink (2006)	*Five Minds for the Future* by Howard Gardner (2007)	*The Global Achievement Gap: Why Even Our Best Schools Don't Teach the New Survival Skills Our Children Need—and What We Can Do About It* by Tony Wagner (2008)
"Six Senses"	"Five Minds"	"Seven Survival Skills"
1. Design	1. Disciplined Mind	1. Critical Thinking and Problem Solving
2. Story-Telling	2. Synthesizing Mind	2. Collaboration Across Networks and Leading by Influence
3. Empathy	3. Creating Mind	3. Agility and Adaptability
4. Play	4. Respectful Mind	4. Initiative and Entrepreneurialism
5. Symphony	5. Ethical Mind	5. Effective Oral and Written Communication
6. Meaning		6. Accessing and Analyzing Information
		7. Curiosity and Imagination

Bolded "Senses," "Minds," and "Skills" are met through an oral history project depending on the learning objectives.

In a growing number of schools across the country, however, students are doing more than transcribing their interviews. They are converting their interviews into museum exhibits, short plays, and historical documentaries (using software such as iMovie and Final Cut). Hip Hop artists Jay-Z and Fort Minor have incorporated oral history interviews into such songs as "December 4" and "Kenji." The song "December 4" begins with a quote from Jay-Z's mother in her own voice and focuses on important events in the artist's life. "Kenji" uses live voices of Japanese Americans to highlight their imprisonment during World War II.[21] Students are finding innovative ways to adapt oral history to the language they speak. Their comfort with bringing sound to the Web allows them to bring to life their interview in ways a transcript cannot. "Published" projects on the Internet can include both the transcription and audio. Individual voices differentiate oral history from other historical methodologies and twenty-first-century technology, along with the twenty-first-century student, will make the voices of the past more prominent and more accessible, restoring aurality to oral history.

In the case of the American Century Oral History Project, if it were not for the technological skills of students, and their desire to apply those skills to their learning, then the more than 750 interviews collected since 1997 would be inaccessible to researchers as well to the interviewees who wanted to share their stories. Students designed and built its Web site (http://www.americancenturyproject.org). The virtual archive (http://www.mdch.org) that makes nearly the project's entire collection available online was digitized and uploaded by motivated students who are more at ease with such technology and who saw the value of sharing their work with the world.

Motivating the Twenty-first-Century Student

When educators are motivated to enrich their teaching through oral history, the next challenge becomes how to motivate students who will be asked to work harder and think differently as oral historians. Usually, the most authentic opportunity for students to think like a historian comes through writing a research paper, which will be read by an audience of one—the teacher—and is complete once it earns a grade. With an oral history project, the research paper is just an early step in a process that engages students in many dimensions and can potentially bring their work to a wide public audience. Educators who assign students a project that empowers them with their own learning and challenges them to make a permanent contribution to the historical record will see a different approach to learning regardless of a student's ability and interest. Howard Levin, who directs "Telling Their Stories" (http://www.tellingstories.org), has said that students using oral history "have a very clear sense of the importance of their work due to the permanent nature of their production. For many of our students the result moves far beyond the question of whether or not the work is more highly motivating. The work is truly meaningful, deeply felt, and fully understood by the students as vitally important. They are naturally motivated, motivation is not the problem in this case, and not the primary outcome, but rather priding work that has authentic meaning sure beyond the classroom."

Another educator commented: "I've felt that oral history allows students to have direct involvement in the creation of history. If taught well—to get students to buy into the project—students can see that history is active, current, alive not static, boring, and dead." When assessing the value of an oral history project one St. Andrew's Episcopal School student said:

> The oral history project stood out among all my other high school learning experiences because it was unique in its completeness. It wasn't just an interview, or just a research paper, or just a biography. It was each of those things and in combining them together, we created a story that helped us to understand the great story of history. We weren't just learning a lesson in school, we were learning empathy and emotion, fear and elation and despair. History became personalized—the Holocaust survivor was not defined solely as a survivor, but also as a mother, a writer, and a Romanian American, not just a number, but a living, breathing person. The politician was not just an ambitious hypocrite, but a person with a family and his own struggles. The African American civil rights' advocate's experiences with discrimination were not confined to the 1960s. The oral history project gave us the world in a sense, and taught us that everyone has a story.

Begin an oral history project by providing students an opportunity to choose their topics and/or interviewee, a process that "returns responsibility for learning to the student."[22] Students should understand that for an oral history project, there are some guidelines and restrictions. In particular, a potential interviewee must be available and (in the case of our project) not a family member. Selecting their interviewees or interview topics empowers students. One student combined his interests in baseball and civil rights. While the modern civil rights movement receives significant coverage in the standard history curriculum, baseball receives scant coverage except for a mention of Jackie Robinson. The student secured an interview with Ernest Burke, who had once played in the Negro Leagues. The student found that "staying unemotional and focused on my questions was difficult as Mr. Burke discussed the most intimate details of his childhood and that pain, suffering, and humiliation of discrimination in segregated America. However, once we started discussing the Negro Leagues and baseball, I became more comfortable and realized that our mutual passion for the game transcended our age and other differences." Beyond giving the student a chance to pursue his passions, the interview took on additional importance when Ernest Burke died a few months later. The interview is now in the National Baseball Hall of Fame in Cooperstown, New York.

Another student was interested in the 1969 Stonewall Riots in Greenwich Village, in Manhattan, which she could not find in her textbook. She tracked down

Warren Allan Smith, traveled to New York City, and conducted her interview with him. One self-declared feminist interviewed a 1950s housewife. She reported that her interview totally contradicted her research and perceptions: "I could not understand why this woman did not hate staying at home raising five children with no career or educational opportunities. I thought that I had done something wrong. What I learned, however, is that her story was one that had [rarely] been told. I told her story."

Even without direction from teachers, most students understand the value of oral history as primary source material. Across the United States each year, students participating in the National History Day contest create a "convergence of evidence" in their presentations by incorporating oral history interviews. When one contestant was asked her method for securing an interview with former Los Angeles Dodger manager Tommy Lasorda, for a project on Jackie Robinson, she replied, "I dialed information, got his number, and called him." Another St. Andrew's Episcopal student, when asked, "In what ways does an oral history project motivate you differently than other learning opportunities?" replied:

> The oral history project motivated me because it was real. The student who has studied physics, chemistry, and math thrills when he realizes that he can use these skills to build a suspension bridge, but this practical application rarely appears until college or afterward. Our projects, like the suspension bridge, had a purpose. We had the chance to preserve a story that might have disappeared untold. The oral history project enabled us to be not just students, but historians. That gave us a professional level that we strove to achieve and found that we could.

Most academic activity involves two people, the student and the teacher. What makes an oral history project different from other types of learning opportunities is that it brings in another player, the interviewee. The students now bear the responsibility of preserving the story of that person's life. A unique aspect of a student-driven oral history project is the role each of the major participants—educator, student interviewer, and interviewee—plays in the project. Each brings a degree of authority, all of which is essential to ensuring the quality and utility of the final product. By its nature, oral history is then a shared experience between interviewer and interviewee.[23]

One of the strongest motivating factors for students is the realization that they are not just preserving a record of someone's life, but that they are doing so potentially for future research use. At the beginning of the project, I highlight the professional nature of the students' work by distributing the Oral History Association's Principles and Standards. Realizing that they are doing the work of "professionals" enhances the students' commitment to the project. They also read Charles Morrissey's "Asking Hard Questions: Harvey the Historian as Colleague."[24] Morrissey reminds them to ask the questions—especially the controversial ones—that future historians would have wanted to ask interviewees who are no longer present. The student is doing oral history today for the historians of tomorrow.

An especially rewarding factor in an oral history project is the opportunity for students to use their emerging skills as historians to give something back to their communities, by making people feel that their personal history is worthwhile. In the end, an oral history project offers a "real-world component" by involving the community, and that motivates students to want to acquire the academic skills to produce that product.[25]

As one of my students at St. Andrew's Episcopal School commented:

> The aspect that I find the most satisfying about the oral history project is that we as students make a difference in our communities and societies by preserving stories and perspectives that in most cases would otherwise be left untold and unwritten. It felt rewarding to provide my interviewee with a substantive report about himself and what he witnessed. He had not been interviewed before and he was touched that what he had to say was being preserved. Human behavior dictates that every person brings a unique perspective to what they witness.

The Rich Narrative of History

James Baldwin once declared that the history of the United States "is longer, larger, more various, more beautiful, and more terrible than anything anyone has ever said about it."[26] Too often, the experience most students have in their history classes does not reflect this rich narrative. With the guidance of dedicated educators, however, students can see history more fully. In 2000, a St. Andrew's Episcopal School student interviewed an individual about his military service in Europe during World War II. Eight years later, in order to get legal permission to add the interview to the school's online collection, a copy of the transcript was sent to the interviewee and his wife. She returned the permission to upload the project along with a letter that highlighted the value of the project:

> As soon as the transcript arrived I read it to my husband, and it jogged his memory at a time when it badly needs jogging. He has Alzheimer's disease and doesn't remember much. But he did recall some of the things he spoke about in the interview and was pleased to think again about this very important time in his life. I, in turn, was happy to see that, at least for a time, he was quite responsive.

At the end of the project, students reflect on their initial—and possibly only—experience of being oral historians. Many acknowledge the power of oral history "to captivate the imagination and to inspire emotion."[27] Doing interviews brought meaning and purpose to their school work. One student's reflection continues to motivate me as an educator:

> Looking back, it seems to me that the oral history project was unique not only because it allowed for an alternative perspective on history, but also because it demanded a significant amount of individual initiative and independent thought. Much more so than other high school assignments. Taking a tape recorder out

into the "field," prepared, yet ultimately vulnerable, cemented the transformation from high school student to oral historian.

If all our students leave our classrooms thinking like that, we will have done more than train the next generation of oral historians. We will have trained the next generation of mindful citizens.

NOTES

1. *New York Times*, Mar. 26, 1997.
2. Barbara Tuchman, *Practicing History* (New York: Ballantine Books, 1981), 57.
3. James Loewen, foreword to *Dialogue with the Past: Engaging Students and Meeting Standards through Oral History*, by Glenn Whitman (Walnut Creek, Calif.: AltaMira Press, 2004), x.
4. http://www.loc.gov/vets/
5. Barry A. Lanman and Laura M. Wendling, *Preparing the Next Generation of Oral Historians: An Anthology of Oral History Education* (Lanham, Md.: AltaMira Press, 2006), ix.
6. David Kennedy, "The Art of the Tale: Story-Telling and History Teaching," *History Teacher* 31 (May 1998): 318.
7. Michael Brooks, "Long, Long Ago: Recipe for a Middle School Oral History Program," *OAH Magazine of History* 11 (Spring 1997): 32.
8. Daniel A. Kelin II, *To Feel as Our Ancestors Did: Collecting and Performing Oral Histories* (Portsmouth, N.H.: Heinemann, 2005).
9. *Linking Literature: Using Oral History to Connect Books to the World* (New York: The Student Press Initiative, 2004), ix.
10. Thorn Markham, John Larmer, and Jason Ravitz, *Project Based Learning Handbook: A Guide to Standards-Focused Project Based Learning for Middle and High School Teachers*, 2nd ed. (Novato: Calif.: Buck Institute for Education, 2003), 4.
11. Barry Lanman, "Oral History as an Educational Tool for Teaching Immigration and Black History in American High Schools: Findings and Queries," *International Oral History Review* (June 1987): 128.
12. Lanman, "Oral History," 129–30.
13. Ibid., 134.
14. Eliot Wigginton and Christopher Crawford, "Foxfire and the Educational Mainstream," in *The Past Meets the Present: Essays on Oral History*, ed. Rebecca Sharpless and David Stricklin, 101–18 (Lanham, Md.: University Press of America, 1988). Available at Baylor University's Institute for Oral History's Workshop on the Web http://www3.baylor.edu/Oral_History/pmp%20webpage/pmp.htm.
15. Barbara Allen and William Lynwood Montell, *From Memory to History: Using Oral Sources in Local Historical Research* (Nashville, Tenn.: American Association for State and Local History, 1981), 3, 15.
16. Barbara Tuchman, *The Guns of August* (New York: Ballantine Books, 1962), xi.
17. Arthur M. Schlesinger, "History as a Weapon," in *The Disuniting of America: Reflections on a Multicultural Society* (New York: W. W. Norton and Company, 1998), 52.

18. Tony Wagner, *The Global Achievement Gap: Why Even the Best Schools Don't Teach the New Survival Skills Our Children Need—and What We Can do About It* (New York: Basic Books, 2008), 169–70.

19. Ibid., 1–2.

20. Daniel Goleman, *Emotional Intelligence: Why It Can Matter More Than IQ?* (New York: Bantam Books, 1997).

21. Mark Naison, "Hip Hop and Oral History: Turning Students into 'Griots' for a New Age," *Magazine of History* 22, no. 3 (July 2008): 46–48.

22. Mary Tedrow, "Best Practices: The Miracle of Choices," *Teacher Magazine*, http://www.teachermagazine.org/tm/articles/, May 5, 2008.

23. Ronald J. Grele, *Envelopes of Sound: The Art of Oral History* (New York: Praeger, 1991), xv.

24. Charles Morrissey, "Asking Hard Questions: Harvey the Historian as Colleague. *OHA Newsletter* (Fall 2004): 8.

25. Barbara Combs and Christy Stevens with Linda Koch, eds., *Considering Assessment and Evaluation: A Foxfire Teacher Reader* (Mountain City, Ga.: The Foxfire Fund, Inc., 1999), 109. See also *From Thinking to Doing: Constructing a Framework to Teach Mandates Through Experience-Based Learning, Considering Reflection*, and *Considering Imagination and Creativity*, available through Foxfire Inc. at http://www.foxfire.org.

26. James Baldwin, "A Talk to Teachers," *Saturday Review*, Dec. 21, 1963.

27. This phrase is taken from Doris Kearns Goodwin's *Team of Rivals. The Political Genius of Abraham Lincoln* (New York: Simon and Schuster, 2005), xix. Goodwin is describing the compelling story of Lincoln, which she researched using primary sources that included oral history interviews collected following Lincoln's assassination.

BIBLIOGRAPHY

Kelin, Daniel A., II. *To Feel as Our Ancestors Did: Collecting and Performing Oral Histories.* Portsmouth, N.H.: Heinemann, 2005.

Lanman, Barry A., and Laura M. Wendling. *Preparing the Next Generation of Oral Historians: An Anthology of Oral History Education.* Lanham, Md.: AltaMira Press, 2006.

Markham, Thorn, John Larmer, and Jason Ravitz. *Project Based Learning Handbook: A Guide to Standards-Focused Project Based Learning for Middle and High School Teachers.* Novato, Calif.: Buck Institute for Education, 2003.

Wagner, Tony. *The Global Achievement Gap: Why Even the Best Schools Don't Teach the New Survival Skills Our Children Need—and What We Can Do About It.* New York: Basic Books, 2008.

Whitman, Glenn. *Dialogue with the Past: Engaging Students and Meeting Standards Through Oral History.* Walnut Creek, Calif.: AltaMira Press, 2004.

CHAPTER 31

ORAL HISTORY IN UNIVERSITIES: FROM MARGINS TO MAINSTREAM

JANIS WILTON

WHEN I stumbled into the beginnings of my life as an oral historian in the late 1970s, in Australia, oral history was primarily an activity that happened outside universities. When pursued within universities, it was considered a fairly unsophisticated method for research projects. My own initiation came as a research assistant on a project to record the experiences of European refugees who had made their way to Australia in the years immediately preceding and following the Second World War. I went to my first interview armed with a tape recorder, some background on the topic, and no specific training in oral history. That initiation was not unusual since at the time there was limited, if any, oral history training offered at universities in Australia. There was also a deep skepticism directed at oral history by some academic historians.[1] For those who did venture into the field, it was often with the belief that oral history interviewing was simply about asking questions and recording answers. It was seen as, after all, "just common sense."[2]

The skepticism—though now both more refined and more filtered—and the commonsense view can still be found within universities.[3] However, the growth in university oral history courses, research projects, archives and other activities, their diversity and innovative nature, and the burgeoning literature on the teaching of oral history in tertiary institutions all suggest that oral history has moved from the margins to the mainstream, and that it is recognized as grounded in complex and sophisticated theories and methods.

There is now a richness of oral history in universities, in Australia and elsewhere, that deserves exploring: its different practices and approaches adopted across disciplines, its literature, and its impact on students, staff, and on the relations between universities and their surrounding communities. In considering the role of oral history in universities past, present, and future, this survey makes no claims to be exhaustive or comprehensive and is limited by a focus primarily on English-language literature and on the programs, networks, and examples with which I am familiar, including my own teaching and learning practices.[4] It aims, however, to provide an overview of key achievements, issues, strategies, and challenges, and to provoke thinking about ongoing and future issues, strategies, and concerns.

A note on terminology: a single unit of study (lasting for one or two semesters) is described as a course; a series of courses (usually toward a degree) is described as a program; and teaching staff are described as staff or teachers.

Oral History Courses

In 1973, the new University of Papua New Guinea (established in 1966) created a sequence of oral history courses. As Roderic Lacey explained, the impetus came from a variety of directions. There was the reality that for the majority of the population, oral sources were the only means to document and access their experiences and histories. The documentary sources, as in other colonized nations, were those of the colonizers. There was a recognition that the students attending the university were being educated within a Western tradition that was moving them away from village life and, consequently, away from the value of oral sources and oral traditions. There was also the specific trigger of a visit from "an African scholar" who had conducted staff seminars in oral history. There were some misgivings that oral history might be seen as somehow different to and separate from history, but the decision was made to initiate courses that required students to learn by doing.[5] The features and learning outcomes of the courses, as described by Lacey, included balancing content and practice, the importance of training, learning by experience, awareness of the value of oral sources, respect for others, an appreciation of different worldviews, publishing student work, creating an archive, and closer relations between the university and the communities from which its students came.[6]

The University of Papua New Guinea was an early participant in a movement that has seen an increase in the number of oral history courses offered at undergraduate and postgraduate levels, from a variety of disciplines and with a range of different emphases and objectives. In 2008, for example, there are individual oral history courses taught within history majors, women's studies, sociology, teacher training, archaeology, and in cross-disciplinary offerings at the undergraduate level. At postgraduate level, there are individual courses within programs, and there are entire programs devoted to oral history and related studies. There are also courses at both levels that have come and gone.

The extent and range of activity has produced a growing literature on the teaching of oral history in universities. There are contributions such as those by Tracey K'Meyer and Alistair Thomson that have surveyed the field and focus on drawing together the common threads to present overviews of teaching practices and strategies.[7] There are overviews like those given by Donald Ritchie in his *Doing Oral History* that ask questions and suggest answers about the place and status of oral history in universities.[8] More numerous are the contributions that offer reflective and analytical accounts about particular courses and individual experiences.[9]

Through all this literature and through the variety of oral history courses in universities, particular issues are surfacing as central for the development of contemporary and forward looking oral history teaching and learning.

Reflective Teaching and Learning

Reflective learning is a core element of oral history courses, just as reflexivity has become a core issue in oral history scholarship. Within this paradigm, students are encouraged to keep journals in which they reflect and write critically about all aspects of the processes involved in their oral history work.[10] Feelings, ideas stimulated by the literature, mistakes, revelations, imagined outcomes for an interview, actual outcomes, failures, challenges, concepts understood, concepts applied, concepts misunderstood, relations between student and interviewee, between students, between student and teacher—all of these go into the journals. For assistance, there are the rich and thought-provoking examples within oral history scholarship that demonstrate how reflexivity can inform but also reshape thinking about a topic, interview, or end product. Valerie Yow's article tracing the evolution of intersubjectivity and reflexivity in the literature provides an effective and stimulating starting point.[11] There are many specific examples suited to particular topics.

In my teaching practice, favorite examples include Heather Goodall's reflections on her own research agendas when recording memories about the impact of nuclear testing on Aboriginal communities in South Australia and her more recent reflective writing on the process of working with Isabel Flick to create her life story, and Katherine Borland's incisive exposure of how listening to her grandmother challenged and refined her understanding of her grandmother's experiences.[12] These examples of researchers reflecting are flanked by examples of authors who have integrated critiques of the oral history process and of their role in the process alongside the uncovering of their narrators' life and family stories. The possibilities are wide-ranging. Among those I use are Mark Baker's *The Fiftieth Gate*, Susan Varga's *Heddy and Me*, and Arnold Zable's *Jewels and Ashes*.[13] Then there is the power of reflexivity driven home by access to students' own evaluations and demonstrations of its impact. Vicki Ruiz uses the self-ethnographies of three students to illustrate the nature and effectiveness of reflexivity. Renate Prescott presents a detailed account of one student's journey of self-discovery through initiating oral history interviews about the Vietnam War with family members. Gerri Sorenson provides an account of her group oral history learning experience and the process that resulted in the creation of quilts as the focus for their presentation. Barry Lanman and Laura Wendling highlight the importance of capturing students' observations on their learning experiences by including reflective commentaries from three students.[14]

An emphasis on reflexivity does not stop at urging the practice among students. Teachers of oral history are also thinking and writing reflectively about their teaching. Alan Booth, in his treatise on teaching history at universities, has advocated the importance of reflective inquiry on the part of both staff and students in order to engage fully with each other and with their subject material.[15] As teachers reflect, their teaching practices and their own learning evolve. Sandy Polishuk openly admitted that her initial incentive in establishing an oral history course at Portland State University was to create an archive of oral history interviews with activists, her "radical elders." She used students to provide part of the labor force, but by reflecting on and evaluating her teaching practice, Polishuk came to appreciate the importance of the students'—and her own—learning experiences. She watched, and learned, as students engaged with their narrators and improved their listening skills and their "ability to think on their feet." The archival objective remained, but her twin objective was now to see her students "grow, learn to appreciate the lessons of the past, and be inspired by the commitment and impact of their narrators."[16] Anne Butler revealed the evolution of her use of oral history within a women's studies course, writing about the ideas borrowed from other scholars and practices; her reactions to and adaptations of demonstrated strategies; and her incorporation of learning from previous teaching of different cohorts of students. Butler demonstrated how her approach to teaching oral history had grown from reflective and critical thinking about the literature, other peoples' examples, and her own experiences.[17]

Active Learning

Reflexivity connects readily to another strong feature of oral history courses in universities: the emphasis on active learning. Oral history became seen as a means whereby students do not just read about history, they *do* history.[18] For Kimberley Porter, her students at the University of North Dakota actually participated in the gathering of history, "collaborating with their narrators to create materials found nowhere else."[19] Derek De Bruyn, in reflecting on the growing place of oral history in the teaching of history in South Africa, took it a step further by noting that the attractiveness of oral history lies partly in its contrast to outdated teaching methods that depended on the "transmission" model, the idea that students are provided with information that they only *have* to learn.[20]

At the core of active learning is the experience of conducting interviews and all the preparation and processing entailed. Ronald Grele, who headed the Columbia Oral History Research Office, succinctly argued that "Any course in oral history is, at heart, a fieldwork course."[21] The challenge, then, is how to balance practice with theory. Repeatedly, the literature on teaching oral history in universities has emphasized the need to introduce students to the rich and often complex scholarship on oral history while also providing them with training for conducting and processing interviews.[22] Different strategies and resources have been offered. Grele focused on how the various oral history texts can be used as the focus for debate on historiographical issues in a graduate class, and how those debates also feed into the development of students' interviewing skills and their awareness of the challenges when research involves working with people.[23] An exchange on teaching education at the post-secondary level held at the 1997 annual gathering of the American Oral History Association, indicated a mixing of texts on theory and fieldwork, and a mixing of teaching and learning strategies for fieldwork preparation with actual fieldwork. Courses with different emphases and at different levels have employed different strategies.[24]

To provide a specific example, in my oral history course, students begin with an immersion in oral history products (books, Web sites, films, and radio programs) and in selected scholarship. They draw on that immersion to write an analytical piece on how and why oral history has contributed to our understanding of a particular aspect of the past. The aspect selected will be the focus of the interviews they subsequently conduct. The practical preparation for the interview experience includes strategies and activities familiar in the literature on teaching oral history skills: practice interviews with each other and/or with family members, listening to and evaluating the interview skills of existing oral history interviews, being interviewed themselves, spending time thinking about and experiencing how our memories work, confronting ethical issues, and role-playing the unexpected as well as how to handle "difficult" interviews. These practical experiences are flanked by excursions into the scholarly literature that discusses, analyzes, and evaluates specific research experiences and practices in oral history interviewing. This balancing of theory and practice is reflected by the current choice of prescribed texts for the course: Rob Perks and Alistair Thomson's *The Oral History Reader*, and Beth Robertson's *Oral History Handbook*.[25] These are supplemented by a range of articles, readings, and other resources provided online. As in other oral history courses, students are expected to read, think, practice and then read, think, practice in order to prepare for and conduct their interviews.

A similar mixing of theory and practice, underwritten by active learning and reflexivity, characterizes the strategies adopted in oral history courses regarding students' work after they have conducted interviews. Some courses have as a primary object the inclusion of student interviews in an archival collection, or the introduction of students training to be librarians or archivists to the specific requirements of oral history collections. In these instances, the skills learned and practiced in processing interviews include those of particular relevance for collecting agencies. At the University of New South Wales, in Sydney, Australia, for example, an oral history course was offered within the postgraduate diploma in library and archive studies. After familiarizing students with the nature of oral history and oral history interviews, it examined conservation, information management, and storage issues.[26]

Courses that encourage applied uses of the interviews—in performance, creative writing, visual art, digital storytelling, in primary and secondary classrooms, for example—necessarily incorporate readings and tasks specific to these formats and purposes.[27] Courses with history as a focus tend to look more closely at the layered nature of the historical evidence and insights that can be read from the interviews, and how these can be interpreted and presented.[28] There are common emphases, concerns, and challenges in all these, depending on course objectives and on the level of the course, whether undergraduate or graduate, introductory or advanced.

When focusing on strategies and guides for processing and evaluating interviews, and for working with narrators, reflexivity is called upon by having students summarize and evaluate the interview and their role in it. Oral history literature and handbooks offer some guidance. My students are first directed to Beth Robertson's *Oral History Handbook* with its examples of summaries constructed immediately after an interview that capture the essence of the content, and of the ways in which the interaction between narrator and interviewer influenced the interview while also creating a document suitable for deposit in a public collection.[29] Samples of more evaluative reflections are then available through a series of vignettes of "most memorable interviews" and "most frustrating interviews" from the International Oral History Association's *Words and Silences/Palabras y silencios*.[30] These provide digestible and accessible examples, reassuring students that oral history interviews present challenges and delights for even practiced oral historians, while also illustrating the power of reflexivity. Other courses use different texts and examples, but the purpose is the same: to have students think about their experiences in the context of broader interviewing skills, and with theoretical and ethical issues.

The impact of this emphasis on reflection and evaluation as a learning strategy is borne out by students' observations. A student in Sue Bruley's oral history course in women's studies reflected on how her first interview made her feel awkward and confronted her with ethical issues about privacy:

> I felt like an intruder.... I left the interview asking myself a whole new set of questions about what moral right we had to ask such personal questions of these women?... the interviews showed us how delicate a matter oral history is, because of its subjectivity.[31]

Others among Bruley's students came away from their interviews with a better understanding of the negotiated spaces that exist between interviewer and interviewee, their different agendas, and the need to recognize the interview as a jointly authored and owned experience. After realizing that her interviewee chose what and how she answered, one student observed:

> The relationship between interviewer and interviewee is not one of simple manipulation...but one between two autonomous adults....The interviewee can control and manipulate the interview by refusing to answer questions; by portraying themselves in what they consider their best light; by telling the interviewer what they think she wants to hear or by reconstructing an imaginary past.[32]

By reflecting on and evaluating their interview experiences students learn to apply and adapt the knowledge gained through reading the literature. Theory informs practice informs theory.

In courses where print versions of interviews are required, the experience of transcribing and editing is usually prefaced by readings and discussion about the issues involved in moving from the "aurality" of a recorded interview to the one-dimensional form of print. These discussions and debates necessarily mix the practical (format, punctuation, skills, levels, and style of editing) with the theoretical and analytical. The close and time-consuming labor, and the listening and hearing required for creating verbatim transcripts, as Ron Grele has emphasized, not only exposes students to the skills and challenges of transcribing but also has them noticing and evaluating in more detail their own interview skills, narrative structures within the interviews, silences, and the use of language.[33]

The decisions involved about the format of a final presentation invite further confrontation with issues of ownership and control, with the degree to which narrators and interviewers can experience that "shared authority" introduced by Michael Frisch and now central to oral history, and with examples of the ethical, conceptual, interpretive, and literary challenges in working with oral history material.[34] There is a growing selection of resources to trigger thinking and debate as, increasingly, oral historians share their commentaries on the process of converting raw oral history material into products for different audiences. The impact of this literature on students' work is evident in publications by students and former students. There are, for example, Lorraine Sitzia's account of the difficulties involved in trying to implement Michael Frisch's "shared authority"; Katharine Elise Perry's explanation of why she decided to use a poetry format to present her mother's memories; and Denise Phillips's analysis of the ethical and intellectual issues involved in recording and presenting the memories of trauma of a Hazara refugee from Afghanistan.[35]

Learning and Other Outcomes

Reflexivity, active learning, and mixing theory and practice—these are hallmarks of oral history teaching and learning in universities. As such, courses take students from initial thinking and reading about oral history through the experience of preparing, conducting, and processing oral history interviews to the creation of a variety of end products. Integral to all this are the ways in which the learning activities are linked to assessment tasks and to other outcomes that students can expect from oral history courses.

In thinking through and identifying assessment tasks and learning outcomes, there is an awareness of the diversity of backgrounds from which students come and the reasons why they elect to pursue an oral history course. Tracey K'Meyer identifies those who do an oral history course because it is a requirement of their program of study; those who see it as a "springboard" for research in a postgraduate degree; and those who—for a variety of reasons—choose it as an elective.[36] Among the last category, K'Meyer and others recognize that some students see such a course as an easy option, a way to fill up their degrees. Others come to such an elective because they have been introduced to oral history in foundation courses and want to learn more or because they see it as offering particular or different skills, a different emphasis to more traditional subjects, an opportunity to record the stories of a relative or friend. Students enrolling in one of my oral history courses, for example, cited the following reasons: "The chance to document a family member's memories"; "I found this practical opportunity [to do an interview] a rarity"; "It might assist me in a possible future study in which interviews will play a major part"; "To enhance the studies I have already completed in archaeology and palaeoanthropology"; "I have an interest in local museums and see oral history as a very useful tool in this area"; "I was drawn to this subject as it is totally different to other history subjects that I have studied"; "I'm hoping to incorporate the skills learned in this unit into the primary classroom"; and "My background is in Indian (South Asian) history, so I am another who plans to research the immigrant experience."[37]

A thread running through the expectations my students expressed, and those recorded for other oral history courses, is the desire to conduct an interview as a way to learn skills, record stories and memories at risk of being lost, and to share the results of their work, at least with family if not beyond. Alongside these hopes, there is also trepidation: a realization that oral history is not just common sense and an easy path; the time and effort to be consumed; the confrontation of working with people; the challenge of putting theory into practice; the fear of getting a poor grade because interview skills are not up to scratch or an interviewee proves difficult; the diverse range of tasks and skills involved; nervousness at the prospect of conducting, processing, and presenting interviews; and unease at the range and level of oral history scholarship.

Student expectations and fears, their diverse backgrounds, and their different skills are factored into assessment tasks. Rather than making interview skills an assessable task, many courses focus on evaluating how and what students learn from the oral history process. Reflexivity again surfaces. What is assessed are students' self-evaluations of an interview experience, their use of oral history literature to comment on that experience, their ability to recognize strengths and weaknesses, and their areas that need improvement. They are also measured for completing and addressing the various steps or stages involved in the oral history process, the forms, the issues—practical and theoretical. There are research proposals, short exercises, reports, forms, analytical annotations of resources and readings, oral presentations, essays, and, in most cases, an end product of some sort.[38]

The emphasis on the creation of an end product requires an adequate matching of student backgrounds, expectations, and fears with desired learning outcomes, and the need for assessment. It is desirable to have an end product that goes beyond its life as an assessable piece of work for a university course. This is what Howard Levin and Kimberly Porter have referred to as "authentic doing" or "authentic task learning," projects that go beyond the classroom.[39] This approach is based on the belief that with the appropriate teaching and learning strategies, both undergraduate and postgraduate students can produce work of a quality that can be presented to audiences other than their teacher and for purposes other than only as an assessable task. It is a belief that counters the reservations Leonora Ritter expressed in the early 1980s as she contemplated her students' oral history experiments; she wondered whether she should "succumb to the lecturers' suspicion of the student method and regard it only as a useful exercise, dismissing the possible value of the content?"[40] It is also a belief that offers reassurance for the student from Sue Bruley's course in southern England who was concerned that she was doing an injustice to her interviewee because the interview was only for a university project.[41]

This belief in students' abilities, coupled with a belief in the teaching and learning strategies within oral history courses, has resulted in some startling end products. University and community oral history archives and collections have acquired significant additions. The Virginia Tech University Library, for example, is now home to a collection of oral history interviews about the experiences of school principals with full-text transcripts available online.[42] Students who participated in Susan Douglass's oral history course documenting destroyer escorts in World War II contributed to a specialist collection in the university archives, and those students can view results of their work online.[43]

Students have also had the satisfaction of seeing their work performed, displayed, published. In his video history courses, Albert Lichtblau's students can create one of three different types of short films.[44] Students who participated in Debra Sutphen's Historical Reasoning course, during the year she focused on oral histories with Japanese Americans about their experiences of internment during the Second World War, have their contributions in a book produced from the project.[45] Students from my oral history course have published versions of their final assignments and have presented papers to conferences.[46]

The impact of this "authentic learning" is well captured by students' reactions and comments. It is an impact that highlights the variety of the learning outcomes experienced by students more broadly through the active learning involved in pursuing an oral history project, however small, however discrete, however different, from beginning to end. They are learning outcomes relating to skills but also to awareness, self-identity, engagement with learning, and an increased knowledge of the complexities, challenges, and satisfactions of oral history scholarship and practice.[47]

- [The presentation at the end of the course] ... broke a barrier for me as far as confidence goes.... I feel far more capable.[48]
- This experience brought me back to life as a student. I miss tangible learning, you can only sit and listen to a lecture for so long.[49]
- I have learned that oral history is a highly dynamic, refined art of intuitive reasoning, held together by the science of a well-thought out research theme.[50]
- It was ... a life altering experience.... The insight and strength shown to us through the stories of everyday people inspired us all; the anger and resentment that many of us espoused when we heard the stories was a surprise to us all; and the compassion and understanding that we gained because of another's life has changed us all.[51]

Oral History in the Curriculum

There are obviously rich and diverse practices in teaching oral history in the university sector. Students who take the courses extol their learning outcomes. Staff comment on the stimulation and insights gained, and on the levels of student engagement. Archives, communities, history, and other disciplines benefit. However, where do oral history courses sit within and across the various disciplines in universities?

In reflecting on his newly initiated oral history course at the University of New South Wales in 1990, Martin Lyons noted the skepticism with which oral history was frequently met. He commented on the "strong consumer resistance to the notion that history is about assumptions, values and attitudes, as well as about 'what actually happened.'" He also lamented that "so many academic historians still regard oral testimony as an inherently inferior source, afflicted as they are by what Marc Bloch called "the document fetish."[52] To what extent do his concerns still apply? Has oral history become a part of mainstream curricula or does it remain as an add-on elective?

The answers are varied. In some countries, oral history, let alone oral history courses, have yet to be accepted as appropriate for universities. A powerful example comes from the leading and internationally recognized oral history scholar, Alessandro Portelli. In his reflections on oral history presented at a round table at the Fourteenth International Oral History Conference held in Sydney in 2006, Portelli observed that despite Italy being the only country to have hosted three international oral history conferences and being home to some leading oral historians:

> Italy is one nation where no one makes a living by working in oral history, just nobody. I teach American literature. Luisa Passerini was refused a professorship until she wrote a couple of books in which she did not use oral sources. One of the founders of the Italian oral history movement, Cesare Bermani, is unemployed. Others work in different capacities.[53]

In such a climate, oral history as a focus for students enters universities only through research projects. By contrast, there are universities where oral history has a clear presence in named courses and even in named programs, and where scholars could claim to make their living at least partly as oral historians who are able to share their skills and knowledge through teaching. Examples include the well-established and long-standing postgraduate oral history courses at Columbia University in New York.[54] In 2009 there was also a new Master of Oral History and Historical Memory at Monash University in Melbourne, Australia, and a new MA in Oral History at the University of Huddersfield in Great Britain.[55] There are, as well, individual research methods courses or oral history components of such courses within more traditional postgraduate and honors degrees. At the University of Cape Town in South Africa, for example, there is an optional postgraduate course titled "Oral History: Method, Practice and Theory", and in the MA in History program at Wright State University in Dayton, Ohio, there is an optional reading seminar in oral history.[56]

At the undergraduate level, the tendency has been toward offering one or two individual courses within a degree program. These courses sometimes sit quite forlornly among fairly traditional offerings and sometimes are flanked by other similarly forward-looking and less traditional courses. The history offerings at the University of Papua New Guinea continue to include an oral history course in the company of courses on Pacific history, modern Europe, Australian history, U.S. history, and war and peace in the twentieth century.[57] At my own University of New England, the oral history course sits among a mixture of other applied history courses and more traditional history courses.[58] Within the Women's and Gender Studies Program at Victoria University of Wellington in New Zealand, Alison Laurie offered a sequence of two oral history courses, the first focusing on existing oral histories and autobiographies, the second on the methods of conducting original oral history research. They are located comfortably in a range of women's- and gender-studies courses that invite undergraduates to explore, among other things, feminist perspectives, the analysis of representation and images, and queer studies.[59]

The courses initiated by Matts Greiff at the University of Malmö in Sweden indicate a more integrated approach. Greiff explains that in developing their history curriculum at the new university, oral history was seen not just as method "but also a perspective on historical studies." It was a way "to reach people," to engage students—many of whom would go on to be school teachers—with history as a discipline and, at the same time, with their surrounding communities. Oral history became a foundation course in the curriculum.[60]

At the University of Malmö and other universities that are integrating oral history into their curricula not just as electives or add-ons but as elements in the foundation perspectives and content that are being taught, there is strong evidence that oral history is being accepted as an essential and inspiring component of a curriculum. Oral history also has gained an increasingly obvious profile as more clearly identifiable oral history courses and programs are being introduced and expanded. They still tend, however, to be clustered as part of research methods courses, in or near public history programs, and in those universities that have oral history collections or research offices.[61] There are also oral history courses that have come and gone, the victims of programs being withdrawn, staff attrition, and the tenuous hold that oral history teaching and learning has had, particularly within traditional universities. There remains some way to go before oral history is seen as an unavoidable element in history—or other disciplinary and interdisciplinary—programs. Yet, its innovative teaching and learning strategies sit at the frontiers of university teaching.

Research, Archives, Communities

To leave a discussion of oral history in universities as a discussion primarily about how and where it is taught, and the skills, assessment, and recognition attached to that teaching and learning, would neglect a significant aspect of the presence and status of oral history in tertiary education institutions. There are staff and postgraduate research projects that overtly utilize oral history, oral history archival collections, and oral history projects that enable universities to engage with their surrounding communities. There are also conferences, seminars, and workshops that reach outside the university. Indeed, these activities have the higher public profile. Coupled with the offering of oral history courses, they are creating a university culture in which oral history has a more secure place, since it offers a unique way to combine teaching, learning, research, collecting, service, and community relations.

Oral history research projects are evident across universities. They exist in those universities that overtly teach or collect oral histories and in those that do not. They are pursued by people steeped in oral history scholarship and training, and by those who come to oral history with little training or background—and by some who continue to believe that oral history is simply about getting out there with recording equipment and collecting information or stories. Within these parameters, the range and quantity of postgraduate theses and academic staff research projects are boundless. A glance at the programs of national and international oral history conferences or through the indexes of oral history journals attests to the different disciplinary bases, different topics, and different issues, which have preoccupied university-based researchers.[62] Familiarity with postgraduate theses and staff projects within schools where modern history is taught and researched reveals oral history embedded in different topics and issues. In my own school, for example, there are honors and postgraduate theses with oral history as a central source and methodology in areas such as refugee experiences, indigenous studies, food history, adult education, volunteer organizations, and rural settlement plans.

These wide-ranging oral history research projects, even where oral history is used in an unproblematic way, are contributing to a growing culture in which oral history is an acceptable component—or at least a tolerated component—of universities. This is bolstered, and possibly spearheaded, by the role of universities in supporting oral history collections within their own archives and libraries, and as new initiatives. Oral history collections like those at Columbia University, which started collecting in 1948, and the Baylor Institute for Oral History at Baylor University in Texas, which began its collection in 1970, are relatively early examples of the archival collection-based projects that are located in universities around the world.[63]

Some university archives include among their collections oral history interviews with past and present members of the university. Implicit in these collections, and the projects that generated them, is a recognition that remembered experiences are a vital aspect of institutional history. Since 1980 the University of New South Wales has been recording and archiving oral histories with staff members.[64] The Edith Cowan University Archives in Perth, Australia has audio tape recordings dating from 1987, focusing particularly on the institution's role in teacher education and education more broadly in the university's home state of Western Australia.[65] Nanzan University in Nagoya, Japan has been collecting oral history interviews with professors since 1990.[66] These collections largely focus on the achievements of academic staff, especially staff at the upper levels of the profession, and are essentially elite oral history collections.

A different type of institutional focus is found in those collections, largely initiated in concert with oral history courses, that record the experiences of current students, especially those from minority backgrounds. Collections accommodate that important strand that has existed within oral history from its beginning: an emphasis on recording and conserving the experiences of people and groups who would otherwise be omitted from the records. Examples include "First Black Women @ Virginia Tech," housed in the university archives of Virginia Tech, which is identifying, recording, and presenting the experiences of "the first black women—students, staff and faculty" to enter the university.[67] Another is the Oral History and Community Memory Archive at California State University–Monterey Bay, which is building collections of interviews with and by first-generation college students.[68]

Universities also host oral history collections that move beyond their own institutions' histories. Some are overt research projects connected to the research interests of particular staff; others are generated through a concern to work closely with communities surrounding the university or to collate material that has a wider significance. Among the huge range of possibilities, specific examples include the Iranian Oral History Archive at Harvard University's Center for Middle Eastern Studies, established in 1981;[69] the Bali Oral History Archive at Murdoch University in Perth;[70] and the oral history collection in the University of Wollongong Archives in New South Wales.[71]

A key feature of these archives and collections is their online presence. Underpinning that is their intention to publicize the collections and make them publicly available. This sharing of resources through the Internet is indicative of another important strand typifying oral history in universities: the extent to which they share resources and expertise, and, in sharing, learn to work in partnership with community groups and other agencies. Strong examples of this come from South Africa. In its early years, History Workshop at the University of Witwatersand in Johannesberg, initiated a series of community oral history activities. On reflecting on the evolution of these outreach activities, Belinda Bozzoli observed:

> In earlier times we believed—naïve intellectuals, as we were—that we were "bringing history" to the audience. But we had not taken into account the cultural and social assertiveness which accompanied the "revolution from below" taking place in South Africa in the 1980s. We had a taste of "counter-hegemony"—for the audience commandeered the history, music and entertainment.[72]

History Workshop now runs its outreach programs in cooperation with local organizations and museums. Its teacher training and curriculum development work are done in close consultation with the teachers who are responsible for initiating oral history projects within school curricula.[73] From the University of Cape Town, the Centre for Popular Memory emphasizes that it recognizes who owns the past. Its 2009 mission statement declares:

> People in South Africa have a dynamic, but largely unrecorded heritage. The Centre creates spaces for these stories to be heard, seen and remembered.[74]

It conducts projects with community and government organizations; publishes and presents the material in a variety of formats; has an archive, some of which can be accessed online for registered users; and shares resources both online and through workshops. At the University of Natal, the Sinomlando Centre for Oral History and Memory Work has moved from a focus on recovering the "silenced memories of the Christian communities, particularly those which suffered under apartheid" to applied research and training in relation to "HIV/AIDS, gender issues, African traditional religion, township and life and family history."[75] The Centre's Memory Box Program typifies the form of working together—in this case with people with HIV/AIDS and their families—that sits at the core of the Centre's community work.[76]

This concern with placing community and individuals' perspectives and ownership at a central place in outreach programs, and in creating partnerships with organizations and groups outside universities, reflects the evolution in oral history thinking more broadly. There is a recognition that there is a shared authority, knowledge, and expertise. There are different perspectives and issues of ownership that should be acknowledged and addressed. For universities steeped in traditions of academic elitism and a focus on the expertise of university staff, these requirements are often challenging. Yet, inroads have been made, and not just in South Africa. University-based oral history projects are working in cooperation with community groups, sharing their resources and the products of their work, and in the process helping not only to bring down barriers between tertiary institutions and their surrounding communities, but to establish networks that extend nationally and internationally.

A few more examples illustrate the point. The East Midlands Oral History Archive in Great Britain is a joint initiative between the University of Leicester and the local government authorities. It provides an archive for oral histories from the surrounding region, showcases specific projects online, offers training for community groups, and provides a series of "how to" information sheets online.[77] MATRIX: The Center for Humane Arts, Letters, and Social Sciences Online at Michigan State University hosts two significant projects. The first is an ambitious Historical Voices project, working in cooperation with community and government organizations, and with other universities and research institutes to "create a federated archives and trans-institutional resources." Its aim is to provide an online sharing of oral history projects, digital resources and training, and educational resources.[78] The second MATRIX hosted project is the H-Net online network and, within it, H-Oralhist, an online forum and collection of resources that bring together scholars and practitioners of oral history around the world, within and outside universities.[79] MATRIX's role in hosting H-Net is akin to that played by other universities that host oral history associations and conferences. In so doing, they enhance the presence of oral history within universities and, as importantly, ensure that oral history is connected not just across a worldwide university sector but also well beyond.

The Presence of Oral History

Oral history in universities in the early twenty-first century consists of a web of interrelated activities. There are oral history courses taught at different levels, within and across different disciplines, and with varying degrees of visibility. Teaching and learning oral history in tertiary institutions has produced a growing body of literature that has emphasized features associated with reflective practices, active learning, the mixing of theory and practice, and the relationship between learning outcomes, assessment, and the variety of end products, which students are able to create. The vitality and presence of oral history are enhanced by the research, archival, and community projects in all their diversity. The sharing of resources through training, partnership projects, and online is indicative of that long-standing core focus of oral history: to give voice and recognition to those whose experiences have, whether in history or within traditional academic life, often been ignored.

A cautionary note is needed: although there are some long-standing oral history programs, and a growing number of academics who have accepted oral history as at least part of their culture, there remain many universities where oral history activities remain outside their doors or where its hold is tenuous. Yet, where they do exist, oral history teaching and projects have helped bring down barriers between universities and their communities. They have challenged university thinking that once placed the knowledge and expertise of academic staff on a pedestal. Through the Internet and through outreach programs, they have opened university resources to the public, locally and worldwide. We need to make sure this trend continues.

NOTES

1. In Australia, this was colorfully evident in the critiques presented by Patrick O'Farrell, for example, "Oral History: Facts and Fiction," *Oral History Association of Australia Journal* 5 (1982/83): 3–9.

2. The survival of this view provided the trigger for Tracey K'Meyer, "'It's Not Just Common Sense': A Blueprint for Teaching Oral History," *Oral History Review* 25, nos. 1/2 (1998): 35–57.

3. Derrick De Bruyn's article, "Teaching Oral History: A South African Perspective," in *Proceedings of the Twelfth International Oral History Conference: The Power of Oral History—Memory, Healing and Development*, vol. 3, ed. Philippe Denis and James Worthington, 1493–509 (Pietermaritzburg, S.A.: International Oral History Association and Sinomlando Project, University of Natal, 2002), identifies one of the problems in teaching oral history is that it is still regarded as "outside the curriculum."

4. Within these networks I acknowledge in particular the significance of those created through the International Oral History Association (http://www.iohanet.org) and the Oral History Association of Australia (http://www.ohaa.net.au).

5. Roderic Lacey, "Teaching Oral History in a New Nation: Experiences and Prospects," *OHAA Journal* 1 (1978–79): 43–45.

6. Ibid., 45–49.

7. K'Meyer, "It's Not Just Common Sense," and Alistair Thomson, "Teaching Oral History to Undergraduate Researchers," in *The Handbook of University History Teaching*, ed. Alan Booth and Paul Hyland, 154–65 (Manchester, U.K.: Manchester University Press, 2000); see also Timothy P. Fong, and Ava F. Kahn, "An Educational Exchange: Teaching Oral History in the Post-Secondary Level," *Oral History Review* 25, nos. 1/2 (1998): 9–35.

8. Donald A. Ritchie, *Doing Oral History* (New York: Oxford University Press, 2003), 207–14.

9. A good example of the range of writing on teaching oral history at universities is available in Barry Lanman and Laura Wendling, eds., *Preparing the Next Generation of Oral Historians* (Lanham, Md.: AltaMira Press, 2006), pt. 4.

10. For example, Kahn in Fong and Kahn, "An Educational Exchange," 22; and Janis Wilton, "Share and Compare: Ideas for Teaching Oral History," *OHAA Journal* 18 (1996): 17–19.

11. Valerie Yow, "Do I Like Them Too Much? Effects of the Oral History Interview on the Interviewer and Vice-Versa," *Oral History Review* 24, no. 1 (1997): 55–79.

12. Heather Goodall, "Colonialism and Catastrophe: Contested Memories of Nuclear Testing and Measles Epidemics at Ernabella," in *Memory and History in Twentieth Century Australia*, ed. Kate Darian-Smith and Paula Hamilton, 55–76 (Oxford: Oxford University Press, 1994); Heather Goodall, "Writing a Life with Isabel Flick: An Exploration in Cross-Cultural Collaboration," *Public Historian* 27, no. 4 (2005): 65–82; and Katherine Borland, "'That's not what I said': Interpretive Conflict in Oral Narrative Research," in *Women's Words*, ed. Sherna Berger Gluck and Daphne Patai, 63–75 (London: Routledge, 1991).

13. Mark Baker, *The Fiftieth Gate* (Sydney: Flamingo, 1997); Susan Varga, *Heddy and Me* (Melbourne: Penguin, 1994); and Arnold Zable, *Jewels and Ashes* (Melbourne: Scribe, 1991). For a context for these books, see Janis Wilton, "Generations of Journeys," in *Speaking to Immigrants: Oral Testimony and the History of Australian Immigration*, ed. A. James Hammerton and Eric Richards, 149–69 (Canberra: Research School of Social Sciences, ANU, 2002).

14. Vicki L. Ruiz, "Situating Stories: The Surprising Consequences of Oral History," *Oral History Review* 25, nos. 1/2 (1998): 71–81; Renate W. Prescott, "The Vietnam War and the Teaching and Writing of Oral History: The Reliability of the Narrator," *Oral History Review* 26, no. 2 (1999): 47–64; Anne M. Butler and Gerri W. Sorenson, "Patching the Past: Students and Oral History," *Frontiers: A Journal of Women's Studies* 19, no. 3 (1998): 205–12; and Jennifer Braithwait Darrow, Ronald Simon, and John D. Willard, "Learning Oral History: Reflections on a Graduate School Education," in Lanman and Wendling, *Preparing the Next Generation*, 407–15.

15. Alan Booth, *Teaching History at Universities* (London: Routledge, 2003), 11–13.

16. Sandy Polishuk, "Interviewing Radical Elders," in Lanman and Wendling, *Preparing the Next Generation*, 399–405.

17. Butler and Sorenson, "Patching the Past," 200–205.

18. Erin McCarthy wrote that oral history is "about doing history instead of reading about it," in "Oral History in the Undergraduate Classroom: Getting Students into History," in Lanman and Wendling, *Preparing the Next Generation*, 321.

19. Kimberley K. Porter, "Oral History: Authentic Task Learning for the College Classroom," in Lanman and Wendling, *Preparing the Next Generation*, 303.

20. De Bruyn, "Teaching Oral History," 1493–94.

21. Ronald Grele, "Values and Methods in the Classroom Transformation of Oral History," *Oral History Review* 25, nos. 1/2 (1998): 61. Also available in Lanman and Welding, *Preparing the Next Generation*, 327–38.

22. See, for example, Fong and Kahn, "An Educational Exchange," 27–29; Grele, "Values and Methods in the Classroom Transformation of Oral History"; K'Meyer, "It's Not Just Common Sense," 37; Martin Lyons, "Teaching Oral History at the University of New South Wales," *Australian Historical Studies Association Bulletin* 62 (1990): 47; and Wilton, "Share and Compare," 17–18.

23. Grele, "Values and Methods."

24. Fong and Kahn, "An Educational Exchange," 13–17.

25. Robert Perks and Alistair Thomson, eds., *The Oral History Reader* (New York/London: Routledge, 2006), and Beth M. Robertson, *Oral History Handbook*, 5th ed. (Adelaide: Oral History Association of Australia, South Australian Branch, 2006). See also Fong and Kahn, "An Educational Exchange," and Grele, "Values and Methods in the Classroom Transformation of Oral History" for discussions and examples of readings and resources, and the sample syllabus from the Oral History Research Office at Columbia University in Lanman and Wendling, *Preparing the Next Generation*, 437–43.

26. Course brochure provided by Rosemary Block, Curator of Oral History at the State Library of NSW and one of the course coordinators.

27. See, for example, Edric C. Johnson, "Involving Pre-Service Teachers in Collecting and Performing Oral History," *Social Studies* (Sept./Oct. 2007): 197–99; Howard Levin, "Telling Their Stories: Student Production and Delivery of Digital Video Interviews via the Internet," in *Proceedings of the Fourteenth International Oral History Conference: Dancing with Memory*, ed. Rosemary Block, Paula Hamilton, and Janis Wilton (International Oral History Association and Oral History Association of Australia, Sydney, 2006) (CDRom); Albert Lichtblau, "Teaching Video History," *Proceedings of the Eleventh International Oral History Conference: Communicating Crossroads of Experience*, vol. 1 (International Oral History Association and Dept. of History, Boğaziçi University, Turkey, 2000), 336–40; David Sidwell, "All the World's a Stage: Oral History Performance in the Classroom," in Lanman and Wendling, *Preparing the Next Generation*, 347–54; and Tracey M. Weis, Rina Benmayor, Cecilia O'Leary, and Bret Eynon, "Digital Technologies and Pedagogies," *Social Justice* 29, no. 4 (2002): 153–67.

28. See for example, Sue Bruley, "Women's History, Oral History and Active Learning: An Experience from Southern England," *Women's History Review* 5, no. 1 (1996), especially 119–22; Grele, "Values and Methods in the Classroom Transformation of Oral History"; Lyons, "Teaching Oral History at the University of New South Wales"; and Prescott, "The Vietnam War and the Teaching and Writing of Oral History."

29. Robertson, *Oral History Handbook*, 74–77.

30. *Words and Silences/Palabras y silencios* 2, no. 1 (Aug. 1999): 5–32, and no. 2 (June 2004): 3–10.

31. Quoted in Bruley, "Women's History, Oral History and Active Learning," 117.

32. Ibid., 118.

33. Grele, "Values and Methods," 68–69.

34. Michael Frisch, *A Shared Authority: Essays on the Craft and Meaning of Oral and Public History* (Albany: State University of New York Press, 1990).

35. Lorraine Sitzia, "Telling Arthur's Story: Oral History Relationships and Shared Authority," *Oral History* 27, no. 2 (1999): 58–59; Katharine Elise Perry, "Tales Full of Music and Strong and Resourceful Women," *OHAA Journal* 27 (2005): 1–7; and Denise Phillips, "'I'm 21 and Have No Any Happy Days': An Oral History Narrative from the Hazara Refugee Community," *OHAA Journal* 27 (2005): 28–33.

36. K'Meyer, "It's Not Just Common Sense," 38.

37. Comments posted during July 2008 to an online discussion in which students introduced themselves and what attracted them to the oral history course. The course is taught by distance education. There are sixty-eight enrollments this semester. Many are older students and, as the comments suggest, come from a variety of backgrounds. The oral history unit is offered across a range of degrees including teaching degrees, urban planning, local family and applied history awards, as well as the Bachelor of Arts.

38. For examples, see K'Meyer, "It's Not Just Common Sense," 46–48, and Thomson, "Teaching Oral History to Undergraduate Researchers."

39. Levin, "Telling Their Stories," 2; and Porter, "Authentic Task Learning."

40. Leonora Ritter, "Introducing Oral History to First Year Tertiary Students," *OHAA Journal* 5 (1982–1983): 114.

41. Bruley, "Women's History, Oral History and Active Learning," 118.

42. Patrick Carlton, "Oral History as an Engine to the Power of Education," in Lanman and Wendling, *Preparing the Next Generation*, 381–92.

43. http://library.monmouth.edu/spcol/DESA/index.htm. The course and project are discussed in Susan Douglass, "Destroyer Escorts in World War II—'The LittleWarship That Could,'" in Lanman and Wendling, *Preparing the Next Generation*, 393–97.

44. Albert Lichtblau, "Teaching Video History."

45. Debra Sutphen, "Sierra College's 'Standing Guard' Japanese American Internment Oral History Project," in Lanman and Wendling, *Preparing the Next Generation*, 371–79.

46. See, for example, Perry, "Tales Full of Music and Strong and Resourceful Women," and Phillips, "'I'm 21 and Have No Any Happy Days.'"

47. For other summaries of learning outcomes see Thomson, "Teaching Oral History to Undergraduate Researchers."

48. Quoted in Bruley, "Women's History, Oral History and Active Learning," 190.

49. Butler and Sorenson, "Patching the Past," 211.

50. Darrow et al., "Learning Oral History," 412–13.

51. Lucinda Willis, "Experiencing Oral Histories of Another Generation and Another World: A Student's Perspective," in Denis and Worthington, *Proceedings of the Twelfth International Oral History Conference*, vol. 3, 1603.

52. Lyons, "Teaching Oral History at the University of New South Wales," 47–48.

53. Taken from the recording of the roundtable discussion.

54. Lanman and Wendling, *Preparing the Next Generation*, 416–17, 437–43, and http://iserp.columbia.edu/education-programs/ohma.

55. http://www.arts.monash.edu.au/historical-studies/pgrad/coursework/oral-history.php; and http://www.hud.ac.uk/mh/history/courses/ma-history.php

56. web.uct.ac.za/depts/history/newsite/electives.htm. The syllabus for the "Readings in oral history" seminar at Wright State University is available at http://www.oralhistory.org/wiki/index.php/Readings_in_Oral_History_Graduate_Seminar.

57. http://www.upng.ac.pg/shss_hgp.html.

58. http://www.une.edu.au/study/history/.

59. http://www.victoria.ac.nz/education/courses/gender-women/index.aspx.

60. Matts Greiff, "Oral History at Malmö University," in Denis and Worthington, *Proceedings of the Twelfth International Oral History Conference*, vol. 3, 1510–23.

61. K'Meyer, "It's Not Just Common Sense," 37; and Ritchie, *Doing Oral History*, 207.

62. For information on international conferences visit the Web site of the International Oral History Association (http://www.iohanet.org). *IOHA News*, which is published on the Web site, allows readers to browse the contents lists of oral history journals from around the world.

63. http://www.columbia.edu/cu/lweb/indiv/oral/; and http://www.baylor.edu/oral_history.

64. http://www.recordkeeping.unsw.edu.au/Collections/oral_history.html.

65. http://www.archivists.org.au/edith-cowan-university-archives.

66. Eriko Yamamoto, "Oral History in Japan," *Words and Silences/Palabras y silencios* 1, no. 1 (June 2002): 44.

67. Black Women @ Virginia Tech: http://spec.lib.vt.edu/blackwom/

68. http://hcom.csumb.edu/oralhistory/.

69. http://fas.harvard.edu/~iohp/about/.

70. http://wwwlib.murdoch.edu.au/boha/.

71. http://www.library.uow.edu.au/archives/collections/bcoll.html.

72. Quoted in Cynthia Kros and Nicole Ulrich, "Oral Testimony, Teaching History and Social History in South Africa," in Block, Hamilton, and Wilton, *Proceedings of the Fourteenth International Oral History Conference: Dancing with Memory*, 3–4.

73. Ibid.

74. http://www.popularmemory.org.za.

75. http://www.sinomlando.ukzn.ac.za/.

76. See Philippe Denis and Nokhaya Makiwane, "Stories of Love, Pain and Courage: AIDS Orphans and Memory Boxes," *Oral History* 31, no. 2 (2003): 66–74.

77. http://www.le.ac.uk/emoha/.

78. http://www.historicalvoices.org/.

79. http://www.h-net.org/~oralhist/.

BIBLIOGRAPHY

Booth, Alan. *Teaching History at University: Enhancing Learning and Understanding.* London: Routledge, 2003.

Booth, Alan, and Paul Hyland, eds. *The Handbook of University History Teaching.* Manchester, UK: Manchester University Press, 2000.

Lanman, Barry, and Laura Wendling, eds. *Preparing the Next Generation of Oral Historians.* Lanham, Md.: AltaMira Press, 2006.

Perks, Rob, and Alistair Thomson, eds. *The Oral History Reader.* London: Routledge, 2006.

Ritchie, Donald A. *Doing Oral History.* New York: Oxford University Press, 2003.

Robertson, Beth. *The Oral History Handbook.* Adelaide: Oral History Association of Australia, South Australian Branch, 2006.

CHAPTER 32

CASE STUDY: ENGAGING INTERPRETATION THROUGH DIGITAL TECHNOLOGIES

RINA BENMAYOR

ALMOST a decade ago, I began experimenting with digital technology in my undergraduate oral history class. I focused on designing simple digital tools that would help students transcribe their interviews, write better reflective journals, and submit work and receive comments electronically.[1] At that time, communicating with students via email, using electronic tools to receive and comment on student work, and designing templates to facilitate journaling and transcribing seemed "cutting edge." From today's vantage point, my "high-tech" strategies are quaint and rather obsolete. Faculty have more sophisticated electronic tools at our disposal for oral history instruction, including digital transcription programs, multimedia programs that integrate voice, image, and word, and learning management systems where we can post course materials, communicate with students, organize group communication and receive, comment on, grade, and return student work electronically.

In addition to advances in teaching technologies, today's students come with higher degrees of technological literacy than a decade ago. They are equipped with computers, iPods, and cell phones, and many know how to use digital audio and video recorders. Where once we had to teach how to use specialized software programs, faculty now take for granted that students know how to make slide presentations. Some are already familiar with sound or video editing processes, and a few may even have multimedia production experience.

As the 2008 meeting of the Oral History Association affirmed, oral history and digital technologies are converging.[2] The new "Digital and Community Showcase" inaugurated at that meeting featured more than thirty projects, including digital application and publishing platforms, Web and Internet applications, GIS memory mapping, social networking tools, transcription and preservation programs, fully researchable online oral history archives, and digital tools for teaching oral history. We are beginning to see the emergence of online oral history journals with rich hypertext environments.[3] Already it is becoming hard to keep up with the many and varied ways that digital technology is having an impact on the practice and teaching of oral history.

My interest in this landscape of digital possibilities is pedagogical, and my aim is to share some recent experiences and thoughts on the benefits and limitations of digital formats for interpretation and presentation of oral history. Digital strategies engage students in creative ways, allow them to represent interviews through full image and sound, and make more visible the cognitive steps involved in analysis and interpretation of oral histories. However, digital strategies in teaching oral history require the same level of close pedagogical attention as traditional learning methods. Technology is a tool, not a substitute, for pedagogy.

Context: The Undergraduate Oral History Course

The context for these reflections is the undergraduate oral history course, "Oral History and Community Memory," that I offer in an interdisciplinary humanities and communication major at a state university campus. The course meets a major breadth requirement, so it is likely to have up to thirty-five members in the class, whose concentrations may include journalism, rhetoric, literature, philosophy, history, creative writing, women's studies, or ethnic studies. My students are not traditional history majors and do not have a particular interest or disciplinary commitment to oral history. My job is to excite them about oral history.

To do so, I engage students in the full oral history process, including designing, conducting, recording, archiving, and interpreting one or more original oral history interviews. I usually organize the class around a theme, such as memories of growing up Asian American in Salinas, California; the experience of first-generation college students; or family history. It is a project-based course that asks participants to develop intellectual, organizational, and communication skills. The class is organized sequentially in three parts: (1) a general introduction to oral history and preparation of interviews, (2) recording and conducting interviews, preparation for the archive, and (3) interpretation and presentation of the projects.

To model the interpretive process, I assign a selection of critical essays that are accessible to a nonspecialized readership. These include classics like Alessandro Portelli's "What Makes Oral History Different," Kathryn Anderson and Dana C. Jack's "Learning to Listen," Alistair Thomson's "Anzac Memories," Katherine Borland's "'That's Not What I Said,'" Ruth Finnegan's "Family Myths, Memories and Interviewing," and others that expose students to the range of interpretive possibilities in oral history.[4] The readings provide examples of critical analysis around issues of memory, representation, standpoint, and performance that students can apply to the analysis and interpretation of their own interviews.

Students report that the two aspects of the class they most enjoy are conducting their interviews and presenting them to the class at the end of the semester. It is no coincidence that both of these activities involve either direct human interaction or use of technology, rather than critical reading and writing. Most students in the class have little or no training in historical or symbolic analysis, and they often flounder when asked to derive larger meanings from their narratives or to consider their interviews as constructions of memory. Consequently, the two main pedagogical questions that challenge me are: How to better engage students in oral history interpretation? How to encourage them to move beyond "show and tell" in presenting their interviews to the class? My most recent experiments with digital technologies address both these questions, with varied results, and invite contemplation about the opportunities, benefits, and costs of using digital formats for interpreting interviews.

Interpretation through Technology

Digital technologies present various opportunities for oral history in the classroom. To begin with, they have the potential to refocus our attention on orality/aurality and performativity. while written transcripts remain important and very useful in certain archival contexts, our ability to reproduce and stream audio and video interviews with relative ease has changed the way we access, share, examine, analyze, and interpret oral narratives. The Web and the Internet can bring us complete oral history collections, combining sound, image, and word. We can now listen to or watch full interviews n the classroom, with and without the mediation of the written transcript.[5] As Portelli emphasizes, we can better attend to the centrality of form to meaning, to examine how a story is told as well as how it is remembered.[6]

Yet, digital teaching strategies cannot be considered uncritically, as the very nature of the medium necessarily affects the process of critical inquiry and reflection. Regarding digital storytelling as a format for critical analysis, the cultural historian Michael Coventry asks: How does a digital telling of a story relate to the practice of critical reflection?[7] Where do digital strategies enhance critical reflection, and where do they hinder it? With regard to the presentation of critical analysis we also ask: What are the benefits and limitations of the digital performance of an analysis, as opposed to the more traditional written essay format? We all appreciate the distinction between reading a paper at a conference session as opposed to presenting one's ideas directly to the audience. One digital presentation tool for oral history that has become commonplace is the PowerPoint slide show, which easily integrates image, sound, and word. Slides organize the presentation of material, but do they also shape the way in which the analysis is achieved? In the context of oral history, how does a digital telling of an oral history relate to the critical practice of its interpretation? Does the use of a digital medium change the way students analyze, argue, interpret, and present their ideas?

The Use of PowerPoint in Oral History Interpretation

The very nature of oral history lends itself to oral and visual formats for critical interpretation and presentation. As a teacher, I encourage the study of oral history in as lively and multisensory a way as possible, including multimedia strategies for students to forge, present, and get feedback on their critical ideas. I use technology to engage group discussion, to facilitate interactive sharing of primary materials and students' final presentations of their projects to the class. In extending use of digital tools to facilitate critical interpretation, I use a pedagogically constructivist model of scaffolded steps to guide students through the analytical and interpretive processes.

In training attention on process, I decided to sacrifice the traditional written essay and instead assigned a final PowerPoint presentation in which audio or video clips of the interview were to be integrated with critical readings and student commentary. Students were asked to use a digital environment to analyze their interviews and present their conclusions to the class. I found the advantages of this shift from the written to the audiovisual were several. First, students approached the assignment differently, as they associate digital tools with creative construction or "play." This had the potential to draw students into the assignment, turning analysis into a dynamic activity. In addition, hypertext capacity enabled a structural interconnection of audio/video text, critical concept, and interpretive reflection. And finally, the format also privileged oral presentation, and occasioned group dialog, collective critique of ideas, and diversity of interpretation. Students were asked to prepare the following series of slides:

1. A title slide
2. Brief biographical highlights about the narrator, derived from the interview
3. A one-paragraph abstract of the interview
4. A five-topic interview guide used during the interview
5. An analysis of some aspect of form in the interview, using one or more critical readings on oral history form

6. An analysis of one important piece of content in the interview, using one or more critical readings in oral history
7. A final reflection on what one learned about oral history.

In steps 5 and 6, students were asked to make explicit connections between the clips they showed, critical interpretive concepts about oral history and memory, and the meanings they discovered in their interviews.

On the surface, the assignment might appear simple, but to be used successfully it actually required a series of cognitive steps: careful thinking and preparation; reading and review of assigned essays; selecting appropriate and significant excerpts on form and content for analysis; applying the critical concepts to the chosen excerpts; compressing critical points into slide-appropriate phrases, and finally, explaining, elaborating, and defending their critical interpretation orally in class. My experiment with PowerPoint was intended, as Coventry suggests, to engage students in representing "a theoretically informed understanding of texts and contexts in a form other than 'traditional' writing."[8] My intention was to make the steps of critical interpretation more visible to students, to encourage the application of critical concepts to their narratives, to help them to take notice of the performance of oral history, and to engage an aural/oral/visual mode of critical presentation.

An example of student work illustrates some of the successes and problems I encountered. Ironically, I am restricted here to the written word to make my points. The following examples are drawn from an interview conducted by three students with a family member of one of the Jonestown Massacre victims.[9] In the slide, on form, they chose to apply Anderson and Jack's observation about the importance of performance to more fully grasp the significance of the narrative.[10]

Form

Critical Reading

"Some of us found discrepancies between our memories of interviews and the transcripts because the meaning we remembered hearing had been expressed through intense vocal quality and body language, not through words alone" (Anderson and Jack 158).

Interpretation

"Writing down what Elizabeth said does not convey the meaning of her words. When you listen to her and watch her in the video, she is looking into why she made the decision she did and really looking at the effect the death of her sister had on her. Her body language and the changes in her voice, and especially the silences show Elizabeth in a very different light that cannot be transcribed through the written word. While watching her, she looks off into the distance and this shows that she is piecing all of these memories together and applying them to her life today. When she questions if she has lived her life because of her sister or because of herself, she slows down the speed of her voice and she has moments of silence that tell the audience that she is reflecting on something that she has never really thought about before. The video of the interview provides detail that only audio could simply not have provided."

The accompanying video clip showed Elizabeth, the narrator, reflecting on her own thoughts as she told her story. Students' interpretation demonstrated an awareness of Elizabeth's own search for meaning during the interview process. ("She looks off into the distance and this shows that she is piecing all of these memories together and applying them to her life today.") They experienced and described the way in oral history caused the narrator to step back from her "story," to discover or express some new realization, a prelude, perhaps, to what Anderson and Jack call the "meta-statement." The commentary also addressed the class audience directly in the process. ("If *you* listen to her and *you* watch her... and she has moments of silence *that tell the audience...*" [italics are mine].) They "showed" the evidence to support their interpretation and opened the space for class dialog around differing perspectives.

For their content slide, students chose a critical reading from Alessandro Portelli's "What Makes Oral History Different?":

Content

Critical Reading

"The first thing that makes oral history different, therefore, is that it tells us less about events than about their meaning. This does not imply that oral history has no factual validity. Interviews often reveal unknown events or unknown aspects of known events; they always cast new light on unexplored areas of the daily life of the non-hegemonic classes (Portelli, "What Makes..." 67)

Intepretation

"Elizabeth provided this entire story that you will never find in a textbook. We have discussed our surprise about the difference between what we found in our research and what we learned from Elizabeth. We learned that Elizabeth almost went to Jonestown with her father, but didn't because she wanted to perform in a play at school, *The Miracle Worker*. The 'book history' of Jonestown provides the basics of what happened, but Elizabeth's story tells about the details and what happened to those left behind. You would never find through research that she had almost gone to Guyana, and how she feels about that."

The students' commentary however, missed the key point. Portelli's quote is intended to move interpretation away from facts and events and more toward the interpretation of their meaning. They focused, however, more on the idea of "unknown aspects of known events" rather than on an interpretation of the meaning of these unknown aspects. They explained how their interview allowed for the emergence of a larger story around Jonestown, concerning the ways in which the events impacted family members and what they did or did not do in response. But they stopped short of reflecting on the meaning of Elizabeth's decision not to accompany her father, rather than simply discovering the fact of it. They do not elaborate on the significance of this example to the narrator's own understanding of her experience.

Shortcomings aside, these two examples demonstrate a serious engagement with the assignment with mixed results in the quality of the interpretation. As often happens when asked to draw on critical readings to support their interpretations, students select a particular phrase or sentence that pops out but may fail to examine the phrase in the context of the argument being made. Consequently, the phrase "unknown aspects of unknown events" was not understood in the larger context of form and meaning-making. What became apparent was that even though the students were able to make connections between their own interviews and critical concepts in oral history, the scaffolded form of the PowerPoint itself did not necessarily avoid the pitfalls of the quick, decontextualized use of concepts. In fact, the abbreviated form of the PowerPoint may have served to shortcut the analysis.

Part of the decision to use PowerPoint was to facilitate a dynamic presentation of critical ideas to the class. Students produced visually organized and esthetically pleasing slide shows and some were able to "speak" their interpretations, although many simply read the words on the slide. Nonetheless, the presentations led to good group discussions and occasional challenges to particular interpretations. The class was visibly engaged, in no small degree due to the multimedia format. However, digital presentations are not without their own dangers. The most evident of these is the temptation to fall back into a simple and uncritical "show and tell" mode learned in elementary school. Making a nice looking slide with bells and whistles can easily overshadow the more difficult task of critical reflection.

I offer these examples to emphasize that, regardless of the tool, close pedagogical attention still needs to be paid to the way students understand and interpret assignments. At worst, digital formats can lead students to simplistic abbreviation of ideas or avoidance of critical thought. At best, they can be used productively to model cognitive steps. While I intend to continue using PowerPoint to help structure the interpretive and presentation processes, I do not believe that the digital format is a substitute for the more developed interpretive essay. In fact, my PowerPoint assignment might best serve as a preparatory step in constructing a fuller written reflection. That is, an "and/and" rather than an "either/or" approach to the pedagogical use of digital technology.

In sum, the opportunities digital tools offer are many. They can help model, breakdown, and make more visible to students the kinds of cognitive/interpretive steps involved in oral history. They can enable a more vivid shared interpretive experience by enabling others to see or hear an interpretive point, rather than having to rely on the limited dimension of the written description. Bulent Dogan and Bernard Robin, who study instructional technology, report that "teachers who implemented the digital storytelling [a practice related to oral history] into their classroom activities reported significantly higher levels of student engagement and motivation, and also believed that their students displayed improved technical, presentation, research, organizational skills, and writing."[11] They imply that digital formats do not exclude and may actually enhance more traditional pedagogical goals and interpretive practices. There is no guarantee that the mere use of digital formats necessarily achieves the desired quality of interpretive skill. As I learned through this use of PowerPoint, without sufficient attention to the fundamental processes of close reading, synthesizing, and understanding concepts (steps which might also be approached through digital tools), students are just as likely to fall short of the mark in the digital format as they do in the written essay.

Digital media are useful in preserving and conveying the dynamic and living nature of oral history and the meaning of performance. Within the decade, it is possible that our students may be much more proficient in using digital multimedia and may be able to create digital essays with complex hyperlinked critical meanings. Even then, more sophisticated use of digital strategies does not by itself insure effective critical interpretation of oral history.

NOTES

1. Rina Benmayor, "Cyber Teaching in the Oral History Classroom," in *The Oral History Reader,* edited by Robert Perks and Alistair Thomson, 434–45 (New York: Routledge, 2006).
2. The 2008 Oral History Association Annual Meeting, held in Pittsburgh, Pa., was organized around the theme of "A Convergence of Interests: Oral History in the Digital Age." For details, see the conference program at http://www.oralhistory.org/annual-meeting/past-annual-meeting.
3. See, for example, the new Canadian Oral History Forum d'histoire orale (http://journal.canoha.ca/index.php/ohf).
4. All these articles are contained in Perks and Thomson, *Oral History Reader.*
5. A good example of a fully researchable online archive is Sherna Gluck's Virtual Oral/Aural History Archive at California State University–Long Beach (http://salticid.nmc.csulb.edu/cgi-bin/WebObjects/OralAural.woa/).
6. Alessandro Portelli, "What Makes Oral History Different?" in Perks and Thomson, *Oral History Reader,* 32–42.
7. Michael Coventry, "Cross-Currents of Pedagogy and Technology: A Forum on Digital Storytelling and Cultural Critique—Introduction," *Arts and Humanities in Higher Education* 7, no. 2: 166.

8. Ibid.

9. Excerpts from a student PowerPoint presentation delivered in spring 2008, Oral History and Community Memory, California State University–Monterey Bay.

10. See Kathryn Anderson and Dana Jack, "Learning to Listen," in Perks and Thomson, *Oral History Reader*, 129–42.

11. Bulent Dogan and Bernard Robin, "Implementation of digital storytelling in the classroom by teachers trained in a digital storytelling workshop." From http://digitalstorytelling.coe.uh.edu/pdfs/Dogan-DS-Research-2008.pdf

BIBLIOGRAPHY

Benmayor, Rina. "Cyber Teaching in the Oral History Classroom." In *The Oral History Reader*, 2nd ed., edited by Robert Perks and Alistair Thomson, 434–45. New York: Routledge, 2006.

Coventry, Michael. "Cross-Currents of Pedagogy and Technology: A Forum on Digital Storytelling and Cultural Critique—Introduction." *Arts and Humanities in Higher Education* 7, no. 2:188–204.

CHAPTER 33

ORAL HISTORY IN THE DIGITAL AGE

KELLY SCHRUM

SHEILA BRENNAN

JAMES HALABUK

SHARON M. LEON

TOM SCHEINFELDT

You do not need to visit quilter Mamie Lee Bryan at her home in North Carolina to hear about her constant need to keep her hands busy, or track down Maj. Rhonda Cornum to listen to her experiences as a U.S. Army flight surgeon captured during the Gulf War. With a few keystrokes and a click of the mouse, you can move from reading about the Great Depression or looking at photographs of bread lines to listening to the voices of individuals who experienced these things, often in very different ways. "They couldn't see any hope for a better tomorrow," recalled one woman whose husband participated in the Bonus March in 1932 and who witnessed the suicide rate rise as despair and hunger set in. Manny Diaz, however, who grew up in New York City during the Depression, remembered the strong sense of community, "You know, when everybody's poor, nobody feels poor."[1]

Oral history means many things. It is a record of oral tradition, compiled of stories handed down from one generation to the next, as well as the recording of personal history or experiences. It can involve a formal interview examining a particular topic, such as the history of the space telescope, or a moment in time, such as the partial meltdown at the Three Mile Island commercial nuclear power plant near Middletown, Pennsylvania, on March 28, 1979. A kind of oral history can also occur informally, when family members share stories around a kitchen table or when a high school student interviews his grandmother about immigrating to the United States.[2]

The task of categorizing oral history has become even more challenging in the digital age. It is possible to define online oral history in broad terms, as resources are available via the Internet that are related to the collecting, cataloging, preserving, or sharing of oral history. Much beyond that, however, the more specific characteristics are difficult to identify. Oral history resources online can mean many things and serve many purposes, depending on the content, format, and presentation. Materials range from descriptions of oral history content to transcriptions of formal interviews, from the filmed musings of a relative about growing up in a small town presented via *You Tube* to surveys completed online about recent presidential politics.[3]

At one end of the spectrum are catalogs, presented as a list or a searchable database with metadata about oral histories that are primarily available only by request or in person. The United States Holocaust Memorial Museum, for example, provides the *International Database of Oral History Testimonies*, a tool for locating oral history collections related to the Holocaust at museums, universities, and local and national institutions around the world. Bringing together information on major repositories as well as small collections with no Web presence, this database presents basic information on finding aids, the general scope of the interviews available, and access. The oral histories themselves are not accessible via the catalog, but the tool serves as a valuable starting point that can save many hours of research or allow for an examination of the scope and diversity of the available oral histories.[4]

Other projects place the content of traditional oral histories online as text, audio, or video. Before the Internet, oral histories most commonly circulated as written transcripts. Transcripts, now widely available online, still offer powerful testimony of individual experiences. One can read, for example, as Miriam Allen DeFord describes her early involvement in the suffrage movement to interviewer Sherna Gluck: "Ever since I can remember, my mother was for 'votes for women'—which was the thing then. When I was fourteen she sent me down to suffrage headquarters to stuff envelopes." The full transcript is available and searchable, either alone or as part of a significant collection of stories about the suffrage movement, "The Suffragists: From Tea-Parties to Prison." An audio clip from one of these interviews on the Web site *History Matters* presents the voice of Laura Ellsworth Seiler recalling her campaign work via automobile tour, with her mother in tow as chaperon. Hearing Seiler's voice provides an additional layer of information, as does her laughter as she describes her "small and charming and utterly Victorian" mother inviting men from local bars to come listen to her speech on women's suffrage. This audio clip, however, is only part of the longer interview that is available and searchable in written form.[5]

On the other end of the continuum are projects conceived for the Web that present content online in varying ways. The "Seventh Ward Speaks" Oral History Project, part of the *Neighborhood Story Project* in New Orleans, Louisiana, was designed to encourage neighbors to share their personal experiences with each other. Oral histories become posters and are displayed in the neighborhood and mounted online. Barbara Trevigne, for example, reflected on the changing meaning of community: "Everyone used to be involved. Everyone sat on the porch. You told stories, you listened, and you asked." Each online poster presents a snippet, a few lines from the interview, and a series of images, while the longer stories are being compiled for a book.[6]

New media technology has the power to expand the reach and exposure of oral history exponentially. According to the most recent survey by the Pew Internet and American Life project, home adoption of broadband rose to a remarkable rate of 55 percent in 2008, up from 47 percent in 2007.[7] This expanded capacity means that more individuals will have the ability to easily watch and listen to high-quality audio and video over the Internet, opening vast possibilities for oral historians. Another survey by the Pew project revealed that 57 percent of Internet users have watched video online and that a significant portion of them share what they find with other users. These numbers should continue to grow, indicating even more opportunity for digital history projects.[8] This expanded reach and exposure demands that we consider carefully the questions of presentation and of audience when designing, delivering, and collecting oral history online.

Audiences for Online Oral History

Identifying primary and secondary audiences for an oral history web project is key to success. Generally, the audiences for Web projects fall into three categories: (1) scholars, (2) students and teachers, and (3) interested members of the general public. Each group has unique needs and concerns when approaching oral history online.

Researchers and Scholars

Scholars are perhaps the audience with which oral historians and archivists are most familiar. These users often seek archives of raw material to mine for research purposes and want access to complete recordings of interviews with minimal editing. The Internet has dramatically increased their access to oral history collections, bringing valuable information about the past to new and ever-growing audiences in the present. For example, the Library of Congress American Memory collections offer a large archive of interviews dealing with a wide range of topics. While a Google search on "oral history" returns more than 13 million results, the savvy search-engine user can refine and filter the parameters to quickly locate reliable resources.[9]

There are also new tools for engaging with oral history, from searching the full text of a transcript to text-mining a large collection of oral histories, looking for anticipated and unanticipated patterns. Excerpts are easily linked to longer interviews, allowing users to examine the full context of a selection or to locate multiple interviews related to a topic. Audio and video interviews also allow users to ask about the relationship between interviewer and interviewee, to hear the questions asked, and to listen for tone and emotion—locating surprise or irony not always transparent in a written text.

Most oral historians do not think of themselves as librarians or archivists, but carefully considering issues of metadata and cataloging when presenting their work on the Web makes it most useful to scholars. Libraries use highly articulated metadata systems to catalog their collections that go far beyond the basic information of title, author, subject, and description. Historians need not emulate the detail and specificity of a Machine-Readable Catalogue (MARC) record or the Encoded Archival Description (EAD) system, but a more streamlined metadata standard, such as that developed by the Dublin Core Metadata Initiative (DCMI), provides users with enough contextual data about each record to navigate the materials efficiently.[10] Exposing complete metadata significantly increases the ability of search engines to locate specific oral histories within a large collection.

Equally essential to making oral history materials discoverable for research are issues of accessibility for users of different abilities. Web accessibility has been of central concern to Web designers ever since the community embraced standards in the move to separate style from content using cascading style sheets (CSS). This effort to make content available regardless of the style elements means, for example, that text is available to screen readers for those with visual impairments. These users, however, make up only one of a host of audiences that require special accommodations to fully experience Web content.

In 1998, when congress amended the 1973 Rehabilitation Act (29 U.S.C. 794d), Section 508 called for accessibility accommodations for users of electronic and information technology, with the goal of providing information for those with disabilities that is comparable to the information accessed by other users.[11] Although the law applies to federal agencies, the standards established for compliance with Section 508 have come to serve as the base of all Web accessibility work. The community of Web designers and developers also adopted the cause of accessibility as they worked to create technical specifications for building Web sites. Thus, the World Wide Web Consortium has also issued a set of Web Content Accessibility Guidelines (WCAG).[12]

For the oral historian constructing a digital project, the most important of these standards involve the delivery of audio and video content. Section 508 standards and the WCAG 2.0 standards both call for a text equivalent for every nontext item, allowing users to convert that content to larger print, braille, speech, symbols, or simpler language. Primarily these standards refer to images, but they logically lead to the next set of guidelines about time-based media. Web developers need to present a synchronized alternative to prerecorded audio or video, which provides the equivalent information. The content of the alternative should include not only a rendering of the speech or the audio but also a description of the imagery and titles on video. Generally, captioning for audio and video is the preferred method for providing this alternative, although video of sign interpretation is another option.[13]

At the very least, the best practice is to present full, time-coded transcripts of all audio and video content in close proximity to the multimedia versions.

The Internet also serves as a medium for communication about oral history for scholars engaged in oral history projects or looking for oral history research. From easy access to guides for conceptualizing and conducting oral history to journal articles and blog postings about the practice, the Internet provides a wealth of informational resources on the practice and business of oral history. The Oral History Association, for example, presents a wiki and a blog as well as a host of more traditional resources. Other online offerings include the Southern Oral History Program guidebook *Resources for Planning and Conducting Oral History Interviews*, the *Do History* "Step-by-Step Guide to Oral History," and the Minnesota Historical Society guidelines for creating, transcribing, or editing oral histories. In addition, academics have initiated virtual conversations about oral history by posting videos on a range of topics, from definitions to research methods.[14] Teachers and students can also raise questions, post announcements, and share curricular, readings lists, and sundry other items on H-ORALHIST, an interactive forum conducted via email.[15]

Students and Teachers

Students and teachers are another key audience for digital oral history projects. With the plethora of written, audio, and video oral histories online, teachers can now bring voices of the past directly into the classroom, connecting students to the past and linking past events to individual lives. Students can read Turkish folk tales collected to preserve centuries of oral tradition in a rapidly changing area of the world, listen to interviews on the experiences of Koreans and Korean Americans in the United States between 1903 and 1965, or browse the recollections of men and women who participated in the British colonial experience in India.[16]

Oral histories, however, are a specific kind of historical evidence. When students and teachers ask questions based on the nature of oral history, such as the relationship between the interviewer and the interviewee, they are better able to construct meaningful historical knowledge. *Making Sense of Oral History*, by Linda Shopes, models this process by introducing the field of oral history and presenting specific questions to ask when reading or listening to oral history interviews. Careful selection of manageable segments of the sources, and ample contextual framing, also encourage thoughtful use of oral histories. Narratives can be juxtaposed to illuminate the importance of perspective, change over time, the need for corroboration, and other elements of the craft of history. The *National Visionary Leadership Project* presents a large collection of video interviews with African American community leaders, along with lesson plans that integrate carefully chosen interview excerpts and associated primary source materials.[17]

Engaging students of all ages in conducting oral histories to actively recover stories of the past is a powerful teaching tool; presenting the materials they collect online, even more so. Placing oral history projects online allows students to not only learn from their families or communities and share those stories in the classroom, it also allows them to share what they are learning with those outside the classroom, with their families both locally and globally.

"What Did You Do In The War, Grandma?" was the central question asked by high school students in South Kingston, Rhode Island, in the 1990s as part of an oral history project to document the lives of women during World War II. In this early example of an online student oral history project, twenty-six interviews are presented as written transcripts with brief introductions. Eileen Hughes wanted to join the Women's Auxiliary Army Corps (WAAC), but just as she was turning eighteen, they raised the minimum age to twenty-one. "I was very angry because I really, really planned on going," Hughes remembered. "I wrote to the President of the United States and said I just wanted to go and I didn't think it was fair."[18]

Lisa Morehouse, a former English teacher in San Francisco and rural Georgia, described the process as magic: "Collecting oral histories, or documenting the experiences of people who have lived through a particular aspect of history, allows students to see themselves as storytellers and historians. The process taught my students skills from across the standards spectrum, and it made them conduits between history and a person's life—an experience that stayed with them well beyond the assignment." She told of an at-risk student whose interview with his mother, a refuge from the Khmer Rouge, not only changed his understanding of his family history but helped him connect to school and learning in a new way. *The Making: Oral History Project* offers further evidence of the impact of conducting oral history research. Conducted by a high school class at the John F. Kennedy bilingual, bicultural school in Germany, the project documents the process of conducting oral histories for a book about the Berlin Wall. Students share their experiences and the lessons they learned by interviewing relatives, neighbors, and others about life before and after the fall of the Berlin Wall.[19]

Teaching with oral history can mean creating, using, or integrating interviews into student projects. All three are happening in classrooms and are changing the ways that teachers and students relate to the past. They allow students to access stories and to tell stories that do not appear in textbook narratives. New formats, such as podcasts, and venues for presenting audio and video, such as YouTube, make it possible for students to share their work as amateur oral historians with a broader audience. Students have put their own projects online individually. Standing in front of an empty towel rack and a closed door, a young man discussed the advantages of conducting a first-person interview and added, "I did this for social studies and language arts. I got a 90."[20]

General Audiences

Beyond the specialized audiences of scholars and the education community, interested members of the general public form a potential audience for oral history work. Prior to the significant expansion of new media projects, the public had limited access to oral history work outside of popular histories, scholarly monographs, and documentary films. Now we have the possibility of presenting oral history with a supplementary context of images, documents, and film footage. American Radio Work's *Remembering Jim Crow* presents a rich historical context that includes excerpts of interviews with individuals who lived through segregation, historical images, and secondary perspective from historians.[21] Community histories also provide excellent examples of this type of crafted narrative presentation of oral history. The Library of Congress's American Folklife Center's project, *Working in Paterson: Occupational Heritage in an Urban Setting*, contains 470 interview excerpts and almost 4,000 images from a four-month study of occupational culture in Paterson, New Jersey. The site also includes six interpretive essays to provide context.[22]

Web sites are by far the most prevalent means by which oral historians reach these general audiences in the digital age, but they are not the only Internet channel available. The iPod's signature white earbud headphones are nearly ubiquitous accessories on city sidewalks and public transit systems. "Podcasting"—Internet broadcasting—makes each and every one of those headphoned commuters a potential oral history listener, subject, or interviewer.

Through its partnership with National Public Radio (NPR), StoryCorps has garnered tremendous attention and expanded its pool of interviewers and interviewees. With podcasting, every oral history project can enjoy many of the same distribution services, if not the same audience size.[23] By making it easy for oral historians to broadcast digital audio files to large audiences and for those audiences to access audio content when and where they please, podcasts present particular opportunities to oral historians. Literally within minutes, and at little or no cost, oral historians can produce a serial audio program that listeners can easily find, subscribe to, and listen to on their computers, iPods, MP3 players, and other portable digital audio devices.

Barely ten years after the first blog was posted, blogs are now a familiar part of mainstream media with major news organizations, scholarly associations, and government agencies all maintaining these quick, chronologically ordered Web publications. Essentially audio blogs, podcasts are likewise growing in popularity. Avoiding as much technical jargon as possible, a podcast is no more and no less than a digital audio file attached to an RSS ("really simple syndication") feed. The combination of audio and RSS is exceedingly easy to produce—attaching an MP3 file to a blog post does the trick—and doing so creates a broadcast that other Web services (feed readers, search engines, and music directories) can read, automatically detecting when new audio is added to the feed. It is this combination of technologies, for instance, that enables iTunes to "watch" a sound project's feed—its podcast—so that every time a new audio file is added, iTunes automatically downloads it to the user's music library and iPod. Podcast technology essentially enables listeners to "subscribe" to Internet audio programs, download new audio content as soon as it becomes available, and listen to it later at their convenience.

The first step in starting a podcast most often involves creating a blog, a remarkably simple operation. Most popular blogging services and software packages include the two essential technologies of podcasting, a way to mount MP3s online and an RSS feed to syndicate them. Free hosted blog services such as *Blogger*,

WordPress.com, or *TypePad* are relatively easy to set up. Alternatively, if you have access to a Web server, a blogging package such as *MovableType* or *WordPress* allows you to host your own blog.[24]

The benefits of simple, affordable audio broadcasting technology to oral historians are obvious. Yet oral history podcasting remains in its infancy. A 2009 search of the iTunes podcast directory for "oral history" yielded fewer than fifty podcasts. Nevertheless, a growing number of small oral history projects are using podcasting to great effect. These early adopters have pioneered several different models. Some projects, such as the *Stony Brook University Oral History Project*, have chosen to publish full, unedited interviews from their back catalog. Others, such as the *Los Alamos Historical Society Podcast* project introduce short "teaser" clips with a headnote from project staff directing listeners to the physical archives for access to full transcripts and audiotapes. Still others are more heavily edited and produced. Each *Mozilla Digital Memory Bank* podcast sets off interview clips with introductory music, a thorough headnote, intervening commentary, and links back to full interview transcripts and downloadable digital audio. In this case, and also in the case of the *Hurricane Digital Memory Bank* project, podcasts encourage visitors and contributions to the online collecting site.[25] Used in this way, podcasting can be an effective way not only of disseminating historical content but also of increasing participation in the project.

Varieties of Online Oral Histories

The continuum of online oral history runs from catalogs of traditional materials to full access, from online text transcripts and audio recordings completed by traditional oral historians to newfangled oral history projects generated in the digital age and intended for Web presentation and engagement—"born digital" projects of the twenty-first century. In between, are projects that started in one era and are finding new audiences in another.

Adapting the Past for the Present: Putting Traditional Archives Online

An online archive is fundamentally a collection of digital files to share with other people. For the oral historian with a predigital collection, making resources available online is largely a function of conversion. Oral histories that are intended for online distribution are recorded, collected, and organized according to a preset architecture based on the technical considerations of the project. The more than five hundred oral histories collected for the *Bracero History Archive*, for example, were recorded with the goal of creating an online archive. Interviews were recorded using digital equipment, and all material was collected digitally. The project can then focus on organization and presentation.[26]

When a historian builds a digital archive using nondigital resources, however, additional steps and questions are involved. One example is *Greensboro VOICES: Voicing Observations in Civil Rights and Equality Struggles*, created by the Greensboro Public Library and the University Libraries of the University of North Carolina–Greensboro. The project Web site presents written transcripts of 140 oral history interviews conducted from the late 1970s to the early 1990s and focused on the civil rights movement in Guilford County, North Carolina. Interviews cover a range of topics, from sit-ins such as the Woolworth's protest to various marches, and from school desegregation to local NAACP and Congress of Racial Equality (CORE) chapters. The project existed as a traditional oral history project for many years, and the original audio recordings and transcripts are held in a brick-and-mortar archive at the University of North Carolina–Greensboro. However, the materials were limited to those who traveled to the archives, and the audio files were in danger of deteriorating. This prompted a decision to go digital. Audio files were digitized and paper transcripts were scanned and converted via optical character recognition (OCR) software; they were then edited thoroughly in a multistep process and presented via the Greensboro VOICES Web site.[27]

This lengthy process is representative of the steps involved in converting oral histories to the digital age. One key step is the conversion of files from analog to digital formats. Although it may sound daunting, the technical process is not complicated. Commercial services are available, and there are many hardware and software solutions—both free and paid—that will convert analog files into digital. In principle, they work the same way: identify the files to convert and select the output format; the program does the rest. There are many digital sound formats, but the two most prevalent are MP3 and wav.[28] Each has its strengths and limitations. Wav files are often the highest quality, but usually represent large file sizes. MP3 files retain slightly less of the original file data but are significantly smaller. For typical voice recordings, the difference in quality can be minimal.[29] Deciding which format to use means deciding whether the project or the user will need the higher detail and fidelity of a wav file, or whether a smaller, more servable, MP3 file would be acceptable.

One compromise is to use both, converting master analog files to both formats. The larger wav files may be stored on a server in case there is a genuine need for researchers to examine those files, while an archive features the MP3 versions for convenience. The *Greensboro VOICES* project saved the converted audio in both formats, higher quality wav files and compressed MP3 user copies, although neither are available via the Web site. The *Bracero History Archive* provides MP3 versions of oral histories via the Web, but wav versions of all files are maintained on a separate server for backup.

The first step is importing analog files onto a computer. Most computers have sound cards that are capable of making the analog-to-digital conversions. This requires appropriate equipment to play the analog files, such as a phonograph or cassette player, as well as an (inexpensive) 3.5 mm male-to-male stereo patch cord. One end of the cord plugs into the output jack of the media player, the jack normally used for headphones. The other end of the cord plugs into the audio input jack on the computer, the jack normally used for plugging in a microphone. Software to make the conversion is the next requirement, and there are dozens of programs that will import and convert files. In each case, the process is similar: using analog equipment, the stereo patch cord, and sound editing software, the computer imports and converts files. Converted files can be used in multiple ways to populate online archives.

Beyond Text and Audio: Online Video

For practical reasons of cost and portability, most oral historians until recently worked primarily with text and audio. Video, however, has provided yet another layer of information. The *Densho Digital Archive* was created to record the history of Japanese American internment camps before, during, and after World War II. The project has collected more than six hundred hours of videotaped oral history interviews as well as supporting documents and photographs. The interviews, presented as video, are divided into segments and are accompanied by full transcriptions and keyword definitions. Designed as a resource for teachers, students, and researchers, a free registration process regulates access to the archive. Watching Kara Kondo as she describes the night she and her family were sent to an internment camp is a powerful learning and research tool, her hesitations as telling as her words: "I'll always remember the sound of the gate clanging…knowing that…you had barbed wires around you and you were really being interned."[30]

The *Densho* project, started in the late 1990s, collected interviews with the Web in mind and specifically requested permission for online use of video. This is not the case for oral histories collected in previous decades before the technology for sharing audio or video, or even of freely distributing transcripts, was conceivable. Some interviewers recorded oral histories by taking handwritten notes during interviews and later, as audio recording equipment became more affordable, with audiotapes. The wide-ranging technologies and processes present a number of challenges in the twenty-first century. Permissions signed decades ago may not address current methods of distribution, thus raising ethical questions for written transcripts as well as audio records. Preservation is another challenging issue, as tapes deteriorate and new machines are no longer compatible with older recordings.

Even with the technical ability to reach large audiences and to share oral history interviews with researchers, teachers, and students around the world, questions remain about how they are used. *Densho* worked to balance the goal of protecting interviewees with its aim to reach a large audience and to deepen the study of Japanese American internment. The project presented eleven compelling video excerpts on YouTube, including an introduction to the project. The *Tibet Oral History Project* similarly uses YouTube as a medium for reaching out to the general public with an introductory movie explaining the goal of the project—"to preserve the true history of the Tibetan people"—and short clips from oral history interviews. These clips offer links back to the main project Web site.[31]

Collecting Oral History Online

Over time, people have grown even more willing and eager to tell their stories. Viewers interact with the media they consume, and they want to be heard. Individuals around the world share their ideas and memories every day, uploading text, photographs, audio, and video to an ever-growing host of online repositories. YouTube, a novelty only a few years ago, receives ten hours of video every minute: people around the world watch hundreds of millions of these videos daily.[32] Only a small percentage of these videos present formal oral histories, but many more record the voices of individuals who want to share their opinions and thoughts on the latest song as well as on major political events around the world. People of all ages are creating records of their own histories, their thoughts on elections and natural disasters as well as on significant events in their personal lives, such as the daily routine on a farm, learning to read, or experiences on the road as a political campaign worker.

It is common today for a host of organizations, from media outlets to museums, to tap into this new openness, to ask for input, comments, or stories from online visitors, in addition to the ubiquitous personal blogs and online repositories for chronicling life's details. On a 2009 visit to CNN.com, online visitors were asked to share their experiences trying to survive the economic downturn, as well as their thoughts on how they will remember the outgoing president George W. Bush. Similarly, several years before the doors are scheduled to open at the National Museum of African American History and Culture, the museum launched a digital memory book to generate community and audience interest in this newest Smithsonian. When inviting contributions, the museum states, "You can connect your stories and oral histories with friends, family, and new acquaintances through the NMAAHC virtual Memory Book."[33]

The Internet offers many resources connected with the collecting and sharing of oral history, as well as a growing dialog about its practices and uses, but it has also played a role in shaping the definition of oral history. In the late 1990s, the notion of collecting history online was relatively new. One of the first Web sites designed with this explicit goal, the *Blackout History Project* invited visitors to complete a lengthy online survey in 1998 about their experiences during the New York City blackouts of 1965 and 1977.[34] It also asked contributors to provide a phone number so researchers could call and conduct a longer, more traditional oral history interview. *Blackout* offers a good example of how historians explored the transition to digital collection methods, experimenting with a new format but retaining a traditional format as a key part of the process.

Another early example, *Brainerd, Kansas: Time, Place, and Memory on the Prairie Plains*, launched in 2000, focused on a broader chronology connected to a specific place. A former bustling railroad town, Brainerd today boasts a population of forty to fifty residents "varying according to the weather, the state of the local economy, and the fortunes of the nearby high school football team." Memories emailed by former residents were added to more traditional in-person interviews to create the collective record of Brainerd's history. On a larger scale, between 2003 and 2006, the British Broadcasting Corporation's *WW2 People's War* gathered 47,000 stories and 15,000 images from Britain's World War II veterans and survivors of the London Blitz.[35] Another good example is the *September 11 Digital Archive*, designed to digitally collect, preserve, and present the history of the September 11, 2001, attacks in New York, Virginia, and Pennsylvania. It launched with little fanfare in January 2002, simply by asking users to "share their story." Since its launch, the site has collected and archived more than 150,000 digital objects and was the first digital collection accessioned by the Library of Congress.[36]

More recently, StoryCorps has explored a mixed-media strategy of in-person interviews, online collecting, Web dissemination, and podcasting to capture a huge range of stories from tremendously diverse audiences and to foster communication. "By recording the stories of our lives with the people we care about," its organizers note, "we experience our history, hopes, and humanity... creating a growing portrait of who we really are as Americans." Topics range from poignant personal moments with stories of love or childbirth to individual experiences within larger historical events, such as leaving Cuba in 1963, participating in civil rights marches, walking the picket line during the Memphis sanitation strike of 1968, or surviving daily life as a prisoner of war. For each story, StoryCorps includes a photograph of the interviewee and in some cases, the interviewer, a brief description of the topic and the individuals, a quote, and an audio file. The stories are grouped by theme and the keyword search examines the full text, although there are no written transcripts available. The quotes and topics draw in the listener, but this online archive is primarily designed for browsing.[37]

The key differences between a traditional oral history project and a digital one include process, metadata, and verification. A trained oral historian conducting an interview brings a number of tools and strategies to the process, including background knowledge and careful collection of basic information, such as demographics, locations, names, and dates. A Web site, in contrast, collects what users choose to offer, be it thorough or fragmentary. Most digital archives do not edit postings for grammar or check for "accuracy," so each contribution stands as originally created by the individual contributor, although some projects provide contributors with access to copies of their materials and with the ability to edit submissions. Nevertheless, it is important in the digital realm, just as it is in the physical realm, to consider issues such as privacy, permissions, vetting, and preservation. Devices such as "terms of service" notices, clear copyright terms, and electronic consent forms can mitigate some of these problems.[38]

Despite these challenges, it is possible to create a rich digital archive that encourages public participation in saving the past without compromising the integrity of the evidence collected or the privacy of contributors. Digital collecting need not be expensive or complicated, but it should be designed to fit your intended audience and potential size of collected materials. Collecting data can be as simple as communicating over email or as complex as a large-scale digital history repository.

When targeting a small group, creating a questionnaire with online survey software, such as *Survey Monkey* or *Poll Daddy*, may be a good option. Starting a blog, through a hosted service or locally managed, provides space for receiving lengthy comments. Moving to a multi-user environment gives a small, contained group of individuals the opportunity to upload photos and share stories at will. Using Web phone services, such as Skype, allows a historian to conduct a traditional interview over phone or video that can be recorded, saved, and uploaded to a digital archive. Even Internet chat services that allow for real-time conversations may be archived as digital oral histories. For larger projects, the most flexible and powerful way to manage digital collecting is to develop a Web site. A number of free or inexpensive platforms offer tools and modules for building robust database-driven websites, contribution forms, and ways to display and share submissions, such as *Joomla*, *Drupal*, and *Omeka*.[39]

When designing a Web site for collecting history online, strive to build something that is easy to navigate, loads quickly in a variety of browsers, provides a simple way for people to share with the archive, and helps contributors feel comfortable sharing personal stories and images. Provide basic site navigation for browsing, contributing, and learning more about the project. Make the project's mission clear, state your intended audience, and provide information about project partners, staff, or community connections. Create a simple way for people to contribute to the site by designing a short form and easy process for sharing and uploading images, podcasts, or other born-digital files. Clearly state file size limitations, which is particularly an issue with high-resolution photographs and video clips, and provide alternative ways for interested contributors to share their materials. While you may want to generate a form with detailed questions about experiences of the subject, let the individual decide what they want to contribute by making most fields optional. The more that is required, the less likely the person is to finish and submit the form. Try to reach as many potential contributors and to make the process as comfortable and easy to use as possible.

Building a Web site can be the easiest part of a collecting project. Finding contributors requires significant legwork and staff time. In its early stages, it is important to line up individuals to share with the archive, so that there are materials to browse when the project goes public. Partners can also help promote a project. Distributing publicity materials, flyers, postcards, and bookmarks with the site's URL at meetings and conferences helps attract traffic to the site. Promote the project in the digital world by reaching out to bloggers, posting notices on discussion lists, contacting the news media, writing articles in relevant journals or magazines, and discussing and sharing the URL on social networking services such as Twitter, Facebook, or Digg.

While a project can reach many people with a Web interface, the targeted audience may also include populations who are "unwired," requiring additional outreach. First, set up a local phone number through Skype or other online telephone service that will provide the opportunity to contribute via voicemail. Those audio files can then be uploaded directly into the archive. Print prepaid reply cards for short written responses, or if the site relates to a physical museum exhibit, offer comment cards in the gallery. Those cards can be scanned and uploaded, as happened with the *September 11: Bearing Witness to History* exhibition at the National Museum of American History.[40] Make use of Web terminals at public libraries and community wifi hotspots by leaving publicity materials nearby or introducing the project and helping the audience to contribute. Making a digital collecting site a true grassroots effort requires considerable outreach.

At the Crossroads

Oral history sits at the crossroads of the convergence of old and new media. Parts of it are an artifact of the past. A well-known example is the Works Progress Administration (WPA) Federal Writers' Project that set out to record the experiences of more than two thousand former slaves in the mid-1930s. Interviewers recorded stories in seventeen states and asked ex-slaves to share personal accounts of their lives during slavery. When questions arose, however, about the accuracy of some of the records, handwritten by the interviewers during or after the conversations, there was no audio or video record available for verification. Audio records, for example, would help researchers today try to understand the relationship between interviewer and interviewee, including how former slaves perceived government employees who asked them about memories of a painful topic more than seventy years in the past.[41]

In the digital age, these problems are unlikely to repeat. There will be new problems, such as long-term storage of digital files, but the Internet has greatly expanded the capacity of oral historians to record and disseminate ordinary voices from around the world on an almost limitless array of topics. Oral history, a powerful tool for researching, teaching, and learning about the past is not new, but widespread access to it is. From presenting catalog information to collecting oral histories, from displaying video of interviewees reflecting on the past to capturing responses to current events via podcasts, the Internet is unquestioningly reshaping the field of oral history.

NOTES

1. Library of Congress, American Memory, *Quilts and Quiltmaking in America*, http://memory.loc.gov/ammem/qlthtml/qlthome.html; Frontline and WGBH, *The Gulf War: War Stories*, http://www.pbs.org/wgbh/pages/frontline/gulf/war/; Chicago History Museum, *Studs Terkel, Conversations with America*, http://www.studsterkel.org/htimes.php (accessed Jan. 5, 2009); StoryCorps, "Manny Diaz," http://www.storycorps.net/listen/stories/manny-diaz-and-blanca-vazquez.

2. Smithsonian National Air and Space Museum, *Oral History on Space, Science, and Technology*, http://www.nasm.si.edu/research/dsh/ohp-introduction.html; Center for History and New Media, *The Accident at Three Mile Island*, http://echo.gmu.edu/tmi/index.php.

3. "Chapman Cousins Oral History: Growing Up in a Small Town," YouTube, http://youtube.com/watch?v=42uEx6dk_V8.

4. United States Holocaust Memorial Museum, "Oral History Catalog Search," http://www.ushmm.org/research/collections/oralhistory/search/.

5. Bancroft Library, Regional Oral History Office, "The Suffragists," http://www.archive.org/stream/teapartiesprisonooglucrich/teapartiesprisonooglucrich_djvu.txt; Center for History and New Media, *History Matters*, "Auto Tours for Women's Suffrage: An Oral Memoir," http://historymatters.gmu.edu/d/5334.

6. *Neighborhood Story Project*, http://www.neighborhoodstoryproject.org/seventh.html.

7. John B. Horrigan, "Home Broadband Adoption 2008," *Pew Internet and American Life Project*, July 2008, i, http://www.pewinternet.org/pdfs/PIP_Broadband_2008.pdf.

8. Mary Madden, "Online Video," *Pew Internet and American Life Project*, July 25, 2007, i–iv, http://www.pewinternet.org/pdfs/PIP_Online_Video_2007.pdf; Lee Rainie, "Pew Internet Project Data Memo: Video Sharing Websites," *Pew Internet and American Life Project*, Jan. 9, 2008, http://www.pewinternet.org/pdfs/Pew_Videosharing_memo_Jan08.pdf.

9. American Memory, Library of Congress, http://memory.loc.gov/ammem/index.html. See, for example, *American Life Histories: Manuscripts from the Federal Writers' Project, 1936–1940*, http://memory.loc.gov/ammem/wpaintro/wpahome.html, with approximately 2,900 life histories addressing topics such as family, education, income, occupation, political views, religion and mores, medical needs, and diet, as well as observations on society and culture.

10. Library of Congress, *Understanding MARC Bibliographic: Machine-Readable Cataloging* (5th ed.) http://www.loc.gov/marc/umb/; Library of Congress, *Encoded Archival Description (EAD) Official Web Site* http://lcweb.loc.gov/ead/; *Dublin Core Metadata Initiative*, http://dublincore.org/.

11. Section 508, http://www.section508.gov/index.cfm?FuseAction=Content&ID=3. For a summary of accessibility issues, see Trenton Moss, "What Is Web Accessibility?" *A List Apart*, Apr. 30, 2004, http://www.alistapart.com/articles/wiwa.

12. World Wide Web Consortium, "Web Content Accessibility Guidelines," http://www.w3.org/TR/WCAG20/. See also World Wide Web Consortium, *Web Accessibility Initiative*, http://www.w3.org/WAI/.

13. Section 508, 1194.22 and WACG 2.0 Guidelines 1.1, and 1.2. See also Lisa Herrod, "Deafness and the User Experience," *A List Apart*, Aug. 12, 2008, http://www.alistapart.com/articles/deafnessandtheuserexperience/.

14. Oral History Association, *Oral History Association,* http://www.oralhistory.org/; University of North Carolina-Chapel Hill, *Southern Oral History Project*, http://www.sohp.org/howto/index.html; Judith Moyer, "Step-by-Step Guide to Oral History" http://dohistory.org/on_your_own/toolkit/oralHistory.html; Minnesota Historical Society, *Oral History Collection*, http://www.mnhs.org/collections/oralhistory/oralhistory.htm.

15. Listserv@h-net.msu.edu.

16. Texas Tech University, Special Collections Library, *Uysal-Walker Archive of Turkish Oral Narrative*, http://aton.ttu.edu/; University of Southern California, *Korean American Digital Archive*, http://www.usc.edu/libraries/collections/korean_american/; Louisiana State University, T. Harry Williams Oral History Center, *British Voices from South Asia*, http://chnm.gmu.edu/worldhistorysources/d/61/whm.html.

17. Linda Shopes, "Making Sense of Oral History," *History Matters* historymatters.gmu.edu/mse/oral; *National Visionary Leadership Project*, http://www.visionaryproject.org/education/.

18. Linda Wood, Judi Scott, and Brown University, *What Did You Do in the War, Grandma?* http://www.stg.brown.edu/projects/WWII_Women/TeenageVolunteer.html.

19. Lisa Morehouse, "Living Legends: Oral History Projects Bring Core Subjects to Life," *Edutopia,* http://www.edutopia.org/oral-history-projects; AMack Studios, "The Making, Part I: Oral History Project," http://www.youtube.com/watch?v=tILFdICHYTU&feature=related; AMack Studios, "The Making, Part 2: Oral History Project," http://www.youtube.com/watch?v=V66Y4SC_gpU&feature=channel.

20. chehade9999, "Oral History," http://www.youtube.com/watch?v=3q2zoxJolmI.

21. Stephen Smith, Kate Ellis, and Sasha Aslanian, American RadioWorks, *Remembering Jim Crow*, http://americanradioworks.publicradio.org/features/remembering.

22. Library of Congress, American Folklife Center, *Working in Paterson: Occupational Heritage in an Urban Setting,* http://memory.loc.gov/ammem/collections/paterson/.

23. Indeed, NPR itself publishes StoryCorp interviews as a podcast http://www.npr.org/rss/podcast/podcast_detail.php?siteId=9157743.

24. Several good online tutorials can help get you started. Common Craft provides simple, introductory cartoons explaining the basic elements of blogs http://www.commoncraft.com/blogs, RSS http://www.commoncraft.com/rss_plain_english, and podcasting described here at http://www.commoncraft.com/podcasting. Apple provides guidance for new podcasters http://www.apple.com/itunes/whatson/podcasts/specs.html.

25. Stony Brook University Oral History Project, https://podcast.ic.sunysb.edu/weblog/oralhistory/; Los Alamos Historical Society Podcast project http://www.losalamoshistory.org/pods.htm; Mozilla Digital Memory Bank Podcast, for example, http://mozillamemory.org/blog/category/oral-history/; Hurricane Digital Memory Bank project, http://hurricanearchive.org/news/?cat=12.

26. *The Bracero History Archive,* bracerohistory.org.

27. Greensboro Public Library and the University Libraries of the University of North Carolina-Greensboro, *Greensboro VOICES*, http://library.uncg.edu/depts/archives/civrights/index.asp.

28. MP3 stands for MPEG-1 Audio Layer 3, and files in this format will end in that suffix—sample.mp3; likewise, wav stands for Waveform, and those files will end with the. wav suffix.

29. GMG Classical Music Forum did a blind survey in 2007 to see whether a group of classical music enthusiasts could tell the difference between MP3 and wav recordings. Of the nearly two hundred respondents, only about forty could distinguish a difference between MP3 and wav versions of Berlioz's *Symphonie fantastique*. Clearly this exercise

suggests that the quality lost by compression to MP3 may be acceptable in many circumstances.

30. Densho, *Densho: The Japanese American Legacy Project*, "Kara Kondo Interview Segment 26," http://archive.densho.org/main.aspx.

31. Densho, "About the Densho Project," http://www.youtube.com/watch?v=hq4sBSsuJDQ&feature=PlayList&p=761F41590740EC6D&index=4 (accessed Dec. 28, 2008); Tibet Oral History Project, "Tibet Oral History Project," http://www.youtube.com/watch?v=iGj5AWXadLA.

32. YouTube, *YouTube*, http://www.youtube.com/t/fact_sheet.

33. *CNN.com* points online visitors to their *iReport* section, where they collect comments and stories about recent news, such as the section on "Surviving a Tough Economy," http://www.ireport.com/ir-topic-stories.jspa?topicId=178151 and "How Will you Remember Bush?" http://www.ireport.com/ir-topic-stories.jspa?topicId=179723; National Museum of African American History and Culture, "Memories," http://nmaahc.si.edu/memories.

34. Center for History and New Media, *Blackout History Project*, http://blackout.gmu.edu/.

35. *Brainerd, Kansas: Time, Place, and Memory on the Prairie Plains*, http://www.rootinaround.com/brainerd/; BBC, *WW2 People's War*, http://www.bbc.co.uk/ww2peopleswar/.

36. Dan Cohen and Roy Rosenzweig, *Digital History: A Guide to Gathering, Preserving, and Presenting the Past on the Web* (Philadelphia: University of Pennsylvania Press, 2005) and also online at http://chnm.gmu.edu/digitalhistory/; *September 11 Digital Archive*, http://911digitialarchive.org.

37. StoryCorps, *StoryCorps*, http://www.storycorps.net/.

38. For a thoroughgoing discussion of technical, ethical, and legal issues pertaining to online collecting, see Cohen and Rosenzweig, *Digital History*, chap. 6, and James T. Sparrow, "On the Web: The September 11 Digital Archive," in *Public History: Essays from the Field*, ed. James B. Gardner and Peter S. Lapaglia (Malabar, Fla.: Krieger, 2004).

39. L-soft provides Listserv email list hosting, http://www.lsoft.com/, and H-net remains a widely used forum for creating and finding lists on a variety of history topics, http://www.h-net.org/. Yahoo Groups offers free email group hosting for thousands of groups, http://groups.yahoo.com/. Survey Monkey, http://surveymonkey.com and Poll Daddy, http://polldaddy.com are just two examples of online survey software. There are a number of free and low-cost blogging services, for example, Blogger, owned by Google which offers a free blogging platform and hosting, http://www.blogger.com; Moveable Type is an open-source package available for hosting on your own server, http://www.movabletype.org; WordPress is another open-source product that provides free software, hosted accounts, and a multi-user environment: http://wordpress.com/ and http://wordpress.org. For examples on collecting and posting digital oral histories gathered through Instant Messenger and Skype see these examples from the Mozilla Digital Memory Bank: Mozilla Digital Memory Bank, Object #7285, Aug. 14, 2007, http://mozillamemory.org/detailview.php?id=7285; CHNM MDMB Content Team, Mozilla Digital Memory Bank, Object #7591, July 18, 2008, http://mozillamemory.org/detailview.php?id=7591. Open-source site construction and content management systems include: Drupal, http://drupal.org/, Joomla, http://www.joomla.org/, and Omeka, http://omeka.org.

40. To see postcards scanned from the exhibition September 11: Bearing Witness to History, (Sept. 11, 2002 to July 6, 2003), see http://911digitalarchive.org/galleries.php?collection_id=31

41. Library of Congress, American Memory, *Born in Slavery: Slave Narratives from the Federal Writers' Project, 1936–1938*, http://memory.loc.gov/ammem/snhtml/snhome.html.

BIBLIOGRAPHY

Cohen, Dan, and Roy Rosenzweig. *Digital History: A Guide to Gathering, Preserving, and Presenting the Past on the Web*. Philadelphia: University of Pennsylvania Press, 2005.

Shopes, Linda. "Making Sense of Oral History." History Matters, http://www.historymatters.gmu.edu/mse/oral.

Sparrow, James T. "On the Web: The September 11 Digital Archive." In *Public History: Essays from the Field*, edited by James B. Gardner and Peter S. Lapaglia. Malabar, Fla.: Krieger, 2004.

Index

Note: Page numbers in *italics* indicate tables and charts.

abolitionism, 188
abortion, 179
Abu Ghraib prison, 121
academic freedom, 436
access issues
  and archives, 291–99, 326–27, 506–8
  and cataloging, 398–401
  and the digital revolution, 291–99, 326–27, 347–48
  and funding, 292–93
  and indexing practices, 339, 341
  and interview restrictions, 354–55
  and the media, 303
  and media technology, 501
  and online standards, 502
  and online transcripts, 292, 500
  and public domain, 363
  and "raw" vs. "cooked" documents, 334–35
  and scholarship, 27–28
  and students of oral history, 464, 478, 504
  and time codes, *298*
  and university-based oral history programs, 422
  and unprocessed materials, 401
acetates, 404
acquisitions appraisal, 395–98
actual malice, 357
adult education movement, 5
"Advocacy Oral History: Palestinian Women in Resistance" (Gluck), 175
Afghanistan War, 5
Africa, 176. *See also specific countries*
African American Odyssey: The Stewarts, 1853–1963 (Broussard), 190–91
African Americans
  and American slavery, 186–90
  and the civil rights movement, 186, 193–95, 465
  and community studies, 190–93
  and cultural heritage, 61
  and group identity, 68
  and illiteracy research, *67*
  and racial interview dynamics, 32–33
  and the Tuskegee Syphilis Study, 364
  and voting rights, 69
  and women's oral history, 170
African National Congress (ANC), 152, 153
After School Writers Club, 452–53
age issues
  and generational divides, 43, 44
  and gentrification, 227–29
  and gerontology, 203–7
  and intergenerational interaction, 282
  and later life, 202–15
  and memory, 82
  and negotiating remembrance, 282
Agee, Arthur, 197
agricultural extension, 172
AIDS in the UK: The Making of Policy, 1981–1994 (Berridge), 376–77
AIDS Social History Programme, 376
Aintree Hospital, 380
Akenfield (Blythe), 5
Albertelli, Guido, 118
Alemanno, Gianni, 119
Alexander Street Press, 181
Alfonsín, Raúl, 132–35
Alice's Adventures in Wonderland and Through the Looking Glass (Carroll), 104
All Saints Heritage Project, 380
Alleanza Nazionale, 113
Allison, Jay, 310
alternative frameworks, 440
alternative histories, 445n19
Amazon, 299
American Archivist, 322
American Century Oral History Program, 456–57, 457–58, 458–59
American Folklife Center, 15, 311, 451, 505
American Historical Association, 364
American Historical Review, 374
American Legion, 14
American Negro Slavery (Phillips), 187
American Oral History Association, 474
American Revolutionary War, 3
analog recordings, 287, 394, 402, 404–5, 406n4, 508
analysis of interviews, 40
anarchism, *67*, 69
ancestor worship, 52
and women's oral history, 171
Anderson, Kathryn, 173, 175, 182, 492, 494–95
Anderson Valley Oral History Project, 452
Andrew W. Mellon Foundation, 414
Anglo-American Cataloging Rules, 2nd edition (AACR2), 398
Ant Follower conjecture, *72*, *73*

anthropology
  and African culture, 187–88
  and audio recording, 286–87, 316
  and autobiographical memory, 106
  and cultural retention, 188
  dialogic, 56
  and linguistics, 101
  and memory biases, 79
  palaeoanthropology, 477
  and positivism, 81
  and postmodernism, 174, 176
  and the sensory revolution, 219–20, 221
  and women's oral history, 176, 177
anti-Communism, 41, 120
anti-Fascism, 113–14, 119–20, 122nn2–3, 298–99, 344
anti-imperialism, 134–37
antilynching movement, 410
"Anzac Memories" (Thomson), 432, 492
apartheid, 6, 435
Apple, 9, 290, 299
archaeology, 477
archival institutions
  and accessibility issues, 291–99
  and acquisitions appraisal, 395–98
  archival vs. oral evidence, 79
  and cataloging, 398–401
  dark archives, 301
  defined, 406n1
  and digital technology, 295, 315–16, 324–27, 506–8, 510–11
  and funding issues, 393–94, 395–98, 398–401, 401–5, 405–6
  and Holocaust survivors, 248
  and House of Memory and History, 114
  and model for oral history, 420
  and practice of oral history, 315–16
  and preservation, 401–5
  and "raw" vs. "cooked" documents, 334
  and recording technology, 8, 319–24
  and reflective teaching, 473
  role of, 393–94
  and university-based oral history programs, 481–84
An Archives Approach to Oral History (Lance), 320–21
Argentina, 9, 121, 125, 130–31, 143, 434
artifact-based recording, 325
artifact-free recording, 325, 326
artificial intelligence, 344
Artists With Disabilities Oral History Project, 34
Ashton, Paul, 440
Ask the Fellows Who Cut the Hay (Evans), 97, 317
"Asking Hard Questions: Harvey the Historian as Colleague" (Morrisey), 466
Assmann, Aleida, 250
Association of American Historians of Medicine, 373
associative memory, 280
Associazione Italiana di Storia Orale (AISO), 118
Associazione Nazionale Ex Internati (ANEI), 113
Associazione Nazionale ex-Deportati (ANED), 113, 118
Associazione Nazionale Partigiani Italiani (ANPI), 113, 115, 117, 119, 122n6
Associazione Nazionale Perseguitati Politici Antifascisti (ANPPIA), 113, 118
Atlanta History Center, 304
Atlanta Race Riot, 305
Attica prison, 121
Auburn University, 301
audiences for oral history, 501–6
audio cassettes. *See* cassette recorders
audio installations, 309
audio recordings. *See also specific audio formats*
  and development of recording techniques, 277
  and digital technology, 9–11, 286–90, 299, 490, 514n29
  and the Federal Writers' Project, 5
  and growth of oral history, 79
  and life expectancy of media, 324
  and preservation issues, 404
  and transcription, 7
audiovisual history, 277–83
audiovisual recordings, 399, 402, 406n5
"Aural History and Historical Audio Documentary Production," 308
Auschwitz, 225
Australia. *See also* University of New South Wales
  and aboriginal peoples, 6, 434, 472
  British migration to, 77–78
  and community nursing, 380
  and community-based oral history projects, 224
  and digitization of collections, 407n13
  and growth of oral history, 470–71
  and Holocaust survivors, 246
  and the International Oral History Association, 9
  National Library of Australia, 401, 403, 405, 407n13
  and oral history programs, 475, 480
  and Pickett, 86–90
  politics of, 433
  and Project Jukebox, 308
  and reconciliation processes, 322, 435
  State Library of South Australia, 395–96, 400, 402–4, 406n6, 407n15
  and "testimonies of resistance,"379
  and vicarious creating, 395–96, *400*, 400–401, 402–5, 406n6
  and World War I, 432–33
  and World War II, 470
Australian Centre for Oral History, 308

authentic doing, 478
authentic learning, 478–79
authoritarianism, 137, 138, 148
authorship issues, 58
autobiographical memory, 12–13, 83, 93n24, 96–97, 106, 107–8, 439
autobiographies, 375, 385
automated format migration, 300
Azaustre, Manuel, 71
Azaustre conjecture, 71, *72*

background of oral history, 3–6
backlogs, 399–400
Baker, Mark, 472
Bal, Mieke, 103
Baldwin, James, 467
Bali Oral History Archive, 482
Balmain, Sydney, 227–29
Baltimore, Maryland, 66, *67*, 68, 69
Bancroft Library, 198, 422
bandwidth issues, 289, 292–93
Banfield, Theresa, 170
Barcelona, Spain, 66, 68–70
Barker, Robin, 57
Barzun, Jacques, 4
baseball, 465
basketball, 197–98
batch conversions, 300
Battle of Crete, 234
Baum, Willa, 170, 394, 411
Bayer, Ronald, 376
Baylor Institute for Oral History, 482
BBC, 44, 209–10, 310, 316, 510
Bearman, Peter, 258, 260
Beaver, Alaska, 57–58
Been in the Storm So Long: The Aftermath of Slavery (Litwack), 189
"Beginning Where We Are: Feminist Methodology in Oral History" (Anderson, Armitage, and Jack), 173–74
Behar, Ruth, 177–78
Belenky, Mary Field, 173
Belgrave, Michael, 445n27
Beloved (Morrison), 117
benign neglect, 404
Benison, Saul, 35, 373, 374
Bergson, Henri, 220
Berliner, Emile, 316
Berlusconi, Silvio, 113, 114, 119, 120
Bernal, Dolores Delgado, 178–79
Berridge, Virginia, 376–77
Berry, John, 225–26
Best Practices for Oral History (OHA), 365
Billy Graham Center Archives, 307
Bing, Leon, 196–97
Binney, Judith, 445n27
biography, 58, 373, 458. *See also* autobiographies
Black Oral History Collection, 193–94
Black Panther Party, 196, 358
Black Women Oral History Project, 172
Blackman, Margaret, 59
Blackout History Project, 509–10
Bloch, Marc, 479
Blogger, 505–6, 515n39
blogging, 503, 505–6, 511, 512, 515n39
Blood of Spain: An Oral History of the Spanish Civil War (Fraser), 447n51
Bloods (gang), 197
Bloods (Terry), 451–52
Bloom, Benjamin, 453–56, *454*, *455*
Blythe, Ronald, 5
Boder, David, 245, 246
Bodfish, Waldo, Sr., 59
body language, 31, 281
Bond, Julian, 410
Bonus March, 499
Boog, Kathryn, 386
Booth, Alan, 473
Borland, Katherine, 472, 492
Bornant, Joanna, 323
Boschma, Geertje, 386
bottom-up approach to history, 4–5, 8, 191, 411
Boulanger, Ghislaine, 264n4
Bowers, Samuel H., 355
Boyd, Nan Alamilla, 198–99
Bozzoli, Belinda, 483
Bracero History Archive, 507
Bradley, Tom, 193
Bragg, Janet Harmon, 275
brain physiology, 222
Brainerd, Kansas: Time, Place, and Memory on the Prairie Plains, 510
Braithwaite, Yvonne, 193
Branch, Taylor, 194
Brazil, 9, 69
Brennan, Sheryl, 380
Brief Encounter (1945), 78, 88
Britain
  and archival institutions, 320, 321–22, 324
  and the digital revolution, 315–16
  and the Falklands War, 5, 125
  and medical oral history, 373, 375, 382
  and oral history education, 97
  and public oral history, 432, 436, 439, 441–42
  Survey of English Dialects, 317
British Association of Sound Collections (BASC), 322
British Institute of Recorded Sound (BIRS), 320, 329n30
British Library, 322, 326, 329n30, 379
British Medical Journal, 378
British Museum, 316
British Oral History Society, 9, 320
broadband access, 501

Brookdale Center on Aging, 204, 206
Brooks, Michael, 452
Brotherhood of Sleeping Car Porters, 193
Brown's Subject Headings for African American History, 337
browsing, 341–43, 346
Bruley, Sue, 475, 478
Bruner, Jerome, 89
Bryan, Mamie Lee, 499
Bryant, Diana, 228–29
Bryant, Kobe, 197
Buchenwald concentration camp, 66
budgetary issues. *See* funding and budgetary issues
Buenos Aires, Argentina, 138, 435
Bühler, Charlotte, 205
Bull, Michael, 227
Burawoy, Michael, 443
Burke, Ernest, 465
Burnham, John C., 373
Bush, George W., 355–56, 509
Buss, Fran Leeper, 177
Butler, Anne, 473
Butler, Judith, 101
Butler, Robert, 12–13, 203, 204, 209, 211
Butler Library, 420
Byatt, A. S., 83
Bynum, North Carolina, 412

Cairo, Egypt, 236
Calata, Nomonde, 144
California State University, Long Beach, 181, 308
California State University, Monterey Bay, 482
California Supreme Court, 357
Cambodia, 434
camcorders, 269. *See also* video recordings
camera techniques, 269, 270–72, 276n2
"camera's eye," 278–79, 281–82
"Can There Be a Feminist Ethnography?" (Stacey), 174
Canada, 9, 321, 322, 323, 363, 434
Cannery Women (Ruiz), 172
Cano, Alejandro, 129
Canti lontani dal centro (2008), 122n13
Cao Zhuxiang, 180
Capaci, Christine, 452
Capture Wales, 310
caregivers, 160, 161–63, 212, 214
Carnegie Mellon University, 338, 344, 345–46
Carr, Leroy, 348
Casa della Memoria e della Storia. *See* House of Memory and History
cascading style sheets (CSS), 502
cassette recorders, 8, 287–89, 299, 318, 324, 394, 404–5
Castellanoz, Eva, 53
cataloging, 335–38, 339, 340–41, 398–401, *400*
Catalonia, 68
Catholic Church, 119, 160
Cavill, Rhoda, 224
CBS, 360
Center for Civil Rights, 414
Center for Documentary Studies, 194
Center for History and New Media, 309
Center for Malvinas War Veterans, 134
Center for Middle Eastern Studies, 482
Center for Oral History (COH), 40
Center for the Study of the American South, 409, 414
Central Committee (Communist Party of Czechoslovakia), 45, 46–47
Centralia, Washington, 14
Centre for Contemporary Cultural Studies, 80
Centre for Popular Memory, 435, 442, 483
Cerboni, Susanna, 122n13
Chafe, William, 195
Cham Muslim Oral History Project, 434
Chamberlain, Mary, 88, 91
Chapman, Audrey, 146
Chapman, Joan, 228
Charter 77, 42, 43
"Ch'eghwetsen'", 54
Chesneaux, Jean, 126
Chew, Ron, 305
children, 68, 159–64
Chile, 143, 434, 435
choice theory, 107
Christel, Michael, 338
Christianity, 99–100, 146–47, 150–51
chronological memory, 85, 162, 263
Churchill, Winston, 439
cinematic language, 283
Circolo Gianni Bosio, 116–18, 119, 120
City University of New York (CUNY), 181
Civil Rights Documentation Project, 193, 307
Civil Rights in Kentucky Oral History Project Digital Media Database, 293–94
civil rights movement
  and African American history, 186, 193–95, 465
  and broadcast media, 303, 304–5
  and digital technologies, 414
  and *Greensboro VOICES*, 507
  and historical revisionism, 120
  and Holocaust survivors, 246
  and illiteracy, 70, 72
  and the Institute for Southern Studies, 410
  and the Kentucky History Society, 293–394
  and "Listening for a Change," 414
  and Marshall, 352
  and race relations, 193–95
  and student oral history work, 465
  and Terkel, 451
  and trials, 355
  and web resources, 310
  in Wichita, Kansas, 191
  women's role in, 192

Civil Rights Movement Veterans, 310
Civil Rights Project, 293
civil society, 153
Civil War, 188, 189
civilians, 130–31, 132, 238
Clark, Helen, 234
class issues, 4–5, 139, 175
Classen, Constance, 221, 226
classroom environment, 450–56
Clemens, Roger, 355
Clinton, Bill, 412, 414
close-ups, 274
cloud mechanisms, 347
CNN, 509, 515n33
Coates, Roy, 236
coding issues, 342. *See also* cataloging; indexing
Cohen, Daniel, 310
coherence of concepts, 104
Coleman, Peter, 205, 207, 214
collaboration, 59–61, 343–44. *See also* community-based oral history
collective memory
  and collective consciousness, 423–24
  and conceptual vocabulary, 104–7
  described, 13
  and historical inquiry, 96–97
  interdisciplinary research on, 12
  manipulation of, 13–14
  and memory studies, 97–98
  and national identity, 130
  and Native American culture, 58
  personal memory contrasted with, 107–8
  and September 11 oral history project, 256
  social creation of, 99–100
  and social identity, 101–4
  subjective dimension of, 79–80, 89, 100–101, 108, 263
  and trauma, 14, 256, 261
  and war memories, 241–42
Columbia Oral History Research Office, 7, 256, 262
Columbia University
  and institutional review boards, 365
  and Nevins, 3–4, 170, 317
  and oral history archives, 3–4, 97, 482
  postgraduate oral history courses, 480
  and the Regional Oral History Office, 420
  and September 11 oral history project, 15, 28
commemoration, 133, 241–42, 251–52, 258, 282
commercial market, 283, 292
Committee of Liberated Jews (CHC), 244
Common Rule, 364–65
communal memory, 263. *See also* collective memory
Communism, 41, 120
Communist Party of Czechoslovakia (CPC), 38, 44, 45–49
Communist Party of Italy, 113
Community of Memories, 308
community-based oral history
  and audience for oral history, 504–5
  contributions to oral history field, 440–43
  and family histories, 190–93
  political and social goals, 27
  and presentation of interviews, 431
  and university-based programs, 422, 481–84
  and unsolicited materials, 396
compact cassette tape recorders, 8. *See also* micro-cassettes
compact discs (CDs), 9, 288–90, 299–300, 324–25
Compact Flash memory, 405
compound objects, 295
compression algorithms, 289, 301, 514n29
computer hard drives, 299–300
Computer Output Microfilm (COM), 406n5
Condrau, Flurin, 378
conflict interviews, 37–49
conflicting accounts, 30–31. *See also* verification
Congress of Industrial Organizations (CIO), 192
Congress of Racial Equality (CORE), 507
consent forms, 511
containerization, 228–29
CONTENTdm, 295, 339
context of interviews, 51–52, 62, 458
contraception, 377
contracts, 369
control vocabularies, 337, 344
Convention Relative to the Treatment of Prisoners of War, 239
conversational narratives, 161
"cooked" documents, 334–35
Cooter, Roger, 375
Copeland, Peter, 325
copying recordings, 273, 287
Copyright Act, 353, 360–62
copyright issues, 351–52, 359–63, 511
Cornum, Rhonda, 499
counterfactual histories, 445n19
Coventry, Michael, 492, 494
Cowgirls (Jordan), 171
Craib, Ian, 149, 153
Cree people, 434
Crellin, John, 383
Crete, 236
Crips, 197
critical reading, 494–96
critics of oral history, 79
cross-cultural settings, 51–53, 53–59, 59–61, 61–62, 377
cross-disciplinary work. *See* interdisciplinary work
cross-referencing, 341–42, 343
Crowell, Aron, 55
Cruikshank, Julie, 62n1, 177
Cruikshank, Moses, 59
Cuba, 435

cultural issues
  and collective memory, 101, 105, 106–7
  and cross-cultural settings, 51–53, 53–59, 59–61, 60–61, 61–62, 377
  cultural memory, 87–88, 96, 102
  and House of Memory and History, 112
  and negotiating remembrance, 282
  and public policy, 114
  and the sensory revolution, 219–20
  and storytelling styles, 88
  and taboos, 52–53
  and traditions, 188
  and trauma, 148
  and the Truth and Reconciliation Commission, 146–47
  and women's oral history, 173–74, 174–75, 180
Cunningham, Rosa Lee, 196
curricula of oral history programs, 450, 462–64, 479–81
Curry, Constance, 195
"CVS" approach, 340–41
Czech Association of Oral History, 40
Czech Children, 43
Czech Republic/Czechoslovakia, 9, 38, 39–40, 437

Dahmer, Vernon, 355
Daley, Christina, 94n41
Daly, Christopher B., 172, 413
Danziger, Kurt, 222
Darfur, 251
dark archives, 301
Dash, Leon, 196
data integrity, 300
databases, 293, 340, 511
Davidson, Florence Edenshaw, 59
Davies, Kerry, 378
Davies, Stuart, 442
Davis, Walter Royal, 413
Day, Annette, 437
Day of Memory, 123n17
Day of Remembrance, 123n17
Day of the Dead celebration, 53
De Berg, Hazel, 402
De Bruyn, Derek, 473
De Klerk, Willem, 142
De Simone, Mariano, 117
Deans, Dixie, 238
death camps, 72
death squads, 142
"December 4" (song), 464
Decker, Sola, 386
declarative memory, 93n24
deeds of gift, 352–53, *367*, *368*
defamation, 355–58
defense industries, 192
DeFord, Miriam Allen, 500
Dellums, C. L., 193
dementia, 212, 213
democracy
  and Argentina, 127–28, 131, 132, 133–34
  democratization of oral history, 325–26, 423, 425, 443, 450 (*see also* community-based oral history)
  and "Do It Yourself" (DIY) interview movement, 182
  and illiteracy, 65, 66–68, *67*, 68–70, 70–71, 71–73
  and university-based oral history programs, 422
  and war memories, 133, 135–36
Democratic Kampuchea, 434
Democratic Party, 69
Denis, Philippe, 380
Densho Digital Archive, 308, 508–9
Department of Health and Social Security (DHSS), 208–9
Depression, 3, 7, 32, 451, 499. *See also* Federal Writers' Project
depression, psychological, 12, 204, 213, 214
desegregation, 414
Desert Storm Oral History Project, 369
Diack, H. Leslie, 377
dialogic anthropology, 56
The Diary of Anne Frank, 247
Diaz, Manny, 499
Dickinson College, 449
dictatorships
  and Argentina, 124–25, 126–29, 130–31, 134–35, 137
  and failures of democracy, 73
  and Franco, 66, *67*, 73
  and public oral history, 436
  and state revisionism, 322, 435, 436–37
Diderot, 219
Digital and Community Showcase, 491
Digital Audio Tape (DAT)
  and the digital revolution, 324–25
  introduction of, 9
  and life expectancy of media, 324
  obsolescence of, 11
  and preservation issues, 401, 404
  recording system described, 289
"The Digital Black Hole" (Palm), 406n5
digital technology. *See also specific media*
  and access issues, 291–99, 326–27, 347–48
  and analog recordings, 118, 406n4
  and archives, 295, 315–16, 324–27, 506–8, 510–11
  and audio recording, 9–11, 286–90, 299, 490, 514n29
  and cataloging, 399
  and collection of oral histories, 509–12, 515n39
  and content of oral histories, 495–97
  and conversion technology, 288
  described, 285–86
  digital collections, 394
  digital object management, 326
  digitizing resources, 118, 296, 299–308, 402, 404–5, 406n5, 407n13, 407n15

and forms of oral histories, 494–95
impact on oral history practice, 512
and indexing, 292, 324, 327, 333–35, 336, 341
and interpretation issues, 492–96
and *Living Atlanta*, 304
and online collections, 506, 508–9, 510–11
and oral history audiences, 501–3, 504–6
and photograph-sharing sites, 297
and presentation, 493–94
and preservation issues, 299–308, 401–2, 404–5, 406n5, 407n13, 407n15
and researchers, 501–3
and the sensory revolution, 222
and the Southern Oral History Program, 414
and storytelling, 309–12
student and teacher resources, 503–4
and undergraduate education, 491–92
and women's oral history, 181–82
Dillinger, John, 360
Directory of British Oral History Collections, 321
disabilities, 379, 442
disappearances, 125, 127, 128, 139n9
disc recorders, 287
discrepancies between the written and oral sources, 12
discrimination, 170
discussion lists, 512. *See also* forums
disembodied modes, 283
disengagement theory, 205–6
Displaced Persons (DP) camps, 245
dissidents, 41–45
dissociative senses, 228
distance education, 487n37
District Six Museum, 441
Dittmer, John, 195
Do History, 503
"Do It Yourself" (DIY) interview movement, 181–82
Dobrof, Rose, 203, 204, 206–7, 211, 212–14
documentaries, 35, 79, 251–52, 361
Documenting the American South project, 311
Dogan, Bulent, 497
Doing History (Ritchie), 472
Doing Oral History (Ritchie), 457
Doña Maria's Story: Life History, Memory, and Political Identity (James), 180
donated materials, 354, 361, 396–98, 403
Doncaster Gate Hospital Heritage Project, 380
Douglass, Frederick, 188
Douglass, Susan, 478
Drobnick, Jim, 223
Drupal, 511
Dubček, Aleksandr, 47
Dublin Core Metadata Initiative (DCMI), 339, 502
DuBois, Lindsay, 435, 445n30
Duke University, 8, 194
Dunaway, David, 441–42
Durkheim, Émile, 100
DVD cameras, 10
dynamic range, 287

Earl Warren Oral History Program, 193
East Midlands Oral History Archive, 483–84
Eastern Europe, 249, 251, 322. *See also specific countries*
economic conditions, 70, 152–53
Edinburgh University, 320
Edison, Thomas, 316
Edith Cowan University Archives, 482
The Edwardians: The Remaking of British Society (Thompson), 447n51
Egypt, 236
Eichmann, Adolf, 246
Eick, Gretchen, 191
eight-track recorders, 287–88
El Alamein (battle), 235
elitism, 441
Ellis Island, 82, 117, 121, 305
Elsasser, Nan, 171
email, 9, 10, 490, 503, 516n39
Embacher, Helga, 278
embodied memory, 437
embodied modes, 283
emerging crises, 28
EMI "Midget" recorders, 317
emigration, 246
Encoded Archival Description (EAD), 502
end-of-life interviewing, 384
Envelopes of Sound, 161
environment of interviews, 28
episodic memory, 93n24, 104
The Era of the Witness (Wieviorka), 249–50
Erikson, Erik, 205
Eskimo culture, 58, 59–61
Essex County Record Offices, 320
ethics issues
and dated permissions, 508
and history of medicine, 372–87
and informed consent, 383
and institutional review boards, 364–65
and interviewing techniques, 58
and legal issues, 351
professional standards, 26, 27
and public oral history, 431
and shared authority, 380–85
and therapeutic oral history, 383–84
and university-based oral history programs, 475
and war memories, 241
ethnicity. *See* race and ethnicity
Evaluation Guidelines (Oral History Association), 27
Evans, George Ewart, 97, 317
exploitation of subjects, 27, 32

Eyes on the Prize (film), 195
eyewitness accounts, 4, 260, 432

faceted referencing, 340
facial expressions, 268, 271
Fahrenheit 9/11 (2004), 355
fair use, 362–63, 364
Falklands War. *See* Malvinas War
false associations, 358
false light, 358
family histories, 190–92, 280–81
"Family Myths, Memories and Interviewing" (Finnegan), 492
Fascism, 113–14, 119–20, 122nn2–3, 122n15, 298–99, 344
Federal Circuit Courts of Appeal, 357
Federal Writers' Project
 and audio recordings, 5
 and "bottom up" oral history, 411
 and former slave narratives, 3, 32–33
 and interview practices, 32–33
 Library of Congress collections, 187
 and Lomax, 187
 and note-taking practices, 6–7, 317, 512
 and Terkel, 5
 and video recordings, 5
Federation of Freedom Volunteers, 113
Federazione Italiana Volontari della Libertà (FIAVL), 113
feminism, 171, 173–74
Fentress, James, 103
Fewkes, Jesse Walter, 286, 316
fictional characters, 360
fieldwork, 6–7, 316, 404–5, 474
The Fifties: A Women's Oral History (Harvey), 451–52
The Fiftieth Gate (Baker), 472
film and filmmaking, 171–72, 269, 277, 281–82
Finnegan, Ruth, 492
First Amendment, 357
Five Minds for the Future (Gardner), 462
flash memory, 289–90, 325, 405
Flick, Isabel, 472
Flickr, 297
Flint, Bill, 240
Flippin, Katherine Stewart, 190–91
Florence, Italy, 239–40
Flowers, Ruth, 170
flu epidemic, 14
Fogerty, James, 322, 323
foibe massacres, 120, 123n17
folk songs, 286, 316
folksonomy, 344
Forged Under the Sun (Buss), 177
forgiveness, 146. *See also* Truth and Reconciliation Commission (TRC)
Forstchen, William R., 445n19
Fort Minor, 464
Fortier, Normand, 323
Fortunoff Video Archive for Holocaust Testimonies, 247, 248
forums, 484, 503, 516n39
Forza Italia, 113
Fosse Ardeatine massacre, 112, 114–15, 118–20
four-track recorders, 287–88, 304
Framing Public Memory (Phillips), 440
Franco, Francisco, 67
Franco Coggiola sound archive, 118
Frankton Junction, New Zealand, 306
Fraser, Ronald, 447n51
free speech movement, 424
Freedmen's Bureau, 189
freedom of expression, 436
Freedom of Information Act (FOIA), 354, 355
French Ministry of Culture, 69–70
French Revolution, 97, 373
Freund, Alexander, 312
Freyberg, Bernard, 239
Fried, Rob, 462
Friedländer, Saul, 250
Frisch, Michael
 and public memory work, 438–39
 and public oral history, 431, 438
 and shared authority concept, 88, 306, 381, 431, 476
 and study of memory, 80, 438
 on subjectivity, 81
From Parlor to Prison (Gluck), 171
Frontiers: A Journal of Women Studies, 169–72, 176, 178
Full Stop Law, 133
funding and budgetary issues
 and accessibility, 292–93
 and archival institutions, 393–94, 395–98, 398–401, 401–5, 405–6
 and the House of Memory and History, 119
 and online video, 508
 and preservation of collections, 299–300, 401, 404, 405–6, 406n5
 and reminiscence therapy, 211
 and September 11 project, 260
 and the Southern Oral History Program, 413–15
 and storage of recordings, 7
 and university programs, 171
 and vicarious creating, 406n6
 and video recordings, 406n3
 and women's oral history, 181
future-use clauses, 353

Galileo conjecture, 71, 72
Gallipoli, Turkey, 234
gangs, 197
Garbo, Greta, 281
Garden of the Finzi-Continis (1970), 247
Gardner, Howard, 453–56, *454*, *455*, 462, *463*

Garrow, David, 194
Gaston, Paul, 410
gatekeepers, 45
Gates, William, 197
Gauguin, Paul, 10
gay communities, 198, 465–66
Gaza, 121
Geiger, Susan, 176
gender. *See* women's oral history
"The Gender of Memory: Rural Chinese Women and the 1950s" (Hershatter), 180
general audiences, 504–6
generational divides, 43, 44
genocide, 251, 434–35
gentrification, 227–29
geographic representation, 235
George Magoon and the Down East Game Wars (Ives), 61
George Mason University, 309
Germany death camps, 66, 67
gerontology, 203–7
Gerring, John, 104
Gertner, Alexander, 245
gestures, 268
Gettysburg Address, 4
ghettos, 42, 115
"The Giant Footprints,"52
Gibson, Faith, 213
Gielen, Helga, 280–81
Gielen, Michael, 280–81
gifted materials, 354, 361, 396–98, 403
Gilbert, Peter, 197
Gill, Paul, 383
Gilligan, Carol, 173
Gingrich, Newt, 433, 445n19
glasnost, 47
Glass, Brent, 412
Glassberg, David, 436, 439
The Global Achievement Gap (Wagner), 462
Glover, Tini, 236, 237, 239–40
Gluck, Sherna, 170–72, 174–75, 181–82, 500
GMG Classical Music Forum, 514n29
Goffman, Erving, 281–82
Goleman, Daniel, 463
Goniwe, Nyameka, 145–46, 151
Good Times, Bad Times: Women with Learning Difficulties Telling Their Stories (Atkinson, et al.), 378–79
The "Good War" (Terkel), 5
Goodall, Heather, 472
Google, 299, 312, 342–43, 452
Gorbachev, Mikhail, 47
Gore, Al, 412
Gould, Joe, 3
Graff, Henry F., 4
Grainger, Percy, 316
Gramophone Company, 316
Grand Central Terminal, 311
Granshaw, Lindsay, 374
Graves, Robert, 124
Graybill, Lyn, 150
Great Britain. *See* Britain
Great Depression, 3
Greece, 240
Greenblatt, Stephen, 107
Greene, Christina, 192
Greene, Mark, 398–99
Greensboro, North Carolina, 195
Greensboro Public Library, 507
Greensboro VOICES: Voicing Observations in Civil Rights and Equality Struggles, 507
Greenwich Village, 465–66
Greiff, Matts, 480
Grele, Ronald
  on archivists, 319
  and "bottom up" oral history, 5
  definition of oral history, 161
  on oral history education, 474, 476
  on the SOHP, 411
  on study of memory, 438
  on subjectivity, 81
  on transcription, 476
Griggs, Cynthia, 194
Grim, Valerie, 179
Grossberg, Mimi, 278–79
group identification, 105
Guam, 377
Guber, Rosana, 136
guerilla movements, 132, 134
Guguletu Seven, 149–50
Gullah people, 188
Gulledge, Judy, 452

Haddon, Alfred Cort, 316
Haight, Barbara, 214
Halbwachs, Maurice, 98, 99–100, 102–3, 105–7
Hale, Sondra, 174–75
Haley, Alex, 190
Hall, Bob, 410
Hall, Jacquelyn Dowd, 172, 409–15
Hamer, Fannie Lou, 195
Hamilton, Paula, 438–39, 440
Hamlin, Susan, 190
Hampton, Henry, 195
Hampton High School, 452–53
Hard Times (Terkel), 5
Hardy, Charles, 441
Hartman, Geoffrey, 248
Harvard University, 482
Hattori, Anne Perez, 377
Havel, Václav, 42, 47
Hawaii, 191
Hazara refugees, 476
Healey, Chadwyck, 422
healing value of oral history, 147–51, 159–64, 241, 383–84. *See also* Truth and Reconciliation Commission (TRC)

health care policy, 206, 215
Heart to Heart: The Twentieth-Century Battle against Cardiac Disease: An Oral History (Weisse), 376
Heddy and Me (Varga), 472
Help the Aged (charity), 211
Hendricks, Shirley, 214
herding culture, 60–61
Heritage Lottery Fund (HLF), 324, 331n58, 380, 442
Herodotus, 417
Hershatter, Gail, 180
Herskovits, Melville J., 188
Higginson, Thomas Wentworth, 188
high-definition video, 290
Higher School of Mechanics of the Navy (ESMA), 128, 138, 139n9
high-fidelity sound archives, 325
high-tech exhibits, 307
Hillbilly Women (Kahn), 171
Hilliard, David, 196
Hine, Darlene Clark, 192
Historical Voices project, 484
history and historians
  and accessibility of research, 291
  and educational standards, *460–61*
  historic characters, 360
  historical analysis, 357, 459
  historical memory, 263
  Historical Reasoning (course), 478
  and historiography, 433–34
  history wars, 433
  and medicine, 372–87
  and revisionism, 119, 136
  and subject specialists, 421
  and university-based oral history programs, 475
History and Memory, 96
History Makers, Inc., 335–38, 341–42, 344–47
History Matters (web site), 308, 500
History of Hospital Infection, 383
A History of Medicine (Major), 373
History Project in Boston, 198
History Workshop movement, 5, 320, 483
Hitchlock, Karen, 379
Hitler, Adolf, 71, *72*, 73
HIV/AIDS, 153, 159–64, 198, 376–77, 381, 483
H-Net online network, 484
Holocaust
  and Italian politics, 120
  Jewish Holocaust project, 224
  and oral history education, 465
  and the Shoah Visual History Foundation, 11, 248–51, 253n15
  and survivor narratives, 11, 244–52
  and testimony-based studies, 148
  United States Holocaust Memorial Museum, 248, 306, 500
Holocaust and Genocide Studies, 247
Holocaust Martyrs' and Heroes' Remembrance Authority, 244
homeless population, 431
homosexuality and homophobia, 198, 199, 359
Honey, Michael, 192
Hong Kong, 436
Hoop Dreams (1994), 197
H-ORALHIST listserv, 10, 484, 503
Horváth, Rita, 250
hospice care, 387
House of Memory and History, 112–22
"How Crane Got His Blue Eyes" (Lind), 57
Howard, John, 433
Howard Hughes Medical Center, 222
Howard University, 193
Howarth, Ken, 321
Howes, Douglas, 220
Hradilek, Adam, 437
Hudson, Jean, 224
Hughes, Eileen, 504
Huillet, Danièle, 281
human rights
  and the House of Memory, 121
  ideology of, 247
  and the Malvinas War, 125, 126–27, 128, 129, 136
  and public oral history, 434–35
  and trauma response, 256–57
  and Truth and Reconciliation Commission, 143–47
Human Rights Victim (HRV) hearings, 143
Humanities Councils, 171
Hunt, Nigel, 384
Hurricane Digital Memory Bank, 506
Hurricane Katrina, 14, 28, 301

Idaho Statesman, 359
idealism, 71, *72*
"Ideologies of the Twentieth Century" (seminar), 117
Ignatieff, Michael, 144, 153
Illinois Institute of Technology, 245
illiteracy, 65–73
immigrants
  and access to interviews, 354
  and audiovisual recordings, 278, 282
  and curriculum standards, 453
  and displaced persons, 245
  Italian, 117, 121
  Latino, 413–14
  and nontraditional oral histories, 309
  and North Carolina, 413
  and September 11 oral history project, 258, 259
  and students of oral history, 477, 500
  Ukrainian, 436
  and women's oral history, 171
  World War II refugees, 470
impartiality, 436
imperialism, 134–37
"The Implications of Oral History for Librarians" (Zachert), 319
In a Different Voice (Gilligan), 173

indexing
  and digital technologies, 292, 324, 327, 333–35, 336, 341
  and History Makers Childhood Stories Project, 335–38
  and keyword searching, 401
  multidimensional referencing, 340–41
  and passage referencing, 339
  and the Shoah Foundation, 249, 252, 253n17
  sorting vs. exploring, 341–43
  and sound recordings, 7, 10
  subject-based indexes, 292, 293
  and thematic coding project, 344–47
  thematic indexing, 343, 344–47
  and vernacular referencing, 343–44
indigenous people, 6, 433, 434, 472. *See also* Native Americans
individual memory, 437, 440
industrialization, 227–29, 412–13
influenza epidemic, 14
informal oral histories, 500
information technology (IT) departments, 294
informed consent, 365, 383
Informedia Digital Video Library, 338, 344, 345
Instant Messenger, 515n39
instantaneous discs, 404
Institute for Contemporary History (ICH), 39–40
Institute for Southern Studies, 410
Institute for the Documentation of the Crimes of Communism, 45–46
Institute for the Study of Totalitarian Regimes (USTR), 437
Institute of Museum and Library Services (IMLS), 301, 338
institutional ethnography, 173
institutional review boards, 351, 364–65
intellectual evolution of oral history, 11–16
intellectual property, 58, 360, 362
interactivity, 343–44
InterClipper, 335, 337, 340, 341, 345
inter-coder reliability, 346
interdisciplinary work
  and memory research, 81–82, 96
  and public oral history, 438–39
  and reminiscence therapy, 209
  and social identity, 102
  and "traveling concepts,"103
  and undergraduate courses, 491–92
  and university-based oral history, 471
  and women's oral history, 173
intergenerational interaction, 282
International Association of Sound and Audiovisual Archives (IASA), 322, 404
International Conference on Oral History, 9
International Database of Oral History Testimonies, 500
International Oral History Association (IOHA), 9, 16, 39–40, 115, 351, 435, 475
International Oral History Conference, 479–80
International Women's Year conference, 181
International Workers of the World, 14
Internet and online resources
  and accessibility issues, 27, 291, 292, 326–27
  archival delivery systems, 298–99
  and archival institutions, 393–94
  and audio broadcasting, 506–8
  and broadband access rates, 501
  and cataloging, 339, 398
  and collective memory, 106
  and copyright issues, 363–64
  and digital video, 290–91
  and discussion forums, 484, 503, 514n29, 515n39
  and indexing, 339, 341, 342–43
  and the IOHA, 9
  and legal issues, 363–64
  and long-term storage, 512
  and practice of oral history, 316
  and privacy issues, 10
  and "raw" vs. "cooked" documents, 334
  and remote users, 326–27
  and scholarship, 10, 27
  and students of oral history, 464, 478, 492
  and survival of oral history collections, 406
  and tagging methods, 297
  and telephone services, 511, 512, 515n39
  and thematic coding, 347
  and transcripts, 500
  and university-based oral history programs, 420, 482
  variety of oral history resources, 24–25, 307–9
  and Web 2.0, 324, 327
  and Web cameras, 290
  and web site development, 511–12
interpretation of oral histories, 40, 56–57, 194–95, 495–97
interviewing practices
  and copyright issues, 360–61
  and cross-cultural settings, 51–62
  documenting interviews, 35
  dynamics of, 23–35
  and end-of-life interviewing, 384
  environment of interviews, 28
  and ethics issues, 58
  factor affecting interviews, 27–29
  and Holocaust survivors, 251–52
  and illiteracy, 65–73
  impact of video recording on, 273
  interview-based research, 25–26
  interviewer/narrator pairings, 32–34
  and post-conflict situations, 37–49
  preparation for interviews, 29–34
  rapport with interview subjects, 30, 34
  resources on, 24
  restrictions on, 354–55
  two-person interviews, 271
  and university-based oral history, 418–19
  variety of, 16
  and women's oral history, 175

The Intolerable Burden (film), 195
Inupiaq Eskimos, 59
invented traditions, 437
involuntary memory, 220
Iphofen, Ron, 386
iPods, 9, 290, 505
Iranian Oral History Archive, 482
Iraq War, 5, 9
iReport, 515n33
Irish Folklore Commission, 317
Isaac, Andrew, 54
Isay, David, 310–11
Istituto Romano per la storia d'Italia dal Fascismo alla Resistenza (IRSIFAR), 116–20
Istituto Storico della Resistenza, 115–16
Italian Association of former Deported Persons, 113
iTunes, 290, 299, 505
Iverson, Allen, 197
Ives, Edward, 61
Ives, Sandy, 170

Jack, Dana C., 173, 175, 492, 494–95
Jackson, Jim, 238–39
Jakeš, Miloš, 45, 47, 48
James, Daniel, 180
James, Lebron, 197
James, Steve, 197
Japan, 9, 237, 239
Japanese-American internment camps, 305, 508
Jay-Z, 464
Jefferson, Alphine, 192
Jennings, Cedric, 196
Jewels and Ashes (Zable), 472
Jewish Holocaust project, 224
Jimmy Carter Boyhood Home National Historic Site, 306
John, Peter, 54–55, 62
Johnson, Samuel, 3, 355
Johnston, Ian, 236
Johnston, Susanna, 211, 213
joint-work doctrine, 361
Jones, Anne Hudson, 385
Jones, Greta, 383
Jones, Lu Ann, 172, 413
Jonestown Massacre, 494
Joomla, 511
Jordan, Michael, 197
Jordan, Teresa, 171
Jordanova, Ludmilla, 374, 430, 440
Josselson, Ruthellen, 89
Journal of Gerontological Social Work, 204
Journal of Multimedia History, 309
Journal of the Society of Archivists, 322
journalism, 28, 29, 31, 35
Joye, Harlon, 303
Judge Horton and the Scottsboro Boys (television), 357

Kahn, Kathy, 171
Kakar, Sanjiv, 378
Keen, Beryl, 190–91
Kelin, Daniel, 453
Kemp, Mick, 208–11
"Kenji" (song), 464
Kentuckiana Digital Library (KDL), 296, *298*
Kentucky Educational Television, 293
Kentucky Historical Society, 293, 294–95
Kentucky Oral History Commission, 194, 293
Kentucky Oral History Project, 194, 294
Kerr, Daniel, 431
Khmer Rouge, 434, 504
King, Martin Luther, Jr., 194
Kirchner, Néstor, 128
The Kitchen Sisters, 310
K'Meyer, Tracey, 472, 477
Kondo, Kara, 508
Korean War, 5, 70, 451
Korstad, Robert, 172, 192, 413
Ku Klux Klan, 33, 71, *72*, 355
Kuhn, Clifford, 450
Kulumani, 152
Kundera, Milan, 437

La Classe operaia va in paradiso (Petri), 117
La Falange, 71
labor history, 191, 192, 439
LaCapra, Dominic, 147
Lacey, Roderic, 471
lacquers, 404
Lancashire Record Office, 320
Lance, David, 320–21
Lane, Lunsford, 188
Langer, Lawrence, 245
Lanman, Barry, 473
Lanzmann, Claude, 247, 283
lapel microphones, 270, 318
Larson, Mary, 294
Las Mujeres: Conversations from a Hispanic Community (Elsasser, MacKenzie and Tixier y Vigil), 171
Lasorda, Tommy, 466
later life, 202–15
Latin America, 322
Latino community, 258, 259, 413–14
Laurie, Alison, 480
lavalieres (lapel microphones), 270, 318
lawsuits, 355–58, 363
"Learning to Listen" (Anderson and Jack), 175, 492
Lee, Chana Kai, 194
Lee, Harper, 453
Leeds University, 317
legal issues
  consent of subjects, 45
  copyright, 351–52, 359–63, 511
  defamation, 355–58

and institutional review boards, 364–65
and the Internet, 363–64
interview restrictions, 354–55
legal ramifications of oral history, 351–69
patient rights, 378
privacy torts, 358–59
release agreements, 57, 307, 351–53, 360–61, 363, *367, 368, 369*
rights to stories, 57
safeguards, 365–66
and standards of practice, 15–16
and the Truth and Reconciliation Commission, 150
"The Legendary Topography of the Gospels in the Holy Land" (Halbwachs), 99
Lehna, Carlee, 386
Leloudis, James, 172, 413
Lemke-Santangelo, Gretchen, 191
Letter on the Blind (Diderot), 219
Letterman, David, 359
Levi, Primo, 247
Levin, Howard, 464–65, 478
Levine, Lawrence, 187
liability, 366. *See also* legal issues
libel, 355
librarians, 334, 352
Library of Congress
American Folklife Center, 15, 311, 451, 505
American Memory collection, 501
and digitization, 407n13
and the Federal Writers Project, 187
and Holocaust survivor testimony, 245
and legal issues, 352, 353
and the Marshall donation, 352
and preservation, 401
and *StoryCorps*, 198
and subject headings, 337
Veterans History Project, 15, 16, 351, 451
Lichtblau, Albert, 478
Liddington, Jill, 443
Lieblich, Amia, 89
Life Behind a Veil (Wright), 195
life caching, 326
life expectancy of media, 299, 324
life histories, 384–85, 386
Life Lived Like a Story: Life Stories of Three Yukon Native Elders (Cruikshank), 62n1, 177
Life Review, 12–13, 204, 206–7, 207–12
life stages, 82, 205. *See also* age issues
lighting, 269, 272
Like a Family: The Making of a Southern Cotton Mill World (Hall, et al.), 172, 409, 412–13
Lincoln, Abraham, 4
Lind, Maggie, 57
Linked project, 309
"Listening for a Change" project, 414
Listening Is an Act of Love: A Celebration of American Life from the StoryCorps Project (StoryCorps), 311
Listservs, 516n39
literary theory, 101
litigation, 365–66. *See also* legal issues
Litwack, Leon, 189
Living Atlanta: An Oral History of the City, 1914–1948 (radio program), 304–5
Living the Story: The Civil Rights Movement in Kentucky (documentary), 194, 293
Living Through the Hoop: High School Basketball, Race, and the American Dream (May), 197–98
Lloyd, David, 154
Local People: The Struggle for Civil Rights in Mississippi (Dittmer), 195
Lochead, Richard, 322
LOCKSS ("Lots of Copies Keep Stuff Safe"), 301
Loewen, James, 450–51
Lomax, Alan, 317
Lomax, John, 187, 199, 286
London Metropolitan University, 441
London's Voices, 309
"The Long Civil Rights Movement: The South Since the 1960s" (Hall), 414
longevity of media, 299, 324
longitudinal studies, 214, 258
long-term storage, 512
Longview Historical Center, 367
Lorenz, Federico Guillermo, 435
Los Alamos Historical Society Podcast, 506
lossy and lossless compression, 289
Loudon, Irvine, 381
Louie B. Nunn Center for Oral History, 293, 296
Louisville, Kentucky, 195
Lowes, Leslie, 383
L-soft, 516n39
Lucas, Maria Elena, 177
Lyon, Gloria, 224–25
Lyons, Martin, 479

MacColl, Ewan, 317
Machine Readable Cataloging (MARC), *400*, 502
Macintyre, Stuart, 433
MacKenzie, Kyle, 171
Mackintosh, Carolyn, 380
Madison, Indiana, 191
Madondo, Cliford, 161
Magna Carta, 353
magnetic tape recorders. *See* tape recorders
Magoon, George, 61
Maine, 61
Major, Ralph, 373
The Making: Oral History Project (class project), 504
Making Sense of Oral History (Shopes), 503
Makiwane, Nokhaya, 161
Malacrida, Claudia, 378, 383

Malvinas War
  described, 124–25
  differing views of, 129
  heroes of, 132–34
  and historian's role, 135–39
  and human rights violations, 125–26, 126–27, 128, 129, 136
  interview subjects from, 5
  and military dictatorship, 126–29
  and military failings, 140n11
  and patriotism, 130–31
  and political memory, 125–26
  soldiers' memories, 134–35
  and state terrorism, 125, 127–29, 132, 135–36, 138
  victims of, 131–32
Mandela, Nelson, 142, 153
Manzoor, Farhat, 383
Maoism, 180
MapQuest, 342
Marantz cassette recorders, 287, 405
Marantz Superscope, 318
Marcotulli, Marco, 122n13
marginalized groups, 70–71, 199, 306. *See also specific groups*
Margules, Gabriele, 279
Marini, Giovanna, 117, 121
market trends, 288
Marshall, Thurgood, 352, 353
Martin Luther King National Historic Site, 305
Martin-Smith, Ted, 240
Marx, Frederick, 197
Marxism-Leninism, 39
Masons, 66
mass media, 259
Maternal Thinking (Ruddick), 173
Mather, Elsie, 56
Matibhe, Ike, 52
MATRIX: The Center for Humane Arts, Letters, and Social Sciences Online, 308, 484
Mauthausen concentration camp, 66, 282
Mauthausen conjecture, 66, *72*
May, Reuben A., 197
Mbeki, Thabo, 153
McDougal, Rona, 380
McEwan, Watt, 239
McKeller, Shelley, 376
McKenna, James, 383
McKeown, Thomas, 373
McKibbin, Kerry, 453
McMahon, A. W., 205
McNeil, William, 14
medicine
  history of medical profession, 373–77
  medical sociology, 377
  nurses' stories, 379–80
  patient stories, 377–79
  role of oral history in, 385–87
  and shared authority, 380–85
medium close-up (MCU) shots, 271
Mein Kampf (Hitler), 71, *72*
Meissner, Dennis, 398–99
memoirs, 420
"Memory and Globalization" conference, 115
memory (biological). *See also* collective memory
  associative memory, 280
  autobiographical memory, 12–13, 83, 93n24, 96–97, 106, 107–8, 439
  and the "camera's eye," 278–79
  and children affected by HIV/AIDS, 159–64
  and cinematic language, 282–83
  and contemporary oral history, 77–82
  and cultural influences, 121–22
  declarative memory, 93n24
  defined, 104
  and dictatorships, 126–29
  embodied memory, 437
  episodic memory, 93n24, 104
  of former soldiers, 134–35
  and individual perceptions, 12
  and interview preparation, 30
  involuntary memory, 220
  memory entrepreneurs, 126
  and the memory paradox, 90–91
  and military conflict, 13, 105, 129–39, 233–34
  and national oral histories, 446n51
  and negotiation of remembrance, 281–82
  and nostalgia, 237
  official memory, 440
  passive memory, 98
  and patriotism, 130–31, 132–34
  personal memory, 107–8, 250
  and politics, 114–16, 119–21, 124–25, 125–26, 256
  procedural memory, 93n24
  and public events, 116–18
  and public oral history, 437–40
  and reminiscence therapy, 13, 202–15
  scientific research on, 82–90, 93n24, 135
  semantic memory, 93n24, 104
  and the senses, 83, 220, 221–23
  sensory memories, 83
  short-term memory, 83–84
  social memory, 96, 102, 435, 437–40
  symbolic memory, 102
  and trauma, 14, 245, 256, 259, 261
  triggers for, 251, 279–81
  and truth and reconciliation commissions, 142–43, 143–47, 147–51, 151–54
  unreliability of, 79–80
Memory Box program, 160–61, 483
memory (computer), 277–83, 289–90, 326
Memory Studies, 96
Memoryscape, 309
Mendosa, Mitch, 452
mental health, 202–15, 256, 378
Merriam, Alan, 286–87
metadata, 292, 294, 297, 502, 510

metaphor, 55
meta-statements, 495
Mexican Americans, 53
Meyer, Renate, 435
Mhlawuli, Nombuyiselo, 144–45
Michaels, Paula, 372
Michelet, Jules, 97
Michigan State University, 308, 484
micro-cassettes, 404
microfilm, 406n5
microphones, 269–70, 318
Microsoft SQL, 293
migration studies, 191, 192. *See also* immigrants
Miles, Jean, 226–27
Miles of Smiles, Years of Struggle (Santino), 61
military
  and conscription, 138–39, 140n11
  and dictatorships, 124, 138
  historians of, 9
  juntas, 137
  military service, 130, 275, 467, 499, 510
  and national narratives, 130
  and repression, 121
  and state terrorism, 125, 127–29, 132, 135–36, 138, 322, 435
Miller, Daniel, 106
Miller, Graeme, 309
Mills, Kay, 194
Millwood, Beth, 412
Milwaukee Neighborhoods Project, 368
MiniDisc (MD), 9, 11, 289, 324–25, 401, 404
Ministry for Culture and Heritage (New Zealand), 234
Ministry of Cultural Heritage (Italy), 118
Minnesota Historical Society, 198, 503
Minqar Qa'im (battle), 235
Mississippi Department of Archives and History, 355
Mitchell, Duncan, 380
Mkhonto, Sindiswa, 145
The Modern Researcher (Barzun and Graff), 4
Modigliani, Sara, 117, 121
Monash University, 480
Montana, 179
Moore, Michael, 355
Moore, Shirley Ann, 191–92
Moorland-Spingarn Research Collection, 193
moral discourses, 430
moral witnesses, 253n27
A More Perfect Union (exhibit), 305
Morehouse, Lisa, 504
Morris, Errol, 283
Morrison, Toni, 117
Morrissey, Charles, 318, 411, 430, 466
Morrow, Phyllis, 56
Moses and Aaron (Schönberg), 281
Mothers of Plaza de Mayo, 126
Moveable Type, 506, 515n39
Mozilla Digital Memory Bank, 506
MP3s, 289, 505–6
Muckamore Abbey Hospital, 380
Mulcahy, Joanne, 53
multidimensional referencing, 340–41
multidisciplinary foundation of oral history, 11
multimedia technology, 312, 493–94, 496
multiple intelligences, 453–56, *454*, *455*
Multiple Intelligences: The Theory in Practice (Gardner), 456
municipal museums, 306
Murdoch University, 482
Murphy, Mary, 172, 413
Murray, Donald Walter Gordon, 376
Museum of London, 309, 441
Museum of the American Indian, 306
music industry, 6
Muslim Women in Mombasa, 1890–1975 (Strobel), 176
Muslims, 176, 258, 259
Musselman, 245–46
My American Century (Terkel), 451, 457
Myerhoff, Barbara, 206
Mystic Seaport, 306
mythology, 150

Nanzan University, 482
Napster, 290
narrative
  and active remembering, 279
  conversational narratives, 161
  and interview terminology, 26
  narrative flow, 241
  narrative psychology, 87–88
  narrative theory, 89–90
  narrative therapy, 159
  national narratives, 130
  and public oral history, 437–40
  subaltern narratives, 435, 445n30
  and video production, 269
The Narrative Study of Lives (Josselson and Lieblich), 89
Nasstrom, Kathryn, 409–15
nation building, 149
National Air and Space Museum, 433
National Archives and Records Administration (NARA), 8, 407n13, 459
National Association for the Advancement of Colored People (NAACP), 191, 192, 507
National Association of Italian Partisans, 113
National Baseball Hall of Fame, 465
National Commission on the Disappearance of Peoples (CONADEP), 127
National Community of Women Living with HIV/AIDS (NACWOLA), 160
National Congress (Argentina), 133
National Council of Negro Women, 192
National Endowment for the Humanities (NEH), 172, 303, 304, 412

National History Day, 466
National Humanities Medal, 414
National Library of Australia, 401, 403, 405, 407n13
National Museum of African American History and Culture, 311, 509
National Museum of American History, 305, 512
national parks, 6
National Prosecuting Authority, 152
National Public Radio (NPR), 15, 304, 311, 505
National Sound Archive (NSA), 322, 329n30
National Visionary Leadership Project, 503
nationalism
  and Christian memory, 99
  and cultural symbolism, 105
  and gender issues, 179
  and the Malvinas War, 130, 133–34, 136, 138
  and narcissism, 153
  and totalitarian regimes, 140n17
  and trauma, 259
Native Americans, 52–56, 57–58, 59–61, 316
natural disasters, 14, 28
Navajo culture, 52
Nazism, 38, 67, 69, 72, 364, 436
Ndanbuki, Berida, 179–80
Ned, Annie, 177
neglect of archive materials, 404
Negro Leagues, 465
neighborhood museums, 306
Neighborhood Story Project, 500–501
Neisser, Ulric, 82, 85, 88
Nelson, Davia, 310
networking, 300, 463
neuroscience, 82–87
neutral shots, 274
Nevins, Allan, 3–4, 12, 170, 317–18, 420
New Deal, 187, 317
New Left, 113
New Orleans, Louisiana, 500–501
New York Activist Women's Voices: Oral History Project, 180–81
New York City, 262, 510
New York City Fire Department, 15
New York Times, 4
New York Times Co. v. Sullivan, 357
New York Times Foundation, 257
New Yorker, 3
New Zealand, 9, 234–36, 239, 322, 434
New Zealand Army Division, 236, 239
Newfoundland, 377
Newman, Turak, 59
Ngewu, Cynthia, 146–47, 149
Night (Wiesel), 247
9/11 Digital Archive, 309–10. *See also* September 11, 2001, Oral History Narrative and Memory Project
nongovernmental organizations (NGOs), 126
nontraditional oral history, 309
nonverbal language, 275
Nora, Pierre, 102
normalizace (normalization), 38–39, 41, 43
Normandy Beach, 7
North Coast California Rural Challenge Network Oral History Project, 452
North West Sound Archive, 320, 321
Northeast High School, 197
Northern Ireland, 383
Northern League, 113
Northup, Solomon, 188
nostalgia, 237
November revolution, 38, 39–40, 49
Novick, Peter, 247
nuclear weapons, 433
Number Our Days (Myerhoff), 206
Nunca Más (Never Again), 127, 128–29
Nuremberg Trials, 246
nursing, 379–80
Nursing Voices archive, 380

Obama, Barack, 414
objectivity, 35, 174, 436
Obroda initiative, 47
O'Callaghan, Casey, 226–27
OCLC, 295
O'Farrell, Patrick, 79, 433
Office for Human Research Protection (OHRP), 364–65
Office of Cultural Policy, 117, 119
official memory, 440
Olick, Jeffry, 103
Olsen, Dorothy, 219
Omeka, 511
One Hundred Student Revolutions project, 39–40
O'Neal, Shaquille, 197
Online Public Access Catalog, *400*
online resources. *See* Internet and online resources
Oozevaseuk, Estelle, 55
Open University, 378
open-reel recorders, 317, 394, 404
Operation Crusader, 235
Oppenheimer, Gerald, 376
oppression, 434–35
optical character recognition (OCR), 507
oral biography, 58
oral evidence, 79, 421
Oral History, 9, 97, 377–78, 432
Oral History and Community Memory Institute and Archive, 482
Oral History Association (OHA)
  and cross-cultural settings, 54–55
  and digital technologies, 491, 503
  first national meeting, 8
  and growth of field, 452
  and institutional review boards, 364, 365
  and the Internet, 308
  and media awards, 305
  Principles and Standards, 466
  and recording technology, 317–18

and StoryCorps, 311
support for researchers, 39
website, 308
Oral History Coffeehouse, 459
Oral History for the Local Historical Society (Baum), 170
Oral History Handbook (Robertson), 474, 475
"Oral History Movement: Seeking Out the Voices of Women, Blacks, Radicals, and Workers for a Better-Balanced Story" (Hall), 411
"An Oral History of Our Time" (Gould), 3
Oral History Online, 308
The Oral History Reader (Thomson), 474
Oral History Research Office, 3, 317, 474
Oral History Review, 81, 97
Oral History Society, 9, 321, 322, 442, 447n65
O'Regan, Harley, 224
outsourcing, 404

Pacific Northwest, 194
Pacific War, 237
"painted faces" crisis, 134
palaeoanthropology, 477
Palazzo della Cultura, 115
Palestine, 121, 175
palliative care, 384, 387
Palm, Jonas, 406n5
Parker, Charles, 317, 321
Parr, Joy, 223
partisanship, 433
passage referencing, 339
Passerini, Luisa, 80, 81, 100, 438, 441
passive memory, 98
Patai, Daphne, 174–75
Paterson, Mark, 224
patient stories, 377–79
patriotism, 130–31, 154. *See also* nationalism
The Pawnbroker (1964), 247
peace movement, 121
peer review, 10, 381
Peleliu, 233
Peloponnesian Wars, 3, 449
Pennington, T. Hugh, 377
Pennywinkle: Oral Histories from Tylerton, Smith Island in the Chesapeake Bay, 452
perestroika, 43, 47
Perks, Robert, 382, 474
permissions, 364, 508, 511
Perry, Katharine Elise, 476
persecution, 43
Persian Gulf War, 451
personal memory, 87, 107–8, 250
Petri, Elio, 117
Pew Internet and American Life project, 501
philanthropy, 352–53
Philips Company, 287
Phillips, Denise, 476
Phillips, Kendall, 440
Phillips, U. B., 186–87
Phoenix, Arizona, 191
phonograph, 316
photographs, 272, 279–80, 295
physical environment of interviews, 28
physical gestures, 268
physically active remembering, 279
Pickett, Joan, 77–78, 85–86, 88–90, 91
Piet, Christopher, 146–47
Pietrangeli, Paolo, 117
Pink, Daniel, 462, *463*
Pinochet, Augusto, 435
Pius XII, Pope, 122n15
Placák, Petr, 43
Plaza de Mayo, 133
podcasting, 280, 309, 379, 504, 505–6, 510–11, 512
poetry, 476
Poland, 436, 439
Polish Hill Remembered, 453
Polishuk, Sandy, 473
"Political Élites and Dissidents in the So-called Normalization Period in Czechoslovakia: Autobiographical Interviews" (project), 40–41
politics
and archival institutions, 323–24
and campus climate, 419
and days of remembrance, 123n17
and disputes over memory, 128
and HIV/AIDS, 153
and interview restrictions, 354
and the Malvinas War, 125–26
political affiliations, 34, 41–45, 66
political history, 102
political memory, 124–39, 256
and public oral history, 430–31, 433, 434–35, 436, 437
and repression, 126–27, 134
and Rome's House of Memory, 112–22
and the Truth and Reconciliation Commission, 149, 151, 152
and war memories, 124–39
women in, 181
Poll Daddy, 511, 516n39
Pollock, Della, 413
Polyani, Michael, 223
Pompeii, 238
Popular Memory Group, 80–81, 87–88, 441, 445n30
populism, 136, 438
Portelli, Alessandro
and digital technologies, 492
and dynamics of memory, 13–14, 77, 80–81, 82, 86, 90, 100, 438
on "history-telling," 425n4
on House of Memory and History, 112–22
on interviewing techniques, 46
on oral history curriculums, 491–92, 495–96
on status of oral history in universities, 479
Porter, Dorothy, 374
Porter, Kimberley, 473, 478

Porter, Roy, 378
positivism, 79, 81, 100
Post Traumatic Stress Disorder (PTSD), 245, 259
postcolonial theory, 174–76
postgraduate oral history courses, 480, 481. *See also* university-based oral history
postmodernism
  and archival issues, 323
  and Australian politics, 433
  and linguistics, 101
  and public oral history, 438
  and women's oral history, 174–76, 178, 179–80
poststructuralism, 101
potlatch songs, 54
Potsdam conference, 38
PowerPoint, 493–94, 496
Practicing History (Tuchman), 450
Prague Spring, 38
Prescott, Renate, 473
preservation of materials. *See also* archival institutions
  and digital technology, 299–308, 401–2, 404–5, 406n5, 407n13, 407n15
  and format changes, 325
  and online collection of histories, 511
  and selection criteria, 401–5
  and video recordings, 290–91
Price, Victoria, 357
Prichard, Edward F., Jr., 354
Priebke, Erich, 118
primary source material, 334
Primo de Rivera, José Antonio, 71
Principles and Standards (Oral History Association), 27
print resources, 24, 25
prisoners of war, 5, 113, 235, 238–40, 253n15, 464, 510
privacy issues, 10, 278, 358–59, 511
privatization, 113
procedural memory, 93n24
Process of National Reorganization (Argentina), 125, 127
Project Based Learning, 453
Project Jukebox, 308
Promotion of National Unity and Reconciliation Act, 143
propaganda, 128
property rights, 58
Protectorate of Bohemia and Moravia, 38
protocol issues, 52
Proust effect, 219–29
psychiatry, 204
psychology
  and aged populations, 204, 207–8
  and memory research, 82, 84–85, 87–89
  narrative psychology, 87–88
  and psycho-acoustics, 289
  and psychoanalysis, 101, 264n4
  and the sensory revolution, 222
  social psychology, 79, 101–4, 207–8
  and trauma, 240, 256, 261 (*see also* Post Traumatic Stress Disorder)
  and the Truth and Reconciliation Commission, 151
  and war memories, 241
public disclosure of private facts, 358
public domain, 360, 363
public figures, 357
The Public Historian (Frisch), 438–39
public institutions, 112–22
public opinion, 126, 131
public oral history. *See also* community-based oral history
  and common sensibilities, 430–31
  described, 429–30
  and the international setting, 432–37
  and public memory, 12
  and Rome's House of Memory and History, 112–22
  and social remembering, 437–40
  and women's oral history, 170–71
publicity, 512
Pulitzer Prize, 206

questionnaires, 235, 396–97

Rabel, Roberto, 233
race and ethnicity
  and access to court materials, 355
  Atlanta Race Riot, 305
  and the civil rights movement, 193–95
  and community studies, 190–93
  ethnic museums, 306
  ethnographic studies, 4, 26, 106, 286–87
  and family history, 190–92
  and human rights ideology, 247
  insights from oral history, 195–99
  and interviewer/narrator pairings, 32–33
  and marginalized groups, 70–71, 199, 306
  and military service, 275
  and new insights, 195–99
  and public oral history, 442
  and segregation, 72, 170
  and slavery, 186–90
  and women's oral history, 174
  and World War II, 237, 275
Radcliffe College, 172
Radio Ballads, 317
Radio Free Europe, 44
Radio Work, 505
radiography, 386
Radstone, Susannah, 98
Rafferty, Anne-Marie, 380
Ragsdale, Eleanor, 191
Ragsdale, Lincoln, 191
Ralph J. Bunche Collection, 193

Randforce Associates, 333, 345
Randolph, A. Philip, 61
rapport with interview subjects, 30, 34
Ravensbruck concentration camp, 66
"raw" documents, 334–35
Rawes, Peg, 223
Read, Peter, 435
Recall, 211, 212, 213
recession, economic, 152–53
reconciliation, 142–54, 434–35
Recording Industry Association of America (RIAA), 288
recordings. *See* audio recordings; video recordings; *specific technologies*
recreations/reenactments, 274–75
Red Brigades, 120
Red Cross, 238
Red Was the Midnight, 305
reel-to-reel recorders, 7, 299, 303, 304, 317
reference librarians, 344
Reflections of the Silver Screen: A History of Allegany County Movie Theatres, 452
reflective teaching, 472–73
reflexivity, 477
refugee communities
  Hazara refugees, 476
  Holocaust survivors, 244
  Hurricane Katrina victims, 14
  and oral history curriculums, 481
  as oral history subject, 5
  Refugee Stories project, 441
  and September 11 terrorist attacks, 259
  in South Africa, 153
  World War II refugees, 470
regional identities, 34
Regional Oral History Office (ROHO)
  Artists With Disabilities Oral History Project, 31
  and civil rights collections, 193
  and defamation lawsuits, 356–57
  and digital technologies, 10, 317
  scope and goals of, 417–18, 420–24
Rehabilitation Act (1973), 502
Rehnquist, William, 352
release agreements, 57, 307, 351–53, 360–61, 363, *367, 368, 369*
religion
  and African American identity, 68
  and African-Christian hybrids, 187
  and Czech dissidents, 42
  and interview dynamics, 34
  and Mexican American culture, 53
  and persecution, *67*
  and the Truth and Reconciliation Commission, 146–47, 150–51
  and *ubuntu*, 54
Remembering Jim Crow, 505
reminiscence therapy, 13, 202–15
Rendina, Massimo, 118
reparations, 152
repetition, 86–87
repression, political, 126–27, 134
Republican Party, 69
Resistance History Institutes, 115–16
resistance organizations, 113, 115–16
resource allocation, 215
Resource Description and Access (RDA), 398
Resources for Planning and Conducting Oral History Interviews, 503
restorative interventions, 386
retribution, 434–35, 436
Revenue Cutter Service, 55
revisionism, 186, 434, 436–37
Revival initiative, 44
Rhudick, P. J., 205
Richardson, Julieanna, 345
Richman, Joe, 310
Rickard, Wendy, 263, 381
Rico, Aldo, 133
Riggs, Marlon T., 198, 199
Rights Management and Digital Preservation, 405
Riksarkivet, 406n5
Ritchie, Donald
  and memory research, 82, 84, 91
  and oral history education, 157, 458–59, 472
  and public history, 429, 436
Rivers, Tom, 374
Robbins, Ian, 384
Roberts, Alan, 233
Roberts, Dmae, 310
Robertson, Beth, 474, 475
Robertson, Claire, 176, 179
Robin, Bernard, 497
Robinson, Jackie, 465, 466
Robinson, Theodore, 275
Rock 'n' Soul Museum, 306
Rockefeller Foundation, 412
Roediger, Henry L., 96
Romaine, Howard, 410
Rome Cinema Festival, 120
Rome Film Festival, 114, 116
Rome Institute for Italian History from Fascism to Resistance, 115–16
Romero, Luis Alberto, 136
Roots: The Saga of a Black Family (Haley), 190
Roots: The Triumph of a Black Family (television), 190, 247
Rose, Jacqueline, 153–54
Rose, Stephen, 82, 84, 86–87
Rosenzweig, Roy, 310
Rosie the Riveter Revisited: Women, The War and Social Change (Gluck), 172
Ross, Martha, 34
Rowland, Steve, 310
Royal Albert Hospital Archive, 380
Royal College of Nursing Archive, 380
Royal Phillips Electronics, Inc. (Phillips), 8
RSS (Really Simple Syndication), 505
Rubens, Lisa, 418–19

Ruddick, Sara, 173
Ruiz, Vicki, 172, 473
Ruskin College, 5
Russa, Ignazio La, 122n15
Russell, David, 380
Russell, Elizabeth M., 377
Ruweisat Ridge (battle), 235
Rwanda, 121, 251

Sacks, Oliver, 90, 224
Salat, Solomon J., 282
Salonika, Greece, 14
Salvatore, Nick, 199
Samuel, Raphael, 7, 320, 321
San Francisco, California, 195, 198–99
San Francisco Oral History Archive, 224
Sanders, Mark, 150
Sands, Diane, 178–79
Santino, Jack, 61
Sayigh, Rosemary, 179
Scalfaro, Oscar Luigi, 115
Scarpino, Philip V., 430
Schacter, Daniel, 83, 84, 85
Schindler's List (1995), 248
Schlesinger, Arthur, Jr., 459
Schlesinger Library, 172
Schnapper, Dominique, 126
Schönberg, Arnold, 281
School of Scottish Studies, 317, 320
School of Sergeant Majors, 133
Schudson, Michael, 102–3
Schweitzer, Pam, 208, 213–14
scientific method, 13
Sea Islands, 188
Seale, Bobby, 358
searching, 341–46
Second Face (video), 180
Second New Zealand Expeditionary Force, 239
secondary witnesses, 253n27
segregation, *72*, 170
Seiler, Laura Ellsworth, 500
Seinfeld, Jerry, 355
self-consciousness, 273
self-ethnographies, 473
semantic memory, 93n24, 104
senses, 219–29
sensory memories, 83
September 11, 2001, Oral History Narrative and Memory Project, 15, 28, 255–63
September 11: Bearing Witness to History, 512
September 11 Digital Archive, 510
settings of interviews, 28
"Seventh Ward Speaks" project, 500–501
Sexual Orientation and Social Conflict Collection, 198
sexuality and sexual orientation, 198, 359, 378, 442
Shadbolt, Maurice, 234
shared authority, 88, 306, 380–85, 431, 476, 483
Sharing the Same Bowl: A Socio-Economic History of Women and Class in Accra, Ghana (Robertson), 176
Sharp, Cecil, 316
Sheen, Juliet, 225–26
shellac-based records, 404
Shenandoah Valley Oral History Project, 453
Shoah (1985), 247, 283
Shoah Visual History Foundation, 11, 248–51, 253n15
The Shop on Main Street (1965), 247
Shopes, Linda, 310, 438–39, 503
short-term memory, 83–84
Sidney, Angela, 177
sight, 222
Signs: Journal of Women in Culture and Society, 176, 180
Silva, Nikki, 310
Simmel, George, 228
Sinomlando Centre for Oral History and Memory Work, 159, 161–62, 163–64, 483
Sinosizo, 160
situated knowledge, 225
Sitzia, Lorraine, 476
Sivan, Emmanuel, 97–98
skepticism of oral history programs, 470, 479
Skype, 511, 512, 515n39
slander, 355
slavery, 33, 68, 69, *72*, 186–90
slides, 211–12
smell, sense of, 224–26, 228–29
Smith, David, 377
Smith, Dorothy, 173
Smith, Graham, 382
Smith, Kitty, 177
Smith, Mark, 221, 229
Smith, Warren Allen, 466
Smith-Robinson, Ruby Doris, 194
Smithsonian Institution, 55–56, 275, 433, 509
social behaviors, 65, 89, 100–101, 148
social change, 48–49, 68, 202–15
social constructionism, 374–75
Social History of Learning Disability Group, 378
social identity, 101–4
social justice, 196, 433
social memory, 96, 102, 435, 437–40
social movements, 126
social networking, 299, 382
social policy, 206
social psychology, 79, 101–4, 207–8
social sciences, 340, *460–61*
social status, 34
socialism, 79
Socialist Party of Italy, 113
Society for the Social History of Medicine, 373
Society of American Archivists (SAA), 322
Society of Former Agents of the FBI, 26
sociology
  and collective memory, 98

and Lance, 321
medical, 377
and memory research, 79
and oral history education, 450
and public oral history, 443
and social identity, 102
solid-state memory, 325, 405
songs, 188
Sonic Memorial Project, 309
Sony cassette recorders, 287
Sophie's Choice (Styron), 247
Sorenson, Gerri, 473
sound archives, 116, 315–27, 379
Sound Portraits, 311
sound quality, 403
South Africa
and archival institutions, 321, 322
and children affected by HIV/AIDS, 159–64
and collapse of apartheid, 6
and community-based oral history, 441–42, 483
and cross-cultural contexts, 53–54
culture of, 52
and oral history associations, 9
and oral history education, 473–74, 480, 483
and public oral history, 434, 435, 441, 442
and truth commissions, 142–54, 435
South Today, 411
Southern Christian Leadership Conference (SCLC), 194
Southern Exposure, 410
Southern Folklore Quarterly, 286
Southern Historical Collection, 194, 410
Southern Oral History Program, 194, 409–15, 503
Southern Regional Council, 410
Soviet Union, 43, 46–47, 249
Spain, 66–68, 67, 72, 137, 205
Spanish American War, 205
Spanish civil war, 66, 67, 68
spatial arrangements, 278
Speaking for Ourselves (podcast), 379
Spencer, Harry, 240
Spielberg, Steven, 248–49
spontaneity in recordings, 274
Spring Hill College, 301
St. Andrew's Episcopal School, 456, 465, 466–67
St. Fagans National History Museum, 320
St. Lawrence Island, 55
Stacey, Judith, 174, 176
Stalag Luft VI, 238
Stalinism, 436
Stanford University, 301
Stanton, Marie, 226
Starr, Louis, 7
State Library of South Australia, 395–96, 400, 402–4, 406n6, 407n15
State of War, 304
state terrorism
and the Malvinas War, 125, 127–29, 132, 135–36, 138
and manipulation of memory, 322
and social memory, 435
State University of New York, Albany, 308
Statens Ljud och Bild Arkiv, 406n4
Statewide Guide to Oral Histories, 293
statistics, 425n5
Štěpán, Miroslav, 47, 48
"Step-by-Step Guide to Oral History," 503
stereotypes, 205, 238
Stewart, T. McCants, 190
Stewart-Lai, Carlotta, 191
Stonewall Riots, 465–66
Stony Brook University Oral History Project, 506
Storace, Francesco, 122n3
StoryCorps
described, 198, 310–11
and the DIY oral history movement, 182
growth of, 505
and legal issues, 351
and mixed-media strategies, 510
origin of, 15
and the practice of oral history, 24
scope of, 351
storytelling, 85–86, 90, 309–12
Straub, Jean-Marie, 281
Streep, Meryl, 247
Strobel, Margaret, 176
student movements, 39–40, 47–48, 138, 194
Student Nonviolent Coordinating Committee (SNCC), 194
students of oral history
and the American Century Oral History Program, 456–57
as audience, 503–4
and the classroom environment, 450–56
educational benefits of oral history, 424–25
methodological training, 457–61
motivating, 449–68
and technological skills, 462–64
Styron, William, 247
subaltern narratives, 435, 445n30
subconscious, 100
subject specialists, 420
subject-based indexes, 292, 293
subjectivity
and collective memory, 79–80, 89, 100–101, 108, 263
and content analysis, 338
and Holocaust testimony, 250, 252
and medical oral history, 374
and the memory paradox, 90–91
and public oral history, 438
subjective memory, 79–80, 89, 100–101, 263
subjective nature of oral history, 12
and thematic coding, 346–47
and traumatic memories, 261
and the Truth and Reconciliation Commission, 150

subpoenas, 354
"The Suffragists: From Tea-Parties to Prison," 500
"Superbugs and Superdrugs: A History of MRSA,"381
Super-8 film, 280–81
Survey Monkey, 511, 516n39
Survey of English Dialects, 317
Survival in Auschwitz (Levi), 247
Suskind, Ron, 196
Sutphen, Debra, 478
Suva Intermediate School, 452
Sweden, 248
Sweet, Helen, 380
Sydney Harbour Bridge, 226–27
symbolism, 102, 133, 137–38, 138–39, 154
syndication, 505

The Tacit Dimension (Polyani), 223
tags, 297, 344, 345
Takrouna (battle), 235
Tal, Kalil, 148–49
"talking head" interviews, 268
Talking History, 308–9
Tanana Chiefs' region, 54
Tansey, Tilli, 381
tape recorders. *See also* video recordings
  cassette recorders, 8, 287–89, 299, 318, 324, 394, 404
  eight-track recorders, 287–88
  four-track recorders, 287–88, 304
  introduction and adoption of, 79, 315, 417
  and Memory Box program, 160–61, 163–64
  micro-cassettes, 404
  reel-to-reel recorders, 7, 299, 303, 304, 317
  and reminiscence therapy, 203, 211–12
The Tape-Recorded Interview (Ives), 170
Task Force for International Cooperation on Holocaust Education, Commemoration, and Research, 248
taxonomies, 337, 347, 453–56, *454*, *455*
Taylor, Quintard, 195
Te Papa Tongarewa museum, 306
teacher education, 474
Teaching American History (TAH), 335–36
technology. *See specific technologies and devices*
television interviews, 25
Telling Our Stories, 310
"Telling Their Stories: Oral History Archives Project,"452, 464–65
tenure, 436
Terkel, Studs, 5, 304, 318–19, 411, 451, 457
"terms of service" notices, 511
terrorism, 15, 255–63
Terry, Wallace, 196
Tester, Claire, 386
"Testi e testimony" (seminars), 117
testimony collection, 244–52
text messaging, 10
text searching, 346
Thatcher, Margaret, 211
"'That's Not What I Said'" (Borland), 492
thematic indexing, 343, 344–47
therapeutic value of oral history, 147–51, 159–64, 241, 383–84
thesauri, 337
The Thin Blue Line (1988), 283
thin copyright, 360, 362
Thomas, Martin, 225–26
Thomas, Sherry, 171
Thompson, Paul
  and the archival imperative, 320, 321
  and "bottom up" approach to oral history, 5
  and collective memory research, 100
  and medical oral history, 375–76
  and memory research, 78–79, 82–83, 85
  and national oral histories, 447n51
  and recording technology, 7, 317–18
Thompson, Thea, 317
Thomson, Alistair, 118, 180, 432, 472, 474, 492
Thrasher, Sue, 410
Three Mile Island, 499
Thucydides, 3, 417, 449
Tibble, Whiro, 240
Tibet Oral History Project, 509
time codes, 296–97, *298*, 503
time sampling, 288–89
Tindall, George, 410–11
Tixier y Vigil, Yvonne, 171
Tlingit culture, 58
To Kill a Mockingbird (Lee), 453
Tocqueville, Alexis de, 285
Toelken, Barre, 52
Tomes, Nancy, 375–76
Tongues Untied (1989), 198
Tonkiss, Fran, 228
torture, 435
totalitarian regimes, 434. *See also* dictatorships
touch, sense of, 224
traditions, invented, 437
training, 164, 357, 395–98, 420, 447n65
transcription
  and accessibility issues, 292, 500
  and audio recordings, 7
  and digital technology, 296, 327
  and funding issues, 304
  and students of oral history, 458–59
  and thematic coding, 345
  and time codes, 296–97, *298*
  and video recordings, 267
transfer agreements, 352–53
Translated Woman: Crossing the Border with Esperanza's Story (Behar), 177–78
translators, 29
trauma
  and children affected by HIV/AIDS, 159–64
  and collective memory, 14, 256, 261

and end-of-life interviewing, 384
and Holocaust survivors, 250–51
and loss of senses, 225
and negotiating remembrance, 282
and reminiscence therapy, 213
and September 11 oral history project, 255–62
and the Truth and Reconciliation Commission, 147, 151–52, 154
and warfare, 137
Treatment Action Campaign (TAC), 153
Treleven, Dale, 287
Trevigne, Barbara, 501
troubadours, 3
Troy University, 301
Truth and Reconciliation Commission (TRC), 13, 142–54
Tuchman, Barbara, 450, 458
Turner, Lorenzo, 187
Tuskegee Airmen, 275
Tuskegee Syphilis Study, 364
Tutu, Desmond, 54, 144, 146–47, 150
Twin Cities Gay and Lesbian Community Oral History Project, 198
Two Fusiliers (Graves), 124
"two-demon theory,"136
two-person interviews, 271
Tyali, Nomonde, 154
TypePad, 506

ubuntu, 54, 146–47
uchronie, 445n19
Uher Report Monitor, 318
UK Business Archives Council, 321
Ukraine, 9, 436
unauthorized use, 363
Unbound Feet (Yung), 179
Unbound Voices (Yung), 179
unemployment, 196
Union Maids (film), 171–72
unions, 4, 14, 66–69, 106, 120, 171, 192–93
United Kingdom, 202–3, 207–12, 387
United States
and Ant Follower conjecture, 73
and archival institutions, 321–22, 323
Federal Writers' Project, 3, 5, 6–7, 32–33, 187, 317, 411, 512
and medical oral history, 375, 376
and oral history education, 97
and public oral history, 432, 433, 439, 441–42
and reminiscence therapy, 211
scope of oral history practice, 351
United States Holocaust Memorial Museum, 248, 306, 500
University at Buffalo, 333, 345
University of Alabama, 293, 295, 301
University of Alaska, Fairbanks, 308, 396
University of California, Berkeley
and adoption of new technologies, 308, 317
Artists With Disabilities Oral History Project, 34
and defamation lawsuits, 356–57
and oral history archives, 4
and the Regional Oral History Office, 417–18, 419
status of oral history at, 421–22
University of California, Los Angeles (UCLA), 4, 193, 425n5
University of Cape Town, 480, 483
University of Chicago, 4
University of Georgia Press, 304
University of Huddersfield, 480
University of Illinois, 345
University of Kentucky, 194, 293, 296, 297
University of KwaZulu-Natal, 159, 164
University of Leicester, 483–84
University of Malmö, 480
University of Massachusetts, 181
University of Michigan, 365
University of Natal, 483
University of New England, 480
University of New South Wales, 475, 479, 482
University of North Alabama, 301
University of North Carolina, 194, 311, 409–15, 507
University of North Carolina Press, 413, 414
University of Papua New Guinea, 471–72, 480
University of Southern California, 249
University of Southern Mississippi, 307
University of Texas, 365
University of Utah, 182
University of Winnipeg, 312
University of Witwatersand, 483
University of Wollongong Archives, 482
university-based oral history. *See also specific universities*
and active learning, 473–76
and archival institutions, 321
benefits of oral history education, 424–25
and civil rights movement research, 193
and curriculum choices, 479–81
and development of archives, 4–5
graduate programs, 16
and the Internet, 307–9
and the interview process, 418–19
and learning outcomes, 476–79
and online classes, 10
and reflective teaching, 472–73
and the Regional Oral History Office, 420–24
and research in the community, 481–84
and technological advance, 417–18
unprocessed materials, 401
unsolicited oral history, 395–98
Uprising of '34, 304
urban history, 191, 227–29
Urban School, San Francisco, 452
U.S. Army Corps of Engineers, 15

U.S. Army History Center, 369
U.S. Constitution, 360
U.S. Copyright Office, 361
U.S. National Library of Medicine, 374
U.S. Navy, 377
U.S. Oral History Association, 422
U.S. Public Health Service, 364
U.S. Supreme Court, 352
US News & World Report, 16
user-generated tags, 297, 299, 343–44

validity of concepts, 9, 104, 106
Valley of the Kings, 238
Valley Women's History Collaborative of western Massachusetts, 180–81
Varga, Susan, 472
Vause, Clifford, 236–37
Veltroni, Walter, 112, 114, 115
Velvet Revolution, 42
Verdoolaege, Annelies, 146
verification, 4, 11–12, 25, 150, 379, 510, 511, 512
vernacular referencing, 343–44, 347
Veterans History Project, 15, 16, 351, 451
vetting. *See* verification
vicarious creating, 394, 395–98, 399, 406n6
Victoria University of Wellington, 480
The Victors? The Vanquished?, 40
video recordings
  advantages of video, 268–69
  cameras for, 10
  databases of, 335–36
  and digital technology, 290–91, 301, 490
  and the Federal Writers' Project, 5
  and Holocaust testimony, 252
  interviews, 29
  and oral history trends, 267
  and pedagogy, 495
  production techniques, 269–70, 270–72, 276n2
  and storage costs, 406n3
  and tape recording technology, 300–301
  and thematic coding, 345
  video tours, 273–75
  videohistory guidelines, 269–70
Viertel, Salka, 281
Vietnam War, 5, 451
Virginia Tech, 478, 482
virtual memory books, 509
Virtual Oral/Aural History Archive, 308
vision, 222
Voice of America, 44
The Voice of the Past: Oral History (Thompson), 5, 79, 100
voice overs, 274
voice-recognition technology, 327, 394
Voices of Collective Remembering (Wertsch), 105
Voices of Gallipoli (Shadbolt), 234
Voices of the Valley: Volume I, 452
"Voices of Women Homemakers" project, 172
volunteerism, 442
Von Plato, Alexander, 46
Von Ranke, Leopold, 4
voting behaviors, 65, 66, 69

Wachtler, Howard, 338
Wade, Dwayne, 197
Wagner, Tony, 462, *463*
Waitangi Tribunal, 434, 445n27
Wallis, Don, 191
Wallot, Jean-Pierre, 323
war. *See also* military
  combat situations, 233–34
  domestic details of war, 238
  and historians' place, 135–39
  and Holocaust survivors, 244–52
  and illiterates, 70, 71
  and oral histories of returning veterans, 5–6
  typical experiences, 236–41
  veterans of, 15, 16, 130, 131–32, 351, 451
  victims of, 131–32
  and war crimes, 126–27, 131, 280, 436
  war memories, 133, 134–35, 135–39
Warsaw Uprising Museum, 306
Washington, George, 4
Washington Heights, 278
Washington Post, 196
Washington State University, 193–94
Washington Women's History Consortium (WHC), 181
Waterman, Peter, 228–29
Watkins, Thomas, 192
wax cylinder recordings, 316, 404
We Didn't Have Much, but We Sure Had Plenty: Stories of Rural Women (Thomas), 171
"We Only Come Here to Struggle": Stories from Berida's Life (Robertson), 179–80
Web Content Accessibility Guidelines (WCAG), 502
Web pages. *See* Internet and online resources
Webber, Amos, 199
Weberian analysis, 375
Weig, Eric, 296
Weine, Stevan, 255, 256, 259, 262
Weisse, Allen, 376
Wellcome Library, 379
Wellcome Trust, 331n58
Wellcome Witness seminars, 381
Welsh Folk Museum, 317, 320
Wendling, Laura, 473
Wertsch, James V., 96, 105
Wessex Sound and Film Archive, 320
West, Bernard, 303
Westkott, Marcia, 173
whalers, 55–56
"What Did You Do In The War, Grandma?" (project), 504

"What Makes Oral History Different" (Portelli), 80, 492, 495
Wheaton College, 307
Wheeler, Winona, 434
Whitaker, Matthew, 191
White Knights of the Ku Klux Klan, 355
Who Built America?: From the Centennial Celebration of 1876 to the Great War (multimedia project), 305
A Whole New Mind (Pink), 462
Why Survive? Being Old in America (Butler), 206
Wichita, Kansas, 191
Wickham, Chris, 103
Wiesel, Elie, 247
Wieviorka, Annette, 249–50
Wikipedia, 344
wikis, 503
Will the Circle Be Unbroken (radio program), 304–5
Williams, Brian, 355
Williams, Ralph Vaughan, 237, 316
Williams, Raymond, 87
Wilson, Richard, 146
Wilson, William Julius, 196
Windschuttle, Keith, 433
Wing Luke Asian Museum, 305
Winter, Jay, 97–98
wire recorders, 7, 287
Wisconsin Humanities Council, 368
Wise, Leah, 410
With Babies and Banners (film), 171–72
witness testimony, 4, 260, 432
Witnesses to Change: Families, Learning Difficulties and History, 379
Wittner, Judith, 173
"Women, Work, and Cinema" (seminars), 117
Women's Airforce Service Pilots (WASPs), 275
Women's Auxiliary Army Corps (WAAC), 504
"Women's Life Histories: Method and Content" (Geiger), 176
women's oral history
  assessment of women's oral history, 178–79
  and cultural norms, 100, 173–74
  current women's oral history, 179–81
  and the digital revolution, 181–82
  female faculty, 411
  gender roles and memory, 94n41
  and HIV/AIDS, 153, 160
  and military service, 275, 504
  origins of women's oral history, 169, 170–72
  and postmodernism, 174–76
  and race, 174
  and representation issues, 176–78
  and slavery, 187–88, 189
  and women's culture, 173–74
  and women's movements, 120, 171, 172
  and women's studies, 475, 480
  and women's trades, 278–79
Women's Oral History: The Frontiers Reader, 169, 178
Women's Ways of Knowing: The Development of Self, Voice and Mind (Belenky et al.), 173
Women's Words: The Feminist Practice of Oral History (Gluck and Patai), 174, 175
Wood, Nancy, 97–98
Woodard, Ken, 453
WordPress, 506, 515n39
Words and Silences/Palabras y silencios (International Oral History Association), 475
Working in Paterson: Occupational Heritage in an Urban Setting (project), 505
Working Lives Oral History Project, 295
Working (Terkel), 5
"work-made-for-hire" doctrine, 361
Works Progress Administration (WPA). *See* Federal Writers' Project
World Trade Center, 309
World War I, 125, 432, 451
World War II
  and Australia, 470
  BBC oral history project on, 510
  and civil rights, 195
  and collective memory, 13, 105
  and combat memories, 233–34
  and Fosse Ardeatine massacre, 112
  interviews of combat experience, 5
  and propaganda interviews, 38
  and public oral history, 436, 437, 439
  and race issues, 237, 275
  and recording technology, 7
  and students of oral history, 451, 452, 467, 478
  and video recordings, 268
  and women's military service, 275, 504
World Wide Web. *See* Internet and online resources
World Wide Web Consortium, 502
World Women's Conference (Mexico City), 177
WRFG radio station, 303, 304
Wright, George C., 195, 199
Wright State University, 480
Written Document Analysis Worksheets, 459
written vs. oral stories, 55
WW2 People's War, 510

xenophobia, 153, 258, 259
Xhosa culture, 53–54

Yad Vashem, 244, 250, 253n22
Yahoo Groups, 516n39
Yale University, 249
Yalta conference, 38
Yellowman, 52
YIVO Institute for Jewish Research, 244
Young Men's Christian Association (YMCA), 238

Your Mommy Kills Animals (documentary), 361
YourStory Project, 182
YouTube, 500, 504, 509
Yow, Valerie, 81, 83–84, 91, 429, 472
Yung, Judy, 179
Yup'ik culture, 52–56, 57
Z. Smith Reynolds Foundation, 410–11, 414
Zable, Arnold, 472
Zachert, Martha Jane, 319
Zalumas, Jacqueline, 380
Zardini, Mirko, 222
Zerubavel, Yael, 437
Zydowski Instytut Historyczyny (ZIH), 244